THE PLURALISTIC HALAKHAH

PAUL HEGER

STUDIA JUDAICA

FORSCHUNGEN ZUR WISSENSCHAFT
DES JUDENTUMS

HERAUSGEGEBEN VON
E. L. EHRLICH

BAND XXII

WALTER DE GRUYTER · BERLIN · NEW YORK
2003

THE PLURALISTIC HALAKHAH

LEGAL INNOVATIONS IN THE LATE SECOND COMMONWEALTH AND RABBINIC PERIODS

BY
PAUL HEGER

WALTER DE GRUYTER · BERLIN · NEW YORK
2003

♾ Printed on acid-free paper which falls within the guidelines of the ANSI
to ensure permanence and durability.

ISBN 3-11-017636-X

Bibliographic information published by Die Deutsche Bibliothek

Die Deutsche Bibliothek lists this publication in the Deutsche Nationalbibliografie; detailed bibliographic data is available in the Internet at <http://dnb.ddb.de>.

Printed in Germany
Cover Design: Christopher Schneider

In memory of my beloved life-partner and wife, חיה, who devoted her life to raising our admirable children, and who endured with love and patience my winding path of life.

ACKNOWLEDGEMENT

This book represents the outcome of my reflections on the fundamental philosophical-theological ideas of the Sages - the ideas that served as the basis for the creation of the talmud, that magnum opus which has been the continuous guide for Jewish life and cultural survival. I have had the supreme good fortune of being able to reflect on these issues during a lifetime, starting within a strictly orthodox milieu, moving to a modern and less stringent orthodox environment, then carrying on business in a totally secular society. Through extensive travelling I have encountered an array of other cultures and faiths, and, most recently, have had the reward of an academic approach to Talmud. My life experiences are reflected in this work.

I am indebeted, first and foremost, to Professor Harry Fox, of the Department of Near and Middle Eastern Civilizations at the University of Toronto, who introduced me to a critical yet unbiased academic approach to talnudic literatre, and who continually provides me with useful assistance and guidance. It is also my pleasant duty to thank Professor Ernst Ludwig Ehrlich, who steered the first, crucial, phase of this study, and Professor Günter Stemberger, who has dedicated much time and thought toward the final structure and contents of the book. I wish to remember with thanks the friendly and valuable contribution of Professor John Revell, who read the entire manuscript of the book's first version. Last, but not least, I am most thankful to Dr. Diane Kriger, for her assistance in the editing and corrections of the final text.

Toronto, Ontario September 2002

Table of Contents

Introduction

It is my proposition that a pluralistic and tolerant attitude dominated the pre-70 halakhic environment, with one exception: the rules of the Temple cult celebrations. An examination of the halakhic environment in the pre-70 period is thus an essential prerequisite to the wider investigation of the changes engendered by the destruction of the Temple. The destruction generated a unique response by the Jewish people. The Sages created a unique ideology, uprooting ingrained concepts of nationhood, the relationship with the Deity, worship, the priesthood, sacred locations, and the culture in general.

From historical sources it is obvious that sacrificial worship in the Temple had achieved its most venerated status in the period prior to the Temple's destruction. We need not go into detail with respect to the many historical and sociological motives that lay behind this circumstance; for our purposes, it suffices to acknowledge the *opinio communis* that the sacrificial cult in the Temple was the focal point of the Jewish people in Judah and the Diaspora during the last two hundred years of the Temple's existence - that is, from the Maccabean revolt until the destruction. Identification with the Jewish people was expressed in both abstract belief - in one God, and in the Torah as His law bestowed upon the Israelites - and in the concrete sacrificial ritual at the Temple, in the most sacred location of Jerusalem.

As a consequence of the Temple's destruction, the Sages effected a transformation of this ritual: in place of priestly-controlled rites to be performed in a particular sacred place, there developed a sophisticated and intellectually guided system of prayer that was universally accessible. The study of the Torah, and of the halakhah that was its outgrowth, became the beacon of the Jews, and the guarantor of their uniqueness and of their survival as one people despite their wide dispersion. It is in this response to the destruction of the Temple, meticulously designed by the Sages, that we may understand the singularity of this event; its impact on the character of the Jewish people and their particular cultural and political development justify our deeming the destruction "the" primary event of Jewish history.

The study of the Torah and the evolution of the halakhah started prior to the Temple's destruction. This event, however, created a significant change in the character of the halakhah and its practical application, so that there is a distinctive dichotomy between pre- and post-70.[1] The significance of the halakhah in the creation of the Jewish people - the interesting phenomenon of a nation defined exclusively by a collective ideology - cannot be underestimated. It is therefore meritorious, in my opinion, to analyze the philosophical foundation of the halakhah, the theological beliefs and intentions of its authors, and its stages of development, with particular emphasis on the impact of the Temple's destruction on that complex and protracted path.

Detailed Postulates with respect to Halakhic Development

The most outstanding difference between the pre- and post-70 periods is the pluralism of the halakhic environment, with respect to both doctrine and practice, which characterized the pre-70 period, as opposed to the quest for a fixed halakhah in the post-70 period. This thesis runs counter to opinion that has been predominant until quite recently, and I shall substantiate it by assessing the following postulates that constitute its main elements:

a) Pre-70, religious rules were determined by tradition, and by the *ad hoc* decisions pronounced by various erudite men who enjoyed respect and obeisance in their respective communities. These men had no titles or public functions; the titles Rabban, Rabbi, and the generic denomination Sages were a later development. For convenience, I shall use the collective term "Sages."

b) Contradictory halakhic decisions by different Sages were of no concern to the functioning of public institutions. Decisions were not archived, nor were they considered final and binding on all the people. Certain decisions may have become a permanent part of the general Israelite tradition; others, however, were likely practised solely within their restricted communities and for a limited time.

In such circumstances, it is little wonder that we have no reliable data from the pre-70 period concerning halakhic decisions, or the names of their authors.[2] Nor were the contradictory decisions perceived, either by their authors or by the public, as disputes. They were seen as legitimate variations in the obligation to fulfill the divine commands expressed in the Torah.

c) There was no intention to establish one final and definitive legal codex, and the performance of the Torah's precepts in everyday life was,

---

1 For reasons of brevity, I shall use "pre-70" and "post-70" to refer to the periods before and after the Temple's destruction.

2 In some cases, as we shall see (chap. 4, n. 13 and text), the names of early authors of ethical declarations are preserved.

therefore, quite unregulated with respect to minute details. The lack of a consistent and comprehensive legal system in that period in fact left an extended imprint on the subsequent developmental stages of Jewish law, allowing the preservation of a flexible legal system. This also explains the prohibition against preserving the halakhot in writing.

d) Differences in daily rules and customs did not, therefore, provoke serious divisions, and disparate practices could co-exist in the daily social-political sphere.

e) These circumstances stand in complete contrast to the post-70 period, when Rabban Gamaliel, the first acknowledged leader and assumed Patriarch of the post-destruction period, attempted, for political motives, to establish a single, fixed halakhah.

f) The Sages were resolutely opposed to this revolutionary method, which in effect curtailed the independence that they had, up to then, enjoyed.

g) The creation and implementation of a single fixed codex, from its inception to its general acceptance, thus constituted a lengthy process, continuing over many centuries.

Methodology: General Remarks

The cornerstones of this study will be the concepts and methods of rabbinic legislation, its relation to tradition and to Scripture, and its different stages of development. To substantiate the thesis and its various postulates, I shall critically analyze and evaluate relevant citations from the general corpus of rabbinic literature.

This study comprises a broad investigation, rather than a detailed study of particular subjects. I have, in other words, attempted to integrate relevant historical and social circumstances. I have thus aimed at reaching a balance between two equally meritorious and intellectually rewarding quests: an in-depth analysis of every aspect of each issue, and a holistic portrayal of the prevailing ideology and circumstances that influenced the creation of the rabbinic legal corpus.

My main task in writing this book consists of posing new questions with respect to the influence of historical events and outstanding personalities on the development and shifts in rabbinic ideology and creativity. My aim is to offer different perspectives on the various elements of this topic, postulating reasonable hypotheses on these issues, as well as on issues that have already been raised. With this scope in mind, I do not see it as imperative to record in detail the wealth of scholarly opinion and discussion that has preceded my study. The quotation of all scholarly publications on such a wide array of topics would exceed my intellectual capacity, as well as the boundary of a monograph. I shall also avoid giving scholarly citations for those opinions on which there is general agreement. As compensation, I shall be able to present a broader picture of the overall ideology of the Sages and their *Weltanschauung*, which induced them to create an unrestricted, adaptable method of law-making, without being confined by the rigid rules of a closed system. I attempt to present, through a critical analysis of the relevant texts, a portrayal of Israelite "culture," in the widest definition of that term; I shall set out the overall conditions pertaining in each period, and their developmental stages. It is certainly not my intention to disregard the significance of the current "reductionist" method of analyzing a specific topic in great depth, a valuable contribution from the specialist's perspective. I wish to offer instead an overarching description of the complex issues that motivated the Sages, in their goal to create an open, flexible environment - an environment that was, on the one hand, unmarked by confrontation or schism within their own group, and, on the other hand, in apparent utter conformity with the unchanging words of God as expressed in Scripture.

In my opinion, the study of biblical historiography in particular has been negatively affected by the narrow viewpoint of many of the scholars who are involved in the evaluation of textual authenticity. A similar attitude is also manifest with regard to rabbinic literature. We currently encounter either "minimalist" or "maximalist" approaches to the examination of texts; the flawed consequence of this trend is that adherents of one school utterly exclude the conclusions of the other. One may say that there is never a single determinant or event that dominates the life of an individual or of a society to the exclusion of all others. A wide range of factors and occurrences will motivate the thoughts and deeds of a single person, and likewise of a people, and incite shifts in ideology and action. We must therefore consider this range of factors, according to our contemporary understanding and *Weltanschauung*, and analyze them according to a variety of scholarly methods. I have attempted, in my scrutiny of biblical and rabbinic sources, to take the "middle" road, a multiform *modus operandi*, without assuming that there is only one correct method, or taking an extreme position. R. Rendtorff would call such an approach a "methodological pluralism."[3] Though I need not agree with all of B. Halperin's views concerning the authenticity of biblical narratives, I do concur with his statement that the historical question is "what is more probable, not the certain, cause of events and causation to posit."[4]

My aim is to present an objective and critical investigation of the rabbinic halakhah and the underlying philosophy and beliefs of the Sages.

---

3 R. Rendtorff, "Paradigm," p. 63.

4 B. Halperin, "The State of Israelite History," p. 545.

Such an investigation will necessarily involve a meticulous scrutiny of the underlying literature - halakhic, narrative and aggadic[5] - and particularly of the all-embracing "harmonization" system in which the Sages smoothed off or neutralized contradictory dicta with (often far-fetched) hermeneutics. Nonetheless, I wish to emphasize my great respect and reverence for the Sages' wide-ranging considerations in their quest for the survival of the Jewish people. They were, in my opinion, most progressive and "modern" in their thought-processes, and attempted, with all the intellectual resources at their disposal, to adapt the laws to contemporary conditions and conceptions, while still maintaining the broad spirit of the Torah. The intricate and sophisticated "harmonization" system constituted an essential and successful tool for this task. The ultimate realization of their quest certainly attests to their great foresight.

Studies of the rabbinic legal system, as it is expressed in the Talmud, have usually been undertaken by scholars with a traditional background. There is some degree of restraint in their critical examination, conditioned by their religious beliefs;[6] a "fig leaf" of varying dimensions, concealing a reluctance to break open the last confines of unrestricted criticism, is always present in their discussions.[7] This reluctance tends to obstruct the perception of the whole picture, and hinders an unqualified investigation into the entire issue.[8] One may detect some affinity between this reluctance and the concept of the unseen God, whose divine nature and attributes can never be fully grasped, and whose motives can never be fully understood. Something must and will forever remain hidden from the human mind, and one must not attempt to fathom the uttermost bounds of these metaphysical concepts.[9] Hence, for these scholars a certain limit to

---

5 See P. Schäfer, *Studien*, p. 11

6 I. Englard, "Research in Jewish Law," p. 37 and note 55, asserts that a religious approach impedes objective historical research of religiously inspired law. L. H. Schiffman, "Contribution," p. 206, writes that ideological considerations are still apparent in talmudic research.

7 V. A. Harvey, *Confrontation*, p. 115 writes: "All of our judgments and inferences [including historical ones] take place...against a background of beliefs. We bring to our perceptions and interpretations a world of existing knowledge, categories and judgments."

8 See for example the essay of S. Z. Havlin, על החתימה הספרותית. My proposal that the Amoraim, the Sages who came after the Mishnah, were reluctant to use their authority to amend prior halakhot would likely seem too radical to this excellent talmudic scholar at the traditional Bar Ilan University. He conceives this phenomenon to be the result of a self-imposed decision by the Amoraim, and by the subsequent generations of Rabbis, to avoid contradicting halakhic decisions of the earlier masters.

9 We read in mHagigah 2: 1: כל המסתכל בארבעה דברים ראוי לו כאילו לא בא לעולם מה למעלה מה למטה מה לפנים ומה לאחור וכל שלא חס על כבוד קונו ראוי לו שלא בא לעולם "If one ponders on [the following] four matters, it

their investigation is preferable and appropriate. On the other side of the boundary, we encounter those scholars who consider it their duty to demonstrate the dichotomy between Scripture and Talmud and the deficiencies of the rabbinic method and hermeneutics. I trust that my particular prejudgment[10] is neither restricted by any religiously influenced opinion, nor biased by any denigrating prejudice[11] against the rabbinic legal *modus operandi*. I thus hope to present to the reader an overview of rabbinic halakhic literature that is somewhat different than either of the views above.

There appears to be an inherent methodological paradox in using talmudic texts. Certain passages are invoked to substantiate a thesis, on the one hand; on the other hand, the authenticity of other passages, or of their significant details,[12] is denied, and it is assumed that their formulation had some purpose other than the conveyance of accurate historical information. This problem also affects biblical criticism, and we cannot escape it. We do not reject *a priori* the authenticity of every biblical narrative; we examine the text critically, and consequent upon a meticulous assessment of the relevant circumstances, we may employ some of its elements and reject others.[13] It is a matter of careful judgment

---

would have been better had he not been born: What is upward, what is below, what is in front and in the rear" - that is, metaphysical questions. The next dictum enlightens us as to the reason for this apparently odd maxim: "Whoever has no consideration for the honour of his Creator is not worthy of having been born." We perceive that these metaphysical questions concerning the beginning of the world and its structure are deemed to be exclusively within divine jurisdiction, and human aspirations to infringe upon this privilege are seen as *lèse majesté*, an offense against God's glory. See also Maimonides' philosophical interpretation of Moses' two requests in Exod 33: 12 - 23: "teach me your ways so I may know you [v. 13]" and "show me your glory [v. 18]," and the tension between these two demands (*The Guide of the Perplexed*, book 1, chap. 54).

10 Heidegger coined the concept of "fore-understanding," a formal condition of all understanding (H. G. Gadamer, *Truth and Method*, p. 261).

11 Gadamer, ibid. p. 263, distinguishes between productive prejudices that make understanding possible, and prejudices that hinder understanding and lead to misunderstanding.

12 See J. Neusner's essay "Attributions."

13 The scholarly debate regarding objectivity and subjectivity in biblical research is also unquestionably linked to a theistic or atheistic approach, but it is my opinion that one can and should adopt a "middle of the road," compromising stance. A theistic understanding need not absolutely imply a *maximalist*, fundamentalist approach, since the Bible allows a wide range of interpretation and adjustment to contemporary circumstances; we shall see that this approach was in fact adopted by the theistic Sages. On the other hand, an atheistic approach still allows the acknowledgment of the authenticity, entirely or partially, of many biblical narratives, and does not compel an *a priori minimalist* approach, denying any authenticity to biblical literature. A diachronic approach to resolving inconsistencies and contradictions in biblical

of all aspects of the passage, using various methodological criteria. Nevertheless, despite this academic process of evaluation, we observe different, often conflicting, scholarly conjectures about the passages in question. The same consideration applies to the critical examination of the talmudic narratives.[14] We must not simply deny any authenticity to rabbinic narratives, but must analyze them critically and assess whether we have adequate reason to question their authenticity. In some instances, we are indeed able to detect a kernel of truth hidden in narratives suspected to be fictitious, or formulated with a deliberate facade. We must also base our conclusions about the validity of rabbinic narratives and their general underlying philosophy upon numerous talmudic citations, rather than upon individual contrary quotations. Although, as I have written above, the focus of my study is the underlying theological-philosophical foundation of the halakhah, and not an assessment of the authenticity of historical events, I have granted this problem my most serious consideration, and have proceeded, as far as possible, with an objective assessment.

Another dilemma faces the scholar who wishes to investigate the ideological-philosophical background of the rabbinic literature. The great pluralism of the rabbinic dicta, and the diversity of their often conflicting declarations, impede our assigning them to one particular philosophical foundation. The only common concept underlying the Sages' utterances was their belief in the infallibility of the Torah and its teachings, in the broadest sense. The Tannaim, the generators of the rules and decrees under review, proclaimed neither their underlying philosophy nor the motives that induced them to decide one way or another. The Amoraim, in their quest to understand the foundations of the tannaitic decisions, attempted to categorize many of these rules according to general principles, or attributed them to different interpretations of biblical verses; but this classification was the result of their own imagination and speculation, lacking any explicit indication by the Tannaim.

It is fascinating to investigate in this respect the attempted classification of the disputes between Beit Hillel and Beit Shammai. There is a general proposition that attributes leniency to Beit Hillel and strictness to Beit Shammai. This does not, however, hold up to scrutiny, since in a number of occurrences Beit Shammai were the lenient party and Beit Hillel the stricter one. There was also a maxim that the halakhah was to

---

narratives and commands seems to me an appropriate method; it concedes a qualified authenticity to biblical narratives, without infringing upon any theistic or atheistic understanding. See Otto Kaiser, *Studien zur Literaturgeschichte des Alten Testamentes*, pp. 183 ff.

[14] Even J. Neusner, whose criticism of the authenticity of rabbinic narratives is well-known, concludes (*Pharisees, Part I*, p. 357): "We are no better off in deciding they *never* [the author's emphasis] are reliable."

follow Beit Hillel in all cases; this too could not be sustained, and various devices were applied to circumvent this sweeping resolution. We must also not suppose that Beit Shammai adhered more to the straightforward understanding of the biblical text while Beit Hillel proffered a broader range of exegesis. Neither Shammai nor his disciples, for instance, opposed Hillel's ordinance of the *prosbul*,[15] an institution utterly in contrast to the scriptural law. In point of fact, the Houses constitute a unique phenomenon in rabbinic literature. Nothing is known about their identity, organization, or date of inception and disintegration. Though particular Sages are known to have been disciples of Hillel or Shammai, the decisions of these Houses are never attributed to a particular individual. Furthermore, it is perplexing that the disputes between the Houses never provoked the sort of schism that existed between the Pharisees and "dissidents." I shall propose in the Appendix an unconventional hypothesis that the Houses were actually a fictitious construction.

The same pluralism and contrasting ideologies are clearly evident in the rabbinic homilies, indicating the vast range of their philosophical thought. One can, therefore, only attempt to comprehend the range of the Sages' perceptions of their own authority. They shared a belief of the Torah's supremacy as the blueprint for the life of the Jewish people. From this axiom ensued their engagement in attempting to understand the divine will and purpose expressed in the Torah, and to inculcate its message among the people. I attempt to detect the motivations of the Sages; but this is rather difficult and speculative, given that they did not consider it necessary to reveal their philosophical-theological foundations. I must admit that my personal intuition remains a crucial factor in the formulation of my assumptions in this respect, as I believe intuition has likewise informed the opinions of other scholars who have approached this subject.

Methodology in Detail

The first impediment we must surmount in a study of this nature is the lack of first-hand accounts regarding the halakhah of the Pharisees (or pre-70 Sages). It is usual to deplore the fact that we do not have authentic documentation of the Sadducees and statements from their own sources; I complain, in contrast, that we do not possess authentic decrees of these pre-70 Sages. What we do possess was written much later. This material conveys, at best, how the compilers perceived the pharisaic decrees, or how they thought it advisable to transmit them. The only authentic data from the pre-70 period in our possession are the halakhot and ideologies of

15 Cf. I. Ben-Shalom, בית שמאי, p. 79.

the Dead Sea Scrolls. This is a very large obstacle that will probably not be corrected; we cannot expect to find ancient pharisaic scrolls.[16]

Considering these circumstances, a creative approach must be used to reconstruct the halakhic environment of the pre-70 period. I propose to do this from an extrapolation of the post-70 conditions, for which we do possess adequate data in rabbinic literature. I believe that in this way we may derive a plausible portrayal of the halakhic and ideological-philosophical perspective of the Pharisees. I do not intend to take a general position in this study with respect to the association between the pre-70 Pharisees and the post-70 Sages. My interest in their connection is limited[17] to the halakhic component of that relationship, and it is of *opinio communis* that in this respect the Sages considered themselves followers of the Pharisees.[18] This approach will also allow us to create a plausible line of continuity between the pre- and post-70 periods; in this way, we may obtain an integrated picture of the halakhic environment in Israel[19] in the last period of the Second Temple, the era of the sects, in its ideological and political setting.

A thorough examination of post-70 rabbinic literature, to reveal its developmental stages and to retroject these to the pre-70 period, thus constitutes a significant component of this study. Such an extensive examination is indispensable, given the fact that the Sages did not communicate their underlying philosophies or the historical circumstances that influenced their decisions. By this method, I shall attempt to substantiate my proposal that the pre-70 period was dominated by a pluralistic and tolerant halakhic environment, with the exception of the rules regarding the Temple cult.[20]

---

16 Jay M. Harris, "From Inner-Biblical Interpretation to Early Rabbinic Exegesis," states on p. 257: "The Pharisees themselves left us no literature."

17 J. Neusner is an outspoken critic of the use of rabbinic data for the establishment of historical facts, considering this to be imputing a scope to such data for which they were not intended. He writes in "Evidence," p. 220, that a notion that is correct for theological inquiry may be false for historical inquiry. I conclude, conversely, that a notion that may be false for historical inquiry is correct for a theological inquiry, which is an essential element of our study (see nn. 22-23 and text).

18 See the extended deliberation on this issue in chap. 4, "Excursus: The Association between Pharisees and 'Rabbis.'"

19 J. Neusner, "Evidence," p. 21, declares: "No one will claim that a fifth century source by definition tells us nothing whatsoever about the first century." He continues that such a position is absurd, as is the position that everything said in the fifth century about the first century must automatically be perceived as historical fact. On particular issues, however, it is possible to deduce earlier circumstances from later narratives.

20 This exception is amply substantiated in the second part of the study.

In so deducing patterns of ideology and conduct, it seems to me indispensable to derive the intellectual methods and techniques that were generally applied in the creation of halakhic decisions, and the philosophical background of such methods. The study investigates the legal environment, and its developmental stages, in specific periods, and does not constitute an integrated examination of the overarching characteristics and implications of Jewish law.[21]

The study will also concentrate on the theology underlying specific rabbinic beliefs related to the halakhic process, and the continuous adaptation implicit within it. The study does not aspire to deduce from rabbinic literature the general theology of the Sages - that is, issues such as the nature of monotheism and divine immanence.[22] It will, however, address the methods and scope of Torah interpretation, rabbinic authority, the multivocality[23] of the divine utterances, and similar issues.[24] Jewish law, founded upon the Torah, has a philosophical - theological foundation, which necessarily informed the halakhic decisions of the Sages on both ritual and civil issues. We must attempt to reveal their meta-halakhic convictions, in order to discern the intent of their decisions, understand the mechanisms they used, and perceive the theological justification for the changes and adjustments effected in the law. It is the existence of this "common theological denominator" that explains the Sages' belief that completely opposing decisions may be derived from the same divine utterance. Similarly, the perception that apparent adaptations and adjustments of the law, as well as completely new ordinances, actually have their root in the Sinai revelation can only be rationalized on the basis of this shared theological foundation. Further, it is this particular commonality between the Sages and the pre-70 Pharisees, as argued above, that allows the extrapolation of post-70 approaches to halakhah to the pre-70 period.

Finally, it must be noted that rabbinic citations encompass both legal and philosophical aspects. I shall not, therefore, distinguish in my evaluation between these two aspects; both elements will be used, without distinction, to deduce whether the Sages tended toward an open, pluralistic and flexible approach to halakhah, or toward a fixed approach.

---

21 On this topic see J. Neusner, *Judaic Law*, and particularly his debate with Sanders.

22 This contrasts to the approach of J. Neusner, who does attempt to extract rabbinic theology from his examination of halakhah; see, e.g. his *History*, pp. 220 ff.

23 See the various discussions in this study of the maxim אלו ואלו דברי אלהים חיים "Both [conflicting halakhic decisions] are the words of the living God," found in bEruvin 13b and other sources.

24 I do not address the question of whether the rabbinic laws were actually practised by the masses. See the Introduction to C. Hezser, *Social Structure*, on this topic.

To summarize: I shall start with an exposition of rabbinic declarations from both tannaitic and amoraic literature in the post-70 period, and deduce from these the method of legal decision-making. I shall then proceed to extrapolate the circumstances prevailing in the pre-70 era. Investigation of the philosophical opinions of the Sages is thus founded upon interpretation of, and logical deduction from, such texts. Given the dearth of texts relevant to the halakhic environment in the pre-70 period and our need to make plausible conjectures based on the later texts, it is essential to quote abundantly from such texts and comment upon them extensively.

Further, given that the Sages did not divulge the theological foundation underlying their halakhic decisions, and that we must reveal this by a meticulous analysis of their literature, it is evident that to best achieve this objective we must examine each and every genre of declaration within this immense corpus.[25] It is equally indisputable that narratives and rhetorical debates lend themselves to a much wider and deeper analysis of their underlying ideology, and offer greater scope for revealing their underlying intentions, than do simple and unembellished halakhic declarations. I shall therefore use such narratives, whenever available, as the basis from which to derive a portrayal of the rabbinic mind and intentions.

With respect to the use of multiple sources, current scholarly opinion tends to assess rabbinic sources within a hierarchy of authenticity. Mishnaic citations are granted the greatest reliability, toseftan citations less, and so on down through Midreshei Halakhah, Y. T. and B. T. This hierarchy of citation is the rule in modern studies, with a manifest preference for Y.T. quotations as against those of the B. T., with respect to rhetorical discussions and narratives referring to Palestinian circumstances. I do not intend to question this contemporary method,[26] which may[27] be appropriate for the verification of historical facts and

---

25 See the citations of various scholarly opinions on this premise in chap. 4, nn. 23-4.

26 See I. Gafni, "Talmudic Research," on the preference for the reliability of the Y.T. over the B. T.

27 The questionable authenticity of all rabbinic literature is now an *opinio communis*, thoroughly substantiated in many scholarly publications. G. Stemberger, *Introduction to the Talmud and Midrash*, presents a survey of scholarship on this issue, and concludes (p. 58) that the attribution of a particular document to the tannaitic or amoraic period is sometimes problematic. D. Goodblatt, "The Babylonian Talmud," notes various fictitious baraitot in the B. T. J. Neusner, *Purities, Part XXI*, p. 246, states: "The Mishna is the work of tradent - redactors." W. S. Green, "Biography," declares more explicitly: "[The] chain of tradents, only occasionally mentioned by name, the redactors and the editors who stand behind the present form of both discrete pericopae and entire documents substantively revised, embellished and refined received materials, and sometimes invented new ones, to suit their various agendas. We know from the documents what the redactors wanted us to know and in the way

events. I suggest, however, that this method is largely irrelevant for the purposes of my study. My aim, as I said, is to reveal the rabbinic motives behind the halakhic decisions. It is the rabbinic philosophical - theological ideology, and how this influenced their decisions and their exposition of debates and events, that is crucial to my scrutiny, not whether the incidents that are described really occurred. This goal affects my methodology in two ways. First, the examination of material other than rabbinic sources is irrelevant to the core of the study. I shall thus concentrate on the exploration of appropriate citations from rabbinic literature.[28] Second, I shall make extensive use of B. T. narratives and rhetorical discussions (in addition to the usually straightforward halakhic pronouncements of the Mishnah). I often prefer such B.T. sources because they present, as a rule, a wealth of detail that is often missing in parallel sources;[29] their superior redaction[30] thus offers greater scope for analysis, especially as this concerns the mindset of the redactor. More efficient redaction may in fact correlate with a deficiency of authenticity; this issue, however, does not negatively influence my investigation. Further, the lack of a Y.T. source is usually not critical.

As one example, we may take the B. T. narrative concerning the dispute between Rabbi Eliezer and the Sages over the "Akhnai oven," and the specific mention of Rabban Gamaliel's "sudden" death being the

they wanted us to know" (p. 80). This is precisely what I am attempting to retrieve from their narratives.

28 C. Hezser, *Social Structure*, p. 43 writes: "Rabbinic literature is the most important source of information on the rabbinic movement." This scholar, we may note, is utterly critical of the authenticity of this literature; she must still acknowledge, however, that it is the only source from which we may deduce the underlying rabbinic philosophy.

29 For example, the narrative of the Akhnai hearth appears in an extended, detailed and instructive fashion in bBava Metzi'a 59b. Excerpts of this event in mKelim 5: 10 and tEduyyot 2: 1, on the other hand, lack details. The version in yMo'ed Qatan 3: 1, 81d also lacks a number of important details, and does not allow for the deduction of significant conclusions. For instance, the divine acquiescence to the Sages' judgment in this narrative, symbolizing a capitulation to their authority on earth, is missing in the Y. T. version. Similarly, the passage that connects Rabban Gamaliel to the dispute with Rabbi Eliezer, with respect to his direct and significant involvement in the process of establishing a fixed halakhah, is missing in the Y.T. version. I therefore prefer to use the extensive B. T. version in my analysis of this narrative in sections 1.4 and 4.2.2.2. See J. Rubenstein, *Talmudic Stories*, pp. 48 ff., who meticulously compares the Y. T. and B. T. versions. I shall comment on Rubenstein's deductions from this narrative further below in nn. 36 and 39.

30 J. Rubenstein, *Talmudic Stories*, pp. 49-50, in comparing the Y.T. and B.T. versions of the Akhnai narrative, states regarding the Y. T. version: "Moreover, the plot is disjointed to such a degree that it is difficult to determine the causal and temporal sequence."

result of Rabbi Eliezer's ire and evil eye.[31] The latter point does not appear in the Y.T.; yet the authenticity of this narrative would not be enhanced if it did. The same conclusion may be reached regarding the absence in the Y. T. of the divine acquiescence to the Sages' judgment in this case, though it was in conflict with the divine intent. J. Neusner[32] has distinguished between earlier, supposedly more reliable, traditions relating to a Sage, and apocryphal narratives conceived by the imagination of later generations. In our case, however, both the Y. T. and the B. T. record legendary occurrences, and both attempt to conceal the real motive of the struggle.[33] The quotations in the B. T. thus provide a medium for significant deductions. It is also possible that the traditions that are missing in this and other Y. T. passages were in fact known to the Y. T. redactors, and were simply omitted in the interest of brevity.[34] At any rate, the authenticity of these and similar narrative elements is irrelevant for our purposes[35] - that is, the revelation of the rabbinic (amoraic) vision of

---

31 See a description and analysis of this point in sections 1.4 and 4.2.2.2.

32 J. Neusner, *Yohanan ben Zakkai*, p. 297.

33 The earlier sources already seem determined to hide the real story behind their abbreviated report. In mKelim 5: 10 the dispute between Rabbi Eliezer and the Sages is quoted; the mishnah adds זה תנורו של עכנאי "this is the oven of Akhnai," which seems to hint at some well-known event. This mishnah stands in contrast to other halakhic disputes between Sages, which do not mention any linkage to a specific occurrence or person; yet it does not indicate why this dispute is remembered as being connected to a particular person. The enigma is deepened by tEduyyot 2: 1, which complements the dispute with the statement: והיה נקרא תנור של עכנאי שעליו רבו מחלוקות בישראל "and [this dispute] was named Akhnai's oven, a topic on which many conflicts occurred in Israel." The toseftan passage thus adds a detail regarding the occurrence of conflicts, but gives no indication of the particular character of this halakhic dispute, or of the motive behind the accretion of conflicts. One would not, of course, expect the rabbinic redactor to record expressly a power struggle between Rabban Gamaliel and Rabbi Eliezer, possibly with personal undertones, that was exacerbated by the Akhnai oven incident into open, fierce confrontation.

34 Another factor that must be considered is the existence of different manuscript traditions, which may explain the omission of some details in the currently available text. P. Schäfer, "Status Quaestionis," p. 147 writes that the Talmud Yerushalmi used by the redactor of Genesis Rabbah "was decidedly different from the Yerushalmi in existence today." Similarly, the quotation of a narrative in a source assumed to be later-redacted does not unquestionably establish its late origin. Schäfer's discussion on the relationship between Mishnah and Tosefta (pp. 147 ff.) suggests a similar problem regarding the relationship between Y. T. and B. T.

35 Similar circumstances governed my decision to quote amply from the B. T. narrative of Hillel's encounter with the Bene Bathyra regarding the Passover offering on Sabbath, particularly as it refers to an ahistorical event. For our purposes, it is even irrelevant whether there is a kernel of truth in the narrative or it is utterly fictitious. The significance of the narrative lies in its intended message; the later, larger version

halakhah, and of their belief in the divine endorsement of their own authority, as well as that of the Tannaim, to decree laws according to their interpretation of the Torah.

Further, the fact that the Y. T. redactors seem unaware of such traditions does not serve as evidence that they disagreed with the Babylonian redactors on this matter, as this would be nothing other than argumentation *ex silentio*. There are embellishments and additions in the B. T., but the relevant question is whether there is a conflict in the underlying ideology between the Y. T. and B. T. versions with respect to the issue under investigation.[36] There is no doubt that in our case above the Palestinian Sages believed they had divine authority to proclaim halakhot founded upon their interpretation of Scripture, exactly like their Babylonian peers. This is evident, for example, in Rabbi Ishmael's dictum in yQiddushin 1: 2, 59d, that in three instances the halakhah (that is, a rabbinic decision) dislodges Scripture. In yGittin 4: 1, 45c, there is a similar rhetorical declaration that rabbinic decrees uproot the Torah's commands.[37] The usually greater number of details in the B. T. narratives simply indicate more clearly the thoughts of the tradents and later redactors, and their understanding of the traditions received from their

---

is more pertinent to this point. The shorter Tosefta version may have had a narrower motive, that of linking the hermeneutic method and its rules to a charismatic personality such as Hillel. The later Amoraim, at a time when the wide range of exegetical methods was already commonplace and uncontroverted, wished to convey other messages, through their addition of details to the narrative. We thus have the opportunity to analyze the issues that concerned them. I have drawn attention to the possibility of different attitudes in the Y. T. and the B. T. versions regarding the tension between logic and tradition: chap. 1, n. 13.

36 We may pose the same question with respect to J. Rubenstein's perception (*Talmudic Stories*, p. 60) that the B. T. narrative was "interested not only in the legal process but in the human interactions that inhere in that process." The fact that the Y. T. version ignores this aspect, as Rubenstein asserts, does not indicate that the Y. T. authors and redactors opposed the rabbinic decrees, founded upon scriptural hermeneutics, which forbid a person to shame someone else. In mBava Metzi'a 4: 10, for instance, it is prohibited to shame a repentant person and a proselyte for their prior deeds. We also read in yHagigah 2: 1, 77c: המתכבד בקלון חבירו אין לו חלק לעולם הבא "One who enhances his own honour by shaming his neighbour has no part in the world to come." Rubenstein also notes that the Y. T. version ends optimistically with the forgiving of Rabbi Eliezer and the annulment of his excommunication, a fact that is missing in the B. T. This absence may indicate a difference in attitude. In the earlier period in which the Y. T. was redacted, there was no application of a fixed halakhah; in contrast, the Stammaim, the alleged redactors of the narrative in the B. T., were active in the period when the imposition of a fixed halakhah was already far advanced. This historical difference may explain the lenient attitude of the Y. T. versus the stricter approach of the B. T on the question of Rabbi Eliezer's excommunication.

37 These dicta are quoted and explained *in extenso* in section 1.4.

ideological forefathers; a shorter version, in other words, is not absolute evidence of enhanced authenticity.[38]

Nonetheless, I shall cite, where available, parallel sources from the two Talmudim and duly comment on occurrences in which these parallels seem to reflect different conceptions.[39] I believe that this method of citing from various sources, and emphasizing their similarities and differences, allows for a fairly reasonable deduction of the underlying rabbinic philosophy. Those instances in which B. T. citations have no parallels in other sources should not be deemed *a priori* the work of the later redactors. They may, in fact, represent much earlier thought, appropriately edited by later redactors, who believed themselves to be simply expressing the ideas of their predecessors.

---

38 P. Schäfer, "Johanan b. Zakkai und Jabneh," offers an example of the analysis of a narrative that exists in four different versions. It is not evident from his examination that the earlier and shorter versions are always the closest to historical truth.

39 The debate regarding the methodological approach to rabbinic documents, particularly with respect to the relationship between the various sources, and their evaluation on the redactional or source critical level, has been stimulated by two recent and notable books. S. J. D. Cohen has edited a collection of papers in *The Synoptic Problem in Rabbinic Literature*, and J. Rubenstein has published *Talmudic Stories: Narrative Art, Composition, and Culture*. It is not within the scope of this study to extensively review the various nuances regarding the problematic of the rabbinic texts; this has been efficiently done by Carol Bakhos in her review of Cohen and Rubenstein in *JBL* 120. I will simply cite several quotations that represent the general trend of these books, which is, as Bakhos notes, "to debunk the documentary hypothesis... espoused by Jacob Neusner" (ibid., p. 785). S.J.D. Cohen states (as quoted by Bakhos, ibid.): "Much of ancient rabbinic literature is as synoptic as Matthew, Mark, and Luke; because of their extensive parallels in structure, content, and wording, rabbinic texts should be 'seen together.'" Robert Goldenberg observes (as quoted by Bakhos, ibid. pp. 785-6) that there are "pre-existing materials that have been incorporated in the canonical documents M. T,Y, and B....The really creative minds in the early history of rabbinic Judaism were the authors of these ingredients, not the compilers who mechanically assembled them." Judith Hauptman's paper discusses, in particular, the relationship between Mishnah and Tosefta, but the following comment by Bakhos (ibid, p. 786) can serve as a paradigm, *mutatis mutandis*, to the relationship between other sources, as for example between Y.T. and B.T: "Paragraphs not found in the Tosefta, yet found in the Mishna, are not necessarily the creation of the redactor of the Mishna." Shamma Friedman (quoted by Bakhos, ibid. p. 787) maintains that "the edited parallel" model is more reliable "in providing a more realistic concept for talmudic literature"; the analysis of parallel sources fosters an understanding of the cultural context and its developmental stages. C. Hayes (as summarized in ibid. pp. 787, 788) proposes the application of both the documentary and source-critical approaches, a combination of synchronic and diachronic perspectives. Finally, the review notes that J. Rubenstein's work attempts to disclose the rabbinic cultural milieu from the analysis of six talmudic narratives. Bakhos (ibid. p. 791) rightfully questions the assumption that one may extrapolate an entire cultural context from six stories. I have attempted, on the other hand, to restrict my deductions from each narrative that I have cited to a particular element of rabbinic ideology, and believe that this is a responsible approach.

Furthermore, I believe that the Amoraim, in both Palestine and Babylon, understood better than we do the essence of the tannaitic pronouncements and their underlying philosophy. The Amoraim shared with the Tannaim a common theological perspective, the "prime mover" of their deliberations and conjectures. Our perception of the way that thought and circumstance interacted in ancient periods is powerfully shaped by contemporary opinions, which naturally differ, in some cases vastly, from the rationales applied by the Sages. The Amoraim were chronologically closer to the preceding generations of Sages than we are, and thus less likely to have been influenced by alterations in circumstances. They aspired to walk in the footsteps of their predecessors, and believed that in their own considerations and conclusions they were actually doing so. I therefore think that an analysis of their extensive literature, replete as it is with a great variety of rhetorical and narrative types, along with the more concise tannaitic utterances, constitutes an appropriate method to deduce patterns of ideology and conduct.[40] Historical development can be assessed either on the basis of the presumed chronological order of the sources that are cited, or, in their absence, through logical deduction of plausible patterns. On the basis of these patterns, it is then feasible to extrapolate the circumstances of earlier periods, for which we do not possess authentic data.[41]

The same consideration may be applied to the question of the connection between the Pharisees and the later Sages. As I shall argue in an Excursus, the latter perceived themselves ideologically as the followers of the Pharisees, and we can therefore deduce from an analysis of relevant rabbinic passages a plausible picture of the pre-70 halakhic environment. The political and social associations between the Pharisees and the later Sages, widely debated among scholars, are beyond the scope of this study; the diverse proposals on this topic are irrelevant to our focus on the

[40] J. Neusner, "Rabbinic Sources," attempts to understand and translate the Mishnah as an independent and coherent corpus. For the purpose, however, of researching the generation and unfolding of the law, it is appropriate to analyze the amoraic literature. The Amoraim assumed that the Mishnah was addressed to them; further, their understanding of the Mishnah was certainly closer to the intentions of the mishnaic redactors than our analyses of the Mishnah. If we exclude the amoraic attempts at harmonizing the Mishnah's inconsistencies and contradictions, I think we may grant a high degree of acuity to their understanding of the Mishnah. A synthesis, therefore, between an independent consideration of the Mishnah and the amoraic understanding of the Mishnah is necessary for a reliable analysis.

[41] D. Goodblatt, *The Monarchic Principle*, takes a similar approach to a comparable problem regarding the status of the Patriarchate in an earlier period; he declares (p. 132): "It is easiest to write the history of the Patriarchate backwards," because the most reliable evidence comes from the later period.

halakhic environment.[42] Though I use such terms as "Patriarch," "Sanhedrin," "Council," and "Academy" in this study, I make no claim that these institutions indeed existed in the relevant periods with the configurations and functions cited in rabbinic literature, or that they possessed any particular types of authority.[43] I use the terms in the same manner as they are used in rabbinic literature, since they represent the rabbinic view; as this study attempts to reveal the Sages' perceptions and beliefs, it must analyze both the style and content of their own sources.[44]

Main Topics of Study

I should like now to present an outline of the most significant (and in some cases unconventional) propositions of the study.

a) Halakhic Development

As stated, the foundation of my thesis is the existence of an open, tolerant and pluralistic halakhic environment in the pre-70 period, and an examination of this topic constitutes the current study. The movement toward institutionalization of a codex of law, and its imposition upon and diffusion among both public and private sectors, is necessarily a protracted process. This book portrays the developmental stages of Jewish law in the transition period from the pre-70 to the post- 70 period. I perceive three stages in this development, based on certain characteristics relevant to the institutionalization of the halakhah: the pre-70 period, the tannaitic period, and the amoraic era.[45]

In the first period there was no aspiration to establish a fixed halakhah. The people practised their religious and civil obligations according to their accustomed traditions; if new problems developed, or there was a lack of information, they approached their local Sage, an erudite person who delivered his decision according to the way he

---

42 See further arguments and a summary of scholarly deliberations in chap. 4, "Excursus: The Association between Pharisees and 'Rabbis.'"

43 See below, nn. 51 ff. and related text, on the term "authority" as utilized in this study.

44 See chap. 4, "Excursus: The Title and Authority of the Patriarch (Nasi) and the President of the Academy/Court (Av Beit Din)," for scholarly opinions on the issue of the Patriarchate.

45 J. Neusner, *Judaic Law*, p. 25 perceives three different stages: pre-70, 70 to 130, and 140 to 170. He bases this division on a different criterion than I have used; he attempts to reveal, from a historical perspective, which laws would likely have been debated and decided in each of the above periods. My study concentrates on the question of whether, at a given time, there existed either a pluralistic halakhic environment or an attempt to fix a unitary halakhah; my division into stages and their component phases is thus different.

understood the divine precepts of the Torah. Some of these *ad hoc* decisions that eventually became a permanent part of Israelite tradition remained anonymous; we know neither the names of their authors, nor the names of the Sages who declared opposing decisions in the same or in other localities.[46] None of the decisions were actively archived, either orally or in written form, to serve as precedents, and therefore the names of their authors were unimportant.[47] I perceive them as being at this stage a collection of *ad hoc* decisions on various subjects, rather than a methodically arranged "whole," like the Mishnah. For various reasons, some decisions were permanently accepted by the majority of the Israelite people, and became statutory; others, however, quickly entered into oblivion, likely because they were accepted solely within the restricted area of the Sage's activity, or were invalidated by later decisions.

One must assume that in the quest to correctly fulfill the Torah commands, many problems arose because of the gaps and inconsistencies in the text. In the absence of a central legal institution, each Sage, whatever his status or title, attempted to interpret the relevant scriptural commands as best he could according to his imagination and philosophical disposition. The Mishnah in fact records opposing traditions. These have their roots in the different decisions of the pre-70 period. Josephus' statement that the Pharisees were the most accurate interpreters of the laws (*J.W.* 2: 162) indicates the dynamism of halakhic decision-making in his period. As new problems required answers, the Pharisees continued to interpret Scripture in ways that were considered to be expressing the divine intention. This process can also be observed in the earlier period of Ezra and Nehemiah; the activities of these leaders may in fact have served as a paradigm to the later Sages. Though Scripture, for instance, does not

---

46 Though it is not within the scope of this essay to analyze J. Neusner's book *Judaic Law*, I would like for the sake of clarity to make two comments. Neusner attempts to demonstrate that disparate laws were practised among different groups. In contrast, I attempt to prove that even within the same group, as, for example, among the pharisaic element of Israelite society, one might find an array of diverse rules. This occurred as a result of differing decisions by the Sages, or by earlier authorities. Neusner's example of the marriage contract (ibid., p. 14) does not seem to me relevant for establishing the pattern of Judaic law. One must consider that marriage was not, and still is not - despite its later ritualization - considered a sacramental act, but simply a civil contract. Like deeds of sale and acquisition, its formalities were thus not religiously regulated. Over time, it became invested with a religious aspect, as all aspects of Israelite life became ritualized in the Mishnah. The Sages bestowed divine inspiration and Torah foundation even on their civil and financial rules, and consequently established exact ritual forms for every transaction, including the marriage contract. A comparison of fifth century B.C.E. Elephantine marriage contracts with second century C.E. rabbinic deeds seems to me inappropriate.

47 According to J. Neusner, *Purities, Part XXI*, p. 315, names were indicated when they were important, and omitted if of no significance.

prohibit trading on Sabbath, Nehemiah extended the restrictions against Sabbath work to include trade (Neh 13:17). In a similar spirit of extending the scriptural rules, marriage to any alien woman was prohibited (Ezra 10: 10-11, Neh 13: 23), and many more new rules were promulgated on the basis of a fluid interpretation of Scripture (Ezra 7: 6, 10).[48] The later Sages, we may note, considered Ezra equal in status to Moses (tSanhedrin 4: 7), as he taught the interpretation of the Torah to the Israelites.

In the second period, that of the Tannaim, Rabban Gamaliel the Patriarch initiated the movement toward a fixed halakhah, based on political motives. The identification of the authors of halakhic decisions became important, in order to establish the final halakhah as the pronouncement of one Tanna or another.[49] During the slow process of working out a system of a fixed halakhah, there was still much liberty for autonomous legislation. Allegedly rejected opinions were zealously memorized and archived for possible modification of previous decisions. The final halakhah was still not exclusively binding; the courts could still deliver judgments according to "accepted" or "rejected" halakhah, and the individual Israelite still had the liberty to judge which halakhic decision to accept and to conduct himself according to that decision.

In the third, amoraic, era, the trend toward fixed halakhah triumphed. Prior decisions were perceived as final and immutable. In consequence, legal creativity was constrained by the decisions of the previous generations, and the necessity of following the one and only fixed halakhah narrowed the freedom of the individual and his personal judgment.

b) The Nature and Implications of Rabbinic Authority

As stated above, we do not possess adequate data for the consideration of the halakhic environment in the pre-70 period, and I have therefore joined together the examination of the first two stages. Since the main goal in reviewing the developmental stages of Jewish law is to detect patterns of movement from a pluralistic *modus operandi* to a closed, restrictive and

---

48 See further on this issue section 2.1. This fluidity of decision-making is also evident, for instance, with respect to the procedure for raising funds for the building of the sanctuary, the performance of the sacrifices, and the remuneration of the clerics. Exod 25: 2 mentions simply that the people were encouraged to bring offerings for the construction of the Tabernacle. Solomon, in contrast, did not request donations for the building of the Temple; he conscripted labourers (1 Kgs 5: 27; 5: 13 in KJV) and financed the building of the Temple from the royal treasury. For the rebuilding of the Temple by Ezra, only some heads of families gave offerings (Ezra 2: 68), though the general population had the necessary means to do so (Hag 1: 4).

49 Rabbinic literature has not disclosed any consistent reasons for the establishment of disputed halakhot according to the opinion of one Sage or another. Reasons have been occasionally proffered, but without any effort to present them as rational and convincing solutions.

fixed halakhah, I have extended the investigation to the amoraic period. This afforded me the opportunity to elaborate on the dissimilar approaches of the Tannaim and the Amoraim; this difference had consequential implications for the subsequent development of Jewish law, as the Gemara, not the Mishnah, became the primary halakhic document.[50] We may note in particular the difference in attitude to the question of authority. This issue seems to me to be a fundamental element of the Sages' decision-making and interpretive activity, as I shall illustrate below.

I propose that the Sages believed that they had ample authority bestowed upon them by divine will[51] for the creation of new laws and the adaptation of prior rules to new circumstances; this activity, of course, took place within the broad boundaries of the Torah, the *Grundnorm* of Jewish law.[52] The Sages' credo of free choice, the antithesis of the Greek philosophy of predestination,[53] was the foundation of their authority to make decisions according to their understanding of the Torah. This belief in human freedom is embodied in the scriptural statement: "I have set before you blessings and curses. Now choose life [Deut 30: 19]," and was so perceived by the earlier and later Sages[54] and the traditional

---

50 See J. Roth, *Halakhic Process*, p. 174, n. 12. An examination of the succeeding stages of this development, as set out by Roth, is not essential for our purposes.

51 Deut 17: 10 - 11, and the relevant talmudic interpretations. See next note, and section 1.4.

52 The citation from Sifre and Midrash Tannaim (section 1.4) that "One must obey them [the judges] even when they tell you that left is right and right is left" - that is, even in the case of a blatantly erroneous decision - appears in a different form in yHorayot, 1:1, 45d. There it is stated that one need not obey when the judges' decision is manifestly wrong. Even this exception, however, does not affect their almost unrestricted authority; it is limited to an obviously false decision, such as a statement that left is right and right is left.

53 It is not within the scope of this study to elaborate upon Josephus' somewhat ambiguous portrayal of the pharisaic philosophy in this respect. His description of subtle philosophical matters, particularly when written for alien readers, is at times exaggerated, inconsistent, and sloppy. See in this respect: S. J. D. Cohen, *Josephus*. L. H. Vincent and A. M. Steve, *Jérusalem de l'Ancien Testament I*, p. 144, n. 2, write that Josephus' records are an "excellent approximation" of facts, but not of ideas. G. Baumbach, "The Sadducees in Josephus," p. 175, expresses major doubts "regarding Josephus' manner of presentation" of the question of predestination and free will.

54 We read in Sifre Deut 53: החיים והמות נתתי לפניך.. שמא יאמרו ישראל הואיל ונתן המקום לפנינו שני דרכים דרך חיים ודרך מות נלך באיזו מהם שנרצה תלמוד לומר ובחרת בחיים "'I have set before you life and death [Deut 30: 19]'...lest the people of Israel interpret [this to mean] since God has offered us two ways, the way of life and the way of death, let us go the way we wish, [the second part of the verse] teaches us: 'Now choose life.'" A similar homily appears in *Pirqe d'Rabbi Eliezer*, 15; there the reference is to a good way and a bad way. *Midrash Tanhuma, Pequde 3*, expresses this crucial rabbinic dictum differently. The

commentators.[55] They understood that the Torah was intentionally given in such a manner to grant humans the duty and privilege of interpreting it. They certainly did not perceive their authority as an infringement of the divine commands; nor did they critically analyze the divine rules.[56] They believed that the Torah and its underlying philosophy could be interpreted in different ways,[57] and God had bestowed upon them[58] the authority to define His will and intentions pragmatically[59] in any given historical circumstances and contingencies.[60] The flexibility of the law and its intrinsic faculty for adaptation is the logical and categorical consequence

---

deuteronomic verse is taken to affirm the predestination of humans in all respects, with one exception: אבל אם צדיק אם רשע לא אלא הדבר ההוא נתנו בידו של אדם בלבד "Whether one will be a villain or a righteous person is exclusively within the individual's power."

55 We read in Maimonides, *Mishneh Torah, Hilkhot Teshuvah* 5: 3: כלומר שהרשות בידכם וכל שיחפוץ האדם לעשות ממעשה בני האדם עושה בין טובים בין רעים "That is, you have the privilege, and whatever human acts a man desires to do, whether good ones or bad ones, he does."

56 By this phrase, I mean that the Sages did not apply unfavourable criticism. They carefully examined every apparent contradiction in Scripture, and harmonized such contradictions with suitable hermeneutics; they strongly believed that there could be no contradictions in the divine opus, and any apparent contradiction was simply a result of human inability to perceive correctly. See also R. Kasher, "Interpretation," p. 575 on this subject

57 We read in bQiddushin 20a: מכדי הני קראי איכא למידרשינהו לקולא ואיכא למידרשינהו לחומרא מאי חזית דדרשינהו לקולא נידרשינהו לחומרא "Since these [biblical] verses can be interpreted both in a lenient and in a strict way, why have you chosen to interpret them in a lenient way; let's interpret them in a strict way."

58 In bBava Metzi'a 59b we read Rabbi Yehoshua's pronouncement: לא בשמים היא "[The Torah] is [no longer] in heaven," and the divine consent: נצחוני בני "My children were victorious over me [defeated me]."

59 We read in Sifre Deut 122, yQiddushin 1: 2, 59d, and bSotah 16a: בשלשה מקומות הלכה עוקבת מקרא "In three instances [rabbinic] halakhah uproots Scripture." Examining the three laws, we may note that the Sages' alterations are not really an elimination of the scriptural regulations, but rather an adjustment, an extension of their intrinsic principles. The Torah states, for instance, that the blood of a slaughtered animal must be covered with earth .The Sages perceived the covering of the blood to be the core of the divine decree. They thus extended the definition of the incidentally-used term "earth" to include every other substance that could cover the blood. The other rabbinic rules are of similar character. In modern language, one might say that they did not read the sacred text in a "fundamentalist" manner. See further section 1.4 on the question of "uprooting Scripture."

60 The most notable proclamation on this topic is the homiletic interpretation of the verse עת לעשות לה' הפרו תורתך (Ps 119: 126) as implying "It is time to do the will of God, and for that, one may breach the law of the Torah" (mBerakhot 9: 5, yBerakhot 9: 5, 12d ,14c, 14d; bTemurah 14b; bGittin 60a; and other citations).

of the aforesaid philosophy, as well as a crucial element of the Sages' authority.

The Sages were at the same time "in authority" and "an authority."[61] The term "authority" as used in this study encompasses three concepts: a) The general idea of human authority to interpret the Torah. b) The Sages' authority, sanctioned by God, to correctly interpret the Torah - that is, they were "the" authority. (As I posit in the study, the Amoraim were reluctant to use this authority.) c) The voluntary consent of the Sages to accept a leader's authority (though sometimes, they opposed him). The study does not examine the political significance of this term - that is, whether the authority of the Sages and their courts was confirmed by the Romans, and whether the bulk of the Israelite community accepted the rabbinic halakhic decisions in their daily life with respect to ritual and economic issues.[62]

The cognizance that the Torah could be interpreted in many ways,[63] that it was not given in a final form but rather "in the making,"[64] to be appropriately interpreted by the Israelites, created a halakhic environment of tolerance and pluralism. The awareness of these circumstances, together with the humility of the Sages, averted the contingency of anyone declaring that he knew best[65] the ultimate divine will and intentions.[66] There was thus no exigency to establish one fixed halakhah; that, in fact, would be against the divine design,[67] and against the pronouncement by a Voice of Heaven (found in baraitot in yYevamot 1: 6, 3b and bEruvin

---

61 M. S. Berger, *Rabbinic Authority*, p. 153.

62 See D. Goodblatt, *The Monarchic Principle*, pp. 133 ff. on the practical legal powers of the Sages.

63 T. Frymer-Kensky, "The Emergence of Jewish Biblical Theologies," p. 114, calls it "the multivocality of the Bible."

64 We read in ySanhedrin 4: 2, 22a: אמר רבי ינאי אילו ניתנה התורה חתוכה לא היתה לרגל עמידה "Rabbi Yannai said: If the Torah had been given 'cut-off' [with every matter defined exactly], it could not have stood [i.e. it would have no operative effect]."

65 Avi Sagi, "Pluralism," p. 135, states: "There is a paramount difference between an approach arguing there is one halakhic truth, and one acknowledging a multiplicity of options."

66 The narratives concerning Sages who categorically opposed halakhic decisions, as we learn from the record of Rabbi Eliezer (see chap. 1, nn. 57 ff. and related text), refer to events from the post-70 period; it was then that efforts were undertaken, due to political motives, to abrogate this pluralistic attitude. These Sages were indeed resisting a radical deviation from existing practice.

67 Avi Sagi, "Pluralism," writes on p. 106: "The metaphysical status of God's word is pluralistic." He states further on p. 121: "Halakhic values do not reflect a fixed metaphysical order."

13b): אלו ואלו דברי אלהים חיים "Both [conflicting halakhic decisions] are the words of the living God]." [68]

Though I perceive a great difference in the attitude of the Tannaim and Amoraim with respect to authority, as I shall discuss in the study, I wish to emphasize here that the Amoraim too believed that the Torah could be interpreted in many ways, though they had no authority to interpret the text in opposition to the tannaitic way of reading. This can be observed in their deliberations, in the numerous instances in which they attempt to reveal the biblical sources of the tannaitic dicta in the Mishnah. In some cases the Amoraim assumed that the Tannaim deduced their conflicting decisions from different verses: "What is the foundation of their dispute? The [conflicting interpretation] of that verse." In other instances, we encounter a more complex debate with respect to a tannaitic conflict, as for example in bYoma 7b-8a, cited in the study.[69] I will quote here only an excerpt. The deliberation starts with Abbaye's assumption that Rabbi X deduced his opinion from a phrase of a particular scriptural verse, and that Rabbi Y derived his conflicting opinion from another phrase of the same verse. It is then asked: How does Rabbi X interpret the apparently opposing phrase, and the answer is: He deduces another halakhah from that phrase. Then the question turns to Rabbi Y: How does he interpret that phrase, and so on. This discussion and many like it confirm that the Amoraim were conscious of the multiplicity of different interpretations possible for the Torah texts, and had no theological or legal concerns about such contrary interpretations when rendered by the Tannaim; though they established the fixed halakhah, they never perceived the rejected opinions as erroneous or false. They did not, however, consider themselves competent to proffer any reading of the Torah text contrary to that assumed to have been at the foundation of the tannaitic dispute. The quest for fixing a definite halakhah almost completely reversed the acceptance of a many-sided reading of the Torah and led ultimately to the establishment of a single, authoritative reading.

The Sages did not perceive their rules to be additions to or subtractions from the divine commands, the *jus divinum*, but considered rather that they were inherent in the Torah.[70] This is the meaning of the

---

68 The above maxim appears in rabbinic literature in connection with a supposed dispute between members of the renowned schools of Beit Hillel and Beit Shammai. It also appears once in bGittin 6b in connection with another dispute.

69 Section 2.3.2.

70 We encounter a remarkably similar conception in Maimonides' *The Guide of the Perplexed*, book 2, chap. 29, regarding the apparent conflict between the supernatural occurrence of miracles and the immutable physical laws underlying the world's creation. Maimonides asserts that the omniscient Deity had already at the time of creation provided for such miracles to occur at the appropriate time.

apparently paradoxical pronouncement in yPe'ah 2: 4, 17a,[71] and bMegillah 19b: "God revealed to Moses the subtleties of the Torah, and those of the Scribes, and what the Scribes would originate." Such additions and subtractions are forbidden,[72] according to rabbinic interpretation of the biblical utterance: "See that you do all I command you; do not add to it or take away from it [Deut 13: 1; 12: 32 in KJV]."[73] They also asserted their authority to interpret scriptural utterances in a manner quite removed from the apparently simple meaning,[74] for the support of their legal pronouncements. Preserving in this way the formal shell of the scriptural declarations, and maintaining the appearance of acting according to the written Torah, they could justify their (at times exceptional) decisions.

The above statement leads us to the much debated issue of whether the halakhah was the product of presumably correct hermeneutics - מדרש

---

71 The text in yPe'ah 2: 4, 17a is slightly different, but evidences the same intent: אפילו מה שתלמיד וותיק עתיד להורות לפני רבו כבר נאמר למשה בסיני "Even what a proficient disciple would declare before his teacher was already recounted to Moses on Sinai." I have chosen the B. T. quotation as the more extended text.

72 It seems that the mediaeval commentators did not perceive significant rabbinic innovations as inherent in the divine decrees. The question of what type of rabbinic rule should be considered an addition therefore created a dilemma, upon which ensued conflicting debates; see J. Roth, *Halakhic Process*, pp. 157 ff. See also S. Z. Havlin, על החתימה הספרותית, pp. 163 ff. He cites a great array of later traditional commentators, who, through the use of a complex classification system, laboriously attempt to reconcile the obvious contradiction between the many rabbinic additions to and annulments of precepts and their own belief that such changes are prohibited. See my example of the rabbinic hermeneutic method that is used with respect to the far-fetched extensions of the meat and milk prohibition (section 2.5). It is plausible that the Sages considered it necessary to proclaim this extension a Torah decree, despite the unquestionable fact that it was a rabbinic conception, precisely to avoid the impression that it was a prohibited addition to a Torah command.

73 The Sages created from this verse two precepts: בל תגרע "do not take away [from the biblical decrees]" and בל תוסיף "do not add [to them]" (mZevahim 8: 10). The mandate not to cancel or diminish a precept is clear, and the rule not to add decrees was strengthened by the Sages with an appropriate homily on the concluding verse of Leviticus (27: 34); we read in in Sifra, *Behuqqotai* 8, yMegillah 1: 4, 70d, and bYoma 80a: אלה המצות שאין נביא רשאי לחדש דבר מעתה "'These are the commands [the Lord gave Moses on Mount Sinai for the Israelites],' and from now on not even a prophet may proclaim new commands."

74 We encounter a remarkable homily in bMenahot 29b recounting that Moses was present at a session in which Rabbi Aqiba presented his teaching to his pupils, and did not recognize Rabbi Aqiba's teaching as originating from the Torah given to Moses at Sinai. This event occurred in God's presence; God learned the Torah on that occasion according to Rabbi Aqiba's hermeneutic methods, and approved it, despite the fact that it was so far from the original utterances that Moses did not understand it (see also section 3.7).

יוצר "creative interpretation" - or the result of a prior ideological decision, subsequently supported or justified by appropriate hermeneutics - מדרש מקיים "integrative interpretation."[75] I take a definite stand on this issue, and declare that the Sages' decisions were founded mainly upon their own conceptual reflections, and that the subsequent hermeneutics served as justification: וקרא אסמכתא בעלמא "the scriptural verses serve only as support."[76] The only exceptions to this proceeding are the rabbinic declarations concerning the sacrificial celebrations. Since there were no practical considerations involved in these halakhot after the Temple's destruction and the abolition of sacrifice, these rules were founded exclusively upon hermeneutics.[77] In his recent study of the significance of ethical considerations in the Sages' halakhic hermeneutics,[78] M. Halbertal does not take a clear position on this issue, though the question is extremely significant for our understanding and evaluation of the entire rabbinic legal system. He does, however, implicitly substantiate my thesis through his simple exposition of the problem - that is, whether the Sages considered ethical values in their halakhic decisions. His assumption that their final judgments were influenced by such extrinsic principles,[79] rather than by appropriate interpretations of the text, conforms with my conclusion as well.

We observe, in fact, that the Sages decreed significant rules and regulations, both lenient and strict, based on external considerations, and then corroborated them through exegesis that was quite remote from the biblical text. Numerous citations in the study will substantiate this statement, and I wish to mention here only a few well known cases: the drastic mutation of the *lex talionis*, the use of "burning" without fire as a mode of execution, and the extension of the prohibition against cooking an animal in its mother's milk to preclude the consumption of any milk products with any meat products. Even if we assume that not all new decrees and changes were created with this method, it is evident that the

---

[75] This is the translation appearing in M. Elon, *Jewish Law, History, Sources, Principles*, vol. 1, p. 283.

[76] This is a common rabbinic declaration at the conclusion of deliberations in which the attempt to reveal the scriptural origin of a law has failed (see chap. 2, n. 129). The orthodox scholar Isaac Halevy, דורות הראשונים, vol. 5 pp. 234 ff., also takes the position that halakhot preceded midrash. He states that this is attested from the style of the tannaitic dicta in the Mishnah; these make it clear that their origin is not in scriptural hermeneutics, but in the basic study and inquiry of the Tannaim.

[77] In my remarks in the second part of the study, I observe the effect of these utterly theoretical conjectures.

[78] M. Halbertal, מהפכות.

[79] W.S. Green, "Biography," p. 79, writes: "The general principles behind [the rabbinic documents] are implicit and rarely spelled out."

Sages believed they had the authority to proceed in this way, and did unquestionably apply this method in many of their decisions. We must also consider the pluralistic attitudes of the Sages and their diversified opinions and ideologies in every aspect of their deliberations; this tolerance for opposing opinions[80] attests to their belief that they had the authority to declare a variety of decisions, with no one decision considered the most legitimate.

I include in the study an example of the rabbinic method of deliberation in the course of deciding a halakhah, with respect to the prohibition against cooking milk and meat together. This will offer the reader an insight into the discursive method used in the exposition of a halakhic decision, without taking a position as to whether the halakhah was founded upon the stated exegesis, or whether the latter served only as justification for a decision founded upon logical and pragmatic considerations. In my opinion, however, the fact that all the Sages involved in the discussion extended the specific biblical prohibition against cooking an animal in its mother's milk to all types of milk, claiming this to be a scriptural precept, indicates that this was an arbitrary decision. The decision could not have been based upon the proffered interpretations; these could serve only as "integrative interpretations."

The rabbinic perception of scriptural decrees in both their "legal" sense and their "common" sense[81] empowered them with extensive legal flexibility. This approach permitted them to maintain the formal framework of the law, and at the same time to modify its practical application. The original, divine laws were thus obeyed, and blatant disrespect toward them was avoided. The application of this legal fiction technique, and the deliberate lack of a restrictive system, were both crucial elements in the development of rabbinic legal procedure. The Sages throve in this environment, despite the obvious tensions and paradoxes. Flexibility, to the extent that it entails change to a prior state, is intrinsically antithetic to a conservative viewpoint that wishes to preserve the status quo. This latter state of mind is a cornerstone of every religion that is founded upon belief, and must have been a basic part of the Sages'

---

80 See H. H. Cohn, "Methodology," p. 129, heading "Fourth." We shall see (section 1.2) that the זקן ממרא, "the rebellious elder," may continue with his legislative pronouncements even when the halakhah is proclaimed against his opinion, and may also conduct himself in accordance with his own conclusions. We may also note Rabbi Yohanan's declaration that Beit Shammai continued to act according to their own convictions, despite the fact that the halakhah was established according to Beit Hillel (see further section 3.4). In my opinion, neither Beit Shammai nor the other Sages considered this a transgression of the law, because they were willing to consider that other conclusions might be correct.

81 See section 2.1.

theology. Moreover, we encounter in rabbinic literature[82] and practice[83] a strong tendency toward the glorification of previous generations. The Sages were able to counterbalance this fossilizing tendency by reevaluating the status of the contemporary Sages,[84] granting them the authority to alter earlier decisions[85] and to proclaim rules that seemed removed from, or even in conflict with, scriptural texts.

At times the Sages proclaimed decisions that apparently obliterated Torah precepts. What philosophical foundation granted them the legal authority to do so? Scripture does not indicate or even hint at any contingency that would permit the transgression of a divine command. On the other hand, the Torah was and still is perceived as the blueprint for a comprehensive way of life and behaviour for the Israelite people. Hence, the Torah must provide a system for resolving situations in which one precept appears to conflict with another one, or is incompatible with some condition of life. I present the proposition that the decision to override the Sabbath law in order to save human life, initiated by the Maccabees and subsequently developed by the Sages, was the source of a future hierarchic principle in the legal system - that is, that some precepts take priority over others in certain circumstances. This Sabbath law decision furnished the philosophical-theological foundation for the general idea of "overriding" in Jewish law, and permitted far-reaching adaptation. As is common, the Sages did not reveal the philosophical foundation of their legal decisions, but one must assume that they indeed based them on their preexisting ideologies, as argued above.

---

82 We read in yDemai 1: 1, 21d and yShegalim, 5: 1, 48d: אין הוון קדמאי בני מלאכים אנן בני נש ואין הוון בני נש אנן חמרין "If [we consider] the previous generations to be angels, we [may consider] ourselves humans; [but] if we consider them to be humans, we should consider ourselves donkeys." The same homily also appears in bShabbat 120b in Hebrew, and in Gen. Rab. 60: 8 in Aramaic.

83 I shall discuss in the study (sections 2.3.2 and 4.1.7) the practical consequences flowing from the distinction between the status of the Tannaim and that of the later Amoraim. We shall also note that decisions of Hillel and Shammai were rejected because of a conflicting tradition assumed to derive from the earlier Sages Shemayah and Abtalion (chap. 4, n. 74 and related text).

84 In Sifre Deut 153 and bRosh HaShanah 25b there is a homily on Eccl 7: 10, אל תאמר מה היה שהימים הראשונים היו טובים מאלה "Do not ask why the old days were better than these," interpreting the verse as referring to the status of contemporary judges. Another homily in mRosh HaShanah 2: 9 confirms the authority of all judges: שכל שלשה ושלשה שעמדו בית דין על ישראל הרי הוא כבית דינו של משה "[Exod 24: 9 comes to teach us] that every three appointed judges in Israel are equal [in their authority] to the court of Moses."

85 See the many feasible methods of legal change outlined in chap. 3, especially regarding repeal provisions in section 3.2.

The Sages could obviously not acknowledge the pragmatic motive behind the decision to override the Sabbath law, as recorded in 1 *Macc.* 2: 33 - 42 and *Ant.* 12: 274 - 276. The acknowledgment of such circumstances would constitute "reform," repudiating the belief in the immutability of the divine words of the Torah. It would also have utterly demolished the doctrine of the direct and continuous transmission[86] of all the Torah precepts and details from Sinai, a cornerstone of rabbinic authority. The Sages thus needed to derive a Torah support for overriding the Sabbath law. Mekilta d'Rabbi Ishmael, *Ki-tissa* 1 and bYoma 85a-b[87] record a question that was posed to a number of Tannaim: "Where do we get the idea [from the Torah] that the saving of a life [פקוח נפש] overrides the Sabbath?"[88] Seven answers are proffered; three are founded upon *ad majorem* considerations,[89] and three upon exegesis of apparently superfluous terms in biblical verses. The seventh proposition, confirmed by the talmudic redactor as the most reliable,[90] interprets a biblical verse in a way that enables the broadest application of the overriding principle to

86 See mAvot 1: 1.

87 This narrative, in a similar style and with some minor reversal of attributions, appears in both sources. The version in Mekilta, however, lacks the last (seventh) utterance, which is significant for my interpretation of this homily. This last homily appears in tShabbat 15: 17, in connection with the question asked and answered by Rabbi Yose (without any introductory narrative, as in B. T. and Mekilta), and was apparently pronounced by Rabbi Aha in the name of Rabbi Aqiba. It also appears anonymously in Sifra *Ahare* 9: 13, connected to a homily by Rabbi Ishmael; the latter deduces from it permission to worship idols when one is in a solitary environment, in order to save one's life. Hence, the homily on the phrase וחי בהם in Lev 18: 5, declaring that God's precepts were given לחיות בהן - that is (as I perceive it), for human benefit - appears already in the earlier sources such as Tosefta and Mekilta. The problem of assessing correct attributions and determining the occasions at which the various dicta were pronounced has no effect on the analysis of the narrative's underlying philosophy. The last utterance in the B.T., which grants preference to the overall proclamation that the divine laws are for human benefit, does not conflict with the philosophy of the antecedent utterances. In terms of literary style, the B.T. version is the best edited, containing all the relevant homilies that are scattered throughout many sources, as well as a conclusive judgment; for this reason, I have chosen this version for analysis. In an unpublished essay, I have demonstrated the various developmental stages of the edict decreeing the overriding of the Sabbath laws for the saving of life. As I illustrated in this essay, it is plausible that the last, conclusive utterance in the B. T. represents the decisive rabbinic decision on this topic, which served as a basis for further development by later commentators.

88 See further chap. 2, nn. 20-21 and related text; chap. 3, nn. 197-198 and related text; and chap. 4, n. 46.

89 These arguments are circular, and their frailty and superficial nature are obvious.

90 The editor quotes Raba's declaration: לכולהו אית להו פירכא בר מדשמואל דלית ליה פרכא "All [six] assumptions can be invalidated, except the one pronounced by Samuel [i.e. the seventh]."

preserve and enhance the quality of life: וחי בהם ולא שימות בהם "[It is written in Lev 18: 5: 'Keep my decrees and laws...] and live according to them,' and that teaches us not to die [by keeping] them."

The overriding formula is used explicitly in rabbinic literature with respect to Sabbath laws, allowing activities that would otherwise be a blatant transgression. Since this type of overriding was already perceived as an acknowledged phenomenon, it was relatively uncomplicated to allow the overriding of the Sabbath laws, even for the new custom of beating the willow branches on Sabbath.[91] I posit, however, that the philosophical essence of the overriding principle, once recognized, was the foundation of many other decisions. As we have just seen, the scriptural mandate in Lev 18: 5 "to live by them [the laws of the Torah]" - that is, to preserve life - stands in particular occurrences in opposition to the Sabbath restrictions; the Sages decided that saving life should have priority over the Sabbath laws, and the latter should therefore be overridden in appropriate cases. This universally acknowledged principle was further extended by later Sages, and a hierarchy of precepts developed. We encounter a remarkable example of this procedure in yShevi'it 4: 2, 35a and bSanhedrin 74a. There it is stated that saving life overrides all biblical precepts, except with respect to three rules that enjoy a higher status in the hierarchy of precepts.[92] The precise circumstances are then debated with respect to the conditions under which an exception is allowed to override the precept "to live by them."[93] We observe here that a ranking formula is

---

91 The dissident groups, who did not acknowledge the overriding principle, opposed the legalization of waging war on Sabbath, and the beating of the willow branches on Sabbath. We read in tSukkah 3: 1 and in bSukkah 43b that the Boethusians had concealed the willow branches brought into the Temple to be beaten on a Sabbath day, because: לפי שאין ביתסין מודין שחבוט ערבה דוחה את השבת "The Boethusians do not agree that the beating of the willow branches overrides the Sabbath [law that would otherwise prohibit such beating]."

92 I have chosen to translate the B. T. version, as its literary style is more appropriate for translation into English; there is no difference in the content of the two versions. We read in the B.T.: אם אומרין לאדם עבור כל עבירות שבתורה ואל תהרג יעבור ואל יהרג חוץ מעבודה זרה וגילוי עריות ושפיכות דמים "If one commands a person: Transgress all the laws of the Torah or you will be killed, he should transgress them and avoid his execution, with the exception of three instances: idolatry, prohibited sexual intercourse [such as incest or adultery] and killing [a person]."

93 We read there: ועבודה זרה לא והא תניא אמר רבי ישמעאל מנין שאם אמרו לו לאדם עבוד עבודה זרה ואל תהרג מנין שיעבוד ואל יהרג תלמוד לומר וחי בהם ולא שימות בהם יכול אפילו בפרהסיא תלמוד לומר ולא תחללו את שם קדשי ונקדשתי בתוך בני ישראל "[Above it was stated that the prohibition of idolatry is not overridden by the precept "to live"], but we have learned from Rabbi Ishmael: How do we know that if one is compelled to practise idolatry [in private] or be killed, he should practise it and avoid being killed? [This is learned from the verse] 'to live by them [and thus not to die by them].' Does this include [a

unmistakably applied in the process of reaching legal decisions; the discussions refer to the particular conditions under which another biblical precept[94] is perceived to have a higher status than the precept "to live by them."

This principle of overriding has the potential for almost unlimited application, within the broad boundaries of the general philosophy and norms of the Torah and the divine intentions expressed therein. The wide application of this principle is indicated in an exegesis of the verse עת לעשות לה׳ הפרו תורתך "It is time for you to act, O Lord, your law is being broken [Ps 119: 126]." In bGittin 60a[95] the verse was pragmatically interpreted to mean: "Since [the regular law] is impracticable in this case, 'It is time to act for God, they broke your law' [and thus we annul the application of the regular law]."[96] It can also be seen in the perceptions of particular Sages. An interesting example is Hillel's assertion that emptying the bowels and washing the body are precepts, since humans are created in God's image and are thus mandated to keep their bodies clean and in good condition.[97] The obligation to preserve the body, perceived in its widest possible meaning,[98] in fact constituted the implicit legal foundation of

---

case in which one is forced to practice idolatry] in public? [No] - because it is said [in Lev 22: 32] 'Do not profane my holy name. I must be acknowledged as holy by the Israelites.'"

94 The precept לא תחללו את שם קדשי ונקדשתי (see the previous note) enjoys a higher status in the hierarchy of precepts than the command "to live by them."

95 This homily also appears, with many variations, in mBerakhot 9: 5, yBerakhot, 9: 5, 12d, and 14d, bTemurah 14b, and other sources.

96 This overriding principle is applied explicitly in mBerakhot 9: 5 with respect to the rule allowing the mention of the divine name, originally prohibited in the Torah in the words לא תשא (Exod 20: 7, Deut 5: 11).

97 In Lev. Rab. 34: 3, we read the following pronouncement by Hillel: אמ׳ לו תלמידיו רבי להיכן אתה הולך א׳ להן לעשות מצוה אמרו לו וכי מה מצוה הלל עושה אמ׳ להן לרחוץ במרחץ... אמ׳ לו וזו היא מצוה אמ׳ להן אין "His disciples asked him: Rabbi, where are you going? He answered them: I am going to perform a precept. They said to him: What precept is Hillel performing? He answered them: To take a bath in the bathhouse...They asked him: Is that a precept; and he replied: Yes." Hillel compares his washing of the human body, created in God's image and likeness, to the attention paid to the statues of kings, which are cleaned, polished and decorated by those appointed for this duty; all the more so are we obligated to render such duty for the human body. The same narrative in ARN, Recension B, chap. 30 declares that Hillel performed all his deeds as divine precepts: וכל מעשיך יהיו לשם שמים כהלל "And all of your deeds should be for the sake of heaven, as Hillel practised."

98 A similar homily on Deut 4: 9 and 15 is encountered in a baraita quoted in bBerakhot 32b. The admonition to "take care and watch yourself" ("yourselves" in v. 15), lest one forget the Sinai revelation and God's commands and indulge in idolatry, is interpreted as a decree against risking one's life. A baraita quoted in bAvodah Zarah

certain halakhot that were apparently in conflict with the simple meaning of the biblical text.

Similar considerations, especially ethical ones, easily deducible from the spirit of the Torah,[99] have also influenced halakhic decisions,

---

12b lists as rabbinic prohibitions a number of dangerous practices, such as drinking uncovered water or water from sources that may have been contaminated, which might result in danger to one's life. The statement in yBerakhot 7: 5, 11c, השותה משקין מזוגין שעבר עליהן הלילה דמו בראשו "One who drinks a mixed beverage from the previous day is endangering himself," is less explicit regarding the character of such a deed. It is not clear whether this is only a rabbinic counsel against danger, or at the same time also a transgression of a decree. Although such a decree is not explicitly associated with a scriptural command, it seems that the Sages considered it as religiously inspired - that is, as an extension of a scriptural command and its intention. There is an interesting dictum in this regard in bAvodah Zarah 30a, after a discussion on boiled wine and wine mixed with water: אמר רבא הלכתא יין מזוג יש בו משום גילוי ויש בו משום יין נסך "Raba said: The halakhah regarding mixed wine is related to [the rule against drinking] uncovered wine, and to [the rule against drinking] wine used for libation to idols." Raba thus links together the definite prohibition against partaking of idolatrous libations with the interdiction against endangering oneself by drinking uncovered liquids; both restrictions are united in his pronouncement of the halakhah. He may have deduced this from the above-mentioned homily in bBerakhot 32b; he could also have deduced it from the scriptural command to build a parapet around the roof (Deut 22: 8), to prevent someone falling from the roof; the extension of this law would similarly be that one must avoid injuring oneself, as well as anyone else. Maimonides in his *Mishneh Torah, Hilkhot Rotze'ah Ushmirat Hanefesh* 11: 5, declares that one is punished for endangering oneself, and we must therefore assume that this amounts to a transgression of a religious decree. We read there: הרבה דברים אסרו חכמים מפני שיש בהם סכנת נפשות וכל העובר עליהן ואמר הריני מסכן בעצמי ומה לאחרים עלי בכך או איני מקפיד על כך מכין אותו מכת מרדות "The Sages prohibited many things because they are dangerous [and all their prohibitions are considered to be laws founded upon the Torah]; if one transgresses them saying: 'I endanger only myself, and what is it to others,' or 'I ignore such things,' he is punished with lashes."

99 The biblical editors emphasized the social laws and ethical obligations as divine precepts. Secular laws and humanitarian attitudes were thus sacralized. See A. Fitzpatrick-McKinley, *The Transformation of Torah*, pp. 32-5, for a concise review of E. Otto, *Rechtsbegründungen*. Otto perceives the theological motive of the phrase כי חנון אני "for I am merciful [Exod 22: 26]" as proclaiming that God has an "open ear for the complaints of his subjects." The Sages then amplified its scope. They stressed the commitment of *imitatio dei*, emulating the divine attribute of social responsibility. We read in yPe'ah, 1: 1,15b, bShabbat 133b and Mekilta d'Rabbi Ishmael, *Beshallah* 3: מה הוא חנון ורחום אף אתה היה חנון ורחום "As He is gracious and compassionate [Exod 34: 6, in reverse order], so should you be gracious and compassionate." A homily in bSotah 14a deduces the duty of emulating God from the words אחרי ה' אלהיכם תלכו "It is the Lord your God you must follow [literally 'go after Him']" in Deut. 13: 5 (v. 4 in KJV); as this is impossible to follow literally, since He is a consuming fire (Deut 4: 24), such imitation is expressed in socially motivated deeds, particularly charitable works.

implicitly and sometimes explicitly. Hillel has again given us an explicit example of the overriding principle in his renowned and innovative *prosbul* ordinance,[100] which invalidated a clear biblical decree that a loan must be forgiven in the seventh year. He decided that the biblical precept in Deut 15: 9, "Be careful not to harbour this wicked thought," overrides the precept to cancel debts in Deut 15: 1. It is not important for our purposes to contemplate whether Hillel's motive in overriding the debt-cancellation ordinance was motivated by his particular exegesis of the apparently conflicting verses, or by a conclusion that he must change the strict law because debt-cancellation would provoke great economic damage and personal distress.[101] What we note is the explicit use of this overriding procedure.

I suggest that we also see the implicit influence of the overriding principle in certain case histories discussed by M. Halbertal,[102] in his inquiry on ethical values as a constituent of rabbinic halakhic decisions. For instance, Halbertal cites[103] an alleged exegesis by anonymous elders of the scriptural phrase "for a woman in her monthly period [Lev. 15: 33],"[104] which concludes that a woman is forbidden to put on cosmetics during her period and the subsequent days of impurity, before her ritual cleansing bath. Rabbi Aqiba opposed this rule, arguing that such a harsh procedure would make the woman ugly in the eyes of her husband and he might divorce her.[105] He therefore allowed her to adorn herself. It is evident from this narrative that the "dispute"[106] is the result not of

---

100 See the text of mShevi'it 10: 3 and relevant discussion in chap. 2, nn. 151 ff. and related text.

101 I believe that Hillel's action constituted a rational response to contemporary social needs; we might perceive his response as quite "modern."

102 M. Halbertal, מהפכות.

103 Ibid., p. 16. This dispute appears, with slight differences, in Sifra, *Metzorah Zavim* 9, bShabbat 64b, and yGittin, 9: 8, 50d.

104 Exegesis interprets this to mean that the menstruating woman should be isolated, kept at a distance from her husband, by prohibiting her embellishment.

105 Rabbi Aqiba declares in mGittin 9: 10 that a man can divorce his wife if he finds a prettier one.

106 The unmistakable implication of this narrative is that an archaic custom (still alive in some societies, for example among the Ethiopian Fallashas) totally isolating the woman during her period was modified by Rabbi Aqiba; the modification may in fact have been simply attributed to him, as a highly revered personality, to enhance its acceptance against the opposition of conservative circles. Num. Rab. 10: 8 and ARN Recension A 2: 3-4, both late sources, still prohibited the woman from adorning herself during her menstrual period. Moreover, certain Sages (probably of the conservative sector) approved of the ancient custom of keeping the woman physically repulsive during her period. We read in these sources: כל המנולת עצמה בימי נדתה רוח חכמים נוחה הימנה וכל המקשטת עצמה בימי נדתה אין רוח

different exegeses of the biblical verse, but of utterly different approaches to a human problem. The rabbinic decree, aimed at avoiding a possible[107] transgression of prohibited sexual contact, was founded upon biblical exegesis;[108] Rabbi Aqiba's decision to override this rabbinic decree was founded upon a desire to avoid frivolous divorces.[109] (In my opinion, it is the Gemara, not Rabbi Aqiba, which asks how "the exegesis" of the relevant phrase is to be reconciled with the contrasting opinion, and then answers that the phrase means: "to remain impure until her ritual bath.") This example corroborates my thesis that rabbinic hermeneutics serve as a subsequent support for decisions adopted for other reasons[110] (i.e. "integrative interpretation"). It also confirms the use of the principle of overriding.

חכמים נוחה הימנה "The Sages appreciate the [woman] who disfigures herself during her menstrual period, and censure the woman who adorns herself during that time." There was no discussion between "the elders" and Rabbi Aqiba, and hence no dispute.

107 The prohibition against the woman making herself attractive, especially in the waiting period after the end of the actual menstruation, must be seen as the preventative "fence around the Torah"; this is a cornerstone of rabbinic legislation, founded upon the exegesis of Lev 18: 30: ושמרתם את משמרתי עשו משמרת למשמרתי "[It is written] 'keep my requirements' - [this means] make a guard for my commands [to ensure their accurate fulfillment]" (bMo'ed Qatan 5a and bYevamot 21a). On the issue of the "fence," see further section 4.1.7.

108 ARN Recension A, 2: 1-4 and Num. Rab. 10: 8 affirm this explicitly as a fence that the Torah itself specified in two distinct verses on the behaviour of the menstruating woman. The above-cited verse in Lev 15: 33 is interpreted as extending the prohibition against sexual intercourse to prohibit the woman washing her face or shading her eyes blue, and Lev 18: 19, ואל אשה בנדת טמאתה לא תקרב "Do not approach a woman during her uncleanness," is interpreted to add interdictions against embracing the woman, kissing her, conversing with her on frivolous matters, and sleeping with her clothed.

109 We do not know the motive behind Rabbi Aqiba's concern about potential divorces. It may have been intended as a counterbalance to his opinion that a man can divorce his wife if he found a prettier one (see n. 105 above). Whatever his motive may have been, he apparently perceived the avoidance of frivolous divorces to be a virtuous goal within the boundary and spirit of the Torah. He certainly might have interpreted mAvot 2: 12, וכל מעשיך יהיו לשם שמים "and all your deeds should be for the sake of heaven" more convincingly than Hillel, who perceived emptying his bowels to be a biblical precept. See above n. 97.

110 I wonder that Halbertal perceives this ordinance concerning the woman's behaviour during her period as the result of a מדרש יוצר a "creative interpretation" (מהפכות, p. 17), and the alleged "dispute" as having an exegetical basis. In view of the above-cited quotations and comments, I maintain that the opposite is obvious. Rabbi Aqiba's exegesis (if indeed it is his and not that of a later editor) constitutes a biblical justification for a predetermined decision, and is thus a מדרש מקיים, an "integrative interpretation."

Another of Halbertal's examples of value considerations in the halakhic decision process illustrates a further aspect of rabbinic legal philosophy. He cites a baraita, from an extended deliberation in bQiddushin 20a,[111] on the method of accounting to be used in calculating the redemption of a slave. The baraita decrees that one must always act in favour of the slave, even to the detriment of his owner. Although the rule is supported in the baraita by appropriate exegesis of biblical verses, it is evident that the decision was determined *a priori* according to the underlying philosophies of the various Sages involved, and then justified with rather frail hermeneutic supports. One Sage challenges the lenient (from the point of view of the slave) decision on the basis of the relevant exegesis, asserting that the biblical verse could be interpreted equally well in the opposite direction.[112] An answer is given that the Torah indicates a bias in favour of the slave; this is in turn supported by a far-fetched exegesis of another biblical verse. In the continuation of the deliberations, however, a bias to the disadvantage of the slave is suggested, again as the result of complex exegesis. This talmudic discussion serves as further confirmation of the thesis that exegesis served solely as a justification for decisions determined according to other motives - in this case, a particular philosophical attitude toward the slave.[113] The essential conflict between the opposing opinions does not depend on divergent exegeses of the quoted verses, but rather on different interpretations of the basic biblical attitude toward the slave. I presume that both ideologies reflected in this passage perceived the underlying philosophy of the Torah to be biased in favour of the destitute and oppressed; the point of contention is limited to a difference in the interpretation of this fundamental principle. One view considered this a fundamental principle that would allow no exception. The other view perceived that human intervention preventing the full

---

[111] מהפכות, p. 17. The relevant exegesis appears in yQiddushin, 1: 2, 59b, and in bQiddushin 20a. There is a lacuna here in MS Leiden of the Y. T. and I will therefore cite the B. T. version: נמכר במנה והשביח ועמד על מאתים מנין שאין מחשבין לו אלא מנה שנאמר מכסף מקנתו נמכר במאתים והכסיף ועמד על מנה מנין שאין מחשבין לו אלא מנה תלמוד לומר כפי שניו "If the slave was sold at a price of one hundred and at the time of his reacquiring his freedom his value went up to two hundred, he must repay only one hundred, because it is written '[he must pay] of the paid price [Lev 25: 51].' If he was sold at a price of two hundred, but at his redemption he is older and worth only one hundred, he must repay only one hundred, because it is written '[he must repay] according to the years [Lev 25: 52].'" The frailty of the logic is clear, and evidently being used to support a pre-existing rabbinic decision for the preferential treatment of the slave. The application of the same privileges to an impoverished person selling his inheritance is deduced in the Gemara by analogy to the slave.

[112] See this citation in n. 57.

[113] In this point I agree with Halbertal.

punishment of a sinner[114] would constitute an infringement upon the divine authority; the overall biblical approach toward the poor must therefore be overridden in this particular occurrence. Since the Sages did not reveal the philosophies underlying their different approaches, we are limited to speculating on what these were. Nonetheless, whatever the different philosophies were that motivated their attitudes, we can deduce that the overriding principle guided their basic legal approach. The rabbinic decision to favour the interest of the slave, and thus harm his owner, goes against the basic Torah law requiring equal treatment of rich and poor [115] and the inviolability of private property.[116] Hence a biblical support, however far-fetched, was necessary to put into effect the overriding principle and grant preference to one biblical precept over another.

The extended exegesis of the verse וחי בהם ולא שימות בהם, and its application in overriding the divine prohibition of work on Sabbath, might in this way have served as the biblical support for a number of lenient rules pertaining to "delicate persons." I believe that a thorough examination of rabbinic halakhic decisions will reveal that the overriding principle was the foundation of many halakhot that apparently conflict

---

114 The assumption behind this opinion in bQiddushin 20a is that the slave was brought to his "condition" because he had sinned by trading in produce grown in the *shemittah* year, and any amelioration of his treatment would constitute an infringement upon the divine authority.

115 We read in Exod 23: 3: ודל לא תהדר בריבו "and do not show favoritism to a poor man in his lawsuit." We note also the requirement to remain strictly impartial with respect to commercial transactions of all kinds, including dealings in real property. Lev 25: 15 - 17 admonishes the buyer and seller of land to be scrupulous in the accurate valuation of the years until Jubilee, when the land returns to its owner. There are no explicit provisions for either the seller's or the buyer's benefit; impartiality is required to avoid fraud. (One might perceive a slightly preferential treatment for the buyer, as, for instance, he could not be compelled to resell the property unless it remained in his use for at least two years). On the other hand, the distress sale by the impoverished countryman described in Lev 25: 25 - 28, in the same impartial style, which is based on a calculation with relation to the number of years in use, is interpreted differently in mArakhin 9: 2. There it is decreed that when the impoverished seller has the means to reacquire his property, he enjoys the same financial privilege as the slave does when acquiring his freedom. That is, if the value of the land has increased, he pays the old low price, and if it decreases, he pays the current low price.

116 We read in bGittin 36b: ומי איכא מידי דמדאורייתא לא משמטא שביעית ותקינו רבנן דתשמט "[Referring to a rabbinic decree for the forfeit of loans, which was not applicable according to the Torah, it is asked] Is there anything that is not forfeited according to the Torah law, and the Sages decreed it as forfeited?" This assertion indicates the acknowledgement of the principle that the Sages must not exercise their authority to cause financial losses to one party for the benefit of another, unless it is explicitly decreed in the Torah.

with biblical precepts, or rely on extremely far-fetched interpretations.[117] Disputes between Sages in such occurrences can therefore be perceived as different opinions about the hierarchy of biblical precepts - that is, which precept is deemed to be more significant according to one's perception of the philosophical foundations of Scripture.

The examination of Halbertal's study leads us finally to the topic of ethical considerations as a constituent of halakhic decisions - or, as he expresses it, the relation between law and morals and halakhah and morals. Though this topic is not within the primary scope of the study, it does offer a further perspective on the Sages' underlying philosphy regarding the halakhah. I suggest that Halbertal's division between law and morals and halakhah and morals is incorrect. I think that in rabbinic theology there is no such distinction; the halakhah is equivalent to the law. Further, there are no rules or guidelines for an Israelite outside the Torah, the divine blueprint of the world.[118] The dictum cited above, to the effect that additions to or decreases from the divine commands are prohibited, indicates the Torah's completeness and perfection, since God is perfect. Nothing can be added to the words of the omniscient Deity; humans have the obligation to study the Torah[119] and reveal[120] its intrinsic and comprehensive[121] directives. As I understand rabbinic philosophy from my reading of their texts, the correct ethical behaviour is to be inferred from

---

117 M. Halbertal, מהפכות, p. 21 perceives a division between the conscious and subconscious influence of ethical values in rabbinic halakhic decisions. I prefer to assume that the Sages were always conscious of their philosophical understanding of the Torah's intentions, which guided their decisions. They sometimes divulged them explicitly in the exegesis of biblical verses, as in the case of the slave's redemption, and in other cases did not reveal them.

118 We read in ARN Recension A, chap. 8, Addition b: חביבין ישר׳ שניתן להם כלי שבו נברא העולם ומה הוא כלי זה זו תורה שבה נברא העולם "The Israelites are favoured [by God] since a plan within which the world was created was given to them. And what is this plan? It is the Torah, the blueprint of the world's creation." A similar homily appears in Gen. Rab. 1: 1: כך היה הקב״ה מביט בתורה ובורא את העולם "Thus the Holy One, Blessed be He, studied the Torah and created the world."

119 We read in mAvot 2: 8 in the name of Rabban Yohanan ben Zakkai: אם למדת תורה הרבה אל תחזיק טובה לעצמך כי לכך נוצרת "Don't boast that you have amply pursued the study of the Torah, because that is the purpose for which you were created."

120 S. A. Handelman, *Interpretation*, p. 88, writes: "The text, for the Rabbis, is a continuous generator of meaning, which arises from the innate logic of the divine language."

121 We read in mAvot 5: 22: הפוך בה והפוך בה דכולה בה "Turn it [the Torah] and turn it again [study it intensely from all aspects] since everything is in it." Max Kadushin, who describes rabbinic concepts as "value concepts," writes in *Understanding the Rabbinic Mind*, p. X: "If Rabbinic Judaism is a criterion, religion and morality have a common, positive character."

the precepts in the Torah and from the divine acts,[122] and there is nothing beyond this.[123]

The scholarly debates in legal and philosophical circles on the relationship between morals and the law - particularly whether the law must be "just" or can be "unjust," both in theory and in application - do not apply, in my opinion, to Jewish law as the Sages perceived it. Deut 4: 8 emphasizes the uniqueness of Jewish law in this respect: "And what other nation is so great as to have such righteous decrees and laws as this body of laws I am setting before you today."[124] The fact that the Sages were both the legislators and the judges helped them to resolve any dilemmas that might arise when "formal" justice clashed with other ideals. They could easily maintain the formal principles, but redress possible hardships by appropriate modifications during the judgment proceedings. Hillel's judicial decision to change the status of someone born of a forbidden marriage[125] is one such example.

In contrast to some theories of secular law, morality is considered an essential element of Jewish law and an intrinsic constituent of the system.[126] The divine origin of Jewish law, and the heavenly surveillance that is deemed to ensure its accuracy in practice, enable the inclusion of moral obligations within the legal and judicial systems. Both such factors have limited, if any, application to the secular law.[127] A particular decree will demonstrate this point. The command in Lev 19: 16, לא תעמד על דם רעך, is vague and undefined. The NIV interprets this: "Do not do anything that endangers your neighbour's life"; the KJV translates:

---

122 As in the concept of *imitatio dei*; see the citation from yPe'ah, 1: 1, 15b, bShabbat 133b, and Mekilta d'Rabbi Ishmael, *Beshallah* 3 in n. 99.

123 Theological, metaphysical and ethical convictions all underlie this philosophy, as well as the general attitude that law reflects the will of the Sovereign (in this case, the Deity). See Dale Patrick, "Studying Biblical Law as a Humanities."

124 To ensure a perfect social and political organization, the law must be perfect. This can only be achieved through divine revelation (i.e. prophecy); human law cannot be perfect and all-encompassing.

125 See citation and explanation in chap. 2, nn. 160-162 and related text.

126 L. E. Newman, *Past Imperatives*, p. 56, states: "It seems that there is no distinction [between law and ethics in Judaism], they are one and the same, both are part of one seamless body of divine instruction, which as a whole constitutes God's revelation to Israel." Marvin Fox, "Maimonides and Aquinas on Natural Law," writes on p. 7: "In ancient Hebrew thought there is only one source of the knowledge of good and evil, the commandments of God as they are revealed to man." See also M. Elon, *Jewish Law*, vol. 1, pp. 142 ff.

127 See J. Bentham, *An Introduction to the Principles of Morals and Legislation*, pp. 285 ff., regarding the relations between private morality and legislation. He writes on p. 285 that although an individual ought to perform acts beneficial to the community of his own accord, the legislator ought not to compel him to do so in all cases.

"Neither shalt thou stand against the blood of thy neighbour." The LXX translates: οὐκ ἐπισυστήσῃ ἐφ' αἷμα τοῦ πλησίον σου "Do not gather against the blood of your neighbour." Sifra *Qedoshim* 2, in contrast, interprets this phrase as a positive obligation,[128] a command to rescue your neighbour from danger, even if you must the kill an aggressor in the process.[129] Such a broad obligation cannot be said to exist in secular law. The biblical verse ends with the maxim: "I am your God," emphasizing the uniqueness of this and similar commands: only God knows whether one really tried to save one's neighbour, or otherwise do what was required, and thus whether one is liable to punishment. Such an assessment cannot be made by a human court.[130]

Consequently, a method must be devised to resolve fairly a situation in which the moral principle underlying a law seems to conflict with its execution in practice. The overriding principle, the hierarchy of the decrees, was the method found suitable to bridge this "apparent" gap - "apparent" because in theory this gap does not exist, since the divine law is perfect. According to the Sages' *Weltanschauung*, the contradiction is apparent only to us, and it is our obligation to seek the true divine intention of the laws in order to resolve it.

---

128 This is not simply a voluntary, extra-legal recommendation to act לפנים משורת הדין "beyond the line of the law" - that is, to do more than the law requires. It is a positive precept, listed by Maimonides in his book of precepts, *Sefer HaMitzvot*, as number 297. It is included with those prohibitory laws the infraction of which invokes severe penalties. The transgressor, however, is not punished with lashes, because it is a passive infraction; see *Mishneh Torah, Hilkhot Rotze'ah Ushmirat Hanefesh* 1: 14.

129 We read there: ומנין שאם אתה יודע לו עדות אין אתה רשאי לשתוק עליה תלמוד לומר לא תעמוד על דם רעך ומנין אם ראית טובע בנהר או ליסטים באים עליו או חיה רעה באה עליו חייב אתה להצילו בנפשו תלמוד לומר לא תעמוד על דם רעך "And how do we know that if you are aware of evidence [that can save the life of a convicted person] you are not allowed to remain silent? We learn this from the verse 'do not stand against the blood of your neighbour.' And how do we know that you have an obligation to save somebody you see drowning, or attacked by robbers, or by a cruel beast, even at the cost of [the aggressor's] life? From '[do not stand against] the blood of your neighbour.' The homily also deduces from this verse the same obligation with respect to saving someone from a murderer or rapist.

130 There are a number of such commands in the same chapter, with respect to, for example, swearing falsely (v. 12); cursing the deaf or putting a stumbling block in front of the blind (v. 14); seeking revenge or bearing a grudge; and the commands to love one's neighbour (v. 18) and use honest measures (v. 36). The fulfillment or violation of these edicts can be determined only by God. The deaf person cannot hear whether he was blessed or cursed; one's neighbour does not know one's true feelings toward him, and can be easily misled by one's outward manner. Following these edicts there appears the exhortation: אני ה' "I am [your] God [i.e. I will know how you behaved]."

Thus, in the Sages' belief, there is no tension between justice and morality in Jewish law, since there is no division between these concepts in the divine law. Only laws framed by humans can be either just or unjust. A judge may be perceived to go beyond the "authoritative" text of the secular law in his or her decisions, by employing his or her own moral views to redress some deemed injustice in the application of the law. The rabbinic Sage, on the other hand, though acting similarly, perceived himself to be adhering faithfully to the divine rules and intentions. One may argue that the secular law is morally neutral, and in effect the resolution of apparent or real conflicts between the formal application of the law and a perceived injustice will depend on the judge's personal ideology. Jewish law is not morally neutral; it is ideology-dependent, based on the comprehensive rules and ethical values of the Torah. The Sages did not consider themselves to be modifying the unalterable scriptural doctrine, but rather to be interpreting the rules according to what they believed was the divine intention. They were at the same time both conservatives and reformers; they revered each and every letter of Scripture,[131] but still interpreted them. They believed that they were acting in accordance with the divine intention in holding that the law was given for the benefit of the people - according to the maxim וחי בהם "to live by them" - and not for the benefit of God.

The Context of the Study

This study is the first part of an extended work on Jewish society that examines the ultimate motive behind the creation of the "sects" in the period just prior to the destruction of the Second Temple. Since the start of critical examination of Israelite history, various scholars have attempted to detect the real motive for the split in Jewish society in the pre-70 period. A host of reasons were offered, generally dependent upon the personal approach of the author to social, political and religious problems, and tainted with contemporary political and social philosophies. J. Neusner offers an extensive list and critical examination of such essays,[132] and I may thus avoid enumerating and discussing them.

---

[131] Cf. J. Neusner, *Judaic Law*, p. 20, who asserts that the Mishnah's authors "have taken from Scripture what they chose," and decided "what they would simply ignore." My assumptions are quite the opposite. Taking the talionic law as one example, the Sages did not ignore the command עין תחת עין "an eye for an eye"; rather, they interpreted it and demonstrated that it must be understood as imposing pecuniary compensation (bBava Qamma 83b).

[132] J. Neusner, "Appendix: Bibliographical Reflections," in *Pharisees, Part I*, especially on pp. 326 ff.

It is a generally accepted premise that the disputes before 70 between the particular groups, or sects, were of a halakhic, and not of a theological, nature.[133] Having offered in this current work a detailed analysis of the pluralism that dominated the halakhic environment until relatively late, I shall go on in the second part of this work to study the circumstances that led, in spite of this pluralism, to the creation of the "sects" in the last period of the Second Temple. As suggested above, pluralism could not be and was not applied regarding the sacrificial cult issues.

Sources

I shall briefly note here the sources, translations and methods of citation that are used in this study. Biblical translations are taken from the NIV. All rabbinic citations are taken from the Bar-Ilan database. The translations of these texts are mine. Citations from the Septuagint are from the Göttingen edition, where available; again, the translations are mine. Citations from Philo and Josephus, and their translations, are taken from the Loeb Classical Library edition. Transliteration and abbreviation of the names of rabbinic and other works follow those used in the *SBL Manual of Style*, edd. P.H. Alexander et al. (Peabody, MA, 1999); names of Sages and places follow the spellings used in G. Stemberger, *Introduction to the Talmud and Midrash*, 2nd edition (1996). Transliterations are generally italicized, with the exceptions of frequently used words such as "halakhah," "baraita," "midrash," and "aggadah." Capitalization is used when referring to works as a whole; thus, for instance, "Mishnah" refers to the entire mishnaic corpus, while "mishnah" refers to a single law within that corpus.

To avoid encumbering those readers who are not overly familiar with the original Hebrew and Aramaic of the rabbinic citations, and to permit a logical flow of the arguments, I shall generally provide only an English translation of these citations in the text; the use of citations in their

133 See, e.g., A. J. Saldarini's deliberations with respect to the interaction between social and religious aspects in the pharisaic - sadducean struggle, in *Pharisees*, p. 370. I argue that there are no accusations in the literature of the "dissidents" or "separatists" (terms that I shall define in the second part of the study) that their opponents were guilty of heresy or wrong belief; rather, accusations refer to the incorrect interpretation of Torah precepts. We must contrast this attitude with the disputes between the general Jewish society and the Jewish Christians, which were of a theological nature. Although Josephus mentions philosophical differences between the Pharisees, Sadducees, and Essenes, there was a common theological denominator among them, that stood in contrast to the theology of the Christian Jews: they all believed that the meticulous fulfillment of the Torah precepts, the expression of the divine will, was their most important duty. There was not a corresponding common denominator of belief or practice within the definition of any other kind of Judaism.

original languages, with English translations, will for the most part be reserved for the footnotes. This will also save much time for the reader familiar with the original languages, who may then form his or her own opinion about the exactness and degree of objectivity of my translations. I will also occasionally repeat citations where they are used to support different propositions, thus avoiding the necessity for the reader to revert to prior sections.

The footnotes have also been used for detailed explanations of concepts contained in the rabbinic citations, especially for those that are not directly associated with the issues of the study, or absolutely necessary for the substantiation of my thesis. This is intended for the convenience of the inquisitive reader who would like to fully understand the theme behind the citation. I also believe that it is worthwhile to offer the reader who is not acquainted with the rabbinic style of contemplation and deliberation a small window on their methods of consideration and decision-making. I do hope that the readers of the "Studia Judaica" Series will appreciate this procedure, and indulge the resulting expansion of the study.

Endnote

Let me now, at the end of my Introduction, make some short personal statements. In a recent review of my last book, my "reconstruction of Israel's customs and laws" was assessed as follows: "His suggestions are interesting, but too often based on postulates in which historical plausibility tends to become assimilated with historical facts." I therefore take advantage of this occasion to assert that I did not declare my assumptions and conjectures to be certitudes. I emphasized their character as hypotheses, but at the same time strove to substantiate them by inferences from textual and other sources, and attempted to present them as "more plausible" than other conjectures. I reiterate this position with respect to the present study. I may quote here a statement of P. R. Davies[134] that knowledge "is a conclusion which data, method and reasoning have led us to assert as knowledge."

Although I attempted to shape my study as objectively as possible, I realize that my construction of the Sages' thoughts and intentions, a fundamental element of my general thesis, is based on my interpretation of rabbinic citations. Others may reach different conclusions from the same sources. I may quote here an avowal of H. D. Preuss:[135] "Each effort to set forth an overview carries with it some of the personal idiosyncracies or peculiarities of the author. This means that the present investigation

[134] P. R. Davies, *Scribes and Schools*, p. 1.

[135] H. D. Preuss, *Old Testament Ideology*, p. 1.

contains my own peculiarities and weaknesses and reflects both the character and the limits of my knowledge." I must similarly acknowledge that my investigation and conclusion are imbued with and driven by the current *Weltanschauung*, the product of our contemporary culture. Common opinion, however, acknowledges that history is always written from the standpoint of the present - that is, what is at present considered important. Finally, I recognize that some of my postulates may be considered controversial, out of line with generally recognized opinion. To justify such a daring step, I wish to quote from a study by L. L. Grabbe. He declares: "There is nothing more dangerous to good scholarship than the comfortable consensus which lies unchallenged...questioning the consensus can only be salutary...." He concludes: "We need to take account of all sources and possibilities."[136]

[136] L. L. Grabbe, "4QMMT and Second Temple Jewish Society," p. 89.

1. The Tension between Tradition and Interpretation

It is my conviction that until the destruction of the Second Temple, the biblical texts and commands were interpreted[1] by competent intellectuals, both individually or as part of a group. Their interpretations were based on their understanding of the texts[2] and of the general principle, the *Grundnorm*,[3] of the Torah, as well as their awareness of the necessity of adapting the traditional rules and customs to actual circumstances. The requirements dictated by contemporary political and economic conditions guided their considerations and decisions. They did not intend, however, to override the divine commands, or grant priority to human interests above them; they simply assumed that their decisions complied with the divine will. The Sages interpreted scriptural utterances in such a way as to connect the primeval divine intention to the specific conclusions they now reached in the current circumstances. Their intensive study of the Torah, and their quest to reveal its concealed messages[4] and manifold rationales, induced them to believe both that they understood the ultimate divine will

---

1 There are many scholarly debates on the question of whether the halakhah was derived by means of tradition or hermeneutics; several of these scholarly views will be discussed in section 2.2.

2 We encounter a relevant homily in yMegillah 1:1, 70a: נאמר כאן דברי שלום ואמת ונאמר להלן אמת קנה ואל תמכור הרי היא כאמיתה של תורה...מה זו ניתנה להידרש אף זו ניתנה להידרש "It is said here [Esth 9: 30], 'Words of goodwill and truth [assurance]' and it is said there [Prov 23: 23], 'Buy the truth and do not sell it.' [This comes to teach us] that the Megillah is as truthful as the Torah…just as the Torah was given to be interpreted, so was the Megillah."

3 In modern language we would say that the "Law" consists of norms of universally accepted principles, and each judge decides its application in each particular case. The Sages perceived themselves as having the same liberty of decision with respect to the norms of the universal divine "Law." J. Roth, *Halakhic Process*, p. 9 calls this divine law the *Grundnorm* (a term used by the legal positivist Kelsen), stating that the Sages considered themselves to be its sole legitimate interpreters.

4 מקרא אחד יוצא כמה טעמים "From one verse many rationales are derived [bSanhedrin 34a]." The maxim is cited there in the name of the school of Rabbi Ishmael. I have not found precisely the same homily in the Y. T; given, however, the many declarations in both Talmudim that שניהן מקרא אחד דרשו "both [Tannaim] have deduced [their conflicting decisions] from [the exegesis of] the same biblical verse," it is evident that this maxim reflects a commonly-held rabbinic opinion.

expressed in the Torah,[5] God's word, and that God had granted them authority to interpret the Torah according to their own perception of its rationales.[6]

There is an interesting assertion in this respect, cited in the name of Rabbi, in Sifre Deut 135 (and in a slightly different literary style in a baraita in bHagigah 18a), regarding the problem of establishing the different types of work prohibited on the full-festival days and half-festival days. The rhetorical deliberation concludes: "Did not Scripture transmit this [Deut. 16: 8] to the Sages to tell you on which days it is prohibited to work, and on which it is permitted, what type of work is prohibited and what type is permitted?"

We may compare the attitude expressed here to the contemporary attitude of orthodox Jews, who follow the rabbinic proclamations in all aspects of life, even with respect to political issues. The Sages were deemed to possess דעת תורה,[7] a thorough comprehension of the Torah, which gave divine instruction in all ways of life, and hence they were able to determine the divine intention in all matters. This legitimacy and authority allowed the Sages to change or override tradition by granting

---

5 E. S. Rosenthal, מסורת הלכה, p. 322, cites a narrative from bEruvin 13b: תלמיד היה לו לרבי מאיר וסומכוס שמו שהיה אומר על כל דבר ודבר של טומאה ארבעים ושמונה טעמי טומאה ועל כל דבר ודבר של טהרה ארבעים ושמונה טעמי טהרה "Rabbi Meir had a disciple, whose name was Sumchus, who brought up forty-eight rationales [for declaring] any polluted item polluted, and forty-eight rationales [for declaring] any pure item pure." This declaration demonstrates the importance attached to perceiving the rationale for every halakhah; one who is competent knows not only the laws decreed in Torah and Mishnah, but also the rationalization of the lawgivers.

6 See Z. Safrai and A. Sagi, סמכות, pp. 10 ff., for an extended deliberation on the different Jewish opinions concerning the source of this authority. Three possible sources are discussed: the Sages' expert insight, divine command, or the people's fundamental consent to obey the Sages. I doubt whether the Sages had in mind the requirement of prior consent, a modern Hegelian concept. They acknowledged public acceptance in a different way, declaring: אין גוזרין גזירה על הצבור אא״כ רוב צבור יכולין לעמוד בה "One does not promulgate an edict that the majority of the people cannot maintain" (tSotah 15: 10), and nullifying edicts which were not accepted by the majority. We read in yAvodah Zarah 2: 7, 41d, and in a slightly different literary style in bAvodah Zarah 36a, that Rabbi invalidated a prior decree prohibiting the use of oil produced by gentiles, because: בדקו ומצאו בגזירתו של שמן ולא מצאו שקיבלו רוב הציבור עליהן "[The Sages] investigated the prohibition against [the use of gentile] oil and did not find that most of the people acceded to it." See further section 3.2.

7 This concept appears in bHullin 90b. The traditional commentator Metzudat David interprets the phrase ודעת אלהים "the knowledge of God" in Prov 2: 5 as הם רזי התורה "they are the secrets of the Torah."

priority to their own creative interpretation of biblical commands, whenever they deemed it necessary for the attainment of greater goals.[8]

A significant detail of the well-known narrative in yPesahim 6: 1, 33a and bPesahim 66a, concerning the issue of whether the performance of the Passover sacrifice overrides the Sabbath, illustrates this point.[9] The Bene Bathyra, leading scholars in Judah, had "forgotten" this specific rule, and asked Hillel whether he knew the correct law by tradition. They had approached him because of his credentials: "since he was a disciple of the two great scholars Shemayah and Abtalion." Hillel disregarded their particular question, and instead based his answer on logical considerations and exegetical rules. He thus emphasized the validity of using the rationale behind the law as an authoritative method for the establishment of halakhah.

I would go further in the analysis of this remarkable narrative and stress the tension that is evident between the two legitimate methods, tradition[10] and creative interpretation, for the establishment of halakhah.[11]

---

8 See sections 2.3.2 and 4.1.7 regarding the different attitudes of the Tannaim and the Amoraim toward the extent of their authority, and their tolerance of contrary opinions. Professor M.D. Herr brought my attention to a certain tension in rabbinic homilies regarding the relationship between the Torah, the divine utterance, and the Sages' function. We may note, in particular, Rabbi Yehoshua's declaration in in yMo'ed Qatan 3: 1, 81d, and bBava Metzi'a 59b, during the renowned dispute between Rabbi Eliezer and the Sages, that the Torah is no longer in heaven, and God's utterance in bMenahot 29b, when Moses did not understand a teaching of Rabbi Aqiba, that it was a halakhah given to Moses from Sinai. Both passages imply that the Sages had the authority to interpret the Torah, which was given to humankind at Sinai. We encounter a more radical attitude in Num. Rab. 19: 7 and Pesiqta d'Rav Kahana 4: בשעה שעלה לשמי מרום שמע קולו של הקב"ה יושב ועוסק בפרשת פרה ואומ' הלכה משם אומרה "When [Moses] came to heaven, he listened to the voice of God studying the pericope of the [Red] Heifer, uttering the [relevant] halakhah in the name of the one who declared it [Rabbi Eliezer in mParah 1: 1]." One may deduce that the author of this homily intended to go a step further, alleging that God studies the rabbinic declarations and determines the halakhot according to their utterances. This homily is of late origin, and I doubt whether this particular attitude was, in reality, the foundation of the rabbinic philosophy with respect to their authority. Such homilies were intended to enhance rabbinic authority and confirm the divine endorsement of rabbinic decisions. The various forms of these narratives reflect the creative imagination of their authors, rather than distinct philosophies.

9 E. S. Rosenthal, מסורת הלכה, p. 327, notes this detail.

10 "Tradition" has different interpretations in Jewish law, as we shall see in section 1.2. A particular behaviour may be perceived as a tradition because prior generations acted in this way; "tradition" may also refer to something received by the oral chain of transmission throughout the generations from Sinai, or from the transmission of a decision by an earlier Sage. All these variations appear in this study. See also the discussion in section 1.6.1 of the ambiguity surrounding the term שמועה.

11 Cf. D. Daube, "Rabbinic Methods of Interpretation and Hellenistic Rhetoric," who

Although the Bene Bathyra asked Hillel for the tradition and he based his answer on his personal logic, they accepted his reply with much enthusiasm: "They immediately seated him at the head [of the table] and nominated him as their Patriarch; and he taught them the halakhot of Passover the whole day."[12] In the next passage, however, we encounter a drastic shift in the tone of Hillel's discourse: "He said to them: What was the reason for my coming from Babylon and my nomination as your Patriarch? Because of your laziness, you did not learn from the two great scholars Shemayah and Abtalion." But Hillel did not formulate his answer on the tradition known by these scholars, and hence his teasing of the Bene Bathyra was unfounded.

I suggest that Hillel, or more likely the redactor of the narrative, intended to confirm by the second part of the story the equivalent validity of tradition in establishing halakhah, in contrast to the purport of the first episode. Hillel was asked how to proceed if one had forgotten to bring the knife for the slaughter of the Passover sacrifice before Sabbath, as it is forbidden to carry anything in public on Sabbath. In contrast to the previous question, the Bene Bathyra did not ask him whether he knew the halakhah on the basis of tradition; yet he answered: "I have heard this halakhah [by tradition], but forgot it." In this case, he did not try to establish the halakhah through logical consideration, as in the first instance, but emphasized the significance of the tradition. Further, to emphasize its importance and extend its practical application, he advised the Bene Bathyra to observe the actual practice, or tradition, of the people. The passage ends on a startling statement: "He observed the [people's] practice, and remembered the halakhah, saying: That is what I learned by tradition from Shemayah and Abtalion." Hillel not only bestowed legitimacy on the people's traditional practice, but also equated it in authority to rabbinic tradition. The authenticity of the story and its many details is obviously a matter of great doubt,[13] but its significance is its

---

perceives in this narrative a contest between pharisaic reliance on tradition and the logical interpretation of Scripture affirmed by the Sadducees. Hillel maintained that traditional decisions were all logical. Regarding the issue of whether the halakhah is founded upon interpretation, or only supported by it, see section 2.2.

12 I have quoted primarily from the B.T. version of this citation, for the reasons explained in the Introduction. The parallel text in yPesahim 6: 1, 33a, has a slightly different literary style, but expresses exactly the same idea.

13 A shortened version appears in tPesahim 4: 13-14, which presents only Hillel's decision and legal justification with respect to the rules of the Passover sacrifice on Sabbath. At its conclusion, the narrative simply adds that later the same day, Hillel was appointed Nasi (Patriarch) and taught the Bene Bathyra the relevant halakhot. This version does not lend itself to an assessment of the motives behind the narrative, as does the B. T. version. Yet another version of this narrative appears in yPesahim 6: 1, 33a. In addition to minor alterations, this passage indicates that the Bene Bathyra did not accept Hillel's decision founded upon his logical considerations, until he told

implicit message: the importance of, and tension between, the two foundations of halakhah, tradition and interpretation. In fact, we may remark that in many occurrences the tension is that between the decisions of previous generations of Sages, which have attained the standing of tradition, and the contrary opinions of contemporary Sages.[14]

1. 1. The Unity of Written and Oral Torah

In the traditional view, the basis of the Israelite legal system is the conviction that the Torah was given in its totality by God on Mount Sinai. Both the written and the oral Torah are integral elements of the divine law, and are equally revered. There is a famous story regarding a gentile who came for conversion (bShabbat 31a, among other sources[15]), which demonstrates their equivalence: "There was the report of a gentile who came before Shammai [with the intent to convert to Judaism] and asked him: How many Torot do you have? And he replied: Two, the written Torah and the oral Torah."[16] We read in Sifra *Behar* 1[17] a passage

---

them: כך שמעתי משמעי׳ ואבטליון "I heard it thus from Shemayah and Abtalion." They then nominated him as Patriarch because of this transmitted knowledge that he possessed. It seems that the editor of this passage in the Y. T. granted more importance to tradition, and did not acknowledge the authority of a Sage to formulate halakhah founded upon his own logic. This fact demonstrates the tension between the two principles, but we shall see in our further deliberations that this constricting, "fundamentalist" opinion was not the common practice in the development of halakhah; the "liberal" attitude of creative interpretation gained the upper hand. The entire story is clouded with doubt: is it possible that both Hillel and other leaders of Judah "forgot" the halakhah on an issue - the implications of the eve of Passover falling on the Sabbath - that one supposes must have arisen quite often? A. Kaminka, "Hillel's Life and Work," has expressed his amazement at this report, since any priest in Jerusalem "could have testified with certainty" as to how such a situation was to be resolved. D. Goodblatt, *The Monarchic Principle*, pp. 185 - 186 quotes a number of scholarly opinions on the authenticity of the narrative (mainly in connection with his examination regarding Hillel's appointment as Nasi), noting (p. 186) Neusner's general declaration that "it is unlikely that the source contains 'a shred of historically usable information.'" Cf. D. Instone Brewer, *Techniques*, p. 47, who writes: "Hillel's dispute is historically believable."

14 M. S. Berger, *Rabbinic Authority*, writes on p. 154: The authority of the talmudic Sages for one generation is transformed generations later into the authority of Jewish tradition."

15 ARN, Recension A, chap. 15, and Recension B, chap. 29.

16 This notion is expressed in different sources, in various styles. We read in Sifra *Behuqqotai* 2: מלמד ששתי תורות ניתנו להם לישראל אחד בכתב ואחד בעל פה "We learn [from the exegesis of a biblical verse] that two Torot were given to Israel, one written and one oral." In Sifre Num. 351, we read: שאל אגניטוס הגמון את רבן גמליאל אמר לו כמה תורות ניתנו לישראל אמר לו שתים אחת בפה

affirming that those rules that are missing in the written Torah nonetheless originate from the Sinaitic revelation: "Were not all the precepts stated at Sinai? But [the text in question teaches that] just as all the rules and all the specific minutiae of the sabbatical year were stated at Sinai [the Sinai revelation], so the specific minutiae of all precepts were stated at Sinai."[18] In yPe'ah 1: 1, 17a, it is in fact asserted that the oral Torah is even more cherished by God than the written Torah:

> Rabbi Haggai [said] in the name of Rabbi Samuel son of Nahman: Oral and written precepts were uttered and we do not know which are more cherished, but from the verse [Exod 34: 27] "for in accordance with these words I have made a

ואחת בכתב "Antigonos the chief asked Rabban Gamaliel [the Patriarch]: How many Torot were given to Israel? He answered him: Two, one oral and one written." In Midrash Tannaim to Deut 33: 10 a similar question is posed by Agrippa to Rabban Yohanan ben Zakkai and the same answer given. Regarding the identification of the Roman official and the authenticity of the narratives that record the same event with two different names, see M. D. Herr, "Dialogues," and P. Schäfer, *Studien*, pp. 181 - 183.

17 A similar but shorter pronouncement appears in Sifra *Tzav* 11. In bHagigah 6a, bSotah 37b and bZevahim 115b, a baraita is cited concerning a dispute between two Tannaim: דתניא רבי ישמעאל אומר כללות נאמרו בסיני ופרטות באהל מועד ורבי עקיבא אומר כללות ופרטות נאמרו בסיני ונשנו באהל מועד ונשתלשו בערבות מואב "We have learned in a baraita: Rabbi Ishmael says: The principle rules were pronounced at Sinai and the details [told to Moses] in the Tent of Meeting. Rabbi Aqiba says: The principle rules and the details were pronounced at Sinai, repeated in the Tent of Meeting and repeated a third time at the Plains of Moab." In yPe'ah 2: 4, 17a, and yHagigah 1: 8, 76d we read: שהרי כמה הלכות נאמרו למשה מסיני וכולהן משוקעות במשנה "Indeed, how many were the halakhot that were declared to Moses at Sinai, and all are incorporated in the Mishnah." This last citation contains in effect the same notion as the more extended citations from the other sources.

18 M. D. Herr, *Encyclopedia Judaica*, s.v. "Oral Law," p. 1440, suggests that the oral law existed before the written law. This is certainly true of a variety of traditions practised by the people, similar to the Greek νόμοι ἄγραφοι, which were put into writing at a certain period of sophistication or institutionalization of prevailing customs. Some of these customs were preserved in the Torah in the spontaneous and unrefined form in which they were practised at the time, and others were preserved without any precise details, since they were not institutionalized and not uniformly performed by all the people. The oral Torah as perceived by the Sages, however, referred to the complex minutiae of all the biblical commands and prohibitions. Their records of the oral Torah comprised both customs originating from earlier traditions and other rules that they devised and perfected, or altered for practical reasons. From the legal point of view, we could compare the Torah to the Roman Twelve Tables that constituted a written composition of prevailing customs, rather than a legal codex. The collection of all the enacted laws and their details was published only by Justinian in the 6th century C.E. in the *Corpus Iuris Civilis*.

covenant with you and with Israel," we know that the oral precepts are more cherished.[19]

The belief that all the minute elements of the oral Torah, applicable to all circumstances and for all time, were transmitted from generation to generation of scholars and religious leaders, is affirmed in the first mishnah of Avot,[20] whose entire text I shall quote below (note 84). But this axiom came blatantly into conflict with the facts of everyday life; disputes were inevitable, and a multitude of different opinions and decisions by the various Sages proliferated. Various rationales were devised to explain these disputes, upon which I shall elaborate in due course.

In particular, this apparent inconsistency[21] with the idea that all rules were determined at Sinai could be reconciled through the sophisticated perspective set out above, that the Sages were deemed to comprehend the ultimate divine will expressed in the Torah, and therefore all their decisions were considered to originate within the confines of God's utterances to Moses. I suspect that a great number of Sages perceived their privilege to interpret the Torah in this way; anchored in this belief, they

---

19 Another midrash emphasizes the advantage bestowed by the oral Torah in separating the Israelites from the gentiles in the Diaspora. We read in Exod. Rab. 47: 1: אלא המקרא אני נותן להם במכתב והמשנה והתלמוד והאגדה אני נותן להם על פה שאם יבואו עובדי כוכבים וישתעבדו בהם יהיו מובדלים מהם "The *miqrah* [Bible] I give them in writing, and the Mishnah, the Talmud and the Aggadah I give them orally, so that when they are in captivity among the gentiles, they will be segregated from them [because the Israelites will live according to the rules of the oral Torah and the gentiles will conduct themselves differently; though they would obviously be able to know Scripture, they would not know the particulars of the oral Torah]." In yPe'ah 2: 4, 17a, a homily on Hos 8: 12 (כמו זר נחשבו "...they regarded them as something alien") declares the same idea in another way: מה בינן לאומות אלו מוציאין ספריהן ואלו מוציאין ספריהן אילו מוציאין דפתריהן ואילו מוציאין דפתריהן. "What [creates the distinction] between them [Israelites] and the other peoples? They bring out their books and they [the others] bring out their books; they bring out their notes and they [the others] bring out their notes...."

20 J. Neusner, *Purities, Part XXI*, p. 326, writes: "The authority of the Mishna, laid down in Aboth, Mishna's first and most compelling apologetic, is that the authority of Mishna rests upon its status as received tradition from God."

21 A. Rosenthal, תורה , pp. 467 ff., draws attention to another inconsistency regarding this issue. Rabbinic law requires the recitation of a benediction before studying the Torah, praising God for giving the Torah to us. Rabbinic literature records a dispute regarding whether the same benediction must also be pronounced before the study of Mishnah, Talmud and Midrash. We observe that although it is declared that God gave both the written and the oral Torah at Sinai - which would comprise all these works - there is still doubt as to whether one may categorically declare this in a benediction.

were granted the freedom of opinion to express their own perceptions of the divine intent. As we shall see, the maxim "Both [opinions] are the words of the living God [yYevamot 1: 6, 3b, bEruvin 13b, and many other occurrences],"[22] offered the philosophical foundation for this course of action.[23]

1.2 The Reverence for Tradition

It is well known that tradition is the basis of much law; at certain points in time, political and spiritual leaders formalize the existing traditions into precise legal formulae. Israelite law has an additional dimension: what the Sages considered to have been received by transmission, either from the divine communication to Moses at Sinai, or from Sages of previous generations. When the Sages formalized these traditions into law, they may also have incorporated new laws, whether assimilated from other cultures (after appropriate adaptation to the Israelite monotheistic faith and history), or from their own creative imaginations. (See definition below, p. 56.) These "new" laws may have been presented as the outcome of the leaders' benevolence and concern for the orderly life of their people, or as the result of divine inspiration. In any event, the laws were characterized as something for the advantage of the

---

[22] The "Voice of Heaven" proclaimed this paradoxical dictum, so that though the halakhah is declared to be in accordance with the opinion of Beit Hillel, the opposing opinion of Beit Shammai is likewise to be perceived as God's word.

[23] Certain fundamentalists, as we would call them today, were probably not content with such a subtle adjustment, and came up with a more definite solution: a great number of instructions given to Moses were forgotten. We read in bTemurah 15b: והאמר רב יהודה אמר שמואל שלשת אלפים הלכות נשתכחו בימי אבלו של משה דאישתכח לדו אישתכח ודגמירן להו הוו גמירי כמשה רבינו "Did not Rav Yehudah say in the name of Samuel that three thousand laws were forgotten during the period of mourning for Moses? [Answer:] What they forgot, they forgot, but whatever they transmitted by tradition corresponded to Moses' teaching." The term גמירי represents here the process of determining decrees and rules on the basis of tradition, conveyed from generation to generation from Moses at Sinai. It must be noted, however, that the deliberations of the Sages who tried to understand the declarations of their predecessors on a broader basis were erroneously associated with the same term. The discussions of the Amoraim and their deliberations on the rules of the Mishnah are thus popularly known under the name of גמרא and appear under this name in the printed editions of the Talmud. I use the term Gemara to refer to situations in which a question is asked and answered in the Talmud without attributions. I do not intend to enter into a discussion as to the author or authors of the סתמא in the Talmud, as I do not think this question is of direct relevance to the specific issues of this study.

people, as we read in Deut 4: 6: "Observe them carefully, for this will show your wisdom and understanding to the nations, who will hear about these decrees and say 'Surely this great nation is a wise and understanding people,'" and in Deut 5: 30 (v. 33 in KJV): "Walk in all the way that the Lord your God has commanded you so that you may live and prosper...."

The formulation of the laws in Israel was not different than in any other ancient society, and the first codification of the law consisted of a more or less systematic collection of existing traditions and customs. No leader could have imposed an entire code of conduct on a people that was in opposition to its deep-rooted traditions.[24] Tradition remained a crucial element of the Israelite legal system in all its developmental stages. The rabbinic declaration that all tradition stems from Sinai,[25] that is, from

---

[24] A midrash that confirms this point is found in Mekilta d'Rabbi Ishmael *Yitro* 5, and Sifre Deut 343 with slightly different wording. The Mekilta states: נגלה על בני עשו הרשע ואמר להם מקבלים אתם עליכ׳ את התורה אמרו מה כתיב בה אמר להם לא תרצח אמרו לו זו היא ירושה שהורישנו אבינו שנאמר ועל חרבך תחיה נגלה על בני עמון ומואב אמר להם מקבלים אתם את התורה אמרו לו מה כתוב בה אמר להם לא תנאף אמרו לו כלנו מניאוף דכתיב ותהרין שתי בנות לוט מאביהם והיאך נקבלה נגלה על בני ישמעאל אמר להם מקבלים אתם עליכם את התורה אמרו לו מה כתוב בה אמר להם אל תגנוב אמרו לו בזו הברכה נתברך אבינו דכתיב והוא יהיה פרא אדם וכתיב כי גנב גנבתי וכשבא אצל ישראל מימינו אש דת למו פתחו כלם פיהם ואמרו כל אשר דבר ה׳ נעשה ונשמע וכן הוא אומר עמד וימודד ארץ ראה ויתר גוים "[God] revealed himself to the children of Esau the wicked and asked them: Do you accept the Torah? They asked: What is written in it? He answered: You shall not murder. They said to Him: [We cannot accept it] since this is our legacy from our ancestor, as it is said: 'You will live by the sword [Gen 27: 40].' [So] He revealed himself to the children of Ammon and Moab and asked them: Do you accept the Torah? They asked: What is written in it? He answered them: You shall not commit adultery. They said to Him: [We cannot accept it] since we all originate from an adulterous relationship, as it is written: 'So both of Lot's daughters became pregnant by their father [Gen 19: 36]' and how could we accept the Torah? [God] revealed himself to the children of Ishmael and asked them: Do you accept the Torah? They asked: What is written in it? He answered: You shall not steal. They said to Him: [We cannot accept it] since this is the blessing our father was blessed with, as it is written: 'And he will be a wild man [Gen 16: 12],' and it is written further: 'For indeed I was stolen away [by the Ishmaelites] [Gen 40: 15].' And when [God] came to the Israelites, '...from his right hand a fiery law for them...[Deut 33: 2],' all opened their mouths and said; 'We will do everything the Lord has said [Exod 19: 8].' And it is also said: 'He stood and measured the earth; He beheld and drove asunder the nations [Hab 3: 6].'" This midrash suggests that even the Deity could not impose laws that were in conflict with a people's legacies and traditions.

[25] Maimonides, in the Introduction to his Mishnah commentary, offers a vivid and imaginative portrayal of the manner of transmission of the oral Torah by Moses. The ingenuity of this outstanding scholar and philosopher is remarkable. He writes (free translation from Hebrew edition of J. Kapah, vol. 1, pp. א-ב): "God gave the Torah

divine origin, obviously enhanced its significance and impact on legal decision-making.

The significance of tradition, and its supremacy in disputes over the use of factual arguments or purely logical deductions, is emphatically stressed in mEduyyot 1: 3. The subject of this passage is the quantity of drawn water that makes a ritual bath unfit. Hillel and Shammai dispute the minimum quantity that effects this disqualification, but the mishnah then states: "But the Sages say: [The halakhah] is neither according to the one nor according to the other. [The decision seems to have been postponed] until two weavers from the Dung Gate of Jerusalem came and testified in the name of Shemayah and Abtalion that three *login* of drawn water make the ritual bath unfit, and the Sages confirmed their testimony [and declared this to be the halakhah]."[26] In tEduyyot 1: 3 the message of our mishnah is

---

to Moses together with its interpretation and explanation of all that was included within the sophisticated Scriptures. This was his method of teaching it to Israel: Aaron entered first into his tent and Moses taught him the Torah and its interpretation; afterwards, he remained seated at his right side. Then Aaron's sons Eleazar and Itamar came in and he taught them the Torah, as he had tutored Aaron; one sat at Moses' left side and the other sat at Aaron's right side. Then the seventy elders entered and they were taught by Moses in the same way as Aaron and his sons. Then the mass of people entered who desired to know the divine teaching, and Moses taught them so that all should hear [directly] from him." Maimonides then goes on to work out the statistics: Aaron heard the Torah from Moses four times, his sons three times, the elders twice, and the masses once. Then Moses left [the tent] and Aaron taught the remaining community and left; then his sons taught them and left; then the elders taught and left. Thus, everyone heard the Torah four times.

26 It is beyond the scope of this study to elaborate upon the many issues raised by this mishnah, which are discussed by the traditional commentators and scholars. The mishnah does not indicate the underlying motive of the dispute. We do not know, for example, whether Hillel and Shammai had different notions with respect to the factual issue of the maximum quantity of a substance (drawn water, in this case) that could be absorbed by spring water without altering its nature. Such types of argument are also found, for instance, in the concept of בטל בששים, the question of whether one egg of an impure bird cooked together with sixty pure eggs renders the whole lot inedible (bHullin 97b), and questions regarding other mixtures of different quantities of pure and impure substances. On the other hand, it is possible that both Hillel and Shammai had different traditions regarding the quantity of drawn water that makes the ritual bath unfit, and the Sages preferred the earlier tradition reported in the name of Shemayah and Abtalion. The Ra'abad in his commentary to the Mishnah takes a different approach, and follows the talmudic method of attributing every dissent to different interpretations of biblical verses and expressions. He argues that Hillel proposed a *hin* as an adequate quantity, because Scripture indicates this as a measure: ושמן זית הין (Exod 30: 24); Shammai argued for nine *kav*, because it is the minimum quantity of water needed for the purification of a man who has a nocturnal emission; while the Sages decided the minimum quantity was three *login*, a quarter of a *hin*, the quantity of the libation for the perpetual daily *tamid* offering (ונסכו רביעית ההין in Num 28: 7). This is quite an inventive proposition, but I do not believe that it was the core of the dispute. It is also remarkable that though Hillel

even more emphatic: "Why did it mention there [in the testimony of the mishnah] their [the weavers'] location and occupation? Since there is no more humiliating occupation than weaving[27] and no more disreputable location in Jerusalem than the Dung Gate. Therefore [this teaches us that] the Fathers of the World [the most illustrious teachers] did not impose their opinion in opposition to tradition; all the more so should any man [not] affirm his opinion in conflict with tradition."[28] The juxtaposition of the opinions of the great scholars Hillel and Shammai with the testimony of the lowest class of weavers emphasizes the absolute dominance of tradition.[29]

---

and Shammai were disciples of Shemayah and Abtalion and had received the tradition from them (as is clearly emphasized in the classic transmission statement in mAvot 1: 12: הלל ושמאי קבלו מהם "Hillel and Shammai received from them [Shemayah and Abtalion]"), they did not in this case have the correct tradition from their teachers; only the two humble weavers knew the exact tradition. The issue is still more complex because the mishnah quotes Hillel as using the term *hin*, the exact word of his teacher, instead of the commonly used three *kav*, (the identical quantity), and that indicates that his declaration was indeed founded upon his teacher's utterance. Another oddity is the fact that according to a narrative in bShabbat 15a: בשלשה מקומות נחלקו שמאי והלל "Shammai and Hillel disputed [only] on three issues" (see further on this issue section 3.4). (In yHagigah 2: 2, 77d, the same point is made in an indirect manner: בראשונה לא היתה מחלוקת בישראל אלא על הסמיכה בלבד ועמדו שמאי והלל ועשו אותן ד "Originally there was only one dispute in Israel, regarding the laying of hands [on the offering]; [but then] Shammai and Hillel made it four [that is, by their additional three disputes].") The Gemara confirms that this statement refers to the three topics cited in the first three mishnayot of Eduyyot; thus the two famous Sages did dispute only on three issues, and in all three cases, the halakhah is not decided according to either of their opinions. We may assume, therefore, that the message of the three mishnayot in Eduyyot was to emphasize the significance of tradition, and to highlight the tension between tradition and a contrary minority opinion. The authenticity of the minutiae of these mishnayot was not the main interest of the redactor, and thus the mishnayot could be presented in a manner that reflected their message rather than their historical accuracy.

27 This term is usually translated as "weavers"; for instance, Ch. Albeck, ששה סדרי משנה, סדר נזיקין, translates אורגים. I think, however, that in this case it should be understood as "scrapers," a lowly task included within the process of weaving, from the root גרד (as in Job 2: 8).

28 See section 4.1.5, regarding the difference between an anonymous tradition and an identifiable one.

29 There is no logical method for establishing the quantity of unsuitable water that spoils the ritual cleansing bath; this is established by tradition. On the other hand, the minimum quantity of water required for the bath is established through logical consideration. We read in Sifra *Metzorah* 3 and bEruvin 4b: מים שכל גופו עולה בהן וכמה הן אמה על אמה ברום שלש אמות ושיערו חכמים מי מקוה ארבעים סאה "[It is written in Lev 15: 16 'he must bathe his whole body with water; this means] his entire body should be immersed in water, and how much is

Further evidence is found in tSanhedrin 7: 2, which outlines the procedure for establishing the halakhah in cases of dispute between an individual and the majority; here, too, the supremacy of tradition is evident:

> [If] one [of the judges] says: [I have based my opinion] on a tradition, and all the others say: We do not possess this tradition, they do not vote [it seems that in this case the halakhah is established according to the tradition reported by the individual judge].[30] But when one [judge] prohibits and another authorizes, one declares [something] polluted and another [considers it] pure, and all declare that they have no tradition for this specific case, then a vote is taken. When one Sage has a tradition from two sources and two have a conflicting tradition from one source, the tradition from two sources overrides the tradition from one source.

We observe that tradition overrides even the opinion of the majority,[31] and not even a vote was necessary to approve a law based on tradition.

---

that? [A volume of] one cubit square and three cubits in height, and the Sages assessed that forty *se'ah* [of water would fill this volume]." This dictum explains mMenahot 12: 4: כל מדות חכמים כן בארבעים סאה הוא טובל בארבעים סאה חסר קרטוב אינו יכול לטבול בהן "All the dimensions [established by] the Sages [are standards]: One may bathe in [a receptacle containing] forty *se'ah*, and must not bathe in forty *se'ah* less a pinch." We observe that logic was a consequential factor in the Sages' decision, as long as it did not conflict with Torah or tradition as they perceived it. See further on this mishnah chap. 2, n. 142.

30 A dictum in yKetubbot 4: 12, 29b apparently conflicts with the concept of the predominance of tradition: אמר ליה אנא אמרי שמועה ואת אמרת מתניתא תבטל שמועה מיקמי מתניתא "He said to him: I based my declaration upon a tradition and you based yours upon a mishnah, let the opinion based upon tradition be suppressed by the one based on the mishnah." The traditional commentators explain that in this specific occurrence the term שמועה does not refer to tradition but to a pronouncement of Rav Hisda. The passage thus affirms that his opinion should be overridden by a baraita of Rabbi Hiyya; a tannaitic baraita takes precedence over a declaration by an Amora, according to the general maxim that an Amora cannot oppose a tannaitic declaration. On the other hand, the passage may indicate a conflicting opinion on this issue, as on many others, expressed within the "pluralistic" environment of the Talmud.

31 The text of this Tosefta passage originates from the Zuckermandel edition, but there are other manuscripts with altered texts, and commentators have attempted to effect emendations to render the text comprehensible. Because of these inconsistencies in the text, it is difficult to interpret the first phrase: "When one says: [I have based my opinion] on a tradition, and all the others say: We do not possess this tradition, they do not vote." What is the opinion of the others? Do some have a conflicting opinion, or no opinion at all? The verification of this fact is crucial for the correct understanding of this dictum. I consider the phrase to mean that the others do have diversified opinions, but founded upon their own reasoning, and not upon tradition. The same phrase לא שמענו in the subsequent instance must be interpreted in this way, and it would be logical to assume that the editor intended them to be equal; the

Although I do not wish to enter into a general discussion of the philosophical aspects of rabbinic theology, I think it is nonetheless important to emphasize this elemental principle of that theology: human logic is overridden by tradition. This is not to say that logic was not used by the Sages as a source of law, or that tradition could not be appropriately interpreted and adjusted to reconcile it with logic. Logic was a significant and valuable element, but only so long as it could be fit within the framework of tradition. The question of whether, and to what extent, it was appropriate to divulge to the public the influence of logical considerations on the Sages' deliberations, is another matter. Josephus, for example, states that the Pharisees were guided in their decisions by λόγος,[32] a term of indeterminate meaning. It is a matter of dispute as to whether the λόγος that guided the Pharisees represents reason or doctrine.

The validity of tradition as against logical deduction is also corroborated by a passage addressing the law of the זקן ממרא, the "rebellious elder." The Sages interpreted the biblical pericope in Deut 17: 8 - 14, "If there arise a matter too hard to judge...," as referring to a dispute between scholars and a "rebellious elder" who does not accept the decision of the Jerusalem court. The punishment in such a case is death: "that man shall die."[33] Nonetheless, we read in bSanhedrin 88a:

> If one says: [I have declared my decision on the basis of] a tradition, and others say: We have a [conflicting] tradition, then he is not liable for the death penalty. When he says [I have declared my decision on the basis of] a logical deduction, and they say: We have a [conflicting] logical inference, he is not liable for the death penalty; and all the more so when he says: [I have declared my decision on the basis of] a tradition, and they say: We have a [conflicting] logical deduction, he is not liable for the death penalty. Only when he says: [I have declared my decision on the basis of] a logical deduction, and they say: We have a [conflicting] tradition, [is he liable to the death penalty].

We observe here that disputes between two conflicting traditions, or between opposing logical deductions, are legitimate; only the opposing of logic to tradition is rigorously condemned. It must be noted, however, that the "majority rule," to be discussed further below, also plays a role in the formulation of this decision, and thus we cannot deduce from this case the absolute supremacy of tradition over logic in all instances. As we have seen above, tension is thus created in the application of the law; and ways

---

second parts of both instances are thus equal, and only the first part is determinative with respect to the requirement to take a vote. According to this passage of Tosefta, therefore, a tradition quoted by one person overrides the opinions of others founded upon their own considerations.

32 *Ant.* 18: 12. I revert to this issue in the second part of this work, regarding the distinct attitudes of the Pharisees and Sadducees toward halakhah.

33 See further on this subject section 2.3.1.

must be devised to reconcile between tradition and interpretation,[34] without invalidating the primary principle of the supremacy of the divine commands. Thus the Sages' fundamental philosophy with respect to human authority to modify the divine law is grounded in a paradoxical approach. A polar tension exists between two axioms: "Were not all the precepts communicated at Sinai...with all their particulars" (Sifra *Behar* 1[35]), and "The entire Torah was also interpreted by the Rabbis" (bYevamot 21a),[36] which indicates just the opposite.[37]

At this point it would be well to point out another difficulty: what exactly is meant by "tradition"?[38] We do not know when Torah rules, other than in matters of ceremonial and public concern, were institutionalized. It is plausible that people adhered to the main biblical decrees in an indefinite way, as they are portrayed in Scripture, and each individual or small community filled in the missing details, as they considered appropriate. Such a process is common, especially in the early development of a legal system,[39] and we can deduce its presence in Israelite society simply from the lack of details with respect to a great number of scriptural laws.

Traditional scholars, on the other hand, assume that established customs have existed from time immemorial, and therefore Scripture had no need to indicate them. They proffer as an example the topic of

---

34 It is also possible that apparently contradictory declarations with respect to the supremacy of tradition versus logic stem from different Sages professing conflicting opinions. We shall examine in section 1.3 the value placed on the broad independence of each Sage to express his personal convictions within the pluralistic environment of early rabbinic society.

35 See n. 17 for the entire text of this declaration as well as a list of other sources.

36 I have not found an exact parallel to this declaration in the Y. T., but there is a passage that in my opinion expresses the same basic idea. A dispute is noted in Mekilta d'Rabbi Simeon b. Yohai, 23: 15: ולא יראו פני ריקם אפלו כל שהוא וחכמים אומרין אין פחות לעולת ראיה ממעה כסף ולחגיגה שתי כסף "[It is written in Exod 34: 20] 'No one is to appear before me empty-handed' [and that means one may bring] even something trivial; but the Sages say: The minimum value of the pilgrimage burnt-offering is one *ma'ah* and of the holiday offering two silver coins." In a rhetorical deliberation on this declaration in yPe'ah, 1: 1, 15a, it is asked: How is this possible? The answer is: ויש כן זו "Indeed, it is so [regarding other issues]"; subsequently it is stated that the Sages established such details for all the biblical precepts.

37 See E. S. Rosenthal, מסורת הלכה, p. 351.

38 See also the discussion of terminology in section 1.6.1.

39 O. Kaiser, *Einleitung in das Alte Testament*, p. 67 emphasizes the distinction between *Gesetzbuch*, "a book of jurisprudence," and *Rechtsbuch*, "a book of laws." The first represents a codex, a system of laws, and the second constitutes a collection of existing laws. He perceives Scripture as a collection of both existing laws and traditions and ideals of what ought to be.

divorce,[40] for which there are no procedural details in Scripture, alleging that such details must always have existed. I would postulate that there was only a fixed rule to write a divorce document, as is written in Deut 24: 1: "He writes her a certificate of divorce, gives it to her and sends her from his house." The exact form and text of this "certificate" were left open, and each man wrote what he considered appropriate. It seems, for instance, that even in later times the mention of the wife's name was a matter of debate. We read in mGittin 9: 3: "The core of the divorce document is: You are free to marry everyone," while in mGittin 4: 2 we read: "And Rabban Gamaliel the Elder has decreed that he [the man] should write his name and every surname he has and the wife's name and every surname, for the public benefit [to avoid false identification of the divorcee]." The requirement for the signatures of witnesses was also instituted later. There was thus a long path from the unregulated manner of writing a divorce document to the institutionalized intricacies of the current document.[41] The same circumstances must have pertained with respect to all other indefinite biblical laws,[42] with the details evolving

---

40 M. D. Herr, *Encyclopedia Judaica*, s.v. "Oral Law," p. 1439, quotes a citation from Judah Halevi on this topic: "The statutes of the Written Law could not have been fulfilled literally even in the generation in which they were given, since 'that which is plain in the Torah is obscure, all the more that which is obscure (Judah Halevi, *Kuzari*, 3, 35).'" In particular he states, "There is no reference to the laws of marriage, while the law of divorce is mentioned only incidentally."

41 See Ch. Albeck, ששה סדרי משנה, סדר נשים, pp. 266-8, in the introduction to Tractate Gittin, concerning the legal development of the text of the divorce document.

42 In the second part of this work I discuss similar circumstances regarding the lack of quantities mentioned in the biblical commands for certain *minhah* offerings, and the precise specifications provided for others. As argued there in more detail, these differences indicate the different periods of origin of the various rules, and consequent differences in description. In earlier times when spontaneous cult worship prevailed there were no precise rules; these were conceived at a later time when the offerings were institutionalized. In this case, it was easy to introduce new regulations, since these were created by the small priestly group for its own benefit; no protest was expected. The rabbinic assumption that פרי עץ הדר "a choice fruit from the trees [Lev 23: 40]" is a particular citrus fruit, the *etrog*, constitutes a similar example. Scripture does not indicate the type of the fruit or of the tree, but simply that it is a beautiful species; one may assume that initially everyone could choose the most beautiful fruit he had in his orchard to honour the Feast of Tabernacles, or Ingathering. Josephus in *Ant.* 3: 245, for instance, states that περσέα "peaches" are the appropriate fruit for Sukkot, but in *Ant.* 13: 372 he mentions χίτριον "citrus fruit." It is plausible that even in his time the exclusive use of the *etrog* was not yet finally established. There are deliberations on the identification of the biblical term עץ הדר (Lev 23: 40) in ySukkah 3: 5, 53d, and in bSukkah 35a. Interestingly, it is not asserted that the use of the *etrog* is a halakhah from Sinai; rather, there is an attempt to deduce its use by a variety of farfetched exegeses. It is even postulated that the term *hadar* has an affinity with the Greek ὕδωρ, "water," as the *etrog* grows on water.

slowly and becoming traditional over the course of time. What had been a pronouncement of a Sage eventually became a tradition.

We must also question how it was possible to introduce into general use a recently established custom and allege that it was an ancient tradition from Sinai. As an example, we may note the rabbinic declaration that the design, pattern, and colour of the phylacteries are a tradition from Sinai. There is no evidence as to when these precise standards were instituted; I think, however, that it would be unreasonable to assume that at the time of the promulgation of the biblical dictum "Tie them as symbols on your hands and bind them on your foreheads [Deut 6: 8]," all these precise[43] instructions were in effect. This is, however, a sociological problem not directly connected to our study, and thus I shall not elaborate upon it; I simply bring the reader's attention to this dilemma.

1. 3 The Value of Free Expression

The above citations reveal rabbinic attempts to attribute the particulars of the law to tradition, tracing their origin to Sinai, that is, the Divinity. This undertaking, however, obviously represents the ideal. The Mishnah, and even more the Talmudim, consist of an endless array of disputes of every possible character. The existence of such disputes invalidates any proposition that a continuous transmission of tradition stands at the core of the Israelite legal system.[44]

The disputes recorded in the Mishnah generally do not indicate the motives behind the different opinions. It was only the later Amoraim, in their deliberations concerning the correct interpretation of the Mishnah, who attempted to detect the reasons behind tannaitic dissension; they, in fact, attributed such dissension to disagreements about the correct interpretation of biblical verses, not to differences in the transmission of tradition. There was also a certain trend of opinion that attempted to deny

---

43 I shall quote only a few of these rules. We read in yMegillah 1: 9, 71d: קשרי תפילין הלכה למשה מסיני "The pattern of the knots of the phylacteries is a halakhah [given] to Moses from Sinai." The same origin is declared in bShabbat 28b regarding the engraving of the character ש on the box of the phylactery for the head, the square pattern of the phylacteries, and the black colour of their straps. In yMegillah 4: 9, 75c, we read: תפילין מרובעות שחורות הלכה למשה מסיני "[The requirement that] the phylacteries be square and black is a halakhah [given] to Moses from Sinai."

44 Conservative ideologues of all times, from the Sages until our days, have attempted to harmonize the logical deductions that were the real motives of the rabbinic disputes with their faith-conditioned belief that all tradition originates from Sinai. *The Epistle of Rav Sherira Gaon* (987 C. E.) is the most renowned early attempt to resolve this dilemma.

the significance of the disputes. Such is evident, for instance, in Mishnah tractate Eduyyot, which (as indicated by both its name[45] and its structure) has as its specific purpose to proffer evidence of correctly transmitted halakhot. Tosefta tractate Eduyyot begins by explaining the scope of the tractate, and of the meeting that generated it. We read in 1: 1: "When the Sages met in the 'vineyard' of Yabneh they deliberated and said: There may come a time when a person searches for the [correct] law of the Torah or of the Scribes [rabbinic Sages] and does not find it." The reason for this situation, as the passage continues, is: "...because one decision would not be similar to another [because of the disputes]. So they said: Let us start with [the disputes] between Hillel and Shammai [so as to decide a uniform and fixed halakhah]."[46]

An entirely different picture, however, is presented in bEruvin 13b:[47]

---

45 The term עדויות originates from the root עוד "to affirm," "to give evidence."

46 Regarding the purpose of the assembly, see section 4.1.2, in particular the quotation from tEduyyot, text at n. 47. In bShabbat 138b, there is an extended deliberation on the scope of this assembly: עתידה אשה שתטול ככר של תרומה ותחזור בבתי כנסיות ובבתי מדרשות לידע אם טמאה היא ואם טהורה היא ואין מבין "[The purpose of the assembly was to avoid, for instance, a situation in which] a woman might take a loaf of *terumah* [that must be eaten in purity] and go back and forth among the synagogues and schools to find out whether it is pure or polluted, and not receive a conclusive answer [because of different opinions]." In Sifre Deut 48, we encounter a similar dictum regarding the degree of uncleanness of something touched by a creeping animal. There then follows a dictum of Rabbi Simeon ben Yohai explaining the circumstances expressed in Amos 8: 12 : אלא איש פלוני אוסר איש פלוני מתיר איש פלוני מטמא איש פלוני מטהר ולא ימצאו דבר ברור "[Amos 8: 12 refers to those who search for the word of the Lord, but will not find it; this does not mean they will forget it, but rather refers to the prospect that] one [Sage] will prohibit [something] and another will permit [it], one will declare [something] unclean and another will declare [it] clean, and they will not find a clear decision." In the quotation of this dictum in bShabbat 138b, the ending is slightly expanded: שלא ימצאו הלכה ברורה ומשנה ברורה "They will not find a clear halakhah or a clear mishnah [that is, as Rashi explains, without a dispute: שלא יהא בה מחלוקת]."

47 The narrative about the "Voice of Heaven" that decided the halakhah according to Beit Hillel also appears in yBerakhot 1: 4, 3b, yYevamot 1: 6, 3b, and ySotah 3: 4, 19a. In those instances it lacks the beginning statement to the effect that the Houses disputed for three years; the number three, however, is a commonly-used number, and is also mentioned in both Talmudim concerning the three disputes between Hillel and Shammai (see above n. 26). The above Y.T. instances also lack the concluding statement giving the motive for establishing the halakhah according to Beit Hillel. This statement, with a significant addition, does appear as a separate explanation in ySukkah 2: 8, 53d (on which I shall elaborate in the Appendix.) The attitude in both Talmudim to the "Voice of Heaven" narrative is identical; I have used the more extended citation from the B. T.

> Rabbi Abba said in the name of Samuel: For three years Beit Shammai and Beit Hillel disputed. The one side said: The halakhah is as we maintain, and the other side said: The halakhah is as we maintain. [Then] the "Voice of Heaven" emerged and said: Both are the words of the Living God, but the halakhah is [to be decided] according to Beit Hillel. [But] since both opinions are "the words of the Living God" [that is, equally truthful and authoritative], why is the halakhah decided according to Beit Hillel? Because they were kind and humble, and not only did they quote both their own opinions and those of Beit Shammai, they also quoted those of Beit Shammai before their own.

There is no suggestion here that Beit Hillel possessed the correct tradition, as opposed to Beit Shammai. There are, moreover, numerous decisions that are in blatant conflict[48] with the above passage, and with other talmudic dicta. It is interesting, therefore, that the Sages' justification for adopting the halakhah of Beit Hillel was that they demonstrated their open-mindedness and readiness to consider conflicting ideas and opinions objectively. They respected their opponents' views, and reached their own decisions only after thorough and unbiased consideration convinced them of the superiority of their opinions over those of their adversaries.

---

[48] The maxim אלו ואלו דברי אלהים חיים "Both are the words of the Living God" is in conflict with the notion that all interpretations and hitherto unrevealed regulations originate from Sinai and were transmitted from generation to generation (see further on this point the citation of mAvot 1: 1 in n. 84). There are also instances of Beit Hillel changing their opinion and agreeing with Beit Shammai's declarations, as for example in mEduyyot 1: 12-14: אלו דברים שחזרו בית הלל להורות כדברי בית שמאי "These were the [conflicting] issues on which Beit Hillel recanted their [previous opinions] and taught according to Beit Shammai." The mishnah clearly indicates that they changed their minds as a result of their open-mindedness; they were convinced by the logical arguments of Beit Shammai, and not because Beit Shammai had a more reliable tradition. In mShabbat 1: 4 there is a record of an instance in which Beit Shammai overpowered Beit Hillel: ואלו מן ההלכות שאמרו בעליית חנניה בן חזקיה בן גוריון כשעלו לבקרו נמנו ורבו ב״ש על ב״ה וי״ח דברים גזרו בו ביום "And these are the halakhot which were declared in the upper chamber of Hananyah son of Hezekiah son of Gurion when they went up to visit him. At the voting, Beit Shammai had the majority over Beit Hillel, and eighteen edicts were decreed on that day." Such a situation is inconceivable if the halakhah was always decided according to Beit Hillel. A dictum in yShabbat 1: 4, 3c, and in bShabbat 14b, שמנה עשר דבר גזרו ובשמנה עשר נחלקו "They decreed eighteen issues [according to Beit Shammai] and on eighteen issues they remained opposed," similarly indicates that the issue of correct tradition is not at the core of these disputes. The significance of this dispute will be discussed more fully below; see section 3.4.

1. 4 Rabbinic Authority to Overrule Even Torah Law

The Rabbis themselves confirmed their own superior authority; they also extended its scope to the maximum, through appropriate exegesis of the biblical verse: ושמרת לעשות ככל אשר יורוך "You must act according to the decisions they give you [Deut 17: 10]."[49] We read in Sifre Deut 154: "If they show you that right is left and left is right, obey them."[50] The Sages' prerogative, though boundless and unrestricted,[51] was thus seen to represent the divine will; any man who acted upon the Sages' decisions was accordingly absolved from any sin, should the judgment have been based on a mistaken consideration on the Sages' part. Their judgment, in other words, was the final expression of the law.[52]

Talmudic dicta and narratives confirm this approach. We read in mHorayot 1: 1: "If the court had ordered a transgression of one of the Torah's precepts and an individual acted according to their judgment in error [not knowing that it was mistakenly decreed by the court and hence a transgression], he is not liable [for a sin offering], since he relied on the court, irrespective of whether he acted together with them, or he followed their action, or even if they did not perform the action." The mishnah

---

49 B. M. Levinson, *Deuteronomy and the Hermeneutics of Legal Innovation*, writes on p. 4 that "Deuteronomy was already a complex hermeneutical work from the beginning; it was the composition of authors who consciously reused and reinterpreted earlier texts to propound and justify their program of cultic and legal reform, even - or particularly when those texts conflicted with the author's agenda." Assuming this postulate is correct, it is no wonder that the command to obey the contemporary religious and legal authorities unconditionally appears in Deuteronomy. The Sages, who analyzed every biblical verse meticulously in all its aspects, may have been similarly convinced of the far-reaching message in these verses, and frankly declared their unlimited authority to be founded upon them.

50 A similar dictum appears in Midrash Tannaim, in a homily on Deut 17: 10: מנין שאם יאמר לך על שמאל שהיא ימין ועל ימין שהיא שמאל שמע לדבריהם ת״ל ככל אשר יורוך "How do we know that if he [the judge] tells you left is right and right is left, you must obey them [the priests and the Levites of the central courts]? This is what we learn from the verse 'whatever they may instruct you.'" There is, however, a conflicting version in yHorayot, 1: 1, 45d (cited in the Introduction n. 52; see also following note), which absolves one from obedience to an obviously incorrect decision.

51 The sole exception would be a mandate to "follow other gods"; similarly, one is commanded "not to listen" to a prophet who preaches such a rule (Deut 13: 2 - 5). In yHorayot 1: 1, 45d, we read a completely opposing interpretation of this verse, demanding obedience to a court decision only when it is evident that the judges were not in error; when they are obviously mistaken, however, one must not obey their decision. I will revert to this contradiction later in the study, chap. 4, n. 295.

52 J. Roth, *Halakhic Process*, writes on p. 133: "Rabbinic interpretation of the Law is, as it were, the never-ending revelation of the will of God."

stresses the principle: "This is the rule: If a man acts upon his own [erroneous deliberation], he is liable, but if he follows [the erroneous decision of] a court, he is not liable." We observe that an unlawful action is legitimated through the mediation of a court; consent is given *ex post facto*, בדיעבד. Further, not only is there no transgression in performing such an improper deed, but one would also be liable for failing to obey the court's dictate.[53]

A passage found in tSukkah 2: 3, yYevamot 1: 6, 3b, and bEruvin 6b-7a[54] reveals that the Sages had the prerogative to override an indisputable Torah law: "The law is always according to Beit Hillel. If one wishes to conduct himself according to the decisions of Beit Shammai, he may do so, or according to the decisions of Beit Hillel, he may do so. But if [someone wants to conduct himself] according to the decisions of Beit Shammai, [he must carry out both] their lenient and their stringent decisions; [if he follows the decisions of] Beit Hillel, [he must likewise carry out both] their lenient and stringent decisions." In contrast to the previous dictum, permission is here given *a priori*, לכתחילה, to perform a direct action against the law intentionally, as long as one follows the decisions of one Sage or one school consistently. It is only prohibited, as the Talmud subsequently says, to choose only the lenient decisions of each school. Since the halakhah, the correct law, is stated to be according to the decisions of Beit Hillel, if one follows decisions of Beit Shammai he will definitely transgress the law in those occurrences in which their decisions are more lenient than those of Beit Hillel;[55] nonetheless, he is allowed *a*

---

[53] See nn. 50-51; if a learned person was aware that the court had unmistakably erred, he must not follow the erroneous decision.

[54] The cited text is from the B. T.; the other sources make the same point, in a less compact way.

[55] In bYevamot 14a there is a dispute between various Amoraim as to whether indeed Beit Shammai accepted the decree that the halakhah is to follow Beit Hillel, or whether they continued to act according to their own opinions. Although some Amoraim assert that the Beit Shammai school conducted themselves according to Beit Hillel, there are a number of talmudic passages that attest to the opposite. Tosafot at bYevamot 14a ד"ה לא עשו ב"ש כדבריהם draw our attention to some of these occurrences. I shall add another citation suggesting that Beit Shammai conducted themselves in conformity with their own halakhah even in matters of extreme significance. We read in mEduyyot 4: 8 and (in a slightly different literary style) in mYevamot 1: 4: ואף על פי שאלו פוסלין ואלו מכשירין לא נמנעו בית שמאי מלישא נשים מבית הלל ולא בית הלל מלישא נשים מבית שמאי וכל הטהרות והטמאות שהיו אלו מטהרין ואלו מטמאין לא נמנעו להיות עושים טהרות אלו על גב אלו "[The mishnah first refers to a particular dispute between the Houses: Beit Shammai require a widow left without children to perform the *halitzah* ceremony instead of entering into a levirate marriage with her brother-in-law; she is thus disqualified, like a divorced woman, from marrying a priest. According to Beit Hillel she is not required to marry her brother-in-law, in this particular

priori to do so, since all rabbinic affirmations could override explicit scriptural law and attain full legality.[56]

The most well-known narrative confirming the supremacy of rabbinic decisions[57] over explicit Torah law is the account of the dispute between

---

circumstance, and thus the *halitzah* ceremony, even if performed, amounts to nothing, and she may consequently marry a priest.] And although they [Beit Shammai] disqualify [such a widow from marrying a priest] and the others [Beit Hillel] allow [her to marry a priest], Beit Shammai did not avoid marrying women from Beit Hillel, and Beit Hillel did not avoid marrying women from Beit Shammai; and [despite] all the issues of purity and impurity [on which they disputed] and these declared pure and the others declared impure, they exchanged vessels from one group to the other." It is evident that even with respect to extremely significant issues in Israelite law, each group continued to act as it thought appropriate. In bYevamot 14a, it is asked how it is possible that the members of Beit Hillel married women from the Shammai group, given the serious repercussions: אלא ב"ה מבית שמאי אמאי לא נמנעו בני חייבי כריתות ממזרים נינהו "They are liable to the punishment of excision, and the children [are considered] *mamzerim*." The answer is that the people of Beit Shammai דמודעי להו ופרשי, informed the others before any wedding that the girl was born of a liaison not permitted according to Beit Hillel's opinion, and the marriage was avoided. The same question is then asked with respect to the issues of pollution and purity, and it is similarly answered that the Beit Shammai members informed the Beit Hillel people about the specific conditions of the utensils, and they avoided using them. It is evident that these are speculative answers; those who asked the questions and answered them could not conceive that the Beit Hillel group acted in a way that would bring them into such blatant conflict with the law, as they perceived it. With respect to the marriage issue, the mishnah indicates only that they intermarried, a fact that does not absolutely preclude the possibility that they avoided marrying someone from a particular family. One cannot assume this kind of possibility, however, regarding the borrowing of utensils; the text of the mishnah, לא נמנעו עושין טהרות, seems to indicate that they accepted as pure all the utensils so declared by Beit Shammai. And indeed, the Y. T. has no record of a dispute concerning whether each House acted according to its own halakhic decisions. Besides the mishnah's indications, both Talmudim (yYevamot, 3: 1, 3d, and bYevamot 27a) quote the failed attempt of Rabbi Yohanan b. Nuri to enact a pragmatic procedure by which both parties could harmonize their practices, without giving up their own conceptions. This seems to indicate that each House acted according to its own opinions. In any event, it is of no significance for our purpose whether these answers are based on reality; they do attest that Beit Shammai definitely acted according to their own convictions, and further, that this right to act contrary to the declared halakhah was granted to everybody.

56 Another rationalization of this apparently paradoxical dictum, the maxim "Both are the words of the living God," is discussed in section 3.4.

57 B. Z. Rosenfeld, "Sage and Temple," quotes on pp. 445-6 a midrash from Song Rab. 1, regarding a stone chair on which Rabbi Eliezer sat and taught his disciples: פעם אחת נכנס ר' יהושע התחיל ונשק אותה האבן ואמר האבן הזאת דומה להר סיני וזה שישב עליה דומה לארון הברית "Once Rabbi Yehoshua entered [the School] and started to kiss that stone, saying: The stone is like Mount Sinai and he [Rabbi Eliezer] who sat on it is like the Ark of the Covenant."

the Sages and Rabbi Eliezer with respect to the pollution of the Akhnai oven. This is narrated *in extenso* in bBava Metzi'a 59b.[58] The story recounts a miraculous divine intervention that sided with Rabbi Eliezer's opinion, demonstrating that his decision was the correct interpretation of the Torah and agreed with God's original intent. When the בת קול, "Voice of Heaven," announced that the law was always as Rabbi Eliezer declared it, Rabbi Yehoshua stood up (in defiance) and said: לא בשמים היא "[The Torah] is [no longer] in heaven [cf. Deut 30: 12]." Rabbi Yirmeyah explained: שכבר נתנה תורה מהר סיני אין אנו משגיחין בבת קול "...since the Torah was already given [to the people of Israel] on Mount Sinai, and one does not [have to] comply with [the dictates of] the Voice of Heaven."[59] Under Torah law, the majority decision should prevail, as it is written in Exod 23: 2: "Tend toward the majority."[60] The climax to the sensational story is the divine agreement with Rabbi Yehoshua's pronouncement. It is stated that Rabbi Nathan met Elijah the prophet and asked him: "How did God react at that time?" And he answered: "He smiled and said: My children were victorious over me, my children were victorious over me."

Several rabbinic declarations will illustrate this explicit authority to override scriptural commands. We read in Sifre Deut 122, yQiddushin 1: 2, 59d, and bSotah 16a:

---

58 It is also recounted in mKelim 5: 10; tEduyyot 2: 1; and bBerakhot 19a; in yMo'ed Qatan 3: 1, 81d, the name appears as חכינאי. I have chosen the B. T. version of the narrative for the reasons set out in the Introduction (nn. 31 ff. and related text.) For a comparison between the Y. T. and the B. T. versions, see J. Neusner, *Biography*, p. 123. See also the discussion of this passage in section 3.4.

59 I. D. Gilat, פרקים, pp. 184-5 quotes a lengthy deliberation from the introduction to קצות החושן, a late publication, concerning a question of Rabbenu Nissim Girondi, a ראשון: how can one explain the Sages' audacity in deciding against the divine truth, which was clearly perceived in Rabbi Eliezer's decision? The answer employs a maxim from bBerakhot 25b: לא נתנה תורה למלאכי השרת "The Torah was not given to angels [but to humankind, on whom intellect was bestowed]." Thus humans understand and interpret the Torah according to their innate capabilities, even if this understanding conflicts with divine truth.

60 The simple interpretation of this verse is different than this homily suggests; there are further interpretations in the Talmud. It is common procedure to interpret a biblical verse in different ways in order to deduce the support needed for necessary decrees. We read in tBerakhot 4: 15, with respect to a dispute between Rabbi Aqiba and Rabban Gamaliel: אמ' לו למדתנו אחרי רבים להטות אע"פ שאתה או' כך וחביריך או' כך הלכה כדברי המרובין "He said to him: You have taught us [to interpret the verse] 'Tend toward the majority': although you say one thing, and your colleagues say the opposite, the law is according to the opinion of the majority."

Rabbi Ishmael says: in three instances, the halakhah [61] dislodges Scripture. The Torah [in Lev 17: 13] states: "Drain out the blood and cover it with earth," and the halakhah states [the blood may be covered] with anything that grows plants [including ground-up stones, flax, fine ceramic shavings, pulverized manure, and powdered sand, but not pulverized metal artifacts, flour, bran, or coarse bran, according to Sifra *Ahare* 8]. The Torah states [in Deut 24: 1] that a man is to write a book of divorce [that is, on parchment or papyrus] and the halakhah states that it may be written on any detached material [even on a leaf, according to mGittin 2: 3, but not on a wall]. The Torah [in Exod 21: 6] states [the ear of the permanent slave is to be pierced] with

---

61 The cited text is from the Sifre version. The main message of this declaration - that is, that the Sages have the authority to change biblical precepts - is identical in all three sources, but the text and some of the examples differ. The Y. T. version states: התורה עוקפת למקרא "The Torah dislodges the biblical verse"; the term הלכה is replaced here by תורה, which may suggest an even stronger emphasis on the Sages' authority. The B. T. version differs in its third example; instead of the piercing of the slave's ear, it refers to the Nazir's prohibition with respect to shaving with a razor, and notes that the Sages prohibit the Nazir from shaving with any instrument. This example does not seem appropriate; it does not fit with the other two cases or with the context of the declaration. The purpose of the latter is to demonstrate that the halakhah may permit something prohibited in Scripture, as demonstrated by the two other instances. To forbid something that is permitted, on the other hand, such as shaving with an instrument other than a razor, does not illustrate the enhanced authority of the halakhah.

The traditional commentators interpreted the term halakhah in this declaration as הלכה למשה מסיני "[given] to Moses from Sinai." I suppose that they were uneasy in assuming that a rabbinic interpretation could uproot an explicit divine rule in Scripture. In my opinion, however, the term halakhah does denote in this case a rabbinic interpretation, and not a transmitted decree or explanation. As I shall discuss more fully below (n. 108, and section 3.5), the phrase הלכה למשה מסיני is usually expressed in full, and refers to decrees that have no explicit support in Scripture. The rules cited in our declaration, as discussed in various talmudic texts, are deduced from midrash, that is, from suitable interpretation of biblical verses. We read in Sifre Deut 269, and in a shorter version in bGittin 21b (cited here): ספר אין לי אלא ספר מנין לרבות כל דבר ת״ל וכתב לה מכל מקום "[Scripture, with respect to the writing of a divorce, refers to] a book. I might think it must be a book; how do we know that [it may be written] on everything? Since it is written 'and he writes [for] her,' [that means] on any material." Similar reasoning is found in Sifra *Ahare* 8 and in a shorter version in bHullin 88b, regarding the covering with blood: ת״ל וכסהו "Since it is written 'and cover it,' this teaches us [that it may be covered] with everything." Mekilta d'Rabbi Simeon b. Yohai, 21: 6 and a shorter version in bBekhorot 51a contain the rationale concerning the piercing of a slave's ear: ת״ל ולקחת "Take [an awl - Deut 15: 17] - whatever you take [to pierce a slave's ear]." In these instances it is obvious that the interpretation of the Sages expands the scriptural text. In a number of instances (e.g. bEruvin 4b), an assertion that rules have originated in an interpretation of biblical verses induces the rebuttal: הלכתא נינהו ואסמכינהו רבנן אקראי "It is really a tradition from Sinai [that is, without any scriptural support], but the Sages alleged a scriptural support." This rebuttal does not appear in the other sources citing the three specific cases of our study; the assertion that they originate from the interpretation of biblical verses is thus not challenged.

an awl, and the halakhah states [this can be done] with anything [that pierces, including a wooden prick, a thorn or glass, according to yQiddushin 1: 2, 59d].

The Sages could easily have derived some illusory biblical support for these dicta,[62] as they often do, or used the exegetical justification that Scripture used a casuistic style and thus included similar cases;[63] it seems, however, that this momentous pronouncement was made deliberately without any such support, to emphasize the Sages' superior authority.

A declaration in bMakkot 22b expresses the superiority of the Sages over Scripture: "Raba said: How stupid some people are, who rise [in honour] of the Torah Scroll and do not rise before a great man [a Sage]. [The Sage's authority is greater], since in the Torah [punishment by flogging is] forty [lashes - Deut 25: 3], and the Sages came and reduced it by one [to thirty-nine lashes]." Talmud Yerushalmi utilizes a more pointed expression in portraying the Sages' authority: ודבריהן עוקרין דברי תורה "and their decrees uproot [עוקרין] the Torah's commands."[64]

The extensive authority of a rabbinic court is further demonstrated by a narrative in mRosh HaShanah 2: 8 - 9, with respect to the fixing of the calendar and consequently the date of the holidays. It is emphasized that the court's authority is paramount even when its decision is manifestly based on false facts;[65] it is the resolution of the court, not cosmological

62 R. Yaron, "Biblical Law: Prolegomena," p. 30 makes a similar statement with respect to the prohibition of usury.

63 The Mekilta, for instance, uses this reasoning to include all animals in the prohibition against cooking [and eating] meat with milk, although Scripture mentions only a kid. See section 2.5.2.

64 This maxim appears in yGittin, 4: 2, 45c, in connection with a particular injunction pronounced by Rabban Gamaliel the Elder in mGittin 4: 2 מפני תיקון העולם "for the public welfare." If, after a man had sent a divorce deed to his wife by proxy, he regretted it, he could annul the divorce by convoking a temporary court of three people, before the original document reached his wife. Thus she was not legally divorced. She, however, was not aware of the annulment, and might marry another man, and consequently her children born of that marriage would be *mamzerim*, and not allowed to marry an Israelite. To avoid such a tragedy, Rabban Gamaliel prohibited this conduct. It happened, however, that someone had proceeded in this manner. Rabbi declared the divorce annulled, but Rabban Gamaliel upheld the validity of the divorce; consequently, if the woman married someone else, her children were not defiled. According to the law of the Torah, she was still married and her children were unfit (as Rabbi declared); but since the Sages had the authority "to uproot" even a Torah decree, Rabban Gamaliel decided to save the children from an affliction which neither they nor their mother provoked and for which they should not be blamed.

65 We read there: ועוד באו שנים ואמרו ראינוהו בזמנו ובליל עיבורו לא נראה וקיבלן רבן גמליאל אמר רבי דוסא בן הורכינס עדי שקר הן היאך מעידים על האשה שילדה ולמחר כריסה בין שיניה אמר לו רבי יהושע רואה אני את דבריך "On another occasion two witnesses came and said: We have seen [the new

reality,[66] that is the decisive element that determines the date of a holiday,[67] an event of the greatest significance in Israelite religious life.[68] The fact that the narrative concerns the inaccurate fixing of the Day of Atonement, the most solemn day in the Israelite calendar at that period, indicates the overwhelming power of the rabbinic court.

In some cases the Sages attempted to justify their radical reforms, either by the logical explanation that contemporary circumstances differed from the conditions anticipated by a biblical command, or by suitably interpreting a

---

moon] at its precise time, but then [the moon] was not seen, and Rabban Gamaliel accepted [their testimony]. Rabbi Dosa ben Hyrcanos said: They are false witnesses! How can one testify with respect to a woman that she delivered, and then see her the next day still bearing the child in her womb? Rabbi Yehoshua said to him: I agree with you." Nevertheless, as the narrative continues, Rabban Gamaliel commanded Rabbi Yehoshua to come to his office with his cane and money on the day that was the Day of Atonement according to Rabbi Yehoshua's calculation (that is, so that he would desecrate what in his opinion was the holiday). I shall revert to this narrative below (chap. 4, text at nn. 292 ff.). Rabbi Yehoshua, as the story proceeds, was aggrieved and probably in a dilemma as to what to decide, but Rabbi Aqiba told him: I can deduce from Scripture that what Rabban Gamaliel has done is indeed done (that is, the holiday is in effect, from the religious point of view, on the day pronounced by Rabban Gamaliel), since it says: אלה מועדי ה' מקראי קדש אשר תקראו אתם בין בזמנן בין שלא בזמנן אין לי מועדות אלא אלו "'These are the Lord's appointed feasts, the sacred assemblies you are to proclaim [Lev 23: 4]'; whether at their [exact] time or not, I have no appointed feasts other than those [proclaimed by a court]." The narrative records that Rabbi Yehoshua obeyed the order (and perhaps Rabbi Aqiba's homily); he came as requested to Rabban Gamaliel on the day that he was convinced, based on the facts, was the Day of Atonement.

66 R. T. Beckwith, *Calendar and Chronology, Jewish and Christian*, pp. 106 - 107, adds a philosophical aspect to this topic: the doctrine that man dominates his destiny and consequently fixes the dates of the holidays is a confrontation with the Greek philosophy of man's predestination.

67 There is a similar assertion in mRosh HaShanah 3: 1: ראוהו בית דין וכל ישראל נחקרו העדים ולא הספיקו לומר מקודש עד שחשיכה הרי זה מעובר "If the court and all of Israel saw [the new moon] and the witnesses were investigated, but [the court] did not have time to pronounce the day as holy [as the new moon] before it got dark, only the next day will be considered the new month." Maimonides in his *Mishneh Torah, Hilkhot Qiddush Hahodesh* 2: 8 adds an explanation to this apparently odd decision: שאין הראייה קובעת אלא בית דין שאמרו מקודש הם שקובעין "It is not the sighting of the moon that establishes the day of the new moon; it is the pronouncement of the court 'It is Holy' that matters."

68 This decision is of a permanent character, not limited to the period of its pronouncement. During the Temple period, there was the possibility that the most solemn celebrations of the Day of Atonement, the specific sacrifices, and the annual entrance of the High Priest into the Holy of Holies for the expected theophany, would be performed on the wrong day. Even following the destruction of the Temple, the rules regarding the Day of Atonement still called for many restrictions; as we have seen, Rabban Gamaliel requested the blatant desecration of the Day of Atonement by Rabbi Yehoshua.

biblical verse to include the specific decree. I shall offer an example of each of these types of justification. Deut 21: 1 - 9 provides for the breaking of a heifer's neck in the case of an unsolved murder, "and it is not known who killed him [v. 1]." This procedure was later cancelled, at least by the end of the Second Temple period, as we read in mSotah 9: 9: "When the number of murderers multiplied, the procedure of breaking the heifer's neck was cancelled." We do not know the real reason for the repeal of this and similar rites, but tSotah 14: 1 offers the following motive declared by Rabbi Yohanan ben Zakkai: "Because it [the breaking of the heifer's neck] is applicable only in cases of doubt [concerning who committed the murder], but now the number of those who murder flagrantly has increased [and thus the original law does not apply]."[69] A logical justification was thus used to explain that the biblical precept was not appropriate in specific circumstances. We further read, in mSotah 9: 9: "When there was an increase in the number of adulterers, the rite of the 'bitter water' was abolished; and it was Rabban Yohanan ben Zakkai who canceled it, as it is said 'I will not punish your daughters when they turn to prostitution nor your daughters-in-law when they commit adultery [Hos 4: 14].'"[70] In this case, a suitable biblical verse, a prophetic dictum, is utilized to justify the abolition of a biblical precept, though again this was likely induced by particular circumstances.[71]

---

69 I doubt whether this was the real reason for the cancellation, since an increase in the number of identifiable murderers does not justify per se the annulment of the biblical precept. From the text of the mishnah it appears that this decree dates from the time of the Great Rebellion.

70 On the issue of whether this ruling was really decreed by Rabbi Yohanan b. Zakkai at the time of the Temple, when the procedure could have taken place, or retrojected to give the impression that it predated the Temple's destruction, see D. Instone Brewer, *Techniques*, p. 77. He suggests that Rabbi Yohanan b. Zakkai's ruling must have been after the Temple's destruction, because the High Priest would not have obeyed it. The style of the narrative was composed so as to give the impression that it predated the Temple's destruction. In that case, the authenticity of the narrative should be doubted.

71 A dispute with respect to the acceptance of Ammonite and Moabite converts reveals the use of biblical verses to justify a politically motivated decree. Deut 23: 4 states: לא יבא עמוני ומואבי בקהל ה׳ "No Ammonite or Moabite may enter the assembly of the Lord." Rabbi Yehoshua tended in the direction of abrogating this restriction, as we read in mYadayim 4: 4: בו ביום בא יהודה גר עמוני ועמד לפניהן בבית המדרש אמר להם מה אני לבא בקהל אמר לו ר״ג אסור אתה אמר לו ר׳ יהושע מותר אתה א״ל ר״ג הכתוב אומר לא יבא עמוני ומואבי בקהל ה׳ גם דור עשירי וגו׳ אמר לו רבי יהושע וכי עמונים ומואבים במקומן הן כבר עלה סנחריב מלך אשור ובלבל את כל האומות שנאמר ואסיר גבולות עמים ועתידותיהם שושתי א״ל ר״ג הכתוב אומר ואחרי כן אשיב את שבות בני עמון וכבר חזרו "On that day, Judah, an Ammonite convert, came and stood before them in the assembly and said to them: May I be accepted as a member of Israel? Rabban Gamaliel said no, Rabbi Yehoshua said yes. Rabban Gamaliel said to Rabbi Yehoshua: [How can you say that,] since Scripture says 'No Ammonite or

I thus propose that the Sages undertook to create or modify laws and regulations based upon considerations of exigency and utility,[72] motivated by their desire to preserve Jewish culture and social organization. These laws were then invested with authority through various techniques, including biblical hermeneutics. I must note here that this proposition is at odds with other scholarly views. J. M. Harris, in particular, completely reverses the relationship between Scripture, midrash and halakhah, declaring that the exegesis of scriptural anomalies is the basis of rabbinic law.[73] That is, the midrash, as an exegetical system to reconcile scriptural inconsistencies and redundancies,[74] can be considered a source of law. I do not dispute that some midrashim have as their purpose such a reconciliation,[75] but I do not agree that in general the anomalies of the

---

Moabite may enter the assembly of the Lord … not even the tenth generation.' Rabbi Yehoshua said to him: There are no longer [genuine] Ammonites and Moabites, since Sennacherib king of Assyria mingled all the peoples, as it is said (Isa 10: 13): 'I removed the boundaries of nations, I plundered their treasures.' Rabban Gamaliel said to him:[But] Scripture says [Jer 49: 6]: 'Yet afterwards I will restore the fortunes of the Ammonites,' and they have returned." It is not within the scope of this study to investigate the relevant political circumstances, and Rabbi Yehoshua's specific viewpoint; we may observe, however, how a practical procedure was discussed not on its political or other merits, but based on a correct application of scriptural verses. The effect is to maintain the appearance that every legal decision is grounded in Scripture, and follows the divine intention.

72 J. Roth, *Halakhic Process,* p. 153 cites similar examples: the rabbinic rule for administering thirty-nine lashes instead of the forty mentioned in Scripture (bMakkot 22b), and the statement that there never was nor ever will be a rebellious son executed for his licentious behaviour (bSanhedrin 71a).

73 J. M. Harris, *How Do We Know This?*, p. 11.

74 Ibid., pp. 14 ff.

75 A characteristic homily is, for example, the aphorism בדיבור אחד נאמרו "they were said in one utterance." We read in Mekilta d' Rabbi Ishmael, *Yitro* 7 (and in slightly different literary styles in Sifre Deut 233, Mekilta d'Rabbi Simeon b. Yohai 20: 8, and yNedarim 3: 2, 37d): זכור ושמור שניהם נאמרו בדיבור אחד "[In Exod 20: 8, the fourth commandment states זכור את יום השבת 'Remember the Sabbath day,' while in the second version of the Ten Commandments in Deut 5: 12, the same commandment states שמור את יום השבת 'Observe the Sabbath day.' To justify this variation the Sages say:] The expressions זכור ושמור pronounced by God were effected in one utterance." This solution is appropriate given the theological doctrine that humans are unable to perceive what it really means "to hear the voice" of the abstract Deity, and we read subsequently in Mekilta d'Rabbi Simeon b. Yohai on 20: 8 (and in a slightly different literary style in the other sources): מה שאי אפשר לפה לדבר ומה שאי אפשר לאוזן יכולה לשמוע "What the mouth is unable to utter and the ear unable to hear." The inconsistency is thus reconciled by a homily. The Sages took advantage of the aphorism thus created to justify a number of rules that they thought it opportune to proclaim. We read in bShevu'ot 20b: נשים חייבות בקידוש היום דבר תורה דאמר קרא זכור ושמור כל שישנו בשמירה

ישנו בזכירה והני נשי הואיל ואיתנהו בשמירה איתנהו נמי בזכירה "Women are obliged by a Torah command to fulfill the precept of consecrating the Sabbath by wine, because of the joining of the commands 'to remember' and 'observe' [in the Ten Commandments]; [this joining is to be understood as requiring that] whoever is liable to observe the Sabbath is liable to remember it, and women, who are [included in the precept of] observing, are also [included in the precept of] consecrating." (In Mekilta d'Rabbi Simeon b. Yohai, 19: 7, the general obligation of women to perform all the divine precepts is deduced from a homily on another verse: את כל הדברים האלה אשר צוהו ה׳ אף לנשים "[It is written in Exod 19: 7] 'all the words the Lord had commanded,' and from this, we learn that women also [are included].") In both versions of the Ten Commandments the term לקדשו appears, and this is interpreted in a baraita quoted in bPesahim 106a: תנו רבנן זכור את יום השבת לקדשו זוכרהו על היין "The Rabbis taught: "[It is written in Exod 20: 8:] 'Remember the Sabbath day to make it holy [to consecrate it]'; you remember it with wine." In Mekilta d'Rabbi Ishmael, *Yitro* 7, the same idea is expressed in different words: לקדשו לקדשו בברכה מכאן אמרו מקדשין על היין בכניסתו "It is written 'to make it holy' - [this means] to consecrate it with a blessing. From this we deduce that one should consecrate [the Sabbath] with wine at its commencement." It is evident that the Sages considered it opportune to enhance the Sabbath's festive character by a benediction with wine, and utilized the existing aphorism to obtain support for their rule. The same method of enhancing the Sabbath is found in Mekilta d'Rabbi Ishmael, *Yitro* 7: זכור ושמור זכור מלפניו ושמור מלאחריו מכאן אמרו מוסיפין מחול על הקדש "[It is written] 'remember' and 'observe': 'remember' first and 'observe' afterwards, and this comes to teach us that one must add from the profane to the sacred [that is, one starts the Sabbath before its precise cosmological time, and extends it beyond its precise expiration]." (In Mekilta d'Rabbi Simeon b. Yohai 23: 12, the obligation to start one's rest before the commencement of the Sabbath is deduced from a rather circular homily based on another biblical verse.) There are further rabbinic rules for the enhancement of the Sabbath based on this method, which it would be redundant to cite.

I wish to quote another example that demonstrates the complete flaw in Harris' insinuation that biblical hermeneutics primarily address inconsistencies in the text. We read in Sifre Deut 233 (and in a slightly different word order in yShevu'ot 3: 8, 34d): לא תלבש שעטנז גדילים תעשה לך שניהם נאמרו בדבור אחד "'Do not wear *sha'atnez* [clothes of wool and linen woven together - Deut 22: 11]' [and] 'Make tassels' [ibid. v. 12] were pronounced in one utterance [and this teaches us that the interdiction of שעטנז does not apply to tassels]." There is no inconsistency to reconcile between these two verses. For pragmatic reasons, the Sages permitted the fastening of woolen tassels to linen cloth, and attempted to derive some hint from the Torah for the vindication of this rule. My proposition is substantiated by the fact that the same invalidation of the *sha'atnez* prohibition is justified in other occurrences through a different homily. We read in bYevamot 4a: דכתיב לא תלבש שעטנז גדילים תעשה לך ואמר רבי אלעזר סמוכים מן התורה מנין שנאמר סמוכים לעד לעולם עשוים באמת וישר "As it is written: 'Do not wear clothes of wool and linen woven together' [and] 'Make tassels.' Rabbi Eleazar said: These are joined in Scripture. From where [do we learn this]? As it is said: 'They are steadfast for ever and ever done in faithfulness and uprightness [Ps 111: 8].'" The homily in this case is based on the term סמוכים, from the root סמך "to adjoin, to lean, to support," and by extension "close, near etc." Thus the adjoining of verses (in our case Deut 22: 11-12)

biblical text induced the Sages to create new laws to solve them. I suggest that the numerous talmudic citations, including those quoted in the study, demonstrate just the opposite: the Sages utilized biblical hermeneutics to validate the decrees, rules, and regulations that they deemed to be necessary,[76] and at the same time would allow them to remain faithful to the divine intent and commands.[77] This is seen, for instance, in the above-cited rabbinic dictum that the halakhah dislodges Scripture in three instances - with respect to the covering of the blood of the slaughtered animal, the writing of a divorce document, and the piercing of a slave's ear.[78]

---

allows a permanent exegesis, upon which is founded the remission of the *sha'atnez* rule. In bNazir 42a it is further explained: הא גדילים תעשה לך מהם "[Do not wear *sha'atnez*], but you may make tassels of it." I am confident that the above examples suffice to invalidate Harris' statement that any Sage might interpret the text in whatever way "struck his fancy." Harris further criticizes the fact that there is no consistent pattern in the application of the hermeneutic techniques, and that seems to him an arbitrary method. He does not realize that this method allowed the Sages to be innovative in their approach to a canonized law, similar to the most modern and liberal legislators. In order to demonstrate that the rabbinic laws have no origin in the Torah, and that therefore one is not compelled to fulfill them, he was constrained to discredit the Sages, the first "reformers" of the Torah. They demonstrated an innovative spirit in their legislative activity and had great courage in admitting it, as I have indicated in section 1.4: ודבריהן עוקרין דברי תורה "and their decrees uproot the Torah's commands." This maxim candidly acknowledges that their rules might contradict the Torah. Such a statement goes much further than a simple acknowledgment that rules might not have an origin in the Torah.

76 This issue is discussed in more detail in section. 2.2.

77 I thus challenge R. Bultmann's assertion in his *Primitive Christianity in its Contemporary Setting*, p. 64 that "there was no attempt to reach a deeper understanding of the context, to discover the ideas underlying the text itself, or the circumstances in which it took shape." It is true that the Sages could not acquiesce to something like the "Documentary Hypothesis" as explaining the sources of Scripture; instead, they turned the issue on its head and assumed the law could be adapted to changing circumstances. The pragmatic consequences of their approach seem to me to be far more important than the implications of the modern theory (with which I happen to agree) that Scripture was created as the result of an extended process and influenced by the dominant circumstances of the relevant periods that shaped it. We must consider that the Sages' main aim was the continued existence of the biblically inspired culture and way of life, and their method was appropriate for the achievement of this goal. The so-called critical approach to Scripture would have induced the opposite effect.

78 See n. 61 and related text above; in the Bavli version the third instance is the Nazir's prohibition against shaving. As noted, the Sages might have based their assertions on the casuistic format in each case, but instead used an exegetical validation. In this way, the divine intention was completely respected in these three occurrences.

1. 5 The Antipathy Toward Written Codification

A written code would obviously have alleviated many of the difficulties that led to disputes, but the Sages vigorously maintained their stern opposition to such an idea, believing it would impose a rigid and inflexible legal[79] system. They were fully aware of the absolute necessity to adapt the law to changing circumstances; their unfettered ability to interpret the biblical verses guaranteed the flexibility of the process. A written code would have been an insurmountable hindrance to this flexibility, and was thus forbidden.[80]

---

79 The Torah was considered an overall code of behaviour with respect to all aspects of life, material and spiritual, secular and religious.

80 There is, in fact, no reliable evidence as to whether, or when, such a prohibition was ever authoritatively promulgated. It is possible that this convention, like many others, was based on actual practice, and only later substantiated with a suitable interpretation of a biblical verse to bestow upon it a divine origin. There is only one quite obscure mention of this prohibition in bGittin 60b: דרש רבי יהודה בר נחמני מתורגמניה דרבי שמעון בן לקיש כתיב כתב לך את הדברים האלה וכתיב כי על פי הדברים האלה הא כיצד דברים שבכתב אי אתה רשאי לאומרן על פה דברים שבעל פה אי אתה רשאי לאומרן בכתב דבי רבי ישמעאל תנא אלה אלה אתה כותב ואי אתה כותב הלכות א״ר יוחנן לא כרת הקב״ה ברית עם ישראל אלא בשביל דברים שבעל פה שנאמר כי על פי הדברים האלה כרתי אתך ברית ואת ישראל "Rabbi Yehudah son of Nahmani, the interpreter of Resh Laqish, expounded: It is written, 'Write down these words [Exod 34: 27],' and then it is written, 'for in accordance with these words [this is the NIV translation, but על פי is presumed to refer to oral declarations, in antithesis to the previous utterance].' How is that possible? [The answer is, there are two distinct commands.] The commands given in writing you are not allowed to recite by heart and those given orally you are prohibited from transmitting in writing. From the school of Rabbi Ishmael it was taught: The term אלה 'these' is written twice [in the same verse], [to teach us] these [the words of God] you write, but you do not write [deduced] laws. Rabbi Yohanan said: God made the Covenant with Israel only because of the oral law, as it is written: 'Because of these words I have made a covenant with you and with Israel.'" The conjunction כי is interpreted by Rabbi Yohanan as "because," as in כי בו שבת "because on it [that day] he rested [Gen 2: 3.]" The LXX in our verse translated this term as γὰρ, and Onkelos also interprets ארי "for," "because." A passage in bTemurah 14b states in the name of Rabbi Yohanan: כותבי הלכות כשורף התורה והלמד מהן אינו נוטל שכר "Those who write laws [are deemed] to be burning the Torah, and one who studies from [the written laws] does not earn [divine] reward." Though these homilies are cited in the names of the Amoraim Rabbi Yohanan and Resh Laqish, we must assume that the prohibition against writing laws was decreed much earlier and was a matter of scrupulously practised tradition. If this were not the case, there would likely have been ancient writings of traditions and practices. The homily in the name of a disciple of the school of Rabbi Ishmael might derive from an earlier date, although we do not know how long this school existed after Rabbi Ishmael's death.

The Sages did appreciate the mistakes that would likely occur during the course of oral transmission, leading to erroneous halakhot, but preferred these blunders to the rigid law that would result from a written codex. We read in tSanhedrin 7: 2, quoted above (section 1: 2): "When one Sage has a tradition from two sources and two have a conflicting tradition from one source, the tradition from two sources overrides the tradition from one source." It is evident that the possibility of a corrupt transmission is at the core of this dictum. If one has received the same tradition from two sources, it is more likely to be genuine and true than a tradition heard by two people, but from the same source. Another passage to the same effect is found in mEduyyot 5: 7:

> [Aqabyah ben Mahalalel was excommunicated because he did not accept the opinion of the majority, but before his death he counselled his son to change his mind and agree to the majority opinion. When his son asked him why he had not done so himself, Aqabyah answered:] I have heard my tradition from many, and the others have heard theirs from many; therefore, I held on to my tradition and they held on to theirs [as both had the same authenticity]. But you heard my version from one [from me] and [the opposite version] from many [Sages], and hence it is judicious to ignore the dicta of the single person and accept the dicta of the many [majority].

Both these citations reflect the great concern for accuracy recognized by the Sages and their acknowledgment of the flaws inherent in oral transmission.

Rabbi Yohanan, an important scholar and religious leader in whose name is cited the prohibition against the writing of laws,[81] does make a distinction between written law and written homilies. Though it is recorded that he and his partner Resh Laqish read from written homilies,[82]

B. Gerhardsson, *Memory and Manuscript*, pp. 157 - 8, attempts to identify various motives for the prohibition against writing. He cites, for example, the ancient custom of learning important literary compositions by heart, and the conservative reluctance to change this practice. He compares this to the Greek custom of learning Homer by heart. I think that this proposition is totally flawed. Significant epic literature is even today learned by heart and intellectuals delight in quoting classic and poetic passages in their discussions and rhetoric. The ancient Greeks, however, had no prohibition against recording these compositions in writing. Further, in the period of Rabbi Yohanan, the second part of the third century C.E., the Graeco-Roman world was brimming with written literature of all types and languages.

81 See the previous note, in which he specifically denounces כותבי הלכות, "those who write laws."

82 We read in the continuation of the above-cited prohibition in bTemurah 14b and in bGittin 60a: רבי יוחנן ור״ל מעייני בסיפרא דאגדתא בשבתא "Rabbi Yohanan and Resh Laqish read the books of homilies on Sabbath." This narrative appears in both these sources as part of a rhetorical sequence. There are different versions in the various MSS (indicating perceived difficulties in the text), and dissimilar endings. In both sources, the idea that these Sages read homilies from written works is questioned

as being in conflict with the rule that forbids the writing of the oral Torah, but the answers are different in each source. In bGittin it is stated: והא לא ניתן ליכתב אלא כיון דלא אפשר עת לעשות לה' הפרו תורתך ה"נ כיון דלא אפשר עת לעשות לה' הפרו תורתך "But it must not be written! [Answer]: Just as it is impracticable, [and we apply the rule] 'It is time to act for God, they broke your law [Ps 119: 126 (this is the interpretation of the Sages, while the NIV interprets: It is time for you to act, O Lord, your law is being broken)],' so here too, since it is impracticable, we break the law [according to the context, we must interpret this phrase in this manner, although the text states: They broke the law]." We observe the obscurity of the text; from the subsequent argument "so here too" we must assume that the declaration "Since it is impracticable" refers to some other occurrence, not indicated in this dictum; we thus have no way of determining whether the two instances are relevant to each other. There is also no hint as to what exactly is impracticable. In bTemurah 14b, again within a discussion concerning the prohibition against writing oral law, it is stated: דהא רבי יוחנן ור"ל מעייני בסיפרא דאגדתא בשבתא ודרשי הכי עת לעשות לה' הפרו תורתך אמרי מוטב תיעקר תורה ואל תשתכח תורה מישראל "Since Rabbi Yohanan and Resh Laqish read the books of homilies on Sabbath, and debated the verse [Ps 119: 126 cited above], and said: It is preferable that [a precept of] the Torah is uprooted, than that the Torah should be forgotten by the Israelites." Rather than the issue of impracticability, the editor or others (one has the distinct impression that the argumentation was not expressed by the two Amoraim, but by later scholars) offer this rationale for the writing of the oral law. They may have founded their idea upon a declaration of Rabbi Yohanan in yBerakhot 5: 1, 9a: ברית כרותה היא הלמד אגדה מתוך הספר לא במהרה הוא משכח "Of necessity, one who learns Aggadah from a book will not forget it." This justification in turn raises further questions. The first is the distinction between writing, and reading from, a written text. It is recorded that Rabbi Yohanan and his partner read the homilies. From the justification in bTemurah we must deduce that one may also write them; in order that something not be forgotten, it has first to be written. Yet we have seen in a previously quoted citation of Rabbi Yohanan in bTemurah 14b (see n. 80) the significant difference between the condemnation of writing and the condemnation of reading. Further, if one may write a certain element of the oral Torah to avert the greater calamity of it being forgotten, the same permission should apply to the entire oral Torah, particularly the halakhot, for which there would be even greater concern. From records of the meeting in Yabneh, at which the codification of the laws was decided (tEduyyot 1: 1, bShabbat 138b and others, to which I shall revert in detail), we observe in fact that the primary concern was reserved for the halakhot, the laws. We read in bShabbat 138b: שלא ימצאו הלכה ברורה ומשנה ברורה במקום אחד "...[the concern is] that they [the people] will not encounter a clear law and a definite mishnah in one place" - that is, they will receive different or even opposing decisions. Rabbi Simeon ben Yohai, the author of this dictum, also reveals this rationale in Sifre Deut 48 (as noted above n. 46), in a homily based on Amos 8: 12: אלא איש פלוני אוסר איש פלוני מתיר איש פלוני מטמא איש פלוני מטהר ולא ימצאו דבר ברור "...one man [scholar] will prohibit [something] while another permits [it], one will declare [something] polluted while another declares [it] purified, and [consequently] they will not encounter any clear decision."

The different attitude of Rabbi Yohanan towards the writing of laws and the writing of homilies must be explained otherwise than by the alleged interpretation of

he forcefully condemned anyone writings laws כשורף התורה, "as [equivalent to] burning the Torah." He gave no reasons for this distinction between homilies and law, and in fact contradicts the Sages' position that all elements of the law are equal. These elements - "Bible, Mishnah, Talmud, and Aggadah [homiletic literature]" - are all considered to have been given to Moses at Sinai.[83] Only the Bible was transmitted in writing,

---

Exod 34: 27 to prohibit generally the writing of all the elements of the oral Torah (see n. 80 above). We may note that another Amora, Rabbi Yehoshua ben Levi, whose dictum against the writing of the oral Torah will be quoted in the next note, is as opposed to the writing of homilies as he is to the writing of other elements of the orally transmitted Torah. We read in yShabbat 16:1, 15c: אמר רבי יהושע בן לוי הדא אגדתא הכותבה אין לו חלק הדורשה (החורשה) מתחרך (מתברך) השומעה אינו מקבל שכר "Rabbi Yehoshua ben Levi said: [With respect to] this Aggadah, the one who writes it has no part [in the world to come], the one who teaches it [or turns it over = studies it profoundly] will be burned [or will be put under ban], the one who listens [to it being read from a written specimen] will not be rewarded." It may be that this Sage, in not distinguishing between the different elements of the oral Torah in his prohibition, was following the common rabbinic method of forbidding something that was originally permitted in order to prevent a possible confusion with similar, but prohibited, deeds. This Amora is also known for his particular prominence in the study of homilies, and this may have induced him not to accept an apparently lesser significance or degree of reverence for this specific branch of the Torah; see אנציקלופדיה לחכמי התלמוד והגאונים, vol. 2, p. 463. His attitude, in any event, does not invalidate the many other talmudic citations indicating a distinction in this respect between the laws and the homilies.

83 We read in yPe'ah 2: 4, 17a: רבי יהושע בן לוי אמר עליהם ועליהם כל ככל דברים הדברים מקרא משנה תלמוד ואגדה אפילו מה שתלמיד וותיק עתיד להורות לפני רבו כבר נאמר למשה בסיני "Rabbi Yehoshua son of Levi said: It is written in Deut 9: 10 [regarding the two tablets with the laws] '**and** on them, **as** all **the** words'; [the highlighted particles are superfluous and come to teach us that] Scripture, the Mishnah, the Talmud and the Aggadah, even what a proficient disciple would declare before his teacher, were already recounted to Moses on Sinai." In bMegillah 19b the biblical verse is interpreted similarly, but in a different context: מלמד שהראהו הקדוש ברוך הוא למשה דקדוקי תורה ודקדוקי סופרים ומה שהסופרים עתידין לחדש ומאי ניהו מקרא מגילה "[The verse] comes to teach us that God revealed to Moses the subtleties of the Torah, and those of the Scribes, and what the Scribes would originate, and what does this include? The reading of the Megillah." The homily is presented here to justify in particular the reading of the Megillah as a divine command, but the message is still expressed in a general manner, encompassing every rabbinic decree as originating from Sinai. There is a later homily on Exod 34: 27 in Exod. Rab. 47: 1: ומה אני עושה להם נותן את המקרא בכתב והמשנה והתלמוד והאגדה בעל פה כתב זה המקרא כי על פי הדברים האלה זו המשנה והתלמוד שהם מבדילים בין ישראל לבין העובדי כוכבים "How do I proceed [says God]? I give Scripture [to the Israelites] in writing, and the Mishnah and the Talmud and the Aggadah orally: 'writing,' this is Scripture; 'according to these words' are the Mishnah and the Talmud, which divide between Israel and the gentiles." The author assumed that Scripture, a written document and thus easily published and diffused, would be universally accepted and its laws obeyed

the rest being transmitted orally from generation to generation;[84] but all the elements were considered God's word,[85] equal parts of Israelite heritage,[86] and thus equally obligatory.[87]

(he probably had in mind the Christian world); but the orally transmitted elements and the correct interpretation of the Torah would remain the exclusive knowledge of the Israelites, and thus the practice of these divine precepts would distinguish them from the other peoples. The same idea is expressed in yPe'ah 2: 4, 17a (see n. 19).

84 The line of transmission of the Torah is recorded in mAvot 1: 1: משה קבל תורה מסיני ומסרה ליהושע ויהושע לזקנים וזקנים לנביאים ונביאים מסרוה לאנשי כנסת הגדולה "Moses received the Torah at Sinai and transmitted it to Joshua, and Joshua to the elders, and the elders to the prophets and the prophets to the members of the Great Assembly." The subsequent mishnayot record the later Sages who received it from them and transmitted it on until it reached Hillel and Shammai. I shall revert to the issue of why the transmission ended there. From the context we must assume that this line of transmission refers to the oral Torah. See also Ch. Albeck, ששה סדרי משנה, סדר נזיקין, p. 347, in the introduction to tractate Avot.

85 All the branches of the Torah are of the same holiness, require similar reverence and are subject to the same rules of purity. We read in tBerakhot 2: 12: מכל מקום הזבין והזבות והנדות והיולדות מותרין לקרות בתורה בנביאים ובכתובים ולשנות במשנה במדרש בהלכות ובאגדות ובעלי קריין אסורין בכולן "At any rate, men and women with a discharge, menstruating women, and women after childbirth are allowed to read the Pentateuch, the Prophets and the Hagiographia, and learn the Mishnah, the interpretations [the Talmud], the laws and the aggadot [homiletic literature]; but men with an emission of semen are prohibited from [reading] all of the above."

86 Since this is a cardinal issue of the thesis, I shall quote a number of rabbinic citations. We read in tSotah 7: 21: הכן בחוץ מלאכתך זו מקרא ועתדה בשדה לך זו משנה אחר ובנית ביתך זה מדרש "[It is written in Prov 24: 27: 'Finish your outdoor work and get your fields ready; after that build your home.'] 'Your outside work' signifies Scripture, 'get your fields ready' is Mishnah, and 'build your home' symbolizes Midrash." (There then follow a number of similar homilies expressing the same idea.) We also read in bHagigah 14a: משען אלו בעלי מקרא משענה אלו בעלי משנה כל משען לחם אלו בעלי תלמוד וכל משען מים אלו בעלי אגדה. "[The homily refers to Isa 3: 1: 'The Lord is about to take from Jerusalem and Judah] sustenance,' these are ones who know Scripture; 'subsistence [there is a play on words here, the first term without a ה and the second with a ה; I have therefore translated them as synonyms],' these are ones who know the Mishnah; 'all supplies of food,' these are ones who know the Talmud; 'and all supplies of water,' these are ones who know the Aggadah." In Gen. Rab. 66: 3 we read a homily on Gen 27: 28, from Isaac's blessings of Jacob: מטל השמים זו מקרא ומשמני הארץ זו משנה דגן זו תלמוד תירוש זה אגדה "'Heaven's dew' is the written Torah, 'earth's richness' is the Mishnah, '[the abundance of] grain' is the Talmud, and 'the new wine' is the Aggadah." In tractate Soferim 16: 5, a proficient disciple of Rabbi Aqiba is praised for his vast and astute knowledge in the interpretation of Torah rules: שהיה חכם במקרא ובקי במשנה וותיק בתלמוד וסבר בהגדה "He was sage in [the understanding of] Scripture, erudite in the Mishnah, high-ranking in the Talmud, and ingenious in the Aggadah." Knowledge of Israelite religion, culture and conduct

The fact that the only explicit dictum that prohibits the writing of the oral Torah originates from the words of Rabbi Yohanan and Resh Laqish (see note 80), and both distinguished between halakhot and homilies, must induce us to explore the motive behind this distinction. I postulate that these two Sages understood the purpose of the requirement as ensuring the flexibility of the law, which might be jeopardized by committing the law to writing. This motive, therefore, was relevant only with respect to legal utterances, not to moral homilies. In this case, as in others, it was the Tannaim who had instituted the custom of not writing halakhot, but had not deemed it necessary to declare the rule explicitly, or justify it with hermeneutic support from the Bible. The Amoraim, as with their approach to all tannaitic utterances, attempted to vindicate the rule, and searched for scriptural hints. It is possible that prior to this distinction between halakhah and homilies, the tannaitic custom was considered all-inclusive, and only the highly-regarded Rabbi Yohanan[88] had the courage to limit this restriction and sanction the harmless writing of homilies.

S. Lieberman[89] also notes a differentiation between the written publication of halakhot, which was prohibited, and the writing of notes for one's personal use, which was permitted. He cites a number of talmudic[90]

---

required the equal study of all branches of Israelite literature. An interesting event is recorded in yBava Qamma, 4: 3, 4b: מעשה ששילח המלכות שני איסרטיוטות ללמוד תורה מרבן גמליאל ולמדו ממנו מקרא משנה תלמוד הלכות ואגדות "It occurred that the [Roman] authorities sent two officers to study the Torah from Rabban Gamaliel [the Patriarch] and they learned from him Scripture, Mishnah, Talmud, laws and *aggadot*." G. Alon, *The Jews*, vol. 1, p. 212, assumes that this narrative attests to the interest of the Roman occupiers in Jewish civil law. Alon agrees in this instance with scholarly opinion that while the Romans in Gamaliel's time did not recognize the authority of Jewish courts, the Jews voluntarily submitted their judicial cases to the Sages.

87 A homily in Sifre Deut 306 amalgamates all branches of the Torah into a single unity. A metaphor there compares the Torah to the rain, which fertilizes all plants: כך דברי תורה כולה אחת ויש בה מקרא ומשנה תלמוד הלכות והגדות "So are the words of the Torah; it is all one entity comprising Scripture and Mishnah, Talmud, halakhot and aggadot." Cf. P. Schäfer, *Studien*, p. 197 concerning Rabbi Yohanan's role in this issue

88 We read in bPesahim 3b that Rabbi Yohanan, as a young student sitting before Rabbi, the Patriarch, answered a certain intricate question. The text continues: מובטח אני בזה שמורה הוראה בישראל ולא היה ימים מועטים עד שהורה הוראה בישראל "[Rabbi proclaimed on that occasion:] 'I am sure that he will be a judge in Israel.' And little time passed before he achieved this status."

89 S. Lieberman, *Hellenism*, p. 87.

90 Among others, he refers to a narrative in bShabbat 6b: דאמר רב מצאתי מגלת סתרים בי רבי חייא וכתוב בה "Since Rab said: I found a secret scroll of Rabbi Hiyya, in which [a rabbinic dictum] was written." This demonstrates that the Sages made some written notes for their personal use, as is indicated by the term "secret."

and other sources to substantiate his thesis. The same motive underlies this distinction: the written publication of a law would render it fixed, and was thus banned, whereas the writing of a memo for private use would have no such consequence, and was permitted. G. Stemberger[91] notes the same distinction, and confirms that written publication was prohibited because it "would have precluded the process of modifying this law in accordance with the peculiar time and conditions in each period."[92]

The fact that the Sadducees, and the sects who composed the Dead Sea Scrolls, did indeed write halakhot offers further substantiation of my thesis. These groups objected to the far-fetched hermeneutic methods of the Pharisees with respect to the establishment of halakhah, and disputed the concept of flexibility of the law. They opted for a rigid approach to the law; they therefore had no reason to prohibit the recording of the halakhot in writing, the most efficient method of preserving them in their original form.[93]

1.6 Rabbinic Terminology

Before proceeding to a detailed examination of the nature of halakhic decision-making, it is best to clarify certain of the terms used by the Sages.

1.6.1 "Tradition": קבלה, מסורה, שמועה

Tradition is taken to mean the laws transmitted from generation to generation, as in mAvot 1: 1: "Moses received the Torah at Sinai and transmitted it to Joshua...."[94] It is implicitly assumed that every tradition originates from God's oral transmission to Moses. Both the terms קבלה and מסורה (from the root מסר, "to hand over") may be used to express this

---

[91] G. Stemberger, *Introduction to the Talmud and Midrash*, p. 37.

[92] H. Fox (Lebeit Yoreh), "Introducing Tosefta," questions the generally accepted position that the Mishnah was an exclusively oral "publication." He writes on p. 4: "It may be that for purpose of public discourse Mishnah was to be cited orally whereas privately one may have consulted or used archival copies of a written text." However we may consider these different propositions, they do not offer an answer to why there was a restriction against writing the Mishnah at all. A requirement of flexibility would explain such a restriction. Various methods were devised for circumventing the restriction for pragmatic reasons.

[93] I revert to this topic in the second part of this work, in connection with the examination of the sectarian disputes with respect to halakhah

[94] For the full citation, see n. 84.

concept, both deriving from the above citation.[95] The term שמועה, or the Aramaic שמועתא, from the root שמע "to hear," may also be used; the term connotes decisions that are heard, that is, received by oral transmission.[96] It is interesting that the term מפי השמועה "by hearing," evolved in some instances to mean "from the Deity." We read in yNazir 7: 2, 56c, in the name of Rabbi Jacob b. Idi in the name of Rabbi Simeon, and in bBekhorot 58a in the name of Rabbi Yohanan: [in B.T. מפי השמועה] מדרש אמרוה מפי חגי זכריה ומלאכי "It was stated from the Deity by [the prophets] Haggai, Zechariah and Malachi."[97]

The Talmud does not explicitly distinguish between a tradition resulting from custom and that based on a decision proclaimed by a prior rabbinic or other qualified authority, such as a prophet,[98] king,[99] or similar

---

95 Cf. W. Bacher, *Terminologie*, who writes on pp. I/165-6 and II/185 that the term קבלה was not used by the Tannaim in their discussions, but only by the Amoraim. The term מסר, in his opinion (p. I/106), applies equally to written and oral Torah; the noun מסורת indicates transmission of data or knowledge, whereas the transmission of law is called הלכה.

96 W. Bacher, ibid. p. I/189 adds that the term שמע is also utilized as "to understand - to deduce," as for example in mSanhedrin 1: 6: ממשמע שנאמר לא תהיה אחרי רבים לרעות שומע אני שאהיה עמהם לטובה אם כן למה נאמר אחרי רבים להטות "From what is said [in Exod 23: 2] 'Do not follow the crowd [majority] in doing wrong,' I deduce that I should follow the majority to do good. If so, why is it said [subsequently] 'side with the majority?'" In *Tradition*, p. 9, Bacher states that a dictum introduced by שמעתי intends to declare: "I have received this halakhah from an authoritative source," thus bestowing upon it the utmost authenticity.

97 That is, since it was received by tradition from the prophets, who received it from the Deity; see Rashi's explanation at bBekhorot 58a and at bHorayot 14a. A similar equation is encountered in yShabbat 1: 2, 3a: שכל השומע פרשה מן בן בנו כאלו הוא שומעה מהר סיני "For everyone who listens to a quote from the Torah from his grandson, it is as if he were hearing it on Mount Sinai." The passage goes on: אם יכול את לשלשל את השמועה עד משה שלשלה ואם לאו תפוש או ראשון ראשון או אחרון אחרון "One who proclaims a tradition should declare its origin and course of transmission from Moses, if known to him, otherwise he should mention the first in the line of transmission, or the last."

98 We read in Sifre Deut 175: אליו תשמעון אפילו אומר לך עבור על אחת מן המצות האמורות בתורה כאליהו בהר הכרמל לפי שעה שמע לו "[It is written in Deut 18: 15] 'you must listen to him [the prophet].' Even if he tells you to transgress one of the precepts stated in the Torah, as Elijah [ruled] at Mount Carmel [1 Kgs chap. 18, when he allegedly performed an illegal act], you must obey him for the moment." A similar limitation of the circumstances in which utter obedience to the prophet is required appears in bSanhedrin 90a: Rabbi Yohanan declares that this precept does not apply to a prophet's command to worship idols.

99 We read in bEruvin 21b: אמר רב יהודה אמר שמואל בשעה שתיקן שלמה עירובין ונטילת ידים "Rav Yehudah said in the name of Samuel: When [king]

personality.[100] We shall examine whether such a distinction is implicit in certain occurrences. For now, we may simply note that the term שמועה, implying a tradition that is heard, does not per se exclude a tradition based on some logical foundation; nor is it always the antithesis of סברא, "reasoning" or "logical consideration." It may thus include a tradition without scriptural support or logical foundation, as well as a rule based on Scripture or on logic.[101]

1.6.2 "Torah": תורה

The expression תורה, from the root ירה "to indicate" or "to teach,"

Solomon decreed the laws of Eruvin [the prohibition against transferring something from the private domain of one person to the private domain of another person] and the washing of the hands [before touching a sacrificial object]…." In Sifre Num 116, this obligation is deduced by tortuous hermeneutics, which conclude: נמצינו למדים נטילת ידים מן התורה "Hence we learn that washing of the hands [before touching a sacrificial object] is a Torah precept."

100 We read in bBava Qamma 82a: עשרה תקנות תיקן עזרא "Ezra decreed ten edicts." In yMegillah 4: 1, 75a, the same ten ordinances promulgated by Ezra are listed, but without the heading "ten edicts." In yBerakhot 4 :1, 7a we read: רבי יהושע בן לוי אמר תפילות מאבות למדום "Rabbi Yehoshua b. Levi said: From the Patriarchs we have learned the [three daily] prayers"; he then lists them with appropriate exegesis of the relevant scriptural verses. Another Amora, however, does not deduce this obligation from the exegesis of a verse, but rather from a cosmological motive: כנגד ג' פעמים שהיום משתנה על הבריות "…from the three cycles of the day that influence humankind." In Gen. Rab. 68: 9, the obligation for three daily prayers is founded upon the exegesis of yet another verse. See further chap. 4, nn. 259-61 and related text.

101 We read, for example, in mYevamot 8: 4: אמר רבי יהושע שמעתי שהסריס חולץ וחולצין לאשתו והסריס לא חולץ ולא חולצין לאשתו ואין לי לפרש אמר ר' עקיבא אני אפרש סריס אדם חולץ וחולצין לאשתו מפני שהיתה לו שעת הכושר סריס חמה לא חולץ ולא חולצין לאשתו מפני שלא היתה לו שעת הכושר "Rabbi Yehoshua said: I heard that a eunuch takes off the sandal [performs the ceremony of refusal of the levirate duty], and one performs the same ceremony for his wife [widow]. And [I have also heard] that a eunuch does not perform the ceremony, nor is it performed for his wife, and I do not know the explanation [for these conflicting decrees]. Rabbi Aqiba said: I shall explain. A castrated man performs the ceremony and it is performed for his widow, because he was at one time [before his castration] able to sire offspring [and the first decree refers to such an instance]; [but someone] born a eunuch does not perform the ceremony, nor is it performed for his widow, because he was never able [to sire offspring]." We observe that although Rabbi Yehoshua refers to a שמועה, Rabbi Aqiba clarifies the apparent contradiction by explaining the logic of the two edicts. There are a number of such clarifications by Rabbi Aqiba; in some of these instances he does not explain the logic of the contrasting edicts, but merely clarifies the distinct circumstances that justify the different decrees. Such an example occurs in mPesahim 9: 6.

comprises the entire legal code that teaches the Israelites the correct conduct of life. Torah comprises, in Israelite understanding, the comprehensive religious tradition; that is, it consists of a written element, תורה שבכתב, and an oral element, anything that was said or written by the Sages, תורה שבעל פה. In this study, I shall use the term "Scripture" to indicate the written element of the Torah.

1.6.3 Methods of Legal Decision: מדרש, סברא

Two significant methods are included in the rabbinic decision-making process: מדרש, from the root דרש, "to examine, question, interpret, explain," which represents the result of the "technical" interpretation of Scripture in accordance with a plethora of set rules, and סברא, from the Aramaic root סבר,[102] "to think, imagine, be of the opinion," which expresses the consequence of the process of reasoning and logical consideration.

1.6.4 "Law": הלכה, תקנה, גזרה

The final stage of any legal controversy, the rule that is ultimately adopted, is called הלכה,[103] halakhah, from the root הלך "to go"; halakhah thus indicates the way in which an Israelite must go, act, or behave himself - in essence, how to live.[104]

The term halakhah does not in itself imply an origin from Sinai.[105] Some of the halakhot, perhaps even the greatest part, may be considered to

---

[102] Onkelos translates יבינו לאחריתם "Discern what their end will be [Deut 32: 29]" as סברו מא יהי בסופהון.

[103] In mMenahot 4: 3, following a dispute between Rabbi Aqiba and Simeon b. Nanas, it is stated: אמר רבי שמעון הלכה כדברי בן ננס "Rabbi Simeon said: The halakhah is according to ben Nanas." We encounter countless such expressions in both Talmudim. Another use of the term is found in the question הלכתא כמאן "Whose opinion was decided to be the halakhah?" This is found, for instance, in bShabbat 129a, following a dispute between two Sages; the answer is given: אמר ליה הלכה כמר זוטרא "He said to him: The halakhah is according to Mar Zutra [in this case]."

[104] In his noted work ספר הערוך, Rabbi Nathan of Rome perceived an additional metaphorical nuance within the rabbinic use of the term הלכה: something that goes with - i.e. accompanies - the Israelite people until eternity.

[105] We must note here the distinction between the dogmatic conception that every later decision or new resolution of the Rabbis, derived by an interpretation of Scripture or by logic, originated from Sinai, and the declaration הלכה למשה מסיני, regarding certain rules and customs with no scriptural support or logical inspiration. See further

have been received at Sinai; others, however, are evidently later rules, contrived to satisfy specific needs, mainly with respect to civil matters (as the Sages themselves attest), or to acknowledge entrenched customs. By the authority of the Sages and the courts, such rules became halakhot; that is, they acquired the status of law and were transmitted to succeeding generations in the same way as the edicts attributed to Sinaitic origin.[106]

We must also note here the nuances of meaning in the specific phrase הלכה למשה מסיני "a halakhah [given] to Moses from Sinai." As all rules are supposed to originate from the divine transmission to Moses on Mount Sinai,[107] the Talmud applies this aphorism to rules or customs for which there is no scriptural evidence of any kind,[108] as a type of *deus ex*

---

n. 108 below, and section 3.5.

106 W. Bacher, *Terminologie*, p. I/42 calls such religious ordinances normative, irrespective of their origin.

107 We read in Sifra *Behar* 1 the explicit declaration: והלא כָל המצות נאמרו מסיני אלא מה שמיטה נאמרו כללותיה ודקדוקיה מסיני אף כולם נאמרו כללותיהם ודקדוקיהם מסיני "Were not all the precepts stated at Sinai? But [the text in question teaches that] just as all the rules and specific minutiae of the sabbatical year were stated at Sinai, so the rules and specific minutiae of all precepts were stated at Sinai." See n. 17 for additional rabbinic sources to the same effect.

108 The controversy between the Pharisees and Boethusians concerning the beating of the willow branch on Sukkot is well known (for a further discussion of this controversy see chap. 3, n. 109). In tSukkah 3: 1 there is a dispute among the Rabbis with respect to the origin of the practice: ערבה הלכה למשה מסיני אבא שאול אר׳ מן התורה שנ׳ וערבי נחל "[One Rabbi said]: The willow is a precept [given] to Moses from Sinai; Abba Saul said: It originates from Scripture, since it is written [You are to take] willows [Lev 23: 40]." The core of the controversy is thus whether the custom of the willow was an ancient tradition, or originated from an interpretation of a scriptural verse. I do not think it necessary to quote the many talmudic citations of this declaration to substantiate the thesis that the declaration הלכה למשה מסיני always refers to a decree for which no scriptural or exegetical basis exists, but whose legitimacy is nonetheless supposed to derive from Sinaitic tradition (or, in modern terms, from ancient custom). Maimonides, in the Introduction to his Mishnah Commentary (J. Kapah, vol. 1, pp. יז-יח), asserts that this attribute refers to a rule for which there is no evidence in or hint from Scripture, which also cannot be deduced by logical deduction, and which is acknowledged without dispute. A few examples will suffice to illustrate this point. Both mPe'ah 2: 6 and bNazir 56b recite the system of transmission of such a rule: אמר נחום הלבלר כך מקובלני מרבי מיאשא שקיבל מאבא שקבל מן הזוגות שקבלו מן הנביאים הלכה למשה מסיני "Nahum the clerk said, I received it from Rabbi Me'asha, who received it from his father, who received it from the pairs, who received it from the prophets, [that it is] a halakhah [given] to Moses from Sinai." Sifra *Tzav* 5 and bMenahot 89a record an illuminating discussion following Rabbi Aqiba's attempt to demonstrate the scriptural origin of a rule regarding the quantities of oil required for the libation with specific offerings: אמר לו רבי אלעזר בן עזריה לרבי עקיבא אפילו אתה מרבה כל היום כולו בשמן בשמן איני שומע לך אלא חצי לוג שמן לתודה ורביעית שמן לנזיר

ואחד עשר יום שבין נדה לנדה הלכה למשה מסיני "Rabbi Eleazar ben Azaryah said to Rabbi Aqiba: Even if you continue to deduce for the entire day the quantity of oil required at the thanksgiving offering [not indicated in Scripture] from the duplication of the term 'in oil,' I do not agree with you, because the requirement of half a *log* of oil at the thanksgiving offering, and of a quarter of a *hin* of wine for the Nazir's libation offering, and the decree that there are only eleven pure days between two menstrual cycles, are all halakhah given to Moses from Sinai [and have no support from Scripture, as Rabbi Aqiba declares]." This passage indicates unquestionably that a rule deemed to be "halakhah from Sinai" is the antithesis of a rule derived from an interpretation of a biblical dictum, and Rabbi Eleazar asserted that one could not deduce these rules from a biblical source. We also observe the essence of those rules to which this attribute is applied: quantities of oil not specified in the Bible, and which cannot be logically derived from the text, and physical characteristics of the menstrual cycle. Many other rules to which this attribute is applied are of a similar nature: for instance, the form and colour of the phylacteries, and the colour of the straps. Less clear is the use of this term by Rabbi Aqiba. This Tanna, who according to bMenahot 29b is known to have interpreted every minute textual oddity - שעתיד לדרוש על כל קוץ וקוץ תילין תילין של הלכות "[a man] who will derive a multitude of rules from every stroke of the letters [of the Torah]" - attempted to detect scriptural support for customs of unknown origin. In the famous narrative in bMenahot 29b concerning Moses' participation at a session of Rabbi Aqiba's school, the Rabbi's disciples asked him: רבי מנין לך אמר להן הלכה למשה מסיני "Rabbi, how do you know it [this rule]?" His answer that it is "halakhah [given] to Moses from Sinai" does not correspond to the particular meaning we have attributed to this phrase. Since Rabbi Aqiba attempted to detect a scriptural support for every rule, what he meant by this phrase was simply that his rule originated in Scripture. He referred to his declaration in bNiddah 45a: כשם שכל התורה הלכה למשה מסיני כך פחותה מבת שלש שנים כשרה לכהונה הלכה למשה מסיני "Just as all the laws of the Torah are halakhot [given] to Moses from Sinai, so [his judgment that] a girl of less than three years who is raped is [still] suitable to marry a priest is halakhah [given] to Moses from Sinai." This fundamental declaration is similar to a citation in yMegillah, 4: 1, 74d: מקרא ומשנה ותלמוד ואגדה ואפילו מה שתלמיד וותיק עתיד להורות לפני רבו כבר נאמר למשה מסיני "Scripture, the Mishnah, the Talmud and the Aggadah, even what a proficient disciple would declare before his teacher, were already recounted to Moses on Sinai." I shall revert to this issue in section 3.5. We may note that yShevi'it 1: 5, 33b states: רבי בא רבי חייא בשם רבי יוחנן ערבה וניסוך המים הלכה למשה מסיני ודלא כרבי עקיבה דרבי עקיבה אמר ניסוך המים דבר תורה "Rabbi Ba, in the name of Rabbi Hiyya, in the name of Rabbi Yohanan [said]: The willow and the water libation [on Sukkot] are halakhah [given] to Moses from Sinai, and that [declaration] is contrary to Rabbi Aqiba, who said that the water libation has its origin in the Torah." The terms הלכה or הלכתא, which generally represent the final decision as to how to act, may indicate in other occurrences (even without the attribute למשה מסיני "[given] to Moses from Sinai") a rule, a decision without scriptural support, or logic. We must come to the conclusion that in this case, as in others, the talmudic terms do not represent a precise concept.

It is not clear whether the phrases גמרא גמירי לה or הלכתא גמירי לה, used in the talmudic rhetoric in occurrences for which no logical or scriptural justifications of a certain rule exist, is equivalent to the declaration הלכה למשה מסיני, or means *machina*, to confirm their legitimacy. It is obvious that these rules consisted in many cases of ancient customs, or solutions to newly arisen problems, or the adaptation of old practices to changed circumstances. To ensure their maximum efficacy, the Sages attributed to them a scriptural origin,[109] whenever an appropriate hermeneutic seemed plausible, or to a divine oral transmission.[110] At the same time, we observe that the Sages did not attribute all of their rules to divine origin: Joshua's regulations concerning Jericho do not bear the divine stamp of authorization from Sinai, nor do certain rules attributed to Solomon and various prophets.[111]

---

simply: "It is a tradition." Rashi interprets the declaration גמרא גמירי לה as הלכה למשה מסיני at bSanhedrin 47a, but in no other occurrences. In bZevahim 13a, Rashi interprets the declaration ובן עזאי גמרא גמיר לה to mean that Simeon ben Azzai knew a tradition from the seventy-two elders, referring to his assertion in mZevahim 1: 3: אמר שמעון בן עזאי מקובל אני מפי שבעים ושנים זקן "Simeon ben Azzai said: I know [the rule by tradition] from seventy-two elders." In this occurrence, it is obvious that the rule has no logical or scriptural origin; it is based solely on tradition, but without any attempt to attribute it to a Sinaitic source, and ben Azzai does not extend its origin back further than the seventy-two elders. The issue discussed in bShabbat 97a ending with גמרא גמירי לה refers to a common rule of practice: כל פחות מג׳ כלבוד דמי "What is [placed] less that three handbreadths [from another entity] is assumed to be joined to it." This principle is applied in a number of occurrences in which it makes a significant difference whether something is deemed attached or severed. It is found, for instance, in bShabbat 97a; the passage reveals no logical or scriptural support for the principle, but resolves the issue with the stereotypical declaration גמרא גמירי לה. The Y. T. expresses this rule with different language: שכל הפחות משלשה כסתום הוא "an opening smaller than three handbreadths is [considered] closed" (Eruvin 7: 1, 24b, and Sukkah 1: 1, 52b); again, no explanation or justification are offered. I would suggest interpreting גמרא גמירי לה as "We know it by tradition," with no further allusion as to its original source. The talmudic rhetoric creates a distinction by using the attribute למשה מסיני only in some instances, and I therefore suggest that we accept this distinction between the two expressions.

109 This system of attributing laws and customs to earlier revered personalities is used already in Scripture. We see, for example, that the supplementary custom of living in booths, added to the ancient harvesting holiday, חג האסף בצאת השנה "Feast of the ingathering at the end of the [agricultural] year [Exod 23: 16]," was attributed to Moses (Neh 8: 14). Similarly, a distinctive style of celebrating the Passover Feast and offering (an analysis of which is beyond the scope of this study) was introduced in the period of Josiah, and was attributed in 2 Kgs 23: 22 to the Judges and in 2 Chr 35: 18 to the prophet Samuel.

110 I. H.Weiss, דור דור ודורשיו, pp. 70 - 71 asserts that since we encounter disputes between the Sages as to whether certain decrees are of this category, we must doubt whether their source was really in tradition. He also suggests that the Sages used the attribute "a halakhah [given] to Moses from Sinai" to encourage the fulfillment of decrees that were not scrupulously obeyed.

111 See nn. 99, 100 and 127 with respect to the decrees of Joshua, Solomon, and others.

In addition to halakhah, which implies a permanent, absolute and conclusive resolution, the rabbinic literature lists two supplementary types of decrees: תקנה,[112] *taqqanah*, from the Aramaic root תקן, "to make good, to straighten, to repair,"[113] and גזרה, *gezeirah*, from the root גזר, "to cut," and by metaphorical extension "to cut off, to separate, to deliver a sentence, to decree an ordinance."[114] Both terms relate to extraordinary edicts decreed by the Sages under the mandate of their divine authority. The term *gezeirah* in reference to alien or hostile authorities usually implies an oppressive edict.

E. E. Urbach reviews these two terms and the stages of their development. He states[115] that the term *gezeirah* implies a preventative

---

[112] We read in mSukkah 3: 12 and mRosh HaShanah 4: 3: משחרב בית המקדש התקין רבן יוחנן בן זכאי שיהא לולב ניטל במדינה שבעה "After the destruction of the Temple, Rabbi Yohanan ben Zakkai decreed the use of the *lulav* [the palm branch] in the land outside Jerusalem for all the seven days [of the Feast of Tabernacles]." W. Bacher, *Terminologie*, interprets the tannaitic term as "to arrange" (p. I/204) and the amoraic term as "to improve, to repair" (p. II/241).

[113] Onkelos translates היטיבו כל אשר דברו "Everything they said was good" in Deut 5: 25 (v. 28 in KJV) as אתקינו דמלילו. W. Bacher, *Terminologie*, p. I/204, also compares this term to סדר "to arrange."

[114] Also, "to cut off," "to cancel something," and, as currently used, "to axe." We encounter an interesting homily in bYoma 67b, based on the term ארץ גזרה "solitary place" in Lev 16: 22 (NIV translation) in reference to the scapegoat: גזירה אין גזירה אלא חתוכה דבר אחר אין גזרה אלא דבר המתגזר ויורד דבר אחר גזרה שמא תאמר מעשה תהו הוא תלמוד לומר אני ה׳ אני ה׳ גזרתיו ואין לך רשות להרהר בהן "[It is written in Lev 16: 22] ארץ גזרה; this indicates 'sliced,' that is, a steeply cut rock. Another interpretation: The goat that is cut to pieces and drops down. Another interpretation: I am God and have so decreed, and you must not ponder it." The first two interpretations consist of basic philological explanations, but the third has a theological message: do not ask questions on the motive behind divine commands. The rabbinic גזירות, "edicts" are presumed to have motives for their promulgation; the rabbinic conception of the divine גזירות, however, is of two natures. Mekilta d' Rabbi Ishmael, *Beshallah* 1, in answering the question as to why the firstborn of donkeys must be redeemed, but not the firstborn of camels or horses, states: גזרת מלך היא שלא היה בידן באותה שעה אלא חמורים בלבד "It is a royal [divine] edict; the [Israelites] possessed only donkeys at that time." Here, the odd restriction in the edict is logically explained. In other occurrences, however, the expression גזרת מלך conveys the idea that the edict is a divine decree and must be performed without questioning its motive or logic. There are many examples in rabbinic literature, in addition to that of the scapegoat cited above. In tSanhedrin 11: 6, for instance, a Tanna states that logically the command regarding the rebellious son should have been applied to a daughter; in response it is stated: אלא גזירת מלך היא "but it is a royal edict [and we must accept it without questioning its logic]." Such examples confirm that rabbinic literature abounds with inexact terminology.

[115] E. E. Urbach, ההלכה, p. 11.

measure - that is, the prohibition of an otherwise permitted act that might lead one to carry out a similar, but prohibited, act.[116] The term certainly includes such edicts, as for example in yShabbat 1: 4, 3d, and in a baraita in bShabbat 14b: "Yose son of Yoezer from Zereida and Yose son of Yohanan of Jerusalem decreed that foreign lands and glass objects are impure."[117] We also encounter the term *gezeirah*, however, with respect to decrees of an affirmative character - that is, a mandate to perform a deed hitherto not imposed. We read of such *gezeirot* in mYadayim 4: 3: "On that day [when Rabbi Eleazar ben Azaryah was nominated Patriarch of the College] it was asked [what is the rule regarding the tithes from the harvest] in the seventh year, in Ammon and Moab. Rabbi Tarfon decreed [that the harvest is liable for] the tithes for the poor and Rabbi Eleazar ben Azaryah decreed [that it is liable for] the second tithe [which must be consumed in Jerusalem]."[118] Another example further substantiates my point. We read in yBerakhot 9: 5, 14c:[119] "In three circumstances the heavenly court agreed with the decrees of the earthly court: the devotion of Jericho to the Lord,[120] the reading of the Esther Scroll,[121] and the

---

[116] I have argued below (section 4.1.7) that the term גזרה as a preventative extension of a prohibition is used only by the Amoraim, and not in the Mishnah. W. Bacher, *Termonologie*, p. I/12 considers this term to be an ordinance, regulation or rule without biblical foundation; he does not designate it as a preventative rule.

[117] This edict is also found in tParah 3: 5, but there is no record of who enacted it. We read there: לא גזרו טומאה בארץ העמים אלא לאחר שעלו מן הגולה "They decreed that foreign lands are impure only after they returned from exile."

[118] See further on this mishnah chap. 3, nn. 100, 120 and 183.

[119] The same dictum appears in bMakkot 23b, but there the term גזר is not found; the non-specific עשר is utilized.

[120] In Josh 6: 18 we read that Joshua decreed the devotion of Jericho to the Lord, without any prior divine command. Nevertheless, the people are accused of transgressing this command as if it had been a divine edict, as we read in Josh 7: 11: חטא ישראל וגם עברו את בריתי אשר צויתי אותם "Israel has sinned; they have violated my covenant, which I commanded them to keep."

[121] We read in yMegillah 1: 5, 70d, that eighty-five elders, including about thirty prophets, deliberated upon the apparent contradiction between the prohibition against prophets enacting new precepts beyond those given to Moses, and the obligation to read the Megillah. After divine enlightenment, they realized that the reading of the Megillah is hinted at in Scripture. Exod 17: 14 states: כתב זאת זכרון בספר "Write this on a scroll," while in Esth 9: 32 it is stated: ונכתב בספר "and it was written in a scroll"; hence, the scroll of the Megillah was included in the scroll written by Moses. Similar homilies appear in bMegillah 7a and in Ruth Rab. 4: 5. In the latter, a subsequent homily derives the scriptural support from the *ketiv* קבל, in singular, in Esth 9: 27: קימו וקבלו היהודים לא כתיב וקבל כתיב רבן של יהודים קיבל "'The Jews took it upon themselves' is not written in plural, but in singular; [this refers] to the master of the Jews [the Deity] who consented [to this precept]."

permission to mention the divine name in a greeting."[122] In both citations the edicts, which are expressed with a form of גזר, are certainly affirmative decrees.

Thus while Urbach is correct that the noun *gezeirah* in the Talmud is usually used to prohibit an otherwise acceptable deed in order to avoid a forbidden one, the above passages, as well as many others,[123] confirm that there are also many exceptions. It is therefore impossible to establish a definite classification of its character.[124] It seems that the Sages were not extremely careful in their use of terms and concepts, as we shall observe in other instances.

I would also like to comment on Urbach's thesis with respect to the term תקנה, *taqqanah*, and its verbal forms, from the root תקן. Urbach

---

[122] The Sages deduce this from Ruth 2: 4: והנה בעז בא מבית לחם ויאמר לקוצרים ה׳ עמכם "Just then Boaz arrived from Bethlehem and greeted the harvesters 'The Lord be with you.'" The divine name is written in the MT in the Tetragrammaton form, and this indicates that Boaz pronounced this name in his greeting, although it is forbidden to utter it.

[123] We read, for example, in bShabbat 30a: מנהגו של עולם שר בשר ודם גוזר גזרה ספק מקיימין אותה ספק אין מקיימין אותה "It generally happens that when a human ruler promulgates a decree, it is not certain that it will be obeyed." In this occurrence the term גזרה is neutral as to the character of the decree, but in other instances the term definitely indicates an unfavourable decree. We read in bSotah 12a: ואמר ר״י בר׳ חנינא שלש גזירות גזר פרעה "And Rabbi Yose son of Hanina said: [Pharaoh] decreed three edicts," and all were wicked proclamations. A homily in Mekilta d' Rabbi Ishmael, *Bo* 13 uses the term in the same sense: שכל גזירות שהיה פרעה גוזר על ישראל היו השבויין שמחין "The prisoners in Egypt rejoiced whenever Pharaoh decreed atrocious edicts against the Israelites." There is a further example in yQiddushin 1: 7, 61a; when Solomon came to kill Joab, he said to him: אביך גזר עלי חמש גזירות "Your father [David] pronounced five grievous rulings against me." In other occurrences the term גזרה implies simply a decision, not connected with a decree or law, as in bShabbat 30a: גזרה היא מלפני שאין מודיעין קצו של בשר ודם "[God said to David]: It is my decision that a person's time of demise not be communicated."

[124] In Sifra *Nedabah* 8: 8 the term גזרה is used in an affirmative, even obligatory, sense: נפש תקריב יכול גזרה תלמוד לומר כי תקריב אינה אלא רשות "[It is written] 'A person shall bring.' We could understand this as he **must** bring; the conjunction כי 'if' comes to teach us that it is a voluntary act." A passage in Mekilta d'Rabbi Ishmael, *Bo* 1 seems to define the outermost boundaries of the term גזירה. We read there: כשהקב״ה גוזר גזרות טובות ורעות על ישראל "[The term refers to] when the Holy One Blessed be He proclaims good and bad judgments on Israel." Here the term is completely neutral, and can be used for every type of decision. S. Zeitlin, *Studies*, p. 22 states that גזרה refers to a temporary ordinance decreed for special circumstances. The use of this term for a rabbinic ordinance appears only in the Gemara, as an amoraic concept; the Tannaim in the Mishnah do not use it. See further section 4.1.7.

treats the two terms *gezeirot* and *taqqanot* together, but whereas he considers that the term *gezeirah* unmistakably refers to issues connected with scriptural law, to create a סייג, a "fence" or "hedge" around the Torah (p. 11), most[125] of his citations of *taqqanot* relate to administrative orders in civil matters. At certain periods these orders were within the ambit of the court's authority,[126] but were not considered halakhah,[127]and were not

[125] The ordinance allowing a combatant to take weapons home on Sabbath after a battle is correctly perceived by Urbach (ההלכה, p. 12) as a decree related to a halakhah, but not the primary legalization of the right to defend oneself on Sabbath; the latter was decided by the Hasmoneans, as also perceived by Urbach. According to bYoma 85a, the Sages were asked: מניין לפקוח נפש שדוחה את השבת "From where [in the Torah] do we know that the saving of life overrides the Sabbath?" A number of Sages proffer appropriate interpretations of biblical verses and logical reflections to provide scriptural support; hence, this is not, as Urbach suggests, a תקנה, according to the rabbinic terminology. Some of the תקנות were also instituted within the ambit of customs; I cited above Rabbi Yohanan ben Zakkai's ordinance that the *lulav*, the palm branch, was to be used after the Temple's destruction during all the seven days of Sukkot in the land outside Jerusalem.

[126] We read in tSheqalim 1: 1: בחמשה עשר בו שלוחי בית דין יוצאין ומתקינין את הדרכים ואת הרחובות שחולחלו בימות הגשמים פרק למועד סמך לעולי רגלים כדי שיהו מותקנין בשלשה רגלים "On the fifteenth [of Adar] the representatives of the court would go out and repair the roads and the streets that were eroded by the rains [during the winter] close to the pilgrimage period, so that they would be in good order for the pilgrimages."

[127] Urbach cites, for example, the method established for the return of lost property, the ceremony for the comforting of mourners (bSanhedrin 19a), and a great number of ordinances attributed to Joshua (bBava Qamma 82a) and to King Solomon (bEruvin 21b) referring to matters of public order and relations between neighbours. It is obvious, as Urbach also assumes, that these are ancient customs that developed over a long period of time, and were attributed to great personalities to enhance their significance and ensure their observance. The fact that the Sages do not attribute them to Moses with the maxim הלכה למשה מסיני, but rather to Joshua or Solomon, demonstrates that they did not consider them within the ambit of halakhah. The same consideration applies to the ordinances attributed to Ezra and Nehemiah, cited by Urbach. It is interesting to note that some of the rules attributed to Ezra in the talmudic narrative are in reality scriptural commands, as the following discussions reveal. These dicta do not represent an authentic historical record of the development of halakhah, but rather a common talmudic approach of bundling together a variety of similar decrees, customs, typologies, etc., in order to create a collection of entities with the same number, such as three, seven, ten (see, e.g., mAvot 1: 3 and 1: 18; bBerakhot 51a, 55a, 57b; bPesahim 54a; bYoma 23a; bHagigah 12a; bQiddushin 82a; bBava Batra 10a; bSanhedrin 17b, 36b; bHorayot 13b; bTamid 31b), thirteen etc. In our case, the main goal was to collect ten decrees, without regard to any common characteristic among them. The further dictum that includes ten specific rules with respect to Jerusalem, cited without a distinct origin, reveals a similar array compiled to reach the number ten. Such rules thus cannot be used to derive some common principle or method of promulgation. Some of these rules might be considered halakhot dealing with religious law; others are evidently issues of civil law.

intended to be part of the continuous transmission process from Sinai. A passage in bBava Metzi'a 112b reveals the distinction between halakhah and *taqqanah*. The passage records a *taqqanah* to the effect that a hired worker has the right to swear that he has not received remuneration for his work, in the event the employer declares that he has been paid, and to receive his compensation: "A hired worker takes the oath and receives his pay, when he had requested it on time [mBava Metzi'a 9: 12]." This ordinance instituted by the Sages is in plain contradiction to the general rule, based on the interpretation of Exod 22: 10 (v. 11 in KJV), that the party who must pay (in this case the employer) should take the oath. In the course of the debate, Rav Yehudah in the name of Samuel states: "Very important halakhot were taught here." It is immediately asked: "Are these halakhot? [i.e. this is the wrong term.] These are *taqqanot* [ordinances decreed by the Sages]!" We observe the distinction between the two terms, and the succeeding discussion changes the wording and confirms: "Important *taqqanot* were taught here." A baraita in bShabbat 14b also records an absolutely clear distinction between the two terms: "Simeon ben Shetah instituted [תיקן] the woman's *ketubbah*, and decreed [וגזר] the impurity of metal vessels."[128] The first stipulation, expressed with the term תקן, consists of an administrative rule, whereas the second, expressed with the term גזר, refers to an extension of the halakhah.

Although we should not expect to find in talmudic literature the sort of precise definitions of legal terms that we do in Greek philosophical writings, I postulate that the general character of the term *taqqanah* indicates a rabbinic edict that has no foundation in Scripture. It may be of temporary or perpetual validity, but in contrast to הלכה למשה מסיני "a halakhah [given] to Moses from Sinai," it refers unequivocally to a traditional edict decreed post-Sinai. The applications of decrees characterized as *taqqanot* are various and unqualified: they are found within the secular and sacred domains, in public administrative matters, and in civil and family issues; they do not depend on oral tradition from Sinai[129] or on exegesis of Scripture,[130] and this is their common attribute.

---

[128] The parallel statement in yPesahim 1: 6, 27d, and yKetubbot 8: 11, 32c, does not list the *ketubbah* ordinance among those promulgated by these Sages. In the subsequent rhetoric, however, we again observe a distinction between the two terms: התקין שמעון בן שטח שלשה דברים שיהא אדם נושא ונותן בכתובת אשתו "Simeon b. Shetah instituted three ordinances: that a man may deal with the assets of his wife's *ketubbah* [and is fully responsible for them]..." and subsequently: גזרו טומאה על ארץ העמים ועל כלי זכוכית "they decreed the impurity of foreign lands and glass vessels."

[129] The retrojection of a תקנה to "grand heroes," as M. Jaffee correctly indicates ("Taqqanah," p. 225), acts as validation. The rule derives not from Sinai, but from a revered personality. For example, I have quoted above yBerakhot 4 :1, 7a: "Rabbi

Yehoshua b. Levi said: From the Patriarchs we have learned the [three daily] prayers." In bBerakhot 26b the rule is quoted in the name of the same Rabbi Yehoshua b. Levi: תפלות כנגד תמידין תקנום "The prayers were instituted corresponding to the [daily] perpetual offerings." In the subsequent rhetoric, it is said that indeed the Patriarchs instituted them, and the Sages supported their performance in relation to the offerings. With respect to the blessings after the meal, we encounter a remarkable dictum in bBerakhot 48b that demonstrates the complexity of the issue: אמר רב נחמן משה תקן לישראל ברכת הזן בשעה שירד להם מן יהושע תקן להם ברכת הארץ כיון שנכנסו לארץ דוד ושלמה תקנו בונה ירושלים דוד תקן על ישראל עמך ועל ירושלים עירך ושלמה תקן על הבית הגדול והקדוש הטוב והמטיב ביבנה תקנוה כנגד הרוגי ביתר "Rabbi Nahman said: Moses established the blessing after the meal for the Israelites when the manna descended for them; Joshua arranged the blessing of the land when the Israelites entered the land; David and Solomon established the [complex] blessing regarding the building of Jerusalem: David established [the prayer for God's mercy] 'on Israel, your people and Jerusalem, your city,' and Solomon established [the phrase] 'the great and holy House [Temple].' The blessing '[God] who is good and beneficent' was established at Yabneh [when the Romans allowed the burial of] those killed in Betar [during the Bar Kokhba rebellion]." This dictum is a paradigm for the use of the legal concept תקן. Scripture commands that one bless God for granting food to the Israelites: ואכלת ושבעת וברכת את ה׳ אלהיך על הארץ הטבה אשר נתן לך "When you have eaten and are satisfied praise the Lord your God for the good land he has given you [Deut 8: 10]." Scripture does not, however, indicate the structure of such a blessing, and thus it is indicated that the blessing was instituted by Moses, in the style it had in the rabbinic period. Scripture also requires blessing God for the land, which Moses could obviously not arrange before entering the land; Joshua was thus said to have completed it in due course. David and Solomon were considered to have instituted the blessings for Jerusalem and the Temple, each in its appropriate period; another blessing was attributed to anonymous personalities with respect to an event in the rebellion. A variety of enactments, possibly effected in different periods, are thus attributed to "heroes"(as Jaffee calls them), though the last attribution does not reflect the "heroic" genealogy of its composer, but rather the reason for the prayer. Such enactments lack either tradition from Sinai or basis in a scriptural verse. The above examples demonstrate the various types of rulings included in the legal term תקנה; in some instances it refers to the institution of edicts without scriptural foundation, such as the blessing before the meal, while in others the תקנה establishes the details of a particular command, such as the blessing after the meal. We may note that in yBerakhot 7: 1, 11a, it is said in the name of Rabbi Ishmael: הטוב והמטיב דבר תורה דכתיב ואכלת ושבעת וברכת זו ברכת הזימון "The blessings [after the meal] are a Torah precept, since it is written [Deut 8: 10] 'when you have eaten and are satisfied, praise the Lord,' and this is the first blessing after the meal." The other blessings are deduced by exegesis from the subsequent words in this verse.

130 While this is the general character of the תקנה, Jaffee ("Taqqanah," p. 216) quotes an instance in Sifre Deut 113 in which a scriptural support is added. See chap. 2, nn. 151-59 and related texts, for my discussion on this specific subject in connection with the *prosbul*. One may note that the Amoraim, as well as the redactor of Sifre in this occurrence, assumed that every decree, and particularly one that appears to be contrary to a Torah law, must be founded upon a scriptural support. Another example of this kind is the precept for washing the hands; see chapter 4, n. 133. See chap. 2, n.

In contrast to Urbach, who is interested in the development of the halakhah in all its aspects, my attention is focused on the development of rules and ordinances assumed by the Sages to be of divine origin, and conveyed to Moses on Sinai for perpetual transmission.

1.7 Conclusion

We may depict the supposedly "immutable" rabbinic legal system as a complex triangle of opposing forces. One side consisted of the trend toward freedom of opinion. Another side consisted of the transmitted oral tradition, which had great significance in the life of the people and was considered to have legal authority.[131] This tradition may often have clashed with the opinions of the Sages, or with current circumstances and requirements. Another difficulty associated with tradition concerned the vagaries of oral transmission. It cannot be assumed that customs and legal decisions would be identically transmitted in all their details; decision-making by local leaders and scholars would result not only in differences of procedure from one place to another, but also in the creation of contrasting and often ambiguous traditions.

The third side of the triangle was simply the unlimited variability of human nature. Judgments regarding the applicability of transmitted traditions to current issues, or the solution of new problems, would inevitably result in divergent propositions and pronouncements by the various Sages. This maze of sources and decisions created apparently permanent rifts among the authors of the various opinions, each tending toward his own general perspective and specific conceptions.

One may, to some extent, compare these competing forces and trends with the perception that modern legal systems constantly change according to shifts in public opinion, which is considered to be the ultimate source of legal authority and the initiator of changes in the law. The intrinsic properties of modern systems allow, and even encourage, change and provide appropriate mechanisms for it. In Israelite theology the ultimate source of legal authority is the Deity. The Deity cannot be asked for advice on how to effect the necessary adjustments, and the

142 with respect to the posing of this question for clearly logical decrees that do not require scriptural support. A similar approach is evident here to that which we have observed above (n. 108) with respect to the term הלכה למשה מסיני. As we noted, certain Tannaim maintained that the water libation on Sukkot is such a decree, while Rabbi Aqiba deduced this rule through a hermeneutic analysis of scriptural verses. See chap. 3, n. 95.

[131] According to mAvot 1: 1, cited above n. 84, it was said to have been transmitted by God to Moses, and from then on, until the period of the Sages.

divine law is assumed to be eternal and immutable,[132] since God is omniscient,[133] knows every future circumstance, and proclaimed His commands accordingly. The Sages, however, could assume that they were carrying out the intent of God, the initiator of changes[134] and the source of their authority, and in this way, their approach may be seen as similar to that of a modern judiciary.

There are also obvious similarities between the type of intervention practised by the Sages and the current, and much-debated, issue of judicial activism. The study will quote in due course a number of examples of rabbinic interpretations and decisions that are entirely contrary to the plain meaning of the biblical texts that were the basis of their deliberations.[135] Again, however, there is a fundamental distinction between the two approaches, of a philosophical rather than a practical nature. The promoters of judicial activism argue that it is impossible and indeed unnecessary to search for the "original" intent of the creators of the Constitution or statute law. One may compare this theory to the debate among those in the literary field as to whether the source of meaning of an oeuvre is the "reader" or the "text." The rabbinic philosophy, in contrast, could not build upon such assumptions. The Sages had to assume that they were in fact ascertaining the Deity's original intent;[136] their belief system

---

[132] We read in Deut 4: 2: לא תספו על הדבר אשר אנכי מצוה אתכם ולא תגרעו ממנו "Do not add to what I command you and do not subtract from it."

[133] See Introduction, n. 70 on Maimonides' explanation of the miracles, which he stated had already been planned by God at the time of creation.

[134] A homily in tSanhedrin 4: 7 endorses this viewpoint: ואומ' וכתב לו את משנה התורה הזאת וגו' תורה עתידה להשתנות "And it says: 'He is to write himself a copy of this law.' [This teaches us that] the Torah will change." The homily is based on the fact that the same root שנה can mean both "to duplicate" and "to change."

[135] S. A. Cohen, *Three Crowns*, p. 70, writes with respect to the Sages' philosophy: "The true understanding of Torah depended not upon irrational inspiration, but upon man's exercise of his critical faculties as manifest in sound philology and diligent exegesis." Cohen's statement is elegantly expressed, but is somewhat obscure. His phrase "critical faculties" is difficult; does it imply a critical analysis of God's utterances, the Torah, or simply an attentive study? Does "diligent" exegesis imply "tireless and persistent," or an assiduous search for intent? I have the impression that he perceives the Sages as reaching their decisions on the basis of careful exegesis, whereas it is my conviction (see section 2.2) that their creative exegesis served as justification for their preconceived opinions, which were in turn based on their need to adapt the law to changing circumstances. Their hermeneutics cannot, in many cases, be considered a "diligent" interpretation of the text.

[136] Cf. J. M. Harris, *How Do We Know This?* p. 7: "One is left with the impression that exegesis represents nothing more than the personal preference of different Sages, and, therefore, we might conclude that the results cannot be considered part of the essential message of the divine lawgiver." Harris perceives a dichotomy between the personal opinion of the Sage and God's will and intentions. From reading other parts of his

would not permit them any exegesis that ignored this intent.[137] Since God is omniscient, the Sages' adaptation of His rules to new circumstances would thus not represent a change of the divine intent, but merely their enlightenment regarding the minutiae of this intent for each specific state of affairs.[138]

A remarkable declaration in yShevi'it 1: 1, 33a, indicates the extent of this belief and attitude. We read there: בשעה שאסרו למקרי סמכו ובשעה שהתירו למקרא סמכו "When they prohibited [the working of improvements in a field just before the onset of the seventh year, when the fields must lie fallow], they relied on scriptural support, and when they permitted it, they relied on scriptural support [halakhic midrash]." I understand this apparently paradoxical statement as conveying the belief that the Sages acted in conformity with God's intent expressed in Scripture in both occurrences. They founded their prohibition, when deemed necessary, on their knowledge of the Torah, and the same knowledge supported the opposite rule, when circumstances required it. Contemporary orthodox Rabbis, we may note, proceed similarly and go so far as to proclaim "religiously founded" rulings on political issues. They derive their authority from דעת תורה "knowledge of the Torah";[139] their intimate and penetrating perception of the Torah bestows upon them a competence to apprehend the divine intent, that is not evident to everyone, for all unforeseen circumstances.[140]

---

book, I have the impression that he himself approached his examination of the Sages' halakhic development with a strongly negative predisposition, or even prejudice, which influenced his conclusion.

137 As we have noted above, the Sages did in some cases seem to consider their authority superior to Scripture, as in yQiddushin 1: 2, 59d: בשלשה מקומות התורה עוקפת למקרא "On three occasions the Torah uproots Scripture." This maxim is nonetheless written in an ambiguous style, so as to suggest that the Sages' interpretations were simply reflecting the original divine intent. "Torah" is used not in the sense of a decision by the Sages, but as God's word.

138 We may note again yPe'ah 2: 4, 17a: אפילו מה שתלמיד וותיק עתיד להורות לפני רבו כבר נאמר למשה בסיני "Even what a proficient disciple would declare before his teacher was already recounted to Moses at Sinai." (See n. 83 for the slightly different version of this assertion in bMegillah 19b.) The philosopher E. Levinas, *Nine Talmudic Readings*, p. 39, expresses this idea in a philosophical manner. He states that while the talmudic spirit goes radically beyond the letter of the Bible, its spirit was nonetheless formed in the very letters it goes beyond, so as to reestablish, despite apparent violence to the text, the permanent meaning within these letters.

139 See n. 7 regarding the traditional understanding of this concept. S. Albeck, "Law and History in Halakhic Research," refers on p. 4 to the perception of "the great general rules and principles."

140 With respect to modern thought on the extent of rabbinic authority based on דעת תורה, see Lawrence Kaplan, דעת תורה: תפישה מודרנית.

2. Characteristics of Rabbinic Decision-Making

2.1 The Sages' Method of "Legal" Sense

The specific features of Israelite law that I have discussed in Chapter One compelled the Sages to devise a method for legal change that could accommodate the following challenges:

a) to reveal the divine intentions implicit in Scripture through creative exegesis, thus implying that each and every one of their decisions originated in God's words,[1] transmitted either in Scripture itself or orally;

b) to maintain the formal framework of the law, its external shell, even when modifying its practical application, so as to maintain the appearance of obeying the original, divine law and avoiding any blatant disrespect toward it.

For the first task, the Sages employed מדרש, "midrash," the diversified methods of midrashic exegesis of Scripture. The establishment of rules for the interpretation of the Torah, such as the seven rules of Hillel,[2] the thirteen rules of R. Ishmael,[3] and the רבוי-מיעוט

---

1 The issue of whether the halakhah was created through a midrashic method, or whether midrash served as a subsequent scriptural validation of decisions made by the Sages on other grounds, will be discussed in section 2. 2.

2 We read in tSanhedrin 7: 11: שבעה דברים דרש הילל הזקן לפני זקני פתירא "Hillel lectured on seven principles [of hermeneutics] before the Elders of Pathyra." In ARN Recension A, chap. 37 this narrative appears in a slightly different literary style.

3 The rules of Rabbi Ishmael are enumerated in Sifra, *Baraita d'Rabbi Ishmael* 1. L. Finkelstein, *Sifra*, vol. 1, p. 125 ff., in his introduction to the baraita of the thirteen rules of Rabbi Ishmael, posits some critical questions with respect to the authenticity of Hillel's alleged rules. He notes that: a) none of Hillel's disciples quoted his rules in the period of time from Hillel until Rabbi Ishmael; b) Rabbi Ishmael received these rules from Nehonya ben ha-Qanah (according to bShevu'ot 26a); and c) Rabbi Aqiba ignored Hillel's rules and adopted the rules of Nahum of Gimzo (tShevu'ot 1: 7). Finkelstein does not doubt the authenticity of these attributions and attempts to reconcile the oddities. Gary G. Porton, on the other hand, in *Rabbi Ishmael*, pp. 164 ff., is more critical in his comparison between the rules alleged to have been stated by Rabbi Ishmael and his halakhic deliberations in Sifra. He states on p. 205: "Our sources do not seem to have had a single consistent picture of Ishmael the exegete." Regarding the general issue of authenticity of rabbinic attributions, see J. Neusner,

("amplification-qualification") method of R. Aqiba,[4] as well as the reconciliation of apparent contradictions[5] in the Torah, constituted the logical instruments of the Sages' hermeneutic system. By these techniques they could continue to interpret God's commands, as expressed in the Torah, for the material and spiritual benefit of the Israelite people,[6] even as circumstances changed and new problems arose.

"Attributions" and *Biography*. I hypothesize that these rules may be perceived as similar to grammatical rules. Grammarians establish their definitions and classifications from the analysis of existing languages; they do not create the rules, but simply observe them. Similarly, the many considerations and hermeneutics used in the interpretation of Scripture induced later Sages to define and classify them. The attribution of a literary composition to earlier renowned personalities is not unusual, even with respect to biblical writings, and should not surprise us. We see a similar attempt at arrangement on the part of an Amora who organized and classified a number of tannaitic rules, in bYoma 33a: אביי מסדר מערכה משמיה דגמרא ואליבא דאבא שאול "Abbaye arranged the order [of the daily tasks performed in the Temple] according to tradition that was taught and according to Abba Saul's opinion [who differed in the order of one task]"; the sequence of daily tasks then follows.

4 A homily in bMenahot 29b includes a discussion between God and Moses, in which God says: אדם אחד יש שעתיד להיות בסוף כמה דורות ועקיבא בן יוסף שמו שעתיד לדרוש על כל קוץ וקוץ תילין תילין של הלכות "There will be a man at the end of a number of generations with the name of Aqiba son of Joseph, who will uncover many laws from the interpretation of each stroke of every letter." In yBerakhot 9: 5, 14b we find an explanation of R. Aqiba's system of interpretation as taught to his disciple: נחמיה עימסוני שימש את רבי עקיבא עשרים ושתים שנה ולמדו אתים וגמים ריבויין אכין ורקין מיעוטין "Nehemyah Imsuni was Rabbi Aqiba's disciple for twenty-two years and they learned that [wherever] את and גם [appear in the Torah, the purpose is to express] an expansion, and אך and רק [have the purpose of expressing] limitation." For example, with respect to the apparently superfluous את in Deut 6: 13, it is stated: את ה' אלהיך תירא אמר ליה אותו ואת תורתו "'Fear the Lord your God'; [R. Aqiba] said to him: [Fear] the Lord as well as His Torah [the expansion implied by את]." An example of the limiting function of רק is found in Sifre Deut 126, on Deut 15: 23: רק את דמו לא תאכל שתייה בכלל אכילה רק זו התריית עדים רק ליתן שיעור כזית "'But you must not eat the blood.' Drinking is included in the concept of eating, [and the word] רק 'only' [comes to teach us that before one can be punished for a transgression of this law] one must be forewarned and [must have eaten] at least a quantity the size of an olive." See n. 69 for a further discussion of the use of these hermeneutic rules.

5 For example, one of the above-mentioned thirteen rules of R. Ishmael states: שני כתובים המכחישים זה את זה עד שיבא השלישי ויכריע ביניהם "When two verses contradict one another, let a third verse come and decide between them." See, however, chap. 1 n. 75 for my repudiation of the argument of J. Harris that biblical hermeneutics primarily address inconsistencies in the text.

6 As we read in Deut 4: 1, among many similar biblical dicta: ועתה ישראל שמע אל

For the solution of the second task, the Sages devised a conceptual philosophy that I would characterize as "legal sense," as opposed to "common sense." The laws that prohibit work on the Sabbath offer a comprehensive example of this approach. Common sense would understand the biblical precepts as supporting the Sabbath as a day of rest; hence one would avoid tiring and effort-demanding labour, such as plowing and harvesting (Exod 34: 21), and one would not undertake a long and exhausting voyage out of town (Exod 16: 29). The Sages introduced a legal sense into these two restrictions, a "deconstruction" in modern language. They invalidated the idea that the prevention of tiring work was the sole purpose of the biblical restrictions, and replaced this idea with a legal concept of work: tasks that create something enduring, or complete some assignment, or effect a change in substance, regardless of whether they require any effort or not. The task must also be accomplished in its usual way to be deemed legally as "work."[7] The same deed, moreover, can be deemed a transgression of a scriptural command, and thus punishable, when performed for one purpose, and exempt from punishment when performed for another purpose.[8] Writing two characters

---

החקים ואל המשפטים אשר אנכי מלמד אתכם לעשות למען תחיו "Hear now, O Israel, the decrees and laws I am about to teach you. Follow them so that you may live."

7 We read in mShabbat 10: 6: הנוטל צפרניו זו בזו או בשניו וכן שערו וכן שפמו וכן זקנו "If one tears off his nails [not with a utensil, but] with another nail, or with his teeth, and tears his hair [from his head] and his whiskers and his beard [he is not liable for punishment according to the Sages. Rabbi Eliezer considers him liable, but the halakhah is opposed to his opinion]." Although the Torah prohibits the performance of these tasks on Sabbath, it is not considered a transgression when they are not performed in their usual manner; one is deemed not to have performed the work of cutting one's hair or nails. The Sages, however, prohibited such tasks according to the concept of "making a fence around the Torah"; see further on this concept section 4.1.7.

8 A sick person must not drink a special liquid with healing properties on Sabbath, because healing is forbidden on Sabbath, but a healthy person may drink this liquid to quench his thirst, as we read in mShabbat 14: 3: חוץ ממי דקלים וכוס עיקרים מפני שהן לירוקה אבל שותה הוא מי דקלים לצמאו. Several more examples may be cited. One may rinse food with warm water to warm it up or to clean it, but it is prohibited to rinse certain types of small herrings, because the rinsing completes their preparation (mShabbat 22: 2). The act of rinsing is the same in both cases; but in the first instance, it only warms the food and does not effect any change in its status, while in the second instance it accomplishes a change in the legal status of the herring, from an unfinished to a finished product. Another example of classifying a deed according to its purpose is found with respect to the obligation to offer a sin sacrifice. We read in bShabbat 73b: החופר גומא בשבת ואינו צריך אלא לעפרה פטור עליה "One who digs a hole on Sabbath [unintentionally, as in Lev 4: 2] only for the purpose of obtaining earth [to cover his feces, for example, as Rashi suggests] is exempt from bringing a sin offering." If he had dug the hole so as to deposit

close together with ink, or incising two characters, are transgressions; but writing two characters with each one on a separate page, or writing two characters with fruit juice, which is not permanent, are not transgressions requiring a sin offering when done inadvertently (mShabbat 12: 3 - 5). The writing of one letter is also not perceived as writing; nor is a temporary outlining of letters in sand or dust. Although there is no difference from the perspective of the performer between the two acts, as he does the same work and applies the same effort in each instance, the outcome of his work creates the legal difference between them. With this legal sense approach, the Sages could refine the system, and create practical procedures that would promote the observance and sanctification of the Sabbath and at the same time allow the performance of the necessities of life.[9] In a certain

---

something in it, in contrast, he would be liable for an offering because he transgressed the prohibition against building. This and similar halakhot are founded upon the maxim: מלאכה שאין צריכה לגופה פטור עליה "A [prohibited] work done for other than its essential purpose is exempt from a sin offering [when performed unintentionally]." We encounter examples founded upon this rule in mShabbat 10: 5: המוציא אוכלין פחות מכשיעור בכלי פטור אף על הכלי שהכלי טפילה לו את החי במטה פטור אף על המטה שהמטה טפילה לו "If one takes out [from a private to a public domain a quantity of] food less than the standard quantity in a vessel, he is not liable even for the [taking out of the] vessel, because the vessel is of secondary importance [to the food; and the taking out of less than the standard quantity of food is also not a transgression, as it is not considered an actual deed]. [If he takes out] a living person on a bed, he is not liable for the bed, because it is secondary to the person." In other words, he would be liable for taking out the vessel or the bed by themselves; if he takes them out, however, not for themselves but for the sake of carrying out a minimal quantity of food or a living person, which acts are not transgressions, he is also not liable for carrying out the vessel or the bed.

According to the same principle, one would be liable for two sin offerings for the same act of work if two prohibited acts resulted from it. We read (bShabbat 73b): אמר רב כהנא זומר וצריך לעצים חייב שתים אחת משום קוצר ואחת משום נוטע "Rav Kahana said: If one prunes [a tree] and also needs the branches [for example for a fire, he must bring two offerings], one for the transgression of harvesting [the branches] and one for planting [the act of pruning a tree is conceptually analogous to planting]." On the other hand, if he does not intend to use the branches, he has committed only one transgression, planting, and is thus liable for only one sin offering. In yShabbat 2: 5, 5a, we encounter a similar dispute relating to a more specific case: הבעיר ובישל אית תניי תני חייב שתים אית תניי תני חייב אחת מאן דמר חייב שתי׳ אחת משום מבעיר ואחת משום מבשל ומאן דמר אחת היידא היא "If one made a fire and cooked [over it], there are Sages who teach that he is liable for two transgressions and others who teach he is liable only for one. Those who say he is liable for two [deem] one to be the deed of making a fire and the other the deed of cooking; [for] those who say he is liable for one, it is this very thing [that is controverted - it is deemed to be only one action because one makes the fire by blowing on the embers underneath the pot, and it is this action that also brings the food to cook]."

9 There are many such examples of how the Sabbath law was adapted while still maintaining its external form; the following two are particularly interesting as they

sense, this may be deemed a "formalistic" approach. The law is always formally applied, but not in "mechanical" way - that is, not in the identical manner in all circumstances; its application is altered according to the relevant circumstances of each case.

We may observe the significant conceptual change effected by the Sages through the operation of this legal sense, by noting the contrast between the Sages' attitude toward the Sabbath laws and that of Nehemiah. Scripture prohibits concrete work and toil on Sabbath (Exod 20: 10), such as plowing and harvesting (Exod 34: 21), similar work connected with the gathering and preparation of food (Exod 16: 23- 30),

---

have New Testament parallels: 1) If an animal falls into a water canal, one brings pillows and quilts (or similar objects) and puts them beneath it, to enable the animal to step over them and climb up; it may then go up on its own, but one may not raise it in the usual way (bShabbat 128b). This principle also appears in mShabbat 18: 2: כופין את הסל לפני האפרוחים כדי שיעלו וירדו "One may [carry] and tilt a basket before chicks to allow them to go up and down." This permission is founded upon the maxim that one may carry an allowed vessel, for the use of another object that one is not allowed to carry. In our cases, one is not allowed to carry chicks on Sabbath, or to carry or raise an animal that fell into a canal; but one may carry the artifacts necessary to assist them. (I have chosen the example from the B. T. because of its similarity to an occurrence mentioned in the New Testament, to be discussed below). 2) Rabbi Yehudah permits one to clip off a seed of grain with one's hand and eat it, but one may not, as is usually done, use an implement. Further, one may separate the husks and eat the grain, but to prepare a great quantity to collect in a container would be a transgression of the Sabbath laws. The specific method of separation of the husks, different than the common procedure, is mandated to avoid a manifest transgression of the prohibition to thresh cereals on Sabbath (tShabbat 14: 11). We may compare these examples to their NT parallels, Matt 12: 8 -12 and Luke 14: 1 - 6 for the first, and Matt 12: 1 - 8, Mark 2: 23 - 28 and Luke 6: 1 - 5 for the second. Both Jesus and the Sages (Pharisees) were of the opinion that the animal must be rescued, and that one is allowed to clip some grain on Sabbath to satisfy a need for food; the dispute between their viewpoints, I suggest, has to do with their approaches to the law. Contrary to the rabbinic system, whose purpose was to avoid a direct confrontation with the law, Jesus deduced from his comprehension of the divine law an authorization to act unreservedly against the law in order to alleviate suffering. Jesus also asserted obedience to the law (Matt 5: 17), but I would say (to use modern language) that he pleaded for the relativity of the law and was not concerned with its formal disregard, when such disregard was perceived as necessary and justified. The Sages were extremely disturbed by an explicit indifference to or neglect of the law. I do not intend to make a qualitative judgment on the two philosophical conceptions, but I wish to point out their different consequences. The Sages refined and expanded to the utmost their system of adaptation, preserving at the same time the formal law, whereas Paul, in the second generation after Jesus, negated altogether the significance of observing the law and declared instead righteousness through faith (Rom 3: 20 - 26). The Jews actualized their religious life by investigation of and obedience to the minutiae of the law, while the Christians focused their study on the determination of correct dogma and faith. Cf. S. Zeitlin, "The Pharisees and the Gospels," who suggests the divergent political viewpoints of Jesus and the Pharisees as the reason behind the strict or lenient adherence to the law.

gathering wood (Num 15: 32 - 36), and making fire (Exod 35: 3).[10] Nehemiah adopted a common-sense approach to Sabbath holiness, in his interpretation of the words זכור את יום השבת לקדשו "Remember the Sabbath day by keeping it holy [Exod 20. 8]." He maintained that trading on Sabbath would amount to its desecration, although the latter verse does not specify any particular type of work. He therefore rebuked those nobles who traded on Sabbath, accusing them of a severe transgression: ומחללים את יום השבת "[they are] desecrating the Sabbath day [Neh 13: 17]." This particular violation of the Sabbath is, according to Scripture, a capital offense, punishable by death, as we read in Exod 31: 14: מחלליה מות יומת "Anyone who desecrates [the Sabbath] must be put to death."[11]

The Sages, on the other hand, did not perceive trading to be included within the range of work prohibited by the Bible. Trading on the Sabbath is therefore not considered to be a transgression of a Torah decree, and does not appear in the thirty-nine principal kinds of prohibited work enumerated in mShabbat 7: 2.[12] The prohibition against trading is regarded as solely a rabbinic edict, designed as a preventative measure: "[It is] an injunction [lest one forget that it is the Sabbath] and write [a note of the transaction]."[13] The legal sense of the Sages thus allowed leniency, in

---

10 Since this issue is not the main purpose of our study, I refrain from investigating further the components of these verses, which may be considered of post-exilic origin.

11 This is the only occurrence in the Pentateuch in which a transgression of the Sabbath is described with the term חלל "desecration." Further, outside of Nehemiah, it is only in Ezekiel and Deutero-Isaiah that this term appears with respect to a transgression of the Sabbath laws, which indicates the late origin of this specific infraction. Ezekiel does not disclose his conception of "Sabbath desecration," but accuses the Israelites of having already desecrated the Sabbath in the desert (Ezek 20: 13). Isaiah's conception of Sabbath desecration (Isa 58: 13) seems to be similar to that of Nehemiah. See Heger, *Altars*, pp. 407 - 410 for an extended deliberation on the extension of the Sabbath restrictions by Ezra and Nehemiah, and the scholarly conjectures regarding Jeremiah's admonition (Jer 17: 27) concerning the character of the Sabbath transgression.

12 As we shall see below (n. 185), the Sages developed a list of thirty-nine works prohibited on the Sabbath, which were based on work performed in the Temple. Trading is not included in this list. I do not believe that trading was excluded because it was not performed in the Temple. First, this homily was obviously not the basis for the inclusion of the other works in the list. (I. Gilat, איסורי שבות, discusses the composition of this list.) Second, if it had been desired to include it, the Sages would have found some dialectical justification, just as they found a way to justify the inclusion of sowing and reaping, despite the obvious fact that these agricultural tasks were not performed in the Temple.

13 We read in Maimonides' *Mishneh Torah*, *Hilkhot Shabbat* 23: 12: כותב מאבות מלאכות לפיכך אסור ללוות ולהלוות גזירה שמא יכתוב וכן אסור לקנות ולמכור ולשכור ולהשכיר גזירה שמא יכתוב "Writing is a primary work…therefore it is forbidden to borrow and loan, to prevent a possible writing, and

contrast to Nehemiah's common-sense approach. These differing attitudes toward the practical application of a biblical prohibition on this matter[14]

---

likewise it is forbidden to buy and sell, to rent and lease, to prevent a possible writing." There is no explicit dictum in the talmudic literature to this effect, and it seems that Maimonides, and Rashi in his comments to bBetzah 37a, rely on mShabbat 23: 1: וכן ערב פסח בירושלים שחל להיות בשבת מניח טליתו אצלו ונוטל את פסחו ועושה עמו חשבון לאחר יום טוב "And likewise if the eve of Passover in Jerusalem falls on Sabbath [and one forgot to provide for himself a lamb before Sabbath], one leaves [the seller] his robe [as a pawn], takes his animal, and completes the accounting after the holiday." The prohibition against such a business transaction is only a rabbinic prohibition, and is therefore overridden by the precept to offer the Passover lamb. One must be careful, however, to prevent any writing by the seller; giving him a pawn, without fixing the price, ensures that the seller will not commit a possible error by writing the amount of the debt, as he might do if a price had been established. Similarly, when the eve of Passover fell on Sabbath (see the passage cited above, chap. 1, pp. 45-6), we observe that one was not allowed to carry the slaughtering knife on Sabbath. It had to be placed in the lamb's wool, or between the goat's horns, as stated in yPesahim, 6: 1, 33a (and with slightly different wording in bPesahim 66a): מיד כל מי שהיה פסחו טלה היה תוחבה בגיזתו גדי היה קושרה בין קרניו. Carrying the knife would have been a transgression of a Torah edict, and therefore some way to circumvent the prohibition had to be found to allow fulfillment of the precept of the Passover lamb. That is, one was allowed to transgress the rabbinic edict against trading on Sabbath so as to buy the lamb, and had only to be careful to avoid a written note of the debt.

14 This rabbinic concept raised a difficult question regarding the death penalty inflicted upon the man who gathered wood on Sabbath (Num 15: 32 - 36). Scripture describes his action with the term מקשש "gathers"; this is not, however, a work included in the thirty-nine works prohibited by the Torah, according to the rabbinic interpretation in mShabbat 7: 2 (see further below section 2.4). The term מקשש is translated by Targum Onkelos as מגבב "gathers," similar to the translation of וקששו להם תבן "let them gather their own straw [Exod 5: 7]." Collecting straw is an operation performed after the grain is reaped, and does not imply that any cutting has been done by the person doing the collecting. Targum Pseudo-Jonathan, aware of the problem and following the talmudic discussions on this issue, states: תליש ועקר קיסין "he tore and uprooted wood," but this interpretation does not correspond to the simple meaning of the biblical text. The LXX translates מקשש as συλλέγοντα "collecting" or " gathering," as opposed to tearing or uprooting. In bShabbat 96b, three different opinions are proposed with respect to the transgression for which the man was sentenced to death: a) carrying the wood in the public domain for more than four cubits; 2) tearing the branches from the tree (work that is not explicitly mentioned among the thirty-nine works in mShabbat 7: 2, but is deemed to be conceptually identical to קוצר "reaping," in tShabbat 9: 17; and 3) piling sheaves (or piling the collected wood). The Y. T. version in Sanhedrin 5: 1, 22d, while not as extensive, also has an Amora asking: מקושש משום מאי מיחייב משום תולש או משום קוצר "For which transgression was the gatherer convicted, the uprooting or the reaping?" We observe the concern of the Sages to expose the type of the transgression, since collecting wood, according to the mishnah, would not be a violation of a Torah command calling for a death sentence. Philo also expresses his uncertainty about the character of this infraction, vacillating between ὁ τὴν ἱερὰν

offer a clear view of the crucial conceptual shift effected by the Sages. In contrast, the author of *Jubilees*, and likely the group to which he belonged, did not agree with this hermeneutic method that distorts, in practice, the common-sense comprehension of the biblical text. We read in *Jub*. 50: 8:[15] "And let the man who does anything on it [the Sabbath] die....whoever will discuss a matter that he will do on it so that he might make on it a journey for any buying or selling...let him die." This group did not conceive of any liberty to change the manifest intent of the law, contrary to the rabbinic Sages.

Another example illustrates the Sages' attitude, in this case with respect to the consequences and implications of the legal maxim "a disqualified slaughter is not deemed to be a slaughter." This issue affects in particular the command to cover the blood of any animal or bird that may be eaten, which appears in Lev 17: 13: "[you] must drain out the blood and cover it with earth." The question is therefore whether the blood of an animal in the case of a disqualified slaughter is to be covered. Scripture indicates explicitly its motive: "Because the life of **every** creature is its blood [emphasis added]." Nonetheless, Rabbi Simeon declared that with respect to a disqualified slaughter this command does not apply; a disqualified slaughter is, in legal terms, not a slaughter, and the command refers to an animal legally slaughtered.[16] We observe that the explicit ethical command to treat the blood of a creature, its life element, with respect, by covering it, is annulled as the result of a legal principle.

This legal sense of the Sages, as I have defined it as an element of rabbinic hermeneutics, is to be distinguished from "legalism." My thesis thus has no bearing on the debate as to whether Judaism is an ethical - prophetic or legalistic religion. The ethical commands of the Torah must be fulfilled in practice; when the commands themselves give no hint as to their correct application, they must be interpreted so as to derive the underlying legal principle. We may consider, for instance, the ethical harvest law in Lev 19: 9, requiring the edges of the field to be left for the

---

ἑβδόμην βέβηλον "[he] turned the sacred seventh day into a profane thing," and εἰς παρανομίας ἐπίδειξιν "displaying his disobedience to the law," and finally hypothesizing that it was a specific type of work prohibited on the Sabbath: ὡς γάρ οἶμαι πῦρ ἐναύειν ἑβδόμαις οὐκ ἐπιτέτραπται δι' ἣν πρόσθεν αἰτίαν εἶπον οὕτως οὐδὲ τὰ πυρός ἐκκα συλλέγειν "... for the prohibition against lighting a fire on the seventh day, the reason for which I have stated earlier, applies equally, I presume, to collecting the means for kindling fire."

15 Translation from O.S. Wintermute, "Jubilees."

16 Scripture in fact does not mention slaughter at all in this command; Lev 17: 13, however, indicates אשר יאכל "that may be eaten," limiting the application of the command, according to the Sages' interpretation, to a legally sanctioned slaughter that includes the consumption of the slaughtered animal.

poor. In mPe'ah 2: 5 it is specified how this law is to work in practice: "When one sows his field with one type of seed, he must leave only one edge, although he gathers the harvest in two granaries. If he sows two types of seed, he must leave two edges, even if he gathers [both types] in one granary. If one sows two varieties of wheat, he must leave one edge if he gathers them in one granary, and two edges if he gathers them in two [separate] granaries." The biblical ethical command is thus given practical application through the rabbinic method of finding the legal sense of the biblical verses. A rule is derived to decide what is considered legally as one harvest, requiring only one edge to be left, and what is considered two harvests, requiring two edges. The rule does not, however, alter the ethical character of the original biblical command.

The legal sense approach also made possible the adaptation of civil law to the exigencies of a changing world, or to situations apparently not addressed by the Bible. It allowed, for instance, the creation of a *prosbul*, which permits the overriding of the biblical law that a loan was to be cancelled in the seventh year, and made possible commercial loans, not envisaged in the Bible.[17] This adjustment is based on another legal sophistication, that is, on a legal fiction.[18] It is not a change of the law, but a different assessment of the facts; it shifts the issue from a question of law to a question of fact.[19]

---

17 See the detailed discussion below at nn. 151-159 and related text.

18 In yPesahim 3: 1, 30a a dispute is recorded between Tannaim as to whether one may effect a legal fiction in order to achieve a desired result, when the result is perceived as virtuous. In mPesahim 3: 3 it is stated: כיצד מפרישין חלה בטומאה ביום טוב רבי אליעזר אומר לא תקרא לה שם עד שתאפה "How can one separate *hallah* from polluted dough on the [Passover] holiday? [This is a very complex issue. It is a scriptural obligation to separate the *hallah*, the share of the dough due to the priest. Since the dough is polluted, however, neither the priest nor the layperson may eat it. Further, if it cannot be eaten, it may not be baked. On the other hand, one cannot leave it until the end of the Passover holiday, as one could do for any other holiday, because the dough will ferment, and this would be a transgression of Passover law]. Rabbi Eliezer says: Do not call it *hallah* until after the baking." The Y.T. explains this procedure: מערים ואומר זו אני רוצה לוכל וזו אני רוצה לאכול ואופה את כולה וכשהוא רודה מערים ואומר זו אני רוצה ליישן זו אני רוצה ליישן ומשייר אחת "He gets around the law and says: I wish to eat this [part of the dough], and I wish to eat that part; he then bakes all [the dough], and when he removes [the baked dough from the oven] he says: I want to leave this part or that part [to be better baked], and he leaves one [i.e. the one that would be for the *hallah*, to be entirely burned in the oven]."

19 The institution of the עירוב תחומין is another good example of this system. One is prohibited from travelling more than two thousand cubits outside one's town of residence on Sabbath (Exod 16: 29). The Sages determined that if a person, or his agent, deposits food for two meals at the border of the confines within which he may travel, it will be considered as if his residence were on that spot, and he will then be allowed to travel two thousand cubits outside of that point (mEruvin 8: 2). This

As argued above, I speculate that there was a further principle that assisted the Sages in their evaluation: the concept that one precept could override another.[20] Although such a principle is not indicated in Scripture,[21] I conjecture that the well-known maxim "the saving of life overrides the Sabbath," induced the Sages to consider that other precepts could be overridden. This philosophy then came to be applied in other deliberations, even though this reasoning is not explicitly stated.

---

example uses two fictions: first, the placing of food in some spot on the eve of Sabbath is considered as establishing one's residence there, and second, if the act is performed by one's agent, it is deemed to be his own act, and still establishes his residence there. This second fiction is based on the maxim: מפני ששלוחו של אדם כמותו "... [an act performed by] a man's agent is [considered] as if [performed by] himself" (mBerakhot 5: 5). In both instances, legal assessment differs from the "real" facts: one's residence is not where food is left, and one's agent is not the same as one's self for the purpose of establishing a residence. See J. Roth, *Halakhic Process*, pp. 50 ff.

20 See the discussion in Introduction, pp. 27 ff.

21 There is no hint in the Torah that a divine command may be transgressed for any reason. We observe that in contrast to the far-reaching rabbinic law that allows warfare on Sabbath (tEruvin 3:7, yEruvin 4: 2, 21d, and bEruvin 45a), the dissident book of *Jubilees* does not permit such a transgression of the divine law. We read at 50:12-13 (translation from O.S. Wintermute): "And (as for) any man who does work ... or who goes on a journey...or makes war on the day of the sabbath, let the man... die so that the children of Israel might keep the sabbath...." In bYoma 85a, there is much circular reasoning and a great variety of justifications for this apparently revolutionary principle. According to Raba's concluding statement, לכולהו אית להו פירכא "all [the] rationalizations are problematic," with the exception of the sweeping dictum by Samuel: "It is written [Lev 18:15]: 'and he shall live by them,' this means he shall not die by them." This is a philosophical statement allowing the overriding of many, if not all, precepts by means of the notion that the law is given for the benefit of humans and for the good life in all respects. The commands of God were not given for God's benefit, unlike the attitude reflected in classical myths that humans were created to serve the gods; rather, God provided beneficial laws to the Israelites to improve their lives. I assume that it was this principle that was decisive regarding the overriding of the Sabbath, and not the fact that the *tamid* offering may be offered on Sabbath, as debated in Mekilta d' Rabbi Ishmael, *Bo* 5: אם ללמד על התמיד שידחה את השבת והלא כבר נאמר וביום השבת שני כבשים בני שנה "[Why is it written in Num 28: 2 to bring the offering at the appointed time?] If it is to indicate that the *tamid* offerings override the Sabbath [restrictions, it is not necessary, for] is it not said [in v. 9] 'and on the Sabbath day two lambs a year old' [which clearly indicates that the Passover sacrifice overrides the Sabbath]." A similar homily appears in yPesahim 7: 4, 34b. In bPesahim 66a, it is asked in the rhetorical discussion: ותמיד גופיה מנלן דדחי שבת "And how do we know that the *tamid* offering overrides the Sabbath [the basis of the justification with respect to other sacrifices]?" The answer is: עלת שבת בשבתו על עלת התמיד "'This is the burnt-offering for every Sabbath, in addition to the perpetual burnt offering.'" On the overriding of Sabbath laws, see further chap. 4, n. 46.

It is thus my contention that the Sages, though they used hermeneutic rules, were not bound by a particular systematic method, but rather were guided by certain principles they deemed important. I shall enumerate a few of these principles that I consider are evident from their decisions. A law had to accord with what the Sages understood to be the divine intent, as expressed in the Torah, the *Grundnorm*.[22] It had to be practical,[23] so as to ensure its acceptance by the people.[24] It had to guarantee the separation of the Jews from the surrounding societies. And, most importantly, it had to be flexible and able to be adapted to change. These principles allowed the Sages to give the appearance of maintaining the existing traditions, while at the same time permitting the adaptation of existing rules and custom to changing circumstances.[25] They could thus establish the minutiae of biblical precepts,[26] and even incorporate an alien belief or

---

22 See the definition in chap. 1, n. 3. J. Neusner, " Hermeneutics," p. 206, declares: "Both the Mishna and the Bavli undertake to uncover and expose, in the laws of the Torah, the philosophy that the Torah reveals."

23 E.E. Urbach, סמכות, writes on p. 462 (free translation from Hebrew): "The Sages of the Mishnah and Talmud created their notable works because they considered all aspects of life in their widest extent." The concept of hierarchy among halakhic rules, allowing one precept to override another (see Introduction, pp. 27 ff.), provided to the Sages a far-reaching philosophical foundation on which to base various rules, even if these were not explicitly indicated. It is possible, for instance, that Hillel's promulgation of the *prosbul* received its impulse from the acknowledged principle that actual predicaments might override an explicit scriptural precept. We read in mGittin 4: 3 that he created this circumvention of loan-forgiveness מפני תיקון העולם "for the benefit of the world." The Amoraim also pondered this apparently unfeasible procedure (see below nn. 151-159 and related text); it seems, however, from Hillel's justification, that his decision was founded upon this principle of overriding. To prevent the Israelites from transgressing one biblical precept, Hillel in effect invalidated another precept.

24 We read in tSotah 15: 10: שאין בית דין גוזרין על הצבור דברים שאין יכולין לעמוד בהן "The court should not promulgate a decree that the public cannot sustain." I have cited above (chap. 1, n. 6) passages from yAvodah Zarah. 2: 7, 41d, and bAvodah Zarah 36a, with slightly different wording, which concern a decree that was annulled for just such a reason: בדקו ומצאו בגזירתו של שמן ולא מצאו שקיבלו רוב הציבור עליהן "[The Sages] investigated the prohibition against [the use of gentile] oil and did not find that most of the people acceded to it."

25 We may compare this procedure to the approach of a modern, liberal superior court. Through creative interpretation of a constitutional document, such a court extends the application of the law to areas that seem utterly alien to its original intent, at least according to conservative principles. It is evident, however, that such a liberal court does not perceive itself as contradicting or obliterating the constitutional document; it intends to uphold the basic principles, but assumes that it has the authority to adapt them in practice to changed circumstances.

26 For example, the Sabbath laws, as we read in mHagigah 1: 8: הלכות שבת חגיגות והמעילות הרי הם כהררים התלויין בשערה שהן מקרא מועט והלכות

custom considered propitious[27] or practical.[28] It seems they were not concerned with the problem of syncretism, because they succeeded in

---

מרובות (translated in n. 38 below).

27 One such example is found in Mekilta d' Rabbi Ishmael, *Beshallah* 1, as an anonymous homily, and in a baraita in the name of Rabbi Meir in bSanhedrin 91b: אמר רבי מאיר מניין לתחיית המתים מן התורה שנאמר אז ישיר משה ובני ישראל את השירה הזאת לה׳ שר לא נאמר אלא ישיר מכאן לתחיית המתים מן התורה "Rabbi Meir said: How do we know of the resurrection of the dead from Scripture? It is written [Exod 15: 1]: 'Then Moses and the Israelites sang this song to the Lord.' It is not written 'He sang' [in the text, this term is written in the imperfect/future tense], but 'He will sing.' Hence [we learn] resurrection from Scripture [because Moses will sing when he is resurrected]." In Sifre Deut 47, the idea of resurrection is derived from exegesis of another verse: למען ירבו ימיכם בעולם הזה וימי בניכם לימות המשיח כימי השמים על הארץ לעולם הבא אשר נשבע ה׳ לאבותיכם לתת לכם אין כתוב כאן אלא לתת להם נמצינו למדים תחיית המתים מן התורה "[It is written in Deut 11: 21:] 'So that your days may be multiplied' [-this refers to] this world; 'and the days of your children' [refers to] the days of the Messiah; 'as the days of heaven and earth' [refers] to the world to come. [With respect to] 'that the Lord swore to give your forefathers,' it is not written here 'to give to you,' but to them [those who are not present, that is, the dead]; we learn from this verse that resurrection originates from the Torah." It is evident that the Jews did not base their belief in resurrection on one particular homily; similar homilies appear in other talmudic sources, deducing resurrection from other verses. In mSanhedrin 10: 1, the belief in resurrection is explicitly acknowledged (though the source of the belief is not indicated): ואלו שאין להם חלק לעולם הבא האומר אין תחיית המתים מן התורה "And these are the ones who will not partake in the world to come: those who declare that resurrection does not originate from the Torah."

28 Putting willow branches around the altar was likely a popular custom, taken over from another culture. The Boethusians thus opposed the desecration of the Sabbath by the performance of a new custom, as we read in tSukkah 3: 1 and in bSukkah 43b: לפי שאין ביתסין מודים שחיבוט ערבה דוחה את השבת. It seems, however, that the masses were enthusiastic about this practice, as we learn from the above narratives that when the Boethusians hid the willow branches under stones, הכירו בהן עמי הארץ ובאו וגררום והוציאום מתחת אבנים בשבת "the people became aware of them [the hidden branches], and came and dragged them out from under the stones on Sabbath." In the B. T. version, the narrative proceeds further: והביאום הכהנים וזקפום בצידי המזבח "...and the priests brought them and propped them at the sides of the altar." Tosefta does not indicate why the precept of the willow branch overrides the Sabbath; but the reason may be understood implicitly from mSukkah 4: 3: ערבה שבעה כיצד יום שביעי של ערבה שחל להיות בשבת ערבה שבעה ושאר כל הימים ששה "When does the [precept of the] willow branch [apply for] seven [days]? When the seventh day [of Sukkoth] occurs on Sabbath, the willow branch applies for seven [days], and six days when it occurs on any other day [since only on the seventh day does the use of the willow branch override the Sabbath]." But in bSukkah 43b, the question is asked: ערבה בשביעי מאי טעמא דחיא שבת אמר רבי יוחנן כדי לפרסמה שהיא מן התורה "Why

bestowing an entirely altered theology upon the alien beliefs and customs they assimilated;[29] they disconnected them so efficiently from any alien concepts that their origin fell completely into oblivion.[30] Avoiding strict adherence to a rigid system of decision-making enabled the development of a multi-faceted approach, which facilitated the creation of a flexible legal system. It also suited the Sages' aspirations toward free and autonomous expression of ideas and principles. An inevitable consequence of such flexibility, however, would be the existence of disputes and disagreements.

A detailed examination of the Sages' approach is now in order. Various scholarly opinions concerning the origin of halakhah and its relations to rabbinic decision-making will be discussed, followed by an overview of the composite nature of rabbinic authority. I shall then

---

does the ceremony of the willow override the Sabbath? Rabbi Yohanan said: To demonstrate that it is a precept originating from the Torah." No source is cited for this statement. See further on this question section 3.5. On the primary question of the origin of the precept to use willow branches for the celebration around the altar, we encounter a number of opinions and attempts at legitimation. In tSukkah 3: 1 two possibilities are given: ערבה הלכה למשה מסיני אבא שאול או' מן התורה שנ' וערבי נחל ערבה [ללולב וערבה] למזבח "The [use of the] willow branch [at the altar] is a halakhah [given] to Moses from Sinai. Abba Saul says: It is a Torah precept; it is written [Lev 23: 40] 'and poplars' [in plural, which indicates] willows for the *lulav* and willows for the altar." The declaration that the willow branch is a halakhah given to Moses from Sinai appears in many instances in the B. T., in the name of Rabbi Yohanan, as originating from Nehonyah, a disciple of Shammai, as well as in yShevi'it 1: 5, 33b in the name of Rabbi Yohanan (see further chap. 3, nn. 113, 115, 116). Other opinions on the origin of the willow branch are found in bSukkah 44a. Rav Zebid states: ערבה דלית לה עיקר מן התורה "The willow has no foundation in Scripture." Other Sages suggest different origins: חד אמר ערבה יסוד נביאים וחד אמר מנהג נביאים "One said that the prophets decreed the willow branch [as an obligation - Rashi], and another said the prophets [simply] introduced the custom [without decreeing it to be obligatory]." As in other occurrences, we observe the many methods employed by the Sages to justify a custom that does not appear in Scripture.

29 Y. F. Baer, היסודות ההיסטוריים של ההלכה, has already drawn attention to this practice employed by the Sages. He quotes (pp. 22 ff.) a number of such examples, indicating the probable alien source. The ceremonies of the water libation and the celebration of the drawing of water on the Feast of Tabernacles are particularly mentioned (note 76), along with relevant scholarly opinions. The ceremonies surrounding the carrying of the first fruits to Jerusalem, portrayed in mBikkurim 3: 3, are evidently of alien origin: והשור הולך לפניהם וקרניו מצופות זהב ועטרת של זית בראשו החליל מכה לפניהם עד שמגיעים קרוב לירושלם "And the bull marches before them with his gilded horns and a crown of olive [branches] on his head. The flute [player] precedes the [convoy] until they approach Jerusalem."

30 S. Lieberman, *Greek*, p. 114, writes that the Sages were the "modern" people of their era, who adapted popular folk beliefs, shaped them appropriately, and presented them to the people in their new-fashioned form.

substantiate in detail my proposal that the development of the halakhah was characterized by the very early existence of disputes and controversies. I shall look particularly at the nature of tannaitic disputes; the so-called majority rule; the value given to individual opinion; the disputes between Beit Hillel and Beit Shammai; and the nature of the authority of the Sanhedrin. These categories do not, of course, exist explicitly within rabbinic literature, but must be extrapolated from relevant passages.

2.2 Scholarly Opinions Concerning Halakhic Midrash and Mishnah as the Basis of Halakhah

As we have discussed briefly above,[31] the question of the development of the Sages' version of the halakhah is a contentious matter among scholars: was it derived from midrash (Torah exegesis), or from tradition and continued debate and analysis? As we may more precisely define the issue: Did the law originate in the Sages' quest to determine, by meticulous exegesis, the details missing in the biblical text; or in the concern of the Sages to address double words, redundancies, inconsistencies and other apparent irregularities in the biblical text? Or did the law originate in tradition (whatever its source) and logical deliberations?

There is no scholarly agreement on this issue. J.N. Epstein[32] declares that interpretation of the biblical verses was not the foundation of the halakhah; such interpretation served only to reveal some hint in Scripture that pointed to already-established laws. The midrashim (exegetical interpretations[33]) in Sifra and Sifre were, in the early period, a method of study designed to reveal such hints, rather than serving to develop the law. In the period of Yose ben Yoezer[34] there began a transition period to the mishnaic style,[35] the establishment of halakhot without any support from Scripture. The Mishnah is thus an independent codex, not an interpretation

---

31 Section 2.2.

32 J. N. Epstein, תנאים, pp. 505 - 515.

33 The terms "midrash," "homily," and "interpretation" are somewhat overlapping. I shall use the term "midrash" for the rabbinic interpretation of scriptural verses.

34 Yose ben Yoezer presented his ancient testimony concerning three halakhot in mEduyyot 8: 4, and from this time on there is evidence of disputes between Sages. In view of this mishnah and other homilies concerning this Tanna, one must assume that his activities and those of his contemporaries represented a turning point in the development of the halakhah. I shall elaborate on this issue in due course.

35 J. N. Epstein, תנאים, p. 508.

of the Torah.[36] At that time there were few disputes, since any midrashic concepts that were actually put into practice did not create halakhah, but simply supported it.[37] In other words, the exegesis of biblical verses was not the basis of halakhah;[38] the midrash might support the halakhah, but did not create it. The earliest Sages knew the halakhot and their rationales; it was only after the Temple's destruction that the great disputes began between the disciples of Hillel and those of Shammai. Epstein does not declare explicitly that the Sages knew these halakhot by tradition,[39] but this is implicit in his argument,[40] and from the fact of his citation of the *Epistle of Rav Sherira Gaon*.[41]

Ch. Albeck[42] declares that those halakhot that are not explicitly mentioned in Scripture, or that are mentioned without any descriptive details, were known by tradition from primeval times. The question of whether the basis of the halakhah was in the exegesis of Scripture[43] is thus

---

36 I am not using the term "codex" here in a precise legal sense (see the definition in chap. 1, n. 39), but to emphasize the Mishnah as an independent document.

37 We read in J. N. Epstein, תנאים, p. 511: המדרש תומך בהלכה אבל אינו יוצר את ההלכה.

38 Epstein also relies on the statement in mHagigah 1: 8: הלכות שבת חגיגות והמעילות הרי הם כהררים התלויין בשערה שהן מקרא מועט והלכות מרובות "The halakhot of the Sabbath, the [offerings] on the holidays and the unlawful use of sacred property are like mountains suspended by a hair, since there are many halakhot supported by a limited scriptural text."

39 It is evident that Epstein's statement is conditioned by the traditional belief that all the halakhot, including all the minutiae of the biblical commands and their anticipated contingencies, were known from time immemorial.

40 Epstein quotes (תנאים, p. 511) from mYevamot 8: 3: אמרו לו אם הלכה נקבל ואם לדין יש תשובה: "They retorted: If your declaration is founded on tradition, we shall accept it, but if it is based on your [own] considerations, there is a rebuttal."

41 We read in the *Epistle of Rav Sherira Gaon* (987 C. E), MS Berlin Qu 685 (Or. 160) fol. 210 a (ed. Schlüter): משום דלית הוה אית בהו מחלוקת אלא טעמי משנה ודאורייתא הו' ידעון להון ידיעה ברורה "[The names of the first Sages at the time of the Temple are unknown, except those of the Patriarchs and the heads of the court] because there were no disputes [among them], since the rationales of the Mishnah and the Torah were known clearly to them." M. Schlüter's German translation of this phrase in §15, p. 52 is slightly different.

42 Ch.. Albeck, מבוא למשנה, pp. 40 ff.

43 Albeck is not very specific in his language. He poses the question in this way: ההלכה קדמה לדרש או שהדרש קדם להלכה "Did the halakhah precede the interpretation, or did the interpretation come before [create] the halakhah?" He then demonstrates that many halakhot are certainly without any scriptural basis and hence were in effect before any midrashim were later posited to justify them. The question is thus relevant only in those cases in which one could assume that the Sage pronouncing a midrash perceived that it offered a definite confirmation of his viewpoint, and he established the halakhah on that basis. Albeck then poses the more

limited to those new halakhot for which there was no prior tradition. He then notes the talmudic opinion that cases that could not be decided on the basis of prior tradition were brought to the Great Court in Jerusalem at the time of the Temple, and the Sages made their decisions on the basis of their study of relevant scriptural verses. This system continued after the Temple's destruction, as the Tannaim established their decisions on the basis of their interpretations. Albeck concludes (p. 53) that some halakhot preceded the midrashim, while others were the outcome of the Sages' exegesis. In contrast to Epstein, who denies any creation of the halakhah through midrash, Albeck considers the midrash as the foundation of the halakhah in those occurrences for which tradition was not available.

Urbach[44] cites the different scholarly opinions on this issue, but criticizes the methodology used and thus the deductions that were reached; he contends that these conclusions were based on partial talmudic citations, and that opposing talmudic passages were not dealt with in a responsible manner. Urbach proposes a historical division between the developmental stages of the halakhah. During the period of the Second Temple, the early Tannaim simply decreed rules based on their own authority, without any indication of their foundation or justification. Precedents, in the form of court rulings that became generally applied law, constituted another origin of the older halakhah. These laws were transmitted by the Sages from generation to generation, and are included in the Mishnah in tractate Eduyyot ("Witnesses"), in which the various Sages bear witness to rules received by transmission. These testimonies also incorporated long-established custom that had come to be considered halakhah. In summary, these older laws were institutionalized edicts, proclaimed by the authority of the Tannaim, and thus we encounter no disputes referring to them. Urbach also quotes from the *Epistle of Rav Sherira Gaon*, and interprets the citations there according to his perspective.

Urbach is aware that he must still explain the basis of these earliest decrees and court decisions, and the role of halakhic midrash in this process. He starts with an explanation of the term דרש, the root of the term midrash, and asserts that in the early stage of development of the halakhah, the expression midrash did not signify a hermeneutic type of exegesis, but rather a method of safeguarding and protecting the law through profound and intense study. A special group of professionals, Soferim ("scribes"), initially copied Scripture and also engaged in teaching the Torah. In this capacity they explained Scripture, and for that

---

specific question: Did the Tannaim determine their halakhot on the basis of their study and interpretation of Scripture? He does not propose any other possible foundation for their decisions.

44 E. E. Urbach, מחקרים, vol. 1, pp. 166 ff.

purpose they learned to compare and contrast different biblical verses; they perceived obscure and ambiguous passages in Scripture as well as inconsistencies. In their quest to elucidate these perplexing pericopes, they generated, as a by-product, many solutions and explanations. Some of their propositions were ratified by the Sages and incorporated within the law as decrees; these eventually became standard elements of tradition. These scribes were considered to be of a lower status than the Sages, and their interpretations and explanations were not the direct basis of the law. It was only the authority of members of the Sanhedrin that could confirm the scribes' opinions and grant them the status of law.

With the increase in the number of scribes and lecturers, according to Urbach, the Sages accustomed themselves to the system of explanation and interpretation, but the shift to the acknowledgment of exegesis as the foundation of halakhah was a slow process. The Sanhedrin's loss of authority and the erosion of communal organization as a result of the political circumstances in the last phase of the Second Temple period facilitated and accelerated this process. The Sages Shemayah and Abtalion[45] were the first renowned Darshanim, lecturers who founded halakhot on midrashic exegesis of biblical verses, but were still reluctant to expand this method.[46] The shift from the authoritative pronouncement of halakhah to an autonomous method of establishing halakhah through individual interpretation of Scripture not surprisingly provoked disputes. In mSheqalim 11: 4, we find that Rabban Yohanan ben Zakkai[47] opposes a priestly halakhah founded upon such a midrashic interpretation, and Urbach assumes that this may have been the first opposition to halakhot based upon this system. He perceives a struggle between groups of Sages who advocated midrash as the foundation of halakhah and those who opposed it, quoting various talmudic witnesses to this struggle.

At the final stage, opposition to the midrashic derivation of halakhah had subsided. The interpretation of Scripture, with the guidance of appropriate hermeneutic rules, prevailed and became the foundation for further development of the halakhah. These derivations and the traditional rules became intermingled in a single system; every new resolution attained through halakhic midrash was perceived as having existed from time immemorial, from Sinai. Urbach thus divides the development of halakhah into two distinct phases: in the first phase the promulgation of laws depended upon the authority of those pronouncing them, and in the second phase, because of the changed historical circumstances, the halakhah was founded upon a hermeneutic analysis of Scripture.

---

45 Late first century B.C.E.

46 We read in bPesahim 70b that Yehudah ben Dorotai questioned the unwillingness of these Sages to apply the midrashic method for the establishment of a halakhah.

47 First century C. E.

J. Neusner[48] asserts that Midreshei Halakhah reflect the priority of Scripture in the creation of laws, in opposition to the style of the Mishnah. As Neusner understands Sifra, midrash thus served the needs of the legal system and had no direct relation to the creation of new laws.

D. Weiss-Halivni[49] classifies Israelite legal history into "imperative" and "vindicatory-justificatory" periods, each with its own style of composition that bears these distinct features. After citation, discussion, and critical examination of a great number of prior scholarly views, he expresses his overall skepticism of them (p. 21). He declares that simple halakhic midrash, with the purpose of understanding God's will through appropriate exegesis of God's word, already existed in the second century B.C.E., before the mishnaic period. The transition from the midrashic method of deriving halakhah to the mishnaic form of a bare statement of law without indication of the biblical source[50] did not take place, in Halivni's opinion, before the Temple's destruction (p. 40)[51] The midrashim were collected in general works of Midreshei Halakhah, such as Sifre and Sifra. The Mishnah must be seen as an abridged midrash,

---

[48] See J. Neusner, *Sifra*, vol. 1, p. 30, in which he states that Sifra argues for the priority of Scripture. See also Neusner's conception of the relationship between midrash and halakhah in "Hermeneutics"; he asserts that the Midrash Halakhah Sifra undertook a polemic against the Mishnah, demonstrating "that the Mishnah's rules required exegetical foundations" (pp. 181 ff.), and criticizing the Mishnah for "its failure to cite Scripture," taking the position that "the Mishnah is wholly dependent upon Scripture."

[49] D. Weiss-Halivni, *Midrash, Mishnah and Gemara*.

[50] Halivni, ibid., p. 40, speculates that this change to a shorter version was effected to facilitate the memorization of the orally transmitted decrees. Contra, J. N. Epstein, תנאים, pp. 505 - 515, who argues that studying with the biblical source facilitated memorization.

[51] I do not dispute this affirmation, but would like to comment on one point of Halivni's evidence for the late change to the mishnaic form. He quotes from Josephus, *Ant.* 4: 196 - 7, in which Josephus excuses himself for the arrangement of the biblical laws according to their subject, ignoring the biblical order. Halivni's argument is that since the Mishnah is also classified according to subject, Josephus would not apologize for this order, if the Mishnah had been widely diffused in Judah. I wish to note here the rabbinic affirmation: אין מוקדם ומאוחר בתורה "There is no earlier or later in the Torah"; that is, though one passage is written prior to another, it does not follow that the events it represents actually occurred earlier. Thus, there is no order in the Torah, and one could not be censured for presenting the laws in a different order. This maxim already appears in Mekilta d'Rabbi Ishmael, *Beshallah* 7. It is most likely of earlier origin, since it is the only way to reconcile many inconsistencies observed by a critical examination of the Bible; we must assume that the midrashic authors perceived these discrepancies and reconciled them with such a principle, rather than admit the Bible consists of different sources and redactions. It is certainly possible, or even probable, that in the sectarian atmosphere of Josephus' period not everyone accepted this rabbinic pretext, and he directed his apology toward such groups.

without the justificatory element of the midrash, with which it originally formed one unit. The Amoraim and the other groups[52] whose discourses comprised the Gemara were the interpreters of the Mishnah, analyzing its sources. They returned to the vindicatory style of Scripture and revived the neglected midrashic elements, omitted in the Mishnah. Although Halivni does not declare this explicitly, one must assume that in his opinion the Midreshei Halakhah were the principal source of the Mishnah, and consequently of the halakhah.

I do not intend to enter into a discussion of Halivni's proposition, which is an interesting hypothesis to explain the lack of justificatory language in the Mishnah, as opposed to other types of rabbinic literature. I wish only to remark here that my postulate with respect to the distinct attitudes of the Tannaim and Amoraim (to be discussed more fully in section 4.1.7) offers a plausible explanation for this profound shift to the mishnaic form. The confidence of the Tannaim in their knowledge and their authority to create new norms encouraged them to formulate, for the first time, a distinct, pragmatic legal codex, as was the custom in other cultures. This codex, however, differed from those in other systems in that its decrees were believed to derive from the divine revelation in Scripture. This view is expressed, for instance, in the maxim לא בשמים היא, "it is not in Heaven," referring to the idea that the Torah is no longer in heaven but has been conveyed to the people of Israel;[53] this implies that the Israelites may analyze the Torah in order to reveal its guiding principles and decide new rules based upon them. This is not a critical analysis, which would be sacrilegious, but solely an investigation into the Torah's principal norms. The Tannaim did not intend to change the character of the law from a sacred, God-given system to a secular one,[54] but considered it unnecessary, or superfluous, to reiterate the divine origin of the mishnaic codex. It was therefore not necessary to cite the biblical source of each law. The Mishnah was a distinct composition, a codex dependent on, but detached from, the Bible.

Nor was the Mishnah's particular classification system seen as a departure from the Bible. The maxim אין מוקדם ומאוחר בתורה, "there is no earlier or later in the Torah," which the Sages judiciously considered to be divinely inspired, absolved them from any censure for changing the biblical order of the decrees; further, the lack of biblical citation in the Mishnah would forestall any such criticism. I would speculate that two

---

[52] In addition to the earlier-known Sevoraim, an additional group, the Stammaim, is suggested to have taken part in the final editing of the Gemara.

[53] See Introduction n. 58.

[54] For scholarly opinions with respect to the relationship between secular and sacred law in the development of biblical law, see A. Fitzpatrick-McKinley, *The Transformation of Torah*, pp. 23 - 53.

practical motives induced the Tannaim to arrange the classification of the Mishnah according to subjects. One was simply efficiency, as would be apparent from observation of Roman law. The other was a result of the oral repetition method practised by the Tannaim. To become proficient in memorizing the legal dicta, a Tanna[55] would specialize in one or more particular subjects,[56] thus generating as a by-product a classification according to subject.[57] When Rabbi (Yehudah the Patriarch) made the final editing touches to the Mishnah, he already had before him a reasonably well-organized classification.[58]

---

55 Mnemonic devices are widely used in the Talmud; their use was rendered imperative by the fact that the Talmud was originally transmitted orally. The term תנא "teacher" derives from the root תני "to repeat," and was the origin of the title Tanna. For a more elaborate essay on this term, see Ch. Albeck, מבוא למשנה, pp. 1 - 2. See also M. Elon, *Jewish Law*, vol. 3, p. 1042.

56 There is an engaging narrative in Midrash Tanhuma (Buber) *Terumah*, 1, concerning the advantages of this method for the study and memorization of the (oral) Torah: אבל תורה אינה כן זה שונה סדר זרעים וזה שונה סדר נזיקין עמדו שניהם זה עם זה אמר אחד לחבירו השנה לי סדר זרעים ואני אשנה לך סדר נזיקים נמצא ביד זה שנים וביד זה שנים "But it is different with respect to [the study of the] Torah. One [Tanna] repeats [for himself] the Order of Seeds, and another repeats the Order of Damages. Then they meet and one proposes to the other: Teach me the Order of Seeds and I will teach you the Order of Damages, and so both will know the two Orders." It seems that the names of the Tannaim who repeated the halakhot declared by others were not considered significant enough to quote when the Mishnah was finally redacted. See S. Lieberman, *Hellenism*, p. 88. We do encounter, on the other hand, some reference when the Tanna was probably also the redactor of the tractate, or significant elements of it. We read in yYoma 2: 2, 39d, in the name of Rabbi Yohanan, and in bYoma 14b, in a slightly different style, in the name of Rabbi Huna: תמיד דרבי שמעון איש המצפה היא "[Tractate] Tamid is the work of Rabbi Simeon of Mitzpah." Another Amora declares both in these passages and in bYoma 16b: מדות דר׳ אליעזר בן יעקב היא "Middot is the work of Rabbi Eliezer b. Jacob." Following a rhetorical discussion in bYoma indicating that Tamid could not be the work of Simeon, because one of his declarations would then conflict with a statement in Tamid, it is said in the name of Rabbi Yohanan: מאן תנא סדר יומא רבי שמעון איש המצפה הוא "Rabbi Simeon of Mitzpah was the Tanna of the tractate Yoma." This rhetoric is not found in the Y.T.; there, however, the potential dilemma is elegantly resolved with the declaration: ולא כולה אלא מילין דצריכין לרבנן "It is not all [tractate Tamid that is the work of Rabbi Simeon] but only where the Sages found it necessary [as they did not know anyone else to whom to attribute such parts; other declarations are thus from different Sages]." On the question of the editing of Tamid, see L. Ginzberg, "Tamid. The Oldest Treatise of the Mishna," and J. N. Epstein, תנאים, pp. 27 - 31, who challenges Ginzberg. Regarding the general issue of the authenticity of rabbinic attributions, see J. Neusner, "Attributions."

57 Tractate Eduyyot is an exception, since its editing had a particular motive; this is explained in tEduyyot 1: 3, cited in chap. 1, pp. 52-3.

58 The degree of classification and the style of the legal data that Rabbi had before him

I would also suggest that there is a methodological flaw in the approach of a number of the above-cited scholars. They founded their deductions and conclusions upon the data that appears in the talmudic literature, without submitting these to a critical examination regarding their historical authenticity. There is generally no scholarly disagreement with respect to the limited historical value of the bulk of the talmudic narratives. The disagreements on this topic are indeed limited to the question of whether or not one can discern a kernel of truth in most of the narratives.[59] The want of historical accuracy in talmudic literature should not, however, be considered as "criticism," in a pejorative sense. We must consider that the storytellers undertook to inspire and inculcate a message to their own or later generations, rather then to transmit the exact details of actual events. This circumstance should induce us to adopt a most "critical" approach to talmudic statements concerning the continuous and unimpaired transmission of traditions originating from Sinai, and to the sometimes farfetched efforts of halakhic midrashim to treat certain concepts as genuine Torah precepts.[60] I believe that the above scholars have ignored this significant dilemma in their considerations and conclusions.

Moreover, these scholars, as well as others whom they cite, attempt to identify an orderly, planned development of the rabbinic halakhah for those subjects without any entrenched tradition from bygone times; they differ solely in their characterization of the phases of this system. I shall argue against this perspective and in particular against the imposition of a rigid systematization on the rabbinic development of halakhah. We should not attempt, *a priori*, to discern in the patterns of Jewish thought the type of systematic approach[61] characteristic of Greek logic.[62] The difference in

---

have been matters of discussion among the traditional Jewish scholars and commentators up to the present. See Ch. Albeck, מבוא למשנה, pp. 63 ff. concerning the various opinions.

59 See J. Neusner, *Judaism*, p. 325, who expresses a radical viewpoint: those "who invoke the distinction between the historical kernel of truth and the ahistorical husk, produce capricious and subjective results."

60 See section 2.5.4 for a discussion of the rabbinic assertion that the broadening of the biblical prohibition against cooking a kid in its mother's milk is a Torah precept, and not a rabbinic innovation.

61 P. Schäfer, *Studien*, p. 25, writes: "Systematisches Denken und systematische Entwürfe sucht man bei den Rabbinen ohnehin vergeblich" ("It is futile to seek for systematic thought and design on the part of the Sages").

62 Maimonides, the first Jewish scholar who introduced a codification system for Jewish law in his monumental *Mishneh Torah*, was criticized for this activity. It is interesting to quote in this connection the Israeli historian H. H. Ben-Sasson's portrayal of Maimonides' enterprise, in his article "Maimonidean Controversy" in the *Encyclopedia Judaica*. He writes (p. 746): "[It was] an attempt to impose Greek systematic modes of codification in place of the traditional many-voiced flow of

perspective may be seen, for example, in the Bible itself, in the apparently unsystematic way in which its various elements were amalgamated,[63] and in its innumerable ambiguities and inconsistencies. In the Books of Kings we note the unusual method of dating the royal reigns of one kingdom by relating them to the reigns of the other kingdom, indicating a disregard for a systematic approach even to historical events.[64] This characteristic lack of system[65] is explicable if we consider that Scripture has a distinct historical message[66] and purpose: God is the primary mover of history, and Israel's destiny is decided by the actions of its ancestors; other aims are secondary and inconsequential. Even more significantly, the Bible itself indicates the value placed on pluralism, and respect for disparate views and ideas, in the quest to fulfill the divine intent. The same spirit that influenced the development of this plurivocal reading of the Bible continued its productive activity in the initial stages of biblical exegesis.

In addition to this distinctive and intentional lack of system in Israelite character and culture, I suggest that the Sages' passionate adherence to their autonomous right of judgment[67] influenced subsequent development. This autonomy created an almost "anarchic" mode of deliberation and decision,[68] with each case decided on its specific merits.[69]

---

talmudic discussion." See also S. A. Handelman, *Interpretation*, p. 51, who reviews "the structural differences between rabbinic and Greek thought."

63 The Sages had to acknowledge this circumstance, but declared without hesitation or the slightest criticism that there is no sequential pattern in Scripture: אין מוקדם ומאוחר בתורה See further on this concept n. 51 above.

64 Even Ben Sira's *Wisdom*, written at the peak of the Hellenistic period with the aim of emulating the style of Greek wisdom literature, demonstrates a lack of systematization in its various topics. A. Kahane, הספרים החיצונים, vol. 2, pp. 436-437, went so far as to arrange the topics in alphabetical order and indicate in which chapters and verses they appear in the work.

65 It is not my intention to make any qualitative judgment as to whether this specific social trait is a fault or merit.

66 P. Schäfer, *Studien*, pp. 13 ff. emphasizes the difference between the writing of history, *Geschichtsschreibung* (historiography), in which the Sages had no interest, and the perception of historical events, *Geschichtsauffassung* (sense of history), which the Sages possessed to an acute degree.

67 The fact that scholarly opinion is so divided - as we have seen above - on the analysis of talmudic dicta and the stages of their evolution is itself an indication of a lack of any fixed system guiding the Sages in their deliberations in the process of developing halakhah. Scholars have attempted to detect an orderly system within a disorderly composition, and the many divergent assumptions are the consequences of this impossible task.

68 A typical example is the issue of certain types of "work," such as riding and trading on Sabbath, that were forbidden in an earlier period as being transgressions against Torah precepts and later "downgraded" to rabbinic restrictions. These changes appear as inconsistencies in rabbinic literature, and have led to intensive and varied efforts on

the part of the later commentators to reconcile them. As their intention was to create a coherent, fixed system, it was understandably difficult for them to subsume under one principle these opposing declarations deriving from different times and circumstances. See section 4.1.7 on this issue; see also an extended study of the issue with all its complexities by I. Gilat, איסורי שבות.

69 The Sages found ways, when necessary, to circumvent even the established hermeneutic rules. Sifra, *Baraita d'Rabbi Ishmael* 1 outlines the thirteen rules of biblical hermeneutics. The first two are מקל וחומר מגזרה שוה, "*a minori ad majorem* [and the use of] analogy," giving the impression that the two rules are equal in their consequences and application. A distinction is made, however, in yPesahim 6: 1, 33a and (in a slightly more extensive version) in bPesahim 66a, quoted here: דאין אדם דן גזירה שוה מעצמו אלא קל וחומר דאדם דן מעצמו "...since one does not deduce [a legal decision] from an analogy formulated by oneself [unless he received it from his teacher, as Tosafot at bSukkah 31a clarifies it], but [why hasn't the rule] *a minori ad majorem* [been applied in the case at hand, since that is] a rule that one may formulate oneself ?" The answer is: קל וחומר פריכא הוא "[The application of the rule] *a minori ad majorem* does not hold water in this specific case [though no explanation is given]." The Y. T. version, however, does proffer a justification for the rejection of the *a minori ad majorem* rule: קל וחומר שאמרת יש לו תשובה לא אם אמרת בתמיד שהוא קדשי קדשים תאמר בפסח שהוא קדשים קלין "The *a minori ad majorem* argument you raised has an answer: [the subjects compared are not equivalent, since] the *tamid* is a most holy offering, and the Passover is only a holy offering."

Yet even the *a minori ad majorem* formula is not applied consistently. In some instances its authority is limited; we are told in yYevamot 11: 1, 11d: דר' ישמעאל אמר למידין מקל וחומר ואין עונשין מקל וחומר "Because Rabbi Ishmael said: We deduce a halakhah by the *a minori ad majorem* formula, but we do not punish [for the transgression of a prohibition deduced by the] *a minori ad majorem* formula." Although this rule seems to be generally accepted, as in tShevu'ot 3: 5, Sifra *Qedoshim* 10, Mekilta d' Rabbi Ishmael, *Mishpatim* 7, and many occurrences in both Talmudim, we see an inconsistency regarding its application with respect to punishment. In some occurrences, such as tShevu'ot 3: 5, bSanhedrin 73a and others, we encounter a question: וכי עונשין מן הדין "Does one punish for [a transgression deduced by the] *a minori ad majorem* formula?" In bMakkot 5b and 14a we encounter a definite negative: אין עונשין מן הדין "One does not punish for [a transgression deduced by the] *a minori ad majorem* formula." In bSanhedrin 54a, 74a and bMakkot 17b, it is declared that this issue is in dispute. In the rhetorical discussion in bSanhedrin 54a we read: "He [Rabbi Simeon ben Yohai] believes that one does [punish based on a transgression deduced by the *a minori ad majorem* formula]." Subsequently, a halakhic declaration by Rabbi Simeon's son is quoted, with the conclusion: סבר לה כאבוה דאמר עונשין מן הדין "He is of the same opinion as his father, who said: One punishes [for a transgression] deduced by the *a minori ad majorem* formula." We observe that there is a marked difference in the effectiveness of the rules, and there always exists a method of circumventing an affirmed rule. The assertion that a deduction by analogy is only applicable when received by transmission is in itself vague, since it does not indicate who was ever entitled to apply it; yet it is included in the thirteen legitimate rules of interpretation, and does not explicitly derive from Sinai, contrary to the maxim in Sifra *Behar* 1: כל המצות נאמרו מסיני, cited in chap. 1 at n. 17. On the other hand, the Sages

I also suggest that the Sages were far-sighted in their approach to law, and deliberately avoided a systematic and rigid approach that would bind and limit them and prevent the possibility of distinct and sometimes opposing resolutions.[70] They did not attempt to reveal comprehensive and detailed principles;[71] they favoured a flexible application of the divine law, allowing them to adapt it to any kind of changing circumstances.[72]

I shall offer two final examples of rabbinic decisions to demonstrate the undoubted practical foundation of their decisions, and the function of

---

logically discerned the persuasive strength of the *a minori ad majorem* rule, in contrast to the fragile and unconvincing nature of a conjecture founded upon an analogy between words in verses on completely distinct topics. As in other instances, the formal unity of the thirteen rules is preserved, but the different practical consequences of the two rules are considered on their own merits. J. Neusner, "Scripture and Tradition," p. 188, writes with respect to an analysis of the particular character of the Mishnah: "We find everything and its opposite."

70 An example of such an occurrence concerns the general prohibition against shaving the beard and the Nazir's interdiction against cutting his hair. In Lev 19: 27 we read: ולא תשחית את פאת זקנך "do not clip off the edges of your beard." In bNazir 40b, this verse is interpreted as referring only to shaving with a razor; any other means of cutting the beard is permitted. Lev 21: 5, ופאת זקנם לא יגלחו "[Priests must not] shave off the edges of their beards," is similarly interpreted, from a comparison to Lev 19: 27. On the other hand, the Nazir's prohibition in Num 6: 5, תער לא יעבר על ראשו "no razor may be used on his head," is interpreted in Sifre Num 25, yNazir 6: 3, 55a, and bNazir 39b to mean that cutting the hair with other implements is also prohibited. From the wording, one would have expected the opposite. The explicit mention of the razor in this case should have been interpreted to exclude other implements, whereas the lack of any specific implement in the other two occurrences should prohibit shaving by any means. It is obvious that the Sages understood that they must make a distinction between these three prohibitions, probably because the Nazir had to burn his hair at the conclusion of his vow (Num 6: 18), and construed the text accordingly, prohibiting even the tearing out of his hair. They may also have wanted to avoid the imposition of an absolute prohibition on the general public. Even at the stage of fixing a final halakhah, decisions were not founded upon a consistent principle. In the analyses of many mishnayot, the Gemara often proclaims in amazement, with such expressions as רישא וסיפא רבי שמעון מציעתא רבי יהודה "[How is it possible that Rabbi decided to establish the halakhah] in the first and third dicta according to Rabbi Simeon [in this case] and in the middle one according to Rabbi Yehudah?" In the case referred to, the dispute between Rabbi Yehudah and Rabbi Simeon concerns the principle of whether one may override a rabbinic prohibition to avoid the desecration of a holy scroll. Rabbi decided in two instances to confirm such a principle, and in another to reject it.

71 Gary G. Porton, *Rabbi Ishmael*, p. 204 notes that even Rabbi Ishmael, the alleged author of the thirteen principles of exegesis, did not necessarily follow these rules: "Ishmael was not limited to one set of exegetical principles or to one style of biblical exegesis."

72 G. Stemberger, *Introduction to the Talmud and Midrash*, p. 32, suggests that this consideration was behind the prohibition against writing down the halakhot. See chap. 1, at n. 91.

midrash in this process. The first is the radical replacement of the literal application of the *lex talionis* of Exod 21: 23 - 25, Lev 24: 19 - 20, and Deut 19: 21 with pecuniary compensation. The scriptural texts unmistakably require infliction of the same punishment on the offender that he had inflicted on his peer,[73] but the Sages entirely transmuted this principle and applied instead an obligation of compensation (mBava Qamma 8: 1)[74] We do not know the precise event or the general ethical

---

[73] The text explicitly contrasts compensation for bodily harm inflicted upon one's slave, who is considered property (Exod 21: 26 - 27), with corporal punishment for the same damage inflicted upon one's peers (vv. 24 - 25). (The latter rule follows the command for a punishment of death, "you are to take life for life [v. 23]," that clearly distinguishes between compensation for bodily harm when no death has occurred, in v. 22, and capital punishment for homicide.) The distinction between compensation for loss of property and equivalent punishment for bodily harm is more explicitly emphasized in Lev 24: 17 - 21. There is a clear juxtaposition of the two types of occurrences, killing a person in Lev 24: 17 and killing an animal in v. 18, and reiterated in v. 21: ומכה בהמה ישלמנה ומכה אדם יומת "Whoever kills an animal must make restitution, but whoever kills a man must be put to death." Scripture then declares explicitly: כאשר עשה כן יעשה לו "Whatever he has done must be done to him [v. 19]." This rule is again repeated in v. 20: כאשר יתן מום באדם כן ינתן בו "As he injured the other, so he is to be injured." The assigning of מדה כנגד מדה "equivalent retribution," to both good and evil deeds is a divine attribute, and therefore a sacred guiding principle in Jewish theology and practice. We read in bSanhedrin 90a and in other sources: שכל מדותיו של הקדוש ברוך הוא מדה כנגד מדה "All of the practices of the Holy One, Blessed be He, are [applied] measure for measure [against the deeds of humans]."

[74] We read in mBava Qamma 8: 1: החובל בחברו חייב עליו משום חמשה דברים בנזק בצער ברפוי בשבת ובבשת בנזק כיצד סימא את עינו קטע את ידו שיבר את רגלו "One who injures his neighbour is liable for five components [of compensation]: loss, pain, [cost of] healing, [loss of income, due to enforced] idleness, and humiliation. How [is this decree applied]? If he blinded his eye, cut off his hand, broke his leg ... [compensation is assessed according to a particular system of adjudication of damages.]" This mishnah is in blatant conflict with the scriptural command, as is noted in bBava Qamma 83b: אמאי עין תחת עין אמר רחמנא אימא עין ממש לא סלקא דעתך דתניא "Why [should this be so]? The Torah states [Exod 21: 24 and Lev 24: 20] 'an eye for an eye.' I would say [this is] literally an eye. No, you cannot think so, as we learned in a baraita." The baraita is then quoted (it is also found in Mekilta d' Rabbi Ishmael, *Mishpatim* 8 in the name of Rabbi Ishmael): הרי הוא אומר מכה בהמה ישלמנה ומכה אדם יומת הקיש הכתוב נזקי אדם לנזקי בהמה ונזקי בהמה לנזקי אדם מה נזקי בהמה לתשלומין אף נזקי אדם לתשלומין "It is stated [Lev 24: 21]: 'Whoever kills an animal must make restitution, but whoever kills a man must be put to death.' Scripture compared the injuring of a man to the injuring of an animal, the injuring of an animal to the injuring of a man; just as the injuring of an animal [requires] pecuniary compensation, the injuring of a man requires pecuniary compensation." The same exegesis is quoted in Sifra *Emor* 14; there, however, the author was aware of the frailty of his hermeneutics, and added a further exegetical justification: אם

environment that induced the Sages to officially proclaim this law. It is plausible that both practices, that is punishment and compensation, were exercised contemporaneously for some time,[75] with the remedy at the

---

נפשך לומר לא תקחו כופר לנפש רוצח לרוצח אין את נוטל כופר נוטל את לאיברים כופר "If you wish [I could say that it is written]: 'Do not accept a ransom for the life of a murderer [Num 35: 31]'; [this means] you do not accept a ransom for a murder, but you accept a ransom for [injuring] limbs." It is interesting that the Y.T. does not attempt to reconcile the conflict between the mishnaic dictum and Scripture, but instead offers a logical argument that the scriptural decree must be interpreted as requiring compensation. We read in yBava Qamma 8: 1, 6b: שאם היה סומא וסימא את עינו קיטע וקיטע את ידו היאך זה מתקיים ועשיתם לו כאשר זמם לעשות לאחיו מגיד שאינו משלם אלא ממון "How can this [talion] be applied if a blind man blinded the eye of another, [or] a man without a hand cut off the hand of another? [It is written, in Deut 19: 19]: 'Do to him as he intended to do to his brother'; this tells us that he only pays pecuniary compensation." The verse in Deut does not refer to bodily injury, but to the punishment of false witnesses; the talmudic author, however, perceives it as a general rule of retribution, and applies it to our subject. His conclusion is in turn founded upon another maxim, that the law must be applied equally in all cases; thus, if it is impossible to apply it in every occurrence, it must not be applied at all. We read in bBava Qamma 83b: התורה אמרה משפט אחד יהיה לכם משפט השוה לכולכם "Scripture stated [Lev 24: 22]: 'You are to have the same law' - [this means] a law that is equal for everybody." Similar arguments founded upon the requirement of an equal application of the law in all circumstances are cited in a baraita in bBava Qamma 83b. As one example, an argument cited in the name of Rabbi Dostai b. Yehudah is founded upon the impossibility of applying talion for the loss of an eye when the eye of the guilty person is smaller than the eye of the injured person. It is therefore concluded that only pecuniary compensation can be applied equally in all instances.

75 G. von Rad, *Deuteronomy, A Commentary*, p. 129 hints at such a possibility, which is apparent from the literary style of the text. This restriction to compensation stands in contrast to the choice offered in Exod 21: 29 - 30, in which the injured party can choose to accept pecuniary contribution from the offender, or require his punishment. The owner of the goring ox is personally responsible for the damage caused by the animal, since he was warned and should have put the animal to death; but "if payment is demanded of him [though Scripture does not indicate who demands it, it is probably the injured party's relatives] he may redeem his life by paying whatever is demanded [v. 30]." The Sages changed this rule, however, and decreed that only pecuniary compensation was due for death caused by the goring ox, and its owner was never executed. Various types of exegesis were used to justify this ruling. Mekilta d' Rabbi Simeon b. Yohai 21: 29 addresses the conceptual contradiction by which pecuniary compensation is allowed in this case of death, instead of the capital punishment of the owner that would be required by Num 35: 21. The following exegesis is used: לפי שהוא אומ׳ וגם בעליו יומת יכול כשם שהשור נסקל כך בעליו נסקלין ת״ל השור יסקל השור נסקל ואין בעליו נסקלין "Since it says: 'and the owner also must be put to death [Exod 21: 29]' we might assume that since the bull is stoned, its owner should also be stoned. [But the antecedent phrase of the verse] 'the bull must be stoned' teaches us that [only] the bull should be stoned, and not its owner." B. T. Bava Qamma 83b has another exegesis: אי בעי עינו ניתיב ואי בעי דמי עינו ניתיב קמ״ל מבהמה מה מכה בהמה לתשלומין מכה אדם

לתשלומין "We might say if one [whose eye was destroyed] wishes to have his eye [that is, the eye of the culpable party taken out], we shall give this to him, and if he wishes compensation for his eye, we shall give this to him. [The use of the term מכה for the killing of an animal and for the killing of a man in Lev 24: 21] comes to teach us [that this is not acceptable, but] that just as damage to an animal must be compensated by payment, so must the damage inflicted on a man." In bSanhedrin 15b, the same conclusion is deduced from a far-fetched exegesis of another biblical verse: על רציחתו אתה הורגו ואי אתה הורגו על רציחת שורו "[Scripture states: 'that person shall be put to death, he is a murderer (Num 35: 21)'; this means] you execute him for a murder carried out by himself, but you do not kill him for a murder performed by his bull." Mekilta d'Rabbi Ishmael, *Mishpatim* 10 also attempts to reconcile the apparent contradiction, and at the same time amend the law so as to achieve a just result: וגם בעליו יומת יומת בידי שמים "[The scriptural command that] the owner must be put to death [Exod 21: 29] [means] death by heaven [not by humans]." The commentator Rashi follows the midrashic exegesis in his interpretation of this verse. He declares that the conjunction "if" in v. 30 does not in this case have the usual conditional meaning, but is intended as an apodictic command; that is, the court must establish the amount of reparation, but the owner must not be killed. (This is also found in Mekilta d'Rabbi Simeon bar Yohai on Exod 21: 30.) It is odd, in contrast, that while the Mekilta d'Rabbi Ishmael, *Yitro* 11 states: רבי ישמעאל אומר כל אם ואם שבתורה רשות חוץ משלשה "R. Ishmael says: Every [use of the] term אם "if" in the Torah is a conditional expression, except in three occurrences," this verse is not included in the list. We encounter an interesting narrative on this topic in ySanhedrin 1: 2, 19b: אגנטוס הגמון שאל לרבי יוחנן בן זכאי השור יסקל וגם בעליו יומת אמר ליה שותף ליסטים כליסטים וכשיצא אמרו לו תלמידיו רבי לזה דחיתה בקנה לנו מה את משיב אמר להן כתיב השור יסקל וגם בעליו יומת כמיתת הבעלים כן מיתת השור הקיש מיתת בעלים למיתת השור מה מיתת בעלים בדרישה וחקירה בעשרים ושלשה אף מיתת השור בדרישה וחקירה בעשרים ושלשה "Agnetos the Hegemon asked Rabbi Yohanan b. Zakkai [why the owner of the goring ox should be killed for the harmful action of his ox, as written in Exod 21: 29:] 'The bull must be stoned and the owner also must be put to death.' He answered him: The associate of a robber is deemed to be a robber. And when he left, his [R. Yohanan's] disciples said to him: You have rebuffed him with a reed, but how do you answer us? He said to them: It is written: 'the bull must be stoned and the owner also must be put to death' - the death of the ox is like the death of the owners. [Scripture] compares the death sentence on the owners [in other cases] to the death sentence on the ox [in this occurrence]; just as the death of the owner is effected through investigation and examination by a court of twenty-three members, so the death of the ox is effected through investigation and examination by a court of twenty-three members." This is how I understand this narrative, based on the clear declarations in the above-cited rabbinic sources that the owner is not liable to the death penalty. The Roman interlocutor (whether indeed the narrative is based on real facts, or simply uses, as seems to be indicated in the succeeding narrative, an interesting literary framework within which to convey an opinion on a paradoxical and unpalatable topic) was apparently satisfied with the legal answer that the owner is deemed to be an accomplice to a crime and as such is liable for the same punishment. He would not have understood the intricate and far-fetched hermeneutics, utilized by Rabbi Yohanan b. Zakkai, to reverse the explicit scriptural law. His disciples, on the other hand, considered it morally unacceptable to

choice of the offended party,[76] before the Sages promulgated the restriction to compensation. They could not, therefore, justify this restriction by reference to tradition; they were thus faced with the task of devising scriptural support[77] for such a manifest reversal of a clear biblical command[78] that was founded upon an ancient tradition of vengeance and equivalent retaliation. The *lex talionis* must have been so deeply entrenched in society[79] that the Sages would not have dared to present

---

execute a person for a deed not performed by himself. They therefore asked for a better explanation. And indeed, Rabbi Yohanan b. Zakkai answered according to their expectation that the owner is not liable to the death penalty. He reconciled this rule with the apparently contradictory scriptural text through rather far-fetched hermeneutics. These in fact are legally invalid, as we read in yPesahim 6: 1, 33a, and bPesahim 66a: שאין אדם דן גזירה שוה מעצמו "One cannot deduce a halakhah from a comparison of similar words [that is received solely by tradition]." Cf. D. Instone Brewer, *Techniques*, pp. 80 ff., who in my opinion did not understand this narrative; he assumed that Rabbi Yohanan b. Zakkai answered his pupils that the owner would be executed, which is patently against all rabbinic sources. He ends his analysis: "Just as the man is executed after a proper trial, so also the ox had its own trial before 23 Judges." Following the above narrative in ySanhedrin 1: 2, 19b, there is an interesting dispute referring to v. 30: ונתן פדיון נפשו [פדיון נפשו] של מומת דברי רבי ישמעאל רבי עקיבא אומר פדיון נפשו של ממית "[It is written] 'He may redeem his life' - this means the value of the life of the one killed, according to Rabbi Ishmael, but Rabbi Aqiba says the value of the killer's life." Rabbi Aqiba's philosophical argument is that since he is liable to death by heaven, the killer redeems his life by payment of his own value.

76 Josephus, in *Ant.* 4: 280, maintains that this was the law presented by Moses to the Israelites. The *lex talionis* was practised, unless the injured party consented to receive pecuniary compensation instead of physical punishment. Philo, it seems, maintained the literal interpretation of the Torah law (*Spec. Laws* 3: 195); the *lex talionis* is applied to the maiming of freemen, while a slave who is maimed is freed, according to Exod 21: 26.

77 G. Vermes, *Studies*, p. 62 would call this "applied exegesis." Cf. H. H. Cohn, "Methodology," p. 128, Heading "Third."

78 See Mekilta d'Rabbi Ishmael, *Misphatim* 8, and the extremely protracted discussion and argumentation in the various rabbinic sources cited in nn. 74-75 above, which attempt to justify the total reversal of the explicit intent of Scripture. The radical alteration of the biblical text is also noticeable in the exegesis of Lev 24: 21, mentioned in the above notes. Scripture expressly differentiates between the consequences of harming an animal and the consequences of harming a man: ומכה בהמה ישלמנה ומכה אדם יומת "Whoever kills an animal must make restitution, but whoever kills a man must be put to death"; the exegesis, however, equates them, decreeing compensation in both occurrences.

79 We read in bBava Qamma 84a: תניא ר"א אומר עין תחת עין ממש "We learned in a baraita: Rabbi Eliezer says: [The biblical edict of] an eye for an eye is a literal command." We observe that, in the period of this early Tanna (about 90 C.E.), the drastic alteration of this law was not yet universally accepted. The Gemara in Bava Qamma attempts to reconcile Rabbi Eliezer's declaration with the contemporary halakhah; in the view of the Amoraim, compensation was the original intent of the

their alteration as inherent in their authority to "dislodge Scripture" (yQiddushin 1: 2, 59d, and bSotah 16a; see section 1.4). They needed to find scriptural support, which they accomplished with a far-fetched exegesis.[80] The practical foundation of this rabbinic decree is evident, and the exegesis an obvious cover.[81]

The second example is the virtual repudiation of capital punishment, a penalty that is required in Scripture for a great variety of transgressions. This was done in an elaborate way: the offender was required to be warned by two witnesses, before his transgression, of the gravity of the offence and the punishment to which he would be subjected. Only if he persisted in committing the transgression despite the warning would he be condemned to death.[82] One may assume that such a procedure in effect

---

law given at Sinai, and it would be impossible for them to allege that Rabbi Eliezer contradicted it. We, on the other hand, may assume that he understood the edict literally.

80 In mHagigah 1: 8, as we have seen (n. 38), there is a blatant admission of the fact that many rabbinic rules are without scriptural foundation. A number of biblical citations are quoted in yHagigah 1: 8, 76c, and bHagigah 10a in the name of various Tannaim, in an attempt to detect such scriptural support, but it is evident that they are far-fetched. It is interesting to note that in the B. T. Rabbi Eliezer is connected with the exegesis of a different biblical verse than that quoted in the Y. T., and thus there is also the problem of correct attributions. See Z. W. Falk, "Binding and Loosing." M. Halberthal, מהפכות, p. 171, asserts that the lenient decrees decided upon ethical considerations were generated by the early Tannaim, in the period of Yabneh and Usha.

81 Concerning the question of the priority of mishnah or midrash, it is relevant to note here an assertion by G. Vermes (*Studies*, p. 81): "Wherever their [in this case, the Pharisees'] doctrine departed from the accepted norm they were obliged to defend it with argument solidly backed by Scripture." I must contest his characterization of such defence as "**solidly** backed by Scripture [emphasis mine]." A great number of the halakhic midrashim are far removed from the simple and plain understanding of the relevant scriptural text; an example that indisputably contradicts any idea of the solidity of the midrashic support is the metamorphosis of the *lex talionis*, described above. D. Instone Brewer, *Techniques*, p. 5, remarks concerning the priority of mishnah or midrash: "Ultimately this is a 'chicken and egg' question; exegesis produces new halakot, and new halakot provoke exegesis, and it is meaningless to discuss which one has the priority or to determine the time when either of them emerged."

82 We read in tSanhedrin, 11: 1: ושאר חייבי מיתות בית דין אין מחייבין אותן אלא על פי עדים והתראה ועד שיודיעוהו שחייב מיתה בבית דין ר׳ יוסי בר׳ יהודה אומ׳ עד שיודיעוהו באיזו מיתה הוא מת "And anyone who would be liable to execution by the court is not liable unless [the court convicted him] on the basis of witnesses and prior warning, and informed him that he would be liable to execution by the court [not by a divine act]. Rabbi Yose b. Yehudah says: Unless he was informed of the exact method of execution." The required question is specified in mSanhedrin 5: 1, which describes the procedure in court: התריתם בו "Did you warn him?" A dispute among the Tannaim refers solely to the question of whether the witnesses to the transgression must be the same people who warned the transgressor.

amounted to an abolition of capital punishment. The Sages effected this drastic reform by maintaining, through far-fetched hermeneutics, that this was the real intent of Scripture.[83]

All agree that without prior warning, the transgressor is not executed, even for a deed performed before witnesses. The procedure is elaborated in bSanhedrin 40b: קיבל עליו התראה התיר עצמו למיתה "He confirmed the warning [saying: I know that it is a transgression for which I may be executed], and committed himself to the death penalty." Hence, the transgressor must explicitly confirm his determination to accept the penalty of which he has been forewarned. We read in tSanhedrin 8: 3 a vivid portrayal of such an event, narrated by Simeon ben Shetah: ראיתי אחד שרץ אחר חבירו והסייף בידו נבנס מפניו לחורבה נבנס אחריו ונבנסתי אחריו ומצאתיו הרוג והסייף ביד הרוצח ומנטף דם ואמרתי לו רשע מי הרגו לזה "I saw a man running after his colleague with a sword in his hand. The man ran into a ruin, the other [with the sword] followed him. I entered after them and found the man [who had been pursued] killed and the sword, dripping blood, in the hand of the killer, and said to him: You wicked man, who killed him?" And although it was evident that the man with the sword had killed him, Simeon said to him: אבל מה אעשה לך שאין דינך מסור בידי שהרי אמרה תורה על פי שנים עדים או על פי שלש' עדים יומת המת "What can I do? Your case is not under my authority [to convict you] because the Torah said: 'On the testimony of two or three witnesses a man shall be put to death [Deut 17: 6].'" We see that even in such an obvious case of murder the death penalty could not be applied. The narrative notifies us that the killer was nonetheless punished by God; a snake bit him and he died.

83 There is no mention in Scripture of any prerequisite warning. The relevant passages in Mishnah and Tosefta, as is common, do not enlighten us as to the connection with any scriptural verse; they simply decree the need for warning. Both the Y. T. and B. T. attempt to reveal the biblical support, with rather far-fetched connections. We read in ySanhedrin 5: 1, 22c the usual question: מניין להתרייה "Where [in Scripture] is the warning [derived from]?" None of the answers gives an explicit connection to Scripture. The following, in a baraita, is typical: תני רבי שמעון בן יוחי אומר על פי שנים עדים יומת המת המת מת אלא להודיעו באי זו מיתה מת "Rabbi Simeon b. Yohai says: [It is written] 'on the testimony of two…the man [literally: the dead man] shall be put to death.' 'The dead man' is already dead [that is, how can a dead man be put to death], and hence Scripture teaches us that a man must be warned of the type of execution by which he will punished." In bSanhedrin 40b-41a, we read: אמר עולא מניין להתראה מן התורה שנאמר ואיש אשר יקח את אחתו בת אביו או בת אמו וראה את ערותה אטו בראיה תליא מילתא אלא עד שיראוהו טעמו של דבר אם אינו ענין לכרת תנהו ענין למלקות "Ulla said: Where do we know from the Torah the requirement of pre-warning? [A.] It is written [Lev 20: 17]: 'If a man has sexual relations with his sister, [whether she is] the daughter of his father or of his mother, and he sees her nakedness [it is a disgrace].' [Q.] Does the matter depend on his seeing [her nakedness, rather than his having intercourse]? [If so, we must interpret this odd expression differently, and this means that he cannot be punished] unless he was informed about the outcome of his deed [i.e the punishment]. And if this [requirement] is not relevant to the punishment of excision [a punishment from heaven], it is relevant to lashes [and other punishments inflicted by a human court.]" These two examples offer insight into the gap between the scriptural verses and rabbinic exegesis; as mentioned, the rest of the arguments in

The above two examples seem indisputable, but I should like to add another example that is less straightforward. In my opinion, however, it reveals a significant rabbinic ideology and the Sages' attitude toward radical reforms, and is thus most relevant to this study. I refer to the momentous decision by the Sages to abolish sacrificial worship after the Temple's destruction.[84] The Torah commands the offering of the daily perpetual sacrifices (*tamid*) and of particular sacrifices for the various holy days; the violation of these commands amounts to a grave transgression of the divine law. To support such a radical change, the prophetic verse ונשלמה פרים שפתנו (Hos 14: 3)[85] was interpreted to mean "We may offer our lips as sacrifices of bulls," to imply that the recital of prayers would be equivalent to a sin offering.[86] Further, the study of the Torah, as

---

both Talmudim are of a similar character.

84 See P. Heger, *Altars*, pp. 372 - 374 on this subject. There are no records to the effect that the Jews, under the spiritual control of the Sages, attempted to perform sacrifices after the Temple's destruction. We do encounter many narratives in the rabbinic literature that glorify the Sages who gave their lives for the fulfillment of the divine precepts and also for teaching the Torah. We would also expect here some mention of any aborted attempts to offer sacrifices, and the total absence of such a reference tends to confirm the thesis that there was never any attempt to perform sacrifices post-70. See also B. Z. Rosenfeld, "Sage and Temple," pp. 449-50, who adds a further element to the commonly known list of replacements for sacrifice that was created by the Rabbis: "Sage and Torah had inherited certain functions of the Temple...pilgrimage[s] to the Sage during the festivals...were a substitute for pilgrimage to the Temple during the three Pilgrimage Festivals." Lee Levine, "Judaism," p. 127, states that "there was no attempt [by the Romans] to annihilate the Jewish people or their Judaism."

85 The NIV translates this phrase: "that we may offer the fruit of our lips," following the LXX (14: 3) ἀνταποδώσομεν καρπὸν χειλέων ἡμῶν.

86 We read in Num. Rab. 18: 21: ונשלמה פרים שפתינו אמרו ישראל רבש״ע בזמן שבהמ״ק קיים היינו מקריבים קרבן ומתכפר ועכשיו אין בידינו אלא תפלה "'Our lips instead of calves [Hos 14: 3]' - The Israelites said to the Master of the World: When the Temple existed we used to offer sacrifices and [our sins] were forgiven, but now we have only our prayer." There is a similar homily in Pesiqta d'Rav Kahana 24: א״ר אבהו מי משלם אותם הפרים שהיינו מקריבים לפניך שפתינו בתפילה שאנו מתפללים לפניך "Rav Abbahu said: Who replaces those bulls we used to offer You? Our lips reciting the prayers to You." Exod. Rab. 38: 4 lists various examples of deeds that are considered to replace offerings: עניים אנו ואין לנו להביא קרבנות א״ל דברים אני מבקש שנאמר קחו עמכם דברים ושובו אל ה׳ ואני מוחל על כל עונתיכם ואין דברים אלא דברי תורה "[The Israelites complain]: We are poor and cannot bring offerings. [God] replies: I ask only for words, as it is said: 'Take words with you and return to the Lord [Hos 14: 3, v. 2 in KJV],' and I will forgive you all your sins. 'Words' means Torah [as it says: 'These are the words Moses spoke to all of Israel (Deut 1: 1)']." The homily continues: אמרו לו אין אנו יודעין אמר להם בכו והתפללו לפני ואני מקבל "The Israelites said to Him: We are not proficient in studying the Torah. He answered: Weep and pray before me and I will accept it [as if you were offering

well as other meritorious deeds[87] and behaviour,[88] were endowed with greater eminence than the offering of the daily perpetual offerings.[89] The consumption of the *terumah* tithe by the priests was deemed equivalent to the offering of the daily *tamid*.[90] As with the *lex talionis*, it is evident that the replacement of the sacrifices could not logically be justified simply through a hermeneutic exercise. The Sages perceived that both these decisions were necessary[91] and beneficial and thus enacted them;

---

sacrifices]." This assertion is substantiated by references to events and relevant scriptural verses in which God aided Joshua, the Judges, Samuel, and the people of Jerusalem, when they approached Him with tears and prayers.

87 Sifra *Emor* 10 responds to an assumed question: why does the command to leave the edges of the field and the gleanings of the harvest for the poor appear in Lev 23: 22 in the midst of commands regulating the offerings for the holidays (for Passover and the Feast of Weeks in 23: 4 - 21, and for the Feast of Trumpets and Day of Atonement at 23: 23)? The answer is given : אלא ללמד שכל מי שהוא מרציא לקט שכחה ופיאה ומעשר עני מעלים עליו כאילו בית המקדש קיים והוא מקריב קרבנותיו לתוכו "... to teach that if one performs [the rules regarding] gleaning, the forgotten sheaf, and the tithes for the poor, he is deemed to be [in the same position] as if the Temple were functioning and he were sacrificing his offerings in it."

88 We read in ySheqalim 2: 5, 47a: חביב עלי צדקה ומשפט שאתה עושה יותר מן הקרבן שנאמר עשה צדקה ומשפט נבחר ליי׳ מזבח "The righteousness and justice that you do is more agreeable to me than sacrifice, as it is said: 'To do what is right and just is more acceptable to the Lord than sacrifice [Prov 21: 3].'" A homily in bSotah 5b speaks of the high regard in which the humble are viewed in the eyes of God: מי שדעתו שפלה מעלה עליו הכתוב כאילו הקריב כל הקרבנות כולם שנאמר זבחי אלהים רוח נשברה "If one has a humble spirit, Scripture deems it as if he were offering all the offerings, as it is written: 'the sacrifices of God are a broken spirit [Ps 51: 19, v. 17 in KJV].'"

89 We read in bEruvin 63b: גדול תלמוד תורה יותר מהקרבת תמידין "The study of the Torah is greater than the offering of the perpetual sacrifices."

90 See the relevant talmudic quotations in P. Heger, *Altars*, p. 374, n. 193.

91 A remarkable narrative in Gen. Rab. 64: 10 seems to corroborate, in its essence, this attitude of the Sages. We read there that in the period of Rabbi Yehoshua ben Hananyah, the occupying government decreed that the Temple must be built. As in the Ezra narrative, the *Kutim* (a byword for Samaritans) slandered the Jews, and as the result of a legal trick the Temple could not be built. The Jews were disappointed, the story continues, and were on the brink of rebellion against the Romans. Desiring to avoid rebellion, the Sages sent Rabbi Yehoshua ben Hananyah, a Tanna who lived during the period of the destruction of the Temple, to pacify the masses, which he did with a suitable parable. The authenticity of the details is doubtful, given its "stock scene" of hostile elements slandering the Jews with the particular accusation of not being loyal to the dominant authorities, thus attempting to provoke retaliation against them; this "scene" also appears in Ezra (chap. 4) and in the renowned story of Qamtza and Bar Qamtza (bGittin 55b-56a). On the other hand, we know that the Roman emperor Hadrian did indeed plan to rebuild Jerusalem; see G. Alon, *The Jews*, vol. 2, p. 435. Whether he also had in mind to rebuild the Temple is a debated issue, but there is no doubt a kernel of truth in this narrative about the commendable intentions of the Romans regarding Jerusalem's rehabilitation. The use in the narrative of the

eventually scriptural support was derived for them.[92] Rabbinic dicta regarding the sacrificial system, unlike those regarding the *lex talionis*, could be founded entirely upon interpretation, since sacrifice was no longer relevant. Decisions regarding sacrifice could thus avoid any reflection on pragmatic consequences.[93]

2.3 Rabbinic Authority

2.3.1 "Judicial" versus "Legislative"

A comment is necessary on the different types of authority within the rabbinic system.[94] Unlike modern systems with clear divisions of power, we encounter in rabbinic practice a unity between legislative and judicial[95]

---

term גזרה (from the root גזר) to describe the government's edict to build the Temple thus seems quite bizarre; this term often denotes a harmful, not a meritorious, decree (though see section 1.6.4). Reading between the lines, there may be an implicit message that the Sages did not encourage the building of the Temple with its focus on the sacrificial ceremonies. See on this issue P. Heger, *Altars*, pp. 377 ff. and particularly p. 383, n. 213.

92 This is not to say that all halakhot were created in this way. As a result of the pluralistic approach in the tannaitic period, permitting and encouraging individual opinion, and the lack of systematization, it is plausible that some Tannaim were not so bluntly authoritative in their deliberations.

93 In the second part of this work, I cite an example of the impractical effects of this procedure, with respect to the *minhah* offering.

94 M. S. Berger, *Rabbinic Authority*, explains rabbinic authority as to be both "in authority," and "an authority." He writes on p. 153: "The different spheres of the rabbinic complex project were not always separated, but were blended in ways suggesting that certain rabbinic rules were really mergers or fusions of multiple rabbinic roles."

95 It is not within the scope of this study to extend the discussion on this issue, but I have the impression from statements in mSanhedrin chap. 6 that the Sages who constituted a court were also involved in executing the punishment they proclaimed. In mSheqalim 1: 2 the involvement of the court in the execution of its decrees is more explicit. We read there: אמר רבי יהודה בראשונה היו עוקרין ומשליכין לפניהם משרבו עוברי עברה היו עוקרין ומשליכין על הדרכים התקינו שיהו מפקירין כל השדה כולה "Rabbi Yehudah said: At first they [the agents of the court] tore out and threw in front of them [illegally mixed plants they found in a field]; when the number of transgressors multiplied they tore them out and threw them on the road [to avoid having them used as fodder], and [when this did not eliminate the transgressions] [the court] declared the harvest of the entire field confiscated [including the lawful plants]." Although the mishnah does not explicitly identify the persons who carried out these penalties, tSheqalim 1: 3 does so and provides the legal basis: בחמשה עשר בו שלוחי בית דין יוצאין ומפקירין את הכלאים שהפקר בית דין הפקר "On the fifteenth [of Adar] the agents of the court go [to the

authority, with no effective distinction between them.[96] We often observe abstract theoretical discussions among the Sages with respect to a legal problem; such occurrences would be similar to a legislative committee debating the theoretical aspects of a proposed law, and the Sages in such cases thus acted in the capacity of legislators. There are, however, other occurrences in which we observe discussions and opposing arguments about a concrete case, and a subsequent final decision.[97] In that case, the Sages were acting in both a legislative and a judicial capacity,[98] since they promulgated a new law simultaneously with the act of rendering a decision.[99]

---

respective fields] and confiscate the illegally mixed plants, since the court has the authority to confiscate individual property [by revoking individual ownership]." The Patriarch (Nasi), as for example Rabban Gamaliel, certainly wore various hats: he was endowed with political and executive authority, and mYadayim 4: 4 confirms that he was involved in the debate and the decision regarding the conversion of an Ammonite, functioning as both legislator and judge.

96 The first textual evidence of judges acting on the basis of an established law is encountered in Ezra 7: 25: מני שפטין ודינין די להון דאנין לכל עמה די בעבר נהרה לכל ידעי דתי אלהך ודי לא ידע תהודעון "...appoint magistrates and judges to administer justice to all the people of Trans-Euphrates - all who know the laws of your God. And you are to teach any who do not know them." References to judges in the earlier books of Judges through Kings do not link them with law, but rather with wisdom. Solomon asked God: ונתת לעבדך לב שמע לשפט את עמך להבין בין טוב לרע "So give your servant a discerning heart to govern your people and to distinguish between right and wrong [1 Kgs 3: 9]." 1 Kgs 3: 28 records that the people saw כי חכמת אלהים בקרבו לעשות משפט "that he had wisdom from God to administer justice." Censure arose not because a judgment was legally incorrect but because, as Micah complained, ישפטו ראשיה בשחד "Her leaders judge for a bribe [3: 11]." In Mic 6: 8, the prophet communicates God's authentic will: עשות משפט ואהבת חסד "To act justly and to love mercy." There is no indication that the judges tried cases according to specific legal procedures. Though I am not able to undertake a detailed analysis of the broad semantic range of the term שפט, the use of this term within the book of Judges suggests a meaning of "to lead" rather than "to judge."

97 We have seen, for example (chap. 1, n. 71) the case in mYadayim 4: 4 of an Ammonite who wanted to be converted to Judaism, although this would be contrary to a biblical restriction (Deut 23: 4). After intense discussions pro and con, a conclusion was reached: מיד התירוהו לבא בקהל "Right away they allowed him to convert"; after Sennacherib's policy of forced deportations, the ancient law restricting the Ammonites and Moabites from joining the community of Israel was deemed no longer relevant. See also S. Safrai, *The Literature of the Sages*, p. 154.

98 B. Gerhardsson, *Memory and Manuscript*, writes on p. 105: "The boundary between בית המדרש and בית דין is not easy to draw." See also chap. 4, n. 209 and related text.

99 Whether their discussion amounted to the creation of a new law, or to an interpretation of an existing law due to changed conditions, is not specified, but does

On the other hand, we cannot assert that the Sages were not aware of the difference between a body that acts in a legislative capacity and one acting in a judicial capacity.[100] In bBava Batra 130b a dispute is recorded regarding whether a theoretical discussion or a judicial decision offers a more reliable source for establishing halakhah for the future.[101] We read there: "One [Sage] considered that a legislative pronouncement [הלכה] is preferable [as a source of law], and the other considered that practice [מעשה, i.e. a judicial decision on a particular case] offers more [reliability]."[102] A baraita is then cited that emphasizes the Sages' awareness of the differences between concrete and theoretical decisions:[103] "One does not learn a halakhah from learning [למוד - the opinions of a Sage] or from a judicial decision [מעשה]; one may deduce the halakhah only [when he asks for a decision] regarding a concrete occurrence [הלכה למעשה]."[104]

---

not in fact matter. One who renders a judgment on the basis of a particular interpretation of a principle or a precedent is in a certain sense also a lawmaker. The degree of "lawmaking" depends on the extent of his interpretational autonomy.

100 It must be noted, however, that since the Sages were not concerned with the creation of a consistent legal system, we are unable to discern from their records when a decision was considered the result of a judicial process and when it was deemed the result of a deliberation in the academy. Maimonides, in the introduction to his Mishnah commentary, states that the disputes among the Sages were settled after a decision was taken, and all then accepted it. He discusses the prohibition against eating fowl with milk, and states that all Israel accepted it. Maimonides obviously wanted to overlook the rabbinic record that long after Rabbi Yose ha-Gelili's death people living in his town did in fact eat fowl and milk products together (bShabbat 130a); see the more detailed discussion of this issue in section 2.5 below, especially 2.5.4.

101 I. Englard, "Research in Jewish Law," p. 40, perceives this as a tension between theory and practice.

102 The commentator Rashbam explains the different concepts. The first Sage conceives that a judicial decision may be dependent upon the particulars of the adjudicated case, and the same decision would not be appropriate in another occurrence in which the circumstances might be slightly different. A theoretical decision is therefore more reliable and does not permit an erroneous interpretation. The other Sage perceives that a decision on a concrete issue before a court is deliberated with much more attention and judicious reasoning than a theoretical question, and is therefore more reliable as a precedent for future halakhah.

103 A similar but less explicit dictum is found in yHagigah 1: 8, 76d: ר' חנניה בשם שמואל אין למידין מן ההורייה הכל מודין שאין למידין מן המעשה "Rabbi Hananyah [said] in the name of Samuel: One does not learn a halakhah from another halakhic decision; all agree that one does not learn a halakhah from an occurrence [in which such a halakhah was practised]." It is not entirely clear from this text whether the term ההורייה refers to a concrete court decision, or to an abstract halakhic dictum; I therefore chose to discuss the B.T. version.

104 I do not intend to deny the plausibility of Rashbam's explanation, cited in n. 102, but

The rule of the "rebellious elder" also confirms the rabbinic consciousness of the difference between legislative and judicial activity. We read in tSanhedrin 14: 12: "A rebellious elder who decided [in conflict with the decision of the majority] is liable to punishment, when his pronouncement was acted upon; if it was not acted upon, he is not liable. [On the other hand] if he commanded his judgment to be acted upon, he is liable to punishment even if it was not acted upon." In effect, the rebellious elder may continue with his legislative pronouncements against the decisions of the majority, but not with his judicial pronouncements. The distinction between the two activities is emphasized when we consider that for the judicial activity, he is liable to capital punishment;[105] at the same time, he is free to spread his legislative opinions. Notwithstanding the Sages' undoubted sensitivity to the difference between the legislative and judicial aspects of their opinions, they were not concerned with the separation of these functions among different individuals, even within the context of a concrete lawsuit. I speculate that this attitude was also due to the Sages' aversion to any established organization.

2.3.2 Tannaitic versus Amoraic Attitudes to Authority

A comment is also necessary here on whether the Sages found it necessary to justify their authority.[106] Our evidence has indicated that there is no consistency in this respect. As a general observation, however, we may note that most of the tannaitic dicta in the Mishnah do not disclose their supporting reasons.[107] The Amoraim, in contrast, endeavoured to

---

propose another rationalization. The possibility exists that in a concrete case circumstances might come to light that would not be apparent in a theoretical deliberation. The Sages seem to have been aware of this difference in perspective, as we see in the following maxim in bBava Batra 131a: דאין לדיין אלא מה שעיניו רואות "The judge must decide on what he sees before him."

105 We read in mSanhedrin 11: 4: אין ממיתין אותו לא בבית דין שבעירו ולא בבית דין שביבנה אלא מעלין אותו לבית דין הגדול שבירושלים "One does not execute him at the court of his town, nor in the court of Yabneh, but one brings him to the Superior Court in Jerusalem." This mishnah refers to the זקן ממרא "the rebellious elder," and forms part of a discussion of the legal procedure to be followed in such a case, starting in mishnah 11: 2. See also on this topic chap. 1, text at n. 33.

106 S. J. D. Cohen, "Judaism," writes on pp. 223-4 that the Mishnah presents itself as a source of authority, endowing its human authors with the right to debate and legislate.

107 We must doubt the authenticity of those occurrences in which the exegesis of a scriptural verse is cited as a justification for the declaration. One should not automatically assume that the exegesis is the utterance of the Tanna; it may have been added later (following the current scholarly approach to the problem of attributions). If we cannot rely upon the authenticity of the names associated with a dictum, we

reveal the motives of the Tannaim, usually by deriving the biblical sources of their statements. I posit that the Tannaim had complete confidence in their knowledge, their understanding of the Torah's ultimate intention, and

---

must also question the content, particularly as this is not the usual style of tannaitic declarations. We observe similar additions in the Mishnah, in which alleged discussions between Beit Hillel and Beit Shammai were later attributed to the Houses (see further the Appendix). Even M. Weiss, האוטתנטיות, who tries hard to validate the authenticity of these discussions, admits that in many occurrences one must doubt their authenticity. Because he attempts, in his opinion successfully, to validate the discussions in some occurrences, he proposes to assume that tradition was the basis of all the discussions, and in some cases was added later as something that probably could have taken place. The examples that he cites as being authentic, and representative of the others, however, seem to me problematic. The different discussions quoted in mBetzah 1: 6, and subsequently enlarged upon in tBetzah 1: 10, yBetzah 1: 8, 59d, and bBetzah 12b, suggest a conclusion opposite to that assumed by Weiss. The fact that there are three opinions about the exact circumstances of a dispute between Beit Shammai and Beit Hillel is not unusual; this is a common procedure to clarify missing details, similar to the common question במאי קמפלגי "what are the exact circumstances of the dispute." But in our case, Rabbi Yehudah and Rabbi Yose are compelled to change the text and facts of the assumed discussion between the Houses. Since we must admit that there is an intrinsic doubt as to what the Houses allegedly said, there is similar doubt as to whether anything was said by them at all. The odd expressions used in the alleged debate also add to the difficulty of attribution. The use of the term גזרה שוה is inappropriate here, as Rashi explains, and the use of the expression זכאי בהרמתה to mean that one may act on the holiday seems strange. The fact that a third, anonymous party proposed another view of the circumstances of the dispute, without any mention of a justifying debate, enhances the probability that there was no such debate in the original tradition and *Vorlage* of the Mishnah. Weiss, in fact, maintains the opposite. He suggests (p. 64) that since the "alleged debate between Beit Shammai and Beit Hillel on this issue appears in both the Tosefta and in Babli, it makes it less doubtful that it is an addition by later Sages." The simple fact that a text of a baraita is mentioned in the Gemara, with the introduction דתניא, can certainly not serve as evidence that the debate indeed occurred between Beit Shammai and Beit Hillel, and is not a later addition by the redactor. Weiss' second argument is that the declaration attributed to the anonymous אחרים אומרים that appears in tBetzah 1: 13, without mention of any debate, indicates that the other citations that do mention debates are authentic; if the debate were only an invention, this third anonymous source could have invented a debate as well. Weiss himself declares this evidence to be secondary, and I need not add my opinion of its feebleness. Hence, this argument does not seem to me convincing, and is certainly not decisive for other, more doubtful, cases. The evidence quoted from mZavim 1: 1 and tZavim 1: 4 - 6 is even shakier. It is said that Rabbi Aqiba understood the circumstances of a dispute between the Houses differently than did Rabbi Simeon in the name of Rabbi Eleazar b. Yehudah. Rabbi Simeon alleged: כך אמרו ב"ה לב"ש "this is what Beit Hillel said to Beit Shammai," and convinced Rabbi Aqiba of the correctness of his opinion. That R. Simeon used the expression "this is what Beit Hillel said" does not indicate that this was indeed said by them, but suggests rather "this is what they would have said." Weiss in fact accepts that in other instances this is what such expressions are intended to indicate, as opposed to being explicit statements that something was actually said..

the correctness of their decisions, and therefore did not consider it essential to divulge any justifications[108] for their opinions.[109] Certain Tannaim went to the utmost lengths to defend their particular opinions and statements, even to the point of risking excommunication.[110] The Amoraim lacked such confidence and deemed it essential to validate their declarations with appropriate biblical support. Reverence for earlier ideas and for the intellectuals who generated them is at the core of every conservative *Weltanschauung* and custom; religion and its concrete expressions are especially crucial to a conservative way of life. We may note that this perspective is already displayed in mEduyyot 1: 3; even the opinions of Hillel and Shammai were not accepted by the Sages when there was a tradition originating from the earlier renowned pair of Shemayah and Abtalion.[111] The humility of the Amoraim with respect to

---

[108] J. Neusner, *Purities, Part XXI*, p. 312, writes: "Our Order [of the Mishna] is remarkably uninterested in Scriptural proofs for its propositions." He asserts that the mishnaic writings were used for "the transmission of teachings on behalf of which is claimed divine revelation." I perceive them rather as reflecting the Sages' understanding of the Torah's ultimate intention, and not as the transmission of a particular revelation. The Dead Sea Scrolls group attributed such a revelation to their Teacher of Righteousness.

[109] This crucial distinction between the Tannaim and Amoraim is discussed further in the Conclusion, nn. 49 ff. and related text.

[110] There is, for instance, the story of Rabbi Eliezer who defied the majority of Sages and suffered excommunication (yMo'ed Qatan 3: 1, 81d and bBava Metzi'a 59b). We note also the remarkable declaration of another Tanna in mEduyyot 5: 6: עקביא בן מהללאל העיד ארבעה דברים אמרו לו עקביא חזור בך בארבעה דברים שהיית אומר ונעשך אב בית דין לישראל אמר להן מוטב לי להקרא שוטה כל ימי ולא ליעשות שעה אחת רשע לפני המקום שלא יהיו אומרים בשביל שררה חזר בו "Aqabyah ben Mahalalel gave witness [conflicting with the opinion of the majority] on four halakhot. So they said to him: Aqabyah, retract your decisions on those four issues and we shall appoint you the Chief of the Superior Court of Israel. He answered: I prefer to be considered a fool all my life [to have renounced such an honourable office in order not to compromise my principles], than to be a wicked man one hour before God; they should not say that I recanted [my opinions] for the sake of a position of power." See also mEduyyot 5: 7, quoted in chap. 1, p. 73. Regarding the authenticity of this narrative, see chap. 4, n. 133; though the details of the story may not completely concur with reality, the narrative attests to the tension between the opinion of the individual and the authority of the majority, and bears witness to the tenacity of individual Sages in persisting in their conclusions.

[111] This tannaitic decision indicates the significance of tradition, as discussed in chapter 1. The Tannaim did not reject this important rule per se, but they believed it could be altered, whenever it was deemed necessary. In this particular occurrence, they did not perceive any compelling reason to reject a tradition from a reliable source. The Amoraim, on the other hand, believed that they had no authority to annul prior tannaitic dicta or earlier traditions.

the primary Sages, the Tannaim, is thus only natural.[112] While the Tannaim were confident in their authority to make changes, even those contrary to Torah ordinances, the later Amoraim were hesitant to take responsibility for such drastic innovations.

I postulate that Rabbi's closing of the Mishnah[113] constituted a dominant factor in the creation of this significant difference between the Tannaim and Amoraim. Rabbi's drafting of the conclusive edition of the Mishnah[114] proclaimed, whether intentionally or unintentionally, the

---

112 This attitude is evident in a passage in bBerakhot 35b: בא וראה שלא כדורות הראשונים דורות האחרונים דורות הראשונים עשו תורתן קבע ומלאכתן עראי זו וזו נתקיימה בידן דורות האחרונים שעשו מלאכתן קבע ותורתן עראי זו וזו לא נתקיימה בידן "Come and see that the previous generations are not like the later ones. The previous generations made their [study of the] Torah their permanent occupation, and their work sporadic, and both survived; the later generations made their work permanent and Torah [study] sporadic, and neither subsisted." There is a similar statement on the decline of later generations in yMa'aserot 3: 1, 50c: היו מכניסים את הכלכלה לאחורי הגגות ראה אותן רבי יודה בי רבי אלעאי אמר להן ראו מה ביניכם לראשונים רבי עקיבה היה לוקח שלשה מינין בפרוטה בשביל לעשר מכל מין ומין ואתם מכניסין את הכלכלה לאחורי הגגות "[Certain Sages] were carrying [non-tithed] food onto the roofs [to avoid tithing, according to a dictum that the obligation of tithing is not due in this case]. Rabbi Yehudah b. Elai saw them and said to them: See the difference between you and the previous generations: Rabbi Aqiba would bring small quantities of three different kinds [of fruits], to enable him to tithe each one separately, and you carry in food onto the roof [in order to avoid tithing]." The extent to which their own inferiority, in comparison to their forefathers, was assumed and accepted by later generations is perceptible in the following dramatic aphorism, found in Aramaic in yDemai 1: 1, 21d and ySheqalim 5: 1, 48d: אין הוון קדמאי בני מלאכים אנן בני נש ואין הוון בני נש אנן חמרין, and in Hebrew in bShabbat 120b: אם ראשונים בני מלאכים אנו בני אנשים ואם ראשונים בני אנשים אנו כחמורים "If [we consider] the previous generations as angels, we [may consider] ourselves as humans, [but] if we consider them as humans, we should consider ourselves as donkeys." See S. Z. Havlin, על החתימה הספרותית, who writes on p. 150: "It is well known that the amoraic Sages do not contest the tannaitic Sages." Cf. J. Neusner, "Hermeneutics," who declares that though the Mishnah "was not received in a spirit of humble acceptance" by the Amoraim (p. 191), they accepted the Mishnah's authority (p. 195).

113 Cf. H. Fox (Lebeit Yoreh), "Introducing Tosefta," p. 3, who questions the likelihood that Rabbi Yehudah I (Rabbi the Partriarch) was responsible for the redaction of either Mishnah or Tosefta.

114 See I. Gafni, "היצירה הרוחנית-ספרותית" on the nature and extent of Rabbi's editing of the Mishnah and its repercussions on the future of halakhah (particularly pp. 483 - 485). See also S. Safrai, *The Literature of the Sages*, p. 73, who confirms the gaonic opinion that the Mishnah "was committed to writing in the days of Rabbi." (It is not within the scope of this study to elaborate upon the relationship between the strict admonition of Rabbi Yohanan against writing halakhot and the writing of the Mishnah; see chap. 1, n. 82). The passage of time between the Tannaim and Amoraim

termination of the tannaitic era of halakhic creativity. Rabbi thus put an end to tannaitic innovation,[115] offering no explanations for tannaitic reforms and no scriptural justifications. The consequences of Rabbi's exercise was the generation of a "second class" of Sages, the Amoraim, whose authority was drastically curtailed. They could not pronounce innovative halakhot in conflict with tannaitic decisions; any innovations they declared had to be founded strictly upon prior tannaitic pronouncements. The functions and authority of the Amoraim were restricted to a narrow range of activity: they could only interpret the Mishnah,[116] the definite law; they could attempt to understand the motives of the Tannaim, reconciling apparent contradictions between different mishnayot, or between the pronouncements of the same Tanna in different sources. They did not strive to interpret the Torah itself, and certainly did not consider themselves as possessing the authority to interpret the Torah in a different way than that alleged to be at the foundation of the tannaitic halakhah in the Mishnah.[117] They were constrained from opposing halakhic pronouncements of Tannaim,[118] in contrast to the Tannaim, who could repudiate[119] and oppose declarations of other Tannaim.[120]

---

encompassed the end of the previous flexibility. Safrai declares: "....the creative process of Oral Tora evolved towards its gradual consummation," initiating a process whose consequences were perceived "...only afterwards as the closing of a period."

115 S. J. D. Cohen, "Judaism to the Mishna 135 - 220 CE," (pp. 222-3) declares that Rabbi had imposed his "authority over the rabbinic movement."

116 J. Neusner, "Hermeneutics," writes on p. 201: "Most of the Bavli is a systematic exposition of the Mishnah." H. Fox (Lebeit Yoreh) provides an elegant summary: The Amoraim replaced the מדרש הלכה by the מדרש המשנה. Rashi in bSotah 22b explains the purpose of studying the Gemara, the amoraic opus: ללמוד סברת הגמרא בטעמי המשנה "to study the understanding of the Gemara [that is, of the Amoraim] regarding the Mishnah's motives [that is, those of the Tannaim]." In fact, however, the Amoraim did not attempt to reveal the logical principles behind the tannaitic declarations and controversies, but rather assumed that different interpretations of biblical verses were the bases of the tannaitic dicta.

117 See T. Frymer-Kensky, "The Emergence of Jewish Biblical Theologies," particularly p. 111.

118 There is no explicit dictum to this effect, but this is the common practice. This practice is also implicitly referred to in bSanhedrin 6a, where we read, with respect to a particular halakhah being debated: תרי תנאי ותרי אמוראי דפליגי אהדדי "Two Tannaim or two Amoraim contradict one another." This dictum assumes that disputes can only be conceived of among members of the same category. Another implicit statement is found in bEruvin 50b: רב תנא הוא ופליג "Rab [an Amora of the first generation] is [considered to enjoy the status of] a Tanna, and therefore he may dispute [the dictum of a Tanna]." J. Roth, *Halakhic Process*, p. 62, discusses "the systemic principle that later scholars (*amora'im*) are not at liberty to disagree with earlier scholars (*tanna'im*)." Cf., however, S. Z. Havlin, מחקרים, pp. 166-7. While he agrees that the Amoraim did not contradict the Tannaim, he alleges that they

The Amoraim did not attempt to refine and further develop the legal principles of tannaitic law.[121] Their allegedly restricted authority hindered them from formulating new rules or modifying existing ones based upon their own logic; they avoided taking responsibility for any creative innovation.[122] Their lack of confidence in their own authority in turn gave rise to their supposition that the Tannaim also founded their halakhic decisions upon scriptural exegesis,[123] an assumption in fact contrary to the

---

imposed upon themselves this limitation not to contradict the Tannaim, although they were well aware of their authority to contest prior decisions. Havlin admits that there is no explicit indication of when or by whom such a decision was taken. His study focuses on the dilemma of why later generations did not contradict the earlier Sages, since legally they were empowered to change earlier decisions. It is a fact that the first emergence of a difference in classification among the Sages, in essence and in name, is documented at the transition from the Tannaim of the Mishnah to the Amoraim of the Gemara. I therefore propose that we are justified in assuming that the closure of the Mishnah by Rabbi precipitated this different classification of the Sages.

119 Although this is the common method of the Mishnah, we observe that according to the amoraic attitudes even this prerogative might be curtailed when the prior Tanna was deemed to possess a preeminent reputation. We read in bAvodah Zarah 36a: ור' יהודה הנשיא היכי מצי למישרא תקנתא דתלמידי שמאי והלל "How could Rabbi [the Patriarch and compiler of the Mishnah] repeal a decree promulgated by Beit Shammai and Beit Hillel?" In effect, we observe that most of the disputes in the Mishnah are between Tannaim of the same generation. It is possible that the Mishnah records the actual debates between two Tannaim of the same generation, but it is nevertheless remarkable that we do not encounter declarations by later Tannaim conflicting with opinions pronounced by earlier Sages. We encounter the same pattern regarding the Amoraim. The disputes recorded as between one Amora and another are between Rabbi Yohanan and Resh Laqish (as for example in yPe'ah 4: 6, 18b, bYevamot 36a), Rab and Samuel (yBerakhot 4: 3, 8a, bBekhorot 49b), Abbaye and Raba (bQiddushin 52a). Such disputes are found in numerous instances; similarly, there are disputes between other pairs of Amoraim of the same generation. There are exceptions, which are explained by complex interpretations; this fact simply reflects the innate lack of system in rabbinic halakhah, as I shall outline at the end of this section. In those instances in which the Amoraim did not accept Rabbi's decisions, as described in chap. 3, nn. 12-13, they did not suggest the acceptance of their own conflicting opinions; they merely preferred to establish the halakhah as declared by another Tanna rather than the one favoured by Rabbi, or found other justifications. As the Amoraim deemed all the Tannaim their superiors in every aspect of knowledge, they considered it inadmissible to contradict them.

120 S. J. D. Cohen, "Judaism," writes on p. 221: "The Mishna does not give any obvious indication which opinion is to be followed."

121 See S. J. D. Cohen, ibid., p. 220.

122 J. Roth, *Halakhic Process*, p. 133, attributes the conservative attitude of the rabbinic authorities to their shying away from the awesome responsibility implied in declaring that their opinion reflected the will of God.

123 This constituted a formalist approach rather than the logical approach of the Tannaim. E. E. Urbach, בעלי התוספות, refers to a tension between a formalist tendency versus a functionalist tendency in the later rabbinic deliberations. I think that the same

tannaitic perspective.[124]

It is possible that the Amoraim did indeed perceive that the higher status Tannaim based their decisions on their logical understanding of the divine intention, rather than on far-fetched hermeneutics. In questioning mishnaic pronouncements with the formulaic "How do we know it [from the Torah]," they were thus simply engaging in intellectual exercises, within the overall obligation to study the Torah; within this framework, they diligently examined all its aspects, and undertook to reveal its intrinsic meanings and intentions. The Amoraim, as we observe from their deliberations, were highly intelligent and creative personalities; but ultimately, by declining to take responsibility for halakhic decisions, they were compelled to utilize their imagination and creativity in one direction only, in a more rigorous and severe interpretation of the mishnaic rulings.[125] By maintaining this attitude of restriction, and forsaking leniency, their perspective was ultimately narrowed, putting a halt to the creative development of rabbinic halakhah. The consequences of this situation affect us even today, as each generation continued to limit itself to the restrictive interpretation of the halakhic decisions and guidelines of its antecedents.[126] The maxim כח דהתירא עדיף ליה "the power of

---

categorization can be applied with respect to the different approaches of the Tannaim and Amoraim.

124 See the example quoted in the text below at n. 181. A dispute is recorded in ySukkah 1: 1, 52a (in bSukkah 6b it is quoted as a baraita) on the issue of whether a sukkah must have at least two perfect walls, with a third allowed to be of the size of one *tefah*, or whether there must be three perfect walls and only one partial wall. The dispute between the Tannaim is undoubtedly based on an evaluation of what is considered to be a "temporary" dwelling. The Amoraim nonetheless attempt to derive a complex and far-fetched hermeneutic argument as the foundation of the dispute.

125 They could, theoretically, also find ways and means to interpret the Mishnah - that is, the motives behind the Mishnah's declarations - using a lenient approach, and this was actually done in some cases; the general trend, however, was toward a stricter approach. As we shall see below (n. 222 and related text), Rab, the prominent Amora of the first generation, and Rabbi's disciple, who lived at the time of the inception of the Mishnah (see Ch. Albeck, מבוא לתלמודים pp. 170 ff.), considered it expedient to decree stricter rules when the basic ones were not obeyed. A homily in yQiddushin 1: 9, 61d, based on the exegesis of Prov 13: 21, does not explicitly declare this principle, but may have served as a symbolic guidepost: וסייגין סייגא ותרעין תריעה "One reinforces a fenced-in place and one widens a breach." I. Englard, "Research in Jewish Law," p. 39 writes: "The religious scholar who must in principle attribute binding force to all texts, cases and precedents, cannot freely shape comprehensive abstract principles or create broad legal categories." Englard refers to modern scholars of Jewish law, but his statement is equally appropriate, in my opinion, to the Amoraim.

126 J. Roth, *Halakhic Process*, p. 317, writes: "The early rabbinic Sages interpreted the Bible, the Amoraim interpreted the Mishna of Judah the Prince (ca. 220 C. E.), the early commentators interpreted the Talmud, the later legalists interpreted the

leniency is preferable" neatly summarizes my postulate concerning the attitude of the post-tannaitic Sages. This maxim would at first sight appear to reinforce the value of leniency. It actually indicates the opposite, however, when correctly interpreted in its context,[127] and as both Rashi and Tosafot understood it;[128] it is intended to mean that a lenient pronouncement can only be declared on the basis of tradition, that is, if received from a previous Sage, but a stricter pronouncement may be decreed by anyone.

The distinctive approaches of the Tannaim and Amoraimn are reflected in the different characteristics of the Mishnah and the Gemara. The Tannaim of the Mishnah did not deem it necessary to demonstrate how they reached their decisions; I also assume that they were often well aware of the feebleness[129] of the midrashic method for the creation of

---

commentaries, codes, and Responsa of the earlier."

127 In B. T. Betzah 2b, the Gemara ponders the precise circumstances of a dispute between Beit Shammai and Beit Hillel. The discussion contemplates whether to interpret the dispute in a way that would demonstrate the extent of the strictness of Beit Hillel, or in a way that would demonstrate the extent of the leniency of Beit Shammai. (This dispute is one of the few in which Beit Shammai take the lenient position and Beit Hillel the stricter one). In the rhetoric, the maxim "the power of leniency is preferable" is used to justify a lenient interpretation.

128 Rashi explains: טוב לו להשמיענו כח דברי המתיר שהוא סומך על שמועתו ואינו ירא להתיר אבל כח האוסרין אינה ראיה שהכל יכולין להחמיר ואפילו בדבר המותר "It is preferable to let us know the authority of the lenient [Sage] because he relies on his transmitted learning and is therefore not afraid to be lenient. But the strictness of a pronouncement does not serve as evidence of its authority, since everyone can prohibit something that is permitted." Tosafot emphasize Rashi's explanation and declare: כשאדם מתיר סומך על שמועתו וצריך להביא ראיה לדבריו אבל אדם יכול להחמיר עליו בלא טעם "When a person permits [something] he relies on his transmitted learning and must bring evidence for his pronouncement, but a person can simply be strict and prohibit [something that is permitted] without any reason." It is clear that the maxim "the power of leniency is preferable" means that a lenient decision must be corroborated by a decision that has been transmitted from a previous generation, whereas there is no such limitation on strict decisions.

129 Numerous citations of halakhic midrashim in this study indicate this weakness. I have hinted at this aspect in several instances, but I think that their character is self-evident and does not require additional emphasis. The oft-quoted maxim: מדרבנן וקרא אסמכתא בעלמא "It is a rabbinic edict, and the mention of the scriptural origin is just a support," indicates the Sages' own recognition of the deficiency of midrash as a basis of halakhah. Although this maxim considers the particular halakhot mentioned in the deliberations as rabbinic edicts, I contemplate that the Tannaim may actually have used halakhic midrashim to declare some of their decrees to be Torah edicts. See the discussion below concerning the extension of the prohibition against mixing meat with milk, section 2.5, and section 4.1.7 regarding the different approaches of the Tannaim and Amoraim.

halakhah.[130] The Amoraim of the Gemara simply attempted to derive biblical support for the tannaitic declarations. They could not envision that the Tannaim had a different approach than their own; they were entrenched in their opinion and belief that all rabbinic decrees have a definite biblical source. The tannaitic approach can be clearly perceived in the following example. A determination is made, as I perceive it, that a transgression, if carried out by two people, exempts both of them from punishment, or from bringing a sin offering when it was unintentionally committed. We read in Sifra *Vayyiqra Hovah* 7: "[It is written in Lev 4: 27, with respect to the sin offering for unintentional transgressions]: 'and does one' [of the things that are forbidden - the term 'one' is then interpreted, by Rabbi Simeon, to refer not to the precepts, as is the plain intention of the verse, but to one person, who performed the transgression; this means that] when one person transgressed, he is liable [for a sin offering, but] when two or three persons transgressed, they are absolved."[131] On the basis of this legal principle we read in mShabbat 10: 5: "When one man carries [something] out into the public domain [it is forbidden on the Sabbath to change the status of an object by taking it from a private domain to the public domain] he is guilty. When two men carried it out, they are not liable. If one man alone could not have carried it out and two have carried it out, both are guilty. Rabbi Simeon exempts them." The logic of this distinction, when the object can only be carried by more than one person, is obvious and unquestionable. Rabbi Simeon, it seems, does not agree to this exception, and adheres to the legal principle that a deed performed by two people exempts them from guilt. In mShabbat 11: 2 another criterion is proposed in considering whether two perpetrators are liable or absolved when the effort of both is required for a particular job: are their actions equivalent to "work"? We read there: "If there is one [private] balcony facing another over a public road, one who hands over or throws [an object] from one to the other is not liable [for a sin offering]. If the two [balconies] are side by side, the one who hands over [the object] is liable, but the one who throws it is absolved, because that is how the Levites performed their work [in the period when the

130 See the discussion of Urbach's theory above (section 2. 2) concerning the purpose of midrash in its early stages. He asserts that the expression midrash did not signify a hermeneutic type of exegesis, but rather a method of safeguarding and protecting the law through profound and intense study by the Soferim.

131 A similar principle appears in yShabbat 1: 1, 2c. In bShabbat 3a there is a different approach: תניא רבי אומר מעם הארץ בעשתה העושה את כולה ולא העושה את מקצתה יחיד ועשה אותה חייב שנים ועשו אותה פטורין "We learned in a baraita: Rabbi said [it is written with respect to the sin offering for unintentional transgressions in Lev 4: 27] 'and does' [in singular]. [The rule applies only to] one who carries out the entire [transgression] but not a part of it; if one individual acted, he is guilty, two who acted are not liable."

Levites transported the components of the Tent of Meeting]." Although work carried out by two persons should not be liable, liability is incurred in this particular case because this specific action was performed as part of the cult, and hence constituted "real" work.[132] As I shall argue (in section 3.5), the Temple service served as a model for the concept of "work."[133]

The following dicta in mZevahim 13: 3 further demonstrate the practical application of the above distinction. We read: "When two persons held the knife and slaughtered [an offering outside the Temple's court, which was forbidden] they are not guilty; when two persons grasped a part [of the offering] and raised it upon the altar, they are guilty." The distinction between the two acts is easily understood, if we consider that in the Temple it was the usual practice for two people[134] to throw the pieces of meat upon the altar; thus the two in this case who raised the offering acted in the usual way and were guilty. One person, in contrast, usually performed the slaughtering, and therefore if the deed were performed by two they were not liable. This is a perfect case to demonstrate the tannaitic style of decision.

In contrast, the Amoraim of the Gemara, and the later traditional commentators, did not search for the logical principles inherent in the mishnaic rules, but attempted to detect hermeneutic justifications of all kinds to justify the basic legal principles and to rationalize any disputes.[135]

---

[132] See further on this mishnah chap. 3, n. 97.

[133] In yShabbat 11: 2, 13a the reason for this exception is clarified: שנים שעשו פטורין והכא את אמר שנים שעשו חייבין שנייא היא שכך היתה עבודת הלוים "[It is stated elsewhere that] when two have committed a transgression they are not liable, but here you say that when two have committed it both are guilty. [A.] Here there is a different circumstance, since this was the usual way the Levites executed their work [the case refers to work prohibited because it was performed in the Temple, and this was the regular manner of its execution]."

[134] We read in mTamid 7: 3: ובזמן שהוא רוצה הוא סומך ואחרים זורקין "And when he [the High Priest] so desires, he lays his hands [on the pieces of meat] and others throw it on the altar." Although the mishnah earlier states: וסמך עלידהם וזרקן "[If he desires to accomplish the whole deed by himself] he lays his hands [upon the pieces] and throws them," I perceive that this is written in singular for stylistic reasons, to portray the entire deed as being performed by the High Priest. It does not exclude the possibility, however, that the common priests, who brought up the pieces of meat and served them to the High Priest, also helped him in the strenuous duty of throwing the large pieces. The particular issue is not concerned with whether one man or two must throw the pieces, and therefore the use of the singular or plural is not to be taken as indicating precisely how this act was performed. Indeed, in the *Letter of Aristeas* 93 it is explicitly stated that more than one priest threw the pieces of meat upon the alter. We read: ἀναρρίπτουσιν ἑκατέραις θαυμασίως ὕψος ἱκανὸν καὶ οὐχ ἁμαπτάνουσι τῆς ἐπιθέεως "and they throw each wonderfully high and do not miss the place."

[135] Although it is clear from mZevahim 13: 3 that Rabbi Simeon and Rabbi Yose dispute on the specific issue of whether one is liable for a sin offering for each raising of meat

There is a clearly different approach between the Tannaim and Amoraim to the halakhah. Comparable to the redactors of the Books of Chronicles, who deemed it their responsibility to correct the "flaws" in the Books of Kings,[136] the Amoraim believed that they must determine the motive behind the tannaitic statements. They assumed that the Tannaim certainly founded their decisions upon biblical verses, but did not explicitly quote them, for reasons that they were not to investigate.[137] They also searched to understand a Tanna's declaration when it seemed to them to be in opposition to a biblical decree. Such concerns may be deduced from the amoraic reflections on the Mishnah. Above all, it is certain that when the Amoraim (as well as the redactor of Tosefta)[138] emended the Mishnah, they did not intend to contradict or change the tannaitic decisions.

---

upon the altar, or for only one sin offering in total, the Gemara alleges a wider dispute between them. In the discussion it is assumed that Rabbi Simeon deduces the liability of two people raising the meat from an exegesis of the double expression איש איש in Lev 17: 3, the introductory verse of the prohibition against performing offerings outside the Tabernacle: גבי העלאה נמי כתיב איש איש מיבעי ליה לשנים שהעלו באבר חייבין. The dictum that two people slaughtering together are not guilty is deduced from the expression ההוא in Lev 17: 4: ונכרת האיש ההוא "this man [in singular] must be cut off from his people." The Amoraim ignored the above-cited exegesis on Lev 4: 27, quoted in Sifra and in bShabbat 3a.

136 For example, 2 Chr 4: 1 records that Solomon "made a bronze altar," a datum that is lacking in 2 Kgs in the narrative detailing Solomon's building of the Temple and its accessories. The redactor of Chronicles did not intend to transform what was written in Kings; he simply assumed that, for reasons beyond his knowledge, there was a lacuna in Scripture and it was his duty to correct it. See P. Heger, *Altars*, pp. 314 - 319 on "The Emendation System of the Biblical Editors and Redactors."

137 Cf. J. Neusner, "Hermeneutics," p. 223, who perceives the amoraic question "How do we know it?" - that is, what is its biblical source - as a "devastating critique to the Mishnah."

138 I refer by this statement to M. Jaffee, "Taqqanah," who reviews the textual changes in Tosefta and Gemara with respect to the texts of the Mishnah. It is not my intention to discuss the relationship(s) between the Mishnah and Tosefta, a much-debated issue not directly related to our study. I merely wish to emphasize the different comprehension of this phenomenon by Jaffee, who calls it "reframing." He conceives such changes as "transformations," a concept that indicates intent to produce a change, whereas, in my opinion, they consist rather of an attempt to complement the Mishnah. They may represent the supplementing of a perceived lacuna, or may offer an explanation of an unclear passage in the Mishnah as the redactor of the Tosefta or Gemara comprehended it, or constitute an adaptation to altered circumstances. Jaffee's example of the different texts in mMegillah 3: 5-6 and tMegillah 3: 5-9, regarding the duty to read the relevant Torah commandments in their season, indicates the Tosefta redactors' understanding: what Moses really intended and what he actually did (Lev 23: 44) was to teach the people the minutiae of the relevant rules and regulations. The redactors comprehended that the teaching of the Torah has a practical purpose. Moses therefore induced the Israelites to raise questions about the commandments, and not simply to read the text, to enable him to put forward thorough explanations and ensure the correct fulfillment of each rule. Based on the

We thus often observe in the Gemara's discussion of a mishnaic decree that its opening question is מנא הני מילי (B. T.), מניין or מנלן (Y. T.);[139] these phrases mean "How do we know it?"[140] - that is, what is its biblical source?[141] To the same effect, a Tanna's source will be questioned, with the expression מאי טעמא, "what is his motive," or his scriptural hermeneutics simply assumed, with a phrase such as טעמא דרבי "the motive of Rabbi X's declaration is…." This question of source is posed whether the matter refers to a complex decree that justifies such a question, or to a simple logical rule,[142] or to a custom. In mTamid 1: 1, for example, it is stated: "The priests keep guard at three positions in the Temple," relating to the perfectly common-sense consideration that the Temple should be guarded against intruders. But the Gemara (bTamid 26a) poses the question "How do we know this?" and it is clear from the context that the question refers to the general decree to guard the Temple,

---

maxim כולם נאמרו כללותיהם ודקדוקיהם מסיני "all the rules and particulars of all precepts were pronounced at Sinai," the Tosefta redactors believed they were revealing the real intent of the Mishnah, not "transforming" it. Adaptations of mishnaic edicts to changed circumstances were also seen to have their origins at Sinai; these too were intrinsic elements of the Sinaitic revelation. Although there seems to be an affinity between הלכה למשה מסיני and the above maxim that all the rules were pronounced at Sinai, the Talmud discerns them as distinct concepts; see section 3. 5. A similar interpretation would apply to the other examples cited by Jaffee, but are outside the scope of our investigation. Nor is it my intent to criticize his thoughtful study that elucidates an interesting phenomenon of rabbinic literature; we differ only in our assessment of the philosophy behind the rabbinic practice of changing earlier dicta.

139 We also find מאי טעמא in the B. T. and מה טעמון in the Y. T., meaning "What is the reason [for this dictum]?" The answer generally quotes a scriptural verse, which indicates that the point of these questions is to identify the biblical source.

140 In contrast, J. Neusner, "Hermeneutics," as we have noted above (n. 137), perceives the amoraic question "How do we know it" as indicating criticism of the tannaitic authorities, and the amoraic method of detecting the biblical sources behind tannaitic pronouncements as a form of apologetic. My examination of the amoraic deliberations detects no such criticism of the Mishnah.

141 This expression, as well as the similar מנלן, is translated into English in various ways. See on this issue H. Fox, "*Horayot*," p. 236.

142 A pertinent example concerns the issue of standards. In mMenahot 12: 4 it is declared: "One may bathe in [a receptacle containing] forty *se'ah*, and must not bathe in forty *se'ah* less a pinch." This standard is established on the basis of logic. The Sages reasoned that forty *se'ah* of water would allow one's entire body to be immersed (Sifra *Metzorah* 3 and bEruvin 4b). But the Amoraim in bEruvin 4a attempt to deduce a support from Scripture: שיעורין דאורייתא הוא דכתיב "the standards are of scriptural origin, as it is written…." followed by a far-fetched exegesis to substantiate this statement. In yPe'ah 1: 1, 15b and bYoma 80a, however, Rabbi Yohanan alleges that the standards are הלכה למשה מסיני "halakhah [given] to Moses from Sinai."

not to the number of locations. Abbaye quotes from Num 3: 38: "Moses and Aaron and his sons guard the watching station of the Temple to keep guard for the sons of Israel."[143] There follows a rather niggling series of arguments pointing out that this biblical verse indicates that the Levites (Moses) and the priests (Aaron and his sons) should keep guard together, whereas the mishnah tells us that groups of priests and Levites guard separately, at different locations. A complex and unconventional hermeneutic analysis of the verse is proffered to reconcile the mishnah with the text of the verse.

When there is a dispute in the Mishnah between two or more Tannaim, the Gemara attempts in many instances to understand the exact circumstances behind the disputed issue.[144] In most occurrences the Amoraim venture to reveal the explanation for the differing opinions. This is done either by proposing that each Tanna had a different interpretation of the same biblical verse that was conceived to be the foundation of the tannaitic rule,[145] or by stating that each Tanna deduced his opinion from a

---

143 This is a somewhat clumsy, word-for-word translation, to reflect the interpretation of Abbaye regarding a duty to keep watch at the Temple. This interpretation corresponds to the translation of Onkelos and of the LXX. Onkelos has: נטרין מטרת מקדשא למטרת בני ישראל; all the terms from the root שמר are translated with forms of the root נטר "to guard." The LXX translates: φυλάσσοντες τὰς φυλακὰς τοῦ ἁγίου εἰς τὰς φυλακάς. Here, too, the term φυλάσσω means "to keep watch." The NIV interprets "they were responsible for the care of the sanctuary on behalf of the Israelites."

144 The quest for a thorough examination raises a host of different questions and deductions. I shall quote a few examples from both Talmudim: לימא בהא קמיפליגי "Let us assume that they dispute on this principle"; or אלא ב... פליגי "they dispute on ..."; במאי קמיפליגי or מאי בינייהו "What is the [conceptual] difference," or "What are the practical consequences between the opposing [opinions] of the Tannaim [in the Mishnah]?"; מה פליג מה דמר... מה דמר... "What are the circumstances of the dispute," or "What the one said refers to... and what the other said refers to...." Similarly, the examination of a mishnah raises such questions and deductions as: הכא במאי עסקינן "What are the precise circumstances to which the mishnah refers?"; or כולי עלמא לא פליגי "[In such circumstances] no one [i.e. none of the contenders] disputes," but כי פליגי "their dispute refers to particular circumstances"; ב... איתפליגו אבל ב... כל עמא מודו "On ...they dispute, but on ... all agree"; אף על גב דרבי פליג ב... מודה הוא הכא "although Rabbi X disputes on ..., he agrees here...." An investigation might also result in the following type of statement: רבי שמעון בן אלעזר ותנא דבי רבי ישמעאל אמרו דבר אחד "Rabbi Simeon ben Eleazar and the Tanna of Rabbi Ishmael's school said the same thing [maintain identical opinions]"; ולא פליגי מאן דמר ... ומאן דמר... "And they do not dispute; what the one said referred to ...and what the other said referred [to another situation]."

145 In some cases, such an explanation appears in the Mishnah, as for example in mTerumot 6: 6: ממקום שרבי אליעזר מקל משם ר"ע מחמיר שנאמר "From the

different verse. Such a conclusion can initiate a series of hairsplitting deliberations, as for example in bYoma 7b - 8a, which concerns a dispute between two Tannaim recorded in a baraita. Although according to the text in the baraita, each Tanna uses a logical argument to defend his case, Abbaye attempts to reveal what he considers to have been the "real" motive of their dispute. He postulates that each Tanna deduced his opinion from the interpretation of a different biblical phrase, declaring: "Rabbi Yehudah reasoned from the words מצח ונשא and Rabbi Simeon reasoned from the words תמיד לרצון לפני ה'." Both Tannaim, in other words, deduced their decision from the same verse (Exod 28: 38), but from different phrases, Rabbi Yehudah from the combination of מצח ונשא and Rabbi Simeon from the term תמיד.[146] Next follows the question: "How does Rabbi Yehudah interpret the phrase תמיד," and the answer is: "He deduces another halakhah from that phrase; he should not dismiss from his mind [that Aaron wears the gold plate on his forehead]." Then, as one expects, comes the parallel question: "How does Rabbi Simeon interpret the phrase מצחו ונשא," which, according to Abbaye, was the basis for Rabbi Yehudah's opinion. The answer is: "He requires this phrase to teach us where [the plate should be worn]." The questioning now returns to Rabbi Yehudah: "If Rabbi Yehudah needs [the phrase מצחו ונשא] to deduce [his primary opinion], how does he deduce where [the plate should be worn]?" And this type of argument goes on and on until, at some point, a method is found to conclude it.

In other instances the Amoraim assume: "and both deduced [their conflicting opinions] from the exegesis of the same verse [in some cases, even from the same words]."[147] The Amoraim also attempt to resolve

---

place [i.e the biblical verse] at which Rabbi Eliezer is [induced by his exegesis to be] lenient, Rabbi Aqiba is [induced to be] severe, as is said....."; the divergent hermeneutics of the verse are then cited. From the literary style of this mishnah, it is evident that this explanation of the dispute is a later addition, and should not be attributed to the Tannaim.

146 We encounter similar deliberations and assumptions in both Talmudim. I shall quote one occurrence from yTerumot 7: 2, 44d, which deliberates on a dispute in the Mishnah between Rabbi Meir and the anonymous Sages concerning the punishment to be meted out to the married daughter of a priest who becomes a prostitute. The rhetoric begins by asking: מה טעמא דרבי מאיר "What is Rabbi Meir's reason?" and answers that he deduces his opinion based on exegesis of Lev 21: 9, כי תחל לזנות בית אביה "[a priest's daughter] who becomes a prostitute in her father's house." The question is then posed, מה טעמא דרבנין "What is the reason of the Sages?" and the answer is that they deduce their opinion based on exegesis of the first phrase of the same verse: ובת איש כהן "and a priest's daughter." That is, both contenders derive their conflicting decisions based on exegesis of the same biblical verse.

147 Such examples abound in both Talmudim; see, e.g. yPe'ah 6: 4, 19c, and bBerakhot

apparent inconsistencies between different sources.[148] They strive to determine the halakhah based on due consideration and judicious reasoning,[149] or according to certain guidelines.[150]

4b.

[148] For example: קשיא דרבי אליעזר אדרבי אליעזר "[In this case] the statement of Rabbi Eliezer [or of any other Tanna] is in conflict with another of his statements." A frequently used phrase indicating that one source is in conflict with another is והתניא "We learned a conflicting declaration in a baraita," or והתנן "Is there not [a conflicting declaration in] a mishnah." In certain cases the Sages question what they perceive to be different concepts in the same mishnah: מאי שנא רישא ומאי שנא סיפא, or, קשיא רישא אסיפא "There is an inconsistency between the first element and the second element of the mishnah."

[149] We read for example in yMa'aser Sheni 1: 1, 52c: הלכה כרבי במעות וכרבן שמעון בן גמליאל בפירות "The halakhah is according to Rabbi with respect to [an illegal spending of] money [the proceeds of a swap of the tithe of fruits to be carried to Jerusalem for consumption there], and according to Rabban Simeon b. Gamaliel with respect to [an illegal consumption of the] fruits [in *natura*]." We observe that this decision, like many similar ones, is based upon a serious consideration of the conceptual differences between the two occurrences, and a preference for the more logical solution and balanced halakhah, rather than upon the personalities of the Tannaim. In bEruvin 43a there is explicit emphasis on the effort to decide a halakhah upon logical considerations: כל אותו היום ישבו ודנו בדבר הלכה אמש הכריע אחי אבא הלכה כרבן גמליאל בספינה והלכה כרבי עקיבא בדיר וסהר "They sat all day and deliberated the correct halakhah [regarding the permission to walk after having been brought to a place more than two thousand cubits away from one's residence, the distance it is permitted to walk on Sabbath]. Last night, my father's brother decided that the halakhah is according to Rabban Gamaliel [when one is] on a boat [far from home, and one may move within its area] and according to Rabbi Aqiba [when one was brought and placed] in a shed, or other great enclosure [and there one is permitted to move only four cubits from the spot where one was placed]." Thus, though the Amoraim were reluctant to declare a halakhah founded upon their own logical considerations, rather than on a scriptural support, they did in these cases evaluate the logic of the tannaic disputants when attempting to fix the halakhah according to one or the other opinion. And here again we observe the want of systematization; other rules for fixing the correct halakhah lack such an evaluation.

The dictum in bEruvin 81b: אלא כל מקום ששנה רבי יהודה בעירובין הלכה כמותו "Everywhere Rabbi Yehudah taught about Eruvin, the halakhah is as he declared," is not a trivial decision. It is based on the conceptual viewpoint that one should be lenient with respect to the rules of Eruvin, as we observe from yEruvin 1: 7, 18b: הלכה כרבי יודה דלא כן מה אנן אמרין רבי יודה וחכמים תהא הלכה כרבי יודה אלא בגין דאמר רבי יעקב בר אידי בשם רבי יהושע בן לוי הלכה כדברי המיקל בהילכות עירובין "The halakhah is according to Rabbi Yehudah; the reason why we say that [in a dispute between] Rabbi Yehudah and the Sages the halakhah is according to Rabbi Yehudah is because Rabbi Jacob b. Idi said, in the name of Rabbi Yehoshua b. Levi, that the halakhah is according to the lenient opinion with respect to the rules of Eruvin." This rule was not, however, consistently applied; see the discussion in chap. 3, nn. 44-8 and related text.

[150] See, e.g., yTerumot 3: 1, 42a, and bEruvin 46b (citations in chap. 4, nn. 88-9 and

With respect to a tannaitic decree that apparently opposes a biblical decree, we encounter an interesting talmudic deliberation. In mGittin 4: 3, there is cited, among other rabbinic ordinances: "Hillel instituted the *prosbul* for the public welfare." In mShevi'it 10: 3, the motive for this innovation is thoroughly explained;[151] it is portrayed as the result of an acute necessity to facilitate the supply of capital, either to assist individuals in overcoming financial difficulties, or to provide investment funds for the benefit of the entire society. We must assume that Hillel disclosed the practical reason for his innovation, but not its legal foundation or justification within the ambit of a biblical decree.[152] The Amoraim, on the other hand, could not conceive that Hillel considered himself to have the authority to invalidate a biblical law, and questioned his decision. We read in bGittin 36a: "Is it possible that the Torah decreed [that a loan be cancelled] in the seventh year, and Hillel decreed that it is not cancelled? Abbaye said: [Hillel's ordinance] refers to the contemporary law of the cancellation of loans in the seventh year [which is solely a rabbinic decree, not a Torah decree, and hence Hillel could reverse it.]" Abbaye's attempt to vindicate Hillel's action does not represent an effective solution, since Hillel the Elder lived at the time of the Second Temple, and it seems that the biblical law was enforced at that period.[153] Abbaye has further difficulties in maintaining his position, and must come up with an emendation to his initial postulate. Raba offers another solution to the issue of rabbinic authority to promulgate a decree contrary to biblical law: הפקר ב״ד היה הפקר "Any confiscation by the court is valid."[154] We observe that Hillel introduced a radical innovation

---

related text).

[151] We read there: פרוזבול אינו משמט זה אחד מן הדברים שהתקין הלל הזקן כשראה שנמנעו העם מלהלוות זה את זה ועוברין על מה שכתוב בתורה השמר לך פן יהיה דבר עם לבבך בליעל וגו׳ התקין הלל לפרוזבול "[Deut 15: 1 decrees that at the end of every seven years any debt is cancelled. A loan arranged with a] *prosbul* avoids its cancellation. This is one of the ordinances instituted by Hillel the Elder. When he perceived that people avoided granting loans among themselves, transgressing the biblical decree [Deut 15: 9]: 'Be careful not to harbour this wicked thought [the seventh year, the year for cancelling debts is near, so that you do not show ill will toward your needy brother and give him nothing],' he instituted the *prosbul*." B. T. Gittin 36a describes the formalities of this document; it is signed and deposited at the court, thus ensuring the continued validity of the loan.

[152] See n. 23 above regarding the application of the principle of overriding in this case.

[153] See Rashi's explanation and the comments of Tosafot.

[154] The same rhetorical question is asked in yGittin 4: 3, 45c - d: והילל מתקין על דבר תורה "How could Hillel institute a decree contrary to a Torah law?" The discussion there takes another twist; after various questions and proposed solutions, the final answer is stated: השמט כספים נוהג בין בארץ בין בחוצה לארץ מדבריהן "The cancellation of loans in Israel and outside Israel is only a rabbinic edict." It is not

because he thought it was in the public interest, and was confident of his authority to accomplish this without being required to offer a justification;[155] the Amoraim, in contrast, initiated the search for such a justification. Abbaye could not offer a valid solution in his attempt to maintain his position that Hillel could not decree a rule against the Torah.[156] Raba's solution, on the other hand, avoids a direct confrontation with a Torah law, circumventing it by introducing another legal dictum, the authority of the court to confiscate someone's property. As an Amora, requiring a Torah foundation for every rabbinic rule and regulation, he offers exegeses of two biblical verses to justify this exceptional, almost unlimited, authority. We may note that this same dictum, שהפקר בית דין הפקר, which is of tannaitic origin, is quoted in tSheqalim 1: 3 without any support from the Torah. From Raba's proposition we thus observe that the rabbinic rule granting considerable authority to the court to confiscate property can in effect invalidate the biblical law regarding the cancellation of debts;[157] further, we note that this Amora, in contrast to the Tosefta,[158] attempts to detect a Torah support for the rule.[159]

In another instance, Hillel's decision was not perceived as blatantly conflicting with a Torah decree, or granting extraordinary authority to the

---

clear whether the text refers to an edict from the period of the Second Temple, or after the Temple's destruction. It is not within the scope of this study to elaborate on this complex issue; I have chosen the more explicit B. T. text, which (at least as Rashi understands it) refers to the period after the Temple's destruction.

155 See Conclusion, nn. 53 ff. and related text, for a discussion of the attitude that allowed such radical modifications of biblical laws.

156 I. D. Gilat, פרקים, pp. 191 - 204, devotes a chapter to the discussion of the rabbinic authority לעקור דבר מן התורה "to uproot a Torah decree." He deduces from the numerous citations a distinction between the attitude of the Tannaim and that of the Amoraim on this delicate topic. The former considered their authority to be very broadly based, whereas the Amoraim applied serious limitations to this prerogative. We again observe a differentiation between the two classes of Sages with respect to their self-confidence in their processes of decision-making, as reflected in their relative degrees of constraint or autonomy.

157 We have no way to establish whether Raba considered these extreme consequences of the dictum, and whether he was aware of the legal fiction resulting from the application of the dictum in the cancellation of debts.

158 Sifre Deut 113, on the other hand, attempts to detect a scriptural support, and we read there: את אחיך תשמט ידך ולא המוסר שטרותיו לבית דין מיכן אמרו התקין הלל פרוסבול "[It is written: 'You must cancel any debt your brother owes you [Deut 15: 3]' but not when one assigns the bills to the court. On the basis of this [exegesis] Hillel instituted the *prosbul*."

159 The two exegeses cited by Raba, or by the later redactor of the Talmud, are quoted in the name of Rabbi Yitzhak and Rabbi Eleazar; though these names seem to refer to Amoraim, this cannot be asserted without doubt, since there were also Tannaim bearing the same names. At any rate, the dictum in Sheqalim is quoted as a generally recognized rule, with no justification or biblical support.

court; here the Amoraim did not question his decision, despite its more serious consequences. We read in tKetubbot 4: 9, yYevamot 15: 3, 14d, and bBava Metzi'a 104a: "Hillel the Elder considered the vernacular legally valid."[160] By this legal fiction,[161] he changed the status of someone born of a forbidden marriage,[162] declaring him legitimate and a member of the "assembly of the Lord" (Deut 23: 3, 23: 2 in KJV). The Amoraim did not query this far-reaching decision, perceiving it as founded upon an innocuous logical judgment. Again we note the distinction between the authoritative[163] pronouncements of the Tannaim and the vindicatory style

---

[160] I am indebted to a lecture of Prof. S. Ettinger, Faculty of Law, Bar-Ilan University, which drew my attention to this extraordinary resolution of Hillel.

[161] I. D. Gilat, פרקים, p. 184 describes this as a type of legal dualism, as perceived by M. Feinstein, אגרות משה, אורח חיים, Part I, Introduction: אמת ממש "the real truth," that is known by the Deity, and להוראה אמת, "the truth of the judge," reached after the judge's best efforts and study of the sources. The judges are induced by their awe to attempt to attain the "real truth"; a judge is absolved of guilt if he does not reach this truth, when he has done everything in his intellectual power to attain it. This indicates, nevertheless, the authority and legitimacy of the judge's decision, even in the event he does not reach the level of the divine truth.

[162] The narrative is identical in its essence and details in the three sources indicated above, with only slight stylistic differences among them. I shall quote from B. T. text, which, as is generally the case, is the best edited: אנשי אלכסנדריא היו מקדשין את נשותיהם ובשעת כניסתן לחופה באין אחרים וחוטפים אותם מהן ובקשו חכמים לעשות בניהם ממזרים אמר להן הלל הזקן הביאו לי כתובת אמכם הביאו לו כתובת אמן ומצא שכתוב בהן לכשתכנסי לחופה הוי לי לאינתו ולא עשו בניהם ממזרים "The Alexandrines betrothed their women [and wrote a legal contract, thus making the women forbidden to any other man. But] before their marriage, other men came and seized them [and they bore them children]. The Sages intended to declare those children as born from a forbidden marriage, [but] Hillel the Elder said to them [to the children]: Bring me your mothers' contracts. They did so, and he noticed written in them [the crucial phrase]: 'You will be my wife, when you will be married [according to the appropriate ceremony],' and declared them [the children] legitimate." In fact, this phrase was erroneously written using the people's jargon, and did not conform to the "legal" phrasing; but Hillel, known as a kind Sage with a lenient attitude, deemed the inaccurate text to be valid. Hillel's decision thus seems to me extremely radical. One may assume that the bridegrooms really intended the betrothal contracts to be binding, and to prohibit their brides to others, from the very moment the contracts were written, as is clearly evident in those contracts written by proficient scribes. Thus, the children were "in reality" illegitimate; but the compassionate Hillel sought a way to prevent the imposition of such an affliction on innocent children, and succeeded with the help of a legal fiction to overrule the harshness of the rigid law. The concept of לשון הדיוט has a great array of applications in the talmudic deliberations. In my opinion, however, these are distinct from Hillel's application in our subject case, and thus we need not extend the examination of this topic.

[163] I have offered above (nn. 45-7 and related text) an explanation of Urbach's statement of the authoritative style of the halakhot attributed to the first Tannaim.

of the Amoraic declarations, reflecting their different levels of confidence in their own authority.

My proposition is supported by the conclusion of Peter Schäfer,[164] who asserts that the dogma concerning the oral Torah tradition is to be set at the end of the process, and not at its beginning. In other words, there was no deliberate project for the creation of a corpus of oral Torah. This corpus was gradually formed within the process of promulgating legal rules and edicts; only at a late stage were the extant ancient traditions and subsequent decrees, collected over centuries, deemed to constitute oral Torah given to Moses at Sinai. In Schäfer's opinion this was an amoraic enterprise, accomplished under the leadership of Rabbi Yohanan, who granted the oral Torah a preference over the written Torah, and prohibited its writing. Schäfer conceives this dogmatization to have occurred during the course of a Jewish - Gentile controversy. I need not agree with all of his assumptions,[165] but his main point regarding the amoraic attitudes to oral Torah harmonizes with and complements my own point. The Tannaim did not consider it necessary to attribute their declarations to a superior authority, but the Amoraim, due to their lack of confidence in their own decision-making competence, did perceive such a necessity.[166] They thus collected and institutionalized the various edicts and rules and endowed them with a superior authority, under the aegis "given to Moses from Sinai."

D. Weiss-Halivni[167] offers an entirely different explanation for the distinct methods of the Tannaim, observed in the Mishnah and baraitot, and that of the Amoraim, manifested in the Gemara. Halivni constructs a non-linear path from Scripture to Gemara based on the theme of "justificatory law" versus "apodictic law." In his opinion, Scripture, with its motive clauses, has a comprehensive vindicatory character, while the Mishnah, in contrast, is authoritative in style. The Amoraim, in his view, returned to the justificatory method of Scripture. Although such a difference in style is perceptible, we do in fact encounter authoritative decrees in the Torah, and similarly, motive clauses in the Mishnah. It seems that Halivni considers Scripture to have originated from one source, and therefore conceives that a single, basic underlying philosophy may be

---

[164] P. Schäfer, *Studien*, p. 194.

[165] In the well-known narrative in bShabbat 31a concerning the gentile who approached Hillel for conversion, the existence of both Torot is declared by Hillel. Schäfer's assumption must therefore be narrowly restricted. The authenticity of the narrative is also more than doubtful. On the general issue of authenticity, see J. Neusner, "Attributions."

[166] Cf. J. Neusner, " Hermeneutics," who states on p. 187 that the "Talmud's primary point of interest is the demonstration that the Oral Torah, the Mishnah, rests upon the written Torah."

[167] D. Weiss-Halivni, *Midrash, Mishnah and Gemara*. See also nn. 49-52 and related text.

defined for the entire opus. Attempting to reconcile the various contradictions to such a general thesis is, however, not always possible. If, on the other hand, we consider Scripture to have originated from many sources, from different periods, and to have been redacted by a number of hands, we have less difficulty in identifying the distinct approaches and basic philosophies apparent in the text; we would not, however, be able to construct a single philosophy, as suggested by Halivni. Halivni summarizes this philosophical foundation of Scripture as "God is interested in man's opinion" and "He seeks man's approval."[168] Yet these aphorisms do not seem to me reconcilable with the statement "the Israelites belong to me as servants. They are my servants, whom I brought out of Egypt [Lev 25: 55]." A master does not seek his slave's approval for his commands. The obligation of the Israelites to carry out God's precepts, because of their status as His slaves, or because "I brought you out of Egypt, the land of slavery"[169] (found in Exod 20: 2 and numerous other instances as a motive for obeying commands and admonitions), does not suggest divine interest in human opinion or the deity's aspiration to secure human approval. We may also note, however, that this "tit for tat" character of many pericopes, particularly Lev 26 and Deut 27 - 28, does not harmonize with other language found in Scripture: the mandate to understand the divine laws,[170] taught to the Israelites[171] because they were

---

168 Ibid., p. 16.

169 I do not agree with Halivni that the motive of "having delivered the Israelites from Egyptian slavery" is a justificatory one, in accordance with the idea that God is interested in man's approval. This claim may serve as the legal basis for obligating the unconditional worship of one exclusive God and master (Exod 20: 4; v. 5 in KJV) and absolute obedience to all His commands, but does not indicate God's interest in human opinion, or that the laws are for human benefit. The author of a Jewish liturgy read after the dramatic *shofar* - blowing on Rosh Hashanah, the Day of Judgment, has acknowledged this duality in the relationship of God to Israel. The Israelites approach God on two distinct levels: אם כבנים אם כעבדים "as children [to a father] and as slaves [to a master]." Even within a father-son relationship, we may observe two distinct approaches. One father counsels his son to abide by his advice, because it will be to the son's benefit in future; another commands his son to obey his commands, because he is the father and such obeisance befits his status. The motive "because God delivered the Israelites from slavery" accords with the style of the second father, and does not seem to me as expressing a justificatory manner of persuasion.

170 The literary style of the verses in Deut chap. 4 is characteristic of the distinctive message of this work. The chapter is introduced (4: 1) with the phrase שמע אל החקים "Hear now the decrees." The term שמע has the notion of "understand," in contrast to the usual צוה "to command" utilized in the other books of the Pentateuch to convey laws and rules.

171 The use in Deut 4: 1 of the term למד "to teach," in reference to the divine laws אנכי מלמד אתכם לעשות, also reflects a kind, compassionate, educative approach, characteristic of Deuteronomy. The term appears eight times in chaps. 4 - 6, which

wise,[172] and the various suggestions that the laws were decreed for the Israelites' benefit.[173] The same inconsistency of approach is suggested in the fact that some laws have a motive[174] while others do not,[175] or are devoid of any sensible motive.[176] Further, in contrast to Halivni's assertion of the amoraic preference for the disclosure of the law's motives, we do encounter dicta that emphasize the negative consequences of knowing such motives.[177] We must therefore acknowledge the "pluralistic"

---

should be considered one extended pericope, attempting to convince the Israelites of the superior merit of the law granted by God, and the advantage resulting to them if they fulfill it.

172 We read in Deut 4: 6: כי הוא חכמתכם ובינתכם לעיני העמים ואמרו רק עם חכם ונבון הגוי הגדול הזה "This will show your wisdom and understanding to the nations…[who will] say: Surely this great nation is a wise and understanding people." We read further in 4: 8: ומי גוי גדול אשר לו חקים ומשפטים צדיקם ככל התורה הזאת "And what other nation is so great to have such righteous decrees and laws as this body of laws."

173 We read in Deut 4: 1: למען תחיו "so that you may live." That the laws of God are for the people's benefit is more explicitly emphasized in Deut 10: 13: לשמר את מצות ה' ואת חקתיו אשר אנבי מצוך היום לטוב לך "to observe the Lord's commands and decrees that I am giving you today for your own good." I consider that this notable declaration constitutes the foremost change of direction in Israelite theology, against the idolatrous belief that humans must serve the gods for the gods' benefit and enjoyment.

174 We read in Exod 20: 22 (v. 25 in KJV): כי חרבך הנפת עליה ותחללה "[If you make an altar of stones for me, do not build it with dressed stones] for you wielded your sword upon it and defiled it." Most of the social laws are either self-evident, or indicate the motive, when motivation seems necessary, such as: "Do not oppress an alien; you yourself know how it feels to be aliens, because you were aliens in Egypt [Exod 23: 9]."

175 The prohibition against eating certain animals, for example, is explained only with the obscure phrase טמא הוא לכם "it is unclean for you [Lev 11: 4]." Similarly, there is no justification for the command: ועניתם את נפשתיכם "You shall afflict your souls" on the tenth day of the seventh month. It would be extremely tenuous to connect the affliction of the people with the atonement procedure, since the text associates responsibility and credit for atonement with the cult celebrations of the priest.

176 The cleansing water with the ashes of the Red Heifer (Lev chap. 19) is a good example.

177 We read in bSanhedrin 21b: אמר רבי יצחק מפני מה לא נתגלו טעמי תורה שהרי שתי מקראות נתגלו טעמן נבשל בהן גדול העולם "Rabbi Isaac said: Why were the reasons for the Torah ['s precepts] not disclosed? Because the most illustrious [person] in the world [King Solomon] transgressed the prohibitions of two verses in which the reasons were disclosed [in Deut 17: 16 - 17, the reasons for the interdiction against the king acquiring a great number of horses, and taking many wives, are disclosed. Solomon transgressed both, as indicated in 1 Kgs 10: 29 and 11: 10]." A somewhat obscure homily on this topic appears in ySanhedrin 2: 6, 20c: אמר שלמה שלשה דברים שסחקה עליהן מידת הדין חיללתים "Solomon said: I

character both of Scripture and of the rabbinic literature in general, particularly its legal declarations. The substantiation of this proposition will be discussed throughout this work.

2.4 The Nature of Tannaitic Disputes

The nature of rabbinic disputes varies considerably. Controversies may result from differences in the interpretation of a relevant biblical verse (as often argued by the Amoraim), or give the impression of doing so. One such example is the number of lashes to be administered to one sentenced to this punishment. We read in mMakkot 3: 10: "How many lashes does one administer to him? Thirty-nine lashes, since it is said 'in the number of forty [Deut 25: 2 - 3, the last word of v. 2 and first word of v. 3]'; that means a number close to forty [that is, thirty-nine]. Rabbi Yehudah says he is struck with the full forty lashes. And where is the fortieth lash administered? Between his shoulders." This is one of the infrequent occurrences in the Mishnah in which the Sages' interpretation of a biblical verse is indicated. The Mishnah does not indicate that Rabbi Yehudah had an alternative interpretation, or a different verse that prompted his conflicting opinion, and we can only assume that he did not agree to the Sages' strained exegesis of Deut 25: 2-3, so removed from its simple meaning. The Gemara, which usually attempts to reveal the conflicting interpretations that it deemed were at the basis of the tannaitic disputes, does not indicate in this case the motive behind Rabbi Yehudah's decision. We find only a comment, in bMakkot 22b, on the second part of his pronouncement, that is, the spot where the fortieth lash should be administered: "What is the reason for Rabbi Yehudah's declaration? Because it is written: 'What are these wounds between your hands [Zech 13: 6].'" The real reason for this dispute may have been the intention of

---

violated three matters upon which the measure of the law took sport." The dispute between Rabbi Simeon and Rabbi Yehudah in bBava Metzi'a 115a as to whether דריש טעמא דקרא "one interprets the reason for [a law] in Scripture," has no relationship to the dictum of Rabbi Isaac. This dispute refers to the question of whether one may deduce a further decision from the exegesis of the scriptural motive. For example, Rabbi Yehudah asserts that a king may take more women if they do not turn his heart to other gods, the motive indicated in Scripture for the prohibition of polygamy. Maimonides attempted to explain the purpose of the biblical commands and prohibitions in *The Guide of the Perplexed*. In book 3, chaps. 26 - 34, he discusses their general underlying philosophy, and in chaps. 35 - 49 he enumerates the particular motives of the individual mitzvot, classified into fourteen categories. His enterprise raised much deliberation and opposition among traditional Jewish scholars and philosophers in the Middle Ages.

the Sage[178] who was the author of the majority opinion to mitigate the severe punishment somewhat, by eliminating one lash. It was, however, presented as a result of the interpretation of a biblical command, concealing the social compassion that may have been a contentious motive.[179]

Other disputes arise from divergent opinions on "factual" issues, such as the quantity of food one must consume to be considered as having eaten a meal that requires the performance of the special prayer of thanks, or the minimum quantity of flour in the preparation of dough that obligates the contribution of חלה, "*hallah*."[180] We read in mBerakhot 7: 2: "What is [the minimum amount of food one has to eat] to obligate the saying of the prayer? The size of an olive. Rabbi Yehudah says: The size of an egg." The Amora Abbaye attempts to explain the nature of this controversy as dependent on a different interpretation of the biblical command "When you have eaten and are satisfied, praise the Lord your God [Deut 8: 10]." We read in bBerakhot 49b: "Rabbi Meir [the presumed author of the mishnaic rule] perceives 'eaten' as indicating food, 'are satisfied' as indicating drink, and the consumption of food in the size of an olive is considered as having eaten, but Rabbi Yehudah interprets both terms as indicating a meal that has satisfied, and that is [an amount in the quantity of] an egg." Although Abbaye attempts to explain the controversy between Rabbi Meir and Rabbi Yehudah as a disputation about the interpretation of a biblical verse, it is clear that their differences really

---

178 I use here the singular instead of the plural that would correspond to the term חכמים in the text, because in many instances it is obvious that the term חכמים in the Mishnah in fact reflects the opinion of one particular Tanna. For the substantiation and explanation of this proposition, see section 3. 1.

179 We are unaware of the social circumstances in this period that might have induced a distinction between thirty-nine and forty lashes. One cannot perceive a difference in the amount of pain suffered in each case. I suggest that the number forty had a great symbolic significance in Jewish mythology, and may have penetrated as a consequence into daily life. In the Gilgamesh legend, the flood continued for six days, but in Gen 7: 17 it persisted for forty days. Moses remained for forty days on Mount Sinai, Jesus fasted forty days (Matt 4: 2), Elijah continued his journey for forty days (1 Kgs 19: 8), and it took the explorers forty days to investigate the land of Canaan (Num 13: 25). Forty days are required to accomplish an event; forty years are required for a lasting kingship (David and Solomon); anything less than this number is not deemed to be a completed act. Analogously, thirty-nine lashes were possibly deemed a less humiliating punishment. Today there are, similarly, prison terms of two years less a day that make a great difference in the future social status of the convicted person.

180 This offering, the share of the dough due to the priest, is based on Num 15: 20: ראשית ערסתכם חלה תרימו תרומה "Present a cake from the first of your ground meal." The interpretation of this verse appears in tEduyyot 1: 1. There is no minimum quantity requirement for this offering; the cited dispute refers to the minimum quantity of dough that requires the contribution.

concern the factual issue of the minimum quantity of food considered a meal. This is corroborated by another talmudic dictum in bBerakhot 20b: "[God says] I have commanded them in the Torah: 'When you have eaten and are satisfied, praise the Lord your God.' But they are more punctilious [in their striving to fulfill my command], and praise [me] after [having eaten only the quantity of] an olive or an egg." The suggestion here, in other words, is that food in the quantity of an egg does not satisfy a person's hunger, contrary to the opinion attributed to Rabbi Yehudah. In fact, the plain meaning of Scripture is that praise is required only after one has eaten to satisfaction; the obligation to praise the Lord after having eaten only the quantity of an olive or an egg is a decree of the Sages. This is confirmed in bBerakhot 20b: "...for example, when he ate the quantity fixed by the Sages [that is, the obligation to praise the Lord is a decree of the Sages]." The disagreement of the Sages thus concerns the factual question of the minimum quantity of food equal to a meal (contrary, for example, to merely a taste); the Sages decreed the duty to praise the Lord as an extension of the scriptural command, which requires praise only after having eaten to satisfaction.[181]

The controversy with respect to the obligation to dedicate *hallah* is encountered in mEduyyot 1: 2: "Shammai says that dough in the amount of one *kav* of flour requires the dedication of *hallah*; Hillel says [only] two *kav*, and the Sages say it is neither according to the one nor according to the other, but [the minimum quantity is] one *kav* and one half." This is again a dispute on a factual issue, the minimum quantity of flour deemed a preparation of dough. The mishnah does not indicate the reasons behind the dissension between Hillel and Shammai, but tEduyyot 1: 1 elaborates on the Sages' declaration: "But one *kav* and one half requires the dedication of *hallah*, because it said 'Present a cake from the first of your ground meal [dough] [Num 15: 20]'; 'your dough' - and how much is your dough? Like the dough of the desert, and how much is that? Like the quantity of the *omer*, as it is said: 'the *omer* is a tenth of an *efah* [Exod 16: 36].'" A baraita in bEruvin 83a also cites these verses as a justification for one *kav* and one half. We still, however, have no indication as to the real reason for the controversy between Hillel and Shammai. The mishnah

[181] The entire issue of whether the institution of שיעורין, the minimum and maximum standards that appear in the halakhah in various applications, was fixed by the Sages, or is a הלכה למשה מסיני, that is, an old tradition, is itself a matter of dispute among the Tannaim and Amoraim. See I. D. Gilat, פרקים, pp. 63 ff. The Sages were concerned with the conceptual problem of what can logically be deemed the fulfillment of a particular deed, such as eating or accomplishing a task, or the minimum dimensions of an object, and the like. Such standards reveal the Sages' lack of concern with respect to the generation and historical source of significant halakhic rules; they often ignored established standards that may have been fixed by their own rabbinic rank..

obviously does not reflect a dispute regarding the interpretation of the above verses. One has the impression that they differ concerning the factual issue of the minimum quantity to be deemed a preparation of dough. The complementary texts of the baraita and the Tosefta passage seem to be later opinions not originating from Hillel and Shammai; it is inconceivable that neither Hillel nor Shammai would possess a correct tradition concerning the minimum quantity, and that both would contradict a plausible interpretation of a biblical verse, the supposed basis of the Sages' decision, had they been aware of it. One is tempted to contemplate that this mishnaic "narrative," and the two others with similar concluding phrases in the adjacent mishnayot, were set out in this distinctive manner[182] to emphasize the particular messages[183] conveyed by these mishnayot. The style in which they were ultimately redacted does not reflect, in my opinion, absolute authenticity. For this and similar dicta, one must assume that the message, rather than the details of the narrative, constitutes the real purpose.

In mSukkah 1: 9 there is another example of a dispute concerning a purely factual issue: since a structure ten *tefahim* high is deemed to be a wall (of a Sukkah), is it still considered a wall if detached from the ground more than three *tefahim*? There is no attempt in the Gemara in this case to see the controversy as originating in differing interpretations of biblical verses.[184]

The next example may be considered as a halakhah decided on either "factual" or "logical" considerations. I do not intend to resolve this semantic issue, but wish nevertheless to cite the example; it refers to a significant part of the Israelite way of life, the Sabbath law. We read in mShabbat 7: 2: "There are thirty-nine cardinal works [that one is prohibited to perform on Sabbath]." The mishnah subsequently enumerates them. The Gemara in bShabbat 49b asks: "To what do they correspond?" The Amoraim understood that the precise number of thirty-nine could not be the result of a logical consideration, but must

---

[182] "The Sages say: It is neither according to the one nor according to the other."

[183] The "narrative" at the end of mEduyyot 1: 3 emphasizes the superiority of tradition, even when transmitted by the most humble person, and even if it opposes the opinion of such giants as Hillel and Shammai (see chap. 1, pp. 52-3, concerning tEduyyot 1: 3). Mishnayot 4 - 6 convey significant rabbinic principles. For instance, the rabbinic giants, "the Patriarchs of the World" Hillel and Shammai, accepted the tradition communicated by the humble weavers and gave up their own opinions; everyone should thus follow their example (mishnah 4). The following mishnayot 5 and 6 refer to the strategic and delicate relationships between minority and majority opinions, and the regulations for effecting changes of prior legal rulings. These messages are pillars of the rabbinic legal system, and the communication of these principles was the main purpose for their citation in this specific manner; the communication of the specific laws contained in these mishnayot was of secondary purpose.

[184] See n. 124.

represent some symbolic number, and proposed two answers, befitting the question: it represents the thirty-nine works performed as part of the Temple service;[185] the number corresponds to the phrases "work", "his work" and "the work of," which appear 39 times in the Torah.

The character of the question and answers demonstrates the stretch between the law and its justification. And indeed, mHagigah 1: 8 confirms the dearth of biblical supports for many of the Sabbath laws. We read there: "The laws of Sabbath, of the offerings on the holidays, and for inappropriate use of sacred property, are like mountains suspended on a hair, since there are many halakhot supported by a limited scriptural text." I. D. Gilat[186] writes (in free translation): "There were Sages, contemporaries of Rabbi Aqiba, who were aware that the list [of the forbidden works] and their number [39] are not definite and do not obligate at all. This is because [they were aware] that the list was edited by the Sages, who selected the substance of the works according to their [logical] understanding, founded upon customary work procedures, such as the arrangement regarding [baking] bread, preparing a meat meal, preparation of garments and similar [chores]. They therefore felt entitled not to accept the list as submitted, but to add to or subtract from it, according to their comprehension and the tradition in their possession." Gilat competently expresses the conceptual foundation of the rabbinic Sabbath laws.

Different attitudes to "social policy" seem to be at the core of a dispute between Rabbi Tarfon and Rabbi Aqiba in mKetubbot 9: 2: "If a man passed away leaving behind a wife [who demands the payment of her *ketubbah*], a creditor, and heirs, and he had given a deposit or a loan to a third party, [who should receive this asset?] Rabbi Tarfon says: It should be given to the weakest party. Rabbi Aqiba says: Compassion is not applied in a legal case; the asset should be given to the heirs since the other parties have to take an oath to establish their debt in order to receive payment, while the heirs do not need an oath to establish their rights." The Tannaim of the mishnah do not explain the term "the weakest party," and thus we do not know Rabbi Tarfon's intention or reasoning; this issue is disputed by two Amoraim in bKetubbot 84a. I suggest that Rabbi Tarfon was motivated by "social policy" - that is, a desire to give the asset to the most needy. Rabbi Aqiba's comment about compassion, apparently superfluous since he pronounced his decision on a purely legal point, corroborates my assumption; Rabbi Aqiba adhered strictly to the legal viewpoint, and thus disputed the decision of Rabbi Tarfon that was founded upon a social, rather than a legal, basis.[187]

---

[185] For a theological exegesis of this passage, see chap. 3, nn. 96-9 and related text.

[186] פרקים, p. 43.

[187] On the specific issue of whether ethical values played a role in the Sages'

A noteworthy problem arises with respect to the scriptural law and punishment for prohibited intercourse in Lev 20: 14: "If a man marries both a woman and her mother, it is wicked. Both he and they must be burned." The simple understanding of this verse would indicate that the man married both women together and they agreed; therefore all three are equally responsible and deserve punishment. It seems, however, that the Sages envisaged another circumstance, that the man married his mother-in-law after having married his wife, based on the fact that Scripture states "her mother" after "his wife." Hence, his (first) wife cannot be blamed for a sin executed by others and should not be punished. A baraita to this effect is quoted in bSanhedrin 76b: "[It is written:] 'He and they [must be burned].' [What it really means is] he and one [of the women], according to Rabbi Ishmael; Rabbi Aqiba said: He and both [women must be burned]." As with many quoted baraitot, we are unaware of the occasion at which the matter was pronounced, or the real intention of Rabbi Aqiba - that is, whether his dictum referred to the same situation as that envisaged by Rabbi Ishmael, or whether he intended to say that Scripture refers to an actual *ménage à trois* agreed to by all three, and therefore all were liable for punishment. The Amoraim treat both dicta as discussing the same circumstances, and find highly speculative solutions[188] in order to avoid any possibility that an innocent person might be punished, as might result from Rabbi Aqiba's declaration. They could not conceive that either Scripture or a Sage would adjudicate contrary to this fundamental idea of justice.

These examples thus reveal that certain disputes were based on differences of opinion on practical matters, rather than differences in transmission or interpretations of biblical verses.[189] Other disputes resulted from different philosophical approaches with respect to the solutions of new problems, which definitely did not originate from Scripture. We read in bShabbat 21b of a dispute concerning the manner of kindling the Hanukkah lights: "Beit Shammai say: One kindles eight [lights] on the first day and subsequently decreases [one light each day]. Beit Hillel say: One kindles one light the first day and subsequently increases [one light each day]." It is obvious that the issue of kindling Hanukkah lights, a non-biblical custom, did not involve a dispute concerning an ancient tradition from Sinai, or a controversy with respect to the interpretation of a

hermeneutics and the development of halakhah, see Moshe Halbertal, מהפכות, and Introduction, nn. 102 ff. and related text.

188 Abbaye suggests, for example, that Rabbi Ishmael considers the term אתהן to indicate "one" because in the Greek language ἕν means "one" (the neuter form of εἷς). He suggests that Rabbi Aqiba understands that if he married both, both had a similar intention.

189 I certainly do not exclude the possibility that controversies may result from differences in the interpretation of a relevant biblical verse, as I have written above.

biblical verse. The contenders do not indicate the motives for their different decisions;[190] it seems they did not consider it necessary. As is common, however, the Amoraim attempted to detect their motives, and attributed the dispute to conceptual differences. We read in the B.T.: "[One Amora said] Beit Shammai's reason is [that the arrangement of the lights] corresponds to the remaining number [of days in the holiday] and Beit Hillel's reason is that it corresponds to the elapsed number of days. And the other said: Beit Shammai's reason corresponds to the [daily decreasing number of] bull offerings [on the Feast of Tabernacles, as commanded in Num 29: 12 - 38]. Beit Hillel's decision corresponds to the maxim, 'One enhances the degree of holiness and one does not downgrade it.'" This is a very clear example of the different approaches of the Tannaim and Amoraim discussed above (section 2.3.2), since the disputed rules cannot be linked to halakhic midrash or any other exegetical method. Through a subtle examination of the argument of the second Amora, who compares the mode of kindling the Hanukkah lights to certain offerings commanded in the Torah, however, we can deduce that he attempted to apply the principle behind that Torah rule to another halakhic issue for which there is not the slightest indication in the Torah; just as the sacrifices for an eight-day festival decrease, so the number of Hanukkah lights should decrease.[191] The Amoraim could not concede that purely logical insight and philosophical consideration of the Torah narratives and commands were at the core of tannaitic decisions, and the cause of dissension.

---

190 We might speculate that based on this late dispute, which must not have been earlier than the beginning of the common era, the custom of kindling eight lights on Hanukkah was a recent institution, and the method of its performance had not yet become a tradition. The span of time between the Maccabean revolt and the eight-day consecration of the Temple, and the period of the Tannaim of the Schools of Shammai and Hillel, was at least one hundred and fifty years. The consecration of the Temple was in 164 B.C.E. and Hillel lived at the turn of the century; hence his school must have been active later. If the kindling of lights had been instituted at the time of the Maccabees, it is not likely that one hundred and fifty years later there was still no fixed method of performing this custom.

191 It was also necessary to maintain that no one had the authority to promulgate new laws, in order to repel proposals for renewal by false prophets. We read in bYoma 80a: אלה המצות שאין נביא רשאי לחדש דבר מעתה "'These are the commands [the Lord gave Moses on Mount Sinai - Lev 27: 34]' - no prophet may create anything new from now on."

2.5 "Do Not Cook a Kid in its Mother's Milk": An Example of Rabbinic Methods

Exod 23: 19 contains a prohibition of an apparently compassionate nature: "Do not cook [i.e., boil or seethe] a young goat in its mother's milk." This restriction appears twice more, in Exod 34: 26 and Deut 14: 21. These passages gave rise to diverse rabbinic opinions, and ultimately an extended prohibition against the use of any milk with any meat products. An examination of the development of this broad prohibition and the various opinions and scriptural justifications supporting it makes an interesting case study of rabbinic methods.

2.5.1 Exegesis of the Three Instances

In bQiddushin 57b, a homily from the school of Rabbi Ishmael[192] is cited, regarding the three repetitions of the rule: "One [instance teaches us] the interdiction against eating [the two products together], one the interdiction against benefiting [from the two products together], and one the interdiction against cooking [the two products together]." According to this homily, the threefold repetition serves the purpose of extending the restrictions. Rabbi Aqiba drew a different deduction from the three instances: "Scripture does not include the meat of wild beasts and fowl. Since [the command], 'Do not cook a young goat in its mother's milk' is written three times, this excludes wild beasts, fowl, and unclean [ritually unfit] domestic animals.[193]" Rabbi Aqiba thus deduces that the purpose of every repetition of the prohibition is to exclude (!) something from the application of the rule.

Further exegeses are found in the Mekilta d'Rabbi Ishmael, *Mishpatim* 20: "Abba Hanan says in the name of Rabbi Eliezer: Why is [this prohibition] repeated three times? One[194] for [the inclusion of] cattle, one for goats, and one for sheep." It is odd that this Sage needs separate verses for the inclusion of goats and sheep, which are usually included in

[192] In the Mekilta this homily appears in the name of Rabbi Simeon bar Yohai.

[193] Referred to in mHullin 8: 4, cited below.

[194] Although the term אחת "one" appears three times in the midrash, analogous to the three biblical quotations, I interpret the midrash as a justification for the two superfluous citations. The first biblical quotation has its own scope and does not need any justification. We encounter this rational argument in the Mekilta: רבי יונתן אומר הראשון תחלה נאמר ואין דורשין תחלות "Rabbi Jonathan says: The first [quotation] was uttered initially and [one] does not need [to justify the initial statement by an] interpretation."

the term בהמה דקה "small animals," the antonym of בהמה גסה, "large animals/cattle."[195] Yet another exegesis follows: "Rabbi Simeon ben Eleazer says: Why is [this prohibition] repeated three times? One for [the inclusion of] cattle, one for small animals, and one for wild beasts." In total opposition to Rabbi Aqiba's homily, cited above, we then read: "Rabbi Yoshiyyah says: Why is [this prohibition] repeated three times? One for the inclusion of domestic animals, one for wild beasts, and one for fowl."[196] An anonymous homily then suggests that the repetition of the prohibition renders it eternal: "Another matter: One instance [to establish the prohibition] both in Israel and outside, one [to establish the prohibition as effective] during the period of the Temple, and one [to establish the prohibition as effective] in the absence of the Temple."[197] In the same Mekilta pericope, Rabbi Ishmael interprets the repetition of these verses in a manner entirely disconnected from the idea of prohibition: "[The repetition] corresponds to the three covenants that the Holy One, Blessed Be He, made with Israel: one at Sinai, one on the Plains of Moab and one at the Mountains of Ebal and Gerizim."[198]

---

195 We read in tSotah 6: 8 a precise classification of the types of animals: אם תתן להם בשר בהמה גסה יאמרו בשר בהמה דקה בקשנו אנו תתן בשר בהמ׳ דקה יאמרו בשר חייה ועוף אנו מבקשי׳ תתן בשר חיה ועופות יאמרו בשר דגים וחגבים אנו מבקשין "[The homily refers to Moses' criticism of the Israelites' behaviour in Num 11: 22.] If you give them meat [of cattle], they would say: We desired meat of small animals; if you give them meat of small animals, they would say: We desire meat of fowl and wild beasts; if you give them meat of fowl and wild beasts, they would say; We desire meat of fish and locusts."

196 We can observe from Rabbi Yoshiyyah's dictum that the purpose of the midrash was to justify the prohibition of all meat and milk. As is obvious from Scripture, and as we shall see later in the study, the prohibition could not include fowl, because this species has no milk. But Rabbi Yoshiyyah probably interpreted the scriptural oddity of the threefold repetition in Scripture as justifying the halakhah that prevailed at the time, which also prohibited fowl.

197 In fact, it does not make sense to require a specific command for the validity of the rule during the period of the Temple, the "normative" situation.

198 It is interesting to observe how the ancient translators tackled this issue, and extended the scriptural prohibition. The LXX has translated the term תבשל in Exod 23: 19 and Deut 14: 21 with the appropriate term ἑψω "to cook," but in Exod 34: 26 it uses the much wider term προσφέρω, "to bring to, to add, to use," and similar meanings. Another extension of the prohibition is seen in the use of the term ἀρνός "lamb" instead of αἰγός "kid," the equivalent of the scriptural גדי. We observe an early extension of the prohibition (before rabbinic interference), to include all meat of animals (whether wild animals or domesticated animals only is unclear), and probably to include eating as well as cooking. On the other hand, we do not know whether the ancient tradition also forbade every mixture of meat and milk, or restricted the prohibition to the scriptural "in its mother's milk," which is left unchanged in the LXX. Targum Onkelos followed the rabbinic homilies, on the one hand, and interpreted in all three occurrences לא תיכלון בשר בחלב "You must not eat meat

2.5.2 Types of Meat

We thus have a remarkable array of seven exegetical discussions on the problem of the threefold repetition of a verse. One extends the cooking prohibition cited in Scripture to other uses of meat and milk, such as eating and profiting, without concern as to whether all types of meat and milk are included,[199] while four interpret the repetition as including or excluding particular kinds of meat. Before analyzing the different halakhic deductions derived from the scriptural exegeses,[200] we may note two further discussions on the type of meat prohibited. We read in the same Mekilta: "[It is written], 'Do not cook a young goat in its mother's milk.' I would assume this refers solely to a young goat, how do we know that [the meat of] all animals [is similarly forbidden]? [Answer] Scripture used [a casuistic style - i.e. it does not expressly exclude other animals[201]]." We also read in mHullin 8: 4: "Rabbi Yose ha-Gelili says: It is said 'Do not eat anything you find already dead [Deut 14: 21],' and it says [further in the same verse], 'Do not cook a young goat in its mother's milk.' [Hence we deduce from the adjoining of the two commands that] what is prohibited under the category of a dead animal must also not be cooked in milk. [But] is the fowl that is prohibited under the category of a dead animal also not to be cooked in milk? [No] because it says [not to cook the animal] in its mother's milk; this excludes fowl that has no mother's milk."

We may now summarize the practical differences between the various interpretations:

a) Rabbi Aqiba exempts wild beasts, fowl, and ritually unfit animals from the scriptural prohibition.

b) Abba Hanan explicitly exempts wild beasts and fowl, but does not disclose his opinion with respect to ritually unfit animals.

---

and milk"; but it also adhered to its customary style of not expanding its translation, and did not elaborate further. Targum Pseudo-Jonathan, pursuing its style of introducing rabbinic homilies, interprets: לית אתון רשאין לא למבשלא ולא למיכול בשר וחלב מערבין כחדא. "You are allowed neither to cook nor to eat meat with milk mixed together," and then adds certain exhortations and threats to avoid God's anger and consequent punishment.

199 I have cited only one such midrash as an example, since the focus of the study is the halakhic aspect of the midrashim. There is another midrash, found in Pesiqta Rabbati, Pesiqta d'Rav Kahana and Midrash Tanhuma, based on the verses antecedent and subsequent to the prohibition of meat with milk, with slightly different expressions. Since they have no relationship to the halakhah, I will refrain from quoting them.

200 The purpose of these midrashim is to affirm that the prohibitions therein originate in the Torah, although they derive from rabbinic exegesis. In section 2.5.4 we shall discuss later restrictions considered to be of rabbinic origin.

201 The Mekilta relates another reason for specifying a goat: שהחלב מרובה באמו "Because the mother has much milk [after the delivery]."

c) Rabbi Simeon ben Eleazar exempts fowl from the prohibition, but includes wild beasts; he gives no indication concerning the status of ritually unfit animals.

d) Rabbi Yoshiyyah includes both fowl and wild beasts in the prohibition; again there is no indication concerning ritually unfit animals.

e) The final citation from the Mekilta, noted above, does not declare explicitly the types of meat included in the prohibition, but from the term "all other animals," we must assume that wild beasts and fowl are not included in the interdiction. This generic term would also comprise ritually unfit animals, but I do not think that we can definitely deduce that the author of this exegesis intended this extension.

f) Rabbi Yose ha-Gelili includes wild beasts in the prohibition and exempts fowl. From his analogy, we might deduce that ritually unfit animals would be included in the prohibition, since their mothers have milk. Again, however, I would not extend the prohibition in this way; it is not clear that Rabbi Yose ha-Gelili includes the eating of carrion from a ritually unfit animal within the verse "Do not eat anything you find already dead [Deut 14: 21],"[202] and thus we cannot be sure about including ritually unfit animals in the analogy.[203] On the other hand, it is also not

---

[202] There is a rabbinic maxim: אין איסור חל על איסור "a prohibition is not added to another prohibition [bQiddushin 77b]." Although there is some dispute in the Talmud about this maxim, it is not clear whether those who propose it would have it apply in all occurrences or only in particular cases in which there is a difference in the gravity of the transgressions. In our case, we read explicitly in Sifra *Tzav* 10 that the prohibition against eating the meat of a dead animal does not apply to (ritually) unfit animals: יצאת בהמה טמאה שאין לה טריפה "...except a ritually unfit animal, to which the prohibition against eating a dead animal does not apply." In *Mishneh Torah*, *Hilkhot Ma'akhalot Asurot* 4: 2, Maimonides also declares: אין אסור משום נבילה אלא מינים טהורים בלבד "There is no prohibition regarding carrion, except with respect to ritually fit animals."

[203] Regarding the relevance of the prohibition with respect to ritually unfit animals, there is another dictum of Rabbi Jonathan in the Mekilta: אם למדת על טהורה שבשרה אסור להתבשל בחלבה יכול אף טמאה יהא בשרה אסור להתבשל בחלבה תלמוד לומר בחלב אמו ולא בחלב טמאה "If you have learned [from Scripture] that the meat of a ritually fit animal must not be cooked in [its mother's] milk, you might also deduce that the meat of a ritually unfit animal must not be cooked in her milk, so [the phrase] 'in its mother's milk' comes to teach us that [it refers solely to the milk of a ritually fit animal, like a goat, but] it is not relevant to the milk of a ritually unfit animal." The expressions used in this dictum, בחלבה "in [its mother's] milk," and ולא בחלב טמאה "the milk of a ritually unfit animal," are not clear. The dictum may intend to exclude from the restriction only the meat of an unfit animal cooked in the milk of an unfit animal, or the meat of an unfit animal cooked in the milk of any animal, but would prohibit cooking the meat of an unfit animal in the milk of a ritually fit animal. This is not a trivial question, since, as we shall see, similar questions with respect to the particular types of milk are the subject of inquiry in the Mekilta.

clear from Rabbi Yose's exegetical statement in the mishnah whether in his opinion the eating of fowl with milk is nevertheless prohibited by the Sages, or is absolutely permitted.[204]

2.5.3 Further Issues

The above exposition refers exclusively to the issue of the animals to be included in the prohibited mixtures of milk with meat, but many other problems are associated with the rabbinic hermeneutics and halakhic decisions on this topic. We have seen in the first quotation from the Mekilta that it is also prohibited to profit from the mixture of meat and milk; yet there is an opposing dictum in bHullin 116a: "Rabbi Simeon ben Yehudah says in the name of Rabbi Simeon: Meat combined with milk is not to be eaten, but can be used for profit, as it is said, 'you are a holy people [Deut 14: 21]' and it is said, 'you are my holy people [Exod 22: 30; v. 31 in KJV].' Just as the prohibition there [the subsequent prohibition against eating the meat of a dead animal[205]] applies to eating but not to use for profit, here too [with respect to the mixture of meat and milk] it is forbidden to eat but permitted to use for profit."

Both dicta agree that although Scripture forbids only cooking, the restriction also applies to eating, and each is founded upon a different scriptural support. Another scriptural support appears in bHullin 115b, in the name of Rabbi,[206] deduced from a complex exegesis on an apparently superfluous phrase, using one of the thirteen hermeneutic rules. We read there: "[It is written twice], 'Do not eat it [Deut 12: 24 and 25].'You say

---

204 See further section 2.5.4 on this issue. Maimonides, in his commentary to the Mishnah, asserts that Rabbi Yose permits cooking milk and fowl; it is possible, however, that Maimonides deduced this from the later amoraic statement in bHullin 116a, and not from Rabbi Yose's exegesis in the Mishnah.

205 We read in Exod. 22: 30: ובשר בשדה טריפה לא תאכלו "Do not eat the meat of an animal torn by wild beasts." A torn animal is equivalent to a dead animal, as neither is slaughtered according to the correct rules.

206 I have attempted to cite only tannaitic dicta on this topic, since the rhetorical deliberations of the Amoraim would extend this examination beyond what is necessary for the substantiation of the thesis. I nevertheless shall quote here a deduction by Resh Laqish, because he also connects his hermeneutics to the Passover meat. We read in bHullin 115a: אל תאכלו ממנו נא ובשל מבושל שאין תלמוד לומר מבושל מה תלמוד לומר מבושל לומר לך יש לך בישול אחר שהוא כזה ואי זה זה בשר בחלב "[It is written in Exod 12: 9] אל תאכלו ממנו נא ובשל מבושל במים כי אם צלי אש 'Do not eat the [Passover] meat raw or cooked in water, but roast it over fire'; the term ובשל מבושל is tautological, and comes to teach us that there is a similar [prohibited] cooking, and that is meat and milk [i.e. just as the Passover meat cannot be eaten if 'cooked,' so meat cannot be cooked with milk]."

this refers to [the prohibition against cooking] meat in milk, but perhaps it refers to another of the scriptural prohibitions? I answer you: Come and learn from [one of] the thirteen rules of Torah exegesis: you learn [a missing detail] from a similar subject. Just as Scripture [in the preceding v. 22] refers to two distinct species [את הצבי ואת האיל 'gazelle and deer'], so here too it refers to two distinct categories [meat and milk]."

We find yet another method of deduction in the Mekilta, based on the *a minori ad majorem* formula: "[It is written], 'Do not cook' so we know that cooking is prohibited, how do we know that eating is also prohibited? [Answer] We learn it by [reasoning] *a minori ad majorem*. There is no prohibition against cooking the Passover meat, but it is forbidden to eat it cooked [only roasted];[207] all the more so meat and milk, which it is forbidden [even] to cook, are obviously forbidden to be eaten." I need not comment on the extremely strained attempt to link the manner of preparing the Passover meat to the eating of milk and meat, but simply note the different hermeneutic methods used and the various conclusions reached.

2.5.4 Types of Milk

We may now proceed with an investigation of the types of milk included in the prohibition. We read in a baraita quoted in bHullin 114a: "We learn in a baraita: [It is written 'Do not cook a young goat] in its mother's milk,' so we know [that it is forbidden to cook it] in its mother's milk, but how do we know that it also applies to milk of a cow and sheep? We learn it from the *a minori ad majorem* formula. It is forbidden to cook it in the milk of its mother, with whom it is not prohibited from being yoked; all the more so is it forbidden to cook it in the milk of a cow and sheep, with whom it is prohibited from being yoked [because they are heterogeneous]...." There then follows the logical question of why the phrase "its mother's" is written, and a complex answer is offered. Further questions are asked and answered: "How do we know that it is forbidden to cook it in the milk of its older sister?" "How do we know the same applies to the milk of its younger sister?" The rhetoric goes so far as to ask: "How do we know that it is forbidden to cook it in its own milk?"[208]

---

[207] Exod 12: 9, quoted in previous note.

[208] In the Mekilta d'Rabbi Simeon bar Yohai, the passage with respect to the extension of the types of milk appears twice, with certain textual changes. We read in the commentary to Exod 23: 19: לא תבשל גדי בחלב אמו אין לי אלא גדי בחלב אמו פרה בחלב אמה מנין ת״ל בחלב מכל מקום "[It is written] 'do not cook a kid in its mother's milk,' so we know that one must not cook a kid in its mother's milk; how do we know that the same rule applies to a calf in its mother's milk?

Before concluding the portrayal of the complex processes by which the Sages could extend almost without limit the application of a seemingly simple, compassionately-motivated biblical decree,[209] we must note a

---

[Because] it says 'in milk' and that means in every milk." This text is not very precise, since it gives the impression that the extension of the prohibition refers to an animal cooked in the milk of its own mother, but not to milk from any other origin. In the exegesis of Exod 34: 26 the text is more precise, and the question posed indicates its broader application: בשר שור בחלב מנין ת״ל לא תבשל בחלב "How do we know that the meat of a bull [cannot be cooked] with milk? [Because] it says 'do not cook in milk,' and that means in every type of milk."

209 Other decrees also demonstrate this motivation: for instance, the prohibition against taking a bird together with its eggs or chicks (Deut 22: 6 - 7), and the prohibition against slaughtering an animal and its young on the same day (Lev 22: 28). The Sages were aware of the humanitarian significance of these and similar decrees and declared: צער בעלי חיים דאורייתא "[The decree to avoid giving] pain to animals is a Torah precept [bBava Metzi'a 32b]." This consideration is so important that it overrides a rabbinic edict, as we read in bShabbat 128b: צער בעלי חיים דאורייתא ואתי דאורייתא ודחי דרבנן "The decree to avoid giving pain to animals is a Torah precept and overrides a rabbinic edict." The edict in this case was a rabbinic prohibition against performing certain types of work on Sabbath, which is overridden in order to save an animal that fell into a ditch so as to avert its suffering. The Sages could likely not accept that the divine prohibition of meat and milk was also the consequence of humanitarianism, since this would preclude the extension of the scriptural rule to all classes of meat and milk. With respect to the other humanitarian decrees, cited above, we do read further in Deut. Rab. 6: 1: וכשם שרחמיו של הקב״ה על האדם כך רחמיו על הבהמה "And just as God has mercy upon humankind, so he has mercy upon the animals." The traditional commentators also search for reasons for the meat and milk prohibition. Maimonides, the austere and ascetic philosopher remote from any apparent sentimentalism, vacillates between a medically inspired purpose: היותו מזון עב מאד בלא ספק ומוליד מלוי רב "[the mixture] being certainly a heavy and filling food," injurious to health, and: אין רחוק אצלי שיש בו ריח עבודה זרה אולי כך היו עשין בעבודה מעבודתיה או בחג מחגיהם "I have a supposition that it may have reference to idolatry; it is possible that such a custom was performed in one of their ceremonies or at the occasion of some of their holidays" (*The Guide of the Perplexed*, book 3, chap. 48). It is also possible that his philosophical mind discerned a difference in the suffering involved. There is the real pain of the bird when separated from its eggs or chicks, and similarly that of the animal who is separated from its offspring within the first eight days after its birth. In these occurrences, Maimonides accepted the humanitarian aim as the basis of the decrees, declaring: אין הפרש בין צער האדם עליו וצער שאר ב״ח "There is no difference between the pain of humankind and that of other living creatures." In contrast, the cooking of the kid in its mother's milk does not affect the animal, and thus a humanitarian motive is not appropriate. It might, however, indicate a human insensibility to the suffering of the animal, a sense of brutality. Maimonides considers the rejection of brutality as the purpose behind the prohibition against cutting a limb from a living animal and consuming it. It is therefore strange that he does not mention this concept with respect to the meat and milk prohibition; again, this may have been so as not to limit the extension of this prohibition to all meat and milk. Other traditional commentators do propose humanitarian considerations, but with respect to

further rabbinic rule. The above-cited exegeses and resulting halakhic pronouncements relate in various ways to an express biblical prohibition. But the Sages also appended a rabbinic prohibition against the cooking and eating of fowl with milk, which was not included in the biblical decree.[210] We read in mHullin 8: 1: "It is prohibited to cook any meat in milk, except the meat of fish and locusts.... One may put fowl together with cheese on the table, but one must not eat it [together], according to Beit Shammai. Beit Hillel say: One may not put them [together] on the table and one may not eat them...."

There is, however, no explicit exegesis or other justification for the specific prohibition against cooking fowl with milk. The Gemara (bHullin 104a) that discusses this mishnah has lengthy deliberations as to whether eating fowl with milk is a Torah decree or a rabbinic edict, and whether the second part of the mishnah[211] can be reconciled with the first. Rav Ashi achieves this feat and declares: "The mishnah should be interpreted in this way: 'All types of meat must not be cooked in milk.' Some [of the types of meat] are [forbidden] by the Torah and some by the Sages, except the meat of fish and locusts, which are not forbidden either by the Torah or by the Sages." Yet we read in bHullin 104b only a justification for the prohibition against putting fowl and cheese on the table: "If you were to allow fowl and cheese on the table, people might put meat on the table,

---

the impact on humans, rather than the pain to the animal. Rashbam in his commentary to Exod 23: 19 states: וגנאי הוא הדבר ובליעה ורעבתנות לאכול חלב האם עם הבנים ודוגמא זו באותו ואת בנו ושילוח הקן וללמדך דרך תרבות צוה הכתוב "It is a shameful act, gluttony and greed, to eat the mother's milk with its offspring, as is the slaughtering of the mother and its offspring on the same day, and [not] sending away the bird [before taking its eggs or chicks]. Scripture came to teach us the civilized way [of living]." Ramban in his commentary to Deut 14: 21 states: שלא נהיה עם אכזרי לא ירחמו שנחלוב את האם ונציא ממנה החלב שנבשל בו הבן "...we must not be a brutal people and show no mercy by milking the mother and cooking her offspring in it." While the philosophical foundation of this biblical precept is not the aim of this study, I shall briefly note the conjectures of various renowned commentators, which may be of interest to the reader. M. Noth, *Exodus*, p. 192, writes "[This prohibition] presumably forbids a practice usual in foreign cults." G. von Rad, *Deuteronomy*, writes on p. 102, "[It] seems intended to ward off a milk-spell, as has been discovered from an Ugaritic text." He does not indicate the source. T. H. Gaster, *Myth, Legend and Custom in the Old Testament*, pp. 250-263, lists comparative taboos of primitive societies concerning boiling milk in general or mixing it with flesh. These customs are founded upon the belief that the cow remains in direct physical sympathy with her milk. Every act injurious to the milk, such as boiling it, or contaminating it with meat, or mixing it with blood when a menstruating woman consumes it, may harm the cow and stop her flow of milk.

210 As we have seen, only Rabbi Yoshiyyah assumed that fowl was also included in the biblical decree, and his opinion was probably overruled.

211 We read in mHullin 8: 1: הנודר מן הבשר מותר בבשר דגים וחגבים "If one pledges not to eat meat, he may eat the flesh of fish and locusts."

and eating that is a Torah prohibition." This justification is judiciously refuted since it would amount to a rabbinic preventative edict decreed on top of another preventative edict. The mixture of fowl and milk is not forbidden in the Torah, and constitutes only a rabbinic edict to prevent one from (erroneously) eating the meat of cattle or goats with milk, which is itself a rabbinic edict; one cannot (according to a rabbinic maxim) decree one preventative rule on top of another. Various opinions are offered to justify this rule,[212] but we nonetheless observe the twisted routes that were employed by the Sages.

Given that the attempts to extend the prohibition to fowl are so difficult and unconvincing, we can also understand why Rabbi Yose ha-Gelili did not prohibit eating fowl with milk. We read in bHullin 116a: "Rabbi Aqiba believes that [mixing the] meat of wild beasts and of fowl [with milk] is not prohibited in the Torah, but is forbidden by the Sages, and Rabbi Yose ha-Gelili considers that fowl is not prohibited even by a rabbinic decree." It is odd that we have no explicit pronouncement by Rabbi Yose;[213] the above declaration consists only of an allegation expressed by Amoraim in the course of their analysis of the Mishnah. In fact, they do not cite evidence from a clear declaration by Rabbi Yose, but quote a custom associated indirectly with him: "In the town of Rabbi Yose ha-Gelili one ate fowl with milk." This custom continued to be practised in that particular locality after the death of Rabbi Yose ha-Gelili, and possibly also in other places and times. We read subsequently that Rabbi Levi[214] communicated to Rabbi, the Patriarch, that in a certain unidentified location he was offered the head of a peacock cooked in milk. He did not object to it, he said, because: "...it was in the town of Rabbi Yehudah ben Bathyra and I thought that he proclaimed the same exegesis as Rabbi Yose ha-Gelili, who said that fowl, which has no milk, is exempted from the biblical prohibition." We observe that this custom was also practised in the locality of Rabbi Yehudah ben Bathyra, during the period of Rabbi's presidency, about one hundred years later than Rabbi Yose ha-Gelili.[215]

---

[212] In *Mishneh Torah, Hilkhot Ma'akhalot Asurot* 9: 4, Maimonides asserts that eating fowl with milk is a rabbinic prohibition, but his commentators have a problem substantiating this assertion from any talmudic source.

[213] See above at n. 204.

[214] This was a Tanna who lived in the period of Rabbi the Patriarch, but he is usually quoted in the Babylonian Talmud without the title Rabbi.

[215] Rabbi Yose ha-Gelili was a Tanna of the second generation, active in Yabneh, a contemporary of Rabbi Tarfon (tMikva'ot 7: 11) and a disputant with Rabbi Aqiba on many occasions. I. M. Ta-Shma declares that Rabbi Yose apparently died before the Bar Kokhba War (*Encyclopedia Judaica*, s.v. "Yose Ha-gelili"). Hence we must assume that he was active around the turn of the first century, and Rabbi was active around 200 C. E.

We may now summarize the main elements of this complex exposition. The divergent halakhot and tortuous exegetical endeavours applied by the Sages to extend the simple and clear humanitarian biblical decree suggest that each of the cited individuals had his own perception of the extent of the rule. We have noted, for instance, that one dictum interpreted the repetition of the command as allowing the scope of the rule to be extended, whereas another deemed the redundancy to imply just the opposite. We could speculate on the personal philosophy that induced each Tanna to generate his particular decision; it is, however, to be emphasized that each utilized hermeneutics to justify his opinion rather than to derive it. We observe that with respect to the extension of the prohibition to cattle (sheep could be considered included with goats), the exegesis is uncomplicated and the consequences generally accepted. This extension could also be rationally defended; the same compassion is raised for the calf of a cow and the lamb of a sheep as for the kid of a goat. The exclusion of fowl from the prohibition can also be defended rationally; it is an impossible occurrence, as the fowl has no milk. The legal essence of fowl is also in a "gray zone" between animals and fish with respect to other ritual laws.[216] Nor do fowl carry their offspring within their bodies,

---

[216] There is an explicit biblical decree prohibiting the eating of the blood of fowl. We read in Lev 7: 26: כל דם לא תאכלו בכל מושבתיכם לעוף ולבהמה "And wherever you live you must not eat the blood of any bird and animal." A baraita cited in bKeritot 20b concludes that from the phrase כל דם "all blood" we would assume דם חגבים דם דגים הכל בכלל "[the prohibition] also includes the blood of fish and locusts"; therefore Scripture explicitly specifies "bird and animal."

With respect to the precept of ritual slaughter, the situation is different. From the simple understanding of Scripture, birds did not require ritual slaughtering; this is also substantiated in Lev 1: 15, which states, with respect to sacrifices, that the priests is to wring off the bird's head. Yet we read in mHullin 2: 1: השוחט אחד בעוף ושנים בבהמה שחיטתו כשרה "If one slaughters [and cuts] one [of the two pipes, the esophagus and the trachea] of a chicken, and two [both pipes] of an animal, his slaughter is ritually appropriate." Here there is a clear difference between the requirements for fowl and those for animals. The Gemara in bHullin 27b deliberates on this distinction. It begins by quoting Lev 11: 46: זאת תורת הבהמה והעוף "[It is written] 'These are the regulations concerning animals and birds,'" and then goes on: באיזו תורה שוותה בהמה לעוף ועוף לבהמה לומר לך מה בהמה בשחיטה אף עוף בשחיטה אי מה להלן ברוב שנים אף כאן ברוב שנים ת״ל זאת "In which law was the animal compared to the bird and the bird to the animal? This is to tell us that just as an animal must be ritually slaughtered, so must a bird. Would we deduce that just as for the animal more than half of the two pipes must be cut, so it must be for the bird? [No] the term זאת comes to teach us [an exception]: only the animal [requires the cutting of both pipes]." Bar Qappara establishes a connection to fish: תני בר קפרא זאת תורת הבהמה והעוף הטיל הכתוב לעוף בין בהמה לדגים לחייבו בשני סימנין אי אפשר שכבר הוקש לדגים לפוטרו בלא כלום אי אפשר שכבר הוקש לבהמה הא כיצד הכשרו בסימן אחד "[It is

---

written] 'These are the regulations concerning animals and birds [Lev 11: 46]'; Scripture has cast the bird between animals and fish [as we shall see later]. Therefore one cannot require the cutting of two pipes because it is compared to fish, and one cannot altogether dispense with it in ritual slaughter because it is compared to animals, so what can we do? We require the cutting of one pipe." There follows the question: How do we know that fish do not require ritual slaughter, and the answer: הצאן ובקר ישחט להם אם את כל דגי הים יאסף להם באסיפה בעלמא סגי להו "[It is written in Num 11: 22] '...if flocks and herds were slaughtered for them...if all the fish in the sea were caught for them.' [We observe that for animals, slaughter is required, whereas] for the fish one only has to gather them." There follows another rhetorical question: ויאספו את השליו הכי נמי דלאו בשחיטה "[It is written] 'they gathered quail [Num 11: 32]' and here the same term 'to gather' is used, and that would indicate that there is no requirement for the slaughter of birds"; והא אמרת לפוטרו בולא כלום אי אפשר שכבר הוקש לבהמה "but you stated before that one cannot altogether dispense with it in ritual slaughter because it is compared to animals?" The answer is given founded upon a textual analysis: התם לא כתיבא אסיפה במקום שחיטה דאחריני הכא כתיבא אסיפה במקום שחיטה דאחריני "There [in the passage dealing with quail] the term 'to gather' is not written as a contrast to the slaughter of the others [flocks and herds; the passage thus speaks only of gathering and does not exclude the possibility that the quail were slaughtered afterwards], but with respect to the fish, the term 'to gather' is written in contrast to the other animals that do require ritual slaughtering." These passages substantiate the rabbinic positioning of fowl between animals and fish. I suggest that there is a further explanation for this classification, founded upon a "biological" distinction between the three types. The pattern seems similar to what I have argued above regarding the attribution of sensitive feelings to humans, domesticated animals, wild beasts and fowl: דרש עובר גלילאה בהמה שנבראת מן היבשה הכשרה בשני סימנים דגים שנבראו מן המים הכשירן בולא כלום עוף שנברא מן הרקק הכשרו בסימן אחד אמר רב שמואל קפוטקאה תדע שהרי עופות יש להן קשקשת ברגליהם כדגים "Ober of Galilee interpreted: An animal created from the land [as is written in Gen 1: 24: תוצא הארץ נפש חיה 'Let the land produce living creatures'] must be ritually slaughtered by the cutting of two pipes; fish, which were created from the water [as is written in Gen 1: 20: ישרצו המים 'Let the water team with living creatures'] do not require any ritual slaughter; fowl, created from mud [earth and water, as both the elements water and land appear in v. 20, ועוף יעופף על הארץ 'and let birds fly above the earth'] must be ritually slaughtered by the cutting of one pipe. Rav Samuel of Cappadocia [adds physical evidence to the abstract biblical text]: Look! The birds have scales on their legs similar to the fish." From the above deliberations we may deduce that the requirement for the ritual slaughter of birds was represented as a scriptural decree, through the use of various hermenuetics (similar to the way in which the prohibition against mixing all types of meat and milk was represented as a scriptural decree).

As with the issue of cooking and eating fowl with milk, there is a dispute as to whether the obligation to slaughter birds is a Torah precept or a rabbinic edict; again, the concern was likely the making of a "fence," a preventative measure, around a biblical decree. We have read above Bar Qappara's dictum that fowl must be slaughtered because הטיל הכתוב לעוף בין בהמה לדגים "Scripture has cast the bird between animals and fish"; hence it is a Torah precept. (Maimonides, in *Mishneh Torah*, *Hilkhot Shehitah* 1: 1, declares explicitly: מצות עשה שישחוט מי שירצה

which would create a sentimental and compassionate relationship between the mother and its progeny, as with mammals. The inclusion or exclusion of wild beasts might similarly be the result of different judgments

לאכול בשר בהמה חיה ועוף ואחר כך יאכל "It is a Torah precept that one who wants to eat meat of domesticated animals, wild beasts, and fowl must first ritually slaughter them and then he may eat"). On the other hand, we read in bHullin 27b, and in other occurrences: אמר רב יהודה משום ר׳ יצחק בן פנחס אין שחיטה לעוף מן התורה "Rav Yehudah said in the name of Rabbi Isaac ben Pinhas: The slaughtering of fowl is not a Torah precept." The same point is made in yNazir 4: 6, 53c, though somewhat more elusively: אין שחיטת העוף מחוורת מדברי תורה "The [obligation] to [ritually] slaughter fowl does not clearly result from the Torah's words." In this case too, just as with respect to the consumption of fowl and milk, I speculate that those Sages who declared the rule to be a Torah precept wanted to ensure its observance by the people. The fact that the dispute was still extant at the time of Rav Yehudah, an Amora, in the name of a late Tanna, indicates that the issue was not yet finally settled at that late period.

As to birds sacrificed as sin offerings, Scripture does not indicate explicitly what is done with the bird after the sprinkling of its blood on the altar (Lev 5: 9), but one may assume that it was eaten by the priest like every other individual sin offering. In mZevahim 6: 4 and 7 this is stated explicitly: חטאת העוף כיצד היה נעשית...ואין למזבח אלא דמה וכולה לכהנים "How was the sin offering of a bird performed... the altar does not receive anything other than its blood, and all [the offering] belongs to the priests." Mishnah 7 specifies that the priests eat the offering: אחד חטאת העוף ואחד עולת העוף שמלקן ושמיצה את דמן לאכול דבר שדרכו לאכול ולהקטיר דבר שדרכו להקטיר "With respect to the sin offering of a bird and the holocaust offering of a bird, after [its head] is wrung off, what is regularly eaten [the sin offering] is eaten and what is regularly burnt [the holocaust] is burnt." Thus the priests may eat the bird of the sin offering killed in a manner that would make it unfit to be eaten by a layman; as far as I know, this would be the only occasion on which a priest is allowed to eat a נבלה, a carcass of a dead animal, or any other ritually unfit food. The specific biblical prohibition in Lev 7: 26 against eating the blood of fowl, cited above, was decreed in reference to the offerings, because the blood belongs to the altar, as we read in Lev 17: 11: כי נפש הבשר בדם הוא ואני נתתיו לכם על המזבח לכפר על נפשתיכם "For the life of a creature is in its blood, and I have given it to you to make atonement for yourself on the altar." We observe that the fat of the animals that are offered on the altar cannot be eaten, whereas the fat of beasts that are unfit for the altar can be eaten. We read in Lev 7: 23: כל חלב שור וכשב ועז לא תאכלו "Do not eat any of the fat of cattle, sheep or goats," with the reason given in the succeeding v. 25: כי כל אכל חלב מן הבהמה אשר יקריב ממנה אשה לה׳ "Anyone who eats the fat of an animal from which an offering by fire may be made to the Lord...." In this case, even the Sages had to admit that it is permitted to eat the fat of wild beasts. We read in bKeritot 4a: אי לא כתיב שור וכשב ועז ה״א אפילו חלב חיה במשמע להכי כתב שור כשב ועז למימרא דחלב שור וכשב ועז הוא דאסור אבל דחיה שרי "If Scripture had not listed 'cattle, sheep or goats' [in the above-cited verse] we would have assumed that the fat of wild beasts is also prohibited [to eat]; therefore the itemization teaches us that [only] the fat of cattle, sheep or goats is prohibited but that of wild beasts is permitted."

regarding their nature; one Tanna may have contemplated that wild beasts have no subtle feelings, or that humans are not obliged to have compassion for them as they are for the domesticated animals, while another may have considered all mammals as possessing the same feelings and therefore deserving of the same compassionate treatment. These extensions could therefore be deemed as logically included within the biblical command.

The feebleness of the exegesis is, however, evident in the extension of the prohibition to other types of milk, not associated with the mother and its brood.[217] I would speculate that the Sages were well aware that that extension was not intended in the biblical command, but decided nevertheless to bestow upon it a Torah authority in order to ensure its acceptance by the people. We have seen that in at least two communities the prohibition against eating fowl with milk was not observed by scholarly people[218] for a long time after its proclamation, and we can assume that the people were not pleased at having to miss the pleasure of eating meat with cheese, the case portrayed in the Mishnah.[219] There is

---

[217] It seems that the Sages were not concerned with the biblical narrative in Gen 18: 8: ויקח חמאה וחלב ובן הבקר אשר עשה ויתן לפניהם והוא עמד עליהם תחת העץ ויאכלו "He then brought some curds and milk and the calf that had been prepared, and set these before them. While they ate he stood near them under a tree." This verse suggests that Abraham offered the angels a forbidden meal, and they ate it. I can find nothing in the talmudic literature that reflects any amazement at this situation. A homily in bBava Metzi'a 86b, which directs people to behave according to the ways of the society that surrounds them, quotes as evidence the fact that the angels ate when Abraham offered them a meal. The question is posed: 'How is that possible [since angels do not eat]?" The answer is: אלא אימא נראו כמי שאכלו ושתו "Say rather that they gave the impression of eating and drinking." The angels therefore did not transgress, since they did not really eat. The question still remains as to how Abraham dared to offer a forbidden meal to his guests. The solution of a later Rabbi, the Hatam Sofer, is found in his Responsa: חתם סופר חלק ב (יו"ד) סימן יט ד"ה ואל תשיבני. It is based on a homily in bBava Metzi'a 86b, which states that the angels were angry with Abraham, asking: וכי בערביים חשדתנו "Why did you take us for Arabs?" The Hatam Sofer declared that since Abraham considered the angels to be Arabs, and Arabs may eat meat with milk, he could offer them meat and milk products together at the meal. He could not cook them together, but this is not alleged in Scripture. The midrashim in Pesiqta Rabbati, Pesiqta d'Rav Kanaha and Tanhuma, mentioned in n. 199, allege that God did reproach the angels for their consumption of meat and milk at Abraham's meal. It is recounted that the angels tried to prevent God from taking the Torah down from heaven and giving it to the Israelites. God censured them for their wrongdoing, and because they could not instantly come up with a reasonable excuse, He took advantage of this interval and gave the Torah to the Israelites.

[218] We must assume that the Tanna Levi would not have gone to take part in the feast of an unlearned patron, an עם הארץ.

[219] In addition to the above-cited passage from mHullin 8:1, all the casuistic decrees

other talmudic evidence attesting that particular practices of certain Sages were carried on despite being contrary to halakhah, based on the great reverence accorded the Sage during his lifetime;[220] here, however, we

relating to serving meat and milk refer to meat with cheese. The first part of mishnah 1 reads: ואסור להעלות עם הגבינה על השלחן "...and one must not put [meat] together with cheese on the table"; in mishnah 2 we read: צורר אדם בשר וגבינה במטפחת אחת "A person may place meat and cheese in one scarf," and שני אכסנאין אוכלין על שלחן אחד זה בשר וזה גבינה "two guests may eat at one table, with one [eating] meat and the other cheese." In mishnah 3, we read: המעלה את העוף עם הגבינה על השלחן אינו עובר בלא תעשה "One who puts fowl with cheese on the table does not transgress a biblical command." The prohibitions against cooking are illustrated with the cooking of meat and milk, while the restrictions on eating portray the consumption of meat and cheese. The latter was evidently a regular habit, and thus difficult to uproot.

220 We read in bNiddah 7b: כל ימיו של רבי אליעזר היו עושין כרבי יהושע לאחר פטירתו של רבי אליעזר החזיר רבי יהושע את הדבר ליושנו "During Rabbi Eliezer's lifetime, they practised according to Rabbi Yehoshua's declaration; after Rabbi Eliezer's death, Rabbi Yehoshua reversed the halakhah to its previous status [and re-established the halakhah according to Rabbi Eliezer]." This is an entangled story and I need not elaborate upon it here (see the further discussion in chap. 3, pp. 197-8). For our purpose, it suffices to quote Rabbi Yehoshua's motive for his decision: ומשום כבודו דר"א לא מצינן מחינן בהו "and because of the reverence for Rabbi Eliezer, we could not protest against those who acted according to Rabbi Eliezer's opinion." In tTa'anit 2: 5, we read another narrative concerning the reverence accorded a Tanna during his lifetime. Rabbi Yehoshua wanted to reverse a decision of Rabban Gamaliel concerning fasts: כל זמן שהיה רבן גמליאל קיים היתה הלכה נוהגת כדבריו לאחר מיתתו של רבן גמליאל בקש ר' יהושע לבטל את דבריו "During the lifetime of Rabban Gamaliel, the halakhah was [practised] according to his declaration. After his death, Rabbi Yehoshua intended to revoke his declaration." The narrative records an opposition to Rabbi Yehoshua's intent; in the end the halakhah was established according to Rabban Gamaliel's declaration. We must distinguish, however, between this narrative and our case regarding the custom of mixing fowl and milk. In the Tosefta narrative, the circumstances were entirely different. Rabban Gamaliel the Patriarch instituted a rule concerning fasting on Hanukkah, when this holiday occurs during a fast proclaimed for an extended period, such as 30 days. Although one does not proclaim *a priori* a fast day on Hanukkah, Rabban Gamaliel decided that one does not interrupt an extended fast period because of the holiday. His opinion was accepted because he was the Patriarch, as we observe from the argument of Rabbi Yohanan ben Nuri, whose opposition to Rabbi Yehoshua's intention is recorded at length in bEruvin 41a: חזי אנא בתר רישא גופא אזיל כל זמן שהיה רבן גמליאל קיים היתה הלכה נוהגת כדבריו עכשיו שמת בקשתם לבטל את דבריו אמ' ר' יהושע אנו שומעין לך נקבעה הלכה כדברי רבן גמליאל ולא עירער אדם על דבריו "I see that the body follows its head; during Rabban Gamaliel's lifetime, we have established the halakhah as he declared, and now after his death, you wish to repeal it. Rabbi Yehoshua said: We listen to you; the halakhah was established according to Rabban Gamaliel and nobody objected to it." There is no explicit record of a dispute against Rabban Gamaliel's order, and only after his death did Rabbi Yehoshua decide

encounter a dissident practice in two localities, founded in one case upon a pronouncement of Rabbi Yose ha-Gelili, a century after his death,[221] and in the other case, on a pronouncement of his contemporary, Rabbi Yehudah ben Bathyra. It is possible that, because of an entrenched habit of eating meat with cheese, the Sages contemplated that they must also extend the biblical command to include all types and sources of milk, in order to ensure its observance. Having done so, they could then further extend the prohibition and establish a "fence" around the biblical command by also forbidding the cooking and consumption of fowl and milk, as a rabbinic decree. They succeeded in creating a feeling of repugnance in Jewish society toward any mixture of meat and milk, in contrast to the previously common predilection for the consumption of meat and cheese.

I believe that this case study offers an excellent illustration of the rabbinic method and creative halakhic process, founded upon the practical and philosophical preconceptions of each Sage, and effected through an elaborate hermeneutic method. In addition to our observation of rabbinic decision-making, we may also derive some insight into the history of rabbinic halakhah. The style of the Mekilta, for instance, suggests that the deliberations there concerned earlier rabbinic decrees, justified by later homilies. The discussions cited are introduced by the formula: "How do we know?" This gives the impression that the extension of the prohibition of meat and milk was already a familiar fact of daily life, and the inquiry had to do solely with finding scriptural support. Further, we have observed that even in Rabbi's time, the issue of eating fowl and milk was not yet settled, and this indicates that there was no previous tradition on that specific situation. If there were such a tradition, Rabbi Yose ha-Gelili and his followers would not have transgressed it.

We encounter on this issue of halakhic development an odd narrative in bHullin 110a: "Rab happened to be in Tatlefush when he overheard a woman saying to her friend: How much milk does one need to cook a quarter of meat? So he said: Don't they know the halakhah that it is forbidden [to cook or eat] meat with milk? [Therefore] he remained [in the town] and prohibited even the eating of the udder [which it is forbidden to eat without first squeezing out its liquid]." Rab's motivation to decree stricter rules when the basic ones were not obeyed may appear strange to

---

to change the established custom. In our case, the opinions of Rabbi Yose ha-Gelili and Rabbi Yehudah ben Bathyra were minority statements, patently in opposition to the established halakhah; their opinions nevertheless subsisted for a long period.

[221] Jack N. Lightstone, *Yose the Galilean*, p. 111, notes that in mHullin 8: 1 Rabbi Yose appears to contradict a halakhah accepted by both the House of Hillel and the House of Shammai. Lightstone speculates that views and statements of other Sages were "sometimes pseudonymously attributed to the Houses." Yose could thus formally contradict another Tanna's dictum.

our contemporary minds, but seems to concur with the rabbinic logic.[222] Rashi, well aware of this course of thought, confirms it explicitly: "He saw that they were neglecting the prohibition of meat and milk and made it stricter."[223] This passage indicates that even at such a late stage of rabbinic domination of the interpretation of the Torah laws,[224] this expanded rule was not yet fully integrated into Jewish society.[225] Yet the form of Rab's astonishment suggests his innermost, probably deeply hidden, cognition that the overall prohibition of meat and milk was a rabbinic rule and not a Torah precept. He utilized the term לא גמירי, which implies a halakhah founded upon tradition, as in the phrase הלכתא גמירי (and in the name גמרא for the Talmud[226]). It also seems that the Alexandrian Jews at the time of Philo did not know, or did not observe, all the rabbinic extensions to the scriptural law.[227] The above-cited talmudic narrative and Philo's

---

[222] As in other issues, this principle was not upheld rigidly and universally, and there is a contrasting opinion. We read in bAvodah Zarah 36a that one may revoke a decree, even one of the eighteen edicts (see further chap. 3, nn. 21-3 and related text), if the prohibition was not diffused among the majority of Israelites. That is, when a restriction was not accepted by all Israelites, there is an implication that it was wrongly promulgated in the first instance and should be annulled. Another dictum in ARN, Recension A, chap. 1, states that if one extends the confines of a rule, they cannot be complied with (see citation, chap.4, n. 118 and related text).

[223] Rashi acquired this explanation from a declaration in bBetzah 2b: שבת דחמירא ולא אתי לזלזולי בה סתם לן כרבי שמעון דמיקל יום טוב דקיל ואתי לזלזולי ביה סתם לן כרבי יהודה דמחמיר "[The Gemara questions Rabbi's apparent inconsistency: in mShabbat 24: 4, he presented the lenient declaration as an anonymous pronouncement, thus indicating his preference for it, while in a similar occurrence in mBetzah 4: 3 he presented the stricter opinion as anonymous]. [A.] Regarding the laws of the Sabbath that are perceived as severe and not in danger of slack observance, he decided in favour of Rabbi Simeon's lenient opinion, but with respect to the laws of the holidays, deemed lenient and in danger of being neglected, he decided to establish the halakhah in the stricter manner, according to Rabbi Yehudah."

[224] Rab (beginning of the third century C.E.) flourished about one hundred years later than Rabbi Yose ha-Gelili (beginning of the second century C.E.). We have seen that this early Tanna opposed the rabbinic extension of the milk-meat prohibition to fowl. Hence the interdiction against other types of meat with milk must have been successfully established in rabbinic circles at that time; yet a hundred years later it was still not practised among the masses in Babylon. This also demonstrates that the central Jewish authority in Babylon, headed by the Exilarch, did not have sufficient hegemony to impose its legal decisions on the masses.

[225] On this topic see M. Goodman, *Roman Galilee*, p. 102 and G. Stemberger, "Judentums," p. 99, n. 45.

[226] See chap. 1, nn. 23 and 108, regarding this term.

[227] Philo writes in *Virtues* 144, in his explanation of the biblical command against cooking a kid in the milk of its mother: εἰ τιςἐν γάλακτι κρέα συνέψειν ἀξιοῖ μὴ σὺν ὠμότητι χωρὶς δὲ ἀσεβείας ἑψέτω "If indeed anyone thinks it good to boil

advice to his community[228] lead us to consider the historical dilemma: did the masses obey the punctilious and often strict rabbinic legislation, or did the rabbinic rules have more of a theoretical than a practical impact on the daily life of Jewish society in their period? This is an interesting question[229] with relevance to modern issues; it is not, however, within the frame of our investigation, and requires a detailed and separate study. The question is relevant, nonetheless, to my postulate concerning the pluralism of the halakhic environment and consequent diversity of custom and behaviour in pre-70 Judaism.

From this and similar examples,[230] we may hypothesize that similar conditions prevailed with respect to other rabbinic decrees.[231] Induced by

---

flesh in milk, let him do so without cruelty and keeping clear of impiety." He goes on to say that milk is abundantly available; one should not show cruelty by boiling the kid in its mother's milk, but he has no objection to eating meat boiled in the milk of another animal, and one must assume that this was the custom and tradition in Egypt in the pre-70 period.

228 See also other instances mentioned in the study, such as mixing chicken with milk, the cutting of wood on Sabbath to forge an iron tool for circumcision, the excommunication of Rabbi Eleazar ben Hanokh who did not accept the rabbinic concept of טהרת ידים, and the precept of cleaning the hands (see chap. 4, n. 133).

229 M. Goodman, *Roman Galilee*, pp. 102 ff., deliberates on a different aspect of this issue. He refers to the disregard by the עמי הארץ of principal laws such as *kil'ayim*, tithes, purity, and the sabbatical year. In contrast, my interest is in that segment of the Jewish people who did indeed perform these laws; my question is whether they acted in full compliance with all the minutiae of the rabbinic laws, or whether these intricate rules were only theoretical, or eventually followed only by a scant and insignificant minority. Goodman states, for example, on p. 103, that the Sabbath laws were not ignored even by the עמי הארץ. My question would be whether the general masses simply avoided "real" work on Sabbath, as they understood it, such as plowing, reaping, and making fire, or whether they followed all the rabbinic accretions derived from the thirty-nine principal prohibited works. If we presume the authenticity of such narratives as yHagigah 2: 2, 78a, concerning the man who rode a horse on Sabbath, or Matt 12: 1 - 8 concerning Jesus' disciples who plucked grain on Sabbath, it would appear that the masses did not obey the rabbinic extensions of the Sabbath laws.

230 For instance, the dispute as to whether the ritual slaughter of birds is a Torah precept (see n. 216).

231 There is a record of a similar occurrence, though without exact dates, as in our subject case. We have noted above (pp. 155-6) the dispute in bShabbat 21b between Beit Shammai and Beit Hillel regarding the manner of kindling the Hanukkah lights. One opinion required kindling all eight lights on the first day and reducing their number by one each day, while the other required kindling one light on the first day and increasing the lights by one each day to reach the maximum number of eight. The principal contenders did not hint at the reasons behind their contrasting decisions; the Amoraim attempted to detect their motives and, as is common, proposed various explanations. But the most interesting fact is the following declaration: רבה בר בר חנה אמר רבי יוחנן שני זקנים היו בצידן אחד עשה כבית שמאי ואחד עשה

the motive to secure the core of the laws, the Sages and their later followers steadily widened the "fence" around the Torah, as a precaution against the violation of its essential nucleus. They also decreed other new rules and regulations deemed advantageous with respect to many aspects of Jewish life, and appropriate to contemporary circumstances. The Tannaim, confident in their authority, did not consider it imperative to divulge their reasons; the Amoraim attempted to justify their dicta by a variety of hermeneutics, and their later followers vindicated their decisions by appropriate interpretations of the halakhic expositions of their predecessors.

כדברי בית הלל "Rabba bar bar Hana said in the name of Rabbi Yohanan that there were two elders in Sidon, one [of whom] practised according to Beit Shammai and the other according to Beit Hillel." We have no precise dates as to when the era of Beit Shammai ended, but we know that they were considered to be part of the tannaitic group; Rabbi Yohanan was an Amora, though from the earliest generation. Though a certain period of time must have elapsed between the two periods, we observe that the dispute was still not settled and both styles of kindling the lights were still performed.

3. Is There a System in Rabbinic Decision-Making?

3.1 The Use of the Majority Rule

The Mishnah,[1] the first organized rabbinic collection of laws, often quotes opposing halakhot, but seldom declares explicitly which opinion is decisive. Rabbi, the presumed redactor of Mishnah, merely hints at his preferred opinion by attributing it to חכמים "the Sages," or declaring it anonymously.[2] This lack of an outright declaration not only indicates, in my opinion, Rabbi's hesitancy in pronouncing his opinion *ex cathedra*,[3] but also reveals that there was no rigid system for categorically determining the halakhah. Later Sages continued this type of qualified, non-categorical determination, as we shall observe in the analysis of talmudic citations. Nor is there evidence in the Mishnah that decisions were invariably decided according to the majority opinion. The explicit maxim "It is obvious! [In a dispute] between one individual and many,

---

1 In the Gemara, the Amoraim frequently attempt to reveal the rules for the establishment of the halakhah, but nothing similar to this appears in the Mishnah. The Tosefta shows more of a tendency to influence the establishment of halakhah through the use of the expression: נראין דברי ר׳ "the utterances of Rabbi X seem to us acceptable."

2 As. E. E. Urbach states, חכמים, p. 137: שכן הכניס רבי גם את דעותיו למשנה וגם הכריע "...since Rabbi inserted his views in the Mishnah and also decided [the halakhah in a dispute]." See also J. Neusner, "Attributions," p. 141. In this matter I would agree with Neusner's statement that an anonymous declaration "is deemed to speak for a community and to represent, and contribute to, the consensus of that community." I do not agree that the identification of an individual Sage indicates schism (see chap. 4, n. 19).

3 A. Goldberg, "דרכו של רבי יהודה הנשיא בסידור המשנה," p. 260, argues that Rabbi did not attempt to fix the halakhah; rather, his goal was solely the organization of a collection of halakhic declarations. His primary motive was pedagogic - that is, the editing of the halakhot in such a way as to facilitate their oral recital and transmission. On this point Goldberg concurs with Ch. Albeck (מבוא למשנה, pp. 108 - 109), who asserts that Rabbi did not consider himself competent to choose the correct halakhah from among the declarations of earlier Sages. Therefore, according to Albeck, Rabbi wanted to collect and edit all halakhic pronouncements to ensure their preservation. See also J. Neusner, *Purities, Part XXI*, p. 299, who writes that the immediate purpose of the Mishnah's formalization was to facilitate memorization.

the halakhah is according to the many," that appears often in the Gemara, is quoted only once,[4] and indirectly, in the Mishnah: "Why does one mention the opinion of the individual among [those of] the majority, since the halakhah is according to the majority [mEduyyot 1: 5]?"[5] One may

---

4 There is a certain confusion between the concept of majority rule as it relates to a decision of a court in a concrete case, and as it relates to abstract academic deliberations concerning how the correct halakhah should be established. The phrase אחרי רבים להטות "follow the many" in Exod 23: 2 (this is a word-for-word translation, without consideration of the perplexing context, which has provoked many interpretations; my translation follows the rabbinic interpretation) refers to judicial circumstances, and is used in mSanhedrin 1: 6 precisely with respect to that particular purpose. The verse is used as the foundation for a rule that one requires a majority of one vote to acquit a defendant, but a majority of two to convict. This is the sole exegetical treatment of this verse in the Mishnah. The application of this phrase to judicial occurrences also appears in some Toseftot, Mekilta d'Rabbi Simeon bar Yohai and in the Gemara. On the other hand, it also appears in connection with discussions between Rabban Gamaliel and Rabbi Aqiba, apparently regarding abstract halakhic issues rather than concrete cases. There is a definite difference in the style of quotation of the biblical verse as between the citations relating to judicial issues and those referring to the abstract halakhic ones. In those of the first kind, the biblical verse is explicitly cited as justification, and introduced with expressions such as: למה נאמר, הואיל ואמרה תורה, הוסיף עליהן הכתוב "Why does it say," "since the Torah said so," " Scripture added." In the second type of occurrence we read: אמ' לו למדתנו אחרי רבים להטות אע"פ שאתה או' כך וחבירך או' כך הלכה כדברי המרובין "He said to him, you have taught us to follow the majority; although you say one thing and your colleagues say another, the halakhah is as the majority [maintains]." The identical words of the verse are mentioned, but not attributed to Scripture; they are related to an instruction of the teacher. We thus observe the weakness of this attempt to link the majority rule for halakhic decisions to a scriptural origin.

5 With respect to this point, we may note the sequence of citations, questions and answers in mEduyyot chapter 1. The style and structure of these mishnayot already indicate the weakness and vagueness of the issues surrounding the majority rule. Moreover, tEduyyot 1: 2 has a different text that lends itself to an interpretation distinct from that suggested by the text of the mishnah. It is therefore no wonder that the traditional commentators offer divergent interpretations of these questions and answers. They obviously do not attempt to search for an entirely different methodology, or put in question the attempt of the Mishnah to reconcile the various candid and logical questions within the framework of traditional concepts and assumptions.

Following the first three mishnayot of Eduyyot chapter 1, which quote disputes between Shammai and Hillel with the declaration that the halakhah is according to neither, mishnah 4 asks, appropriately, why the rejected opinions were cited at all: ולמה מזכירין את דברי שמאי והלל לבטלה? An answer is given to the question in mishnah 4, which is not particularly straightforward: שהרי אבות העולם לא עמדו על דבריהם "[The rejected opinions are cited to teach one not to insist upon his own opinion] since the 'fathers of the [Torah] world' did not insist upon their viewpoints." This might hint that in the cited disputes between Shammai and Hillel, each had renounced their previous statements; there is, however, no such express

deduce, therefore, that the redactor of the Mishnah deemed it necessary to include such conflicting statements.[6]

---

indication. This mishnaic sequence also shows noticeable stylistic divergences. In the first two mishnayot, there is no indication as to why the opinions of both Shammai and Hillel were rejected; in mishnah 3, in contrast, the repudiation of their statements is justified by a tradition, and bolstered by the phrase: וקימו החכמים את דבריהם "And the Sages enacted their declarations," that is, they pronounced the halakhah according to the testimony of the weavers. The traditional commentators differ in their interpretations of this phrase. Tosefta is more explicit here and declares in 1: 2: מה אבות העולם לא עמדו על דבריהם במקום שמועה "The fathers of the world did not insist on their opinion where there was a [conflicting] tradition," thus indicating that Hillel and Shammai actually renounced their opinions, as well as the reason for the abnegation of their former views. While Tosefta clarifies the circumstances of the dispute in mishnah 3, however, it still leaves us in limbo regarding the questions raised about mishnayot 1 and 2.

In mishnah 5 there then appears the puzzling question: ולמה מזכירין דברי היחיד בין המרובין הואיל ואין הלכה אלא כדברי המרובין "Why are the [rejected] declarations of the individual mentioned [in the Mishnah] among the declarations of the majority, since the halakhah follows the majority?" In fact, no such disputes appear antecedently, and the following mishnayot cite disputes between Beit Shammai and Beit Hillel, not disagreements between an individual and the majority. We are not informed as to which of the two schools had a majority, or how the halakhah was to be decided in disputes between two groups, as opposed to the case of an individual versus a group. Again, the answer is vague: שאם יראה בית דין את דברי היחיד ויסמוך עליו "If a court learns the declaration of the individual they might rely on it." This element of the answer makes no sense at all. It gives the impression that the court's awareness of such an individual opinion would provoke a negative, undesirable effect; in that case the logical solution would be to eliminate it from the legal codex, and not to record it in the codex to ensure its perpetuity. Further, the following subordinate clause, expressing cause with the relative pronoun ש, does not indicate a logical connection with the prior clause, and does not add to the entire response any perceptible comprehensibility. In mishnah 6, Rabbi Yehudah asks the same question posed in the antecedent mishnah, but starts his question with the phrase אם כן "if so," implying that he refers to the previous answer and indicating his disapprobation of it. Maimonides, in his comments to this mishnah, understands that Rabbi Yehudah's question refers to the answer of mishnah 5, but Albeck alleges that he refers to the original statement of mishnah 4, and asks the same question as that posed in mishnah 5. The traditional commentators created diversified and complex structures to impose some sense on these answers. It is not within the scope of this study to extend our deliberations on this specific issue; I wished merely to demonstrate the shortcomings of the answers proffered within the confines of traditional concepts. J. Roth, *Halakhic Process,* pp. 57 ff. elaborates on the complex issue of mEduyyot 1: 4 - 6 as well as on the different manuscripts. He deduces as the legal consequence of these mishnayot that it remained within the authority of the arbiter to decide a case according to the opinion of an individual, even if it were otherwise rejected according to the maxim that the halakhah is to be fixed according to the opinion of the majority.

6 See the next chapter for a hypothesis regarding this extraordinary preservation of rejected opinions.

The maxim "It is obvious! [In a dispute] between one individual and many, the halakhah is according to the many" is in itself a fiction.[7] In a great number of occurrences the Gemara deliberates on a mishnah in which there is a dispute between one Tanna and others referred to with the phrase חכמים אומרים "the Sages say." The Gemara asks: מאן תנא (in the Y.T.) or מאן חכמים (in the B.T.) "Whose opinion is stated under the term חכמים?"[8] The Amoraim were aware that this phrase in fact reflected the opinion of one particular Tanna, and that Rabbi, who thought this opinion to be the correct halakhah, had therefore quoted it in the name of the "many" to give it the benefit of the rule of the majority.[9] For the same

7 G. Alon, *The Jews*, vol. 2, p. 468, confirms a change in this conduct after the Temple's destruction, as I postulate in section 4.2.2.2. He writes: "Except for a few occurrences, the majority did not usually establish, by vote, one halakhah and impose their decision on the Sages and the people. In general, they allowed individual Sages to teach and act in their own way, according to their understanding and to the tradition they followed. The majority did not deprive the Sages and the people of their liberty, although they limited it somewhat after the Temple's destruction." I find in Alon's declaration a conclusive validation of the general elements of my thesis with respect to the pluralism of the tannaitic period, in its early stages. I believe, however, that I have independently substantiated my proposition with an array of talmudic citations. With respect to topics connected with the internal relations among the Sages, as reflected in rabbinic literature, and separate from political issues, I think we may rely upon Alon's conclusions. Cf. A. Oppenheimer, "Gedaliah Alon," p. 180, who also concludes, despite his criticism of Alon's political analysis, that it is legitimate to follow Alon's research into Jewish history in the period of the Mishnah and Talmudim, though also cautioning awareness of its weaknesses. See also C. Hezser, *Social Structure*, p. 245, for her criticisms concerning the issue of the majority rule.

8 I have come across a different interpretation of this phrase, namely: "Whose opinion has been stated by the חכמים?" This translation seems to have been conceived in order to avoid its simple meaning, which would put into question the principle of majority. It is used by the traditional commentator Rashi, who obviously would not admit such an "unorthodox" consequence. Why would Rabbi hide the identity of a Sage who disputed a declaration of another Sage, as disputes are explicitly mentioned on many other occasions? As we have noted above, Rabbi formulated the device of hiding the name, in order to establish halakhah as he conceived it, without declaring explicitly that it was his personal opinion. He used the סתם method for the same purpose.

9 We must nonetheless observe that sometimes Rabbi quoted an opinion conflicting with his own, in the name of חכמים "the many," thus admitting that the halakhah was to be established against his own opinion. We read, for example, in mMakkot 2:1: נשמט הברזל מקתו והרג רבי אומר אינו גולה וחכמים אומרים גולה מן העץ המתבקע רבי אומר גולה וחכמים אומרים אינו גולה "If [one's] ax slipped off its handle and killed [someone inadvertently], Rabbi says he does not have to go into exile [to the Cities of Refuge] and the Sages say he must. If [a person is inadvertently killed] by a piece of wood split off [during the felling of a tree], Rabbi says [the killer] must go into exile and the Sages say he does not have to." In this specific occurrence, we cannot suppose that Rabbi decided the halakhah against his

effect, Rabbi also used the device of quoting the preferred opinion anonymously,[10] giving the impression that it belonged to the majority, although the identity of the single Tanna was well known.[11] We read in yYevamot 4: 11, 6b: "Rabbi Simeon b. Laqish says: Every anonymous declaration in the Mishnah is [the opinion of] Rabbi Meir." In bSanhedrin 86a, a more extended declaration is quoted in the name of Rabbi Yohanan: "An anonymous [declaration in the] Mishnah is [the opinion of] Rabbi Meir; an anonymous [declaration in] Tosefta is Rabbi Nehemyah; an anonymous [declaration in] Sifra is Rabbi Yehudah; an anonymous [declaration in] Sifre is Rabbi Simeon; and all pronounced their declarations according to Rabbi Aqiba's opinion." In bShabbat 46a, and in many other passages in the B. T., there appears the question: "Did not Rabbi Yohanan say: The halakhah follows the anonymous pronouncement?" In the Y. T. this dictum is stated positively, as, for instance, in yPesahim 3: 3, 30b: "Wherever Rabbi taught a dispute in the Mishnah and then recorded [one of these opinions] as [an] anonymous [declaration], the halakhah follows the anonymous [declaration]." In yTa'anit 2: 13, 66a, the dictum is deduced by *a minori ad majorem* logic: "When Rabbi does not record a dispute but others do, and Rabbi records one opinion as anonymous, the halakhah certainly follows the anonymous declaration." But this statement of Rabbi Yohanan was not always upheld by other Amoraim[12] or invariably even by himself. Hence Rabbi's opinion

own opinion because of an existing tradition; the custom of rescuing oneself from the blood avenger by fleeing to a City of Refuge had not been in effect for a long time, and the ancient custom was certainly forgotten at that period. With respect to Rabbi's decisions on fixing the halakhah, see also C. Hezser, *Social Structure*, p. 241.

10 And a suitable maxim was established, as we read in bYevamot 42b: מחלוקת ואחר כך סתם הלכה כסתם "If we encounter [in a mishnah] first a dispute and then later [in another mishnah] an anonymous dictum [as one of the opinions in the dispute], the halakhah follows the opinion cited anonymously." Citations to the same effect are also found in Y. T., as will be seen in the succeeding text.

11 In the Y. T. such assertions are affirmed, without the question common in the B. T.; the Gemara simply declares מתניתא דרבי "the [anonymous declaration in the] Mishnah is [really the opinion] of Rabbi X."

12 E. E. Urbach, חכמים, pp. 45 ff. observes this circumstance, and substantiates it with a number of talmudic citations. He quotes occurrences in which the Mishnah's interpretation is altered from its simple definition, in order to reconcile Rabbi Yohanan's own affirmation with his maxim that the halakhah follows the anonymous utterance in the Mishnah. In other instances, a stratagem is applied of distinguishing between the anonymous statement of a single person and סתמא דרבים "the anonymous [statement] of many [bSanhedrin 34b]." In the Y. T. the same concept is expressed as: אבל ביחיד אצל חכמ׳ לא בדא הלכה כסתם "But in a dispute between a single Sage and anonymous Sages, the halakhah in this case does not follow the anonymous declaration" (Yevamot 4: 11, 6b).

on the halakhah, expressed through his device of anonymous citation, was also not always accepted.[13]

In some occurrences, Rabbi actually explained his resolution of the halakhah between two dissenting declarations, setting out the circumstances in which he sided with one or the other opinion. We read in tMo'ed Qatan 2: 2: "And likewise Rabbi Yehudah said: Those who return from overseas [during the half holidays] must not cut their hair and wash their clothes, while the Sages allow this. Rabbi said: Rabbi Yehudah's pronouncement seems to me reasonable [hence this should be the halakhah] when the person went on an unessential voyage, and the Sages' declaration [to allow these acts should be the halakhah] when he left for an essential cause."[14]

The Amoraim explicitly confirm this "editing" by Rabbi. We read in bHullin 85a: "Rabbi Hiyya son of Abba said in the name of Rabbi Yohanan: Rabbi sided with the opinion of Rabbi Meir on the prohibition against slaughtering a young animal and its mother on the same day,[15] and

---

13 E.E. Urbach, חכמים, p. 143 quotes a particular occurrence in which the anonymous statement conflicts with Rabbi Yehudah's utterance, and states: אמוראי ארץ ישראל תלמידיו של ר' יהודה הנשיא...לא התחשבו בסתימתו של ההלכה במשנה שלא כדעת ר' יהודה "Amoraim of Israel, Rabbi Yehudah the Patriarch's disciples ... did not acquiesce in his anonymous statement of the halakhah in the Mishnah, in conflict with Rabbi Yehudah's opinion." He quotes further examples and concludes on p. 150: מתוך מה שבררנו מתקבל שהכלל 'הלכה כסתם משנה' אינו בעל תוקף מחייב "From what we have clarified, it results that the rule 'the halakhah follows the anonymous utterance in the Mishnah' is not mandatory."

14 The Gemara in yMo'ed Qatan 3: 1, 81c, and bMo'ed Qatan 14a speculate on legitimate reasons for which the Sages would entitle him to wash his clothes and cut his hair during the half holiday, as stated in Tosefta, or to shave, as stated in mMo'ed Qatan 3: 1. It is interesting to note the different possibilities expressed in the various sources. The mishnah assumes a positive permission: מי שנשאל לחכם והותר "One who asked the consent of a Sage and received it [may shave]." The other three sources assume more negative circumstances. The Tosefta declares: שלא נטל רשות "He did not ask for permission"; the Y. T. indicates: ויצא שלא ברצון חכמים "He left against the will of the Sages"; and the B. T. states: שיצא שלא ברשות "He left without permission," an ambiguous expression, which may indicate that he did not ask for permission, or that he left against the explicit interdiction of the Sages.

15 The issue is more complex than it appears. The dispute between Rabbi Meir and Rabbi Simeon consists of a difference in conceptual views as to whether a disqualified slaughter is still deemed a slaughter, and all the precepts and prohibitions relating to the act of slaughter are therefore applicable. Rabbi Meir conceives that they are obligatory. Therefore, if one person slaughtered an animal dedicated for sacrifice, outside the Temple, and then slaughtered its offspring in the same day in the same circumstances, he is liable for excision for the first slaughter (for slaughtering a sacrificial animal outside the Temple precinct), and for thirty-nine lashes (for transgressing the prohibition to slaughter a sacrificial animal outside the Temple precinct). This Tanna maintains that the more severe punishment of excision does not

therefore he presented it [this opinion] as if it were a dictum of the Sages[16] [as a majority opinion, thus establishing the halakhah]. [He sided] with Rabbi Simeon on the command to cover the blood of a slaughtered animal, and presented it as if it were a dictum of the Sages."

There are some instances in which halakhah was in fact established by a majority vote. We read for example in mYadayim 4: 1: "On that day, they counted the votes and decided that a vessel to wash the feet, if it is of a size from two *login* to nine *login*, and is cracked [and no longer fit as a container], will become impure [when sat upon] as a chair [by a person impure with a discharge]. [The decision was taken in opposition to] Rabbi Aqiba who maintains the same rule for a vessel of any size."

Yet even in the case where a real majority decision might apply, there are no explicit regulations as to its practical application. Were votes taken in every case of a dispute? How was the vote taken? Who determined when to take the vote, so as to avoid an arbitrary decision made during a momentary absence of those Sages who maintained an opinion opposed to the majority? Was there an automatic provision for a recount of votes? Various rabbinic deliberations, in fact, demonstrate the problematic aspects of applying this majority rule. We read in yKetubbot 1: 8, 25d, a discussion concerning a dispute in the Mishnah between Rabban Gamaliel and Rabbi Eliezer on the one hand and Rabbi Yehoshua on the other:

> Rabbi Jacob bar Aha in the name of Rabbi Yoshiyyah said: The halakhah is as Rabban Gamaliel and Rabbi Eliezer [declared it], because they were two against

---

absolve him from the punishment of lashes, in contrast to capital punishment, which would discharge that punishment. For slaughtering the second animal, he is only liable for the punishment of lashes, for transgressing the prohibition of slaughtering the mother and its offspring at the same day. Although the slaughtering of the mother was a disqualified slaughter, he is nevertheless, according to Rabbi Meir, liable for slaughtering both animals on the same day. He is not, however, liable for excision for slaughtering an animal and its offspring on the same day. The slaughter of the offspring is a disqualified slaughter, because one is not allowed to offer an animal and its offspring on the same day; that is, the animal was already disqualified from its status as dedicated to sacrifice, because its mother was slaughtered at the same day. Therefore, this animal was no longer suitable to be offered as a sacrifice, and the slaughterer is not deemed to have transgressed the prohibition against offering a sacrifice outside the Temple precinct. He is, however, liable for lashes, for the transgression of slaughtering the mother and its offspring on the same day. Rabbi pronounced this edict in mHullin 5: 1, as Rabbi Meir's opinion in the name of the Sages, thus establishing it as the halakhah. In mHullin 6: 2, however, regarding the requirement to cover the blood of a slaughtered animal, he decided the halakhah according to Rabbi Simeon's principle that a disqualified slaughter is not deemed to be a legal slaughter. In such an occurrence, therefore, the relevant command to cover the blood is not obligatory. Other examples, brought in mishnayot 1 and 2, are yet more complex.

16 A similar occurrence is cited in chap. 2, n. 223. There the Gemara offers an explanation for Rabbi's apparently inconsistent decision.

> one. Rabbi Yose retorted: If you call it halakhah [a term that indicates a rule received by tradition] then why do you need a majority to establish it? [A tradition, in other words, does not need the support of a majority; the attestation of even one person as to its traditional origin would suffice to overrule the opinion of two.] And if you establish the rule as a result of the majority vote, then it is not a halakhah [if this means a rule received by tradition]. [Moreover] how would you decide if Rabbi Yohanan gave his opinion according to Rabbi Yehoshua's opinion; would the halakhah [no longer] be according to Rabban Gamaliel and Rabbi Eliezer, but according to Rabbi Yehoshua?

The text here indicates a conceptual difficulty concerning the axiom that a decision follows the majority, the same issue I posed above: what is actually intended by the rule of majority, and further, how does this relate to tradition, מסורה? The Y.T. passage goes on to explain that the halakhah is according to the opinion of the two Sages, not by virtue of their majority, but because it is founded upon the rule that a woman is fit to give witness on such cases. The talmudic conclusion contradicts both fictitious assumptions.

This dilemma is further reflected, both implicitly and explicitly, in a number of contradictory passages. The following passage in tBerakhot 5: 2, for instance, is an example of a decision that is not based on any explicit method:

> It happened that Rabban Simeon ben Gamaliel [the Patriarch], Rabbi Yehudah and Rabbi Yose were dining in Akko [on Friday afternoon]. Rabban Simeon ben Gamaliel said to Rabbi Yose: Should we stop eating because Sabbath is close? [Rabbi Yose] answered: Usually you prefer my opinion to that of Rabbi Yehudah, but now you prefer Rabbi Yehudah's opinion to mine? [Rabbi Yose disagrees with Rabbi Yehudah as to when one has to stop eating on Friday in order to eat the Sabbath meal with great appetite. Rabbi Yose maintains that one may continue his meal until it gets dark, but Rabbi Yehudah declares that one must stop at the time of the *minhah* offering or prayer, that is, half an hour after midday]. Will you molest the queen while she is with me in the house? [This is a metaphor from Artaxerxes' proclamation in Esth 7: 8; that is, will you embarrass me in his presence?] [Rabban Simeon] answered: Hence we shall not interrupt [our meal], so the halakhah will not be established forever [against Rabbi Yose's ruling, as a result of their conduct contrary to his ruling], and they did not move from their places before establishing the halakhah according to Rabbi Yose.

This passage does not indicate the reason for fixing the halakhah according to Rabbi Yose, and it seems absolutely arbitrary. Rabban Gamaliel the Patriarch was first of a mind to conduct himself according to Rabbi Yehudah's opinion, but then the halakhah was established simply on the basis of Rabbi Yose's opinion, with no further justification or citation of midrash halakhah or tradition.

We read further in bEruvin 46b: "Rabbi Jacob and Rabbi Zeriqa said: [In disputes among Tannaim] the halakhah is according to Rabbi Aqiba [in a dispute] with one Tanna, and according to Rabbi Yose [even in his dispute] with many Tannaim." The maxim that the halakhah is according to the majority is thus declared invalid with respect to Rabbi Yose, with no reasons given. This is an amoraic dictum, and it may be based on the above passage concerning Rabban Gamaliel's conduct. It does, in any event, demonstrate the ambiguity of the majority rule, and puts into question the nature of the considerations that led to the establishment of the halakhah in any particular case in one way rather than another. The supremacy of a majority opinion against a minority opposition is a universally accepted concept, and it is natural that it was adopted as a leading principle with respect to establishing the halakhah in cases of dispute. The Sages, however, in their quest for flexibility, made use of many logical and legal mechanisms to circumvent this maxim. In yBava Metzi'a 3: 9, 9b, for instance, there is a general dictum by Rabbi Yirmeyah, in the name of Rab: "The halakhah is according to Rabbi Aqiba, even when Beit Hillel [who are deemed to be a majority] dispute with his declaration." Such sweeping statements that the halakhah is always according to Rabbi Aqiba in the Y. T.,[17] or according to Rabbi Yose[18] in the B. T., are the complete antithesis of the majority rule, and cannot be defended in any reasonable way; one cannot, for instance, maintain that all of Rabbi Yose's interpretations were more intelligent than those of his opponents, or his logical considerations superior, or his traditions more reliable. Such a decision with respect to Rabbi Yose contradicts the existence of a general and comprehensive majority rule. Similarly, although the "Voice of Heaven" pronounced the halakhah to be according to Beit Hillel in all cases, we encounter many exceptions to this overwhelming utterance.

We shall now examine in detail various techniques used to circumvent the working of the majority rule.

3.2 Repeal Provisions

The rule of the majority is in fact limited, if not rendered completely hollow, by the right of repeal. This rule is promulgated in the above-cited mEduyyot 1: 5, following the statement that the halakhah follows the majority: "...since a court cannot repeal a decision of another court unless

[17] This declaration is also in conflict with the dictum in yBava Metzi'a 3: 9, 9b, and indicates the lack of any systematic procedure. In the B. T. Rabbi Yose's declarations would override those of Rabbi Aqiba, whereas from the Y. T. dictum one would understand by the *a minori ad majorem* logic that Rabbi Aqiba's opinion would certainly be preferred to Rabbi Yose's.

[18] We indeed encounter a declaration by Rav Mesharshiya disputing such a sweeping decision; see bEruvin 46b.

it is greater in knowledge and number [of Sages]; if it were greater in knowledge alone or in number alone, it cannot repeal the former court's decision; this can be effected only if the court is greater than the other in knowledge and number."[19] This rule in effect permits the rebuttal of a prior decision rendered by a majority. There is certainly no difficulty in convening a court with more members than the previous one; regarding the second condition, there are no rules indicating how it is determined that one court has greater knowledge than another. A majority ruling is thus easily overturned.[20]

---

19 As noted in section 2.3.1, there is no separation in the rabbinic sphere between legislative and judicial authority. Mishnah Eduyyot 1: 5 blends the two. This absence of separation is also apparent in Deut 17: 8-12.

20 Maimonides, in his commentary on mEduyyot 1: 15, is aware of this ruling that renders the existence of a rigid majority rule illusory. He therefore qualifies this ruling, stating that only when the first court reached its decision on the basis of the stated rule of a single Sage, could a greater and more knowledgeable body repeal this decision. There is no such limitation, however, in the various talmudic citations of this rule, and we must assume that it was intended by the Sages to be comprehensive. Maimonides also attempts to define the vague term גדול בחכמה "greater in knowledge"; he asserts that the head of the second court should be more proficient than the head of the previous court. From his commentary, it is unclear whether Maimonides is limiting the possibility of annulling the decision of a previous court to such a particular circumstance, or whether it is only in such an instance that a greater court is required. In *Mishneh Torah*, *Hilkhot Mamrim* 2: 2 he limits the requirement of a greater court to particular conditions, and we read there: בית דין שגזרו גזרה או תקנו תקנה והנהיגו מנהג ופשט הדבר בכל ישראל "...a court that had decreed an edict, or instituted an ordinance, and established a custom that was accepted by all of Israel." In 2: 1, on the other hand, he grants great liberty to the contemporary courts in other instances, and writes: ב"ד גדול שדרשו באחת מן המדות כפי מה שנראה בעיניהם שהדין כך ודנו דין ועמד אחריהם ב"ד אחר ונראה לו טעם אחר לסתור אותו הרי זה סותר ודן כפי מה שנראה בעיניו שנאמר אל השופט אשר יהיה בימים ההם אינך חייב ללכת אלא אחר בית דין שבדורך "If a distinguished court interpreted a law as they understood it by the acknowledged hermeneutical procedure, and decided the case accordingly, and then another court came and, reflecting upon it, came to an opposing conclusion, they may contradict [the decision of the previous court] and decide [the case] as they consider correct. This is because it is said 'to the judge who is in office at that time [Deut 17: 9]'; you must follow the decrees of the court of your generation." The traditional commentators, from the Middle Ages until our own day, were and are aware of the inconsistency between their practice of not contradicting decisions of earlier Rabbis and the talmudic dicta that permit such opposition. Various classifications and justifications are used to reconcile this contradiction. It is not within the scope of this study to elaborate upon this particular issue and the rabbinic solutions, which extend beyond our period of interest. I refer the interested reader to the extensive consideration of this problem by S. Z. Havlin, על החתימה הספרותית, pp. 164 ff. We may note that the rabbinic maxim of a constant intellectual diminution over successive generations (see chap. 2, n. 112) is one such solution; Havlin, however, questions its bearing on the problem (pp. 170 - 173).

It seems further that this right of repeal could operate even when these two conditions were not fulfilled. Details of such a repeal, regarding the consumption of gentile oil, are found in yShabbat 1: 4, 3d, and bAvodah Zarah 36a. In essence, both versions convey the same principle, but vary in certain details. The Y. T. records that Rabbi and his court permitted the consumption of gentile oil. The B. T. version adds the interesting detail that a vote was taken by the court to grant this permission. In the Y. T. Rabbi Yohanan asks: "[How is this possible?] Didn't we learn that only a court with greater knowledge and number may repeal a previously proclaimed edict, and how could Rabbi permit what [the prophet] Daniel forbade?" The B. T. asks the same question, assuming the prohibition against gentile oil to have been decreed by Daniel; after a rhetorical deliberation, however, it is concluded that the Houses of Shammai and Hillel were the authors of the restriction, which was one of the renowned eighteen edicts, and the question is posed:

> How could Rabbi [the Patriarch] repeal a decree promulgated by Beit Shammai and Beit Hillel? Was it not taught that only a court with greater knowledge and number may repeal a previously proclaimed edict [and certainly Rabbi did not have more knowledge than Beit Hillel and Beit Shammai]? And moreover, hasn't Rabba bar bar Hana said in the name of Rabbi Yohanan that a court has the authority to repeal any decision of another court, except [a decree] included in the eighteen particular decrees [promulgated by the combined Houses of Shammai and Hillel[21]] that cannot be abrogated even by Elijah and his court?

Both versions indicate an attempt to reconcile the apparent contradiction to the majority rule. Both offer, in principle, the same solution, but vary with respect to both style and the attribution of the relevant dicta. This variance may indicate a difference in the legal basis of the decision,[22] but has no practical ramifications. The Y. T. version records a declaration by Rabbi Yohanan of an ancient tradition, originating from Rabbi Tzadoq, that any edict decreed by a court that obligates the public is invalid if the majority of the public has not accepted it. It goes on to state: "The Sages] investigated the prohibition against [the use of gentile] oil and did not find that most of the people acceded to it." In the B. T. version, Rav Mesharshiya defends Rabbi's action and explains: "The reason [that one of these eighteen decrees cannot be rebutted] is because the prohibitions therein are diffused among the majority of the Israelites [and thus they could be invalidated if this was not the case]; and our Sages investigated, and concluded that the prohibition against using gentile oil was not diffused among the majority of Israelites." It is evident that both answers

---

21 I have written an as yet unpublished paper on these eighteen decrees. There is no general consensus as to the details of the decrees.

22 See pp. 335-6 on this subject.

in the Y. T. and B. T. attempt to resolve an apparent contradiction between Rabbi's action and the presumed existence of an inflexible rule regarding repeals of previous halakhic pronouncements; there is no indication that Rabbi reached his decision based on the circumstances assumed by the two Amoraim.[23]

Much can be deduced from this narrative. It confirms, first of all, the significant rule that any court can overturn any prior decision of another court, apart from some exceptional edicts,[24] without any particular requirements of superiority over the previous court. In contrast to modern procedures, which allow the overturning of prior decisions only within a precisely appointed hierarchical system, there were no exact rules regarding the rabbinic repeal process,[25] or even regarding contradictory utterances, as we shall see below. This lack of precise regulation is in accord with the general rabbinic philosophy of a flexible and unregulated legal process. This allows, in turn, a loose reading of the requirements for setting up a court of appeal or repeal; even the principle that a decree can be repealed only by a court greater in knowledge and number is invalidated when the relevant decree is perceived not to be acknowledged by the majority of the people. The motive is indicated: "One does not promulgate an edict that the majority of the people cannot maintain." The outer form of the majority rule is, it seems to me, still upheld, while the decree is legally annulled.

Moreover, as in other instances, we encounter antithetical rabbinic utterances. In contrast to the above-cited requirement of a court superior in number and knowledge, suggestive of a hierarchical authority, we read in mRosh HaShanah 2: 9: "Why are the names of the elders [who went up to the Lord in Exod. 24: 1] not mentioned [like the names of Aaron, Nadav and Avihu]? To teach us that every court of three people nominated as judges in Israel is equal to the court of Moses." This philosophical utterance reflects an attitude of equality with respect to the authority of a court, without any consideration of the erudition of its members. Rashi, in one of his legal decisions collected by his school,[26] limits the practical application of this dictum to monetary issues; that is, any court is competent "to impose fines and declare property confiscated."

---

23 The style in both Talmudim indicates that the rhetorical deliberations and solutions are of a later origin, and do not convey the actual statements of Rabbi Yohanan.

24 The eighteen decrees were supposedly permanent. As we have seen above, however, even one of these decrees could be revoked, when it was considered advisable for practical reasons.

25 See n. 20.

26 ספר האורה חלק ב׳ [קמא] שאלה בענין שידוך

In summary, the theological principle that the laws of the Torah, the divine instructions of the omniscient God, are eternal and changeless[27] is formally maintained, but pragmatic methods are devised to maintain their flexibility:[28] the resourceful application of the hermeneutic process, and the postulating of changed circumstances[29] that create the requirement for a different decision.

3.3 Preference for Individual Opinion

Although the Sages established a majority rule principle,[30] the opinion of the individual also came to be viewed as indispensable. Such opposing

---

27 Maimonides writes in *Mishneh Torah, Hilkhot Yesode Hatorah* 9: 1: דבר ברור ומפורש בתורה שהיא מצוה עומדת לעולם ולעולמי עולמים אין לה לא שינוי ולא גרעון ולא תוספת שנאמר את כל הדבר אשר אנכי מצוה אתכם אותו תשמרון לעשות לא תוסף עליו ולא תגרע ממנו ונאמר והנגלות לנו ולבנינו עד עולם לעשות את כל דברי התורה הזאת הא למדת שכל דברי תורה מצווין אנו לעשותן עד עולם "It is clearly said in the Torah that it is an eternal codex, without alteration, abatement or accretion, as it is said: 'See that you do all I command you; do not add to it or take away from it [Deut 13: 1; 12: 32 in KJV],' and it is said: 'The things revealed belong to us and to our children forever that we may follow all the words of this law [Deut 29: 28; 29: 29 in KJV].' You deduce from this that we are commanded to fulfill all the Torah's precepts forever."

28 They did not call this method reform or change, but declared it to be an element of the original revelation at Sinai, according to the maxim that God revealed to Moses even what proficient disciples would state before their teachers. See chap. 1, n. 83.

29 Changes in overall conditions, or in the minute details of a situation, create a requirement for a new resolution. Such circumstances remove the new decision from the ambit of the prohibition against changing, abating or augmenting the existing law; as we know from contemporary legal practice, the detection of a slight variance between the case at hand and a similar precedent is a well-known technique. I assume that the narrative concerning the search of the superior court for an unfamiliar halakhah refers to an occurrence in which the circumstances were barely different. It is evident that cases matching perfectly with precedent decisions were known to the local courts and obviously to the Superior Court, and would not require a vote. But we read in tHagigah 2: 9, tSanhedrin 7: 1, ySanhedrin 1: 4, 19c, and bSanhedrin 88b: נשאלה שאלה בפניהם אם שמעו אמרו להם ואם לאו עומדין למנין "[When] a question came up before them, if they knew the answer, they told them, otherwise they voted [and decided by majority]." Their lack of knowledge indicates that they had no tradition of a similar precedent.

30 As we observe in yMo'ed Qatan 3: 1, 81d, and bBava Metzi'a 59b, concerning the Akhnai oven. There is a further interesting dictum in bNiddah 30b: יחיד ורבים הלכה כרבים פשיטא מהו דתימא מסתברא טעמא דרבי ישמעאל דקמסייע ליה קראי קמ"ל "[In a dispute between] an individual and many [Sages] the halakhah is according to [the opinion of] the many. That is obvious, so what does it come to teach us? We would have thought that [in this occurrence] the halakhah

trends sustained a balance between the imposition of a majority rule and respect for the individual expression and opinion of each Sage.[31] This equilibrium may have been reached after a struggle between the two opposing currents, as I shall elaborate upon in due course. The existence of these currents is evident upon an analysis of various talmudic passages.

A major source of these differing trends in any particular case is the fact that many inferences can be learned from a single biblical utterance, as a result of different and sometimes opposing interpretations. This concept is expressed in the maxim "From one verse many rationales are derived [bSanhedrin 34a]."[32] The maxim is quoted in this case with reference to the various arguments used by the judges to condemn or absolve a person based on different conclusions from biblical verses. Its basis is the remarkable verse in Ps 62: 12 (v. 11 in KJV): "One thing God has spoken, two things have I heard."

Another dictum confirms the independence of individual logical arguments: "They [two Amoraim] needed to learn only the conclusive laws [transmitted by tradition] from Rab, their teacher, but not his logical arguments [bSanhedrin 36b]." Rashi explains that with respect to the need for the Amoraim "to find support and elucidate the rationales [behind the laws]...each man is on his own." This passage also reflects the tension and balance between the two pillars on which the rabbinic legal system is based - that is, the concept of מסורה "tradition," and the concept of personal opinion, often expressed as מן דעה[33] "from deliberation," or as כך הוא בעינינו "that is how we see it."[34] I shall revert to this topic.

The Sages struggled to maintain their independence and freedom to interpret the Torah, both during and following the Second Temple period.

---

would be as Rabbi Ishmael taught, because a verse of the Torah supports him; therefore, it comes to teach us [that even in this case, the halakhah is according to the many]."

31 We may deduce evidence of the respect among the Sages for opposing viewpoints from the statement in in bEruvin 13b (cited in chap. 1, at n. 47), that suggests that the halakhah was established according to Beit Hillel because of their courteous attitude toward their opponents, Beit Shammai. This indicates the usual situation, but there were, of course, exceptions. In a baraita in bQiddushin 52b, for instance, we read that Rabbi Yehudah instructed his disciples not to let Rabbi Meir's disciples into his school because they simply wish to heckle; they did not come to study the Torah, but rather to affront him with their halakhot. See citation and comment in chap. 4, n. 56.

32 See chap. 1, n. 4 for the Y. T. version of this concept.

33 We read in yMegillah 3: 4, 74b: אנא אמר מן שמועה ואת אמר מן דיעה "I stated [my opinion] based on hearing [i.e., tradition], and you stated [yours] from your own deliberations."

34 We read in bSanhedrin 88a: הוא אומר מפי השמועה והן אומרין כך הוא בעינינו "He says: [I know it] from tradition, and they say: This is how we see it."

The tension between a desire for uniformity and a flexible[35] system continued even after the Temple's destruction, and its existence can be traced from many passages. The absolute necessity of independence is demonstrated, for example, by the rule that at least one member of a court rendering a conviction in a capital case must have a completely opposing opinion, in order that the judgment of the court be recognized as valid; if the accused is unanimously convicted, the verdict is not valid. We read in bSanhedrin 17a: "If all [the members of] the Sanhedrin consider him guilty, [the accused] is acquitted." A homily in ySanhedrin 1: 2, 18c, goes even further. The passage, part of a discussion attempting to derive the number of 71 judges required for the Sanhedrin from the wording in 2 Kgs 25: 19, declares: "[It is written in 2 Kgs 25: 19] '...and sixty men from the people and one secretary [eunuch] from the city' - this [the derived number of 70 plus the eunuch] equals seventy-one. And why did they call him סריס 'eunuch'? Because he transposes the halakhah [a play on the root סרס, which means both 'to emasculate' and 'to transpose']." This dictum thus requires the inclusion of one judge whose function is to attempt to reverse the halakhah. Only a decision reached after careful consideration of an unprejudiced and opposing opinion guarantees a fair trial. Different opinions are therefore not only allowed, but encouraged, being an absolute necessity in order to reach correct decisions.

Moreover, as the above passage goes on to indicate, it is a cardinal prerequisite for a judge to be open-minded, unbiased, and capable of a broad range of opinions: "Rav Yehudah said in the name of Rab: One does

---

35 I have noted the confusion in the talmudic deliberations concerning the notion of flexibility, in both the legislative and the judicial processes. We encounter an ambiguous declaration in ySanhedrin 4: 2, 22a: אמר רבי ינאי אילו ניתנה התורה חתוכה לא היתה עמידה לרגל "Rabbi Yannai said: If the Torah had been given 'cut-off' [with every matter defined exactly], it could not have stood [i.e. it would have been impossible to apply]." This text is dubious, but the same declaration appears in the name of another Amora in Tractate Soferim 16: 5, with the addition: לא היתה עמידת רגלים למורה שיורה "It would have given the judge nothing to stand upon [to consider different ways to reach his decision, as the commentator פני משה explains]." This additional phrase and the succeeding text in both versions indicate that the dictum refers to the flexibility of the judicial process, as we read: משה אמ׳ לפניו רבונו של עולם הודיעיני היאך היא ההלכ׳ אמר לו אחרי רבים להטות רבו המזכין זכו רבו המחייבין חייבו "Moses said to the Master of the World: Tell me what is the halakhah? He answered him: Follow the majority, if the majority acquits, acquit him, if the majority convicts, convict him." This element of the declaration indicates a judicial process, but then we read: כדי שתהא התור׳ נדרשת מ״ט פנים טמא ומ״ט פנים טהור "to enable the Torah to be interpreted in forty-nine ways [to declare something] polluted, and in forty-nine ways [to declare it] pure"; this explanatory statement hints at a flexible interpretation of Scripture. See section 2.3.1 concerning the later *de facto* differences in attitude in certain instances with respect to the legislative and judicial processes.

not nominate a member of the Sanhedrin if he does not know how to adjudge the body of a creeping animal as pure according to the Torah law [which deems the animal impure]."[36] The following passage in ySanhedrin 4: 1, 22a indicates that this ability of a judge to present an opposing argument is a real, not an ideal, requirement: "Rabbi...[37]said: Rabbi... had a senior disciple, who would purify the creeping animal and [also] declare it polluted in a hundred ways."[38]

Further evidence for the promotion of freedom and diversity of opinion is encountered in mSanhedrin 5: 5; various instances of controversial opinions among the members of the court are cited, followed by the procedure in the case of a stalemate on a question of conviction: "The [opposing groups] argue one against the other until one member of those who condemned is convinced [to change his mind] by those who acquitted." The general trend of the rabbinic legal system tends toward acquittal, but at the same time we observe the significance of a free exchange of ideas and opinions in order to reach a final decision. From these sources we might assume that this method of free discussion was exclusively applicable to convictions entailing severe punishments. Maimonides, however, argued that the same method is applicable to all aspects of Torah law; the majority decision must be reached after rational arguments have been offered to convince those with opposing opinions of the correct understanding of the divine commands. We read Maimonides' codification of the above mishnah in *Mishneh Torah, Hilkhot Sanhedrin* 9: 3: "When dissension occurs within the Superior Court, with respect to capital offences, or civil laws, or Torah [ritual] rules, [the above principle applies]."

---

36 I did not find a precise parallel to this statement in other sources, but there are a number of passages that point implicitly to the same effect. We read in ySanhedrin 4: 1, 22a: אמר רבי יוחנן כל שאינו יודע לדון את השרץ לטהרו ולטמאו ק' פעמים אין יכול לפתוח בזכות "Rabbi Yohanan said: Whoever is unable to adjudge the creeping animal [both] pure and impure in a hundred ways cannot open [the examination of the evidence for] the defence." (Hearing the defence evidence is an obligation of a judge during a court hearing, as in mSanhedrin 5: 4: פותחין בזכות "[the court] starts hearing the defence.") Similarly, we may note the narrative in tHagigah 2: 9, tSanhedrin 7: 1, ySanhedrin 1: 4, 19c, and bSanhedrin 88b, quoted above, n. 29, regarding the Superior Court: רבו המטהרין טיהרו רבו המטמין טימאו "When the majority [of the Superior Court judges] declared [something] pure, they [the entire Court] declared it pure, and when the majority declared it impure, they declared it impure." This indicates that the minority of the judges actually declared it pure, founding their opinion, just like the majority, on the Torah.

37 The Leiden MS shows a lacuna with respect to both names.

38 In bEruvin 13b there is another version: "There was a senior disciple in Yabneh who deemed pure a creeping animal [ordinarily deemed impure according to the Torah, with the support of] one hundred and fifty rationalizations."

The above citations reveal not only the freedom to pronounce opposing opinions and ideas, but in fact encouragement to proceed with such practice. Conflicting conceptions are not deemed to be erroneous; they are legitimate and indeed solicited.

The maxim that the halakhah is established according to the majority decision can also be overridden where there is a perception that the individual's opinion enjoys a logical superiority over the theory held by the majority. Talmudic deliberations characterize such an individual opinion in the following ways: מסתברא טעמא "his motive is intelligible [or rational]," and נמוקו עמו "his depth is with him [i.e. his reasons are deep and penetrating]." It is asked, for instance, in bGittin 67a: "Why has Rabbi established the halakhah according to Rabbi Yose [against the majority]?" The answer is: "Rabbi Yose has depth [in his decisions]." Yet even this apparently sweeping preference for Rabbi Yose's opinion is not consistently applied. We read the following in bBekhorot 37a (a dispute regarding the appropriate procedure with respect to an injured first-born animal): "Rav Hananel said in the name of Rab: The halakhah is not according to Rabbi Yose. [A question is posed:] This is obvious [there was no need to announce it] since [in a dispute] between the many and the one the halakhah is according to the many. [Answer:] [It was necessary to declare it] because you might have said that [the halakhah is according to Rabbi Yose] because 'his depth is with him,' therefore it had to be emphasized [that the halakhah is according to the majority, not Rabbi Yose]." There is no rigorous principle; Rabbi Yose's opinion may be preferred in many, but not in all, occurrences.

It is not only with respect to Rabbi Yose that we encounter deviation from the majority rule. In bBava Qamma 102a, it is stated: "The halakhah is according to Rabbi Yehoshua ben Qarha [against the opinion of the many]." The proclamation is justified as follows: "I would have said that [in a dispute] between the one and the many, the halakhah is according to the many; the proclamation teaches us that [in this case] the halakhah is according to the one." The Gemara does not utilize in this instance the expression "his motive is intelligible," but suggests this implicitly by stating the logic behind R. Yehoshua's decision: "because it has the effect of rescuing [one's money from idolaters]."[39] In other instances, however, an individual opinion does not override the maxim of the majority decision, even when such an opinion has scriptural support. We read in bNiddah 30b, after a declaration that the halakhah is not as Rabbi Ishmael maintains because the halakhah follows the majority: "[Question:] This is obvious! [Why was there a need to state it?] [Answer:] [It was necessary to state it] because you might have said 'his motive is intelligible' since it

39 This refers to the recovery of a loan from an idolater before a feast day dedicated to an idol.

is supported by [an appropriate interpretation of] Scripture; therefore it had to be emphasized [that the halakhah is not as Rabbi Ishmael declared]." The search for rigid rules is in vain.

We encounter other exceptions to the majority rule in favour of the declarations of an individual Sage, based on various reasons. In yBava Batra 10: 8, 17d, such an exception is justified by a vague reference to the apparently superior quality of the Sage's decisions; but even this logical explanation does not ensure its universal application or acceptence.[40] We read: "There [in Babylon] they decided that the halakhah is always according to Rabban Simeon b. Gamaliel except regarding [disputes about the responsibility of] a guarantor, [a condition with respect to the validity of a divorce, regarding an occurrence at] Sidon, and late evidence [at a trial]." An Amora declares the reason: "since he delivered clearly - decided halakhot from his court." The author of the dictum, however, added a condition to the apparently sweeping declaration: ובלבד במשנתינו "but only [his declarations expressed in] our mishnayot [not in baraitot]."

Another exception is found in bMo'ed Qatan 20a:

> Rabba bar bar Hana said in the name of Rabbi Yohanan: Wherever you encounter an individual [Sage proclaiming] a lenient practice, while the many [proclaim] a strict one, the halakhah is according to the many, except in this occurrence. Although Rabbi Aqiba advocates leniency and the Sages proclaim strictness, the halakhah is according to Rabbi Aqiba, because Samuel said: In the matter of mourning [laws], the halakhah is according to the one who promotes leniency.

[40] As with many other apparently sweeping declarations, this dictum was neither universally applied nor accepted. I will quote a few of the numerous exceptions. In yHallah 3: 5, 59b, one Amora in the name of Resh Laqish declares that the halakhah is according to Rabban Simeon b. Gamaliel, but another maintains that the Sages of both Palestine and Babylon affirm the opposite. In yAvodah Zarah 5: 13, 45b, a dispute is recorded between Resh Laqish and Rabbi Yohanan: חד אמר הלכה כרבן שמעון בן גמליאל וחד אמר אין הלכה כרבן שמעון בן גמליאל "One Sage said the halakhah is according to Rabban Simeon b. Gamaliel, and the other said it is not." Further, although the dictum that the halakhah is according to Rabban Simeon b. Gamaliel is recorded in the Y. T. as originating from Babylon, it was not entirely accepted there. We read in bBava Metzi'a 38b: אמר רבי יוחנן הלכה כרבן שמעון בן גמליאל ורבא אמר רב נחמן הלכה כדברי חכמים "[An Amora] in the name of Rabbi Yohanan said that the halakhah is according to Rabban Simeon b. Gamaliel, and Raba, in the name of Rabbi Nahman, said that the halakhah is according to the Sages [the majority]." In bMo'ed Qatan 22a, Rabbi Yohanan declares another rule: הלכה כרבן שמעון בן גמליאל בטריפות והלכה כרבי שמעון באבל "The halakhah is according to Rabban Simeon b. Gamaliel with respect to [rules regarding] organic defects in animals [bHullin 50a], and according to Rabbi Simeon with respect to [rules of] mourning."

In yMo'ed Qatan 3: 1, 82a, we encounter a parallel dictum concerning leniency in mourning rules: "[It is said] in the name of Rabbi Yehoshua b. Levi that the halakhah follows the Sage who is lenient with respect to mourning rules." As with the above passage, we may assume that this decision is based on logic, though it is not clearly exposed. In yShabbat 1: 8, 4a, however, there is a dictum in the name of Rabbi Aha with no clear justification: "[With respect to disputed halakhot] concerning the Sabbath, mourning and idolatry, the halakhah follows Rabbi Simeon b. Eleazar." Rabbi Simeon's opinion on rules of mourning[41] and idolatry[42] happens to be the lenient one, but regarding the Sabbath rulings, [43] he is more severe.

We encounter a similar concept based on leniency in yEruvin 1: 1, 18b, and bEruvin 46a, with respect to the laws of Eruvin: "The halakhah in the matter of Eruvin is always according to the supporter of the lenient practice." But this maxim too is not universally applied. In yEruvin 1: 1, 18b, for instance, despite the declaration in support of leniency, there is also a declaration that the halakhah in mEruvin 1: 1 does not follow Rabbi Yehudah.[44] Yet this stands against two other allegedly general rules: the rule that in a dispute between Rabbi Meir and Rabbi Yehudah, the halakhah follows Rabbi Yehudah,[45] and the statement that regarding the rules of Eruvin, the halakhah always follows the lenient opinion. It also conflicts with a sweeping statement in bEruvin 81b: "Rav Yehudah said in the name of Samuel: The halakhah [regarding a declaration of Rabbi Yehudah in mEruvin 7: 11][46] is according to Rabbi Yehudah, and

41 See a baraita quoted in bMo'ed Qatan 21b.

42 See mAvodah Zarah 4: 11.

43 See yShabbat 1: 8, 4a.

44 We read there: ר' אחא ר' חיננא בשם כהנה אין הלכה כר' יודה. In the Leiden MS the term אין "not" is erased, but the traditional commentators have added it back, since otherwise the following rhetoric makes no sense. Maimonides states the halakhah contrary to Rabbi Yehudah, a decision that goes against the general rule.

45 The rule that the halakhah follows Rabbi Yehudah in a dispute with Rabbi Meir is expressed explicitly in yTerumot, 3: 1, 42a, and bEruvin 46b. In the talmudic discussion in yEruvin 1: 1, it is not expressed explicitly: וכא תהא הלכה כרבי יודה ואפילו חכמים החלוקים "And here [with respect to our mishnah] the halakhah would follow Rabbi Yehudah, even if the Sages [the majority] oppose him." In the relevant mEruvin 1: 1 the opposing halakhah is not quoted in the name of Rabbi Meir, but as an anonymous rule; this is considered to be the majority rule, though originally a declaration by Rabbi Meir. Thus the rule that the halakhah follows Rabbi Yehudah in a dispute with Rabbi Meir is also held by the Gemara to apply against an anonymous declaration that is deemed to be originally from Rabbi Meir. See yYevamot 4: 11, 6b, and bSanhedrin 86a.

46 The Gemara in bEruvin 81b - 82a speculates as to whether Rabbi Yehudah really disputes the opinion of the Sages, or simply explains their opinions and complements them with his own declarations. This question is posed with respect to Samuel's comprehensive statement, which is in opposition to the general rule that the halakhah

moreover, everywhere Rabbi Yehudah taught about Eruvin, the halakhah is as he declared." In mEruvin 4: 5 Rabbi Yohanan ben Nuri's declaration on Eruvin is much more lenient than that of Rabbi Yehudah,[47] and hence should have been the final halakhah.[48]

Nonetheless, the Sages seem generally to confirm lenient interpretations of the law with respect to mourners and Eruvin, as against any other interpretations. The debate as to whether the halakhot were established on the basis of halakhic midrash or tradition seems in this case to be entirely out of place. Neither had any influence on these decisions; they were the result of logical considerations that were, unfortunately, not conveyed to us except through such terms as נימוקו עמו or מסתברא טעמא.

B. T. Erubin 46b gives further evidence of the lack of any rigid principle concerning the determination of halakhah according to a majority rule:

> Rabbi Jacob and Rabbi Zeriqa said: The halakhah [in a dispute between Sages] is [determined] according to Rabbi Aqiba [in a dispute] with a single Sage, and according to Rabbi Yose [in a dispute] with many Sages, and according to Rabbi [in a dispute] with a single Sage. [Question] What are the exact consequences of this statement? Rabbi Assi said: That is the [fixed] halakhah, Rabbi Hiyya bar Abba said: One tends towards this opinion. And Rabbi Yose ben Hanina said:

---

is according to Rabbi Yehudah in a dispute with Rabbi Meir (bEruvin 46b), but not against Rabbi Yose or more than one Sage. A similar declaration with respect to Rabbi Yohanan ben Nuri refers to an explicit dispute in mEruvin 4: 5, and is complemented by the related debate in bEruvin 46a: סלקא דעתך אמינא הני מילי יחיד במקום יחיד ורבים במקום רבים אבל יחיד במקום רבים אימא לא "You may have thought [that the halakhah goes according to the lenient practice] when there is a dispute between two individuals, or between many [Sages on each side], but in a dispute between a single Sage and many, I would say no [the halakhah is according to the many; therefore it had to be stated specifically that the halakhah is according to the individual Sage Rabbi Yohanan ben Nuri, even against the conflicting opinion of the many]."

47 We read there: מי שישן בדרך ולא ידע שחשיכה יש לו אלפים אמה לכל רוח דברי ר' יוחנן בן נורי וחכמים אומרים אין לו אלא ארבע אמות ר' אליעזר אומר והוא באמצען ר' יהודה אומר לאיזה רוח שירצה ילך "One who falls asleep en route, not being aware of impending nightfall [i.e. the arrival of the Sabbath] is permitted to walk two thousand cubits in any direction [from that point]. These are the words of Rabbi Yohanan b. Nuri, but the Sages say that he may walk only four cubits. Rabbi Eliezer says that he is [deemed to stand] in the middle [of these four cubits, and hence he may only walk two cubits in each direction]. Rabbi Yehudah [disputes Rabbi Eliezer, and] says that he may walk four cubits in every direction he wishes to go." Rabbi Yehudah is more lenient that Rabbi Eliezer, but he is definitely much more severe than Rabbi Yohanan b. Nuri.

48 This is in fact stated in yEruvin 1: 1, 18b: הלכה כרבי יוחנן בן נורי ואפילו חכמים החלוקין עליו "The halakhah is according to Rabbi Yohanan b. Nuri, even when the Sages [the majority] dispute him."

[One may decide according to this opinion], because it seems more likely [to be correct].

According to the latter Amora, nothing is ever rigidly determined, and thus a Sage has the liberty to decide even in opposition to an established halakhah. In effect, we see that despite the fact that there is a clear declaration on deciding the halakhah in disputes involving Rabbi Aqiba, Rabbi Yose and Rabbi, conflicting decisions abound.[49] The halakhah is decided according to Rabbi Aqiba only in a dispute with a single Tanna, but not against the opinion of more than one. Yet regarding a dispute between Beit Hillel and Rabbi Aqiba (noted in mBava Metzi'a 3: 9), it is stated in yBava Metzi'a 3: 9, 9b, in the name of Rab, that the halakhah follows Rabbi Aqiba, against the conflicting opinion of Beit Hillel, though such would definitely be considered the opinion of more than one Sage. The same decision, in the name of Samuel, appears in bBava Metzi'a 43b, though only the Y. T. expresses the fact that the decision is contrary to the opinion of Beit Hillel. This point serves to emphasize the unusual deviation from an alleged rule; in similar circumstances it was stated in bAvodah Zarah 36a: "How could Rabbi [the Patriarch] repeal a decree promulgated by Beit Shammai and Beit Hillel?"[50]

An interesting discussion in mMenahot 4: 3 indicates the complexity of the Sages' considerations in establishing halakhah:

[On the Feast of the Weeks, one must offer, among other offerings, two loaves and two sheep, and the mishnah refers to a situation in which one of these components is missing.] The words of Rabbi Aqiba are: If the loaves are missing, one cannot offer the sheep, but if the sheep are missing, one may offer the loaves. Simeon ben Nannos said: It is the opposite; if the sheep are missing, one cannot offer the loaves, but if the loaves are missing, one may offer the sheep. [This rule is justified] because during the forty years of the desert wandering, the sheep were offered without the loaves [since there was no flour in the desert, only the manna], and hence in this case let them similarly offer the sheep without the loaves. Rabbi Simeon said: The halakhah is according to ben Nannos' declaration, but not because of his justification, since all [the offerings commanded] in Num [28 - 29] were offered in the desert, and all the offerings [decreed] in Lev [23, that comprise the particular offering of the loaves and sheep on the Feast of Weeks] were not offered in the desert. When they entered the land [of Canaan] the offerings [required] in both commands were performed. So why do I say that the sheep may be offered without the loaves? Because the sheep can be offered independently as fellowship offerings, and the sprinkling

---

49 See also n. 17 on this issue.

50 This statement refers to Rabbi's decision to allow the use of gentile oil, despite a prohibition by Beit Hillel and Beit Shammai. See above pp. 185-6. It is odd that although the Y. T. in the case above stresses the fact that the halakhah is according to Rabbi Aqiba and against Beit Hillel, it does not question Rabbi's decision on the use of gentile oil in its deliberations on this issue in Shabbat 1: 3, 3d, and Avodah Zarah 2: 8, 41d.

> of the blood and the burning of the fat allow the priests to consume their flesh [since the offering of the due portions on the altar releases the remaining segments to the priest, or to the offerer in the case of a regular fellowship offering], but the loaves alone [that are not offered in any part on the altar, but are released for consumption only because they are waved together with sheep, according to Lev 23: 20] do not undergo any ritual celebration that could release them to the priests.

We may make a number of observations on this passage with respect to the lack of a system for establishing halakhah. As we have noted above, the rule is that in a dispute between Rabbi Aqiba and one Sage, the halakhah is according to Rabbi Aqiba. In mMenahot 4: 3, one of the few occurrences in which the Mishnah actually establishes halakhah, the halakhah is stated to be according to Rabbi Aqiba's opponent, Simeon ben Nannos. With respect to the motives behind the opinions, we encounter a fascinating mixture. Rabbi Aqiba offers no motive for his opinion, whether tradition, halakhic midrash, or logic; it seems that none of these is applicable. Ben Nannos, on the other hand, offers historical evidence as his motive. This is not, however, a simple citing of tradition. The case under discussion, involving an absence of loaves or sheep, is not precisely the same as the situation in the desert; ben Nannos, therefore, uses analogy to derive a correct solution. He does not establish his opinion on the basis of a specific tradition transmitted from generation to generation. Rabbi Simeon, who casts the deciding opinion[51] that the halakhah is according to ben Nannos, establishes his decision based on a logical analysis of the relevant laws. Neither tradition nor exegesis is invoked, and each Sage felt free to establish his opinion on a foundation that he conceived appropriate.

The absence of any attempt to apply a systematic approach is also manifest in the ramifications of a dispute between Rabbi Yehoshua, Rabbi Eliezer and Rabbi Aqiba in mNiddah 10: 3. The case under dispute involved the purity status of a man and a woman who had a discharge, but did not examine themselves to check their condition every day. On this subject, tNiddah 9: 13 refers to a discussion between Rabbi Eliezer and Rabbi Yehoshua, in which each tried to convince the other of the correctness of his opinion, and then continues: "Rabbi Simeon and Rabbi

---

[51] The halakhah is generally decided according to the Sage who casts the "decisive" opinion in a dispute between two others. We read in bBerakhot 43b: אמר רבי יוחנן הלכה כדברי המכריע "Rabbi Yohanan said: The halakhah is according to the utterance of [the Sage] who decides." Moreover, since Rabbi, the compiler of the Mishnah, quoted Rabbi Simeon's pronouncement together with his well-founded motive, he wished to emphasize specifically that the halakhah in this occurrence is according to ben Nannos, not according to Rabbi Aqiba. Maimonides in *Mishneh Torah, Hilkhot Temidin Umusafin* 8: 15 - 16, on the other hand, decides the halakhah according to Rabbi Aqiba, but Ra'abad disputes his decision, stating that the halakhah is reversed.

Yose said: The utterances of Rabbi Eliezer are deemed more acceptable than those of Rabbi Yehoshua, and those of Rabbi Aqiba [are] more acceptable than those of all the others, but the halakhah is according to Rabbi Eliezer." Although the opinion of Rabbi Aqiba is deemed preferable, the halakhah is nonetheless decided according to Rabbi Eliezer, with no indication of the reason. I assume that it was on the basis of this decision in Tosefta and similar occurrences that an attempt was made in bNiddah 7b to systematically set out the instances in which the halakhah follows Rabbi Eliezer. We read there: "Rav Yehudah said in the name of Samuel: The halakhah follows Rabbi Eliezer in four occurrences [and this is one of the four]." But this statement is then immediately denounced with the question: "Aren't there any more [than those four]?" and this is backed up with striking evidence. The reply is: "[The statement that] the halakhah follows Rabbi Eliezer in four [instances] refers solely to those in the Order of Purities, but in other Orders there are many [halakhot that follow Rabbi Eliezer]." There are also two attempts to extend the range of halakhot that are to follow Rabbi Eliezer. We read in yGittin 3: 2, 44d: "Rav Huna in the name of Rab [said] the halakhah follows Rabbi Yehudah regarding [the rules of] divorce, and Rabbi Eliezer regarding promissory notes." In yAvodah Zarah 5: 11, 45a-b, as part of a discussion between Rabbi Mana and Rabbi Yose, there is the sweeping statement: "As you said there [with respect to the leavened bread of the gentile] that the halakhah is according to Rabbi Eliezer, so it is here; he [R.Yose] replied: And the same everywhere."[52]

Notwithstanding the above decisions asserting the halakhah to be according to Rabbi Eliezer, we are confronted by an odd narrative in tNiddah 1: 5, quoted in yNiddah 1: 1, 49a: "During Rabbi Eliezer's lifetime, the halakhah [in a matter of purity] followed Rabbi Yehoshua; but after his death, Rabbi Yehoshua instituted the halakhah as Rabbi Eliezer [had declared]." The Gemara evidently questions the logic of this odd practice, and concludes that Rabbi Yehoshua changed his mind: "He appreciated his [Rabbi Eliezer's] opinion [after serious consideration]." The authors of the B. T. were likely not satisfied with this solution, since it does not fit within the context; there is no reason why Rabbi Yehoshua should have changed his mind at Rabbi Eliezer's death, a fact explicitly emphasized in the narrative. In bNiddah 7b a different solution was proposed: "Why [did Rabbi Yehoshua act in this way]? Wasn't it because Rabbi Eliezer was a Shamuti,[53] and [Rabbi Yehoshua] thought that if we

---

52 In the parallel quotation in yOrlah 2: 6, 62c, the last character of the word דבה has been corrected so that the word reads דבר.

53 Rashi interprets this term as "excommunicated"; based on this, the sentence must be interpreted as a rhetorical question, though there is no answer at the end to the term לא (this term does not fit in, but makes no sense if attached to the antecedent phrase

practise according to what [Rabbi Eliezer] pronounced in one matter, we might also do so in other matters [in which the halakhah is not as he declared]? Out of respect for Rabbi Eliezer, we could not object to his pronouncements, but after his death, we can do so, and, therefore, the matter is restored to the way it was [before his excommunication]." This solution is quite sophisticated and one may obviously doubt whether this was the reason for Rabbi Yehoshua's decision; nonetheless, it does offer a logical answer for the change in the rule after Rabbi Eliezer's death. Two ramifications of this solution are of interest. We note first the apparent hesitation in establishing halakhah according to the declaration of an excommunicated Sage.[54] Second, it is evident that halakhot might be changed for reasons entirely extraneous to the legitimacy or the logic of the halakhah itself. Even if Rabbi Eliezer's decisions were considered by tradition to be decisive, they could still be overturned for motives unrelated to the issue in question.

We observe that in some instances, the halakhah was established according to Rabbi Eliezer, and in others, it was not.[55] It seems that in some instances the decision was influenced by the convincing logic of his arguments, and not simply tradition; in other instances there is no indication of why his opinion was preferred. We must further note that Rabbi Yehoshua in bNiddah decided that the practice in this specific issue should be contrary to the prior halakhah, on the basis of a consideration alien to the matter itself. We thus have further evidence of the unconstrained freedom exercised by the Sages in shaping their halakhic decisions.

This freedom of decision is manifest in the discussion of a dispute between Rabbi Yehoshua and Rabbi Eliezer, in a baraita quoted in yBerakhot 3: 1, 5d, yMo'ed Qatan 3: 5, 82b, and bMo'ed Qatan 21a; the details of the dispute are identical in all sources, but the attribution of the Tannaim is inverted in two sources.[56] One Tanna declares that a mourner may put on phylacteries on the second day of his mourning, but when a

---

מאי טעמא). The explanation decidedly suggests the problem of an excommunicated Sage. On the other hand, the statement in yTerumot 5: 2, 43c, ורבי ליעזר לאו שמותי הוא "and Rabbi Eliezer is not a Shamuti," must be interpreted, in the context, as asserting that Rabbi Eliezer is not a member of the House of Shammai. See Tosafot at bNiddah 7b on this issue.

54 The record of his excommunication appears in yMo'ed Qatan 3: 1, 81d, and bBava Metzi'a 59b.

55 In the subsequent discussion in bNiddah 7b - 8a there appears the statement, discussed on the preceding page, that with respect to four particular issues in the matter of purity, the halakhah is according to Rabbi Eliezer.

56 The opinion of Rabbi Yehoshua in the Y. T. is attributed to Rabbi Eliezer in the B. T., and vice-versa. I have therefore simply summarized the two opposing declarations. See the citations below, n. 58.

stranger enters, he must take them off.[57] The other declares that a mourner may put on phylacteries only on the third day of his mourning, but need not take them off on the arrival of a stranger. The Tannaim do not disclose their reasons, but one may assume that they differ as to whether severe emotional pain lasts one or two days. The Amoraim in the B. T., as is common, attempt to reveal the biblical verses from which they assume the Tannaim deduced their different declarations. It is interesting to note that the final halakhah is identical in essence in both Talmudim, but since the names of the relevant Tannaim are inverted, so are the declarations of the final halakhah.[58] There is no indication as to why the Amoraim decided the halakhah according to one opinion or the other, or as to why they decided in part according to the one and in part according to the other. I would speculate that such declarations of the final halakhah likely followed the common practice at the time, but there were different traditions about the tannaitic attributions. One must conclude that it is impossible to detect any systematic method in such a decision.

There are, in fact, a great number of occurrences in Tosefta and Gemara of the statement: נראין דברי ר' א...ודברי ר' ב... "The utterances of Rabbi A seem to us acceptable with respect to X, and of Rabbi B with respect to Y." A halakhah, in other words, is pronounced without any specific details, but is divided; the opinion of one Sage is preferred with respect to one specific contingency and that of another Sage with respect to another specific circumstance. We may gain a further understanding of this phenomenon from the following example. It is stated in mShevi'it 10: 1: "A debt incurred for purchases from a shop is not cancelled [in the seventh *shemittah* year]; if it is turned into a loan, it is cancelled. Rabbi Yehudah says: The debt regarding any prior purchases is cancelled [but that regarding the last purchase is not cancelled]." In tShevi'it 8: 3, we read Rabbi's pronouncement of the halakhah: "[Regarding the dispute concerning a] debt incurred for purchases in a shop, Rabbi said: The opinion of Rabbi Yehudah is acceptable when [the shop owner] registers the debt in money terms, and that of the Sages [is acceptable] when he

---

57 The stranger may not know that the mourner is already in his second day of mourning and may assume that the mourner is putting on phylacteries on the first day. To avoid this misconception, the mourner must take them off.

58 In the Y. T. we read in the name of Rab: הלכ' כר' אלעז' בנתינה וכר' יהושע בחליצה "The halakhah is according to Rabbi Eliezer with respect to putting them [the phylacteries] on [on the second day] and according to Rabbi Yehoshua with respect to the obligation to take off [the phylacteries when a stranger comes in]." In the B. T., Ulla declares: הלכה כרבי אליעזר בחליצה והלכה כרבי יהושע בהנחה "The halakhah is according to Rabbi Eliezer with respect to the obligation to take off [the phylacteries] and according to Rabbi Yehoshua with respect to putting them on [on the second day.]" The names of the Tannaim are inverted, but the final halakhah is identical.

registers it in kind." It is evident that neither the dispute of the Sages in the mishnah nor Rabbi's decision are founded upon exegesis or tradition, but exclusively on analysis of the law.[59] Rabbi is thus able to decide the halakhah in one circumstance according to Rabbi Yehudah, and in another according to the Sages. There are instances, as in this last declaration, in which the reason for the decision may be inferred; in some instances, Rabbi himself proffers the reason for his decision,[60] in others the Amoraim speculate on his motive,[61] in still others we are left with no indication of Rabbi's considerations,[62] and in some cases we have no rational clue upon which to base a plausible motive. Moreover, though Rabbi might have decided, with the phrase נראין דבריו, that "the opinion of Rabbi X is more acceptable," the halakhah was not necessarily established accordingly. We read in yYevamot 4: 11, 6a, and yNiddah 1: 4, 49b, the following declaration of an Amora: "Wherever Rabbi said: 'The opinion [of Rabbi X] is more acceptable [than that of Rabbi Y],' the matter still remains in dispute, except [in one instance, with respect to a dispute regarding a fig cake, in which Rabbi's statement was accepted and the halakhah was fixed accordingly.]" We have also noted the reversal of a preference for a Sage's opinion: when Rabbi Yehoshua reversed a halakhah after Rabbi Eliezer's death (tNiddah 1: 5, quoted above, p. 197), this is justified in yNiddah 1: 1, 49a, by the simple statement: שראה דעתו "he appreciated his opinion [i.e. Rabbi Yehoshua changed his mind after Rabbi Eliezer's death, considering that Rabbi Eliezer's opinion was correct]." The lack of a comprehensive system is evident.

3.4 Did the Halakhah Always Follow Beit Hillel?

The principle of majority rule is also undermined in various passages regarding the disputes between Shammai and Hillel and their Houses. In this matter, as in others, we encounter total inconsistency. In tSukkah 2: 3, it is stated emphatically: "The halakhah is always according to Beit

59 The Sages regarded a debt arising from a purchase as not equivalent to a loan, and therefore not cancelled under the provision of the seventh year; the latter relates only to a loan of money, not to the borrowing of goods. Rabbi Yehudah considered that the last purchase was equivalent to a borrowing of goods, but the previous unpaid purchases were legally a loan. Rabbi used another criterion to distinguish between a loan and a borrowing. If the debt is registered in terms of the goods sold, it is considered a borrowing of the goods, but when it is registered in the shopkeeper's books in terms of money, then it is a loan and is cancelled in the seventh year.

60 See bEruvin 32a.

61 See ySotah 9: 1, 23c, and bMo'ed Qatan 7b.

62 See yTerumot 3: 2, 42a, and bMo'ed Qatan 31a.

Hillel." As we have seen in chapter 1, a declaration quoted in yBerakhot 1: 4, 3b, yYevamot 1: 6, 3b, ySotah 3: 4, 19a, and bEruvin 13b provides a justification for this all-encompassing declaration: "The Voice of Heaven emerged and said: Both are the words of the living God, [but] the halakhah is according to Beit Hillel."

In the B. T. version, quoted in the name of Samuel, the narrative has a prologue: "For three years Beit Shammai and Beit Hillel disputed. The one side said: The halakhah is as we maintain, and the other side said: The halakhah is as we maintain; [then, or until,[63] the Voice came out]." With respect to the historicity of the account, Rabbi Abba's record that the dispute between these two Houses continued for only three years is perplexing. There is no explicit historical evidence to contest this, but I do not think it is necessary to document the ephemeral character of this statement, consistent with the prevailing character of the rabbinic literature.[64]

We must furthermore ask why no vote was taken to establish the halakhah according to the majority. This was done on other occasions, with respect to disputes between Beit Hillel and Beit Shammai, as well as other disputes. We read in mShabbat 1: 4: "These are the halakhot that were declared in the upper chamber of Hananyah b. Hizkiyyah b. Gorion when they went up to visit him; at the voting, Beit Shammai had the majority over Beit Hillel, and eighteen edicts were decreed on that day." Tosefta Shabbat 1: 16 adds to the above record: "And that day was extremely troublesome for Israel, like the day the golden calf was made." In the Y. T. this report attains still more dramatic proportions, and we read in Shabbat 1: 4, 3c: "Rabbi Yehoshua Onayah taught: The disciples of Beit Shammai stood downstairs and threatened to kill the disciples of Beit Hillel who attempted to go up.[65] It is taught that six of them [from Beit Hillel] went up and the rest were prevented with swords and spears. It is taught that they decreed [by consensus] eighteen edicts, they decided eighteen by a majority vote, and they remained in dispute on eighteen issues."[66] In bShabbat 15a, Rav Yehudah in the name of Samuel reports the same narrative; it is then declared: "[But] we have learned in a baraita that they reached a consensus, and the answer is: on that day they disputed and on the next day they agreed."

---

[63] The conjunctions that I have put in brackets do not appear in the text, but I think that the context requires one or the other.

[64] For a new hypothesis concerning the meanings of the terms "Beit Hillel and Beit Shammai," see the Appendix.

[65] This is the interpretation of the commentator קרבן העדה; the Beit Shammai disciples wanted to prevent their contenders from going up and creating a majority.

[66] This is the traditional interpretation. I have attempted a critical evaluation of these edicts in an as yet unpublished paper.

I need not debate the authenticity of the piquant details of these narratives. The passages are, nonetheless, instructive: they demonstrate, on the one hand, that the method of voting for the establishment of halakhah was legitimate, and, on the other hand, that this method was absolutely impractical in its application. Is it plausible that the result of a coerced vote would not be overturned? Moreover, is it reasonable that edicts decreed under such circumstances would obtain such extraordinary validity that they could never be repealed, as we have seen above (bAvodah Zarah 36a, quoted on pp. 185-6)? The story itself has an intrinsic flaw: if Beit Shammai had a majority, how is it possible that they did not agree on eighteen issues; why did they not take a vote, as they seem to have done in eighteen other cases? As Beit Shammai had to employ an unconventional method in this case to attain their majority, we must assume that Beit Hillel had the regular majority. It is thus not clear why that majority was not sufficient[67] to establish the halakhah according to Beit Hillel, without the intervention of the Voice of Heaven, or why Beit Shammai did not consent to the majority decision.

The decision by the Voice of Heaven is not only a fiction to conceal the real motive (if there was an identifiable one) for establishing the halakhah according to Beit Hillel, but is also contradicted in other occurrences, in which the narrative requires that the Voice of Heaven be disregarded.[68] We may refer again to the well-known story of the Akhnai oven (yMo'ed Qatan 3: 1, 81d, and bBava Metzi'a 59b, cited in more detail in chapter 1[69]). There we read: "Rabbi Yehoshua stood up and said: [The Torah] is [no longer] in heaven." Rabbi Yirmeyah explains the consequence of Rabbi Yehoshua's utterance and its relation to the narrative: "The Torah was already given [to the people of Israel] on Mount Sinai, and one does not [have to] comply with [the dictates of] the Voice of Heaven." We have seen, in fact, that Beit Shammai accepted neither the majority opinion of Beit Hillel, nor the pronouncement of the Voice of Heaven.[70] We must understand that the term Voice of Heaven is an eponym for the opinion of the majority.

---

67 Tosafot at bEruvin 6b in fact ask this question and explain: בית הלל הוו רובא ולא הוצרכו בת קול אלא משום דבית שמאי הוו חריפי טפי "Beit Hillel were in the majority and would not have needed the Voice of Heaven [to establish the halakhah according to their opinion]; [it was necessary] because the Beit Shammai [scholars] were more astute [and would therefore outweigh the majority]." This solution is also cited in bYevamot 14a.

68 Tosafot, cited in the previous note, were aware of this inconsistency. They reconciled the discrepancy by suggesting that with respect to Rabbi Eliezer the Voice of Heaven intervened solely to defend his honour, but not to establish halakhah.

69 See chap. 1, nn. 58-60 and related text. As I argued in the Introduction, nn. 31-5 and related text, I am quoting from the extended B. T. text.

70 As we have seen in chap. 1, n. 48, Beit Hillel affirmations were not always followed,

Although the Mishnah asserts[71] that despite their different opinions members of Beit Hillel and Beit Shammai intermarried and used vessels declared pure by the other House, the Amoraim dispute whether Beit Shammai accepted, in practice, the dictate of the Voice of Heaven establishing the halakhah according to Beit Hillel. Such disputes appear in yYevamot 1: 6, 3b,[72] and in bYevamot 14a.[73] In both sources there are lengthy rhetorical deliberations questioning how it was possible that Beit Shammai acted against the Voice of Heaven. Many possibilities are hypothesized, including the probability that they acted in this way both before and after the publication of the Voice of Heaven. The possibility that Beit Shammai may have rejected the decision of the Voice of Heaven, as Rabbi Yehoshua is supposed to have maintained, is also raised. The preference for the majority is similarly questioned in bYevamot 14a, and a new rule for deciding the halakhah in a dispute is introduced. We read there: "We accept the majority decision when both contenders are equal in their knowledge, but in our case, Beit Shammai are sharper in their deliberations."[74]

---

despite the Voice of Heaven or the fact that they were the majority opinion. We have also seen in chap. 1, n. 55 the passage in mEduyyot 4: 8 and (in a slightly different literary style) in mYevamot 1: 4, attesting that Beit Shammai continued to follow their own rules.

71 mEduyyot 4: 8 and mYevamot 1: 4; see chap. 1 n. 55.

72 We read there: רב ושמואל חד אמר אילו ואילו כהלכה היו עושין וחד אמר אילו כהילכתן ואילו כהילכתן "Rab and Samuel [dispute this issue]; one said they both practised according to the halakhah [established by the Voice of Heaven to be according to Beit Hillel], and the other said that each practised according to his opinion about the [correct] halakhah."

73 The dispute is described there: לא עשו ב"ש כדבריהם ור' יוחנן אמר עשו ועשו "Beit Shammai did not act according to their own opinions, and Rabbi Yohanan said that indeed they did." (Rabbi Yohanan, an early Amora, studied at the school of Rabbi in his youth and possessed many traditions from the tannaitic period: Ch. Albeck, מבוא לתלמודים, p. 184.) On the early lack of fixed rules, see further section 4.1.6. It seems odd that in yYevamot 1: 6, 3b, we encounter a conflicting pronouncement of Rabbi Yohanan: רבי הילא בשם ר' יוחנן אילו ואילו כהלכה היו עושין "Rabbi Hila said in the name of Rabbi Yohanan: Both acted according to the halakhah." According to the general meaning of the term כהלכה, this passage suggests that both conducted themselves according to Beit Hillel, in contrast to the expression אילו כהילכתן ואילו כהילכתן. This would be in conflict with Rabbi Yohanan's declaration in the B. T., cited above. There are some problems with the different MSS containing this discussion, in both yYevamot and yQiddushin, 1: 1, 58d, which influence the context. The commentators suggest interpreting the term כהלכה to mean that both Houses aligned themselves on the severe side; this, however, does not resolve the apparently conflicting declarations by Rabbi Yohanan. Again, there seems to be a problem of contradictory attributions, or of a flawed transmission.

74 We encounter here a rhetorical answer, which is not conclusive, since we never

The discussion ends differently in the B. T. and Y. T. versions. In the B. T., it remains an open question, a dispute between Amoraim of the first rank. As I interpret the deliberations, the assumption is that Beit Shammai practised according to their opinion even after the manifestation of the Voice of Heaven declaring that the halakhah was to follow Beit Hillel. The Gemara in bEruvin 6b - 7a is aware of the incompatibility of such a practice by Beit Shammai after the proclamation of the Voice of Heaven, or at least an overpowering decision in support of Beit Hillel, and cites an amoraic resolution: הלכה ואין מורין כן "This is the halakhah [that one may practise as Beit Shammai declare[75]], but one does not teach this." And, as is common, there is always another Amora who maintains that one may so teach. A further passage reports that Rabbi Aqiba on a particular occasion followed the practices of both Beit Shammai and Beit Hillel; this is rationalized by the common explanation that the event was limited to a particular circumstance, and does not serve as a general principle.[76] A

---

encounter in the rabbinic literature an explicit statement to the effect that the halakhah follows Rabbi X because he is more knowledgeable. Regarding the many disputes between Raba and Abbaye, it was decided that the halakhah always follows Raba, except in six occurrences, in which it follows Abbaye: והלכתא כוותיה דאביי ביע״ל קג״ם (bBava Qamma 73a). There is no indication in such a principle that a superior mind or knowledge was the criterion for establishing halakhah. In tEduyyot 1: 5, there is a general rule: דבר מדברי תורה הולכין אחר המחמיר מדברי סופרים הולכין אחר המיקל "In a dispute regarding a Torah precept, one decides on the severe side, and regarding rabbinic edicts, one decides on the lenient side." As we have seen above (p. 193), a dictum in yEruvin 1: 1, 18b is similarly founded upon a principle: הלכה כדברי המיקל בהילכות עירובין "The halakhah in disputes on the subject of Eruvin follows the lenient side." This declaration indicates that the motive for the decision is related not to the Tanna who declared it, but to the character of the relevant law. The Sages decided that it was advisable to be lenient with respect to these rules, and this maxim is so significant that it overrides the majority rule, as we read there: הלכה כרבי יוחנן בן נורי ואפילו חכמים החלוקין עליו "The halakhah is according to Rabbi Yohanan b. Nuri [who pronounced lenient rules regarding mourning laws] even when the Sages [the majority] oppose him." The concept of גדול הדור "the outstanding Sage of the generation" does appear in the Talmud; it is used, however, in connection with the duty to grant such a Sage the appropriate respect, but not to indicate that his opinion was to be accepted as halakhah in a dispute with another Rabbi. The idea of the supremacy of an outstanding Rabbi, whose judgment and decisions were accepted by most of the Diaspora communities, and to whom questions were sent, is characteristic only of the later Middle Ages, and initiated the creation of the שאלות ותשובות, the Responsa literature.

75 See chap. 1, text at n. 47, for the citation of this rule.

76 In bEruvin 7a there is an explication of the following narrative found in tShevi'it 4: 21: מעשה ברבי עקיבא שליקט אתרוג באחד בשבט ונהג בו שני עישורין אחד כדברי בית שמאי ואחד כדברי בית הלל רבי עקיבא גמריה איסתפיק ליה ולא ידע אי בית הלל בחד בשבט אמור אי בחמיסר בשבט אמור ועבד

homily in tSotah 7: 12[77] effectively delegates to each individual the ability to decide whether to practice according to Beit Shammai or Beit Hillel.[78]

הכא לחומרא והכא לחומרא "It happened that Rabbi Aqiba harvested an *etrog* tree on the first day of the month of Shevat, and took two types of tithes, one according to the opinion of Beit Shammai [who state that the new year with respect to the obligation of tithes starts on the first of Shevat, and therefore one must provide the first tithe for the Levites and the tithe for the poor, mandatory for the third year of the seven year tithing cycle] and one according to the opinion of Beit Hillel [who state that the new year referring to the obligation of tithes starts on the fifteenth of Shevat, and therefore one must provide the first tithe for the Levites and the second tithe to be eaten in Jerusalem, mandated for the second year of the cycle]." The Gemara then continues with the justification for Rabbi Aqiba's practice. The resolution to this irregular conduct of Rabbi Aqiba is stated as follows: "Rabbi Aqiba was not precisely sure of Beit Hillel's halakhah [that is, whether they said that the new year started on the first or on the fifteenth day of Shevat], and therefore he practised according to the strict rule of both [but really he carried out his duty according to the opinion of Beit Hillel]."

77 We read there: ת״ל דברים הדברים אלה הדברים כל הדברים נתנו מרועה אחד אל אחד בראן פרנס אחד נתנן רבון כל המעשים ברוך הוא אמרן אף אתה עשה לכך חדרי חדרים והכניס בה דברי בית שמיי ודברי בית הלל דברי המטמאין ודברי המטהרין "'All these words' [the apparently superfluous expression in the preamble to the Sinai revelation in Exod 20: 1] came to teach us that [all these words - of the Sages] came from one shepherd, one God created them, one chief conferred them, the blessed Master of all pronounced them; so you too should create a secret compartment and install in it the utterances of Beit Shammai and Beit Hillel, the statements of those who declare [something] impure and those who declare it pure [and reflect upon them all and decide how to proceed]." It is interesting that the Tanna did not have the audacity to explicitly declare the categorical consequences of his homily, and left this for his listeners to conclude. Rashi, the traditional commentator, similarly comments at bHagigah 3b, with respect to all rabbinic disputes: עשה אזנך שומעת ולמוד ודע דברי כולן וכשתדע להבחין אי זה יכשר קבע הלכה כמותו "Make your ear listen, learn and study the utterances of all, and when you understand how to determine which one is correct, establish thus the halakhah."

78 This freedom of decision is also substantiated with respect to other disputes. In bYevamot 14a, it is stated: תא שמע במקומו של רבי אליעזר היו כורתים עצים לעשות פחמים בשבת לעשות ברזל במקומו של ר׳ יוסי הגלילי היו אוכלים בשר עוף בחלב "Come and hear: In Rabbi Eliezer's town, they cut trees to produce coal, to make iron [for a circumcision knife] on Sabbath [if there were no knife available, in order to fulfill the precept of circumcision at its required time, although the established halakhah does not allow such actions on Sabbath]. In Rabbi Yose ha-Gelili's town one would eat fowl together with milk [although the established halakhah does not allow this]." Rabbi Aqiba disputes with both these Tannaim: in mShabbat 19: 1, with respect to circumcision, and in mHullin 8: 8 with respect to the prohibiting of meat with milk. According to bEruvin 46b, the halakhah is to be established according to Rabbi Aqiba: הלכה כרבי עקיבא מחבירו "The halakhah is according to Rabbi Aqiba [in a dispute] with one [Tanna]." The Y. T. in Rosh HaShanah 4: 6, 59c, records a divergent custom in different localities: ביהודה נהגו

The Y. T. version, on the other hand, tends in the opposite direction. First, it goes to the extreme, asserting that the Voice of Heaven declared: "Whoever transgresses the decisions of Beit Hillel is liable for the death penalty"; this significant pronouncement is absent in the B. T. version. The conclusion appears to assume that the dispute between Rab and Samuel on the issue refers to the practice of Beit Shammai before the proclamation of the Voice of Heaven, but afterwards they conducted themselves according to Beit Hillel. I believe, nonetheless, that Rab and Samuel did actually dispute about the practice of Beit Shammai even after the decision that the halakhah was to follow Beit Hillel. My assumption is supported by tEduyyot 2: 3, which refers to the circumstances after the decision - "the halakhah is always according to Beit Hillel" - but nonetheless declares that one may practise according to Beit Shammai or Beit Hillel, as long as one does so consistently. It is obviously impossible to reconcile such radically opposing declarations with the existence of a comprehensive and unified system.[79] I may also reiterate here the apparent absence of motive in bEruvin 13b for establishing the halakhah according to Beit Hillel.[80]

We also observe that this fluid state of affairs subsisted for a long time. In bYevamot 14a, it is stated:[81] "[It is written in Deut 14: 1] 'Do not cut yourself' [and that means] Do not create [separate] groups [the homily is founded upon a derivation from אגד, 'to tie,' 'to bundle,' and its relationship to the noun אגודה 'bunch, bundle, group.'] Abbaye said this admonition refers to circumstances in which there are two courts in the same town, and one judges according to Beit Shammai and the other

---

כר׳ עקיבה ובגליל כר׳ יוחנן בן נורי "In Judah they acted [performed a prayer] according to Rabbi Aqiba and in Galilee according to Rabbi Yohanan b. Nuri."

79 Ch. Albeck, ששה סדרי משנה, סדר נשים, p. 332, interprets this declaration to be not a definite decision, but as intending to state that the people conducted themselves according to Beit Hillel.

80 See the citation and translation in chap. 1, text at n. 47. Neither the existence of a majority, nor midrash, nor tradition, supported the preference for Beit Hillel's opinion

81 As we have seen (n. 73), bYevamot 14a also records that Rabbi Yohanan maintained that Beit Shammai continued to follow their own opinions even after the general declaration that the halakhah was to follow Beit Hillel. It is possible that this dispute regarding how Beit Shammai conducted themselves is connected to the issue of whether or not one must obey a court's decision even when one is absolutely convinced that it is erroneous. Rabbi Yohanan thus understood that the obligation to obey a halakhah that conflicted with his own opinion arose only after a court's decision to establish that halakhah. The subsequent deliberation and dispute between Abbaye and Raba indeed refer to such circumstances (that is, decisions of different courts), with respect to the privilege of disobeying even a court decision when it is deemed incorrect, and whether this is legitimate in all circumstances or only when the decision is manifestly erroneous (for instance, that right is left and left is right). See further section 1.4 on this issue.

according to Beit Hillel; but there is no objection to two courts in different towns judging dissimilarly."[82] We observe that even in this later period of Abbaye (first half of the fourth century C. E.) there was still acceptance of the possibility of different judgments in individual towns.[83] We should keep in mind that this statement acknowledging the possibility of court decisions rendered according to Beit Shammai was declared about two hundred years after the decision that the halakhah always followed Beit Hillel. From this statement, which attests to diversity in judgement[84] even in later periods, we may thus infer the similar existence of unrestricted diversity in earlier times, before the "Voice of Heaven" preference for Beit Hillel, and obviously before 70.

In some instances, we learn that halakhah was established simply because of an opposing practice by a Tanna, or an unexplained custom of the people. In tDemai 5: 24, there is reference to an instance in which a halakhah was established according to what Rabbi Aqiba practised, although it was against the opinion of many opponents, and the Patriarch Rabban Gamaliel censured him for his action against the majority.[85]

---

82 It seems that the Y. T. opinion is more restrictive on this issue. We read in Pesahim 4: 1, 30d, that the admonition against creating factions, deduced from the exegesis of the biblical phrase לא תתגודדו, might apply to such a case: בשעה שאילו עושין כבית שמאי ואילו עושין כבית הלל "...when some conduct themselves like Beit Shammai and some like Beit Hillel." In the following discussion, however, it is asserted that such conduct does not indeed fall under this restriction, but must be avoided nonetheless; the halakhah was established according to Beit Hillel, and hence following the opinion of Beit Shammai must be considered a blatant transgression of the relevant law. The deliberation concludes that this restriction against factions refers only to cases in which it is not absolutely clear how the halakhah was really decided, as for example: תרי תניין אינון על דרבי מאיר ותרין תניין אינון על דרבי יוסי "[when] there are two versions of Rabbi Meir's opinion and two versions of Rabbi Yose's opinion"; although according to the general rule the halakhah is to follow Rabbi Yose, one does not know how to decide in this case because of the uncertainty as to which version of Rabbi Yose's declaration is authentic.

83 Raba's attitude on this issue was even more lenient. He objected only to a court within which some members decided according to Beit Shammai and others according to Beit Hillel, but had no objection to two separate courts in the same town that followed different Houses.

84 With respect to diversity in practice, see chap. 4, n. 137.

85 We read there: מעשה שנכנסו רבותינו לעיירות של כותים שעל יד הדרך הביאו לפניהם ירק קפץ ר' עקיבא ועישרן ודאי אמ' לו רבן גמליאל היאך מלאך ליבך לעבור על דברי חביריך או מי נתן לך רשות לעשר א' לו וכי הלכה קבעתי בישראל א' לו ירק שלי עישרתי א' לו תדע שקבעתה הלכה בישראל שעישרתה ירק שלך "It happened that the Sages went into towns of the *Kutim* [probably Samaritans] along the way; they brought vegetables to them [and] Rabbi Aqiba hastened and took tithes as if it were an absolute requirement to do so [the majority of the Sages maintained that many *Kutim* did take tithes, and therefore one should consider their products as dubious]. Rabban Gamaliel [censured him and]

Tosefta Terumot 3: 12 attests to further anarchy:[86] "Rabbi Yehudah said: The halakhah is according to the declarations of Beit Shammai, but the majority of the people practised according to Beit Hillel, and the Sages say [in opposition to both statements[87]]: One takes *terumah* and tithes and one may immediately make [the wine in] the wine-press impure." The halakhah in this specific instance is according to Beit Shammai, despite the general rule that the halakhah is according to Beit Hillel, by virtue of the rule of the majority and of the special Voice of Heaven; the Sages accept neither opinion, while the majority of the people practise according to Beit Hillel.

We need not continue with such rhetorical discussions to observe the dichotomy between theory and practice, with respect to the method used to establish halakhah. None of these citations and deliberations alludes to issues of halakhic midrash, correct interpretations, or tradition as influencing the establishment of the halakhah according to Beit Hillel rather than Beit Shammai, demonstrating again the lack of any systematic approach to this topic. We have also observed that despite the proclamation of the "Voice of Heaven" (or the final decision) that the halakhah was always to follow Beit Hillel, there remained inconsistency with respect to this general obligation. The stereotypical and concluding statement of the book of Judges seems quite appropriate here: "Everyone did as he saw fit [Judg 21: 25]."

3.5 Inconsistent Application of הלכה למשה מסיני

As yet another challenge to the concept of a strict system of rabbinic decision-making, I should like to briefly point out the lack of consistent

said: How did you dare to contravene the declarations of your colleagues, or who granted you authority to set aside tithes? [He] replied: I did not establish halakhah in Israel, I just set aside tithes with respect to my own purchase. [Rabban Gamaliel] retorted: "Be aware that [by your deed] you have established a halakhah [against the majority] in [the entire community of] Israel by the tithing of your vegetables." The text records that although Rabban Gamaliel promulgated the halakhah according to what the majority taught, he realized later שנתקלקלו ועשו כל פירותיהן ודאי "that they [the *Kutim*] had got corrupted in their practice, and declared all their produce liable for tithes."

86 In yTerumot 3: 2, 42a, the utterances of Beit Hillel and Beit Shammai are reversed. For our purpose, this does not change anything, since the concluding statement, regarding what the people practised and what the Sages declared, is the same.

87 In tTerumot 3: 12, the two Houses dispute the issue of when wine can be made impure without impairing the duty to take the tithes that must be in a state of purity: בית שמיי או׳ משיינטל מעשר ראשון בית הלל או׳ משיינטל מעשר שני "Beit Shammai say [it is allowed] after the taking of the first tithe and Beit Hillel say after the second tithe."

application of the term "halakhah [given] to Moses from Sinai." As we have noted in section 1.6.4, this assertion was used frequently in rabbinic deliberations to indicate the origin of a law for which no scriptural support or other justification could be devised; it is a species of *deus ex machina*, advanced when no other motive could be detected to justify a rabbinic decree or an entrenched custom. Such law might consist of a practice that is not recorded at all in Scripture, such as the water libation at the altar on the Feast of the Tabernacles, in the renowned dictum: "The rules of the ten young plants, the willow branch and the water libation [on Sukkot] are halakhot [given] to Moses from Sinai."[88] It is also used for a rabbinic decree that fills in details regarding a biblical precept, as for example with respect to the phylacteries. In the latter case, Scripture simply mandates: "Tie them [God's words] as symbols on your hands [Deut 11: 18]," without any indication as to how this should be performed. The origin of the square form and black colour of the phylacteries is explained in yMegillah 4: 9, 75c: "We learn in a baraita ...[the requirement that] the phylacteries be square and black is a halakhah [given] to Moses from Sinai."[89]

S. Safrai[90] has also commented on the character of "halakhah [given] to Moses from Sinai." Although from a general perspective his thesis does not conflict with mine, I must emphasize the difference between our two approaches. Safrai does not assume that the attribute "given to Moses from Sinai" is a device used to justify an entrenched custom, whose origin was unknown. He declares only that the Sages did not intend this attribute to mean that the rule refers in real historical terms to a tradition received from Sinai.[91] I do agree with him on this point, but I reiterate my thesis that the maxim does refer to entrenched traditions for which no biblical origin was effectively indicated. We observe this point in a dispute

88 In bSukkah 34a and in other passages. In ySukkah 4: 1, 54b, and yShevi'it 1: 5, 33b, only the last two subjects, ערבה "willow branch" and ניסוך המים "water libation," appear. The first rule of the B. T., עשר נטיעות, refers to the general law that prohibits doing any work shortly before the seventh year, to avoid effecting an improvement during the seventh year, in which the fields must remain fallow. The rule of the ten plants is an exception to this law, allowing one to plow, until the New Year's day of the seventh year, the entire surface of a field fifty by fifty cubits in which ten young plants are spread. Otherwise, one may plow only the land around the trees, in order to protect them from drying out.

89 The phrase refers here to an entrenched custom whose source was unknown. In bShabbat 28b, we read: דתניא תפילין מרובעות הלכה למשה מסיני "We learned in a baraita that the [mandate] to make [the phylacteries] in a square form is a halakhah [given] to Moses from Sinai"; the same dictum is then applied to the requirement for black straps.

90 S. Safrai, הלכה למשה מסיני.

91 Ibid., p. 19.

between Rabbi Aqiba and Rabbi Eleazar ben Azaryah with respect to the quantity of oil for the thanksgiving offering (bMenahot 89a), mentioned above.[92] There is no factual dispute between them concerning the halakhah itself, and in particular the belief that all halakhot have their legal origin in the Torah,[93] given to Moses from Sinai. Rabbi Aqiba, who is known to have deduced halakhot from the interpretation of each stroke of every letter, and other complex hermeneutics,[94] attempted to discover a scriptural support for every tradition.[95] Rabbi Eleazar ben Azaryah and others, who did not agree to such literary acrobatics, declared plainly that the rule in question was a "halakhah given to Moses from Sinai" - that is, an ancient tradition - and needed no biblical support. According to my thesis, both parties decided what the halakhah should be, and devised, each in his own fashion, a reasonable manner of justifying it.

---

92 Chap. 1, n. 108.

93 This is how I understand the citation quoted by S. Safrai (ibid., p. 30) from bNiddah 45a, where we read: אמר להם למה הדבר קשה בעיניכם [אמרו ליה] כשם שכל התורה הלכה למשה מסיני כך פחותה מבת שלש שנים כשרה לכהונה הלכה למשה מסיני "[When his disciples were astonished by a decision of Rabbi Aqiba that seemed to them to be against a Torah rule], he said to them: Why does it look strange to you? [They explained to him, and he answered:] Just as all the laws of the Torah are halakhot [given] to Moses from Sinai, so [my decision that] a girl of less than three years who is raped is [still] suitable to marry a priest is halakhah [given] to Moses from Sinai. [In other words, it is not a decision against the Torah, it is how I understand the Torah precept, and every disciple will interpret anew the Torah that was given at Sinai]." He did not mean to say that his decision was "given to Moses from Sinai," an attribute that he did not accept, but that it was founded upon the Torah given at Sinai, which included all future interpretations by the Sages.

94 In bMenahot 29b, cited in chap 1, n. 108.

95 Contrary to the oft-cited declaration (see text above) that the water libation is considered to be halakhah "given to Moses from Sinai," Rabbi Aqiba deduces this precept through hermeneutics. We read in bZevahim 110b: דאמר ניסוך המים דאורייתא דתניא רבי עקיבא אומר ונסכיה בשני ניסוכים הכתוב מדבר אחד ניסוך המים ואחד ניסוך היין "[Rabbi Aqiba] said: Water libation is a Torah precept [that is, deduced from the Torah], as we learned in a baraita: Rabbi Aqiba says: [It is written in Num 29: 31] 'and its drink offerings' [in plural]. Hence, it refers to two libations: one, the water libation and the other, the wine libation." The same homily appears in yRosh HaShanah 1: 3, 57b, ySukkah 4: 1, 54b, and yShevi'it 1: 5, 33b, though in a slightly different literary style, and with no indication of the source: דרבי עקיבה אמר ניסוך המים דבר תורה "...since Rabbi Aqiba said: Water libation is a Torah utterance"; there then follows the identical explanation. I have therefore quoted the B. T. text, which quotes the homily as part of a baraita. Sifre Num 150 quotes the same homily in the name of Rabbi Yehudah b. Bathyra; a homily by Rabbi Nathan deduces its Torah origin based on the exegesis of another scriptural verse.

Safrai bases some of his thesis on the thirty-nine works listed in mShabbat 7: 2 as prohibited on Sabbath.[96] Although, as he notes, there is no supporting evidence for them in the mishnah, they are also not deemed to have been "given to Moses." I suggest that one cannot compare the thirty-nine Sabbath works and other precepts, such as that of the willow branches, that are termed "halakhah [given] to Moses from Sinai." I have already written of this list of works (section 2.4), and its homiletic linkage to the works performed in the Temple, and wish to comment that this topic is entirely different in nature than the rules that are classified as "given to Moses from Sinai." Scripture indicates explicitly that work is forbidden on Sabbath, and the Sages merely established, or explained, what is included in the term מלאכה, "work." The homiletic linkage to the works performed in the Temple is philosophically not incoherent. The Temple, the most significant institution in Israel, served as an archetype of human spirit and activity, and as such, the types of work performed in the Temple served as a pattern for the universal concept of "work."[97] Therefore, all the thirty-nine types of work performed in the Temple are considered Torah precepts, while other types of prohibited activities are rabbinic edicts. The custom of water libation, in contrast, has not the slightest support in Scripture, and therefore had to be justified by the particular attribute "given to Moses from Sinai." The same consideration applies to the willow branches, included with the water libation in the renowned dictum, cited above: "The rules of the ten young plants, the willow branch and the water libation [on Sukkot] are halakhot [given] to Moses from Sinai." The third subject mentioned in this declaration, the rule of the ten plants, could be considered a logical consequence of the *shemittah* law; but it was included, it seems to me, to avoid admitting explicitly that Torah rules are affected by human logic.[98] This is a philosophical and theological issue;

---

96 S. Safrai, הלכה למשה מסיני, p. 19.

97 W.S. Green, "Biography," writes on p. 78: "The Temple rites reflect, shape and indeed constitute that which is truly real."

98 There is an interesting example of this concept relating to the transfer of objects on Sabbath. The transfer of an object from a private precinct to a public domain is forbidden, but the transfer from one private precinct to another is permitted. As we have seen (chap. 2, n. 132 and related text), mShabbat 11: 2 addresses the case of a transfer between balconies: היו שתיהן בדיוטא אחת המושיט חייב והזורק פטור שכך היתה עבודת הלוים שתי עגלות זו אחר זו ברשות הרבים מושיטין הקרשים מזו לזו אבל לא זורקין "If the two [balconies] are side by side, the one who hands over [the object] is liable, but the one who throws it is absolved, because that is how the Levites performed their work [in the period when the Levites transported the components of the Tent of Meeting]; there were two carts in the public domain, and they handed over the boards from one to the other but did not throw them." This is an assumption, because we have no textual evidence of the way in which the Levites loaded the boards onto the carts. There is evidence that the boards

the Talmudim do not express a monolithic opinion on these crucial questions, but this is not within the scope of our study.[99]

The question of whether a halakhah given to Moses from Sinai is מדאורייתא, "a command from the Torah," that is, decreed by God, or a rabbinic stipulation,[100] is quite significant. This distinction has legal

---

were transported by the Merari clan (Num 4: 31), and that they were given four carts (Num 7: 8), but there is no explicit connection between the two verses. We should not, however, wonder at such a comparison. Josephus, in his description of the Tabernacle (*Ant.* 3: 180 -187), perceives a cosmological significance in each of its elements. He declares in 180: ἕκαστα γὰρ τούτων είσ άπομίμησιν καὶ διατύπωσιν τῶν ὅλων "In fact, every one of these objects [the Tabernacle, its vessels and the priestly vestments] is intended to recall and represent the universe." In his portrayal of the Second Temple build by Herod, he concludes (*J.W.* 5: 212): οὐκ ἀθεώρητον δὲ τῆς ὕλης τὴν κρασιν ἔξων ἀλλ' ὥσπερ εἰκονα τῶν ὅλων "Nor was this mixture of materials without its mystic meaning: it typified the universe." Philo, *Spec. Laws* 1: 84 - 95 attributes cosmological significance to the High Priest's garments.

99 We encounter a similar problem regarding another declaration found in bEruvin 4a and other sources: שיעורין חציצין ומחיצין הלכה למשה מסיני "The standards [the minimum size and quantity to be deemed as a transgression of a precept, as for example the minimum quantity eaten of a prohibited food], the law of the intervening object [on the body of a person taking a ritual bath, because he must 'bathe his whole body (Lev 15: 16)' and an intervening object prevents this], and the partitions [to be deemed walls for the construction of a Sukkah], are halakhot [given] to Moses from Sinai." These rules are the result of logical considerations complementing Torah precepts. This is also obvious from the rhetorical questions in the Gemara: חציצין דאורייתא נינהו דכתיב ורחץ את כל בשרו שלא יהא דבר חוצץ בין בשרו למים "The rule of the intervening objects is a Torah precept, since it is written 'he must bathe his whole body,' and that means that nothing must intervene between his body and the water." Extended discussions of each of the three rules follow, with various solutions; though these are of no direct interest to our investigation, they indicate how the Sages perceived these rules as originating from logical considerations of Torah precepts that were seen as problematic, as well as the indiscriminate application of the classification הלכה למשה מסיני. In yHagigah 1: 2, 76b and other sources, the rule on intervening objects in a ritual bath does not appear. Thus the only dispute concerns whether the various standards for each precept or transgression were given at Sinai, or were rabbinically instituted regulations.

100 In chap. 1, n. 118 and related text, we have seen the case of mYadayim 4: 3, which discusses the obligation to give seventh year tithes in the regions of Ammon and Moab: נמנו וגמרו עמון ומואב מעשרים מעשר עני בשביעית "They voted and decided that one gives the tithe of the poor in the seventh year [on produce grown] in Ammon and Moab." This is obviously a rabbinic edict. We read the following assurance, however, as to the correctness of the Sages' decision: צא ואמור להם אל תחושו למנינכם מקובל אני מרבן יוחנן בן זכאי ששמע מרבו ורבו מרבו עד הלכה למשה מסיני שעמון ומואב מעשרין מעשר עני בשביעית "Go and tell them: Do not be hesitant of your vote. I have a tradition from Rabban Yohanan ben Zakkai, who heard it from his Rabbi, and he from his Rabbi, all the way back to a halakhah [given] to Moses from Sinai, that one has to give the tithe of the poor in the

ramifications, particularly in cases of doubt,[101] and in cases involving the question of whether another precept may be overridden.[102] The expression "halakhah [given] to Moses from Sinai" would seem to imply that the rule is a Torah precept, otherwise it would be a contradiction in terms: a rabbinically instituted rule could not have been given to Moses. Nevertheless, this characterization is used indiscriminately, in both rabbinic literature and traditional commentaries,[103] to refer both to rules classified as Torah precepts and to rules classified as rabbinic edicts.[104]

The lack of any systematic classification is evident in yHagigah 1: 2, 76b, and bEruvin 4a,[105] with respect to the establishment of minimum or maximum standards, שיעורין. The B.T. questions the declaration that the establishment of standards is a tradition "from Sinai," alleging that it is a Torah ruling, founded upon the exegesis of a scriptural verse.[106] The succeeding rhetoric ends with the solution: "These are traditions [הלכתא] and the Sages supported them with a scriptural origin." This vague pronouncement does not explicitly declare what is meant by the term הלכתא. Does it refer generally to a rule received by tradition, and the solution thus contradicts the initial classification as "given from Sinai"? Or is it simply an abridgment of the opening phrase, and actually intends to maintain the particular attribute "given from Sinai"? As I have previously asserted, the Talmudim do not grant much attention to a precise classification of the various terms, and this circumstance holds true with

---

seventh year from [produce grown in] Ammon and Moab." In this occurrence the term הלכה למשה מסיני refers to a rabbinic stipulation. The commentators, who maintain that the term corresponds to a Torah precept, explain that it is not meant to express here a determinate הלכה למשה מסיני, but only something that is similar to it. See also section 1.6.4, and nn. 109-10 below. M. Elon, *Jewish Law, History, Sources, Principles,* vol. 1, pp. 205 ff., quotes this talmudic citation on the tithe for the poor to demonstrate that, although it is termed הלכה למשה מסיני, it in fact constitutes a rabbinic decree. He does not, however, analyze the characteristics of the precept in his discussion.

101 We read in yEruvin 3: 4, 21a, and in a slightly different literary style in bBetzah 3b: וספק דבר תור׳ להחמיר... וספק דבריהן להקל "Every doubtful matter regarding a Torah decree is decided on the severe side...and every doubtful matter regarding a rabbinic decree is decided on the lenient side."

102 As we have seen (chap. 2, n. 28), the willow branch precept is such a halakhah; this case will be discussed further below (nn. 109-10 and related text).

103 For an extensive discussion, see האנציקלופדיה התלמודית, vol. 9, שעב-ג, s.v. הלכה למשה מסיני.

104 See S. Safrai, הלכה למשה מסיני, pp. 16 ff., who discusses this issue and quotes the relevant citations.

105 Quoted in n. 99.

106 In bEruvin 4a, the question is posed: שיעורין דאורייתא הוא "Aren't the standards a Torah precept?"

respect to this specific term. We encounter the expression הלכתא גמירי, "we learned that it is a tradition," with respect to many rules that are certainly not deemed to bear the attribute "given from Sinai."[107]

Another complication arises from a different description of the standards in bBerakhot 41b: "It is a rabbinic stipulation, and the [quoted] scriptural verses serve only as support." The term מדרבנן explicitly portrays the establishment of the standards as a rabbinic stipulation, not originating from any tradition. The text in Eruvin, on the other hand, uses the term הלכתא, "tradition," in its closing argument but leaves us in limbo as to whether this also means "from Sinai." Yet even the explicit term הלכה למשה מסיני "a halakhah [given] to Moses from Sinai" is ambiguous and indefinite; is it deemed to be legally a Torah rule, or a tradition with a superior legitimacy to that of regular traditions, or a rabbinic rule? In yHagigah 1: 2, 76b, and yPe'ah 1: 1, 15b, the question of the legal nature of the standards is disputed between Rabbi Yohanan and Rabbi Hoshayah. The first asserts that the established standards are a halakhah from Sinai; the second asserts that they are simply a rabbinic institution, and, what is most significant, that they can be modified.[108] In this particular issue of standards, the established norms would have

---

107 We read in bShabbat 97a: כל פחות משלשה כלבוד דמי הלכתא גמירי לה "[The rule that] whatever is within the limit of less than three handbreadths is deemed to be attached [to the ground] is a halakhah received by tradition." This rule refers to the example cited above (n. 98) of transferring an object from a private domain to another private domain over a public road, without touching the public domain. Since the item does not touch the public domain, the transfer should be permitted, because there was legally and actually no transfer from the private to the public domain. But if it was transferred close to the ground, that is, less than three handbreadths above it, it is deemed to have touched the ground, and hence a legal transfer to the public domain was performed. There is no indication whatsoever that this rule has the attribute "given to Moses from Sinai." In the Y. T. (Sukkah 1: 1, 52b, and many other occurrences) this rule appears as: שכל הפחות משלשה כסתום הוא "everything [separated by a gap of] less than three handbreadths is deemed attached," with no indication of its legal characterization. A similar dictum is encountered in bBava Qamma 17b: לעולם כגופו דמי וחצי נזק צרורות הלכתא גמירי לה "It [the gust of air from a bird's wings] is deemed to be like its body, and the rule that [an owner pays only] half of the damage caused by pebbles [cast up by his animal, thus an indirect act] is a halakhah received by tradition." This refers to the general law that if damage is caused by the direct movement of an animal or bird, the owner must pay full damages; if, in contrast, a rooster flew over an object and the gust created by the flapping of its wings caused the damage, its owner pays for only half the damage. Tradition decrees that although the gust from the rooster's wings, and similar types of indirect actions, such as pebbles tossed up by a walking ox that damage a vessel (mBava Qamma 1: 2), are deemed to be produced directly by the animal's body, there is a halakhah received by tradition that the owner pays half the damages. We must again agree that the term does not refer to a "halakhah [given] to Moses from Sinai."

108 In bYoma 80a, the same dictum is quoted in the name of Rabbi Eliezer.

obvious repercussions if they are deemed Torah precepts. From the rabbinic principles regarding punishment, or liability for a sin offering, as a consequence of a transgression involving the established standards, we must assume that they are deemed to be Torah rules.

With respect to the use of the willow branch, also characterized as "given from Sinai," its legal characterization as a Torah precept or a rabbinic institution also has decisive significance. As a Torah rule it might override another Torah precept, but as a rabbinic institution it has an inferior status and is overruled by a Torah precept. We have seen that the use of the willow branch overrides the Sabbath, if it occurs on the last day of Sukkot.[109] This would again imply that a "halakhah [given] to Moses from Sinai" is considered a Torah precept; yet, as we have seen,[110] this is not always the case.

We must also consider that certain Sages had particular views on the meaning of terms. The ambiguity of the definition of הלכתא brought up above is also discussed in the Talmudim, and seems to be an issue disputed between Amoraim. A statement is made in mOrlah 3: 9: "*Orlah* [the law forbidding use of the fruit of a plant in its first three years] is a halakhah and *kil'ayim* [the prohibition against planting two different kinds of seed together] is a rabbinic stipulation [מדברי סופרים]." (The mishnah discusses the application of these rules outside Israel.) In yOrlah 3: 7, 63b and bQiddushin 38b it is asked: What does the undefined term "halakhah" in the mishnah mean, and the reply is: "Samuel said [in the B. T. it is Rav Yehudah in the name of Samuel]: It is a custom [הלכתא in B.T.[111]] embraced by the people of that country [Syria] [in other words, it is a

---

109 Chap. 2, n. 28. In tSukkah 3: 1, we read: לולב דוחה את השבת בתחלתו וערבה בסופו "The [precept of the] *lulav* overrides the Sabbath at the beginning [the first day of the Feast] and the [precept of the] willow at the end [the last day]." The precept of the willow must be a Torah precept; if it were a rabbinic stipulation, it could not override the Sabbath, a Torah law. Further confirmation of the overriding of the Sabbath is found in tSukkah 3: 1 and bSukkah 43b, in the statement: לפי שאין ביתסין מודין שחבוט ערבה דוחה את השבת "...since the Boethusians do not agree that the beating of the willow branch overrides the Sabbath...."; hence according to those with whom the Boethisians disagreed, the willow branch must be a Torah precept. For an extensive dicussion of this issue, see P. Heger, "Tosefta."

110 We read in ySukkah 4: 1, 54b, in the name of Rabbi Yohanan: ערבה הלכה למשה מסיני ודלא כאבא שאול דאבא שאול אומר ערבה דבר תורה "The [precept of] the willow branch is a halakhah given to Moses from Sinai; this conflicts with Abba Saul's [declaration], since he said that the [precept of] the willow is a Torah utterance." It is further stated: ודלא כרבי עקיבה "[and] not according to Rabbi Aqiba," who also maintains that it is a Torah utterance.

111 As Rashi explains in the B.T.: הלכתא מדינה: הנהיגוהו הם עליהם בחוצה לארץ - that is, the people have undertaken this halakhah upon themselves, and thus it is a lesser obligation than a Torah precept.

tradition]. Rabbi Yohanan said [in the B. T. it is Ulla in Rabbi Yohanan's name]: It is a halakhah given to Moses from Sinai." In equating the concept הלכתא in the Mishnah with "given to Moses from Sinai," it seems that Rabbi Yohanan considers it a Torah rule.[112] And we observe that Rabbi Yohanan is the personality maintaining in other occurrences that "halakhah given to Moses from Sinai" has the validity of a Torah precept.[113] He also sides with Rabbi Eleazar ben Azaryah in his dispute with Rabbi Aqiba (bNiddah 72b)[114] concerning the concept of "halakhah

---

112 Both the Y.T. and B. T. contain, in essence, the same question; as is common, the Y. T. version is extremely short and would require extended interpretation, and I therefore quote here from the B. T. version: בשלמא לדידי דאמינא הלכה למשה מסיני היינו דשני לן בין ספק ערלה לספק כלאים "[Ulla questioned the opposing opinion and said:] According to my declaration that [the rule] is a halakhah given to Moses from Sinai, the distinction in the Mishnah between [the rules regarding] a dubious *orlah* and [those regarding] a dubious *kil'ayim* is justified [because the first is a Torah precept and the second is a rabbinic stipulation; but if, according to your opinion, the term הלכתא in the Mishnah also refers to a rabbinic decree, there is no justification for a distinction with respect to both dubious cases]." A dubious condition with respect to a Torah precept is decided in a stringent manner, but in a lenient manner with respect to a rabbinic decree; see above n. 101.

113 In yPe'ah 1: 1, 15b and bYoma 80a concerning שיעורין, standards, and in ySukkah 4: 1, 54b and bSukkah 34a concerning the willow branches. In the Y. T. versions, however, there is an apparent contradiction, or at least an ambiguous dictum regarding the understanding of the term by the Sages or redactors. The deliberations in Pe'ah contain the following statement by an Amora: רבי יוחנן כדעתיה דרבי יוחנן אמר כל השיעורין הלכה למשה מסיני דו אמר מעה כסף שתי כסף דבר תורה "Rabbi Yohanan [made the declaration] according to his opinion, since he said: All the standards are a halakhah given to Moses from Sinai; therefore he said that [the minimum value of] one silver coin [for the pilgrimage offering] and two silver coins [for the *hagigah* offering] is a Torah utterance." A homily is then quoted in the name of Rabbi Yohanan, giving the same validity to rules not heard at Sinai as if they had actually been uttered there. Thus a "halakhah given to Moses from Sinai" is equated to a Torah utterance. Another passage, however, gives the impression that in Rabbi Yohanan's opinion such a halakhah is not a Torah utterance. We read in ySukkah 4: 1, 54b (quoted in n. 110): רבי יוחנן ערבה הלכה למשה מסיני ודלא כאבא שאול דאבא שאול אומר ערבה דבר תורה "Rabbi Yohanan [said the precept of] the willow branch is a halakhah given to Moses from Sinai; this conflicts with Abba Saul, who said that the willow branch is a Torah utterance." We can conclude only that such imprecise terminology abounds.

114 As we have seen in chap. 1, n. 108: אמר לו רבי אלעזר בן עזריה לר"ע אפי' אתה מרבה בשמן [בשמן] כל היום כולו איני שומע לך אלא חצי לוג שמן לתודה ורביעית יין לנזיר ואחד עשר יום שבין נדה לנדה הלכה למשה מסיני מאי הלכה ר' יוחנן אמר הלכה י"א "Rabbi Eleazar ben Azaryah said to Rabbi Aqiba: Even if you continue to deduce for the entire day the quantity of oil required at the thanksgiving offering [not indicated in Scripture] from the duplication of the term 'in oil,' I do not agree with you, because the requirement of half a *log* of oil at the thanksgiving offering, and of a quarter of a *hin* of wine for the Nazir's libation

given to Moses from Sinai." In other occurrences, as for example with respect to the form and colour of the phylacteries and their straps, we do not encounter Rabbi Yohanan's direct[115] involvement.[116] I would postulate that Rabbi Yohanan made a definite distinction between edicts with the attribute "halakhah given to Moses from Sinai," which were all deemed Torah precepts, and other edicts received by tradition that did not possess this attribute and were considered rabbinic stipulations. The Gemara, as I have previously stated, did not care to distinguish between them, and thus created the confusion.

Logical and social[117] considerations also had a great influence on the Sages' classifications. Such considerations are at the basis of many

---

offering, and the decree that there are only eleven pure days between two menstrual cycles, are all halakhah given to Moses from Sinai [and have no support from Scripture, as Rabbi Aqiba declares]. [Question:] What is the halakhah [regarding the eleventh day?] Rabbi Yohanan said: [The purity cycle consists] of eleven days." In this case we see that Rabbi Yohanan sides with the opinion that these stipulations are "given to Moses from Sinai," and further, that both are equal to Torah precepts. That is, as the eleven day rule is bundled together with the libation rule, and as the quantities of oil and wine must definitely be considered Torah obligations, the eleven day rule is also a Torah precept.

115 In some instances, as for example yPe'ah 1: 1, 15a, we do not encounter the direct involvement of Rabbi Yohanan. Rather, in the deliberations it is suggested that the relevant dictum corresponds with Rabbi Yohanan's opinion. On the issue of the phylacteries and their form, colour and straps, see n. 89.

116 There are the following sources for these rules: yMegillah 1: 9, 71d, and 4: 9, 75c; bShabbat 28b, 62a and 79b; bEruvin 97a; bMakkot 11a; bMenahot 32b and 35a. We encounter one apparent exception in bMegillah 19b: ואמר רבי חייא בר אבא אמר רבי יוחנן שיור התפר הלכה למשה מסיני "Rabbi Hiyya son of Abba said in the name of Rabbi Yohanan: The size of the unattached part of the *megillah* sheets is a halakhah given from Sinai." This is certainly not a Torah precept, and we are subsequently told that the Amora who uttered it ומחו לה אמוחא ולא אמרו אלא כדי שלא יקרע "hit himself on the head [because he made a mistake, since] the Sages only declared this rule to avoid the tearing of the scroll [and it is not a halakhah given from Sinai]." In yMegillah 1: 9, 71d, there is an explicit statement that the rule regarding sewing together the sheets of the Torah scroll and other holy writings was made by an Amora in the name of Rab. Rabbi Yohanan is mentioned in connection with this rule by another Amora, but he quotes only the term הלכה without the attribute "given to Moses from Sinai." Thus it is the Amora himself who wrongly understood the rule as a "halakhah given to Moses from Sinai"; he retracts this idea with the same proclamation as recorded in the B. T. Rabbi Yohanan is thus consistent in his statements.

117 As we have noted (Introduction, pp. 33 ff.), M. Halbertal, מהפכות, discussing the extent to which ethical motives played a role in the Sages' halakhic decisions, quotes (p. 16) Rabbi Aqiba's declaration that a woman is allowed to put on her make-up during her menstrual period, in order to avoid being repulsive to her husband, who might divorce her. According to Halbertal, Rabbi Aqiba's decision was influenced by an ethical consideration. This dictum is of interest for two reasons: a) Rabbi Aqiba reverses an interpretation of a scriptural verse, which was allegedly the foundation for

rabbinic resolutions and declarations that seem odd when they are assessed merely on the basis of the plain biblical commands underlying them. It is interesting to consider again the difference in legal status between the law of *orlah* and the law of *kil'ayim*; according to mOrlah 3: 9, as we have noted above, the first law is considered a Torah precept and the second only a rabbinic decree.[118] In this regard, Safrai has discussed the apparent contradiction in the fact that the laws of *orlah* and of tithing are valid outside Israel, whereas the *shemittah* law (requiring the resting of the land in the seventh year) is invalid outside Israel.[119] I suggest that the distinction between these rules is founded upon practical considerations. The Sages attempted to maintain social order among the Jewish people, and therefore maintained the laws of *terumah* and tithes outside Israel, although this is not decreed in the Torah, as procedures to provide for the clerics and the poor.[120] These socially-inspired rules had a better chance of

---

the opposing view. b) In mKetubbot 9: 2, in contrast, Rabbi Aqiba asserts: אין מרחמין בדין "One does not decide legal issues on compassionate grounds"; this is in opposition to Rabbi Tarfon's decision, which apparently does consider such grounds. Similar to the general tendency in rabbinic legislation, Rabbi Aqiba does not follow a consistent and comprehensive method in his legal decisions, but determines his opinion on the merits of each particular case. It is also plausible that Rabbi Aqiba made concessions on the specific issue of the woman's appearance, given that he had declared that a man may divorce his wife if he found another more beautiful than she (mGittin 9: 10).

118 See the relevant text of mOrlah 3: 9 on pp. 215-6.

119 S. Safrai, הלכה למשה מסיני, pp. 34 and 78.These are laws linked to the land of Israel. We read in mQiddushin 1: 9: כל מצוה שהיא תלויה בארץ אינה נוהגת אלא בארץ ושאינה תלויה בארץ נוהגת בין בארץ בין בחוצה לארץ חוץ מן הערלה וכלאים "All the precepts relevant to the land are valid only in the land [of Israel] and those not relevant to the land are valid both in the land of Israel and outside it, except the laws of *orlah* and *kil'ayim*."

120 We have already noted (section 1.6.4; see also section 4.1.2) the case of mYadayim 4: 3, in which there is a dispute between Rabbi Tarfon and Rabbi Eleazar ben Azariah regarding the allocation of the tithes in Ammon and Moab in the seventh year. Rabbi Tarfon declared that they should be given to the poor, and Rabbi Eleazar declared that they should be consumed in Jerusalem. A long discussion is assumed to have taken place between the two Sages, but we can observe that Rabbi Tarfon, who was not wealthy like Rabbi Eleazar, was more sensitive to the plight of the poor and brought up a social motive for the justification of his opinion. He said: מצרים שהיא קרובה עשאוה מעשר עני שיהיו עניי ישראל נסמכים עליה בשביעית אף עמון ומואב שהם קרובים נעשים מעשר עני שיהיו עניי ישראל נסמכים עליהם בשביעית "Just as in Egypt that is close [to Israel] they have established the tithe for the poor in the seventh year, so that poor Israelites may rely on it for their livelihood, so we should proceed with respect to the tithes of Ammon and Moab, so that poor Israelites may also rely on it for their livelihood in the seventh year." We see from Rabbi Tarfon's argument, not contested by Rabbi Eleazar, that the edict to give the seventh year tithe to the poor in Egypt was instituted by the Sages for social reasons.

being obeyed if presented as a religious rather than a social duty.[121] In addition, all social decrees are considered divine commands; hence their declaration as Torah law was also technically honest. The law of the seventh year, on the other hand, had no such purpose and was therefore not extended beyond its initial scriptural application to the land of Israel.

This explanation may seem a modern, pragmatic approach. Though I believe that the Sages were indeed guided in their decisions by similar reflections, one may also detect theological grounds for this distinction. The law of the seventh year represents a cosmological extension of the seventh day of rest, beginning from God and extending throughout Israel.[122] Just as the weekly Sabbath law applies only to Israelites and not to all other peoples,[123] so the seventh year resting of the land applies exclusively to the land of Israel. The law of *orlah* had the practical purpose of allowing plants to grow and develop in the first three years, but may also have had a theological motive. The Israelite must abandon

---

The end of this mishnah adds further substantiation to my overall thesis. We read there: נמנו וגמרו עמון ומואב מעשרין מעשר עני בשביעית "They voted and decided that the tithes of the seventh year from [the produce of] Ammon and Moab must be given to the poor." We then read that a witness confirmed this decision in the name of Rabban Yohanan ben Zakkai as a "halakhah [given] to Moses from Sinai," a concept I have discussed above. The ideological foundation of the edict was concern for the socially underprivileged, but it was presented to the people as "given from Sinai."

121 S. Lieberman, *Hellenism*, p. 139, draws attention to a dictum in bAvodah Zarah 35a by Ulla: כי גזרי גזירתא במערבא לא מגלו טעמא עד תריסר ירחי שתא דלמא איכא איניש דלא ס״ל ואתי לזלזולי בה "When they decree an edict in the West [i.e. in Israel, as Ulla is in Babylon] they do not divulge the reason [for it] in the first twelve months, because there may be people who would not accept the reason and would disregard it." Lieberman declares that the Sages often indicated a formal motive rather than the real motive behind their edicts to encourage the people to obey them. He quotes, in substantiation of his thesis, an example from mShabbat 6: 2 and the related discussion in bShabbat 60a, concerning the odd prohibition against wearing shoes with iron nails on Sabbath.

122 We read in Mekilta d'Rabbi Simeon bar Yohai, on Exod. 23: 12: מכל מקום מקיש שבת לשביעית "In any event, Sabbath is compared to the seventh year."

123 We read in Mekilta d'Rabbi Ishmael, *Ki-tissa* 1: ושמרו בני ישראל את השבת לעשות את השבת לדורותם ברית עולם ביני ובין בני ישראל ולא ביני ובין אומות העולם "[It is written in Exod 31: 16 - 17] 'The Israelites have to observe the Sabbath, celebrating it for the generations to come as a lasting covenant. It will be a sign between me and the Israelites for ever.' [Thus it is a sign between me and the Israelites], and not between me and the gentiles." In bBetzah 16a, the same idea is expressed by a metaphor: מתנה טובה יש לי בבית גנזי ושבת שמה ואני מבקש ליתנה לישראל "[God said to Moses:] I have a valuable gift in my treasury, called Sabbath, and I wish to give it to Israel." There is also an odd dictum that prohibits a gentile from keeping the Sabbath, as we read in bSanhedrin 58b: נכרי ששבת חייב מיתה "A gentile who kept the Sabbath is liable for the death penalty."

enjoyment of the fruit for the first three years, thus renouncing something precious of his own, the first benefits of fertility; the rule may be considered as a symbolic extension of the circumcision of the foreskin, symbol of fecundity, also termed *orlah*.[124] This nuance of giving away the first fruits is, in fact, confirmed from the status of the fruits of the fourth year, in which "all its fruit will be holy, an offering of praise to the Lord [Lev 19: 24]."

Returning to the difference in legal status between *orlah* and *kil'ayim*, we see that *orlah* is thus a theological precept with the purpose of inculcating a spiritual effect on the Israelite, and therefore has the character of a personal obligation, valid everywhere. The Sages, I hypothesize, were not certain of the philosophical foundation of the prohibition against planting certain plants together. It might be considered as a misdemeanor against the land, and therefore would not apply in a foreign land; or it might be considered an affront to the divine creation of distinct plants, similar to the prohibition against mating "different kinds of animals [Lev 19: 19]," and as such would be valid universally.[125] The Sages thus decided that this prohibition should bear the character of a rabbinic edict, a distinction that, as we have noted, has legal repercussions particularly in cases of doubt.

We observe, as in other instances, the complexity of the legal problems in the rabbinic literature, and the impossibility of establishing a systematic classification of the terms and concepts used.[126] Each dictum must be analyzed on its particular merits as a problem *sui generis*.

We may conclude by noting the distinction between הלכה למשה מסיני "halakhah [given] to Moses from Sinai" and תקנה *taqqanah* (discussed above in section 1.6.4), as on the surface they appear to be similar. Neither depends on scriptural exegesis, but the first retains the highly esteemed attribute of Sinaitic origin, whereas the second is of a lesser pedigree. Since both concepts were devised for the achievement of similar goals, that is, the validation of customs and rules absent in

---

[124] It is not within the scope of this study to examine the anthropological foundation of circumcision, an ancient custom still practised today in certain societies. I shall simply refer to certain hints of this symbolism in Scripture: the circumcision of Moses' sons, in Exod 4: 25; the גבעת הערלות "the hill of the foreskins" at the sanctuary of Gilgal, in Josh 5: 3; the foreskins of the Philistines given by David to Saul as a price for his daughter, in 1 Sam 18: 25 and emphasized again in 2 Sam 3: 14.

[125] The prohibition against wearing "clothing woven of two kinds of material [Lev 19: 19]" is an element of the same verse prohibiting the two other types of mixtures, but is definitely a command directed at humans: ובגד כלאים שעטנז לא יעלה עליך; it is therefore valid perpetually and universally.

[126] S. Albeck, "Law and History in Halakhic Research," p. 1, writes that all halakhot "flow like a river which, like life itself, sweeps on without any system or order."

Scripture, we must assume that the term *taqqanah* was bestowed on such rules that could not be retrojected to Sinai, or that were clearly new temporary or perpetual ordinances.[127] Consequently, as we have seen, the "halakhah given to Moses from Sinai" could be assumed in some occurrences to be a Torah rule, but the *taqqanah* was unmistakably a rabbinic institution with an inferior status.[128] The precept of ערבה, the willow branch, as it was deemed to originate from Sinai, could therefore override the Torah-founded Sabbath law, whereas Hillel's *taqqanah* of the *prosbul* could not.[129] We can only speculate as to why the details regarding the phylacteries, a Torah precept, were granted the attribute "originating from Sinai," while in contrast, the recitation of the blessing after the meal, similarly a Torah precept, had the lower status of a *taqqanah* composed by Moses. We must again acknowledge the want of a precise and systematic definition of rabbinic legal terms; this was not a critical issue on the Sages' agenda.

---

[127] See the detailed discussion of this term in chap. 1, nn. 125 ff. and related text.

[128] It seems that the lower status תקנה did not enjoy the same acceptance as the הלכה למשה מסיני, in particular when its institution was not retrojected to a renowned personality. We may observe the difference between the uttering of the blessing after the meal, which was held to have been composed by Moses, and acknowledged without dispute, and Rabban Yohanan ben Zakkai's תקנה to blow the *shofar* on Sabbath. We read in mRosh HaShanah 4: 1: משחרב בית המקדש התקין רבן יוחנן בן זכאי שיהו תוקעין בכל מקום שיש בו בית דין "After the Temple's destruction, Rabban Yohanan ben Zakkai ordered the blowing of the *shofar* in every locality in which a court is located." A baraita in bRosh HaShanah 29b states that the Bene Bathyra opposed his decree, and he succeeded in overcoming their opposition only by a ruse, creating a *fait accompli* that could not be opposed. We read there: כבר נשמעה קרן ביבנה ואין משיבין לאחר מעשה "[He said] The *shofar* was already blown in Yabneh and one cannot reverse an accomplished fact." Similarly, the rabbinic preventative rules included within the concept of גזרה were not always accepted or obeyed. For example, Rabbi Yose ha-Gelili and the people of his town did not observe the prohibition against mixing fowl with milk (see section 2.5.4).

[129] See the debate in yGittin 4: 3, 45c - d and bGittin 36a (chap. 2, nn. 151-9 and related text), in which the Amoraim attempt to resolve the dilemma of how Hillel could have instituted a תקנה, the *prosbul*, apparently conflicting with a Torah law. In the Y. T. a short general question is asked: "How could Hillel institute a decree contrary to a Torah law"? In the B. T. version, the question is specific to the topic under discussion: "Is it possible that the Torah decreed [that a loan be cancelled] in the seventh year, and Hillel decreed that it is not cancelled"?

3.6 The Role of the Sanhedrin[130]

I am inclined to assume that the scholars who attempted to reveal a system in the rabbinic creation of the law were hesitant to suppose that the Sages, motivated by expedience, were unrestricted in their creation of the law, and not limited by a particular method or principle. The scholars who sought a unified system might also have been influenced by a narrative in tSanhedrin 7: 1, among other places, which implies that the Superior Court in Jerusalem[131] had absolute authority to settle disputes,[132] and by the fact that the ancient mishnayot do not record disputes. They may have

---

130 Scholars debate whether such an institution existed in the pre- and post-70 periods. I shall mention some of these discussions in the course of the study; see especially the scholarly publications listed in n. 145 below, regarding the historicity of the rabbinic accounts of the existence and functions of a Council/ Sanhedrin. I shall continue to use the term "Sanhedrin," following the rabbinic literature, which applies it indiscriminately.

131 The Superior Court in Jerusalem is described in various ways: סנהדרין, בית דין הגדול, בית דין הגדול שבירושלים, בית דין הגדול שבלשכת הגזית, סנהדרין של שבעים, סנהדרין של שבעים ואחד היתה יושבת בלשכת הגזית. It is not within the scope of this study to discuss the various names and functions of the Superior Court, issues that have generated much scholarly debate with respect to the actual number of Superior Courts and their distinct competencies. I shall use indiscriminately the denomination "Superior Court."

132 The following narrative, with slight variations, appears in a number of sources. I shall quote excerpts from tSanhedrin 7: 1: א״ר יוסי בראשנה לא היו מחלוקות בישׂ׳ אלא בבית דין של שבעים בלשכת הגזית "Rabbi Yose said: In previous times, there were no disputes in Israel, but there was the Superior Court of seventy in the *Gazit* Chamber [in Jerusalem]; נצרך אחד מהן הלכה "When one was in need of [a decision and did not know the] halakhah" one went to the lower courts of twenty-three members; אם שמעו אמרו להן ואם לאו אילו ואילו הולכין לבית דין הגדול שבלשכת הגזית "If they knew they told them, and if not they went together to the Superior Court of the *Gazit* Chamber..." של שבעים ואחד "of seventy-one members...." נשאלה שאילה אם שמעו אמרו להם ואם לאו עומדין למינין רבו המטמאין טימאו רבו המטהרין טהרו משם היה יוצאת הלכה ורווחת בישׂ׳ משרבו תלמידי שמאי והילל שלא שימשו כל צורכן הרבו מחלוקות בישראל "The question was posed; if they knew, they told them, and if not they voted; if those who pronounced [something] polluted [or any decision in another matter] were in the majority, they [the entire court] declared it polluted, if those who pronounced it pure were in the majority, they declared it pure. From there the halakhah went out to all of Israel. When the disciples of Shammai and Hillel, who did not adequately attend them [their masters - i.e. study sufficiently], increased in number, disputes increased in Israel." G. Alon, *The Jews*, vol. 1, p. 311, writes that we have no way to authenticate this idyllic description of the period before Shammai and Hillel. S. A. Cohen, *Three Crowns*, p. 50, argues that the narratives concerning the operation of the Sanhedrin are "lacking in realistic detail" and "entirely detached from a clearly defined historical context."

assumed, in other words, that any dissension was resolved by that court, and therefore does not appear in the record. I wish to postulate, first, that the absolute authority of the Superior Court with respect to halakhic decisions is a fiction,[133] and second, that explanations concerning the late origin of disputes are in the nature of apologetics,[134] designed to promote the basic unity of the rabbinic system. I shall demonstrate these propositions based on talmudic citations that appear to be contradictory or illogical. Scholars have in fact questioned the very existence of a Sanhedrin in the pre- and post-70 periods, and whether there was one Sanhedrin or many, and I shall quote some of these opinions in the succeeding notes.

In the pharisaic-tannaitic period, critical questioning was acute, and shook the foundations of the maxim declared in mAvot 1: 1 that all rules and regulations originate from the primeval divine utterance received by Moses and transmitted from generation to generation.[135] Given the level of controversy surrounding almost every rule, it is inconceivable that all law was communicated to Moses and transmitted faithfully through a particular class of people, and only through them. The Sadducees and possibly other splinter groups rightfully contested this unrealistic affirmation.[136] Nonetheless, the existence of dissension and controversy was imputed to an increase in the number of disciples. This pretext is in itself not only extremely vague and undefined, but also conflicts with the pervasive talmudic opinion that such an increase in Torah scholars is desirable. We have only to read the continuation of the above-cited mAvot

---

133 Cf. S. Z. Havlin, על החתימה הספרותית, who endorses this talmudic statement with respect to the Sanhedrin, and therefore posits that decisions taken by this Superior Court could not be contradicted by any other court. He classifies the types of halakhic decisions, other than those delivered by the Sanhedrin, which could be opposed, and the relevant circumstances (pp. 164 ff.). We again observe the self-imposed limitations of a religiously influenced scholar, who dares not contradict an explicit talmudic narrative; as we have noted, in contrast, other scholarly opinions question the authenticity of this narrative.

134 It is quite probable that the Sages, who were used to halakhic disputes on almost every issue, wondered about the lack of such disputes in the pre-70 period. The description of the Sanhedrin establishing halakhah in dubious instances might have been a response to this disturbing question.

135 S. A. Cohen, *Three Crowns*, p. 59, calls this statement "a stunningly audacious piece of propaganda…to authenticate their own perspective." See also G. Stemberger, "Abot," on the redaction of this tractate.

136 I. H. Weiss, דור דור ודורשיו, p. 3, raises a crucial question: Is it not plausible to assume that the Pharisees devised the maxim that all their decisions stemmed from tradition received from Sinai, precisely to confer upon them the legitimacy contested by the Sadducees? Agreement with this assumption would evidently overturn much scholarly assessment of the relationship between tradition and exegesis, a topic discussed above in section 2.2.

1: 1, the core of the tradition, which states the mandate of אנשי כנסת הגדולה "the men of the Great Assembly": "and teach many disciples." Such reasoning also denigrates the renowned[137] members of Beit Hillel and Beit Shammai, the Sages with the most recorded disputes. Moreover, we read in mAvot 5: 17 that controversy between Hillel and Shammai was for the sake of heaven, hence a virtuous occurrence. Halakhic disputes between Tannaim are never described in a deprecatory way.[138] Rav Sherira Gaon was faced with the same quandary as a result of the Karaite movement,[139] which posed the same questions as its forerunners, the Sadducees, had done centuries before. Rav Sherira, however, did not rely on the same pretext of blaming the increase in disciples,[140] possibly perceiving its utter inconsistency; he used instead the stereotypical excuse of the misfortunes following upon the Temple's destruction and the forced transfers of the Sanhedrin.[141] He does mention the disputes between Hillel

---

137 I have cited above (at n. 50) a dictum from bAvodah Zarah 36a affirming the great esteem in which the intellectual capabilities of the disciples of Shammai and Hillel were held: היכי מצי למישרא תקנתא דתלמידי שמאי והלל "How could [Rabbi] repeal a decree promulgated by Beit Shammai and Beit Hillel"? In yHagigah 2: 1, 77d, referring to a controversy between Beit Shammai and Beit Hillel, Rabbi Simeon b. Yohai calls them by the supreme attribute "Fathers of the World": תמיה אני היאך נחלקו אבות העולם על ביריית העולם "I wonder how the 'Fathers of the World' could dispute about the creation of the world?"

138 The following positive statement regarding disputants is found in a discussion in ySheqalim 3: 1, 47b: שכן נחלקו עליה אבות העולם מאן אינון אבות העולם "…since the 'Fathers of the World' disputed about it. Who are these 'Fathers of the World'? [Rabbi Ishmael and Rabbi Aqiba.]" The latter two Tannaim, of course, disputed constantly. Z. Safrai and A. Sagi, סמיכות, p. 25 declare that the Sages "consecrated" the halakhic disputes.

139 See M. Schlüter, *Mishna*, pp. 2 - 4 with respect to the motive of the Kairouan scholar who posed the question to Rav Sherira that resulted in the Epistle; contra Harry Fox, "*Bavli*," pp. 350-3. At any rate, whether the Epistle was a direct response to an ideological crisis in the community due to the Karaite schism, or written simply out of intellectual interest, one must presume that Karaite doctrines played a crucial role in causing these questions to be raised in this particular historical period. We have no evidence of similar inquiries before this period.

140 Maimonides, in the introduction to his Mishnah commentary, is similarly appalled by those who erroneously interpret this statement, and offers a sophisticated understanding that avoids any disparagement of the disciples of Hillel and Shammai.

141 We read in *The Epistle of Rav Sherira Gaon* (987 C. E.) MS Berlin Qu 685 (Or. 160) fol. 210 a, in M. Schlüter, *Mishna*: וכיון דחרב ביהמ״ק ואזלו לביתר וחרבה נמי ואיפלגו רבנן לכל צד ומשום הנך מהומות ושגושי ושמד וצרות לא שמשו כל צורכן נפישו מחלוקת מן כד נחת נפשיה דרבן יוחנן בן זכאי והוה רבן גמ״ל ועדאן הוה איכא ר׳ דוסא בן הרכינס ואחריני נמי מן הנהו ראשונים אע״ג דאידחו בית שמאי ונקבעה כל הלכה כבית הלל בכל מקום הוהי איכא פלוגאתא בדברים אחרים בדורו של רבן גמ״ל "And because the Temple was

and Shammai and their schools, but is careful not to include them explicitly among those Sages (called simply רבנן, Rabbis), who did not study sufficiently.

The Amoraim tried to sustain the fiction that the number of disputes in the period prior to them was limited, and that their manifestation was a late phenomenon. We read in bShabbat 14b: "[But individual members of the houses of] Hillel and Shammai disputed on only three issues."[142] And when this statement is contradicted by evidence of additional disputes, much rhetoric is expended to maintain the original assertion.[143] We must also consider that the idea of charging the disciples with the initiation of the disputes, and thus absolving their teachers, is intrinsically flawed. The

---

destroyed, they [the Sages] went to Betar and [when] it also was destroyed, the Sages were dispersed to every corner. And because of these riots, confusion and religious persecution, and distress, they could not study sufficiently. Many disputes turned up after Rabban Yohanan ben Zakkai's death, at the time of Rabban Gamaliel; and there were still Rabbi Dosa ben Hyrcanos and others from the first generation [of Sages]. And although the [declarations] of Beit Shammai were repealed and [it was agreed] that the halakhah is always according to Beit Hillel, there were still disputes in the period of Rabban Gamaliel." I need not comment on the accuracy of Rav Sherira's records of events and personalities or the degree of historicity in these records. For our purpose, it suffices to observe his sensitivity to the ideological dilemma posed by the talmudic reasoning, which induced him to tamper with the talmudic text and modify his explanation accordingly.

142 In yHagigah 2: 2, 77d, the same declaration appears in an indirect manner (see chap. 1, n. 26). There are a number of occurrences that record Shammai's statements or conduct conflicting with an anonymous declaration. These do not indicate the name of the contender, but we may assume that it was Hillel. Mishnah Sukkah 2: 8, for instance, records Shammai's action to enable a newborn to fulfill the precept of being in the Sukkah; in bQiddushin 43a, Shammai disputes the remarkable law that acquits the person who contracts with somebody else to commit a crime. Whether Shammai disputed these halakhot with Hillel or with other Tannaim, these instances indicate that controversies were common before the increase in the number of disciples. The dispute concerning the responsibility of one who contracts for murder appears only implicitly in the Y. T.; Shammai the Elder is not involved in the confrontation.

143 The selection of the three disputes between Shammai and Hillel is in itself strange, and raises additional questions. These disputes are the first three contested issues quoted in Mishnah Eduyyot, and in all three the halakhah is established neither according to Shammai nor according to Hillel, but according to the anonymous חכמים. These three halakhot were mentioned because of this exceptional feature; unusual attributes also distinguish the succeeding two halakhot. (See also the discussion of these mishnayot above, n. 5.) One may assume that in the other disputes, the halakhah followed Beit Hillel, or Hillel. It is odd that in some mishnayot, Shammai disputes the statement of his disciples, the Beit Shammai, and we must ask whether it was Shammai who opposed his disciples, or the disciples who disputed Shammai's statements. As we have noted, it is strange that Hillel, who was the disciple of Shemayah and Abtalion, did not know their proclamations, and their teachings had to be learned from two humble weavers. The fictional character of this aspect of the narrative casts doubt upon the authenticity of other details.

creation of two distinct schools, each named after its foremost teacher, and each assumed to possess particular characteristics reflective of its general perspective, must have resulted from the conflicting attitudes of the principals. Of course, such a situation would not preclude the disciples pronouncing statements actually received from their teachers, which were then recorded in the name of the group.[144]

Furthermore, there are countless talmudic citations that contradict the assertion that the Sanhedrin[145] settled all disputes between the Sages. In mHagigah 2: 2 there is recorded a dispute between five generations of Patriarchs (נשיאים) and chiefs of the Superior Court (אבות בית דין) from

---

[144] Y. T. Shabbat 1: 8, 4a, gives such an example with respect to the prohibition against boarding a ship before Sabbath: אין מפרישין לים הגדול לא בערב שבת ולא בחמישי בשבת ב״ש אוסרים אפילו ברביעי ובית הלל מתירין "One does not board [a boat sailing] to the Great Sea, either on the eve of Sabbath or on Thursday. Beit Shammai prohibit it even on Wednesday, and Beit Hillel permit it." This dispute is presented as a point of contention between Beit Hillel and Beit Shammai, but in Sifre Num 203 and Midrash Tannaim to Deut 20: 20, we read: זה אחד משלשה דברים שדרש שמיי הזקן אין מפליגים את הספינה לים הגדול אלא קודם לשבת שלשה ימים "This is one of the three utterances pronounced by Shammai the Elder: One does not board a boat [sailing] to the Great Sea less than three days before Sabbath." We observe that the declaration of Beit Shammai was really a statement of Shammai. It would thus be reasonable to assume that many of the statements quoted in the name of Beit Shammai were really declared by Shammai himself. See the Appendix regarding the topic of the two Houses.

[145] I wish to reiterate here that the prerogatives and authority of the Sanhedrin in the pre- and post-70 periods, with respect to what can be ascertained from rabbinic and Greek sources, are matters of great confusion and controversy. Many scholars have debated these issues, and a variety of hypotheses have been posited regarding the number of Superior Courts or Councils, and their specific functions and authority. H. Mantel, *Sanhedrin*, offers in his introduction, p. XII, and in chap. 2, a detailed report of the many scholarly publications and opinions on this topic up to his time. D. Goodblatt, *The Monarchic Principle*, chaps. 4 and 7, discusses conflicting rabbinic traditions on this issue, as well as modern studies on the questions of whether and when such an institution existed, and the extent of its authority. He too concludes (p. 239): "In sum, there is some indication that the court at Yavneh was considered a successor to and near replacement of the (mythical) 'Great Court' in pre-70 Jerusalem. Such a view may be attested as early as Aqiva." On p. 3 he writes that there was no dominant council in the Second Temple period, because of priestly supremacy. J. Efron, *Studies of the Hasmonean Period*, pp. 288 ff., also gives a concise record of scholarly discussions and doubts concerning the authenticity of the talmudic testimonies about the composition and functions of the Sanhedrin; he cites the various contradictions concerning the Sanhedrin and attempts to reconcile them. See also G. Stemberger, "Judentums," pp. 92 ff., who expresses doubt as to the existence of this institution, as it is portrayed in rabbinic literature, in both the pre- and post-70 periods. G. Alon, *The Jews*, vol. 1, p. 185, writes: "Unfortunately for us, there is much about that original Sanhedrin that remains problematical and speculative. We do not really know how it began, or how it developed." For our purposes, it suffices to draw attention to the questionable nature of the rabbinic evidence with respect to this issue.

the period of Yose ben Yoezer until the period of Hillel and Shammai, that is, over one hundred years; the issue concerned the question of whether one may lay hands on the individual offerings on the holidays. Without taking any position regarding the authenticity of this narrative, one must question how such circumstances can be reconciled with the statement that the Sanhedrin decided on every halakhic dispute. In mHagigah 2: 3 a dispute is quoted between Beit Shammai and Beit Hillel regarding the offerings of holocausts on holidays,[146] and tHagigah 2: 11 records an incident concerning this matter in the Temple precinct, in which Hillel the Elder was personally involved.[147] These two citations alone suffice to

---

[146] Beit Shammai assert that one may offer a fellowship offering, because it is eaten on the holiday, and thus included in the permission to prepare food for consumption on a holiday; but one may not offer a holocaust offering, which is not eaten. Beit Hillel allow both fellowship and holocaust offerings.

[147] This story, which confirms the mishnah dispute, is rather unusual: We read there: מעשה בהלל הזקן שסמך על העולה בעזרה וחברו עליו תלמידי שמיי אמ׳ להם בואו וראו שהיא נקבה וצריך אני לעשותה זבחי שלמים הפליגן בדברים והלכו להן מיד גברה ידן של בית שמיי ובקשו לקבוע הלכה כמותן והיה שם בבא בן בוטא שהוא מתלמידי בית שמיי ויודע שהלכה כדברי בית הלל בכל מקום הלך והביא את כל צאן קידר והעמידן בעזרה ואמ׳ כל מי שצריך להביא עולות ושלמים יבוא ויטול ויסמוך באו ונטלו את הבהמה והעלו עולות וסמכו עליהן בו ביום נקבעה הלכה כדברי בית הלל ולא ערער אדם בדבר "It happened that Hillel the Elder laid hands on a holocaust offering in the Temple court and the disciples of Shammai encircled him [protesting his conduct]. He [using a stratagem] told them: Come and see that it is a female animal and I must offer it as a fellowship offering; he pacified them and they left him. Immediately [as a consequence of Hillel's assent to their opinion] the position of Beit Shammai strengthened and they sought to establish the halakhah according to their opinion. [But] a disciple of Beit Shammai, Baba ben Buta, was there, and was aware that the halakhah was according to Beit Hillel, so he went and brought all the sheep from Kedar [Arabia], placed them in the Temple court and proclaimed: Whoever has to offer holocaust and fellowship offerings may come, take [a sheep] and lay his hands upon it. And so they came, took the animal[s], offered holocausts and laid their hands upon them. On that day the halakhah was [finally] established according to Beit Hillel and nobody contested it." There are a number of piquant details in this story. Why did the disciples of Beit Shammai protest, when they should have known, as Baba ben Buta knew, that the halakhah was according to Beit Hillel? Why did Hillel conceal the truth (or lie) and not confront them with the assertion that he was acting correctly, especially as Baba ben Buta felt free to challenge them? The narrative does not tell us how Baba ben Buta knew that the halakhah was according to Beit Hillel, but we must assume that it was common knowledge, established by a majority vote or by the "Voice of Heaven" - that is, generally approved. There is also the question of why the halakhah was finally accepted through the individual action of Baba ben Buta, rather than by the regular method of establishing halakhah. How Baba ben Buta managed to obtain (or buy) many animals from Kedar and bring them to the Temple on a holiday without transgressing the law is another curious question, and adds to the aura of skepticism surrounding this narrative. The narrative does suggest, on the other hand, the fluid circumstances surrounding the establishment of any halakhah.

contest the fictitious assertion that the Sanhedrin had decisive authority to resolve halakhic disputes,[148] but there are many other bits of evidence.[149] We do not possess exact data on the origin of the different groups, or the use of the general "Beit Hillel" and "Beit Shammai."[150] As with the term חכמים, used by Rabbi in the Mishnah to attribute his preferred halakhah to a majority,[151] there may have been similar reasons to conceal the names

---

[148] A. Büchler, who maintains that there were many Superior Courts, writes in הסנהדרין, p. 39 that neither in Josephus nor in the New Testament do there appear any data concerning the halakhic activity of the Sanhedrin. Such activity is only mentioned in the rabbinic literature.

[149] J. Efron, *Studies of the Hasmonean Period*, p. 293 writes that the smoothly functioning system of the Sanhedrin as portrayed in the literature was not fulfilled in practice. Josephus' statement in *Ant*. 4: 218 reflects the utopian nature of this system: ἄν δ' οἱ δικασταὶ μὴ νοῶσι περὶ τῶν ἐπ' αύτοῖσ παρατεταγμένων ἀποφήνασθαι, συμβαίνει δὲ πολλὰ τοιαῦτα τοῖσ ἀνθρώποισ , ἀκέραιον ἀναπεμπέτωσαν τὴν δίκην εἰσ τὴν ἱεράν πόλιν, καὶ συνελθόντεσ ὅ τε ἀρχιερεὺσ καὶ ὁ προφήτησ καὶ ἡ γερουσία τὸ δοκοῦν ἀποφαινέσθωσαν "But if the judges see not how to pronounce upon the matters set before them - and with men such things oft befall - let them send up the case entire to the holy city and let the high priest and the prophet and the council of elders meet and pronounce as they think fit." There were no prophets in Josephus' period; further, the talmudic records do not mention the High Priest's involvement in the process of solving halakhic questions. Moreover, it seems odd that Josephus names the γερουσία, not the συνέδριον, and it is not at all certain that the two names refer to the same institution. Josephus uses the term συνέδριον generally without specification, as a generic name for a council or an assembly of persons with power of decision, such as relatives and friends of the ruler, army commanders, Romans or Jews (the latter in *Ant*. 14: 91). In *Ant*. 14: 167 the term refers to the Jewish Sanhedrin, as a High Court with the authority to deliver death sentences (in relation to Herod's execution of such sentence without a prior judgement of the Sanhedrin). He does not use this term to describe an assembly that decides the correct law.

[150] To the best of my knowledge, there has been no serious investigation of why, when, and by whom it was decided not to mention the names of the individual Sages, and to classify them together in anonymous groups called "Beit Hillel" and "Beit Shammai." In some instances, individual sages are identified: for example, Rabbi Eliezer in bNiddah 7b (see chap. 2, n. 220), Baba ben Buta (cited above n. 147), Rabbi Dostai (mOrlah 2: 5), Yo'ezer Ish HaBirah (mOrlah 2: 12) and Yohanan ben HaHoranit (tSukkah 2: 3). In yNedarim 5: 6, 39b, and in a baraita quoted in bSukkah 28a, we learn that Jonathan ben Uzziel and Yohanan ben Zakkai were two of the eighty disciples (pairs of disciples in the Y. T.) of Hillel. This issue will be discussed further in the Appendix.

[151] We read, for example, in bTa'anit 6a: מאן חכמים אמר רב חסדא רבי יוסי היא "[Whose opinion is stated under the eponym] חכמים? Rav Hisda said: It is Rabbi Yose'[s opinion]." It is interesting to observe Rabbi's twofold system with respect to Rabbi Meir, the author of most anonymous mishnayot. We read in bGittin 46b מאן חכמים ר' מאיר, a statement that Rabbi Meir's opinion is behind the eponym חכמים, while in countless mishnayot we read: דברי ר' מאיר וחכמים אומרים "These are the words of Rabbi Meir but the חכמים [with no indication as to who is

of the individual contenders in a halakhic dispute.[152] It is thus possible that at least some of the disputes between "Beit Shammai and Beit Hillel" originated in the period after the Temple's destruction.[153]

Even in such a case, however, the same question persists: why did the Sanhedrin not resolve such disputes? The Sanhedrin was certainly active[154] in Sepphoris and Beit Shearim at the time of Rabbi[155] and could have resolved the disputes between the Beit Shammai and Beit Hillel groups that were deemed to have created so much chaos in the halakhic world.[156] In mMakkot 1: 10, for instance, it is attested: "The Sanhedrin

---

behind this anonymous term] say [an opposing declaration]." In bQiddushin 76b, we read a similar amoraic statement: זו דברי ר׳ מאיר אבל חכמים אומרים.

152 The usual Y. T. question is: מאן תנא "Who is the Tanna [whose opinion is proclaimed anonymously in the Mishnah]." In other instances, the Gemara states: מתניתא דרבי "The anonymous opinion in the Mishnah is the opinion of Rabbi X," in answer to an implied question.

153 Jack N. Lightstone, *Yose the Galilean*, p. 111. We have seen above that the dispute regarding the offerings of the holocaust on holidays occurred in fact (if the story is authentic) in the period of the Temple, and took place between Beit Shammai and Beit Hillel (the term בית שמאי is used).

154 This statement is based on rabbinic sources, and is thus certainly open to critical analysis. I have mentioned above (n. 145) the existence of scholarly discussions that question the authenticity of such an institution and its functions. On the other hand, there is no question that some type of a primary Council of Sages did exist; its name and precise authority are irrelevant to my thesis. It is obvious that the Sages would voluntarily have accepted its decisions in halakhic disputes, if this had been established practice in the pre-70 period.

155 These locations are recorded in bRosh HaShanah 31b with respect to the transfers of the Sanhedrin: ומבית שערים לצפורי. In bKetubbot 103b we read: ר׳ בבית שערים הוה אלא כיון דחלש אמטיוהי לציפורי " Rabbi was [living] in Beit Shearim, but because he was sick, they moved him to Sepphoris"; the Sanhedrin was thus also moved there. The narrative regarding the transfers of the Sanhedrin does not appear in the Y. T. There is only an indirect suggestion in ySheqalim 5: 1, 48d, that there was a Sanhedrin at Yabneh: תני סנהדרין שיש בה שנים שיודעין לדבר וכולן ראויין לשמוע הרי זו ראויה לסנהדרין שלשה הרי זו בינונית ארבעה הרי זו חכמה וביבנה היו בה ארבעה "We learned in a baraita: If a Sanhedrin has [among its members] two persons who speak [in seventy languages], and all [the others] can understand [them], it is an apt Sanhedrin; [if it has] three [with such knowledge] it is [considered of] average [competence]; [if it has] four, it is [considered] intelligent; and in Yabneh, there were four [members with such knowledge]."

I wish to reiterate that I do not intend to take any position with respect to the institution called Sanhedrin in rabbinic literature. Since I am attempting to demonstrate generally the internal inconsistencies in this literature, I utilize the terms and concepts mentioned therein, without implying any opinion as to their existence, function, or authority in the periods reflected in the narratives.

156 As we have seen in the above-cited tSanhedrin 7: 1 (n. 132). This narrative also appears in other rabbinic sources. A similar record that "From there the halakhah

operates in Israel and outside Israel."[157] There is also a specific dictum to the effect that the requirement to abide by the decisions of the contemporary court is valid for the court at Yabneh,[158] and this rule would

---

went out to all of Israel" appears with respect to the law of the rebellious elder, in mSanhedrin 11: 2.

157 We encounter an apparently conflicting dictum in bSanhedrin 37b: מיום שחרב בית המקדש אף על פי שבטלה סנהדרין ארבע מיתות לא בטלו "From the day of the Temple's destruction, although the Sanhedrin was abolished, the four types of capital punishment were not abolished." It would appear that the Sanhedrin was not active after the Temple's destruction, a fact contradicted by the above-cited quotations and by the accepted wisdom that the Sanhedrin was active after that event. We must interpret this dictum to refer to the abolition of the authority of the Sanhedrin to render death sentences, according to what we know from the New Testament and from bShabbat 15a: ארבעים שנה עד שלא חרב הבית גלתה לה סנהדרין "Forty years before the destruction of the Temple the Sanhedrin was exiled [from the *Gazit* Chamber in the Temple precinct to a חנות 'store']." The consequences of this move are then stated: שלא דנו דיני נפשות "They did not judge cases that involved death sentences." There is an interesting parallel to this narrative in Sifre Zuta 35: 22: ת״ל מות יומת מכל צד אין במשמע אלא בזמן שהסנהדרין במקומה בזמן שאין הסנהדרין במקומה נתחייב אדם סקילה ביתו נופל עליו "It is written [Num 35: 21]: 'He must be put to death.' This means when the Sanhedrin is in its [proper] location; but when it is not in its location, and a person is sentenced to die by stoning, his house falls upon him [and he is killed by divine intervention]." The passage continues with similar accidents that afflict the sinner. We observe that there is no direct reference to the Sanhedrin being abolished; the euphemistic expression "not in its location" is utilized instead. This phrase may relate to a mythological notion of the eternal existence of the Sanhedrin, which is expressed in a homily in Sifre Num 92: אספה לי שתהא סנהדרין לשמי שבכל מקום שנאמר לי הרי זה קיים לעולם ולעולמי עולמים [It is written in Exod 11: 16:] 'Bring me [seventy of Israel's elders]' - so that there will be a Sanhedrin for my name; every occurrence in which it is said 'for me' refers to [something that is in] existence for ever and ever."

158 We read in Sifre Deut 153 and ySanhedrin 11: 3, 30a: ובאת לרבות בית דין שביבנה "[Deut 17: 9 states:] 'Go [to the priests…and to the judge who is in office at that time]' - to include the court [Sanhedrin] in Yabneh." The talmudic writings make no distinction between the Sanhedrin and the Superior Court in their statements and use the terms indiscriminately (see above n. 130). G. Alon goes beyond the simple skepticism of other scholars and reaches his conclusions on the issue of the Sanhedrin based on an analysis of the talmudic narratives. In *The Jews*, vol. 1, p. 230, he writes that according to a dictum in ySanhedrin 11: 3, 30a, the Superior Court of Yabneh had the same function as the Sanhedrin in Jerusalem, except with respect to the law of the rebellious elder. But he attempts to reconcile an apparent contradiction to this declaration with a passage in yShabbat 1: 4, 3d. We must again note Oppenheimer's criticism of Alon (n. 7), with respect to his political analysis. This bias can definitely be seen by contrasting Alon's perception of rabbinic narratives referring to circumstances pre-70 and those post-70. On the issue of the Sanhedrin's activities pre-70, such as the resolution of halakhic disputes, he is skeptical about granting authenticity to any idyllic depiction of the period before Shammai and Hillel (see n. 132). On the other hand, regarding the politically sensitive issue of the rebuilding of

naturally apply with respect to all other locations of the Sanhedrin. Even if we assume, as many scholars do, that the Romans denied all authority to the Sanhedrin to enforce its own rules,[159] one would expect that the internal discipline of the Sages[160] should have subsisted on such a level as to accept the Sanhedrin's decisions in matters of halakhah, if such a practice had been carried out before.[161] It is thus odd that the Sanhedrin would not employ its authority and resolve these myriad disputes between the Sages.[162]

In addition to my arguments contesting the halakhic decision-making of the Sanhedrin, I would like to draw attention to further opposing evidence. Those scholars who assert the existence of only one Sanhedrin must agree that it would actually have been impossible for this body to decide halakhic disputes, as portrayed in the above-cited rabbinic literature. I do not wish to elaborate on the much debated issue of the Sanhedrin's composition and presidency, but one must admit that it was

---

autonomous Jewish institutions after the Temple's destruction, he is eager to acknowledge the validity of rabbinic declarations, as we observe from the above assertion.

159 It is not within the scope of this study to evaluate the historical functions and authority of the Council/Sanhedrin under Roman rule. I am interested only in demonstrating the fictitious nature of the talmudic assertion that the Sanhedrin resolved halakhic disputes in the pre-70 period.

160 Cf. G. Stemberger, "Judentums," who investigates the authority of the leading Sages in the post-70 period. He criticizes Schürer's conception that Rabban Yohanan ben Zakkai was already the leader of the first Rabbis (p. 96), and that members of the rabbinic sphere ("Umfeld der Rabbinen") voluntarily requested rabbinic decisions (p. 98).

161 The same would apply, even if we concur with the assertion of J. Efron, *Studies of the Hasmonean Period*, p. 301, and other scholars, that there was no Sanhedrin after the Temple's destruction. The change of this institution's name to בית דין הגדול that Efron postulates should not have affected its internal discipline. G. Alon, *The Jews*, vol. 1, p. 8, writes that the Superior Court's authority was particularly strong with respect to religious issues. Alon does not define the concept of "religious issues"; I would assume that he refers to decisions on ritual law, which did not depend on Roman recognition of a Jewish judicial system, since they were not perceived as judicial matters. We observe, however, that the alleged Superior Court or Sanhedrin did not consider it absolutely necessary to impose a fixed halakhah in cases of rabbinic disputes on ritual issues, such as those between Beit Shammai and Beit Hillel.

162 G. Alon, *The Jews*, vol. 1, p. 312, who notes the talmudic declarations on this issue and attempts to reconcile the numerous contradictions, suggests that the Sanhedrin did not sit continuously in Yabneh; it therefore did not decide on all halakhic disputes, but only on certain significant issues. Alon does not, however, explain the reason for the extremely severe handling of Rabbi Eliezer during the Akhnai incident - that is, what was so important as to require his excommunication. See also my comments on J. Rubenstein's analysis of this incident, Introduction, nn. 36 and 39. As I have proposed, it is necessary to distinguish between pronouncing a dissenting halakhah, which was legitimate, and opposing the decision of a court, which was deemed illicit.

composed of both Pharisees and Sadducees;[163] further, the High Priest, who enjoyed a prominent status, was at times a Sadducee.[164] Even if we assume, and this is highly debatable, that in matters of Temple worship the High Priests followed only the pharisaic rules, one could certainly not expect them to refrain from expressing their particular opinions on other halakhic disputes. How could one expect that such a mixed body, with opposing ideas and periods of domination by different groups, would have been accepted by the Pharisees as the superior arbiter in all matters of halakhah?[165]

Finally, I would like to refer again to the scholarly debate as to whether there was one Sanhedrin, or many. It seems to me that a practical issue has been overlooked in this debate: on the basis of the dimensions of the עזרה, Temple precinct, and its various chambers, it is highly questionable whether seventy-one judges and their entourage could have sat in the *Gazit* chamber. The narrow dimensions of this area are attested in mMiddot 2: 6: "The Men's Compartment [עזרת ישראל] of the Temple precinct was one hundred and thirty-five cubits long and eleven cubits wide." In mMiddot 5: 4, we read: "On the south side were the wood chamber, the water chamber [and] the *Gazit* chamber." The mishnah then describes the use of each chamber: "In the *Gazit* chamber the Great Sanhedrin of Israel used to sit and pass judgment on the priesthood." In bYoma 19a[166] the order is reversed, and we read there that these chambers

---

163 Acts 23: 1 - 10.

164 There are many citations of this fact and I shall limit myself to three. We read in tParah 3: 8 of a Sadducee High Priest who was supposed to burn the Red Heifer. In tYoma 1: 8, it is recorded that a Sadducee High Priest performed the incense celebration in the Holy of Holies according to Sadducean rules and died after a few days. In yYoma 1: 5, 39a, and ySukkah 4: 6, 54d, an Amora contends that all celebrations performed according to the Sadducean rules (that is, the water libation, the Red Heifer, and the incense ceremony on the Day of Atonement) were performed by one and the same priest. Acts 5: 17 also refers to a Sadducee High Priest.

165 S. Safrai, הבית השני, p. 14 contests the opinion of scholars who argue that there was more than one Sanhedrin; he maintains that there was only one. He also states (p. 15) that the Sanhedrin was composed of two main blocks: the Sadducees and the Pharisees. He maintains (p. 20) that the Sanhedrin did decide disputes in matters of halakhah, between the Pharisees and Sadducees, or between the various pharisaic schools; but he does not explain how this would have worked in practice. Assuming that a majority vote would decide, we may posit that a number of Sadducees might join the minority pharisaic group, and the halakhah would in the end be established as the result of the Sadducean votes. It is difficult, however, to believe that the pharisaic leadership would consent to such a procedure.

166 We read there: שלש שבצפון לשכת העץ לשכת הגולה לשכת הגזית "Three [chambers] were on the north side: the wood chamber, the water chamber, the *Gazit* chamber."

were located on the north side; this would seem to be the correct side,[167] based on efficient organization of the work. In bYoma 25a, we read: "We deduce that the *Gazit* chamber was [located] half in the holy precinct and half in the *Hil*,[168]and also that it had two entrances, one opening into the holy precinct and one into the *Hil*."[169] The above-cited mMiddot 5: 4 does not state in which compartment the three chambers were located, but from the context we understand that they were in the עזרת ישראל, "Men's Compartment."[170] This may also be deduced from the fact that laymen were not allowed to enter into the עזרת כהנים, "Priests' Compartment,"[171] that followed the Men's Compartment from east to west; further, the Sanhedrin could not extend into the Priests' Compartment, because this was two and one-half cubits higher[172] than the Men's Compartment and the seat of the Sanhedrin must have been on level ground.[173] Hence, the *Gazit* chamber, which had to be open to

---

[167] The comments of Maimonides in *Mishneh Torah, Hilkhot Beit HaBehirah* 5: 17 and Tosafot Yom-Tov in his commentary to Mishnah Middot, and their maps of the Temple court, indicate these chambers to be on the north side.

[168] Between the surrounding wall of the Temple court and the entrance into the holy precinct was a space of ten cubits. We read in mMiddot 2: 3: ממנו החיל עשר אמות ושתים עשרה מעלות היו שם רום המעלה חצי אמה ושלחה חצי אמה "From it [the wall] was the *Hil*, ten cubits [wide], and twelve steps were there, each step half a cubit high and half a cubit wide." Hence the twelve steps occupied six cubits and left four cubits of flat space. The mishnah does not tell us whether the steps were at the side of the wall, and the section near the holy precinct was flat, or vice versa.

[169] This was necessary to enable the priests to enter from the south entrance on the side of the holy precinct, and the Israelites to enter from the north entrance, located in the *Hil*.

[170] We read in mMiddot 2: 5: עזרת הנשים היתה אורך מאה ושלשים וחמש על רחב מאה ושלשים וחמש וארבע לשכות היו בארבע מקצעותיה של ארבעים ארבעים אמה "The Women's Compartment was one hundred and thirty-five cubits long by one hundred and thirty-five cubits wide, and four chambers were [located] in its four corners, each forty cubits by forty cubits." Hence, the *Gazit* chamber could not protrude into the Women's Compartment, because of the chambers in the corners.

[171] We read in mKelim 1: 8: עזרת הכהנים מקודשת ממנה שאין ישראל נכנסים לשם אלא בשעת צרכיהם לסמיכה לשחיטה לתנופה "The Priests' Compartment is holier [than the Men's Compartment] and the Israelites may not enter it except for their [specific] requirements [related to the offering, such as] laying the hands [on the animal], slaughtering [which could be done by a layman] and waving [the offering]."

[172] We read in mMiddot 2: 6: נמצאת עזרת הכהנים גבוהה מעזרת ישראל שתי אמות ומחצה "In consequence, the Priests' Compartment was higher than the Men's Compartment by two and one-half cubits."

[173] The *Gazit* chamber could not extend into the Priests' Ccompartment, because there was no free space, due to the presence of the בית המטבחים (mMiddot 3: 5, and the

laymen, must have been located in the Men's Compartment, which was at most[174] eleven cubits wide. The other dimensions of this chamber must be deduced from other rabbinic narratives. We learn in tSanhedrin 4: 4: "All the people stood and he [the king] sat, since only the kings of the House of David may sit down in the holy precinct." The Sanhedrin, whose members were seated, must have been confined to the section of the chamber that was in the *Hil*, whose floor space, as we have seen,[175] was four cubits wide. The total space was thus at most eleven by four cubits, about six meters by two and one-half meters. It is unlikely that seventy-one members and their entourage could sit in a half-circle[176] within such a small space.[177]

It is interesting to note that the group responsible for the Temple Scroll describes (in column 38 of that document) the building of a court that appears to correspond to the Men's Compartment; this was to have a width of 100 cubits,[178] a far more reasonable space within which to locate the chambers, including the *Gazit* chamber, seat of the Sanhedrin. We must conclude that in this case, as elsewhere, the Sages described theoretical structures without granting due attention to practical issues. Similarly, we must treat the idea that the Sanhedrin functioned as the highest authority on halakhic issues as a mythological[179] utopia. The idea

---

maps of the commentators).

174 As we have seen, there were two other chambers in the Men's Compartment, and we do not know whether they were located to the south side of the *Gazit* chamber, thus leaving the entire width of eleven cubits for that chamber, or to the north side of it, reducing the overall width of the *Gazit* chamber.

175 Mishnah Middot 2: 3, cited above in n. 168.

176 This is the correct arrangement of the court, as appears in tSanhedrin 8: 1: סנהדרין היתה כחצי גורן עגולה כדי שיהיו רואין זה את זה "The [seating arrangement of the] Sanhedrin was like a half-circle, so that they [the members] could see each other." The commentators' maps in the printed editions of the Talmud to Mishnah Middot also indicate the form as a half-circle.

177 S. B. Hoenig, *The Great Sanhedrin*, discusses on pp. 74 - 81 the location of *Lishkat ha-Gazit*, the seat of the Sanhedrin. On p. 77, he also reaches the conclusion that this chamber had two entrances, one for the laity entering from the outside and the other for the priests entering from the *Azarah*. He establishes his assumption from the talmudic sources, but does not pursue his examination of the same talmudic sources to investigate the exact dimensions of the chamber.

178 The English translation of M. Wise, M. Abegg and E. Cook, *Dead Sea Scrolls*, p. 473 states: "You shall build a second [c]ourt surrou[nd]ing the [inn]er [court] at a distance of one hundred cubits. The length of its eastern wall shall be four hundred eighty cubits, the same dimensions applying to all its walls: south, west, and north. Its wall is to be [fo]ur cubits thick and twenty-eight cubits high. Chambers must be built into the outside surface of the wall, distant from each three [Col 39] [and one-half cubits…] No woman shall enter it…."

179 The mythological associations are apparent in passages such as ySotah 7: 5, 22a:

was useful in resolving the dilemma created when the ideological statement that all legal traditions originate from Sinai was contrasted with the prevailing environment of disputes among the Sages.

3.7 Conclusion

I am confident that I have demonstrated the lack of any coherent system in the legal procedure of the Sages. I do not intend to elaborate on the semantic range of the concept of "system"; within the widest application of this term, the Sages who deliberated upon God's commands as transmitted in Scripture were acting within the framework of a system.[180] Yet their basic philosophy of allowing flexibility in the application of the law motivated them to avoid any restrictive standards in creating legal answers suitable to both prevailing and future circumstances.[181] To attain this goal, they used every convenient intellectual scheme: appropriate interpretation of Scripture,[182] logic[183] and

---

שהרי עכן חטא ורובה של סנהדרין נפלה "...Akhan sinned and the majority of the Sanhedrin [thirty-six out of seventy members] were killed [at the first attack on Ai - Josh 7: 5]." This narrative is based on a homily on the verse in Joshua, found in Mekilta d'Rabbi Simeon b. Yohai 12: 37, Lev. Rab. 11: 7, and bBava Batra 121b.

180 We may observe a similar attitude in Israelite cultural-religious life in a later period. Maimonides' attempted, as he writes in the introduction to his *Mishneh Torah*, to codify all the laws "so that no other work should be needed for ascertaining any of the laws of Israel." This work encountered stark opposition from most rabbinic authorities for a long period. They objected to his failure to cite the sources and authorities from which his decisions were derived, which thus prevented them from giving different interpretations. The Geonim before him cited long passages of the Gemara in their codex *Halakhot Gedolot*, which allowed the reader to return to the original sources and form their own ideas about the correct interpretation of the texts, or declare their preference for the decision of one Amora over another. Maimonides' opponents were well aware that he deduced his decisions within the framework of the talmudic system, similar to the earlier Sages who acted within the framework of Scripture, but they wished to retain the right to continue the process of dynamic halakhic creativity.

181 J. Neusner, *From Scripture to 70*, pp. 15-16, classifies the rabbinic halakhot into four categories: I) wholly dependent on Scripture, II) entirely autonomous of Scripture, III) of scriptural origin and secondary development, and IV) of scriptural origin but developed in a way not precipitated by Scripture.

182 The Sages, unhampered by rigid rules, applied hermeneutic techniques in such a way as to suit their intended purposes. See p. 93 for the citation of an apparently paradoxical declaration regarding the assertion of biblical support both for a prohibition and its later repeal. Hermeneutics were also used to reconcile textual contradictions, or to circumvent rules. In other instances, the Sages may have used hermeneutics to reveal the divine intent, whenever they had no prior conceptions on a certain subject. We may compare their method to the modern technique of textual criticism, effected by an unrestricted analysis of every possibility. G. Vermes, *Studies*,

deduction applied within the framework of Israelite doctrines and custom, and the adaptation of tradition, popular practice, and alien influence to the Israelite *Sitz im Leben*, conditioned by the Torah's fundamental principles.

The almost unrestricted extent of their exegesis is demonstrated in the well-known narrative in bMenahot 29b, in which Moses sits in on Rabbi Aqiba's lesson to his disciples. We read there: "And [Moses] did not understand what they were saying, and was extremely distressed. When [Rabbi Aqiba] declared a topic, his disciples asked him: Rabbi, how

---

pp. 80 ff., refers to a process of "applied exegesis," which he describes as the discovery of principles by which Scripture can be applied to new problems.

[183] An interesting style of deliberation is encountered in mYadayim 4: 3, with respect to the dispute between Rabbi Eliezer and Rabbi Tarfon on the issue of seventh year tithes in Ammon and Moab, quoted above (nn. 100 and 120; see also chap. 1, text at n. 118, and chap. 4, nn. 64-66 and related text). The first argument, עליך ראיה ללמד שאתה מחמיר שכל המחמיר עליו ראיה ללמד "You must bring a justification for your assertion, because yours is more severe, and one who decides in a more severe manner must justify it," is a legal argument based on logic. The response is built upon the same principle: אני לא שניתי מסדר השנים טרפון אחי שינה ועליו ראיה ללמד "I have not changed the order of the years [in the sixth year one gives the tithe for the poor, hence in the succeeding year, the tithe to be consumed in Jerusalem is due.] My colleague Tarfon, who changed [the regular sequence, and required the giving of the same class of tithe for two consecutive years] must defend his declaration." Rabbi Tarfon accepted the challenge that the one who wishes to modify the existing law must justify it, and proposed his first logical proof, a comparison to a similar, existing rule: מצרים ח"ל עמון ומואב ח"ל מה מצרים מעשר עני בשביעית אף עמון ומואב מעשר עני בשביעית "Egypt is outside Israel and Ammon and Moab are outside Israel [and therefore it is reasonable to compare them]. Just as the rule was established in Egypt to give the tithe for the poor in the seventh year, so the rule in Ammon and Moab [should be established]." Rabbi Eliezer retorted, based on the same logic: בבל ח"ל עמון ומואב ח"ל מה בבל מעשר שני בשביעית אף עמון ומואב מעשר שני בשביעית "[Why should we compare Ammon and Moab to Egypt?] Ammon and Moab are outside Israel and Babylon is outside Israel. Just as in Babylon one sets apart the second tithe in the seventh year, so the rule should be in Ammon and Moab." Since there is no particular logical preference for one argument over the other, Rabbi Tarfon raises another logical argument, addressing the purpose of the law: מצרים שהיא קרובה עשאוה מעשר עני שיהיו עניי ישראל נסמכים עליה בשביעית אף עמון ומואב שהם קרובים נעשים מעשר עני שיהיו עניי ישראל נסמכים עליהם בשביעית "Just as in Egypt, which is close [to Israel], they have established the tithe for the poor in the seventh year, so that poor Israelites may rely on it for their livelihood, so we should proceed with respect to the tithes of Ammon and Moab, so that poor Israelites may also rely on it for their livelihood in the seventh year." The discussion continues with further logical considerations, which we need not analyze in their entirety. It suffices simply to demonstrate the logical approach of the Sages in their deliberations and decisions. As noted above (n. 120), social policy prevailed over other arguments in this case; it was established as the law by the vote of a majority, and by bestowing upon it the fictitious attribute "halakhah given to Moses from Sinai," to indicate divine approval.

do you know this? And when he answered them: This is a halakhah given to Moses from Sinai, Moses' mind was pacified." We observe the paradox: although Rabbi Aqiba referred to the Torah given to Moses, his teachings were so far removed from the original meaning of the laws that Moses no longer understood what he was talking about. Despite this apparent inconsistency, God confirmed that Rabbi Aqiba's teachings were indeed given to Moses, that is, had their origins in the Torah. Moses, too, acknowledged this divine pronouncement.

The Sages may have considered themselves as the spiritual descendants of the prophets,[184] who conveyed God's utterances to the people.[185] As such, the sole restriction on their authority was not to speak in the name of other gods.[186] Only such flexibility could ensure the preservation of a dispersed people living under the pressure of changes in circumstances beyond their control. Rules were conceived with the implicit understanding that they could be adapted[187] or circumvented

---

[184] The organization of the legal and judicial system is described in Deut 16: 18 - 18: 22. There is a hint of inconsistency with respect to the relationship between the authority of the priest, Levite, and judge at the central place "the Lord will choose" (Deut 17: 9 - 10), and the jurisdictional competence of the prophet, who speaks in God's name (Deut 18: 18), and to whom "you must listen" (18: 15). An appropriate reconciliation between these two authorities, and the absence of prophets during the rabbinic period, may have allowed the Sages to believe that they were complying with both prerequisites.

[185] We read in Deut 18: 18: ונתתי דברי בפיו ודבר אליהם את כל אשר אצונו "I will put my word in his mouth, and he will tell everything I command them."

[186] We read in Deut 18: 20: אך הנביא אשר...ידבר בשם אלהים אחרים ומת הנביא ההוא "... or a prophet who speaks in the name of other gods, must be put to death."

[187] There is an interesting talmudic passage that demonstrates the Sages' method of adapting rules to the prevailing circumstances. We read in mMegillah 1: 8 that phylacteries and *mezuzot* may be written only in Hebrew, whereas Scripture may be written in any language. Rabban Simeon ben Gamaliel, however, limits this permission to the Greek language. In bMegillah 9b, Rabbi Yohanan declares that the halakhah follows Rabban Simeon ben Gamaliel, and, as is common, "detects" a biblical verse that is appropriately interpreted to allow the writing of Scripture in Greek. We read: יפת אלהים ליפת וישכן באהלי שם דבריו של יפת יהיו באהלי שם "[It is written in Gen 9: 27:] 'May God extend the Territory of Japhet, may Japhet live in the tents of Shem.' [This means that] the words [i.e. the Greek language] of Japhet should be in the tents of Shem." Rabbi Yohanan explicitly uses this homily to justify his declaration that one may write the Torah in Greek. In yMegillah 1: 9, 71b, bar Qappara interprets this verse less explicitly; he does not declare that the halakhah follows Rabban Simeon b. Gamaliel, and simply states: שיהו מדברין בלשונו של יפת באוהלו של שם "They will speak the language of Japhet [Greek] in the tents of Shem." Rabbi Yehudah offers another motive, the mandate from King Ptolemy to the seventy Sages to translate the Torah into Greek. In yMegillah 1:9, 71c the preference for the Greek language is explained "logically": the Sages are said to have researched the issue and reached the conclusion that an

whenever it was perceived to be appropriate and necessary.[188] There is an inconsistency between the implicit assumption that Moses had presented all the commands and regulations[189] to the Israelites in the two covenants, at Sinai [190] and at the Plains of Moab,[191] and the explicit direction to ask the priests, Levites, and judges for appropriate rules,[192] and to listen to God's "current" commands conveyed through the prophets. We perceive that the later authorities continued to share in the realization of the divine laws in their relevant periods of activity.

It is my conviction, moreover, that the Sages endeavoured to uphold their freedom of expression and decision. This diversity of approaches and opinions facilitated the generation of efficient law. We read in tSotah 7:

---

accurate translation of the Torah can only be made in Greek. It is also stated that the Aramaic translation was made from the Greek translation. Tractate Soferim 1: 7, on the other hand, asserts that the Torah cannot be appropriately translated into any language, and the day when the Seventy translated it at Ptolemy's request was as injurious to the Jewish people as the day when the Golden Calf was made. The above citations undoubtedly demonstrate that for the practical purpose of allowing Greek-speaking Jews to read and study the Torah, the prohibition against writing the Torah in foreign languages was abolished, or appropriately circumvented. We do not know precisely which Rabban Simeon, the Elder at the time of the Temple, or his grandson at Yabneh, declared this rule, but this does not influence our conclusion. Each was a Nasi (Patriarch); in that capacity, each perceived the necessity of adapting the laws to current circumstances, including the dominance of the Greek language within the large Jewish Diaspora. We may note that Maimonides, in *Mishneh Torah, Hilkhot Tefillin* 1: 19, considered that the prohibition against writing the Torah in Greek was again valid in his time, since Greek was no longer dominant among spoken languages. That is, the original law had been adapted to circumstances in the Hellenistic period; it now reverted to its original status, when such circumstances were no longer applicable.

188 We must note here that the Sages adapted the relevant practical rules that were necessary for daily life, but proceeded on a theoretical basis with respect to the sacrificial ordinances; since the latter rules had no operative effect, the Sages could ignore the practical implications. An example of the impracticality of such theoretical pronouncements involves regulations concerning the breaking up of a baked *minhah* into small pieces to enable the taking of a handful for burning on the altar, which I discuss in the second part of this work.

189 We read in Sifra *Behar* 1 that all rules originate from Sinai. See chap. 1 at n. 17 on this citation; I have proposed there various solutions to the apparently conflicting locations for the revelations: Sinai, the Plains of Moab, and the Tent of Meeting.

190 We read in Lev 26: 46: אלה החקים והמשפטים והתורת אשר נתן ה' בינו ובין בני ישראל בהר סיני ביד משה "These are the decrees, the laws and regulations that the Lord established on Mount Sinai between himself and the Israelites, through Moses."

191 We read in Num 36: 13: אלה המצות והמשפטים אשר צוה ה' ביד משה אל בני ישראל בערבת מואב "These are the commands and regulations the Lord gave through Moses to the Israelites in the Plains of Moab."

192 See chap. 1, n. 49 regarding Levinson's postulate that Deuteronomy consists of a conflicting reinterpretation of earlier texts.

11: "[A homily on Eccl 12: 11:] Just as the plant grows and multiplies, so the words of the Torah grow and multiply; 'the masters of collected sayings' are those [Sages] who enter into the schools and sit in groups [and declare ritual decisions]." The verse in Eccl ends: "All [different opinions] were given by one shepherd." This homily concurs with the declaration of the Voice of Heaven cited above: "These and these [opposing dicta] are the words of the living God [yBerakhot 1: 4, 3b, and bEruvin 13b]." In such passages, one thus perceives the Sages' quest for diversity and willingness to grant equal rank to individual disputants.[193]

In conclusion, we must abandon the assumption that talmudic legal development proceeded either by way of the halakhic midrash form or purely as the result of tradition, and accept that the Sages used every suitable approach to reach their goal. In the above-cited narrative in tSanhedrin 7: 1 (note 132) concerning the decision-making process of the Sanhedrin, we must observe that when faced with a lack of knowledge as to how to decide, the Sanhedrin simply voted. Each member decided the issue according to his logical considerations of the issue and his personal convictions;[194] there is no mention of any discussion of disparate

---

[193] S. A. Handelman, *Interpretation*, p. 56, writes: "In the actual decision concerning which law to follow in practice, the law follows the House of Hillel, but both opinions, even the refuted one, are "the words of the living God," and both are recorded and studied; both are Torah." She compares rabbinic thought to the modern scholars Ricoeur and Derrida on this approach to texts. She states further: "...while the Torah represents absolute and ultimate truth, this truth is never simple and single, but is always subject to interpretation; and the interpretation, while also divine, is to a certain degree a provisional and relative process. Interpretation generates further interpretation and further scrutiny of different aspects, possibilities, and situations."

[194] It is interesting to observe the changes in the text of this narrative effected by Maimonides. In the original texts, for example in tHagigah 2: 9, we read: אם שמעו אמרו להם ואם לאו עומדין במנין אם רבו המטמאין (או) [טימאו] רבו המטהרין טיהרו משם הלכה יוצא ורווחת בישראל "If they knew [likely by tradition, since the term *שמע* indicates that they heard data that had been transmitted], they told them, but if not, they voted; if the number of those who decided [in this case that something was] impure was greater [than the number of their opponents], they [all] considered [the item] impure; and when the majority considered [the item] pure, they considered [the item] pure. From there, the halakhah went out to all of Israel." The same substance, with slightly different wording, appears in the other sources (see above n. 36). In essence, the narrative does not disclose whence the Superior Court derived the halakhah, nor the criteria for their decision. Maimonides was sensitive to these two crucial problems and added his interpretation in *Mishneh Torah*, *Hilkhot Mamrim* 1: 4: ידוע אצל בית דין הגדול בין מפי הקבלה בין מפי המדה שדנו בה אומרים מיד אם לא היה הדבר ברור אצל בית דין הגדול דנין בו בשעתן ונושאין ונותנין בדבר עד שיסכימו כולן או יעמדו למנין וילכו אחר הרוב ויאמרו לכל השואלים כך הלכה "If the Superior Court knew [the halakhah] either by tradition or by their method of hermeneutics, they answered immediately; if it was not clear to them, they deliberated

interpretations of Scripture or similar criteria. We must bear in mind the extensive diversity of opinion within the rabbinic group, less manifest in the Mishnah, as the Tannaim usually do not divulge the rationalizations behind their declarations, but quite evident with respect to almost every subject in the Gemara. Not only were their decisions different, but also their methods of attaining such decisions. They also had different and contrasting philosophical conceptions; though this is not the topic of our study, I shall cite one final passage, found in Mekilta d'Rabbi Ishmael, *Ki-tissa* 1, bYoma 85a-b, and tShabbat 15: 17 (in a different literary style),[195] that substantiates this proposition.[196] We have discussed above[197] the question posed to a number of Tannaim: "Where do we get the idea that the saving of a life overrides the Sabbath?" This is a particularly useful passage for study, since the Tannaim are not asked to create halakhah; it is a discussion concerning an existing custom, and they are asked only to offer their views of its justification. We observe that each Tanna has a different idea. The first group of three Tannaim uses the logical method of *ad majorem*, but each member of this group cites a different case that allows the overriding of the Sabbath. The next three Tannaim first disclose their basic philosophy and then support it by a halakhic midrash based on a scriptural verse, in effect following the maxim: "It is a tradition and the [mention of the] biblical verse is only a support [bPesahim 81b and others]." Each uses completely logical considerations,[198] according to his personal convictions. With respect to

---

and discussed [the matter] on the spot, until they reached a collective consensus, or [if they did not reach a consensus], they voted and decided according to the majority and communicated it to all those who asked them." Maimonides, as it seems from his wording, could not conceive that the Sages decided according to their own logical considerations and personal predispositions.

195 See Introduction, nn. 87 ff. and related text for an extended discussion of this narrative and my reason for choosing the B. T. source.

196 G. Alon, תולדות, vol. 1, pp. 309 ff. draws our attention to the contrasting attitudes exhibited with respect to a crucial issue having to do with the personal life and conduct of the Sage. He refers to the problem of whether one must dedicate all one's time and effort to the study of the Torah, renouncing any interest in work and financial matters, or work for subsistence and study at the same time. A pluralistic attitude also dominated this significant discussion, without any attempt to impose any one opinion.

197 See Introduction, nn. 87 ff. and related text, chap. 2, n. 21, and chap. 4, n. 46.

198 Rabbi Yose son of Rabbi Yehudah says: אך את שבתתי תשמרו יכול לכל תלמוד לומר אך חלק "[It is written in Exod 31: 13] 'Only you must observe my Sabbaths.' We might think this means in all circumstances; the text states 'only,' that is, part of the time." The philosophy of this Tanna reflects the novel idea of the hierarchy or relativity of the commandments; that is, sometimes a divine order may be overridden. Rabbi Jonathan ben Joseph says: כי קדש היא לכם היא מסורה בידכם ולא אתם מסורים בידה "[It is written in Exod 31: 14] 'Because it [the Sabbath] is holy to you.' The Sabbath is committed to you and you are not committed

the particular issue at hand, all happen to reach the same result; but their particular rationales have the potential for distinct consequences in the consideration of other topics. This narrative can be considered a paradigm of the great diversity among the ideas of the Sages, and should put to rest any conception of a single and exclusive rabbinic method.

to the Sabbath." He thus goes a step farther in his philosophical approach, stating that the Sabbath was given to humans and not vice versa; it is the humans who decide when and how to fulfill the Sabbath (cf. Mark 2: 27). Simeon ben Menasyah has an entirely different philosophical approach and states: ושמרו בני ישראל את השבת אמרה תורה חלל עליו שבת אחת כדי שישמור שבתות הרבה "'The Israelites must observe the Sabbath,' stated the Torah [Exod 31: 16] - [one may] profane one Sabbath, so that he may keep many Sabbaths." This Tanna had a practical approach to the issue.

4. The Development of the Halakhic System Pre- And Post-Destruction

4.1 The Fixing of a Halakhic Codex: Pre- or Post-70?

We have seen in the previous chapter the great variety of opinions held among the Sages concerning almost every subject, and their efforts to preserve their freedom to express their ideas on matters of halakhah and doctrine. This privilege was considered to have divine validation, as allegedly proclaimed in the utterance[1] of the *Bat Qol*, Voice of Heaven: "Both [opinions] are the words of the Living God [yBerakhot 1: 4, 3b, and bEruvin 13b]."[2] We have observed both the absolute liberty of expression and, what is more significant, the careful preservation of rejected opinions. We have also encountered instances in which minority decisions were actually followed in practice, long after the "endorsement" of the rule that the halakhah followed the majority.

---

1 A vivid narrative concerning the concubine at Gibeah portrays another divine intervention in this respect. We read in bGittin 6b: דכתיב ותזנה עליו פילגשו רבי אביתר אמר זבוב מצא לה ר׳ יונתן אמר נימא מצא לה ואשכחיה ר׳ אביתר לאליהו א״ל מאי קא עביד הקב״ה א״ל עסיק בפילגש בגבעה ומאי קאמר אמר ליה אביתר בני כך הוא אומר יונתן בני כך הוא אומר א״ל ח״ו ומי איכא ספיקא קמי שמיא א״ל אלו ואלו דברי אלהים חיים הן זבוב מצא ולא הקפיד נימא מצא והקפיד "It is written [Judg 19: 2] 'She was unfaithful to him [her mate].' Rabbi Abiatar said: he found a fly [in his food], Rabbi Jonathan said: he found a hair [there is a dispute as to where]. Rabbi Abiatar met Elijah [the prophet] and asked him: What does God do? He answered: He reflects on the narrative of the concubine of Gibeah. And what does he say? He answered: My son Abiatar says [it is] this way, and my son Jonathan says [it is] this way. He said to him: Can it be that there is any doubt [who is right] before [the omniscient] Deity? He answered: Both [opinions] are the words of the Living God; [her mate] found a fly and did not object to it; he found a hair and did object." Thus, God reconciled the paradox by declaring both declarations to be true, and hence both are the words of the Living God.

2 This is the simple meaning of the maxim, but S. Safrai offers a different interpretation. He maintains that the adjective חיים "living" is not the modifier of God, which would be tautological, but refers to the words of God; these are living, that is, adaptable to life like a living entity.

Despite the considerable evidence of independence of opinion, we must assume that at some point there was a fixed halakhah that constituted in general the real code of conduct governing Israelite society.[3] But this proposition is based mainly on what we can deduce from the period after the destruction of the Temple, starting with mishnaic evidence of deliberations concerned with discovering "What is the halakhah."[4] Such deliberations reflect attempts by the later Sages to decide the normative and binding conduct with respect to a given matter.

The tannaitic disputes on almost every subject recorded in the post-destruction period must convince us that the same type of disputes prevailed earlier. I thus disagree with those scholars who argue[5] that pre-destruction, there was authoritative pronouncement of halakhah by the Sanhedrin, and only with the Sanhedrin's loss of authority as a result of political circumstances was there a shift to the autonomous establishment of halakhah through individual interpretation of Scripture. It was the latter situation, in Urbach's opinion, that provoked sectarian disputes. I have

---

3 I am not taking any position on the issue as to whether, or to what extent, the segment of society called עם הארץ "Am Ha'aretz" in talmudic literature followed the Torah precepts according to all the rabbinic interpretations and edicts. I am focusing on those people who were scrupulous in their attitude toward rabbinic rules and regulations.

4 A concern with rendering a conclusive halakhakic decision in disputes between Tannaim does appear occasionally in Mishnah and Tosefta, with respect to Tannaim active after the Temple's destruction. The declaration in mEduyyot 1: 5, ואין הלכה אלא כדברי המרובין "the halakhah is according to the majority," also originates from the post-70 period. I have discussed in the previous chapter the critical problem regarding the authenticity of tHagigah 2: 9 and other sources with respect to the Sanhedrin's decision-making process at its seat in the Temple. The following narrative in tSanhedrin 6: 6 is attributed to a period much before the Temple's destruction: באותה שעה קיבל עליו יהודה בן טבאי שלא יהא מורה הלכה אלא על פי שמעון בן שטח "On that occasion Yehudah ben Tabai [the judge] undertook to pass judgment and teach only according to Simeon ben Shetah['s opinion]." The term halakhah is mentioned there, but does not refer here to a decision concerning a dispute between two Tannaim; it refers instead to a mistaken verdict of Yehudah ben Tabai, who was induced to render it by his urge to contradict the Boethusians. In certain occurrences, as for example in tParah 7: 4 and tMikva'ot 4: 6, the term halakhah is used with respect to people going to Yabneh to ask about the law with respect to special and novel circumstances. There was no issue there regarding a decision in a dispute between two opinions. We do encounter a narrative in tHagigah 9: 12 concerning a dispute at the Temple between Hillel and disciples of Shammai about סמיכה, the laying of hands on the offering. I have questioned the authenticity of this narrative in chap. 3, n. 147. Moreover, the passage refers to an issue regarding the sacrificial worship at the Temple, which was regulated by particular fixed rules. I shall revert to the issue of the disputes regarding the Temple cult in the second part of this work.

5 See, e.g., chap. 3, n. 133.

already demonstrated[6] the skepticism we should apply in the evaluation of the Sanhedrin's role in halakhic decision-making. The Sanhedrin's role is not at all clear and unquestionable; there is considerable debate among scholars[7] regarding the existence of centralized institutions pre- and post-70, and the varied names, functions, and authority of such institutions in each period. I would assume that the rabbinic leadership gained much more respect and authority after the Temple's destruction than it had pre-70. With the collapse of other political and cultic institutions, the people gathered around the Sages' leadership, the only stable anchor of hope and consolation.[8] There was no real rivalry to their primacy and authority, as there had been before the Temple's destruction. The political disputes among the Pharisees documented at the time of the rebellion[9] were also conciliated, if not entirely called off, as some scholars contend.[10] One would therefore expect even more authoritative leadership on the part of the Sanhedrin post-70.[11] It is thus reasonable to propose that if we encounter disputes among the Sages post-70, we may assume that the same circumstances prevailed earlier, despite our dearth of evidence on such disputes.[12]

---

6 See section 3. 6.

7 See chap. 3, n. 145.

8 Z. Safrai and A. Sagi, סמכות, p. 19 state that the Sages had no official authority in the pre-70 period. Contra, S. A. Cohen, *Three Crowns,* p. 49, who states that after the destruction, the Sanhedrin "continued to play a pivotal role in national life," despite its apparent migration.

9 See *Ant.* 18: 23 - 25 concerning the fourth group, the Zealots, radical fighters against the Romans, who originated from the third group, the Pharisees, before the split among them. Although the Patriarch, the Pharisean Rabban Simeon ben Gamaliel, was the leader of the Rebellion at its start, Josephus writes in *J.W.* 4: 159 that he exhorted the people against the Zealots. He was probably already convinced of the futility of the Rebellion, and striving for negotiation with the Romans, a position later achieved by the pharisaic leadership.

10 See G. Alon, *Jewish History*, pp. 318-328, who declares that the priests and certain pharisaic Sages opposed the leadership of Rabban Yohanan ben Zakkai, the personality who allegedly negotiated the agreement with the Romans (p. 325), on political and other bases (p. 318). J. Neusner, *Yohanan ben Zakkai,* detects in a certain mishnaic statement an intense hatred of Rabban Yohanan ben Zakkai. He proposes three possible origins of such hatred: priestly circles, conservative groups who resented his reforms, and anti-Roman circles (p. 52). See also Heger, *Altars*, pp. 377 ff. concerning the voluntary cessation of the sacrificial service initiated by this leader and the consequent shift from a priestly-controlled, concrete ritual to a sophisticated, intellectually-guided ritual. This momentous reform may explain the priestly opposition. A similar conjecture is proposed by Lee Levine, "Judaism," p. 136.

11 For the sake of brevity, I shall utilize this commonly used date to distinguish between the pre- and the post-destruction eras.

12 See chap. 3, text at n. 142 concerning the statement that Shammai and Hillel disputed on only three issues.

In one matter, however, there is a marked difference between the circumstances before and after 70. While we do have in Mishnah Avot records of early[13] moral sayings by particular named Sages, we do not possess similar attributed accounts of early halakhic pronouncements.[14] There are halakhot[15] (mishnayot) deemed by scholars to be of ancient origin; these are, however, generally anonymous,[16] and we do not know whether they were disputed. It seems to me that, in reality, ancient customs were recorded in the Mishnah as halakhic declarations. They represent, as I postulated in the Introduction (p.18), generally accepted halakhic decisions;[17] but in contrast to the later period, in which all pronouncements, whether accepted or rejected, were zealously preserved, there was no real attempt to preserve the identity[18] of any of the authors of these earlier decisions.[19] The anonymity of these earliest halakhot, and the

---

13 G. Stemberger's assertion in "Abot" that the editing of Avot was accomplished at a late date, does not contradict my thesis that moral homilies were indeed declared by the named pre-70 Sages. During the editing process, the editor(s) may have added later declarations to the genuine pre-70 utterances.

14 In general (though there are some exceptions), we possess records of special edicts decreed by the early pharisaic Sages, not reports of halakhic discussions, disputes, or declarations like those encountered in the Mishnah and baraitot. Cf. J. Neusner, "Attributions," who does not consider this oddity in his comparison of the Mishnah with the tradition expressed in Avot.

15 Scholars call this הלכה קדומה.

16 Josephus, for instance, records in *Ant.* 17: 149- 167 and *J.W.* 1: 648 - 650 the story of two noted scholars, Yehudah son of Sepphoraeus and Matthias son of Margalus, who incited young men to remove the large golden eagle that Herod had erected over the great gate of the Temple. Josephus describes them as the most celebrated interpreters of the Jewish laws, well beloved by the people who attended their daily lectures, and we may assume that they declared halakhot; yet they are not mentioned anywhere in rabbinic literature. Cf. H. Lapin, "Early Rabbinic Civil Law and the Literature of the Second Temple Period," p. 181, who does not perceive "strong continuities between Second Temple Jewish texts and early rabbinic literature where questions of civil law are concerned"; he too notes the anonymity that was characteristic of pre-70 literature.

17 S. Safrai, *The Literature of the Sages*, p. 167, describes them as "opinions of individual Sages that gradually became generally accepted."

18 The few pre-70 authors who are identified may be perceived as an exception. There is also room for legitimate doubt as to these attributions, just as there is with respect to post-70 attributions. Later ordinances may have been attributed to earlier charismatic figures to enhance their status and their acceptance by the masses. We observe that even early Tannaim did not know the precise functions of the *zugot* (pairs) of Nasi and Av Beit Din (mHagigah 2: 2, tHagigah 2: 8, yHagigah 2: 2, 77d, and bHagigah 16b).

19 Various scholars discuss this unusual circumstance. J. Neusner, *Pharisees, Part III*, pp. 239 - 248, suggests that within the *ad hoc* nature of the pre-70 halakhic declarations (as I have postulated them), there was no intent to collect and preserve such declarations. The ethical pronouncements, on the other hand, were perceived as

expressing perpetual, unchanging values, and thus deserving of preservation together with the names of their authors. Neusner indicates another purpose for the attribution of individual names in the Mishnah even when the individual's declaration is rejected; in his opinion anonymity indicates consensus, while identification reflects schism (p. 130). A number of the early Tannaim, however, whose individual declarations are cited, founded their decisions on traditions from pre-70 Sages, and hence there must have been disparate opinions among the traditions from that period. We must therefore ask why these pre-70 "schismatic" opinions were not identified, and only the later Tannaim who recorded and declared them are called "schismatics." Neusner's use of this attribute is in fact in blatant contradiction to the maxim: אלו ואלו דברי אלהים חיים "Both [opinions] are the words of the living God" (yBerakhot 1: 4, 3b, bEruvin 13b and many other occurrences.). There is also the problem of whom to classify as "schismatic," when the Mishnah identifies only two or three dissenting Tannaim. S.J.D. Cohen, *From the Maccabees to the Mishna*, p. 158 also questions why we do not possess any legal declarations from the Pharisees of the pre-70 period. G. Stemberger, "Judentums," p. 90, speculates that many pre-70 Sages perished in the revolt, and this is the reason they are not identified.

Two traditional scholars who uncritically accept the "historicity" of rabbinic narratives also address this circumstance. Z. Frankel, דרכי המשנה, p. 5 writes that the halakhic decisions declared by the Sages of the Great Assembly (כנסת הגדולה) were conceived after intense deliberations by many Sages, and were then presented to the people as the creation of the institution, not of an individual person. Although this solution does not answer the question of the drastic shift in the style of attribution from pre-70 to post-70, since the Great Assembly (whose exact period and range of activity is a debated issue) ceased its activity with the start of the *zugot*, "pairs," much before 70, his proposition as such is logical. L. Finkelstein, "The Ethics of Anonymity among the Pharisees," creates an idealization of the Pharisees and asserts that they deliberately chose to remain anonymous, since "posthumous fame seemed an irrational goal in life...sinful" (p. 188). It is obvious that such a statement is utterly contradictory to so many opposing facts and rabbinic utterances, which compel him to make every conceivable effort to "round the square." I do not find it necessary to analyze critically and refute all the rabbinic dicta he interprets as evidence for his allegation, but I wish to comment on one of them, a narrative from bHorayot 13b-14a. There it is recorded that the Patriarch Rabban Simeon ben Gamaliel II punished Rabbi Meir and Rabbi Nathan by declaring that their halakhic declarations would not be quoted in their names. The fact that forced anonymity is here regarded as a punishment is utterly contradictory to his theory; he attempts to reconcile this by alleging that it was a pedagogic procedure, "really a concealed reward" (p. 196). Yet the entire event and the actions of all the contenders are based upon the Sages' concern for their honour, the antithesis of Finkelstein's idealization of their humbleness. Rabban Simeon objected to the fact that the assembly in the school stood up at the entrance of Rabbi Meir and Rabbi Nathan, the two most reputable Sages; he expected that this honour should belong only to him. He therefore decreed that the people should remain seated at the entrance of the two Sages; when they learned of this, they in turn attempted to embarrass him, displaying his ignorance in a certain field, and to depose him. Rabban Simeon succeeded, with the help of another Sage who was sensitive to the loss of honour of the Patriarch, in thwarting their plot, and punished them with anonymity. It is remarkable that such a narrative, which was evidently shaped by the desire of the personalities involved to uphold and defend their honour, is entirely turned on its head in order to corroborate a thesis that the Sages were opposed to the human drive for fame. Finkelstein does in fact confirm certain

apparent lack_of early disputes, lead us to now to the crucial issue of whether the urge to establish a fixed halakhah was also present pre-70. Relying on the method of retrojection, which I shall explain in detail, I shall argue that the role of the assemblies at Yabneh was to attempt to fix halakhah (an attempt that was by no means successful), suggesting the lack of such fixed halakah up to that point. I shall then set out other evidence that confirms the lack of a fixed halakhah before 70: the strong suggestion that early disputes did in fact exist and were carried forward into much later eras; the limited but significant talmudic evidence of pre-70 pluralism in decision-making; the different literary style of early decision-making; and the fact that the development of detailed rules regarding decision-making was a later phenomenon. Finally, as further evidence of the difference in pre- and post-70 thought, I shall also discuss the change in the concepts of דאורייתא and דרבנן.

4.1.1 The Method of Retrojection

As I have noted, for the period prior to the destruction of the Second Temple, we possess little information relevant to our investigation.[20] We must assume, along with most scholars, that this traumatic event would have had a momentous impact on all aspects of Israelite life, ideological and practical. The period prior to the destruction thus constitutes a crucial subject of inquiry. I shall make use of any available data from that period, but I am constrained to rely to a great extent on extrapolation from circumstances in the post-destruction period. Such an extrapolation of pre-70 circumstances from post-70 literature will not be carried out simply through the uncritical retrojection of the rabbinic narratives onto earlier periods;[21] this method usually represents what "ought to have been," according to the belief of the Sages, and is used to substantiate their own ideological preferences by attributing such beliefs to earlier periods. I shall

---

crucial elements of my thesis. He writes that after the fall of Jerusalem, there was "a welter of contradictory local traditions" (p. 193). He does not explain how these "contradictory" traditions suddenly came into being, if not because of the pluralistic environment of pre-70 that I have postulated. In his conclusion (p. 198), which he does not link to the above dilemma, he declares: "Individuals [Sages] may have entered [the halakhic deliberations] with differing views...but in no instance did these differences lead to conflict."

20 J. Neusner, *Pharisees, Part III*, p. 239, states: "Nearly all pre-70 traditions were thoroughly revised at Yabneh and afterward."

21 See E. Regev, "Purity Laws." He criticizes the method of comparing Qumran halakhot from earlier periods with later tannaitic halakhot. This is not a reliable comparison, in his opinion, since it is not at all certain that the pharisaic halakhah was identical to later tannaitic halakhah. He too perceives the probability of differences between the pre- and post-70 periods.

attempt as far as possible to extrapolate to the earlier circumstances by a critical analysis of later conditions, in order to neutralize the type of ideological imposition apparent in the rabbinic narratives.[22]

This reconstruction of pre-70 circumstances is narrowly limited in this study to the question of the halakhic environment among the Pharisees - whether the halakhah was pluralistic and changeable, or rigid and fixed. I believe that a review of all available rabbinic sources referring to these specific issues,[23] with the purpose of discerning the patterns therein and meticulously analyzing such patterns, can reasonably be expected to achieve this particular and limited goal.[24] The earliest Sages of the post-70 era did not start their halakhic and exegetical activity *ex nihilo*. They encountered a given situation and started from there, possibly modifying certain rules and maintaining others. In effect, all our meditations upon and conjectures about past events are founded upon contemporary conceptions, which we then retroject in an attempt to understand and interpret the occurrences and texts of a bygone era. The Sages were close

---

[22] M. Smith, "A Comparison of Early Christian and Early Rabbinic Tradition," p. 169, declares: "To read back into the period before 70 the developed rabbinic technique of the year 200 is a gross anachronism." Being thoroughly aware of this fact, I shall therefore attempt to extrapolate the differing conditions and circumstances of the earlier period, as I have stated, by a critical analysis of the post-70 era.

[23] P. Schäfer, *Studien*, asserts the necessity of analyzing all rabbinic sources in order to understand their world-view. In his opinion, any comprehension of the tannaitic perspective is possible only at the end of such an analysis. He writes on p. 11 that the result will emerge "erst am Ende dieser Arbeit herauskristallisieren werden." Hence, the world-view of the later sources enlightens us about the much earlier tannaitic period. Cf. E. Rivkin, "Defining the Pharisees: The Tannaitic Sources," p. 205, who concentrates "on a single corpus, the tannaitic literature" to "build a definition of the Pharisees from that corpus."

[24] P. Schäfer, *Studien*, p. 25, derives his portrayal of rabbinic Judaism from both Talmudim (implicitly also including the Mishnah), the Midrashim and Targumim, although there is a span of about five hundred years between the inception of these sources and their final redaction. He writes: "Von zahllosen in den Texten verstreute Einzelaussagen kann eine theologische Vorstellung erschlossen werden." ("A theological portrayal can be deduced from countless statements scattered throughout the texts.") J. Neusner, *Purities, Part XXI*, p. 298, writes that the "linguistic and syntactical style and stylization of the Mishna expresses a world view and ethos." On the other hand, in "Yavneh," p. 16, Neusner writes: "Legal sayings [of Mishnah and Tosefta] deal with picayune and inconsequential matters." In other words, since there are almost no narratives in the Mishnah, it would appear to be impossible to deduce from such statements "a world view and ethos." But the later amoraic literature indicates how the mishnaic declarations were understood and interpreted; this literature thus assists us in our quest of visualizing the tannaitic *Weltanschauung*. The Amoraim were close to the tannaitic period and its prevailing attitudes, and their perceptions of the Mishnah are obviously more pertinent than ours. Similarly, a retrojection of the halakhic environment of the Tannaim post-70 can offer us clues to the pre-70 era.

to their predecessors, the Pharisees, and their understanding of the circumstances in the preceding period offers us a reasonably authentic indication of the underlying philosophy of that era. I will demonstrate, on the basis of my analysis of this rabbinic literature, that there was a protracted and strenuous attempt post-70 to establish a fixed system of halakhah; this in itself indicates that a pluralistic, open halakhic environment must have prevailed before this period.

Excursus: The Association between Pharisees and "Rabbis"

As my method of retrojection assumes a connection between the Pharisees and the later Sages/Rabbis, I must note that scholars have amply debated this issue. There is in fact one trend of opinion that denies any continuity between these "denominations." The core of this debate, however, has a political and social perspective, focusing on questions of status and executive power. These issues are irrelevant to my study, which confines itself to the topic of the halakhic environment and its underlying philosophy, and in fact do not contradict my hypothesis of an ideological connection between these groups. A brief review of these opinions will illustrate my proposition.

S. J. D. Cohen, in a much-discussed essay, proposes that the Tannaim dissociated themselves from the Pharisees: "The Tannaim refused to see themselves as Pharisees....[the Rabbis] had no desire to publicize the connection [with the Pharisees]."[25] But these statements refer to the Rabbis' reluctance, for the sake of political expediency, to identify or be identified with the sectarian character of the Pharisees; this point is the cornerstone of Cohen's thesis regarding the disappearance of the sects in the post-70 period. Cohen does not, however, deny that some rabbinic texts - on halakhic issues - do allege an affinity between the Rabbis and the Pharisees.[26] He concludes: "In all likelihood there was some close

[25] S. J. D. Cohen, "The Significance of Yavneh," pp. 29 and 41.

[26] Ibid., p. 40. Cohen does not discuss these texts, which record disputes between Pharisees and Sadducees and Boethusians; he concludes that the link between the Rabbis and the Pharisees is "tenuous" (p. 39). We must consider, however, that the Mishnah, a rabbinic source, defends the pharisaic halakhah against dissident opinion. This fact indicates clearly that the Tannaim (not only the Amoraim, as Cohen suggests) "begin to see themselves more clearly as the descendants of the Pharisees" (ibid.), and that they followed pharisaic halakhah and justified their halakhic approach. This proposition is corroborated by the DSS literature. Rabbinic halakhot regarding the נצוק (mYadayim 4: 7 and mMakhshirin 5: 9), the issue of whether the *minhah* may be eaten throughout the entire night (mZevahim 6: 1) or only until midnight (Sifra *Tzav* 7: 12), and the issue of טבול יום (tParah 3: 8) are all opposed in 4QMMT. This scroll thus proffers bona fide evidence that the Rabbis indeed upheld the pharisaic halakhah. In contrast, the rabbinic records of debates with the

connection between the post-70 rabbis and the pre-70 Pharisees."[27] In fact, nothing in Cohen's specific thesis of the Rabbis' unwillingness to identify as Pharisees would contradict my method of deducing the pre-70 pharisaic circumstances from the rabbinic halakhic environment post-70.

D. Goodblatt discusses at length various scholarly opinions concerning whether pharisaic Judaism constituted normative Judaism in the pre-70 period, and the degree of authenticity of Josephus' statement of their dominant influence on the masses and their power to incite the masses against their rulers.[28] While the core of this debate is not relevant to our study and to the issue of the connection between the pre-70 Pharisees and the post-70 Rabbis, Goodblatt does quote T. Rajak on the subject of Josephus' record of the Pharisees. Rajak asserts: "The consolidation of Judaism undertaken by Rabban Yohanan ben Zakkai at Yavneh was based upon Pharisaism,"[29] and endorses Neusner's statement on this issue. (Neusner[30] perceives an affinity between the rabbinic traditions about the Pharisees and their portrayal in the New Testament.) In a separate article, Goodblatt writes explicitly: "All modern accounts agree that the leadership which emerged after 70 had some connection with the Pharisees."[31] Discussing the presumed pharisaic ancestry of Rabban Gamaliel II, he further states: "No one doubts the pharisaic connection of Gamaliel II."[32] In another of his publications, Goodblatt

---

Sadducees are of doubtful credulity, particularly given the mocking tone of these records in Mishnah tractates Yadayim and Tosefta tractate Parah. See, e.g. G. Stemberger, "Judentums," p. 90, who writes: "Die rabbinische Texte die die Sadduzäer kritisieren und lächerlich machen, sind aus historischer Sicht kaum von Wert." ("The rabbinic texts which chastise and mock the Sadducees are barely of historical merit".) While it is true that the author of 4QMMT does not explicitly mention the Pharisees as his contenders, we must assume that this was the case. Certain scholars associate this scroll with the Sadducees; see, e.g. Y. Sussmann, "4QMMT," and L. Schiffman, "The Place of 4QMMT," p. 85, and *Reclaiming the Dead Sea Scrolls*, pp. 68 - 71. It is of *opinio communis*, however, that the contenders in this scroll are the Pharisees. Schiffman himself writes in "The Place of 4QMMT," p. 87, that "both texts [the Temple Scroll and 4QMMT], in a variety of laws, reject the policy of the Pharisees and later Tannaim."

27 S. J. D. Cohen, "The Significance of Yavneh," p. 38.

28 D. Goodblatt, "The Place of the Pharisees." Goodblatt cites the opposing conclusions of Morton Smith and D. R. Schwartz; he concludes his study by endorsing Smith's thesis, which does not support the previous scholarly consensus that pharisaic Judaism comprised "orthodoxy" in the first century and that the Pharisees "dominated Jewish society in *provincia Iudaea*" (p. 29).

29 Ibid., p. 33, quoting from T. Rajak, *Josephus, The Historian and His Society*.

30 J. Neusner, *From Politics to Piety*, p. 80.

31 D. Goodblatt, "Iudea between the Revolts," p. 114 .

32 Ibid., p. 116. There is wide consensus on the leading status of Rabban Gamaliel in the post-70 Yabnean period. The extent of his authority and political power is debated. Though this issue affects neither the fact of his pharisaic connections nor the fact of

again notes that the Pharisees are commonly seen as being the spiritual ancestors of the Rabbis.[33]

P. Schäfer; asserting an opposing opinion, doubts whether Josephus' tentative association between the Pharisees and the Rabbis corresponds to historical reality.[34] This discussion, however, refers to the political and social connections, as is clear from his exposition and subsequent discussion,[35] and not to the halakhic issue which is the focus of my thesis. G. Stemberger also puts in question the continuity from the Pharisees to the rabbinic tradition.[36] Stemberger in turn cites an opposing assumption of C. Thoma,[37] describing the latter as representing a school which perceives the Rabbis as a continuation of the Pharisees, though operating in different circumstances and with different goals. Again, this disagreement relates to the political and social connections, and thus Stemberger's stance does not preclude an ideological and halakhic connection.[38] J. Neusner[39] declares that while rabbinic Judaism took shape in part out of "the tradition of the fathers associated with Pharisaism," it should be considered "an amalgam of Pharisaism, Scribism and yet its own distinctive interests." S. Safrai, on the hand, declares: "Oral Tora as it is referred to in the literature, contained the teachings of the pharisaic Sages and their successors, the Tannaim and Amoraim."[40] We may note finally the opinion of J. Lightstone, who has concluded: "It does not appear that the road back to the nature of the pre-70 controversy between the Sadducees and the Pharisees is through rabbinic literature."[41] This conclusion, however, relates specifically to Lightstone's doubts on the

---

his leadership, I shall nevertheless review this debate below in section 4.2.2.

33 D. Goodblatt, *The Monarchic Principle*, p. 213.

34 P. Schäfer, "Der Vorrabbinische Pharisäismus," p. 170. M. Hengel, in his subsequent discussion with Schäfer, does affirm such a connection.

35 Ibid., pp. 172 - 175.

36 G. Stemberger, *Jewish Contemporaries of Jesus*, p. 39.

37 "Rabbinism [sic] is Pharisaism that has been drawn out of a group existence and into responsibility for all Judaism." The quote is from C. Thoma, "Der Pharisäismus."

38 In *Jewish Contemporaries of Jesus*, p. 144, he writes: "In rabbinic texts there are points of contact with concepts that we recognize as Pharisaic, yet these are not *exclusively* [author's emphasis] Pharisaic."

39 J. Neusner, "Yavneh," pp. 3 - 4. He also writes (pp. 22 - 24) that "Eliezer was a post-70 continuator of pre-70 Pharisaism," and states explicitly (p. 32) that Eliezer "was a Pharisee." In *Eliezer ben Hyrcanus*, he is even more outspoken. He writes that Eliezer was an important representative of the old Pharisaism (vol. 2, p. 302), and, what is more interesting for our subject: "Eliezer's historically useful sayings provide good evidence about the main outlines of the pharisaic legal tradition at the last half of the first century" (p. 310).

40 S. Safrai, *The Literature of the Sages*, p. 35.

41 J. Lightstone, "Sadducees versus Pharisees," p. 217.

veracity of rabbinic narratives with respect to the sectarian controversy. Thus I do not think his conclusion contradicts my method of retrojecting from the Rabbis to the Pharisees; in fact, he actually substantiates my approach by assuming that the Rabbis did consider themselves as followers of the Pharisees with respect to their halakhic concepts.[42]

Further substantiation of acontinuity between the pre- and post-70 periods with respect to the halakhic environment can be deduced from the similar literary styles of the MMT Scroll[43] and the Mishnah.[44] Both are composed in the same dialect, and are similar in their content and dialectic method. The one is definitely pre-70 and the other post-70, yet the similarity in character of the two halakhic writings is striking, especially when we compare them with the literary style of the other Dead Sea writings. We observe the constancy between the two periods regarding the approach to the formation of halakhah.

In conclusion, I believe I have shown that there is no evidence contradicting my proposition that an ideological connection existed between the Rabbis and Pharisees, or invalidating my method of retrojecting the halakhic patterns evident in rabbinic literature to the antecedent pharisaic environment.

4.1.2. The Role of Yabneh

We have noted the tendency in the Mishnah toward establishing a fixed halakhah,[45] but even that document still quotes disputed opinions with no indication as to whether, or how, a fixed halakhah was determined from among them. Rabbi's use of the generic attribution חכמים, "Sages," with respect to the halakhah that he considered correct is a late event, occurring more than one hundred years after the destruction of the Temple. And as

[42] In his arguments, Lightstone poses two possibilities: a) the Tannaim, when in possession of a pharisaic legal tradition, always adopted it, or b) the Tannaim projected some of their own laws onto the Pharisees, believing such laws to have been the basis of the conflict between the Pharisees and Sadducees. We note that according to both contingencies, Lightstone assumes that the Sages considered themselves as following in the footsteps of the Pharisees with respect to halakhic issues.

[43] This is not the place to discuss the topic of whether Qumran society was a monolithic group or a conglomerate of many groups who differed in their beliefs and practices; I review scholarly opinions on this issue in the second part of my study. It may be noted here, however, that the author of 4QMMT was definitely from a group that had an affinity with the pharisaic manner of devising halakhah. Since this same style is evident in the Mishnah, we may fairly reasonably conclude that there was a connection between the Pharisees and the Rabbis with respect to halakhic elements.

[44] See M. Bernstein, "The Employment and Interpretation of Scripture," pp. 32 - 33, and J. Strugnell, "The Qumran Scrolls," p. 99.

[45] See section 3.1.

we have seen in the previous chapter: "In a dispute between one individual and many, the halakhah is according to the many."

As hinted before, we cannot expect the talmudic literature to inform us explicitly that unqualified "anarchy" prevailed in the Israelite legal system before 70.[46] The Mishnah and Tosefta tractates of Eduyyot refer to the assembly convened at Yabneh, and portray this assembly as being convened to establish halakhah.[47] The stimulus for the convocation of this assembly, according to tEduyyot 1: 1, was dissatisfaction with the prevailing condition of the halakhah: "They said: It will happen that a person will seek for a topic of the Torah and will not find it, [or] for the topic of a rabbinic decree and will not find it." At first glance, this appears to be simply a problem of accessibility, to which the obvious solution would be the publication of all the laws and decrees. The real problem is stated subsequently: "[To avoid a situation in which] one declaration of the Torah [law] would not be the same as another, they said: Let us start

---

46 A good example of the "anarchy" that dominated the Israelite legal system can be seen in the development of the concept פקוח נפש דוחה שבת "the saving of a life overrides the Sabbath" (see Introduction, text at nn. 88 ff., chap. 2, text at n. 21, and chap. 3, text at nn. 197 ff.). In an unpublished lecture presented at the Department for the Study of Religion, University of Toronto, I have demonstrated the long and tortuous path this principle had undergone from its inception in the Maccabean period until its recognition within the larger Israelite society. In bYoma 85a, a question is posed before several Sages: "How do we know that saving a life overrides the Sabbath?" The style of the question indicates that this principle was already a recognized fact, but its source was unknown. Prior to this period, as I argue, there was no clear idea that this principle was to be applied in different circumstances, nor any comprehensive adherence to this principle in the general Israelite society. Cf. H. Weiss, "The Sabbath in the Writings of Josephus," pp. 371 ff., who notes the contradictions in Josephus' narratives regarding the Israelites' conduct in war, with respect to defending themselves or attacking on Sabbath. He therefore proposes not to accept Josephus' portrayal at face value (p. 379). I see these apparent inconsistencies not as contradictions, but as an indication of different stages in attitude that prevailed at different periods, places and circumstances; this is certainly an expected pattern when a firmly rooted law is overridden during the course of time. We have evidence from *Jub.* 50: 12 that the author of this document and his group did not authorize fighting on Sabbath, and we may assume that other segments of society held similar views, or at least did not agree to all the stages of the slowly-developing permission. Weiss states (p. 380): "The refusal of some people to bear arms was more important than the willingness of others." Such a situation could only persist if there were no final fixed halakhah accepted by the people, and corroborates my thesis that pre-70 there was no fixed halakhah. In tEruvin 3: 5 - 8 there are precise rules for many contingencies with respect to the overriding of Sabbath in wartime. See also M.D. Herr, מלחמה.

47 J.N. Epstein, תנאים, p. 428 maintains that the scope of tractate Eduyyot was indeed to establish halakhah. He interprets the phrase: נתחיל מהילל ומשמאי "Let's start with [deciding the final halakhah with respect to the disputes between] Hillel and Shammai," as intending to say: "And then we shall continue with the others."

with [the disputes between] Hillel and Shammai."[48] A similar fear concerning halakhic disputes is observed in tHagigah 2: 9 and ySanhedrin 1: 4, 19c: "[Lest] two Torot are created." In bSanhedrin 88b, this pronouncement is more explicit: ונעשית תורה כשתי תורות "and the Torah became like two [distinct] Torot." This was the real problem to which the assembly addressed itself; it convened to initiate a process for establishing halakhah,[49] by deciding between the opposing opinions and declarations of the various Sages.[50] Once again, we may conclude that the evident purpose of effecting a change in the halakhic environment, through the establishment of a fixed halakhah, is itself evidence of the lack of a fixed halakhah, and the existence of a pluralistic environment, in the earlier period.

A passage in bBerakhot 28a, among other sources,[51] connects the assembly at Yabneh with Rabban Gamaliel's removal from the Presidency

---

48 See Epstein's assertion in the previous note that Eduyyot's purpose was to establish halakhah. The literary structure of this tractate indicates this; it starts with decisions on halakhah with respect to disputes between Hillel and Shammai, the founders of two opposing Schools and initiators of the greatest number of controversies between the Sages. The Tosefta explicitly declares this purpose. Ch. Albeck, ששה סדרי משנה, סדר נזיקין, p. 277, in the introduction to tractate Eduyyot, writes, in contrast to Epstein, that its editors did not intend to establish halakhah, but only to set in order the halakhic data. He emphasizes that many disputes between Beit Hillel and Beit Shammai are not mentioned in the tractate at all, and others remain undecided. In response, I refer to my thesis concerning the complete lack of systematization of the talmudic literature, and propose that this is the reason for the irregularities observed by Albeck. Such lack of systematization is not, however, inconsistent with the purpose intended for the tractate by its initiator, a personality I shall attempt to identify. See A. Aderet, מסכת עדויות, p. 251, note 2, who summarizes the various traditional and scholarly opinions concerning the purpose of tractate Eduyyot. D. Goodblatt, *The Monarchic Principle*, also discusses the character and purpose of the Yabneh assembly (pp. 241 ff).

49 After the short introduction, in the above-cited tEduyyot, of the dire circumstances, we read the pragmatic consequence: אמרו נתחיל מהילל ומשמאי "They said: Let's start with [deciding the final halakhah with respect to the disputes between] Hillel and Shammai."

50 I have already quoted in nn. 47-8 the scholarly opinions concerning the scope of Eduyyot. See also sections 4.2.2.2 and 4.2.3 on the reason for this "Unfinished Symphony."

51 The first four mishnayot of Yadayim must be included in this list, since the story in mishnah 4: 4 of the Ammonite who wanted to be converted to Judaism also appears in the narrative in bBerakhot 27b relating Rabban Gamaliel's dismissal. With respect to the other mishnayot that are said to have occurred בו ביום "on that day" (i.e. the day of Rabban Gamaliel's dismissal), it is not certain that they took place at that particular event. See Ch. Albeck, ששה סדרי משנה, סדר נשים, השלמות, pp. 384 - 385 on this issue. At any rate, this phrase בו ביום appears only in the record of the occurrence in the B. T.; it is absent in the Y. T.

of the Academy,[52] and gives further evidence of the role of the assembly: "[Tractate] Eduyyot was set out on that day [i.e. the day of Rabban Gamaliel's dismissal]; and whenever we say 'on that day,' it is this day [that was meant]." The narrative does not tell us whether the declarations of the witnesses and the subsequent decisions concerning final halakhot occurred before or after Rabban Gamaliel's dismissal; on the other hand, this narrative clearly indicates that the assembly's goal was to establish halakhah, and adjust any differences with the Nasi (Patriarch). Logically, only the Patriarch could have been the initiator of a project of such momentous impact, to organize an inventory of all the halakhot and disputes, and decide their final outcome.[53] A baraita quoted in the above Bavli passage confirms this: "Rabban Gamaliel did not miss even one hour from the academy [during the deliberations to establish the halakhot]." Hence we see that he was fully involved in this activity, although according to the chronological order[54] of the narrative, this happened after his dismissal.

Yet despite the evident intent at Yabneh to systematize the halakhah, this assembly was not entirely successful.[55] Mishnah tractate Eduyyot in fact consists of an unsystematic collection of עדויות, "testimonies," introduced with the term העיד, "he testified," declarations, introduced with the terms אומרים, "they said" or דברי, "the words of," and records of judgments, introduced by מטהרין, "they declare [it] pure," or אוסרים, "they forbid [it]." There is evidence of the use of the majority rule in this tractate; in mEduyyot 1: 6 Rabbi Yehudah states: "The halakhah is [decided] only according to the words of the majority [against the opinion of the individual]." We do not know, however, when this maxim was

---

[52] The narrative there does not explicitly state his title. In the discussion with his successor (27b), however, he is asked whether he agrees to be ריש מתיבתא "the head of the council [academy]"; this was the organization that established halakhot, as the report records. Other rabbinic sources (see the Excursus "The Title and Authority of the Patriarch (Nasi) and the President of the Academy (Av Beit Din)," state that Rabban Gamaliel was a נשיא "Patriarch." As with the various names of the Sanhedrin in the rabbinic literature, we encounter the same disregard for precise names and titles regarding the community's leaders.

[53] As we have seen above, disclosed in the Tosefta.

[54] I reiterate that we do not have to consider as authentic every detail of the narrative. See the extended discussion of this narrative in n. 300.

[55] See S. Safrai, ההכרעה כבית הלל ביבנה, pp. 28-9, who maintains that the establishment of halakhah according to Beit Hillel was not accomplished at the two meetings at Yabneh. He too states that this was a slow process, starting after Rabban Gamaliel's death.

declared, and whether it was applied in practice; Rabbi Yehudah[56] was a Tanna of the fourth generation, a disciple of Rabbi Aqiba, active after 135.[57]

Further, most of the recorded disputes between Beit Shammai and Beit Hillel are quoted without any decision on the final halakhah.[58] Moreover, as we have noted (tSukkah 2: 3, tYevamot 1: 13), Tosefta

---

56 A baraita in bQiddushin 52b demonstrates Rabbi Yehudah's attitude toward a fixed halakhah: לאחר פטירתו של ר' מאיר אמר להם רבי יהודה לתלמידיו אל יכנסו תלמידי רבי מאיר לכאן מפני שקנתרנים הם ולא ללמוד תורה הם באים אלא לקפחני בהלכות הם באים "After the death of Rabbi Meir, Rabbi Yehudah said to his disciples: Rabbi Meir's disciple should not be let in [to study] in my school because they are just heckling. They do not come to study the Torah, but rather to affront me with their halakhot." The narrative proceeds to recount that one disciple succeeded in intruding, and in fact proclaimed: Rabbi Meir taught me so! Rabbi Yehudah was furious, repeating his warning. The narrative also appears in yQiddushin 2: 7, 63a, but Rabbi Yehudah's explanation of his prohibition is not indicated. The remarkable element in Rabbi Yehudah's discourse is the juxtaposition of "studying the Torah" and "halakhot" as two opposing concepts. In other words, studying Scripture and deliberating on its every possible meaning is seen as the appropriate method, rather than the recitation of halakhot. This apparently odd behaviour of Rabbi Yehudah may aid us in explaining his equivocal declaration in mEduyyot 1: 6 (see chap. 3, n. 5). Perceiving his preference for unrestrained debate over fixed halakhot, we may also consider his statement in Eduyyot to be a plea for the recognition of and respect for the individual's autonomy and right to declare his particular viewpoint. The missing consequence in that declaration would then be as follows: "If someone declares, This is my tradition [in opposition to another opinion, one must go along with this and say: You may persist in your opinion,] since it is an utterance of that Sage [whose tradition you quoted]." The effect of this narrative is seen in the fact that the later Amoraim decided that in disputes between Rabbi Meir and Rabbi Yehudah - and there were many - the halakhah is according to Rabbi Yehudah (bEruvin 46b). The decision in favour of Rabbi Yehudah may be traced precisely to his system of unrestrained deliberation and discussion. Moreover, since his viewpoint was ultimately declared authoritative, it is evident that his opposition to the recital of halakhot was not engendered simply by his egocentrism or personal pride. In yShabbat 3: 7, 6c, there is still a dispute between Rab and Samuel as to whether the halakhah is according to Rabbi Yehudah or Rabbi Meir.

57 J. N. Epstein, תנאים, p. 427, contemplates that this assembly took place about forty years after the Temple's destruction. It is evident, however, that Rabbi Yehudah's declaration originates from a later date; there is incontestable indication of a later editing by Rabbi, who, as we have noted, intended to establish the halakhah by replacing the name of the Tanna whose opinion he preferred with the term וחכמים אומרים, to indicate a majority opinion, or using the expression וחכמים מטהרין to indicate a factual judgment.

58 As I have noted in section 3.4, the maxim לעולם הלכה כבית הלל "The halakhah is always according to Beit Hillel" (tYevamot 1: 13) is a late declaration. Ch. Albeck, ששה סדרי משנה, סדר נשים, p. 332, interprets this declaration, not as the result of a decision and a definite rule, but as intending to state that the people conducted themselves according to the opinions of Beit Hillel.

declares that one is allowed to conduct oneself according to either school. We have also observed that at the time of Rabbi Yohanan ben Nuri, a Tanna of the third generation, an extremely important and practical issue[59] that had been disputed between the two schools was not yet definitely settled. Many of the other recorded disputes among the Sages also remained undecided.[60]

We may thus deduce that despite the effort at Yabneh to create and implement a definite codex, this was not realized. Taking this evidence together with the evidence in Chapter 3, we may conclude that the legal environment post-70 was still quite open and tolerant.[61] We have noted

---

59 We read in tYevamot 1: 9: אמ׳ ר׳ יוחנן בן נורי בא וראה היאך הלכה זו רווחת בישראל לקיים כדברי בית שמיי הולד ממז׳ כדברי ב״ה אם לקיים כדברי בית הלל הוולד פגום כדברי בית שמאי אלא בוא ונתקין שיהו הצרות חולצות ולא מתיבמות ולא הספיקו לגמור את הדבר עד שנטרפה שעה "[The passage refers to a dispute between the two Schools regarding the obligation of the levirate; if the dead man had two wives, and one of them is prohibited from wedding the living brother because of incest, then the levir is not allowed to marry either of the two, and is free of his levirate obligation. This is the opinion of Beit Hillel, but Beit Shammai contend that he is permitted to marry the second wife who has no relationship with the living brother; hence he is under obligation to marry her, and she must not marry another man]. Rabbi Yohanan ben Nuri was concerned about the application in practice [of these opinions] in Israelite society. If one acted according to Beit Shammai and married the other wife, his children would be considered bastards by Beit Hillel, and if one proceeded according to Beit Hillel, and would not marry her [and would also not perform the act of חליצה, the ceremony involving the removal of his sandal which would liberate both himself and the wife from the levirate obligation] the child born [of the wife's marriage with a priest] would not be suitable to be a priest [because he was born of an irregular marriage]. He tried to find a solution, but the time was not propitious [because the Bar Kokhba rebellion started]."

60 Rabbi uses the term חכמים in a number of these disputes to indicate his preference, but in others, there is no indication of the halakhah. As noted above (n. 48), Ch. Albeck considers that the editors of Eduyyot did not intend to establish halakhah, but only to set in order the halakhic data. See also A. Aderet, מסכת עדויות. Aderet would widen the scope of the tractate to include the restoration of hope and reconciliation after the trauma of the destruction, but agrees in principle that its purpose was to find a consensus for the establishment of a single halakhah.

61 Certain narratives confirm the tolerance of and respect for opposing decisions by the early Tannaim. For instance, tShabbat 12: 12 relates that Rabbi Meir, who permitted the preparation on Sabbath of a mixture of wine and oil for healing purpose, did not allow the preparation of such a mixture for himself when he was ill. He said to his critics: אע״פ שאני אומ׳ כן לא מלאני לבי מימי לעבור על דברי חבירי "Although I said so [that it is permitted] I never had the audacity [myself] to contravene the declarations of my colleagues." Rabbi Meir's justification may be perceived as being biased toward a stricter decision, as indicated in the citation of his answer in yBerakhot 1: 1, 3a: אף על פי שאני מיקל לאחרים מחמיר אני על עצמי דהא פליגי עלי חברי "Although I am lenient [in this matter], I practice

that several dicta reflect a recommendation to consider all opinions with respect to a contested issue, and the freedom to decide which is correct (probably in accord with the circumstances of each particular case).[62]

4.1.3 The Existence of Early Disputes

The later disputes recorded in Mishnah and Tosefta Eduyyot likely derive in part from different attitudes to newly arisen problems. One must assume, however, that their origin was mainly in opposing traditions from earlier periods. There are numerous decisions explicitly recorded in Eduyyot, and in other talmudic literature, with the expressions: נמנו, נמנו וגמרו, הלכה כרבי "they voted," "voted and decided," "the halakhah is according to...." It would be unreasonable to assume that such decisions all refer to disputes concerning new problems, that had never arisen before.

We read in mYadayim 3: 5, for instance, the long history of a dispute as to whether the books of Ecclesiastes and Song of Songs are considered to be as holy as other biblical books, and pollute the hands. The mishnah ends with the statement: "[The narrative records] how they disputed and how they [finally] decided." There is no doubt that these books were in circulation in Israelite society before 70, as a dispute is recorded between Beit Shammai and Beit Hillel concerning this issue, but a decision was concluded only at the change of the Patriarch in Yabneh.

Another such example is the dispute regarding the disposal of leavened substances at Passover. Although such questions certainly occurred in the pre-70 period, the dispute among the Tannaim, as is

---

strictness on myself, since my colleagues dispute my opinion." Further on the text states: רבי עקיבא פליג על רבנין ולא עבד עבדא כוותיה "Rabbi Aqiba disputed [a halakhah] with the Sages but he did not act according to his [own] opinion"; the narrative then relates that Rabbi Aqiba declared a house pure, against his own declaration that it was polluted, during a vote on the issue: התחילו מרבי עקיבה וטיהר "They started their vote with Rabbi Aqiba, and he declared it pure." We must consider that this deliberation in Y. T. occurred much later than the events related, and the Amoraim perceived the term חכמים as the majority opinion, which was considered the correct halakhah. The Amoraim were puzzled that in some occurrences Rabban Gamaliel or Rabban Simeon proceeded according to their own opinions, whereas Rabbi Meir and Rabbi Aqiba followed the "majority" opinion. We must understand that the term חכמים used to indicate the majority opinion is a later fiction instituted by Rabbi to establish the halakhah according to the alleged "majority." The amoraic puzzlement is anachronistic, but the remembered narratives confirm the environment of tolerance and respect for opposing opinions among the early Tannaim.

62 See particularly the quotations in chap. 3, nn. 77-8.

evident in the Mishnah,[63] must have been the result of different traditions transmitted from the earlier period.

A final example is illustrated in mYadayim 4: 3. As we have noted,[64] this mishnah records a problem that arose on the day Rabbi Eleazar ben Azariah was nominated Patriarch in place of Rabban Gamaliel in Yabneh (i.e., post-70).[65] The question concerned the type of tithe to be assigned in the seventh year from the crops grown in Ammon and Moab, on the east side of the Jordan. Though the law regarding fallow fields did not originally apply in that region, as it was not considered part of Israel, the Sages nevertheless instituted the obligation of tithes. On the other hand, since no tithes were due in Israel in the seventh year,[66] a dispute occurred between two Sages as to the type of tithe to be set aside in Ammon and Moab: "On that day, it was asked: What type of tithe must be set aside in Ammon and Moab? Rabbi Tarfon decreed the tithe for the poor and Rabbi Eleazar ben Azariah decreed the second tithe [which must be consumed in Jerusalem]." It is significant that a fixed rule had not already been established pre-70, since it must be assumed that Jews lived in these regions at that time, and this problem must have arisen earlier. This mishnah in fact ends by quoting a declaration by Rabbi Eleazar, that he had a tradition from Rabban Yohanan ben Zakkai, who had a tradition from his teacher, and so on back to Moses at Sinai, that in the seventh year the tithe for the poor must be set aside in Ammon and Moab. We may

---

63 We read in mTemurah 7: 5, regarding the disposal of leavened and other substances: את שדרכו לישרף ישרף ואת שדרכו ליקבר יקבר "What is usually burned should be burned and what is usually buried should be buried." In mPesahim 2: 1, a dispute is recorded: רבי יהודה אומר אין ביעור חמץ אלא שריפה וחכמים אומרים אף מפרר וזורה לרוח או מטיל לים "Rabbi Yehudah says: The disposal of *hametz* is effected solely by burning, and the Sages say that one may break it into small crumbs and scatter it in the wind, or throw it into the sea." Yet another legitimate method of disposal is recorded in mPesahim 2: 3: חמץ שנפלה עליו מפולת הרי הוא כמבוער רבן שמעון בן גמליאל אומר כל שאין הכלב יכול לחפש אחריו "*Hametz* covered by fallen debris is considered to be disposed of; Rabban Simeon ben Gamaliel says: This is valid only when a dog is unable to search after it [under the debris]."

64 See, e.g., chap. 1, text at n. 118, and chap. 3, nn. 100, 120, and 183.

65 This narrative, an interesting story to which I shall revert in section 4.2.2.2, appears in yBerakhot 4: 1, 7c-d, and bBerakhot 27b. Rabbi Yehoshua was involved in this event and the record undoubtedly portrays an incident after 70.

66 After the dedication of the first tithe for the Levites, an additional tithe was due, but this one was of two different types: מעשר שני to be eaten in Jerusalem and מעשר עני to be donated to the poor. A fixed cycle of six years regulated their sequence; no tithes were given in the seventh year, when the fields lay fallow. In the first, second, fourth and fifth years מעשר שני was due, and in the third and sixth years מעשר עני had to be given to the poor.

therefore assume that a dispute existed about this problem in the earlier period, and that it had remained undecided and was settled only at Yabneh. We may postulate the same situation with respect to the larger scenario: the Sages did not attempt to establish fixed halakhah before 70, and this was only decided later, at conferences in Yabneh on various occasions.

There is also evidence that certain of these disputes were not settled even in later times. We read, for instance, in mMikva'ot 4: 1: "Rabbi Meir said: At a vote, Beit Shammai had the majority over Beit Hillel, but they admitted that when one forgot [a vessel] in the courtyard, [the water collected in it] does not pollute [the ritual bath]. Rabbi Yose said: The dispute is not yet settled[67] [and the halakhah was not yet established]."

4.1.4 Evidence of Pre-70 Pluralism in Decision-Making

Though there is limited evidence of the pre-70 situation, there are several passages that do confirm the flexibility of pre-70 decision-making. I shall quote two passages dealing with extremely grave matters, concerning the death penalty; we may assume that a similar situation prevailed with regard to less significant cases, that were not considered worthy of recording in the talmudic literature. We read in tSanhedrin 6: 6: "[Yehudah ben Tabai had sentenced one false witness to death, contrary to the law that this penalty is applied only when two witnesses are declared false. Reprimanding him,] Rabbi Simeon ben Shetah said: Scripture compares the requirements for conviction of false witnesses to the requirements for a verdict of capital punishment; just as two or three witnesses are required in a capital case, the same applies for the conviction of false witnesses. On that occasion Yehudah ben Tabai undertook to teach the halakhah only in accordance with Simeon ben Shetah." These two Sages[68] were active at the turn of the first century B.C.E., and we observe that each judged according to his opinion even in cases of capital punishment. The fact that Yehudah ben Tabai accepted Simeon's exposition in this case does not challenge the assumption that there was no fixed codex; it simply demonstrates that there were discussions between the Sages, and one might accept the reasoning of another, after convincing evidence. It is possible that the purpose of this narrative was, in fact, to emphasize this virtuous characteristic of the Sages, rather than to point out the flaw in Rabbi Yehudah's judgment.

---

67 The exact interpretation of Rabbi Yose's declaration is not clear, and there are different opinions on this issue. See Ch. Albeck, ששה סדרי משנה, סדר טהרות, p. 578.

68 According to tHagigah 2: 8, one was a Nasi and the other the Av Beit Din.

A further example is found in mSanhedrin 7: 2:[69] "Rabbi Eleazar son of Rabbi Tzadoq said: It happened that a priest's daughter who committed adultery [and was sentenced to die by burning, as in Lev 21: 9] was enveloped with bundles of branches and burned [in conflict with the rabbinic law cited in the mishnah, which provides a different method of execution by burning]. So they said him: [This was not the correct manner, it happened in this way only] because that court was not erudite [they did not know the precise law]." This event must have occurred at least forty years before the Temple's destruction, since post-destruction the Israelite courts could not impose capital punishment.[70] Another version of this event in tSanhedrin 9: 11, quoted in ySanhedrin 7: 2, 24b, confirms that it is to be dated pre-70: "Rabbi Eleazar son of Rabbi Tzadoq said: I was an infant riding on my father's shoulder and I saw [an execution by fire]."[71] Later Amoraim were extremely concerned with this apparent evidence of a non-normative execution; an extended discussion appears in bSanhedrin 52b, in which various explanations are offered. One such opinion states: "Rav Joseph said: It was a Sadducean tribunal."[72] Another suggestion is cited: "They said to him [to Rabbi Eleazar, to deny the authenticity of his testimony]: You were a minor and one does not bring forth the evidence of a minor."

These passages unequivocally demonstrate that different sentences were pronounced by the courts in capital cases in the period before 70. One must assume that each court based its decisions on individual Sages' perceptions of the biblical commands and precepts. It seems that these circumstances were not considered objectionable pre-70; it was only

---

69 There are some discrepancies in the various MSS containing this narrative, but they are of no consequence for our purpose.

70 This issue is a delicate and much debated topic, and it is not within the scope of our study to elaborate upon it. I am therefore relying on the talmudic declarations in this respect. We read in bSanhedrin 41a: ותניא ארבעים שנה קודם חורבן הבית גלתה סנהדרי וישבה לה בחנות ואמר רבי יצחק בר אבודימי לומר שלא דנו דיני קנסות דיני קנסות סלקא דעתך אלא שלא דנו דיני נפשות: "We learned in a baraita that forty years before the Temple's destruction, the Sanhedrin went into exile [from the Temple court] and met in a shop. And Rabbi Isaac ben Ab[u]dimi said: This comes to tell us that [from that period onward] they did not judge issues regarding the payment of fines. [Question] Is that reasonable? [Answer: No, rather] they did not judge matters involving capital punishment."

71 Rabbi Tzadoq lived at the time of the Temple, as we read in bGittin 56a: דר' צדוק יתיב ארבעין שנין בתעניתא דלא ליחרב ירושלים "Rabbi Tzadoq fasted forty years, praying to God that Jerusalem should not be destroyed." On 56b, we read that Rabbi Yohanan ben Zakkai asked Vespasian ואסוותא דמסיין ליה לרבי צדוק "[to provide] medical doctors to heal Rabbi Tzadoq [from the aftermath of this lengthy fast]."

72 Cf. G. Alon, *The Jews*, vol. 1, p. 190 on this subject.

afterwards that questions were raised regarding the legitimacy of independent and contrasting decisions. I suggest that this evidence of the prevailing situation with respect to capital cases confirms the thesis that the same procedure was undoubtedly followed with respect to cases of less critical significance, and with respect to questions regarding the manner of performance of biblical commands.

4.1.5 Differences in Literary Style

It is also remarkable that the dicta of pre-70 Sages that we encounter in rabbinic literature, albeit scant, indicate a style *sui generis*, different than the later tannaitic pronouncements. The latter take the form of explicit declarations for the purpose of conveying halakhot. They are introduced in the Mishnah by the expressions: רבי פלוני אומר, וחכמים אומרים, דברי רבי פלוני "Rabbi X says" or "and the Sages say" or "these are the words of Rabbi X." The traditions conveyed by the pre-70 Sages, on the other hand, are introduced not as their explicit pronouncements, but as narratives about their deeds or casual expressions. We often encounter, for example, the introductory phrases: "I remember what Rabban Gamaliel the Elder did [tShabbat 13: 2]," "It happened that Rabban Gamaliel acted in such a way [tAvodah Zarah 3: 10]," "It happened at the time of Rabbi Tzadoq's father [that they acted in a certain way, and from that we deduced a halakhah - mShabbat 24: 5]," "They recounted that Rabbi Eliezer son of Tzadoq acted in a certain way [tBetzah 3: 8]." We also encounter the introductory phrase: מקובלני מרבן גמליאל הזקן "I have a tradition from Rabban Gamaliel the Elder [that he acted in a certain way]." Many ancient rules and decrees are introduced by the phrase: "Hillel the elder [or Rabban Gamaliel, or Simeon ben Shetah] decreed an ordinance." The style of these traditions indicates that the pre-70 Sages were not concerned with the declaration of abstract laws and rules; people learned such rules by observing the Sages' behaviour, and in some instances, if asked, the Sages pronounced their opinions.[73] Such a situation also

[73] We encounter in mEduyyot 8: 4 the following phrase: העיד רבי יוסי בן יועזר איש צרידה "Yose ben Yoezer gave witness." We must acknowledge, however, that this style was used to match the character of the tractate Eduyyot, and does not attest that this Sage personally came and gave witness. We also read in 5: 6: עקביא בן מהללאל העיד ארבעה דברים "Aqabyah ben Mahalalel gave witness on four issues." Both these Sages lived at the time of the Temple, and could not have taken part in this meeting in Yabneh. Moreover, Rabbi Yehudah rejects the identity of Aqabyah in the narrative and attributes the saying to someone else. Another alleged dictum of Aqabyah in mBekhorot 3: 4 is expressed with the term מתיר "he allows," in opposition to וחכמים אוסרין "and the Sages prohibit." This gives the impression

explains why most of their declarations were not preserved. Such decisions were not intended as final halakhot for posterity, nor as precedents; their validity was strictly *ad hoc*.

The anonymity of the pre-70 halakhic pronouncements, discussed above (at nn. 13 ff.), also serves as strong evidence that the Sages favoured an open, flexible legal system. Had they been required to memorize halakhic declarations (which were the basis of the existing tradition) with the names of their authors, this would likely have impeded any modification at a later time, given the intrinsically conservative perspective of every religious society. The renowned narrative in mEduyyot 1: 3[74] demonstrates that even Shammai and Hillel could not modify a prior tradition so as to contradict a pronouncement of an identified earlier Sage. We must assume that in that specific occurrence, prior anonymous traditions existed but were disputed by Shammai and Hillel. Were it not for the opinion attributed specifically to Shemayah and Abtalion, the opinion of either Hillel or Shammai would have been confirmed as the correct halakhah; thus it was the "credentials" of the earlier opinion that hindered its revision.

The very absence of recorded disputes among the Sages in the pre-70 period[75] also demonstrates the lack of interest in establishing a fixed halakhah.[76] As we have noted, different opinions were undoubtedly expressed.[77] These were not, however, considered disputes, or viewed in a

---

of an actual halakhic dispute, but from the subsequent discussion, we observe that this was not so. The Tannaim Rabbi Yehudah and Rabbi Yose dispute the precise occurrence that Aqabyah allowed; thus they do not refer to a discussion and dispute between Aqabyah and the Sages, but relate a tradition with respect to a particular concrete inquiry in which Aqabyah decided to allow the use of a blemished animal. The traditions regarding the decisions of the pre-70 Sages were not kept as meticulously as were those of the later Tannaim, and therefore we encounter many controversies concerning their actual substance. See also D. Weiss-Halivni, *Midrash, Mishnah and Gemara*, p. 20 on the editor's change with respect to Yose ben Yoezer's testimony in mEduyyot 8: 4.

74 See citation in chap 1, text at n. 26.

75 We have seen that only three disputes were assumed to have occurred between Shammai and Hillel.

76 D. Goodblatt, "Iudaea between the Revolts," p. 117, writes: "In fact, it is likely that pluralism was typical of Judean leadership in Second Temple times as well."

77 Human nature is characterized by different views and opinions, particularly with respect to interpretations of the texts and narratives of others. The authors of the Dead Sea Scrolls disputed in particular the hermeneutic methods used to interpret biblical verses. They denigrated their opponents, presumably the Pharisees, אשר דרשו בחלוקות "who sought easy interpretations" (CD A, Col. I: 12 - 13).

S.J.D. Cohen, "The Significance of Yavneh," p. 29, writes: "For the first time Jews 'agreed to disagree.'" He consequently asserts that there were disagreements on halakhah in the pre-70 period. But it seems from his context that he refers to the disagreements between the different groups, that is, Pharisees, Sadducees and

---

Essenes. I assert in contrast that there were halakhic disputes even between the pharisaic Sages. The fact that the "Voice of Heaven" was heard at Yabneh, shortly after the Temple's destruction, to establish halakhah according to Beit Hillel, indicates that the latter's contention with Beit Shammai originated in the pre-70 period. Such disagreements did not create "disputes" or splits, as did the controversies between the Pharisees and the dissident groups, as I argue in the second part of this work. As detailed in this chapter, rabbinic narratives explicitly and implicitly attest to the existence of different views and opinions on halakhic problems in the pre-70 period. See, for example, the renowned dispute with Aqabyah ben Mahalalel in mEduyyot 5: 6, quoted in chap. 2, n. 110. As I have noted in section 3.6, talmudic records of the Sanhedrin's activity in the pre-70 period include the following statement: אם שמעו אמרו להם ואם לאו עומדין במנין "If they had [an earlier] tradition [about the halakhah in question] they told them; if not, they arranged a vote [among the members of the court and decided by a majority vote]." Hence, it is evident that there were differences of opinion, an entirely natural human characteristic, among the members of the Sanhedrin. I have amply demonstrated the fictive nature of the statement that the Sanhedrin decided on all doubtful halakhot, but we may still trust the informal reference to the existence of different opinions.

Cohen further asserts in the above study (p. 37) that the concept of oral Torah is never attributed to the Pharisees, and he thus confirms Schäfer's assertion that this concept is of late origin. This fact implicitly corroborates my postulate of a pluralistic exegetical and halakhic environment. The essence of oral Torah is intrinsically opposite to tolerance and pluralism, similar to the immutable and inflexible written Torah. A divinely received law, however transmitted - orally or in writing - does not permit conflicting opinions. Sherira Gaon struggled - in answer to an explicit question in this regard - to reconcile the belief in a divine law with the existence of rabbinic disputes. The passage found in tSanhedrin 7: 1 (see chap. 3, n. 132) and other sources seems to undertake the same justification, though not in answer to an explicit question. The absence of a concept of oral Torah in the pre-70 period is thus consistent with the existence of a pluralistic environment regarding biblical interpretation and decision-making in that era.

We do not possess any reliable data of the pharisaic viewpoint from pre-70, and it is no wonder that so many divergent scholarly views have been proffered concerning that period. I need not enter here into a debate with Cohen's assertion of intolerance pre-70 and the opposite post-70, which appears to be the antithesis of my postulate, having validated my conclusions by appropriate interpretation of rabbinic quotations; I would nevertheless offer some short comments. On p. 29, Cohen forges his thesis upon the "fundamental assumption...that the Pharisees were one of these sects" - that is, that they were definitely "a sect." In his study *From the Maccabees to the Mishna*, pp. 154 ff., however, he maintains that according to the rabbinic texts the Pharisees were "not a sect." In his summary of the relevant chapter (p. 162) he writes: "None of the ancient sources views the Pharisees as a sect, and there is no sign that the Pharisees of the first century had that exclusivistic ideology, strict organization, and group oriented eschatology which characterize sects." He is concerned with the semantic interpretation of the term "Pharisee," which means "separatist," a term having a connotation of "sectarian" (a much debated and doubtful interpretation); he characterizes them as "pietists who...separated themselves to some extent...but who saw themselves, and were seen by others, not as exclusive bearers of the truth but as virtuosi and elites." It seems to me that these two assertions are contrasting, and that his above conclusions in *From the Maccabees to the Mishna* are closer to my thesis than to his assertion in the Yabneh essay. Cohen's assertion that the Rabbis did not associate themselves with the Pharisees might in fact serve to corroborate my thesis

negative light[78] - that is, as confrontations between opposing ideas. Thus, in a tolerant environment in which opinions and conclusions are not finally determined,[79] different decisions would not have been perceived as "disputes." We may note that Josephus, who juxtaposes and contrasts the Pharisees and the Sadducees, characterizes the Sadducees as ones who tend "to dispute with the teachers [*Ant.* 18: 16]." On the other hand, he considers the Pharisees "the most accurate interpreters of the laws [*J.W.* 2: 162]";[80] he states further: "Nor do they rashly presume to contradict their [the elders'] proposals [*Ant.* 18: 13]." We have no authentic Sadducean texts to verify Josephus' portrayal of their attitude, but his characterization of the Pharisees is certainly not consistent with the post-70 rabbinic manner of arguing about almost every halakhic topic.

4.1.6 The Development of Detailed Rules as a Later Phenomenon

The proliferation of rules regarding how the halakhah was to be established is apparent only later, in the discussions of the Amoraim in the Gemara. A dictum in tEduyyot 1: 5 attests to the fact that different Sages could and did deliver conflicting halakhic decisions:[81] "If one asked [a

---

that they dramatically changed the *ad hoc* character of the halakhah into a system of fixed halakhah. This represented a substantial shift in the *Sitz im Leben* of Israelite society. The fact that the Rabbis did not "develop heresiology etc." (p. 41) does not imply that the "intolerant" Pharisees engendered the pre-70 sectarian society. There is nowhere any statement that the Pharisees expelled the Sadducees or the Essenes. The Essenes and Qumranites separated themselves from the bulk of society; they never accused others of expelling them. See also G. Boccaccini, "History of Judaism," p. 290, who refers to the "dynamic and pluralistic nature of Judaism." He alludes to the evolution of the sects as an expression of the "pluralism of ancient Judaism" (p. 293). The creation of sects is an outgrowth of a pluralistic environment, in which varied ideas were prevalent; diverse opinions within a society are either mitigated, or intensified and create schism.

78 Jay M. Harris, "From Inner-Biblical Interpretation to Early Rabbinic Exegesis," p. 266, writes on the other hand that "Rabbinic culture is particularly disputatious."

79 L. L. Grabbe, "Hellenistic Judaism," p. 73, asserts that there was no normative Judaism in the Hellenistic period: "There was a great variety of Judaisms in antiquity."

80 The characterization of the Pharisees as interpreters tends to indicate that they were continuously creating new decisions through their interpretations of the Torah; this suggests a continuing legal development, as opposed to the existence of a fixed legal codex.

81 The original text reads: נישאל לחכם אחד וטימא לו לא ישאל לחכם אחר נשאל לחכם וטיהר לו לא ישאל לחכם אחר. The Tosefta continues with rules as to how to proceed when one has asked two Sages, presumably at the same time, and received opposing decisions. In this case, one should ask a third Sage and accept his opinion. In the absence of a third, one should follow the severe decision in matters of

halakhic decision from] a Sage [on a question of purity] and he declared it polluted, he must not ask [a second opinion from] another Sage [who might declare it pure]; if he asked [a halakhic decision from] a Sage and he declared it pure, he must not ask another Sage [who might declare it impure]." We have noted that Rabbi, who arranged the Mishnah, indicated his preference for the correct halakhah by attributing opinions of particular Sages to the generic חכמים, or quoting it anonymously. The move to establish rules for fixing the halakhah started with Rabbi Yohanan, a student of Rabbi's academy.[82]

A number of citations in the Y. T. illustrate the lack of rules for establishing the halakhah in the earlier period. In yTa'anit 2: 14, 66b, the halakhah is established factually, rather than in the usual manner of declaring that the halakhah is according to Rabbi X; the discussion indicates that the attribution to the Tannaim was not certain. In yKil'ayim 6: 1, 30b, it is said in the name of Rab that the halakhah is according to Rabbi Aqiba;[83] this is then modified to the effect that Rabbi Aqiba's lenient decision is valid only outside Israel. In mBerakhot 5: 2, there is a conflict between an anonymous dictum and Rabbi Aqiba and Rabbi Eliezer, regarding a blessing to be recited at night after the Sabbath; this was definitely a custom originating from an earlier period, but not yet settled. In yBerakhot 5: 2, 9b, the matter is still debated; one Amora suggests accepting Rabbi Eliezer's decision in a specific case, and another declares that the halakhah on this general topic always follows Rabbi Eliezer. Both opinions contradict the general rule.[84] There is a peculiar declaration in yShabbat 2: 3, 5a, with respect to a dispute between Rabbi Eleazar, Rabbi Yehoshua and Rabbi Aqiba: "Logically, it would appear that the halakhah should follow Rabbi Aqiba, since his opinion consists of a compromise between Rabbi Yehoshua and Rabbi Eleazar, but in fact, the halakhah follows Rabbi Yehoshua, because of a conflicting declaration by Rab [an Amora]."[85] In yRosh HaShanah 4: 6, 59c, we learn that, even at

---

Torah precepts and the lenient approach in matters of rabbinic decrees.

82 Ch. Albeck, מבוא לתלמודים, p. 184. See further n. 89.

83 This statement conflicts with a statement in the B. T., quoted below (n. 88), that the halakhah follows Rabbi Aqiba only in a dispute with one Tanna; in mKil'ayim 6: 1, however, to which the Y. T. refers, the disputing opinion is quoted anonymously, which would correspond to the majority opinion. The modification of Rabbi Jacob bar Aha, limiting the lenient rule to outside Israel, in effect harmonizes the Y. T. decision with the B. T. rule.

84 The halakhah should follow the majority, and the anonymous dictum in the mishnah, assumed to be that of the majority, opposes the decisions of both Rabbi Aqiba and Rabbi Eliezer. Both the final halakhah and current custom in fact follow the anonymous dictum, contrary to the opinions of the two Amoraim in the Gemara. This is again an indication of the utter lack of uniformity.

85 In addition to the odd explanation, the decision conflicts with the B. T. declaration

the time of the assembly at Usha, there were still different customs in Judah and in Galilee regarding the liturgy on Rosh HaShanah. Similarly, mPesahim 4: 1 - 5 reflects the use of different customs in various localities; from the discussion in yPesahim 4: 1, 30d regarding the rule to adhere to local customs in such cases, we may deduce that such halakhic disputes[86] were not yet definitely settled, although the rhetoric attempts, rather feebly, to indicate the opposite.[87]

There are various examples of attempts to create elaborate rules, as, for instance, in yBava Metzi'a 3: 9, 9b: "Rab Yirmeyah in the name of Rab [said]: The halakhah is [always] according to Rabbi Aqiba, even when Beit Hillel oppose him."[88] Another complex regulation is found in yTerumot 3: 1, 42a, in the name of Rabbi Yohanan:[89] "[In disputes between] Rabbi Meir and Rabbi Simeon, the halakhah is according to Rabbi Simeon. [In disputes between] Rabbi Simeon and Rabbi Yehudah, the halakhah is according to Rabbi Yehudah, and it is obvious that [in a dispute between] Rabbi Meir and Rabbi Yehudah, the halakhah is according to Rabbi Yehudah."[90]

---

that the halakhah follows Rabbi Aqiba in a dispute with a single Tanna (n. 88).

86 The discussion mentions disputes between Beit Hillel and Beit Shammai, Rabbi Meir and Rabbi Yose; though the disputes were presumed to be settled, it seems that people still did not follow any one particular system. See tSukkah 2: 3, quoted in chap. 1, text at n. 54, that one may follow either Beit Hillel or Beit Shammai, despite the fact that the halakhah was allegedly fixed according to Beit Hillel by the Voice of Heaven.

87 For example, it is suggested that there is a reversal of the names of Rabbi Meir and Rabbi Yose, which is evidently a weak solution. There is no attempt to answer the question regarding the dispute between the Houses of Shammai and Hillel. Similarly weak solutions are proffered regarding the other variations in customs that in fact result from opposing tannaitic opinions.

88 In bEruvin 46b, we read: רבי יעקב ורבי זריקא אמרו הלכה כרבי עקיבא מחבירו וכרבי יוסי מחבריו וכרבי מחבירו "Rabbi Aqiba and Rabbi Zeriqa said: [In disputes among Tannaim] the halakhah is according to Rabbi Aqiba [in a dispute] with one Tanna, and according to Rabbi Yose [even if he disputed] with many Tannaim, and according to Rabbi [in a dispute] with one Tanna."

89 The real focus on the establishment of rules for the fixing of halakhot starts with the first Amoraim, Rabbi Yehoshua ben Levi (yShabbat 3: 7, 6c, yEruvin 1: 1, 18b, yYevamot 4: 7, 5d, bEruvin 46a) and Rabbi Yohanan (yDemai 2: 1, 22d, yBikkurim 1: 5, 64a, yTa'anit 1: 2, 64a, bYevamot 42b; bGittin 75a; bHullin 50a), of the first and second generations. Several of these instances have been quoted above.

90 In bEruvin 46b, quoted in n. 56, we encounter a dictum in the name of Rabbi Yohanan: רבי מאיר ורבי יהודה הלכה כרבי יהודה רבי יהודה ורבי יוסי הלכה כרבי יוסי "[In a dispute] between Rabbi Meir and Rabbi Yehudah, the halakhah is according to Rabbi Yehudah; [in a dispute] between Rabbi Yehudah and Rabbi Yose, the halakhah is according to Rabbi Yose." It seems, however, that it was unclear how the halakhah was to be decided in a dispute between Rabbi Simeon and Rabbi Meir: רבי מאיר ורבי שמעון מאי תיקו "...the answer is *teiqu* ['unresolved']."

4.1.7 דאוריתא and דרבנן

As further evidence of the change in attitude pre- and post-70, I wish now to discuss a particular classification of rules that appears in the talmudic literature. While many rules were deemed to be of Torah origin, דאוריתא, others were acknowledged to be of rabbinic origin, מדרבנן. These rules did not contain any explicit declarations of biblical support to establish them as Torah rules, nor were they derived from ancient tradition;[91] they were considered to be rabbinic extensions of the law. A great number of these extensions were based on a philosophy of prevention, a desire to built a גדר / סייג,[92] a "fence/ hedge", or rather a more remote line of defence, around the core of the biblical commands. The idea was to prevent an erroneous transgression of a Torah precept through inattention,[93] or by an incorrect deduction,[94] or as a result of

91 Such as הלכה למשה מסיני "halakhah [given] to Moses on Sinai." Even this attribute does not automatically imply a Torah rule, however, as I have demonstrated in 3. 5. The lack of consistency impedes any attempt at a general classification, and each case must be examined separately according to its explicit categorization in the rabbinic literature. Further, the fact that a certain restriction is deduced by hermeneutics from a scriptural verse does not automatically make it a Torah precept. Cf. I.D. Gilat, פרקים, pp. 239 ff., who concludes that a halakhah deduced from hermeneutic analysis of a scriptural support, in such rabbinic literature as Sifre, Sifra and the Mekiltot, is a Torah precept. Thus, for example, he detects a conflict between rabbinic declarations that the duty of the husband to feed his wife is a rabbinic ordinance, and other citations that deduce this obligation from biblical verses through hermeneutic analysis. In these occurrences, however, there is no explicit declaration that the duty is a Torah precept; the discussion serves only as a homily and as a scriptural support to a rabbinic rule, as in many other instances. The prohibition against riding an animal on Sabbath, discussed in chap. 2, n. 68, is cited in the Mishnah explicitly as שבות, a rabbinic ordinance (see n. 96), while in Sifra, cited in the same note, it is deduced by hermeneutic analysis from Scripture. We thus observe that scriptural support does not necessarily render a rule a Torah precept. The maxim מדרבנן וקרא אסמכתא בעלמא "[The rule is] a rabbinic decree and the [hermeneutic analysis of a] scriptural verse is just a support," is often used in the rabbinic deliberations, when there is an issue of whether a rule is a Torah precept or a rabbinic decree. The exegeses in the Midreshei Halakhah do not discuss this particular issue, and therefore one cannot automatically deduce that the presence of a scriptural support renders the deduced rule a Torah precept.

92 Both terms are used in the rabbinic literature for the same purpose.

93 As for example the decree in mShabbat 1: 3: לא יצא החייט במחטו סמוך לחשכה שמא ישכח ויצא "The tailor should not go out with his needle close to dusk [on Friday] because he may forget and carry it on Sabbath, after nightfall."

94 As for example the prohibition against eating chicken with milk, as we read in bHullin 104b: אי שרית ליה לאסוקי עוף וגבינה אתי לאסוקי בשר וגבינה ומיכל בשר בחלב דאורייתא "If you permitted the serving of fowl and cheese one might offer meat [i.e.of beef or goat], and eating meat and milk is a Torah

events beyond one's foresight or control.[95] The use of this "fence" method is marked by the term שמא - "the possibility [that one might arrive at an erroneous decision]." One such edict is the concept of שבות, the rabbinically-instituted extension of those activities prohibited on the Sabbath and holidays.[96]

This "fence" method is found in both tannaitic and later sources. Interestingly, however, there is a difference in terminology. In Mishnah and Tosefta, we find חוששין שמא ("one takes into consideration the possibility that..."), and its negative אין חוששין שמא ("one does not consider the possibility that...") where no special precaution is necessary. In amoraic sources, on the other hand, we encounter the term גזרה שמא "a decree [promulgated to avoid] the possibility that [one may transgress a law]." We must not assume that this distinction in the terminology explaining the motive of the ordinances is without any significance.[97] As I

[prohibition]."

95 As for example, if an increase in price occurs, independent of his action. We read in mBava Metzi'a 5: 9: וכן היה הלל אומר לא תלוה אשה ככר לחברתה עד שתעשנו דמים שמא יוקירו חטים ונמצאו באות לידי רבית "And so Hillel said: A woman must not lend a loaf [of bread] to her friend, unless she establishes its current value. [This is] because the price of bread may be higher [at the time when she returns a loaf] and thus she may have effected [the transgression of] usury." For example, the friend might borrow a loaf worth ten pennies, and return a loaf at a time when bread is worth eleven pennies; the one penny would be deemed interest. If the value were established at the time of borrowing as ten pennies, she would return a smaller loaf at that exact value, and thus the lender would avoid any profit from usury.

96 It seems that rabbinic extensions of the Sabbath restrictions were classified under the distinct name שבות. We read in mBetzah 5: 2: כל שחייבין עליו משום שבות משום רשות משום מצוה בשבת חייבין עליו ביום טוב "Whoever is liable on account of *shevut*, on account of a permission, or on account of a command on Sabbath, is [also] liable [for the same transgression] on holidays." Rashi expresses this explicitly in his commentary to bEruvin 33a: כל איסור שבת ויום טוב דהוי מדרבנן קרי שבות "Every prohibition on Sabbaths and holidays that [was] instituted by the Sages is called [or, he calls] *shevut*.'"

97 It is significant that the B. T. added the term גזרה in the explanations of mishnaic statements. We read in mBetzah 5: 2: לא עולין באילן ולא רוכבין על גבי בהמה "One must not climb a tree and not ride on an animal [on Sabbath and holidays]." The Gemara in bBetzah 36b, explaining the motive of these and similar prohibitions, states: לא עולין באילן גזרה שמא יתלוש ולא רוכבין על גבי בהמה גזרה שמא יצא חוץ לתחום "One must not climb a tree - it is a *gezeirah* because of the injunction against [inadvertently] tearing apart a branch, and one must not ride on an animal - it is a *gezeirah* because he might go beyond the limit [within which he is allowed to travel out of his locality]." We observe that the Gemara has added the term גזרה, absent in the mishnah, to bestow upon the mishnaic rule the additional severity inherent in this expression. The Y. T. version of this explanation in Betzah 5: 2, 63a,

have argued (section 1.6.4), the term *gezeirah* indicates the enactment of a decree by an authoritative body. This aspect is absent in the mishnaic sources regarding the "fence," and this absence must be taken as attesting to the different character of the mishnaic declarations. The latter give the impression of recording the Sages' deliberations and consequent decisions, rather than the official promulgation of decrees, and lack the uncompromising rigidity implied by the term *gezeirah* in the amoraic dicta. We may thus propose that in the tannaitic period these guiding rules were merely recommendations that one avoid certain activities, lest one transgress a Torah precept, rather than mandatory decrees to avoid these activities.

This proposal would explain the apparently peculiar records that certain renowned Tannaim did not accept these preventative extensions of prohibitions, and that the citizens of the towns in which these Tannaim were active continued to ignore these prohibitions in later times.[98] Such behaviour is reasonable if the rules were merely recommendations; if they had been mandatory, it is highly unlikely that any Sage would have rejected them. The Amoraim, in contrast, zealous to establish fixed halakhot, changed the character of these preventative recommendations and rendered them obligatory, bestowing upon them the character of *gezeirah*, "compulsory decree."

The examination of these differences between the two distinct bodies of law reveals another oddity. In certain instances, as in mBetzah 5: 2,[99] the Mishnah gives no motive for its preventative measure. The Amoraim, who considered such measures to be official decrees, could only speculate concerning the motives behind the mishnaic rules. We read at bBetzah 36b,[100] concerning a prohibition against riding on Sabbath: "[If it is because of] the possibility that one may go beyond the allowed limit,

---

does not add the term גזרה. We read there: מפני מה אמרו אין עולין באילן שמא ישכח ויאכל או שמא ישכח וירעיד "Why have they [the Sages] said that one must not climb a tree [on Sabbath and holidays]? Because one might forget [that it is Sabbath] and [pick and] eat a fruit, or would forget and shake [the tree to cause the fruit to fall, both deeds which it is forbidden to perform on Sabbath]."

98 We read in bYevamot 14a: במקומו של רבי אליעזר היו כורתים עצים לעשות פחמים בשבת לעשות ברזל במקומו של ר׳ יוסי הגלילי היו אוכלים בשר עוף בחלב. (See chap. 3, n. 78 for translation.)

99 Cited in nn. 96-7.

100 The parallel deliberation in Y. T. Betzah, quoted in n. 97 above, does not indicate this preventative idea, but presents other reasons for the precaution: שמא ישכח וירעיד "One may forget and shake [a tree]"; שמא תינוק הבהמה "the animal may feed its young"; and, what seems to be the conclusive reason: שהוא מצווה על שביתת בהמה כמוהו "because he is commanded to ensure the animal's rest just like his own [rest]." It is not clear what this occurrence entails; likely one would have to raise the suckling, which is a prohibited deed.

should we not deduce that this prohibition is a Torah precept [otherwise it would be allowed, because of the maxim that one does not decree גזירה לגזירה, 'one preventative edict on top of another'? [Answer:] It was decreed because one might cut a branch [from a tree] to whip the animal."[101]

As we have seen (section 1.6.4), while the Tannaim did use the term *gezeirah* for a restrictive court decision, promulgated when deemed necessary, they also used the terms התקין *hitqin* or תיקן *tiqen* for positive ordinances promulgated by courts; such edicts are of a totally distinct character from the preventative rules, and do not actually state that a Beit Din promulgated them.

Having established the conceptual distinction between the tannaitic and amoraic attitudes toward the legal status of these rabbinic resolutions, we may now go one step back and examine the character of pre-70 pharisaic declarations. As I have argued above, the limited number of halakhic citations from this period is one indication of the *ad hoc* character of the Sages' decision-making at this time, and the absence of a system aimed at the creation of a body of precedents to guide future decisions. I now postulate that there was no distinction at that time between Torah precepts and rabbinic edicts. Ordinances and judgments were promulgated to address particular exigencies, and were not inferior in the eyes of the Sages to Torah precepts. Some rules were temporary,[102] while others were decreed for eternity. I suggest that classification into the two distinct statuses of Torah edict and rabbinic edict originated in the post-70 period. The *ad hoc* procedure that dominated the pre-70 period is the antithesis of a classificatory mindset. Such a system thus began and developed only

---

101 It is common in rabbinic literature to search for a scriptural support; we encounter such an attempt in this case, in another source. We read in Sifra *Ahare* 5: 7: מנין שלא יעלה באילן ושלא ירכב על גבי בהמה ולא ישוט על המים וגו׳ תלמוד לומר שבתון שבות [קדש] "How do we know that one must not climb a tree, ride on an animal and board a ship [on Sabbath] etc.? [Answer] Scripture came to teach us this [in the words] 'a day of rest a [holy] Sabbath' [a tautology that is interpreted as adding certain deeds that are not included in the typical definition of work]." Cf. I. D. Gilat, פרקים, pp. 87 ff.

102 For example, the ordinance in mSotah 9: 14: בפולמוס של אספסיינוס גזרו על עטרות חתנים ואל האירוס "At the time of the war with Vespasian [before the Temple's destruction] they decreed a prohibition against brides wearing crowns and the sounding of special bells." We read in yShabbat 1: 4, 3d, and in a baraita quoted in bShabbat 14b: יוסף בן יועזר איש צרידה ויוסי בן יוחנן איש ירושלם גזרו טומאה על ארץ העמים ועל כלי זכוכית "Yose ben Yoezer of Tzerida and Yose ben Yohanan of Jerusalem have decreed that the lands outside Israel and glass vessels are polluted." It is not evident whether this ordinance had a political motive and was thus of temporary validity, or rather constituted an enduring decree.

post-70, in consequence of the recording of halakhot and disputes (as witnessed in Mishnah tractate Eduyyot).

As an example, we may consider the confusion related to the decree that a wife-to-be must obtain a *ketubbah*, in effect a written obligation to pay the wife an agreed amount, in the event of divorce or the husband's death. Whether this obligation is a Torah precept or a rabbinic institution is an open question in both Talmudim, and the conflicting texts indicate the confusion with respect to this issue. In a baraita quoted in bShabbat 14b, it is explicitly declared that Simeon b. Shetah instituted this obligation,[103] and hence it would seem that it is a rabbinic decree. The reason for this decree, indicated in the B. T.,[104] also substantiates this assumption. In the Y. T. the issue is more complex. The passage in yKetubbot 8: 11, 32c, regarding the alleged institution of the *ketubbah* by Simeon b. Shetah (quoted in Chapter One, note 128), does not expressly state that he instituted the *ketubbah*; his decree refers only to the extension of an existing regulation regarding the husband's obligation. This leaves open the possibility that the regulation may be considered a Torah precept; there is, in fact, a dispute on this issue in yKetubbot 13: 11, 36b.[105]

---

103 We read there: שמעון בן שטח תיקן כתובה לאשה "Simeon ben Shetah instituted the wife's *ketubbah*." This was evidently a decree of perpetual validity.

104 We read in bYevamot 89a: מאי טעמא תקינו לה רבנן כתובה כדי שלא תהא קלה בעיניו להוציאה "What is the reason for the institution of the *ketubbah* by the Sages? So that it should not be easy for him [the husband] to divorce her."

While it is stated in bKetubbot 56b: קסבר ר׳ מאיר כתובה דאורייתא "Rabbi Meir considered that the [obligation to give a] *ketubbah* is a Torah precept," and there is a similar assumption in bKetubbot 110b regarding Rabban Simeon ben Gamaliel, these passages do not attest that indeed these two Tannaim considered the *ketubbah* a Torah precept. This seems to be simply an assumption in the Gemara, as reflected in the discussion of the statements of these two Tannaim. The term קסבר "he thinks" regarding Rabbi Meir's halakhic declaration does not suggest that he in fact stated that this was his opinion. In bKetubbot 10a, there is reference to two alleged declarations by Rabbi Simeon b. Gamaliel, which appear to contradict each other; the Gemara, as usual, attempts to reconcile them. The declaration of Rav Mesharshiya in bKetubbot 110b, אמר כתובה דאורייתא "[Rabban Simeon b. Gamaliel] said that the *ketubbah* is a Torah precept," is merely his deduction from a halakhic declaration of Rabbi Simeon. The expression רבן שמעון בן גמליאל אומר כתובת אשה מן התורה in bKetubbot 10a is cited without any indication of its source, and probably refers to Rav Mesharshiya's deduction. It is indeed immediately opposed by a conflicting assertion of Rabban Simeon, found in a baraita on the exegesis of a scriptural vers; the text declares: מכאן סמכו חכמים לכתובת אשה מן התורה "from this [verse], the Sages supported [their opinion] that the *ketubbah* is a Torah precept." As usual, the Gemara perceives a disagreement on the basis of an assumption, and constructs farfetched conjectural solutions.

105 We read there: דתני כתובת אשה מדברי תורה רבן שמעון בן גמליאל אומר אין כתובת אשה אלא מדברי סופרים "We learned in a baraita: The *ketubbah* of a wife is a Torah precept; Rabban Simeon b. Gamaliel says: The *ketubbah* is only a

I suggest that the pre-70 Sages not only considered their ordinances as possessing the same legitimacy and merit as Torah commands, but even viewed them as an extension of the Torah decrees. This attitude is particularly evident in the almost unlimited freedom of opinion of earlier Sages regarding the imposition of the death penalty. We read the following attestation, for instance, in yHagigah 2: 2, 78a (and bSanhedrin 46a, with different wording but to the same effect):

> Rabbi Eliezer b. Jacob[106] said: I have heard that the court imposes punishments contrary to the [rules] of the halakhah and not according to Torah [rules]. [Q.][107] To what extent? Rabbi Lezer [Eliezer] b. Rabbi Yose said: Without appropriate interrogation to ensure against false witnesses.[108] Rabbi Yosa says: [The conviction must be founded upon reliable] witnesses, but [one may convict] without [the regularly required] warning. It happened that someone went riding on a horse on Sabbath and they summoned him to the court and pelted him with stones. [Q.] But [was this not simply] a rabbinic prohibition [the transgression of which does not deserve the death penalty]? [A.] [This was done] because it was [considered] necessary at that time. And again there was another occurrence in which a man was travelling with his wife and had intercourse with his wife behind a fence, and they summoned him to the court and gave him lashes. [Q.] But it was his wife [and thus he committed no transgression that would deserve this punishment]. [A.] [This was done] because he acted disgracefully.

The B. T. version replaces the Y.T. justification for the exceptional punishment (because it was [considered] necessary at that time) with the phrase "to make a fence [around the Torah]." With respect to the first offence, Rabbi Eliezer's explanation that the death penalty was applied "to make a fence around the Torah" is not the same as the rabbinic concept of using preventative prohibitions to avoid a real transgression. It is not, in other words, a case of the Sages declaring the death penalty for the transgression of a rabbinic edict, which was a later classification. Rather, it

---

rabbinic institution."

106 It does not matter for our purposes whether this refers to an early Sage who lived during the period of the Temple and after its destruction (see mMiddot 2: 5 and Ch. Albeck, מבוא למשנה, p. 220 regarding this Tanna), or to a later Tanna of the fourth generation, who lived after 70. The testimony of this individual refers to an early period, at the time of Hellenistic influence. One is tempted to conclude that it refers to the later Tanna, since the Sages before 70 had no titles such as Rabbi, and are simply mentioned by name.

107 This question and the two answers do not appear in the B. T. version.

108 The Hebrew term זימזום is unusual, and allows for different interpretations. I have chosen the interpretation that seems to me most reasonable. I suggest that the B. T. version, which does not have this question and the two answers, is more reliable, since the subsequent examples, which are identical in both versions, have no connection with the antecedent answers in the Y. T. version. Other differences in the two versions are insignificant.

is a resolution to maintain obeisance to Torah laws at a time of overwhelming pressure to assimilate; it represents a political decision to ensure the preservation of Jewish law and custom.[109] The court's ruling had the same legitimacy as a Torah law, and therefore was enforceable by the death penalty, just as a serious transgression of Torah law would be.

We must not rule out, however, the possibility that the death sentence was passed and carried out by a sectarian court;[110] according to *Jub.* 50: 12, riding a horse on Sabbath was punishable by death.[111] Rabbi Eliezer may not have been aware of this sectarian law, and therefore assumed another motive for this extraordinary punishment that seemed incompatible with rabbinic law. His assumption was consistent with the later rabbinic concept of decreeing ordinances as preventative procedures. (As we have noted above, a sectarian ruling was deemed to be behind a statement of the Tanna Rabbi Eliezer ben Tzadoq,[112] concerning an execution by burning that was carried out contrary to Torah law.[113] Rav Joseph stated that this sentence was in fact carried out by a Sadducean court, which imposed different modes of execution.) It is also possible that since the legal status of שבות (the rabbinic extension of Sabbath prohibitions) is not evident in the pre-70 period, we may assume that Nehemiah's conception of the Sabbath laws[114] was still enforced;[115] thus

---

[109] It is interesting that yBetzah, 5: 2, 63a, quoted in n. 97 above, cites another reason for the prohibition against riding on Sabbath, which would involve a transgression of Torah law: the precept requiring rest for one's animals. The Amora who made this declaration apparently overlooked the fact that the Mishnah includes the prohibition against riding under the classification of שבות, the typical denomination for rabbinic edicts regarding Sabbath work. See Ch. Albeck, ששה סדרי משנה, סדר מועד, p. 484, השלמות והוספות, and I.D. Gilat, איסורי שבות, pp. 198 ff.

[110] Eyal Regev, "How did the Temple Mount Fall to Pompey," p. 289 speculates that "the Sadducees were also among those who observed the halakha which forbade fighting on the Sabbath under any circumstances." This occurrence would then bear a logical connection to the succeeding narrative, which concerns the execution by burning allegedly performed by a Sadducee court.

[111] See chap. 2, text at n. 15.

[112] As with the Eliezer ben Jacob mentioned in the narrative concerning the man who was executed because he rode on Sabbath, it is difficult to establish which Sage made this declaration. There were two Tannaim by this name, one who lived at the time of the Temple, and a later one; see Ch. Albeck, מבוא למשנה, p. 224.

[113] See text at n. 71.

[114] See chap. 2, text following n. 10.

[115] I. Gilat does not refer to Neh 13: 17, but states that during the Second Temple period the Sabbath laws were observed in an extremely strict way. It was only later, when the Sages defined more precisely the biblical concept of work prohibited on Sabbath through the creation of thirty-nine distinct types, that such activities as trading, riding, and other acts not included in the list were "downgraded" to work forbidden only by the Sages.

riding a horse was considered a חילול שבת, "desecration of the Sabbath," and consequently a transgression punishable by death in a pharisaic court.

The second offence in the above baraita was considered an affront to public morals; again, however, the Sages administered a punishment appropriate for a transgression of a Torah prohibition.

Another example of the flexible boundary between Torah and rabbinic law is encountered in tSanhedrin 6: 6.[116] Yehudah ben Tabai sentenced a false witness to death, "to contradict the Boethusian's ruling." He later regretted this, not because it was a transgression of a rabbinic rule, but because he learned afterwards that it was contrary to correct Torah law.

The concept of the fence around the Torah is also found with respect to earlier courts. It is proclaimed, for instance, in the name of the Great Assembly: "They proclaimed three dicta: Be restrained in judgment, teach many disciples, **and make a fence [or hedge] to the Torah** [emphasis added]." Again, this dictum is not the same as the legal concept later adopted by the Sages as the basis of their preventative rules. The above mishnah does not explain the concept of the "fence." In mAvot 3: 13, however, we do encounter various definitions of the concept: "Tradition is a fence to the Torah, tithes are an incentive to wealth, vows are an aid to chastity, and silence is a support for wisdom." The first phrase is ambiguous and has generated a number of different interpretations by the traditional commentators; one must thus conclude that the concept had a broad range of meanings.[117] In Mekilta d'Rabbi Ishmael *Bo* 6, we read: "Why have the Sages restricted the consumption of the meat of the offering to midnight [although the Torah allows it until sunrise]? [A.] To keep the person away from [unintentionally performing] a transgression, and to make a fence [around] the Torah." This is a purely preventative measure.

In ARN, there are also a number of definitions of the concept of סייג "fence/ hedge" in various homilies referring to mAvot 1: 1. These indicate that there were many types of instances in which this concept was applied. We read in Recension A, chap. 2: "What type of fence has the Torah applied to its edicts? It is written: 'You shall not approach a woman to uncover her nakedness while she is in her menstrual uncleanness [Lev 18: 19]'; could you say that one may embrace and kiss her and enjoy her company? [No!] It says 'do not approach' [and thus every contact is forbidden]." A preventative rule is derived from the Torah itself, and this restriction has the same legal validity as the explicit interdiction against

---

[116] See n. 4.

[117] Rashi, for instance, states: ע״י המסורת יודעין בירור המקראות והלכותיו "With the help of the traditional orthography in the Torah [the Sages] learned how to interpret the Torah and understand all its laws [i.e. through particular exegeses]."

"uncovering her nakedness" (intercourse). The סייג in this occurrence is the antithesis of a minor rule.

Recension A, chap. 1, ד"ה איזהו סייג, contains another homily regarding the term סייג "fence/ hedge" in a dictum of the Great Assembly, in which there is explicit disapproval of the extension of preventative prohibitions. We read there: "Who provoked this [violation] of the [prohibition] against touching [the tree of the knowledge]? [It occurred] because Adam constructed a preventative fence in his declaration [to Eve].[118] [Extrapolating] from that event, they said: If a person extends [the confines] of his rules, he cannot comply with them. Therefore they said: A person must not add [restrictions] to those which he learned. Rabbi Yose said: It is better [to have a fence of] ten handbreadths [that remains] standing, than one of a hundred handbreadths that collapses." This homily suggests that preventative decrees must not proliferate, in order to ensure their acceptance by the public as genuine Torah rules. The multiplication of such prohibitions, and their degradation to the inferior status of rabbinic edicts, would cause them to be neglected; "the wall of a hundred handbreadths," as so vividly portrayed by Rabbi Yose, would collapse.

Another use of the concept סייג "fence/hedge" is encountered in yNiddah 1: 1, 48d, with respect to a dispute between Shammai and Hillel concerning the duty of a menstruant woman who eats *terumah*. We read there: "Shammai said: [With respect to] all women, their time [at which they first observe the onset of their period] is sufficient. [This means that] they do not retroactively render impure any *terumah* touched before having observed their period. [Hillel, in contrast, declared impure any *terumah* touched since the end of her last period.] And the Sages say: [the halakhah] is according to neither the one nor the other; that is, it is not according to Shammai who did not put a fence around his words [that is, he did not consider the possibility that the woman may have started menstruating before she actually observed it], and not according to Hillel

118 The homily refers to God's command to Adam: ומעץ הדעת טוב ורע לא תאכל ממנו כי ביום אכלך ממנו מות תמות "You must not eat from the tree of the knowledge of good and evil, for when you eat it you will surely die [Gen 2: 17]." Scripture does not record when and how Adam conveyed this prohibition to Eve. We read in Gen 3: 3, however, what Eve told the serpent: ומפרי העץ אשר בתוך הגן אמר אלהים לא תאכלו ממנו ולא תגעו בו פן תמותון "God did say: 'You must not eat fruit from the tree that is in the middle of the garden, and you must not touch it. Or you will die.'" The homily conjectures that Adam, in his desire to prevent the eating of the fruit, expanded the Lord's command and told Eve that touching was also prohibited and might cause death. The serpent could therefore deceive Eve by telling her to touch the tree and convincing herself that nothing would happen to her; when she did so, he convinced her to eat the fruit, as that also would not harm her. Thus because of Adam's exaggerated prudence, God's command was transgressed, with severe consequences.

who exaggerated his considerations." However we interpret here the concept of סייג, it has no influence on the legal status of the issue; the *terumah* touched in the period circumscribed by each Tanna is considered impure according to a Torah precept. There is no argument as to whether the impurity is deemed a Torah precept or a rabbinic decree.

Finally, we may note the extraordinary punishments related in yHagigah 2: 2, 78a and bSanhedrin 46a, quoted above. We observed that instead of the "fence/hedge" concept found in the B. T., the Y. T. version states as the reason for these punishments: "because it was [considered] necessary at that time." This suggests a temporary expedient, connected not to the transgression itself but to other, "political," considerations.

I believe that I have adequately substantiated the proposal that the division into two classes of decrees, those of Torah origin and validity, and those of rabbinic origin with their subordinate validity, was not conceived of, or practised, before 70.[119] Each Sage decided the correct interpretation and application of the Torah commands, to the best of his understanding, and such decisions were equivalent to genuine Torah law.

4.1.8 Conclusion

I could continue to quote similar examples to substantiate the thesis of the lack of a unified codex before 70, but I think that from the citations in this and the previous chapter this circumstance appears obvious. We observe that unquestionably the preoccupation with the establishment of a fixed halakhah is a late phenomenon. Pre-70 there was no established codex,[120] nor any attempt to create one,[121] or even to record and remember

---

119 A. Aderet, מסכת עדויות, p. 265 states with respect to the legal character of the early halakhot (הלכות קדומות) that there was no distinction between a prohibition decreed by the Torah and an interdiction ordained by the Sages.

120 In the various passages regarding the issue of overriding the Sabbath law in *Maccabees, Antiquities, Jewish War, Jubilees*, and the rabbinic narratives in Mekilta d'Rabbi Ishmael, *Ki-tissa* 1, bYoma 85a, tPesahim 4: 13, yPesahim 6: 1, 33a, and bPesahim 66a (see the citations above in chap. 1, n. 125, chap. 2, n. 21, and chap. 3, text at nn. 195 ff.), the absence of any fixed codex regarding when the Sabbath law may be overriden is apparent. See also Jay M. Harris, "From Inner-Biblical Interpretation to Early Rabbinic Exegesis," particularly pp. 259 ff.

121 A. Aderet, מסכת עדויות, p. 252, writes that in the last generation before the Temple's destruction, it was acknowledged that the halakhah was practised in many ways. Cf. I. Gafni, היצירה הרוחנית ספרותית, who contends that the editing of the Mishnah was a long process that started at the time of the Temple, and was finally accomplished by Rabbi in 220 C. E. On the other hand, he too admits that the Temple's destruction expedited the codification of the Mishnah. Hence, he agrees that this traumatic event had a radical impact on the codification of rabbinic laws and rules.

the halakhot. We may reasonably assume that a Sage would decide each case brought before him to the best of his knowledge and judgment concerning the real meaning and intention of the scriptural commands. Some of these decisions may have become a permanent part of the general Israelite tradition, while others may have been practised solely within their restricted communities and only for a limited time. In any event, there was no effort made to record the names of the Sages in the pre-70 period,[122] as their decisions were not perceived at that time as final and binding.

The pluralistic approach to the law in the pre-70 period may have been influenced by the pluralistic style of the Pentateuch.[123] The pre-70 Sages were close in time to the redactors of the Pentateuch, and therefore also possessed a better understanding of the motive that induced the redactors of the Pentateuch to leave such an array of contradictions and inconsistencies. They may have perceived these irregularities not as a symptom of imperfection,[124] but rather as an intentional philosophical

---

122 In mEduyyot 1: 3 (see citation and critical examination in chap. 1, pp. 52-3), the halakhah is stated to have been established on the basis of testimony cited in the name of Shemaya and Abtalion. This is highly doubtful, since Hillel, their disciple, was not aware of this halakhah. The tradition was attributed to Shemaya and Abtalion to gain acceptance for it against the conflicting opinions of Hillel and Shammai, but in effect, we must recognize that the tradition had no authentic author. I speculate that the other two decisions by the anonymous חכמים in the first chapter of Eduyyot, again contrary to the opinions of Hillel and Shammai, were also ancient traditions, whose author was unknown. It is otherwise difficult to assume that later Sages would have decided a halakhah against the declarations of Hillel and Shammai, without questioning such improper conduct. Such a circumstance is encountered in bAvodah Zarah 36a (see chap. 3, pp. 185-6). We must consider, however, that in the latter case the reference is to a decree promulgated by the disciples of Hillel and Shammai, while our case above refers to a confrontation with the eminent Hillel and Shammai themselves. This difference in attitude supports my thesis that there was no intention to record the authors of the various halakhic decisions delivered in the pre-70 period.

123 A. Geiger has remarked in his *Urschrift* that the Pentateuch itself is the product of reworking in the light of social and theological concerns. See generally B. M. Levinson, *Deuteronomy and the Hermeneutics of Legal Innovation*, on this issue.

124 One must assume that the redactors of the Pentateuch were highly intellectual personalities who were definitely aware of the discrepancies among the texts of the canon. This assumption remains valid whether we adhere to the Documentary or to the Fragmentary Hypotheses. We observe that the later Sages perceived these discrepancies and attempted to reconcile the differences by harmonizing them. If these Sages noticed such discrepancies, it would be illogical to assume that the redactors of the Pentateuch ignored them or minimized their significance. See also E. Nielsen, *The Ten Commandments in New Perspective*, on the differences in the Decalogue (pp. 35-44). He states on p. 123: "In all this, a desire for synthesis can be discerned." Although many scholars are of the opinion that the biblical texts were edited to adjust inconsistencies and to adapt the texts to contemporary circumstances, a question still remains in that case as to why so many additional discrepancies remain. We observe, for example, that the Chronicles' redactor/editor adjusted and complemented many lacunae of the Kings' narratives according to his contemporary

legacy, supporting the adoption of a pluralistic approach to the interpretation of the law.[125] This concealed but fundamental message of the Torah could have been perceived as originating from God at Sinai, or as the attitude of the redactors;[126] it did not, in other words, necessarily negate a belief in the Torah's divine origin. And if the Torah itself has a pluralistic aspect, the interpretation of its laws and edicts may or even must bear the same character. The opposition to a hegemonic reading of the Torah, and support for the idea of its plurivocality, are expressed in the maxim אלו ואלו דברי אלהים חיים "Both [conflicting declarations] are the words of the living God";[127] opposing declarations can all be considered legitimate representations of the divine intention.[128] This proclamation is the consequence of reflection on Scripture's literary structure, and is applied to both halakhic and ideological aspects of scriptural interpretation.

As I have endeavoured to demonstrate in this and prior chapters, the early Sages opposed a fixed codex and chose instead a flexible legal

---

view as to "what ought to have been," and we perceive similar additions in the Apocrypha. We must, therefore, assume that the Pentateuch editors intentionally allowed some inconsistencies and contradictions to stand. R. Rendtorff, in his programmatic essay "The Paradigm is Changing: Hopes - and Fears," exhorts biblical scholars to read the texts of the redactors carefully and hear their voice and message first. He recommends searching for the synchronic aspect as well as the diachronic insights.

125 H. Cazelles, "Biblical and Pre-biblical Historiography," p. 125, writes: "The Elohist grouped components having different characteristics coming from different local sanctuaries." This statement corroborates the proposition that different views were tolerated even within each particular "editing school," and substantiates the existence of a pluralistic philosophy on the part of the editors. Robert Alter, *The Art of Biblical Narrative*, writes on p. 12: "The essential aim of...the ancient Hebrew writers was to produce a certain indeterminacy of meaning."

126 R. Rendtorff, "The Paradigm is Changing: Hopes - and Fears," p. 67, quotes a declaration by the philosopher Franz Rosenzweig: "The letter 'R' as usually taken for the 'redactor' actually should be read as 'Rabbenu,' 'our master.'" Hence, we must perceive the redactors not only as intellectual personalities, but also as genuine believers in the divine origin of the Torah. It would be preposterous to assume that the redactors, during their process of amalgamation of different *Vorlagen*, approached their task with the same basic philosophy as the modern minimalist biblical critics. I need not speculate as to their precise conjectures, but they certainly believed that the Torah represents God's word.

127 S. A. Handelman, *Interpretation*, p. 56, explains this maxim as meaning that both declarations are recorded, both are Torah, and there is room for difference, conflict and contradiction.

128 Regarding the apparent paradox encompassed by this statement, see the various explanations of later rabbinic commentators quoted in J. Roth, *Halakhic Process*, pp. 129 ff. Avi Sagi, "Pluralism," p. 106, declares that the statement implies parity between the conflicting options.

system, disposed to adaptation and change.[129] This was the reason for the prohibition against recording the halakhot in writing. Though a written law is not absolutely rigid and immutable, it is more difficult to change, particularly a law alleged to originate from the Deity; even an orally preserved law, if fixed and practised universally, would be subject to the same difficulties. In addition, I think it is evident from the entire style of the rabbinic literature, and the opposing opinions of the Sages on almost every issue, that they bestowed great importance and the utmost value upon their personal ideas. Each Sage was confident that he possessed the correct tradition or accurate understanding of God's intention. This belief was the foundation of the Sages' authority to decree laws and rules in God's name, though these might have conflicted with the pronouncements of other Sages. Without that intrinsic conviction, they would not have dared to speak in God's name; with it, they were impelled to assert their pronouncements with vigour and persistence. We have noted the tenacity of such Sages as Rabbi Eliezer (with respect to the Akhnai oven) [130] and Aqabyah ben Mahalalel.[131] Both Sages, mighty pillars of rabbinic tradition and erudition, were excommunicated, yet endured this severe punishment to the time of their deaths[132] rather than renounce their convictions.[133]

---

129 See S. Safrai, *The Literature of the Sages*, p. 69, who states that "...[the] fluidity of their tradition and its openness to change and development, necessitated a prohibition of writing."

130 See chap. 1, n. 58 and p. 73.

131 Concerning Aqabyah, see mEduyyot 5: 6, cited in chap. 2., n. 110. Concerning R. Eliezer we read in yMo'ed Qatan 3: 1, 81d, in the famous Akhnai narrative: ויצאה בת קול ואמרה הלכה כאליעזר בני "A Voice of Heaven came out and said: The halakhah is according Rabbi Eliezer, my son." In bBava Metzi'a 59b, Rabbi Eliezer's authority is even more greatly enhanced: יצאתה בת קול ואמרה מה לכם אצל רבי אליעזר שהלכה כמותו בכל מקום "A Voice of Heaven came out and said: Why do you oppose Rabbi Eliezer, since the halakhah is always as he maintains?"

132 In the Aqabyah narrative in the B. T. version we read: וכשמת שלחו בית דין והניחו אבן על ארונו מלמד שכל המתנדה ומת בנדויו סוקלין את ארונו "At his death, the court sent [an agent] and laid a stone on his coffin; we deduce [from this] that one pelts with stones [symbolic of an execution by stoning] the coffin of an excommunicated person who dies during his excommunication." Concerning Rabbi Eliezer, we read in yShabbat 2: 7, 5b: ובאחרונה אמר טהור ונסתלקה נשמתו אמרין ניכר רבי שהוא טהור אמר רבי מנא ועד כדון ניכר נכנס רבי יהושע וחלץ את תפיליו והיה מגפפו ומנשקו ובוכה ואומר רבי רבי הותר הנדר "His last solution [of the many halakhot they asked him on his death-bed] was: It is pure; and he expired. They said: It is thus [symbolically] acknowledged that he is pure. Rabbi Mana said: How far was this acknowledged? Rabbi Yehoshua came in, took off his phylacteries, embraced him and kissed him and wept saying: Rabbi, Rabbi, the vow [of excommunication] is annulled." In bSanhedrin 68a the narrative is shorter, but with the same content.

---

[133] I wish to comment on the narrative in mEduyyot 5: 6 concerning Aqabyah, who was active before 70, within the scope of my postulate that there was no trend toward a fixed halakhah in that period. First, Rabbi Yehudah denies in that mishnah that the narrative refers to Aqabyah, and suggests another Sage, Eliezer ben Hanokh; the latter appears only once, in this mishnah, and his period of activity is therefore unascertained. There is also a distinct difference between the subject of the supposed disagreement by Aqabyah and that of Eliezer ben Hanokh. Aqabyah argued on issues of halakhah - that is, how to understand the law; such discussions were completely justified, not censurable by excommunication. Eliezer ben Hanokh, on the other hand, opposed a particular edict, a גזרה that was decided and decreed by the court or the assembly to achieve a specific purpose. The opposition to such an edict is legally a radical confrontation with rabbinic authority, conduct that must be dealt with severely; this is utterly different from a disagreement regarding the interpretation of a halakhah. Further, it seems that this specific edict regarding the pollution of the hands had a dubious history. We read in yPesahim 1: 6, 27d: הלל ושמאי גזרו על טהרת ידים "Hillel and Shammai decreed the edict regarding the purification of the hands." In Sifra *Metzorah* 2, we read: וידיו לא שטף במים אפילו לאחר מאה שנים אמר רבי אלעזר בן ערך מיכן סמכו חכמים לטהרת ידים מן התורה "[It is written in Lev 15: 11: 'Whatever one with an issue touches] without rinsing his hands with water' [will be unclean] even after a hundred years. Rabbi Eleazar b. Arakh said: The Sages used this [verse] to support [the idea that] the washing of hands is a Torah precept." This dictum of Rabbi Eleazar is ambiguous, and does not explicitly assert that the washing of hands is a Torah precept. This ambiguity is confirmed by the following amoraic dispute in bHullin 106a: נטילת ידים לחולין מפני סרך תרומה ועוד משום מצוה מאי מצוה אמר אביי מצוה לשמוע דברי חכמים רבא אמר מצוה לשמוע דברי ר"א בן ערך "Washing the hands for [the consumption of] non-sacred food [was instituted] as an extension of [the obligation for] the touching of the *terumah* [tithe] and must be obeyed as a command. What is the command? Abbaye said: To obey the decrees of the Sages. [Thus it is a rabbinic decree]. Raba said: It is a command to obey what Rabbi Eleazar b. Arakh said. [Thus, as cited above, it is a Torah precept; this is also how Rashi understands Raba's opinion]." After further discussion, it is agreed that the scriptural verse serves only as support; Raba's opinion, however, is not repealed, based on Rabbi Eleazar's declaration that washing the hands before eating bread is a Torah precept. We observe the inconsistency between the declaration that Hillel and Shammai decreed this precept, and Rabbi Eleazar b. Arakh's statement that it is a Torah precept. In addition, the quoted verse refers to one with a discharge, and does not serve as evidence of a general command with respect to healthy people.

We may note that the term פקפק, used in mSukkah 1: 7 and other occurrences with the meaning "to loosen," "to shake," is utilized in mEduyyot 5: 6 to convey metaphorically R. Eliezer ben Hanokh's opposition to a rabbinic decree, insinuating his determination to shake the foundation of the rabbinic decisions. The fact that he was excommunicated for this action, however, does not attest to the general fixing of halakhot at that time. Moreover, we may doubt the authenticity of all details of this narrative, just as we are justifiably skeptical with respect to the miraculous details of the Akhnai narrative. Both narratives have the plain purpose of endorsing and imposing the concept of the majority's supremacy over the opinion of an individual, even when his pronouncement is absolutely correct. One may therefore assume that a narrative with a protagonist of vague identity was attributed to the talmudic giant Aqabyah, rather than to an unfamiliar Tanna. See A. J. Saldarini, "The Adoption of a

It is therefore reasonable to conclude, from the various types of evidence that have been cited, that before 70 each Sage and each court delivered their rulings and sentences *ad hoc*. They decided each case on its individual features, and made their decisions based on their consideration and interpretation of the relevant divine commands.[134] There was no pressure upon the courts to decide according to any precise and unified codex. There was no objection on the part of any authority to this freedom of judgment practiced by the courts and by individual Sages, since it was taken for granted that all acted within the framework of the biblical commands and principles.

I thus question the authenticity of the talmudic declarations that there were no disputes[135] before the increase in the number of disciples of the Shammai and Hillel schools.[136] I believe I have substantiated the fact that before 70, there were disputes within the pharisaic group. The primary distinction between the eras before and after 70 was that before 70 the Pharisees did not impose a unified halakhah on the members of their group.[137] Their members believed in the same basic philosophy, and that

---

Dissident," who reaches the same conclusion, after an extensive critical analysis of the narrative and of scholarly discussions that also question its authenticity. Saldarini writes in his conclusion, p. 556: "The statement that he was excommunicated functions well within Eduyyoth where it contributes to the discussion of individual and majority opinions within the rabbinic school."

[134] D. Patrick, "Studying Biblical Law as a Humanities," p. 33, writes that since biblical law does not cover all possible cases, it is unlikely that it had the binding force of codified law. It was designed rather to inculcate the concepts and principles of Israelite law as an intellectual system, for judges to apply according to their assessment of each particular case.

[135] As we read in tSanhedrin 7: 1; in the other sources there is a slightly different wording: בראשנה לא היו מחלוקות "In the beginning [in the past] there were no disputes [between the Sages]."

[136] I have cited in chap. 3, n. 132 this declaration in tSanhedrin 7: 1: משרבו תלמידי שמאי והלל שלא שמשו כל צרכן רבו מחלוקת בישראל. This statement does not indicate when this situation began, but since this narrative and the other sources associate it with the cessation of the Superior Court in the *Gazit* Chamber, one may assume that it refers to the circumstances after the Temple's destruction, rather than the move of the Sanhedrin to the "store." See the Appendix for an hypothesis putting in question the rabbinic portrayal of the disputes between the two schools of Beit Shammai and Beit Hillel.

[137] G. Alon, *The Jews*, vol. 1, p. 198, actually corroborates my thesis with respect to the circumstances before 70, but does not substantiate his declaration with citations. Alon's perception of the internal relations among the Sages, regarding their halakhic approaches, is highly respected; as this perspective is significant for the corroboration of my view, I shall quote some of his statements on this topic. With respect to a general understanding of the Sanhedrin's aspirations and activities. he states: "...the Sanhedrin hardly ever attempted to impose one single interpretation of the Torah on the whole people, except in a few specific instances when critical social and religious issues were at stake." With respect to the independence of the Sages and their

guided them in their halakhic decisions and sentences. This was sufficient to keep this group together; deviations within these broad confines were considered trivial, and therefore admissible.

Aderet uses the modern term "pluralism" to portray the state of the halakhah post-70,[138] suggesting that consensus prevailed prior to that time, and disputes arose as the result of the loss of central authority after the Temple's destruction. My thesis contradicts this idea. It is plausible that the Patriarch lost some of his previous authority on political and administrative issues during the last stages of the war and defeat, but our issue refers to a problem of inner discipline among the Sages.[139] The destruction of the Temple would certainly not have constituted an excuse for the pharisaic Sages, or their rabbinic successors, to disobey or disregard their own leadership and initiate a process of halakhic disputes on almost every issue, if there had been consensus before that period. One must assume that the Sages would have acted in such a manner as to enhance the prestige and authority of their leadership in a time of crisis,[140] and not initiate steps to undermine it.

I. Ben-Shalom proposes that the disputes between Beit Shammai and Beit Hillel were of a political character, reflecting their contrasting

---

authority to decide the correct application of the biblical laws, he quotes Josephus' description of the Pharisees, and declares: "The teacher...the scholar...and the scribe... are the principal sources of the halakhah - hence the wide latitude and diversity, in practice as well as in theory, during the Second Commonwealth." He then explains the legitimacy of the Sages' autonomy: "...any person who devotes himself to the study of the Torah has the right to give his interpretation and to teach his opinion."

138 A. Aderet, מסכת עדויות who also quotes M. Elon, המשפט העברי, vol 3, pp. 876 - 871 to corroborate his statement. Aderet contemplates (p. 252) that the maxim והרוצה לעשות כדברי בית שמאי עושה כדברי בית הלל עושה "and if one wishes to conduct himself according to Beit Shammai, he may do so, and if according to Beit Hillel, he may do so," indicates the pluralistic attitude toward this, and logically toward all other, halakhic disputes among the pharisaic Sages. I reiterate my previous emphasis (see, e.g. chap. 1, text at n. 54) that this permission is given *a priori*; this too substantiates the thesis that such actions were considered a perfectly legitimate way of observing the law, and not a subsequent approval בדיעבד of initially inappropriate conduct.

139 D. Goodblatt, *The Monarchic Principle*, p. 209 writes: "There is widespread, if not unanimous, agreement that Gamaliel's rise to power is to be explained by internal Jewish factors." He states that the Patriarchate was recognized and accepted by the Jews first, and recognition by the Romans, to the extent it occurred, was subsequent to this. For the substantiation of his assertion, he quotes Alon's "influential" work תולדות, vol. 1, p. 78.

140 G. Stemberger, "Judentums," similarly speculates on the voluntary acceptance of the authority of the rabbinic Sages, which he articulates as "geistige Autorität" (p. 99); I would translate this as referring to an acknowledgement of their "intellectual and spiritual authority."

attitudes toward the uprising against Rome.[141] With the exception of the eighteen edicts, however, which may have had a political undertone, the numerous halakhic disputes between the two Schools recorded in the Mishnah have no connection to political issues. They are simply differences in opinion between a severe or a lenient approach to halakhah,[142] and no procedure existed in the earlier period to decide between these approaches. The talmudic description of the passage of the eighteen edicts, in contrast, reflects the severe tension consistent with political conflict. In this connection tShabbat 1: 16 states: "And that day [on which the eighteen edicts were promulgated] was as troublesome to Israel as the day on which the Golden Calf was made." The Tosefta does not elaborate on the nature of these troubles, but the Talmudim portray the severity of the conflict. In yShabbat 1: 4, 3c, a grim picture is painted: "The disciples of Beit Shammai stood downstairs and were killing the disciples of Beit Hillel [who tried to climb up to vote]." The B. T. at Shabbat 17a states: "They stabbed a sword in the school." We need not assess the authenticity of these outrageous details, but we may assume that they accurately reflect the existence of a grave struggle with respect to politically motivated issues.

Yet there is much evidence that attests to the gracious and intimate relationship between the Schools. In addition to mYevamot 1: 4,[143] we may note the friendly relationship portrayed in other rabbinic sources, such as tYevamot 1: 10 and yQiddushin 1: 1, 58d: "Truth and peace prevailed in their relations, as it is said: 'Love truth and peace [Zech 8: 19].'" The B. T. version in Yevamot 14b goes a step further and emphasizes the amicable relations: "...to demonstrate to you that affection and friendliness prevailed among them, to fulfill what is said: 'Love truth and peace.'"[144] We thus see that the disputes concerning halakhic issues were not considered a divisive phenomenon.

It must also be noted that according to recent scholarly analysis of the Dead Sea Scrolls, "pluralism" existed even in the sectarian communities; these had different halakhot,[145] diversified ways of life,[146] and different texts of the Bible.[147] Halakhic variation was an ongoing characteristic of

---

[141] This thesis is put forward in his book בית שמאי.

[142] See the Appendix with respect to my hypothesis regarding the foundation of the Houses and the character of their halakhic disputes.

[143] Quoted in chap. 1, n. 55.

[144] For further discussion of this issue, see the Appendix.

[145] See L. H. Schiffman, " The Zaddokite Fragments and the Temple Scroll."

[146] See J. M. Baumgarten, "A Response to the Discussion on DJD XVIII," who refers on p. 200 to the "bifurcation of life-styles."

[147] See E. Ulrich, "The Scrolls and the Study of the Hebrew Bible." He emphasizes that the different versions of biblical passages discovered in Qumran are not a

Israelite society. We must thus look beyond leadership or political issues to discern the reasons behind the change in rabbinic attitude after the Temple's destruction.

4.2 The Development of Institutionalized Halakhah

4.2.1 The Effect of the Loss of Centralized Authority

Pre-70 Israelite society, according to E. E. Urbach,[148] lacked any bureaucratic organization. There were no titles (the Sages of that period are known only by their names), remuneration, process of investiture, or any other sign of an institutionalized system. The authority of each Sage was grounded in respect for his wisdom, personality, and behaviour. A system built upon the individual merits the term "anarchic," used by me earlier in the study.

The Temple's destruction, and its traumatic impact on the life of the Jewish people, induced a drastic change in these circumstances, instituted by the Jewish political leadership. Following Urbach, we observe that it was only after 70 that the Sages devised an institutionalized system complete with bureaucracy, titles and authority. This situation, in turn, engendered rankings and classes based on genealogy, wealth, and social position,[149] and with it, the need for fixed laws and regulations.[150]

---

consequence of copy errors, but represent actual variants. He refers to a period of "pluriformity" before the period of uniformity (p. 34).

[148] E. E. Urbach, מעמד, p. 37.

[149] In the record of the dismissal of Rabban Gamaliel (see discussion below, 4.2.2.2) quoted in yBerakhot 4: 1, 7d, Rabbi Aqiba was sadly disappointed that his nomination was rejected in favour of Rabbi Eleazar b. Azaryah. He said: לא שהוא בן תורה יותר ממני אלא שהוא בן גדולים יותר ממני אשרי אדם שזכו לו אבותיו "[He was preferred] not because he has a greater knowledge of the Torah, but solely because he has a greater genealogy than I do. Blessed is the man whose forefathers have bestowed privilege upon him." Rabbi Eleazar's genealogy is then cited: שהיה דור עשירי לעזרא "He was of the tenth generation of Ezra." The B. T. version in Berakhot 27b is more elaborate. There we read that the Sages deliberated upon whom to nominate. They discarded the nomination of Rabbi Aqiba, because of his main drawback: דלית ליה זכות אבות "He has no aristocratic genealogy." All of Rabbi Eleazar's advantages are then recorded: אלא נוקמיה לרבי אלעזר בן עזריה דהוא חכם והוא עשיר והוא עשירי לעזרא "But we shall nominate Rabbi Eleazar ben Azaryah, because he is intelligent, he is rich, and he [has an illustrious genealogy: he] is of the tenth generation of [the family of] Ezra." We encounter a similar preference regarding the reception of disciples into the rabbinic schools. ARN, Recension A, chap. 3 sets out a declaration in the name of Beit Shammai: אל ישנה אדם אלא למי שהוא חכם ועניו ובן אבות ועשיר "One should teach [oral Torah] only to a

We must keep in mind two cardinal features characteristic of the Israelite people. First, the Torah was the basis for all aspects of life, ideological and practical, ritual and secular.[151] Second, the Israelite people were already dispersed in this period all over the *oikoumene*,[152] the "inhabited world" according to contemporary perception. The centrality of Jerusalem with its Temple and sacrificial worship was what kept this dispersed people united. Jews from all over the Diaspora went on pilgrimage to Jerusalem,[153] sent money,[154] first-fruits,[155] and sacrifices to the Temple,[156] and took an interest in events there.[157] With the destruction of the Temple, only a unified code of behaviour, founded upon the Torah and regulating all aspects of life, could guarantee the future existence of the Jews as a united people. Deviations in the daily routine of rituals, customs, and secular aspects of life would create serious and irreversible splits between the widely dispersed communities. Over time, such gaps would surely widen, and end in the creation of entirely separate communities.

---

person who is intelligent, modest, of a noble genealogy, and rich."

150 See I. Gafni, שבט ומחוקק, p. 87.

151 The Torah does not limit itself to the relationship between God and human, but instructs the people on the correct relationship between humans, in all aspects of daily life. We read in Deut 4: 8: ומי גוי גדול אשר לו חקים ומשפטים צדיקם ככל התורה הזאת "And what other nation is so great as to have such righteous decrees and laws as this body of laws." An Israelite lives with the maxim: שויתי ה' לנגדי תמיד "I have set the Lord always before me [Ps 16: 8]," and is constantly under divine scrutiny. Many socially motivated laws conclude with the phrase אני ה' אלהיכם "I am the Lord your God," to emphasize their significance and the divine interest in their fulfillment.

152 See *Ant.* 14: 115 and 190 - 264 regarding the many Jewish settlements in the Roman Empire. See also Philo, *Embassy* 281 - 282.

153 *Ant.* 17: 213; Acts 2: 5 - 11; Philo, *Spec. Laws* 1: 69

154 See *Ant.* 14: 110 - 113 and 16: 166 - 173; Matt 17: 24. See also Cicero's defence before the Senate in *Pro Flacco*, (English translation in M. Stern, ed., *Greek and Latin Authors on Jews and Judaism*, Vol. 1, pp. 196 ff.) regarding the confiscation of the gold donated by the Jews for the Temple in Jerusalem.

155 See Philo, *Spec. Laws* 1: 76-8.

156 See *Ant.* 12: 10.

157 See *Ant.* 13: 74 - 79, concerning the polemic with the Samaritans before Ptolomeus as to whether Samaria or Jerusalem was the site of the only holy Temple. The Jews in Alexandria took a great personal risk in this debate. See also *Embassy*, 188 - 196, concerning Philo's anxiety about the Emperor's edict to place his statue in the Temple.

4.2.2 The Role of Rabban Gamaliel

Rabban Gamaliel, the first Nasi or Patriarch[158] of the aristocratic[159] Hillel family[160] after 70, initiated[161] this process of creating a standard codex.[162] Experience has demonstrated that he was correct in his imagination and apprehension.[163]

---

158 Scholars debate whether Rabban Gamaliel II really bore the title Nasi, "Patriarch," and about the extent of his authority. One may note that M. Goodman, *Roman Galillee*, who asserts (pp. 111 - 118) that only Yehudah I was a "figure more like a ruler," and is skeptical as to how far patriarchal influence extended "beyond rabbinic circles" before the fourth century, agrees that Gamaliel II bore the title Nasi. He disputes only the significance of this title, considering it to mean simply "being lifted up above his fellows" (pp. 112 - 115). D. Goodblatt, *The Monarchic Principle*, p. 208, acknowledges that "Gamaliel II occupied a unique position"; he goes further, however, and perceives that there was Roman influence on his behalf, and consent to his leadership in place of the previous priestly dominance (pp. 176 - 231). In "Iudaea between the Revolts," p. 108, he states explicitly: "The Gamalilean patriarchate was created by the Romans."

159 On the significance of genealogy as it affected Rabban Gamaliel's standing as the leading personality in Israel, see D. Goodblatt, *The Monarchic Principle*, p. 225.

160 This is assumed in the later rabbinic literature, as stated implicitly in the narrative in yKil'ayim 9: 3, 32b. For a critical scrutiny of this "alleged" genealogy, see D. Goodblatt, *The Monarchic Principle*, p. 149.

161 Rabban Yohanan ben Zakkai, the first leader in the post-70 period, was concerned with more serious problems after 70 - mitigating the traumatic impact of the destruction of the central and most holy element of the Jewish people, and strengthening the status of Yabneh and its Sages as the intellectual and cultural center instead of the cultic sanctuary of Jerusalem. He also had the difficult task of placating the understandable opposition of the priests to his perspective and procedures. G. Stemberger, *Das Klassische Judentum*, p. 57, perceives ben Zakkai's problems as "grosse Anlaufschwierigkeiten," significant start-up difficulties. See G. Alon, *Jewish History*, pp. 318-328 (and n. 10 above) on the opposition to Rabban Yohanan ben Zakkai from priests and Sages alike, for both politically-motivated reasons and personal interests. It would therefore have been impossible for ben Zakkai, even if he had perceived the exigency for reform of the legal system, to initiate this process in addition to his other struggles. Rabban Gamaliel's enhanced status in the eyes of the priests and Sages, and the stabilization of the political situation after the initial critical period following the Temple's destruction and loss of autonomy, offered him a better chance for success. As we shall see, this was still an arduous task, replete with many hurdles that he had to overcome. See also nn. 278 and 287.

162 On this issue, see Lee Levine, "Judaism," p. 140.

163 I corroborate this statement in the second part of the study. G. F. Moore, *Judaism*, vol. 1, p. 205 asserts that Judaism survived because it achieved a unity of belief and observance, and emphasizes particularly that "the ground of this remarkable unity is to be found not so much in general agreement in fundamental ideas as in community of observance throughout the whole Jewish world." See below my elaboration on the actions and motivations of Rabban Gamaliel.

As the political leader,[164] considering himself responsible for the continued existence of the people, he comprehended that his principal obligation was to undertake the necessary steps toward standardization. He did not justify his conduct with any modern notion of "nationalism," nor was he concerned with devising supporting philosophical formulae; the future of the Jewish nation was, in my opinion, the inducement for his drastic shift in halakhic method and its application in daily life.

Ezra and Nehemiah had acted to similar purpose in a time of crisis,[165] and Rabban Gamaliel may have considered their deeds as paradigmatic. Though it is not within the scope of this study to debate whether the Israelite "religion" began to appropriate its modern form in the pre- or post-exilic period, there is no doubt that a great reform took place in the period of Ezra and Nehemiah. The ultimate goal of Rabban Gamaliel's reform was identical to that of his forerunners, though in different circumstances. Upon the return from exile, the leadership faced the problem of how to impose a demanding type of Torah observance upon the disunited segments of Israelite society and to mold these groups into one distinct people. In Rabban Gamaliel's period, the supremacy of the Torah as the absolute guide for Jewish life was an accepted fact; his burden was to institute and formulate a unified codex, in order to avert the creation of splinter groups.[166]

The establishment of a single standard codex of behaviour and system of decision-making was not the antithesis of flexibility. The new approach was aimed at avoiding the proliferation of disparate customs, and the imposition of dissimilar court sentences in different localities. This approach contemplated that appropriate changes could be made, but should apply simultaneously to all Israelite communities, in Judah and in the Diaspora. The persistence in the rabbinic environment of halakhic disputes, without final resolutions, for an extended period after 70 indicates a determination to maintain the flexibility of the law, as I shall

---

164 Regarding the political activities of Rabban Gamaliel in Judah and in the Jewish Diaspora, and his recognition by the Roman authorities as the Jewish leader, see S. Safrai, "התאוששות," pp. 30 - 33. See also the discussions on the status of the Patriarchs and the extent of their authority in D. Goodblatt, *The Monarchic Principle*, pp. 176 - 183 and M. Goodman, *Roman Galilee*, pp. 111-118, as well as the Excursus "The Title and Authority of the Patriarch (Nasi) and the President of the Academy/Court (Av Beit Din)."

165 The authoritarian measures to prohibit intermarriage, the concern for the persistence of the Hebrew language, and other organizational steps indicate the "nationalistic" purpose of these measures, though they are not explicitly declared as such. For a detailed record of the innovations of Ezra and Nehemiah in this respect, see Heger, *Altars*, pp. 335 ff.

166 He did not attempt to reverse the split with the Jewish Christians after Paul, who did not feel obliged to obey all the precepts of the Torah.

attempt to demonstrate below; and there continued to be a prohibition against putting even commonly-acknowledged halakhot into writing.[167] The flexibility of the law and the institution of a unified codex are two distinct issues. We may compare this situation to that of modern legal systems that are based on fixed codices. Such a codex is enacted after discussion and deliberation by the legislative body, and all courts must deliver their judgments in conformity with that codex; on the other hand, these laws are flexible, and may be changed in part through creative interpretation by the courts, each according to its recognized competence, or changed more radically by the legislative body. I postulate that Rabban Gamaliel attempted to curtail the "anarchic" prerogatives of the individual Sages that had existed pre-70, and create a single, but flexible, law.[168]

Excursus: The Title and Authority of the Patriarch (Nasi) and the President of the Academy/Court (Av Beit Din)

Before reflecting on the particular political and halakhic activities of Rabban Gamaliel II, it seems opportune to review the topic of the status, prerogatives, and authority of the Partriarchate and Academy, and of their leaders. We encounter two titles in rabbinic literature, נשיא "Patriarch" and אב בית דין "Chief of the Superior Court," but their precise characteristics and functions are never defined, and seem to fluctuate. Much scholarly interest has attached to these terms.[169] I wish to underscore that this particular issue of the authority and power attaching to these institutions has no direct bearing on my study; my interest is limited to the willingness of the Sages to acknowledge or deny, totally or in part, the privileges and prerogatives of a recognized leader. Thus, such questions as the nature and status of the rabbinic council,[170] its recognition by the Roman authorities in the early post-70 period, and the authority and

---

167 This is not to deny that conservative antipathy toward drastic change also had an influence on the decision to continue with oral transmission. The dispute with the Sadducees on this issue may have delayed the introduction of a system that had been so vehemently opposed for a long period.

168 See chap. 3, n. 7.

169 See, e.g., M. Jacobs, *Die Institution des jüdischen Patriarchen*, pp. 99 ff., who suggests that the designation Nasi indicated the person enjoying the highest halakhic authority, whereas the Av Beit Bin would be the head of a local court, hierarchically under the sway of the Nasi.

170 Consistent with my conclusion both generally and in this Excursus that there was no express division between the legislative and judicial functions in the early rabbinic period, I use the word "council" or "council/academy" in a general sense - that is, without reference to a specific council, or to the terms ישיבה-מתיבתא found throughout rabbinic literature.

title of its leader, are beyond the limits and concern of my investigation.[171] I shall, nevertheless, proffer my observations on the occurrence in the rabbinic literature of the title "Patriarch" and the title "Chief of the Superior Court," the alleged deputy of the Academy. I shall also briefly note some of the latest scholarly conjectures and debates on this issue.

As I have written elsewhere,[172] the Sages were not interested in recording the exact details or developmental stages of thoughts and customs.[173] There was a comprehensive attempt to present every rule and custom as having been generated in earlier times, particularly at the Sinaitic revelation; this attitude, in turn, influenced the Sages to retroject current conditions to earlier circumstances, without considering the likelihood of ongoing change.

Continuous change also affected the title Nasi, "Patriarch," and the functions, prerogatives and authority associated with this title, influenced by the character of the incumbent, the attitude of the Roman authorities, and general alterations in the political and economic environment over time. These changes are perceptible in the diverse applications of the title Nasi throughout rabbinic literature. The title is indiscriminately[174] used to describe both past and future kings of Israel of Davidic lineage,[175] as well as the Patriarch in the Second Commonwealth[176] and rabbinic periods.[177]

---

171 See D. Goodblatt, "Roman Recognition," on this issue. See also M. Goodman, *Roman Galilee,* pp. 101 - 111 ("The Limitations of Rabbinic Jurisdiction") on the circumstances in this period.

172 See Appendix, n. 77 regarding the rabbinic narratives on the Pharisee - Sadducee dispute. I shall also discuss this issue in detail in the second part of this study.

173 Transmission of the correct message - not historical accuracy - was the purpose of Scripture, and similarly of the rabbinic literature that was both Scripture's commentary and its complement. See M. D. Herr, "תפיסת ההיסטוריה אצל חז"ל."

174 See M. Jacobs, *Die Institution des jüdischen Patriarchen,* pp. 51 ff.

175 We read in mHorayot 3: 3: ואיזהו הנשיא זה המלך "Who is the Nasi? It is the king," and in tHorayot 2: 2: איזהו נשיא נשיא ישראל ולא נשיא שבטים נשיא ישר' נשיא בית דוד "Who is the Nasi? It is the Nasi of all Israel, not the Nasi of tribes; the Nasi of Israel is the Nasi of the House of David." This use of Nasi, referring to the biblical term in Lev 4, is inexact and historically misleading, since we do not encounter such a Nasi of all Israel in the biblical text. It is unreasonable to assume that the Sages considered the rabbinic *Nesi'im* of the late Second Temple period as the subject of Lev 4, or as Ezekiel's Messianic Nasi. The prerogatives of the king in rabbinic halakhah are also inconsistent with his biblical status. In Lev 4, the High Priest is unmistakably of a higher rank than the Nasi - king, whereas in Mishnah Sanhedrin their statuses are reversed; the High Priest could be judged by a court (2: 1) but a king was above the law, and could not be brought to justice (2: 2).

176 See mHagigah 2: 2 and tPesahim 4: 14.

177 There are numerous references to leading rabbinic personalities bearing the title Nasi, as well as halakhot that unmistakably refer to contemporary personalities with this

There is no doubt that the redactors of the Mishnah assumed the existence of a Nasi already at the time of the Second Temple,[178] and that this position had continued into the post-70 period. Since the Mishnah was redacted in the time of Rabbi Yehudah, and scholarly consensus confirms that he bore the title of Nasi,[179] it is plausible that this position was simply retrojected to earlier periods.[180] There is, in my opinion, only one halakhic rule that hints at the existence of a Nasi in earlier periods. We read in mTa'anit 2: 1: "How is a fast day carried out? One takes the Ark to the open place of the town, and one puts ashes from the roasting fire on the Ark and on the heads of the Nasi and the Av Beit Din." While it is possible that this procedure represents a rule established only in the time of Rabbi Yehudah, one may deduce from the literary structure of the mishnah that it reflects the procedure prevailing at earlier fast days.[181] We must assume that fast days were proclaimed before Rabbi Yehudah's period.[182]

On the other hand, we also observe a constant confusion in rabbinic literature between the denominations and functions of the Nasi and the Av Beit Din. In the above citation, there is a clear distinction between these two title bearers; there is no indication of their respective functions, though there is a suggestion that the Nasi was of higher rank. In the antecedent mishnayot 1: 5 - 6, it is set out that the Beit Din proclaims the fast day; the Av Beit Din, however, is not mentioned. It is recorded in mTa'anit 2: 10 that Rabban Gamaliel II in fact instituted a specific halakhic decree with respect to the proclamation of a fast day. Further, from tTa'anit 2: 5 and bEruvin 41a, we learn that Rabban Gamaliel II imposed his decision over Rabbi Yehoshua's opposition. The texts do not specify, however, by what authority Gamaliel effected this coercion; in the course of the narrative, in both sources, it is simply asserted that he imposed his view because he was the הרישא, "the head," a completely unclear term. There is no indication of the character of the institution of which he might have been the head, such as the Beit Din or the Sanhedrin.

Two toseftot indicate a similar lack of precision in terminology. We read in tSanhedrin 7: 8: "When the Nasi enters, all the people stand up, and do not sit until he tells them: Sit! When the Av Beit Din enters, they make two parallel rows [between which he proceeds] until he reaches his

---

title. See, e.g. mTa'anit 2: 1, with respect to the procedure on fast days.

178 See mHagigah 2: 2 and a baraita quoted in bShabbat 15a.

179 See M. Jacobs, *Die Institution des jüdischen Patriarchen*, pp. 115 ff., who expresses some doubt on the consistency of this title in tannaitic literature; contra, M. Goodman, *Roman Galillee*, p. 114.

180 See M. Jacobs, *Die Institution des jüdischen Patriarchen*, pp. 104 ff.

181 Cf. ibid., p. 87.

182 See mTa'anit 2: 10 and bEruvin 41a.

place and takes his seat. When a Sage enters one person stands and one sits [that is, half the assembly stands and the other half sits] until he reaches his place and takes his seat." The text does not indicate where it is that these personalities are entering, but from the context of the antecedent and succeeding halakhot we must assume that the reference is to the Sanhedrin.[183] In tSanhedrin 8: 1 there is a specific reference to the Sanhedrin: כל סנהדרין.[184] There is no reference, however, to the Av Beit Din; the seating order is recorded as: "The Nasi sits in the middle and the elders sit on his right and left side."[185] Further, instead of the term חכם we find זקנים, "elders," another sign of the confusion between titles and functions. From the second element of this halakhah, it appears that Rabban Gamaliel was the Nasi of the Sanhedrin,[186] yet in many other occurrences[187] we encounter the phrase "Rabban Gamaliel and his court," a statement that would attest to his double function as Nasi and Av Beit Din.

This confusion between the two functions is even more apparent with respect to Rabbi Yehudah, an attested Nasi. The expression "Rabbi Yehudah and his court" appears in a number of occurrences,[188] while the explicit title "the Nasi" appears in three occurrences.[189] The Mishnah, as we have seen, definitely attests to two separate functions, Nasi and Av

---

183 M. Jacobs is somewhat ambiguous on this point (*Die Institution des jüdischen Patriarchen*, pp. 64 ff.). There is a parallel citation of this lemma in yBikkurim 3: 3, 65c; in the subsequent narrative concerning the change of custom, the location בית ועדא is indicated. We may assume that this convention hall served as a place for both lecture and judgment. As I have written above (section 2.3.1), there was no division between the legislative and judicial functions in the rabbinic environment.

184 The use of the term Sanhedrin, followed in the second part of this halakhah by a description of the seating pattern at the time of Rabban Gamaliel in Yabneh, does not indicate that there was in fact a court called Sanhedrin in that period. The first part of the halakhah consists of a general rule, unconnected to any particular circumstances, similar to the rules of judgment for the king and High Priest set out in chaps. 2 and 3 in Mishnah Sanhedrin. Given also the lack of precise details in rabbinic literature, as well as the indiscriminate application of terms prevalent in one period to institutions in different times and circumstances, we may assume that here the term Sanhedrin simply refers to a significant session of a court, with the participation of many dignitaries.

185 This narrative also appears in ySanhedrin 1: 4, 19c.

186 See M. Jacobs, *Die Institution des jüdischen Patriarchen*, pp. 62 ff.

187 See mRosh HaShanah 2: 9; tBerakhot 2: 6, tShevi'it 1: 1, 6: 27; yShevi'it 1: 1, 33a; yShabbat 1: 4, 3d; and many occurrences in the B. T.

188 See mAvodah Zarah 2: 6; mOhalot 18: 9; tShevi'it 4: 17; tAvodah Zarah 4: 11; yShabbat, 1: 4, 3d; yAvodah Zarah 2: 8, 41d; bAvodah Zarah 35b and 36a.

189 See yGittin 7: 3, 48d; yNiddah 3: 4, 50d; bAvodah Zarah 38b. The want of precision regarding the titles is quite noticeable in yNiddah 3: 4; both "Rabbi Yehudah the Nasi" and simply "Rabbi Yehudah" appear in the same segment.

Beit Din, yet on the other hand perceives Rabbi Yehudah the Nasi as the head of the court.

The various rabbinic citations with respect to the fixing of the calendar also reflect a similar confusion between the functions of the Nasi and those of the court. We read in a baraita in bSanhedrin 11a: "One may not intercalate the thirteenth month in a year without the Nasi's approval."[190] In this connection, we learn[191] that Rabban Gamaliel convened the required seven elders for this procedure. The fixing of the new moon was equally a calendar issue; in this case, however, although Rabban Gamaliel is clearly mentioned as the authority who fixed the date,[192] it was the Beit Din that legally proclaimed it. We read in mRosh HaShanah 2: 7: "The head of the court [Av Beit Din?] declares: The [first of the month] is holy; and all the people follow with the refrain: Holy, holy." Adding to the confusion, we read in mishnah 9 that "Rabban Gamaliel and his court" proclaimed the new moon that was put into question by Rabbi Yehoshua. Further, in mishnah 3: 1 the procedure of fixing the new moon is under the jurisdiction of the court, with no mention of a Nasi or a head of the court. We read there: "If only the court has seen the new moon, two [of the members] should stand up, serve as witness, and [the court] should declare: Holy, holy. If three men have seen [the new moon] and they are [members of] a court, two stand [as witnesses]; they join two other court members to the [remaining] one [creating the minimum quorum of three judges], they [the two] attest before them, and they [the three] declare: Holy, holy."[193]

A text in ySanhedrin 1: 2, 19a seems to indicate the intrinsic association of the Nasi with the Beit Din, and either the equating of this title with the Av Beit Din or the elimination of the latter. We read there,

---

[190] In yMegillah 1: 5, 71a, we read that one may intercalate an additional month in a year, "on condition," with no indication of the details of the condition. It is not clear that this necessarily refers to the agreement of the Nasi, as stated in the B. T., since tSanhedrin 2: 13 declares in the name of Rabbi Simeon ben Gamaliel and Rabbi Eliezer ben Tzadoq: אין מעברין את השנה ואין עושין כל צורכי ציבור אלא על תנאי כדי שיקבלו רוב ציבור עליהן "One may not intercalate a month in a year, or undertake initiatives in the public domain, except on the condition that the majority of the people accept these [decisions]."

[191] In ySanhedrin 1: 2, 18c, and in bSanhedrin 11a, in which the narrative attributes the title Nasi to Rabban Gamaliel.

[192] See mRosh HaShanah 2: 8 - 9.

[193] In yRosh HaShanah 3: 1, 58d, an Amora states that the maxim אין העד נעשה דיין "a witness cannot be a judge [in the same case]," which is disputed between Tannaim with respect to a criminal case, also applies to the New Moon declaration. But this point does not affect the proposition that no Nasi was required for the declaration of the New Moon.

with respect to the appointment of scholars (who would probably later be nominated to the council of Sages]:[194]

> [After the period in which each Sage appointed his own students], they reversed the procedure and bestowed honour on that House.[195] They said that if a Beit Din made an appointment without the knowledge of the Nasi, the appointment was invalid, but if the Nasi made an appointment without the knowledge of the Beit Din, the appointment was valid. They then made an amendment that the Beit Din should not make an appointment without the knowledge of the Nasi, and the Nasi should not make an appointment without the knowledge of the Beit Din.

The absence of the Av Beit Din in these procedural changes is extremely odd. One would expect him to have been involved in the appointments to

---

[194] M. Jacobs, *Die Institution des jüdischen Patriarchen*, pp. 172 ff. scrutinizes this vague type of designation and the various scholarly opinions on the specific function and status of the appointees. I think that the Sages designated their main students to become members of the first rank, as we read in tSanhedrin 8: 2 (following the description of the seating order in halakhah 8: 1): שלש שורות של תלמידי חכמ' יושבים לפניהם גדולה בראשונה ושניים בשנייה ושלישיים בשלישית "Three rows of students sat before them [the Nasi and the Elders]: the greatest in the first [row], the second-ranked in the second row, and the third-ranked in the third row." We may suppose that, at some stage, these students were appointed as full members of the council, sitting together with the Nasi. The antecedent narrative in the Y. T. citation gives a reasonable indication of the likely development of this procedure. We read there: בראשונה היה כל אחד ואחד ממנה את תלמידיו כגון רבן יוחנן בן זכיי מינה את רבי ליעזר ואת רבי יהושע ורבי יהושע את רבי עקיבה ורבי עקיבא את רבי מאיר ואת רבי שמעון ישב רבי מאיר תחילה נתכרכמו פני רבי שמעון "At first each [Sage] appointed his students; for example, Rabban Yohanan ben Zakkai appointed Rabbi Eliezer and Rabbi Yehoshua, and Rabbi Yehoshua [appointed] Rabbi Aqiba, and Rabbi Aqiba [appointed] Rabbi Meir and Rabbi Simeon. Rabbi Meir sat before Rabbi Simeon [I propose to interpret the term תחילה as indicating the row that was "before" Rabbi Simeon's row], so that his face became pale [with jealousy]." We observe that these appointments were not for any specific function, such as Av Beit Din or Nasi. See Jacobs, pp. 172 ff. for his interpretation of this narrative. He does not mention the issue of the seating order between Rabbi Meir and Rabbi Simeon, a detail that in my opinion aids us in understanding the character of the appointments. See also I. Gafni, 'ישיבה' ו'מתיבתא', pp. 18 ff.

[195] It is unclear to which House this refers. From the succeeding context, one might assume it relates to either the House of the Nasi or to the Beit Din. The preceding narrative does not hint at any offence or affront to either of these institutions. I would suggest that an intermediate stage is missing in this narrative - that is, the second stage in which the Beit Din, not the individual Sages, appointed the future scholars. In the third stage, the Nasi overpowered the Beit Din and seized for himself this prerogative, and in the last stage, a compromise was instituted in which both parties shared this authority. The phrase חזרו וחלקו כבוד לבית הזה thus refers to the Beit Din, which regained its former authority.

his court, and he should particularly have been mentioned in juxtaposition to the mention of the Nasi. One has the impression that the dispute in this case took place directly between the members of the court and the Nasi.

The absence of an Av Beit Din is also notable in a number of the occurrences cited above; one would have expected a mention of him at the proclamation of the new moon (mRosh HaShanah 3: 1), and within the seating routine of the court (tSanhedrin 8: 1), among other instances in rabbinic literature. Such phrases as "Rabban Gamaliel and his court" and "Rabbi Yehudah the Patriarch and his court" also suggest a leadership function of the Nasi (Yehudah), or presumed Nasi (Gamaliel) within the Beit Din, without the existence of an Av Beit Din. The fact that the identity of the personalities performing such significant functions as Nasi and Av Beit Din is disputed by Rabbi Yehudah in tHagigah 2: 8[196] (apart from the dubious authenticity[197] of the narrative) leads us to question the actual existence of these functions. It is interesting that Rabbi Yehudah disputes not the attribution of opinions to Simeon ben Shetah and Yehudah ben Tabai, but their titles, casting doubt on the continuity of these positions.

Another oddity, already noted by many scholars, is the fact that we do not encounter in rabbinic literature the names of any Sages[198] bearing the title Av Beit Din in the period from the last *zugot* "pairs,"[199] to Yabneh, and from Yehudah I to the end of the talmudic period.[200] Such evidence also attests to the lack of stability of this position. In mEduyyot 5: 6 the

196 The same reversal of the titles appears in ySanhedrin 6: 6, 23c, and yHagigah 2: 2, 77d. In both these occurrences the reversal is not stated by Rabbi, but appears as an anonymous controversy between Tannaim.

197 I shall discuss the authenticity of this entire narrative, which relates to an ongoing dispute over a Temple-related halakhah, in the second part of this work. See also M. Jacobs, *Die Institution des jüdischen Patriarchen*, p. 100. He perceives the insertion of the titles and attributions as a redactional element.

198 A rhetorical narrative in bShabbat 55a contains the statement: מר עוקבא אב בית דין "Mar Uqba sits as Av Beit Din," but this certainly refers to his function as the head of a local court in Babylon, and not the central court. In bQiddushin 44b there is in fact a reference to מר עוקבא ובי דיניה בכפרי "Mar Uqba and his court in Kafri." Cf. D. Goodblatt, *Monarchic Principle*, pp. 284 ff.

199 In Mishnah and Tosefta Hagigah, quoted in yHagigah 2: 2, 77d, and ySanhedrin 6: 9, 23c.

200 H. Mantel, *Sanhedrin*, pp. 103 ff. Mantel has overlooked the mention of Rabbi Nathan as bearing this title; this must have been in Usha, not in Yabneh. This mention occurs in a narrative describing the insurrection of Rabbi Meir and Rabbi Nathan; it is possible that Mantel does not consider this narrative authentic, since R. Nathan is named only in the version of the narrative in bHorayot 13b, but not in the parallel version in yBikkurim 3: 3, 65c. Mantel maintains the permanence of the position of Av Beit Din, against opposing scholarly opinion, and thus has to find a way around this oddity.

reward promised to Aqabyah ben Mahalalel is reported: "Aqabyah, retract your opinion on the four declarations you made and we shall appoint you Av Beit Din for Israel." Such a statement again indicates that this position was not continuously filled;[201] otherwise, his appointment would have compelled the dismissal of the incumbent.[202] This, in turn, would have been against established procedure, as reflected in the maxim: מעלין בקודש ואין מורידין "One may heighten the degree of holiness, but not lower it"; this maxim is applied with respect to Rabbi Eleazar's appointment to this function (bBerakhot 28a), in order not to degrade him (as we shall see below), as well as in yBikkurim 3: 3, 65c.

The narratives[203] recording Rabban Gamaliel's dismissal also reflect a confusion between the various titles and functions. Rabban Gamaliel's title is not mentioned in any of these texts, which show a number of significant variations in details and outcome. These circumstances make it more difficult to derive any solid conclusions about the circumstances prevailing both in the period of Rabban Gamaliel and at the time of redaction. Robert Goldenberg'[204] has made a thorough analysis and comparison of the different texts; although such critical examination is not within the scope of this study, I shall make some comments on his statements, in order to clarify my own views on our specific inquiry. Goldenberg perceives a significant difference between the Y.T. and B. T. regarding the appointment of Rabbi Eleazar. He notes that in the Y. T., he was simply appointed to the Academy, but in the B. T., he was invited to become its leader. He bases his conclusion on the use of the title ריש מתיבתא *resh metivta* in the B.T., whereas the Y. T. states: "and they appointed Rabbi Eleazar to the ישיבה *yeshivah*." Goldenberg interprets this phrase to mean that he was simply elected to the Academy as a member.[205] I do not see any difference between the two texts on this particular issue. It is obvious from the Y.T. text that Rabbi Eleazar was appointed instead of Rabban Gamaliel (a fact with which Goldenberg does not disagree), and whatever we may argue about his status, he was

---

[201] Cf. H. Mantel, ibid., who reaches the opposite conclusion from this narrative.

[202] The addendum "for Israel" to the title Av Beit Din indicates the unique feature of the offer - that is, it was to apply for all Israel. A nomination to the head of a local court does not seem to have been, in the circumstances, tempting enough to influence Aqabyah to repeal his halakhic decision.

[203] In yBerakhot 4: 1, 7d, yTa'anit 4: 1, 67d, bBekhorot 36a and bBerakhot 27b.

[204] R. Goldenberg, "The Deposition of Rabban Gamaliel II."

[205] See the report in ySanhedrin 1: 2, 19a, cited above, that Rabban Yohanan ben Zakkai had already appointed Rabbi Eleazar (it is plausible to assume that this is R. Eleazar ben Azaryah; the Y. T. text has ליעזר) as his student and successor in the academy. One may therefore assume with reasonable certitude that Rabbi Eleazar ben Azaryah was already a member of the academy during Rabban Gamaliel's leadership.

definitely of a higher rank than a member of the Academy. An appointment as a member of the Academy, as Goldenberg suggests, would not have been considered a hostile act against Rabban Gamaliel, and the reconciliation with him would then not have required Rabbi Eleazar's demotion. Moreover, the Y.T. text states they did not depose him from his dignity, and appointed him as Av Beit Din. Though this was obviously a lower rank than the one held by Rabban Gamaliel both before and after his dismissal, it certainly denotes a higher status than that of a simple member of the Academy, as we may observe from many rabbinic quotations. The expression לא הורידו אותו מגדולתו may be interpreted as indicating that the Sages did not reduce him to his previous low status of a simple member, but recompensed him with a higher rank by appointing him as Av Beit Din, with its accompanying dignity and privileges.[206] The Y. T., which records this compromise in a way that suggests there was some reduction in rank,[207] does not use the maxim "One may heighten the degree of holiness, but not lower it."[208] This maxim is found in the B. T., which records a compromise that did not diminish his status.

The text of the Y. T. does differ in terminology, as Goldenberg notes, but in reality conveys the same facts (much as the expression בית הוועד "the college house" in the Y.T. conveys the same idea as בית המדרש "the house of study" in the B. T.[209]). The Y. T. describes Rabban Gamaliel with

---

[206] Cf. D. Goodblatt, *The Monarchic Principle*, p. 252.,

[207] In reality, the appointment to the position of Av Beit Din was not a demotion at all. The title of Rabban Gamaliel is not mentioned in the narrative; it is simply stated that he was the chairman of the academy, with no indication of his capacity. After his dismissal, Rabbi Eleazar ben Azaryah was appointed as the chairman, and his nomination as Av Beit Din granted him the privilege of chairing the academy; this is evident in the many references in the Y. T. and B. T. that state that Rabbi Eleazar presided over the academy (see, e.g., n. 65). There is no evidence as to the exact prerogatives of the Av Beit Din, but undoubtedly he was granted some privileges with respect to the chairmanship of the academy.

[208] In my opinion, this maxim originated in the sacrificial cult, and is employed here metaphorically with respect to appointments of Sages to distinguished ranks. See yShevu'ot 1: 5, 33b, with respect to sacrifices, and bMenahot 39a with respect to the garments of the High Priest during the rituals for the Day of Atonement.

[209] See Lee Levine, *The Rabbinic Class of Roman Palestine*, p. 77, on the parallel terms for the amoraic institutions of lecture. In yHorayot 3: 1, 47a, a passage regarding Rabbi Yohanan and Rabbi Yehudah the Nasi states: לבית וועדא אמר ליה למה לית מרי אמר לן מילה דאורייא "[They came] to the house of meetings; [Rabbi Yehudah] said [to Rabbi Yohanan]: Why don't you give us a lecture from the Torah?" We observe that the בית וועדה was the place in which the Sages lectured. We read in yMakkot 2: 6, 31d: שאם היה תלמיד חכם עושים לו בית וועד "If one were a learned man, they make for him a meeting house [in which to lecture]." See also I. Gafni, 'ישיבה' ו'מתיבתא', p. 24, n. 59, who notes that בית וועד in the Y. T. is equivalent to בית המדרש in the B. T. Cf. D. Goodblatt, *Rabbinic Instruction in*

"he was sitting and lecturing." As we see subsequently, all the people were seated, and then stood up in protest: "All the people began to stand up on their feet." Rabban Gamaliel's "sitting" was on a special chair reserved for the chairman of the Academy, and it was his privilege to start and direct the lecture. The "Chair" as a symbol of leadership is used in the Y. T. in the same sense as one refers to the "Chair" of a University or the "Chair" of a meeting.[210] Having indicated the status of Rabban Gamaliel, the Y. T. records that after the accusation of the people - "Who has not felt your endless cruelty [NIV translation]" - they demoted him from his chairmanship,[211] "and appointed Rabbi Eleazar to sit on the 'Chair.'"[212] Contrary to Goldenberg, I do not perceive this difference in expression as a significant controversy between the two texts.

The most significant difference[213] between the texts lies, in my opinion, in the final outcome - that is, in the nature of the compromise.

Sassanian Babylonia, pp. 63 ff. for a thorough analysis of the term *yeshivah*.

210 Though ישיבה can refer to the chairperson, it is also applied both to a regular chair, and to an institute of learning. The context tells us when it refers to the chairperson, the institution or another form of chair. The term מני "to appoint," in its various grammatical forms, is generally used with reference to a chairperson, as for example in the well-known record of Rabbi Eleazar's appointment in place of Rabban Gamaliel.

211 The term ישיבה used by the Y. T. is the equivalent of the Aramaic expression מתיבתא, from the root יתב "to sit." Both expressions, which denote the Jewish schools or academies, are derived from the special seat of the leading teacher. We read in Sifre Deut 16, with reference to Rabbi Yohanan ben Nuri and Eleazar Hisma, that Rabban Gamaliel הושיבם בישיבה. From the continuation of the narrative, we must interpret this expression as meaning that they were granted an official pre-eminence. When they declined to accept the nomination, Rabban Gamaliel criticised them, saying: הרעתם לצבור שאי אתם מבקשים לעשות שררה על הצבור לשעבר הייתם ברשות עצמכם מכאן ואילך הרי אתם עבדים משועבדים לצבור "You have adversely affected the public by your reluctance to exercise authority over them; in the past [prior to your appointment], you were independent, but from now on, you are servants in bondage to the public." This narrative is also found, with some variation, in bHorayot 10a; in particular, the expression נתן דעתו להושיבם בראש "[Rabban Gamaliel] considered seating them at the 'head,'" replaces הושיבם בישיבה in Sifre. We thus see that the latter expression implies putting someone at the head of the assembly.

212 Cf. D. Goodblatt, *The Monarchic Principle*, p. 252, who seconds Goldenberg's interpretation.

213 There are many other differences between the texts, as Goldenberg has shown by juxtaposing them word for word. The Y. T. has a shortened version and includes different details than the B. T. version. Some differences are insignificant, such as whether Rabbi Yehoshua was a coal maker or a needle maker, while others are of greater importance. These differences are, however, irrelevant as far as the deductions to be made from the narrative. It seems to me that there were a number of versions circulating in Babylon, and the Y. T. chose one of them and adapted the record of

This issue directly relates to our problem, the function of the Av Beit Din. As I have argued above, we must explore the possibility that the appointment of a member of the Academy to a position with the honorific Av Beit Din was not a regularly occurring procedure. Many difficulties could be elegantly resolved by the compromise appointment of an Av Beit Din. A typical example is the struggle between Rabban Gamaliel and the Sages, in which Gamaliel had been the *factotum* who seized all the power he could. As confirmed by both texts, he was the פרנס, *parnas*, "the leader" (of the community, or of an organization of the Sages[214]), as well as the Chair of the Academy. We do not know the exact function of the *parnas* (I shall discuss this term in more detail below), but it is evident that the position had a social character and was not related to halakhic procedures or to the giving of lectures. Though the Talmud does not indicate the prerogatives and authority of the Av Beit Din, it is obvious that the appointment of Rabbi Eleazar to this function ultimately decreased Rabban Gamaliel's authority. Recognizing that current scholarly *opinio communis* attributes little authenticity to the details of rabbinic narratives, we are free to speculate that such a procedure of appointing an Av Beit Din, for many possible motives,[215] was common in Judah or Galilee in the period of the redaction of the narrative, or that there was a recollection of such a function from earlier times.[216] It is plausible, on the other hand, that this honorific function was not *en vogue*[217] in Babylon in the period of the redaction of the narrative, or had a different significance,[218] and thus a

---

Rabbi Eleazar's appointment to the local conditions.

214 It is not my intention to enter into the issues regarding Rabban Gamaliel's rank and authority.

215 Certain individuals may have been appointed (or demoted) because of their strong-mindedness or weakness. An individual without adequate halakhic knowledge might be appointed because of his illustrious genealogy. We may note, for instance, the narrative in bHorayot 13b (n. 19 above) in which Rabbi Meir and Rabbi Nathan attempt to humiliate and discredit the Patriarch Rabban Simeon ben Gamaliel because of his inadequate knowledge, and to demote him. Another version of this narrative in yBikkurim 3: 1, 65c, has no reference to the attempted humiliation of Rabban Simeon. See M. Jacobs, *Die Institution des jüdischen Patriarchen*, pp. 66 ff., and D. Goodblatt, קשר, on the comparison of the two versions and the relative authenticity of their details.

216 D. Goodblatt, קשר, p. 370, considers the references to an Av Beit Din in the Yabnean period as authentic.

217 It is not within the scope of this study to elaborate further on the differences in communal and legal organization between Palestine and Babylon, and the respective functioning of the courts. On legal organization in Palestine, see Lee Levine, *The Rabbinic Class of Roman Palestine*, מעמד החכמים, pp. 44 - 52.

218 D. Goodblatt, קשר, pp. 370 ff. maintains that a division of authority among a Nasi, Av Beit Din, and *hakham* was exercised only in Babylon. He also speculates, however, that the *hakham* had a much lower function than the Babylonian Nasi (*rosh*

different compromise was envisaged in the B.T.[219] The honorific position of Chairman of the Academy was divided between Rabban Gamaliel, who would preside for three weeks[220] in every month, and Rabbi Eleazar, who would preside for one week a month.

---

ha-gola); he was either a ראש ישיבה/ריש מתיבתא (ibid, p. 366), or a judge of the gate (*Monarchic Principle*, p. 287). Yet from the context of the B. T. record of Gamaliel's dismissal, we must deduce that the highest authority was the ריש מתיבתא. First, the Sages decide תא ונעבריה "Let's depose him [and hand over his position to someone else]." They then ask Rabbi Eleazar whether he would agree to become ריש מתיבתא. At the conclusion of the matter, Rabbi Eleazar was not demoted to the lower function of Av Beit Din; rather, the highest function was divided between two persons. The Y. T., in contrast, indicates the existence of a lower function, that of an Av Beit Din.

219 We may also consider another solution to the contrasting endings in B. T. and Y. T, regarding Rabbi Eleazar's new position. We must consider that neither version records the real course of events, particularly with respect to the motive. The bare record of a struggle between the leader, Rabban Gamaliel, and the council of Sages allowed the redactors to compose a narrative that provided missing or forgotten details out of their own conjectures, and concealed the real motive behind the outbreak of the crisis. It is possible that they did not know how the struggle actually ended, or that they attempted to conceal the ending from future generations. The Y. T. had no tradition that Rabbi Yehoshua was an Av Beit Din, and therefore, Rabbi Eleazar had to be appointed to this position as the compromise solution. (In yGittin 5: 7, *editio princeps*, we read in the text of the mishnah: רבי יהושע הושיב בית דין "Rabbi Yehoshua constituted a court." The original source of this quotation is probably MS Parma A (Codex de Rossi 138), the Vorlage of MS Leiden from which the mishnayot of the Venice *editio princeps* were copied. As far as I can ascertain, this is the only source in which Rabbi Yehoshua is named; in all the other sources the quotation appears in the name of רבי. At any rate, this quotation does not indicate that Rabbi Yehoshua was an Av Beit Din; it simply records that he constituted a court for the solution of a particular issue, and does not contradict my conjecture. The B. T. had a tradition that Rabbi Yehoshua was an Av Beit Din (Bava Qamma 74b) and therefore such a solution could not have been recorded in the B. T. This version also contains the motive (missing in the Y. T. version) for not substituting Rabbi Yehoshua for Rabban Gamaliel; this would have been expected, given that R. Yehoshua was Gamaliel's most blatant contender in a number of narratives and halakhic disputes, and the trigger for the "mutiny." I would conjecture that the B. T. version is the more accurate in its case history, particularly with respect to its finale, which gives significant insight into the entire narrative. We encounter reports of Rabbi Eleazar presiding over the council /academy of Sages in many other sources, such as tSotah 7: 9; yHagigah 1: 1, 75d; ySotah 3: 4, 18d,; Mekilta d' Rabbi Ishmael, *Bo* 16; this lends the B. T. record credence over the Y. T. version. See also I. Gafni, "Talmudic Research," on this question.

220 R. Goldenberg, "The Deposition of Rabban Gamaliel II," pp. 187 ff., prefers the common translation of שבת in this text as the Sabbath, the seventh day of rest. I think that the correct interpretation here is "week," similar to the biblical phrase שבע שבתות תמימות (Lev 23: 15) that unquestionably refers to weeks; this is also the opinion of Epstein, whom Goldenberg quotes, and Mantel. We also encounter in

In addition to the retrojection of later circumstances to earlier periods that is much evident in rabbinic literature, and the want of attention to exact terminology,[221] we must bear in mind a further factor. I have already discussed (section 2.3.1) the crucial fact of unity between the legislative and judicial functions in rabbinic practice, in contrast to our modern system. This lack of separation among the legislative, judicial and executive powers[222] was reflected in the fact that the same person would study and interpret the Torah, give halakhic decisions, and deliver

---

bMenahot 65b the phrase: כאן ביו"ט שחל להיות באמצע שבת "Here [there is a reference to] the fifteenth [the first day of Passover] that happens to be in the middle of the week." In substantiation of his view, Goldenberg quotes a narrative (that appears with textual variations in a number of rabbinic sources) containing the question: שבת של מי היתה "whose *shabbat* was it," and the answer that it was the *shabbat* of our Rabbi Eleazar ben Azaryah. In this case as well, the term likely means "week." One must assume that the Sages met every day in the Academy, and that there was a chairman who presented the thesis of the day. We would otherwise have to assume that all the meetings of the Academy mentioned in the narratives, including the events that took place at the dismissal of Rabban Gamaliel, occurred on Sabbath, and that is not reasonable. Moreover, some of the activities recorded in this narrative, such as the entrance of the shield-bearers, would be contrary to the Sabbath laws. In yHagigah 1: 1, 75d, also quoted by Goldenberg, we read: אי איפשר לבית המדרש שלא יהא בו דבר חדש בכל יום "Is it possible that there is not a new matter [halakhah] in the academy every day?" We thus observe that there were daily meetings. Following this we read: מי שבת שם אמרו לו ר' לעזר בן עזריה "Who presided there [in that week]? They said to him: Rabbi Eleazar ben Azaryah." We must interpret the question מי שבת שם with reference to the previous phrase referring to בכל יום, "every day." The verbal form does not contradict this interpretation, since verbs may develop from nouns (and vice-versa) in the progression of a language. To quote just one example, the noun "bank," describing the bench of the money changers, became both a noun referring to an institution and a verb referring to the actions performed in it. A careful reading of the above narrative in Hagigah indicates that the two Tannaim were on their way from one town to another, met Rabbi Yehoshua, and asked him: מה חדוש היה לכם בבי' המדרש היום "What new [halakhot] were there in the Academy today?" This could not have happened on Sabbath, since it is prohibited to undertake a long voyage on that day. The parallel texts in tSotah 7: 9 and bHagigah 3a also indicate the same circumstances. The narrative in Mekilta d'Rabbi Ishmael, *Bo* 16 shows a greater variation in the text; there is no indication that the meeting with Rabbi Yehoshua occurred on the same day as their arrival. Nonetheless, I think that the verbal form שבת must similarly be interpreted there as referring to a week, in conformity with the other texts.

221 As I have written elsewhere (chap. 1, p. 89), the Sages had no interest in the abstract philosophical classifications favoured by the Greeks. One encounters the same problem with respect to the identification of the various "dissident" groups; I shall discuss this point the second part of this study.

222 I have speculated on the probability that the Sages also had substantial executive authority in some periods (chap. 2, n. 95).

judgments. In some instances, according to several narratives, these activities might take place in the same location. The different functions performed by the same institution would explain the many inconsistencies in the names and qualifications of the assemblies and their leaders.[223] Adding to this confusion were the changes in the status of the leader, whatever title he happened to bear in any given period,[224] due to the influence of his particular personality and to the prevailing political conditions.

The functions of the Nasi, and those of the council[225] over which he presided, are also inconsistently described. The narratives in B.T. and Y.T.[226] on the deposing of Rabban Gamaliel provide a good illustration of the various factors involved. Rabban Gamaliel opened the session and presented the halakhic issues to be discussed.[227] His most important qualification, therefore, was knowledge of the Torah, and this is confirmed in a number of occurrences.[228] Rabbi Yehudah II, in contrast, whose Torah

---

223 For example, in the record of Rabban Gamaliel's dismissal, the Ammonite convert came to the בית המדרש, "the academy" (tYadayim 2: 17); in the succeeding elements of the narrative, it is clear that abstract questions were debated there. The end result, the judicial decision, is found in 2: 18: הרי אתה מותר לבוא בקהל "You are allowed to join the [Israelite] community." There is no division between the academy and the court, and nothing to discern between them. Circumstances such as these explain the inconsistencies among the many terms used for the assembly of Sages.

224 M. Jacobs, *Die Institution des jüdischen Patriarchen*, pp. 56 ff. demonstrates how the inconsistencies in the various texts make the chronological ordering of the narratives extremely difficult.

225 Here too an inconsistency in terminology is apparent. At this point, I shall simply use the term "council," without distinguishing any of its various functions.

226 I shall use the Y. T. version as the basis for the analysis, and add details from the B.T. version when these do not oppose the Y. T. For our purposes, it is not important whether these details are entirely authentic; the texts serve to indicate how the tradents and redactors perceived matters. Whether Gamaliel II really was a Nasi is therefore irrelevant; it is the assumption that he did indeed bear this title, as reflected in a number of rabbinic citations, that is of interest. See M. Jacobs' critical analysis, *Die Institution des jüdischen Patriarchen*, pp. 197 ff.

227 In yBerakhot 4: 1, 7d we read: והיה רבן גמליאל יושב ודורש "Rabban Gamaliel sat and lectured." He also opened the lecture, as we observe from his asking the inquirer to ask his question כשאיכנס לבית הוועד עמוד ושאול "when I enter the meeting hall [equivalent to בית המדרש in the B. T.], stand up and ask."

228 Hillel was nominated Nasi because of his superior Torah knowledge: tPesahim 4: 14 and yPesahim 6: 1, 33a. M. Jacobs, *Die Institution des jüdischen Patriarchen*, p. 103 and M. Goodman, *Roman Gallilee*, p. 112 contend that in this instance the title Nasi does not imply the office of Patriarch over all of Israel, but is simply an honorific. This interpretation does not negatively affect my proposition; on the contrary, it confirms the indiscriminate use of the title for different functions and positions. Adding to the confusion, yKil'ayim 9: 3, 32b, quotes Rabbi (Yehudah I) as declaring

knowledge was not highly regarded,[229] appointed others to open the lectures at the meetings,[230] and relied on more knowledgeable Sages for halakhic procedure.[231] Abstract halakhic decisions,[232] as well as court[233]

---

that the Bnei Bathyra abandoned their position as Nasi in favour of Hillel, his grandfather. Other citations substantiate the prerequisite of Torah knowledge. This is explicit in bHorayot 13b, in connection with the rebellion of Rabbi Meir and Rabbi Nathan against Rabban Simeon ben Gamaliel. In our narrative regarding Rabban Gamaliel's dismissal and Rabbi Eleazar's appointment (presumably as Nasi), Rabbi Aqiba perceives with sorrow that in this particular occurrence a political requirement overruled the usual requirement of the best knowledge of the Torah.

229 There is a record in yBava Batra 8: 1, 16a of a deprecatory comment made by Rabbi Yohanan about Rabbi Yehudah Nesia II; after a halakhic discussion with the Nasi, he said to Rabbi Yannai: איתא מן תמן לית אהן גוברא בעי מישמע מילה דאורייא "Let's go away from here, this man [the Nasi] is not interested in listening to a Torah utterance." In the parallel version in bBava Batra 111b, Rabbi Yohanan's remark is slightly less offensive. He says: לית דין צבי למילף "This one [the Nasi] does not want to learn." There are other narratives to the same effect. In bAvodah Zarah 33b and bMenahot 29b it is recorded that Rabbi Yehudah II asked Rabbi Ammi halakhic and midrashic questions. In bMenahot 104a there is the interesting statement: מוריינא דבי נשיאה הוה "A scholar was at the Nasi's [House and we were told to obey his halakhic decisions]."

230 We read in yHorayot 3: 1, 47a: סליק רבי יודה נסייא לבית וועדא אמר ליה למה לית מרי אמר לן מילה דאורייא "[When] Rabbi Yehudah, the Nasi, entered the meeting hall, he said to Rabbi Yohanan, Why don't you give us a Torah lecture?" (see also n. 209). From the wording of the narrative, one has the impression that it was common for Rabbi Yohanan to present the Torah topic and lead the discussion. He was prepared to play his role in the show, planned for the return of Resh Laqish.

231 We read in bRosh HaShanah 20a, within a discussion of an opposing opinion: שכל ימיו של רבי יוחנן היה מלמדנו "[The Nasi, Yehudah II declared] that Rabbi Yohanan taught us all his life."

232 In our narrative in Y. T., we read: למחר עמד אותו תלמיד ושאל את רבן גמליאל "The next day this student stood up and asked Rabban Gamaliel [the halakhah]." The Y. T. does not tell us whether a final decision was given (Abayye and Raba still disputed this halakhah in bBerakhot 27b).

233 For instance, on the question regarding the Ammonite's conversion, posed before the council on the occasion of Gamaliel's dismissal (according to the B.T. narrative), a final verdict was handed down. We read there: מיד התירוהו לבא בקהל "Immediately they allowed him [the converted Ammonite] to be part of the community [of Israel]." The narrative relates a dispute between Rabban Gamaliel and Rabbi Yehoshua on the issue of whether an Ammonite may join the community of Israel, despite the biblical prohibition in Deut 23: 4. Rabban Gamaliel prohibited this, while Rabbi Yehoshua permitted it; following Gamaliel's dismissal, the council, under its new leader, decided in favour of Rabbi Yehoshua's opinion. (See also chap. 1, n. 71.) The authority of Gamaliel to establish halakhah was opposed by the Sages, as recorded in bEruvin 41a (see my discussion of this narrative in chap. 2, n. 220.)

sentences, were given by the Council and its leader. The same Sages, in the same location,[234] served as both legislative and judicial authorities.[235]

As we have seen, both the Y.T. and B.T. reflect a fourth function for Rabban Gamaliel, that of *parnas*; this was an "administrator of public interests," an activity unrelated to learning, teaching or judging. In later periods, the Nasi also had the executive authority to impose law and order.[236]

---

[234] See B. Gerhardsson's comment, quoted in chap. 2, n. 98.

[235] We encounter an interesting narrative in bMo'ed Qatan 16b: כי הא דשמואל ומר עוקבא כי הוו יתבי גרסי שמעתא הוה יתיב מר עוקבא קמיה דשמואל ברחוק ארבע אמות וכי הוו יתבי בדינא הוה יתיב שמואל קמיה דמר עוקבא ברחוק ארבע אמות "...as [for example, the comportment of] Samuel and Mar Uqba: when they were sitting and studying, Mar Uqba sat four cubits away from Samuel [as a sign of reverence, since Samuel's erudition was higher than his], [but] when Mar Uqba was presiding over the court session, Samuel sat four cubits away from Mar Uqba [out of respect for his status when he acted in his capacity of Av Beit Din, as cited in n. 198]." D. Goodblatt, *The Monarchic Principle*, pp. 284 ff., quotes scholarly discussions of this narrative, and particularly on the oddity that Uqba was superior to Samuel in judicial settings. Based on a homily on Jer 21: 12 cited in bShabbat 55a, in which Samuel indicts the Judean kings for their complicity in social crimes and admonishes them to carry out justice, speculation has arisen that Uqba was alleged to be of Davidic descent. I would hesitate to reach such a conclusion from this homily; Samuel apparently found it appropriate to justify his passive attitude, asserting that it was the duty of those in authority to administer justice. The proposition that Uqba was a high official of the Exilarchate, or the Exilarch himself, as stated by Sherira Gaon in his Epistle (B. M. Lewin, p. 126), and was therefore superior to Samuel in the Babylonian hierarchy, cannot be justified from the text. The text gives no indication of such superiority; it simply demonstrates Samuel's respect toward the judge of the court in session, while on all other occasions he enjoyed a higher status than that of Uqba. The subsequent text records Uqba's subordinate behaviour toward Samuel; he escorted Samuel to his home daily, and when he omitted to do this one day, he felt censured by Samuel and acted as if he were excommunicated for a day. This narrative does not accord with the behaviour of a Nasi. I shall also quote an example from Sifre Deut 16. The *pisqa* starts with a midrashic interpretation of Deut 1: 16, ואצוה את שפטיכם, which refers to the conduct of judges in court. The narrative then goes on to record that Rabban Gamaliel seated the judges בישיבה, that is, in the council/academy, but they left their assigned place and sat with the תלמידים "students." When Rabban Gamaliel returned, he censured them, saying that they were now servants in bondage to the public and could not abandon their duties (see the extended text of this narrative in n. 211). They are thus associated with the term בישיבה, which has an affinity with learning and teaching, and sit with the students; but then, following upon a midrash about the conduct of judges, they are reminded that their judicial functions are a duty.

[236] We read in bBava Batra 89a: דבי נשיאה אוקימו אגרדמין בין למדות בין לשערים "From the House of the Nasi [in Israel, probably in the period of Yehudah I, since Samuel is involved in this discussion] they appointed a comptroller in the market for both measures and prices." It is odd that in the parallel version in yBava Batra, 5: 5, 15b, this event is recorded as occurring in Babylon, with the ריש גלותא

The title *parnas* for a public administrator is also used indiscriminately for a variety of functions. Rabban Gamaliel's function as *parnas* seems to have been the safeguarding of the economic welfare of the Sages,[237] or of all Israel. But we observe that Rabbi Aqiba was offered the position of *parnas*, and this was obviously for a different function.[238] The requirements for this position are also confusing. In one instance we read that he must be a תלמיד חכם, a "Sage" or "learned man";[239]

"Exilarch" making the appointment. See D. Goodblatt, *The Monarchic Principle*, pp. 293 - 294 on this topic. This peculiar reversal of the person and location weakens the usual assumption of the greater reliability of the Y. T. over the B. T. See I. Gafni, "Talmudic Research," on this question.

237 Rabbi Yehoshua reproached Rabban Gamaliel (in both the Y. T and the B. T accounts): אי לו לדור שאת פרנסו "Woe to the generation of which you are its פרנס," because the latter was not aware of his economic plight. The Y. T. does not list the Sages' reasons for favouring Rabbi Eleazar as Gamaliel's substitute, as the B. T. does, but simply records Rabbi Aqiba's meditation that Eleazar was preferred because of his illustrious genealogy. The B. T lists Eleazar's wealth among his merits; the significance of this wealth is not its potential for philanthropic use, within Elezar's function as a פרנס, but its use in serving Caesar (probably in bribing the Roman authorities).

238 We read in yPe'ah 8: 6, 21a: רבי עקיבה בעון ממניתיה פרנס "They wanted to appoint Rabbi Aqiba to serve as פרנס." The subsequent narrative gives the impression that this is a "stock scene," similar to the narrative in the B. T. version of Gamaliel's dismissal. Aqiba, like Rabbi Eleazar in the latter case, asks the advice of his wife, before accepting or declining the nomination. It is also interesting to note that in both instances, it was the women who were deemed to have practical foresight, and in both instances, it was believed that the nomination would invite disdain. We also read in yPe'ah 8: 6, 21a that Rabbi ליעזר, probably Rabbi Eliezer b. Rabbi Yose, a Palestinian Amora of the fifth generation (see Ch. Albeck, מבוא לתלמודים, p. 386) was a פרנס, and he had encountered contempt. It is obvious that Aqiba was not offered Rabban Gamaliel's position; nor did Rabbi Eleazar have a status and function comparable to those enjoyed by Gamaliel. We must also note that Betzalel, the master craftsman who built the Tabernacle and its furnishings, is called פרנס (bBerakhot 55a), as is Moses (ibid., 32a). In tractate Semahot 10: 13, it is stated that at the Nasi's death, the people should behave as if they had lost their פרנס. In tSotah 7: 12, God is called a פרנס: כל הדברים נתנו מרועה אחד אל אחד בראן פרנס אחד נתנן רבון כל המעשים ברוך הוא "All the words [of the Torah and its interpretations] are conferred by one shepherd, one God created them, one *parnas* gave them, [and that is] the Almighty, blessed be He." The term פרנס here is not used in the common meaning of providing sustenance, which would certainly conform to the idea of divine providence, but is related to God's giving of the Torah. Compare the use of the term in mKetubbot 7: 1: המדיר את אשתו מליהנות לו עד שלשים יום יעמיד פרנס "If one makes a vow depriving his wife of receiving her sustenance [from his assets] for a period of thirty days, he must provide a *parnas* [to maintain her]."

239 There is a statement in bShabbat 114a, in the name of the Palestinian Rabbi Yohanan, that it is appropriate to nominate a תלמיד חכם, Sage, as a *parnas*; this is כל

elsewhere it appears that people of lesser standing might be nominated for the position,[240] or that integrity was the significant prerequisite.[241]

Further citations will illustrate the "gray area" with respect to the functions of the Av Beit Din and his relations with the Nasi, or alleged Nasi. A rhetorical discussion in bHagigah 16b reflects a division of functions between the Nasi and the Av Beit Din, and it is evident that the court's halakhic decisions are within the competence of the latter.[242] The title Av Beit Din itself also indicates that this person was the head of a court. A statement in bSanhedrin 66a explicitly confirms these functions.[243] Other instances, however, indicate just the opposite; it is the Nasi who has the court under his aegis,[244] and who attempts,

---

ששואלין אותו הלכה בכל מקום ואומרה "anyone who is capable of stating the halakhah at all occasions." A parallel statement in yBerakhot 2: 9, 5d, is not as detailed, but does associate the nomination as *parnas* with a תלמיד חכם.

240 We read in tRosh HaShanah 1: 18: אפילו קל שבקלין ונתמנה פרנס על הצבור הרי הוא כאביר שבאבירים "Even if the most worthless of the worthless is nominated as a *parnas* of the community, [he must be obeyed and honoured] as if he were the noblest of the noble."

241 We read in yPe'ah 8: 6, 21a: לא נמצא לאיש פלוני דבר עבירה "[At the investigation of a nominee] no improper deeds were detected." This refers unmistakably to the person's financial integrity, since the text asserts that despite their merit, one must not appoint two brothers to serve together as פרנסים. Elsewhere in Y. T., an appointed *parnas* is described with the attribute ונמצא נאמן "and he was found trustworthy."

242 We read there: הײנו דקא מורי הלכה בפני שמעון בן שטח "That is why [ben Tabai, the Nasi], undertakes to deliver court decisions only under the guidance of Simeon ben Shetah [the Av Beit Din]." My interpretation of this discussion does not follow Rashi's understanding, which is founded, in my opinion, on the traditional assumption of the Nasi's superiority in all aspects and circumstances. I have approached this text without any such preconception, and I believe that a straightforward interpretation of the text tends to my conclusion.

243 We read there: דיין אתה מצווה על הוראתו כראי נשיא שאי אתה מצווה על הוראתו "[The law applicable to a judge is not applicable to the Nasi.] You are obligated to obey the halakhic decisions of a judge, while you are not obligated to obey the Nasi's halakhic decisions." And conversely: שהנשיא אתה מצווה על המראתו כראי דיין שאי אתה מצווה על המראתו "You are commanded not to rebel against the Nasi, while you are not commanded similarly versus the judge." It is obvious that the Av Beit Din would have at least the same authority as a judge.

244 The expression רבן גמליאל ובית דינו "Rabban Gamaliel and his court," is found in tBerakhot 2: 6, and in many other sources in the Y.T and B. T. The expression רבי (רבי יהודה הנשיא, רבי יהודה) ובית דינו "Rabbi (or Rabbi Yehudah, or Rabbi Yehudah the Nasi) and his court."is found in mAvodah Zarah 2: 6, in tShevi'it 4: 17, and in many occurrences in the Y.T. and B. T. In some instances the Nasi's predominance in particular matters of halakhah is explicitly stated. We read in yShabbat, 1: 4, 3d, that Rabbi's court is called בית דין שרייא "a permissive [lenient] court," because it allowed three previous prohibitions. The connection to

successfully[245] or not,[246] to impose his views upon the court (or Council). The well-known narrative in bKetubbot 103a-b on Rabbi's last wishes and instructions before his death again demonstrates the perplexities regarding the different titles and functions. We read there: "My son Simeon [should be] *hakham*, my son Gamaliel Nasi, Hanina bar Hama should be the chairman."[247] The context of the narrative indicates that all three appointments are of great significance both for the designated persons and for the management and guidance of the people. I suggest that we should perceive them as of equally high status,[248] although with some distinction in their precise rank and functions. Yet the listing of the three titles and Rabbi's instructions are not only inadequate for an understanding of their duties, they also seem contrary to the common perception of these positions. His mandate "my son Gamaliel [should be] Nasi," a title which is supposed to represent the highest rank, was uttered after his pronouncement of the title *hakham* for his second son Simeon; one would have expected the reverse. The vague title *hakham* is nowhere defined, but it is certainly of a lower rank than the Nasi.[249] The parental guidance for

---

Rabbi is reinforced by the statement that in these instances Rabbi's name is not disclosed, but his accomplishment is recorded as carried out by רבותנו "our Rabbis."

245 In the record of Rabban Gamaliel's dismissal, we observe that Rabban Gamaliel wanted to impose his opinion regarding the conversion of the Ammonite, and was enraged at Rabbi Yehoshua's reluctance to accept his views. Immediately after Gamaliel's dismissal, the halakhah was established according to Rabbi Yehoshua's opinion. Similarly, we have seen in tTa'anit 2: 5, quoted in chap. 2, n. 220, that following Rabban Gamaliel's death, Rabbi Yehoshua wanted to reverse a decision of his that had been established against contrary opinions. He was opposed by Rabbi Yohanan ben Nuri, who said: כל זמן שהיה רבן גמליאל קיים היתה הלכה נוהגת כדבריו "During all of Rabban Gamaliel's lifetime, the halakhah was practised according to his view."

246 We read in bGitttin 76b: ר' יהודה נשיאה בנו של ר"ג בר רבי הורה ולא הודו לו כל סיעתו "Rabbi Yehudah Nesia, the son of Rabban Gamaliel, son of Rabbi, gave a halakhic decision, but none of his council accepted it." See M. Jacobs, *Die Institution des jüdischen Patriarchen*, p. 123, on the identification of this person.

247 I have used this translation, which is the most common. There are two different MSS of the Hebrew text, and in yTa'anit, 4: 2, 68a, the text reads בראשה , an expression that may imply "the first." See M. Jacobs' comments on this issue, *Die Institution des jüdischen Patriarchen*, pp. 72 ff. and 78.

248 See D. Goodblatt, קשר, pp. 368 - 369, who reaches the same conclusion from an examination of this text.

249 Note the hierarchy implied in the seating order for these dignitaries, as set out in tSanhedrin 7: 8, quoted in the text above at n. 183; the *hakham* is the third in rank after the Nasi. The B. T. redactor definitely concurred with this status, as we see from his record of the "rebellion" by Rabbi Meir and Rabbi Nathan against Rabban Simeon ben Gamaliel. It does not matter for our purposes whether this narrative is authentic, or represents later Babylonian conditions, as D. Goodblatt contends (קשר, pp. 365 ff.); it suffices that the redactor understood the statuses in this way, and the narrative

this function, expressed as סדרי חכמה, "orders of wisdom," neither offers any clarification of his function nor explains why he was nominated by his father before his elder brother, the intended Nasi. The first instruction to the future Nasi, to conduct his Patriarchate with the highest dignity,[250] is certainly comprehensible, and conforms with rabbinic dicta to this effect;[251] the second dictum, זרוק מרה בתלמידים "treat the students with dominance [harshly]," seems, however, inappropriate to the Nasi,[252] and its significance as one of the two most important rules proffered to the future Nasi by his predecessor is puzzling. There is finally the perplexity concerning Rabbi Hanina's title and function,[253] to which many scholars[254] have applied their knowledge and imagination.

There is also conflicting evidence with respect to the honour due to the Nasi. I have cited above the requirement of submission to the Nasi (in bSanhedrin 66a[255]) and the obligation to stand before the Nasi (in bMo'ed Qatan 27b; see n. 251). While certain narratives attest to compliance with these practices,[256] others indicate a lack of due respect, bordering on rebellion.[257]

---

thus indicates his inconsistency.

250 See M. Jacobs, *Die Institution des jüdischen Patriarchen,* p. 75 on the different interpretations of the term ברמים in the text. I would explain the plural form as suggesting: "Carry out actions of the highest dignity." The noun has dropped out, leaving only the adjective.

251 We read in bMo'ed Qatan 27b, in the name of Rabbi Yohanan: הכל חייבין לעמוד מפני נשיא "Everyone must stand up before the Nasi." This and other citations confirm the obligation to honour the Nasi.

252 The dignity associated with the Nasi's status, and the more advanced nature of duties, do not accord with him carrying out the function of disciplining the students.

253 The puzzle is made yet more obscure by the existence of a different version of the narrative in yTa'anit 4: 2, 68a.

254 See the more recent studies by M. Jacobs, *Die Institution des jüdischen Patriarchen,* pp. 70 ff., who quotes previous opinions, and by D. Goodblatt, קשר, pp. 364 ff.

255 I have translated the Hebrew expression המראתו as "rebellion," according to Jastrow, but the intent of this dictum is not the prohibition of an open rebellion; it is rather a command to obey the Nasi and to not contradict him. Similarly, we read in Num 20: 24: מריתם את פי למי מריבה "You rebelled against my command at the waters of Meribah," where there was no open rebellion.

256 Even an especially skilled Sage might not authorize the use of a blemished first-born animal without first receiving approval from the Nasi (yHagigah 1: 8, 76c). But in bYoma 78a we learn the motive behind this rule: דבר זה הניחו להם לבי נשיאה כדי להתגדר בו "This privilege was left to the House of the Nasi so that he could raise himself above others [Jastrow]." Rashi interprets להתגדר בו as לשון גדולה, "language of prominence [or majesty]." A number of citations in this study affirm this motive.

257 The narratives in both Talmudim on the deposing of Rabban Gamaliel, whatever its

These perplexities and confusion regarding the titles and functions of the Nasi and the Av Beit Din in the rabbinic period (from the destruction of the Second Temple to the redaction of both Talmudim) have been much scrutinized by scholars and historians. I have mentioned above the recent studies of M. Jacobs, D. Goodblatt and M. Goodman, who offer their opinions on this issue as well as summaries of prior research, speculations and propositions. Jacobs concentrates his efforts on invalidating the commonly-held assumptions about the titles, functions, and authority of these dignitaries. Goodblatt and Goodman attempt to establish the relevant political and administrative circumstances; a reconciliation of the conflicting data is effected by attributing them to different periods and different locations (particularly Palestine and Babylon). The critical examination of these propositions is not within the scope of my study, and I leave an assessment of these theories to the discretion of the reader. I reiterate that my short exposition on this matter is simply intended to demonstrate once again the utter lack of precise definitions in rabbinic literature. The perspective of this Excursus, and of the study in general, is not the extraction of historical data, but rather an investigation into the *Weltanschauung* of the Sages. As I have written elsewhere in this study, the Sages maintained a belief that the Torah was the blueprint of the world, and all its ultimate implications were revealed at Sinai; at the same time, they nonetheless effected adjustments in response to changing circumstances. They were aware of historical changes, but given the immutability of Torah, they could not openly acknowledge such change. Just as the redactor of Chronicles added data to his historical records that he deemed was missing in Kings, in the belief that such events must have occurred, the Sages could also not envisage that contemporary conditions differed from those in the antecedent generations. This attitude might explain their reluctance and lack of interest in, or even opposition to, a concept of historical development. My short exposition illustrates how this attitude has affected descriptions of communal organization in rabbinic literature.

4.2.2.1 Rabban Gamaliel's Attempts to Unify the Halakhah

Insight into Rabban Gamaliel's role in establishing a fixed halakhah may be gleaned from various narratives that reflect his great foresight in attempting to impose a degree of standardization on halakhic rules. As I

---

real motives, indicate an open rebellion. The redactors' intent seems to have been to demonstrate an insurgence against a Nasi, as they perceived Gamaliel's status. Similarly, the intended deposing of Rabban Simeon ben Gamaliel by Rabbi Meir and Rabbi Nathan, quoted only in the B. T. (see n. 19), attests to the same disrespect and contempt shown toward the Nasi.

stated earlier, Rabban Gamaliel realized that after the loss of the Temple, the symbol of unity of Israel, only a unitary legal codex could guarantee the people's survival as a single, unified entity.[258] In his capacity as Patriarch, and as a scion of a reigning family, his far-reaching political vision was an intrinsic element of his personality. This vision guided his conception of the future of Israel, and the ways in which he proposed to achieve his goal.

An example of his foresight relates to the issue of the evening prayer. According to the rabbinic record, this matter was the subtance of the last incident between Rabban Gamaliel and Rabbi Yehoshua, and induced the dismissal of the former. Rabbi Yehoshua maintained that this prayer was not an explicit obligation, while Rabban Gamaliel declared the opposite. The daily prayers were instituted as replacements for the sacrifices,[259] at a time when the תמיד *tamid*, the perpetual sacrifices, were offered in the Temple "in the morning" and "at twilight" (Exod 29: 38 - 42 and Num 28: 3 - 8). The additional sacrifices on the Sabbaths, the days of the new moon and the holidays were also replaced with prayers called מוספים "additional prayers," and were performed at the same time of the day as the relevant sacrifices. But there were no daily, obligatory sacrifices at evening time, and therefore no prayers were needed to replace them. Rabban Gamaliel's assertion that the evening prayer was obligatory was therefore not reasonable.[260] Even the prayers extant at the time of the

---

258 Though Rabban Gamaliel's goal is not explicitly stated in the rabbinic literature, we may deduce a hint of it from a homily in Lam. Rab., Proem 25: עד שלא גלו ישראל היו עשויים עדרים עדרים... וכיון שגלו נעשו עדר אחד "Before the Israelites were exiled, they were [divided] into many flocks [groups]...but after they were exiled they became one flock."

259 For an extended study on the replacement of the sacrifices, see Heger, *Altars*, pp. 380 ff.

260 In yBerakhot 4: 1, 7a, Rabbi Yehoshua b. Levi states: תפילות מאבות למדום "From the Patriarchs [the Sages] have learned the [three] prayers"; there then follows a homily with the relevant scriptural verses, which indicate, through suitable hermeneutics, that the Patriarchs prayed three times a day. The passage goes on: ורבנן אמרו תפילות מתמידין גמרו תפילת השחר מתמיד של שחר את הכבש אחד תעשה בבקר תפילת המנחה מתמיד של בין הערבים תפילת הערב לא מצאו במה לתלותה ושנו אותה סתם הדא היא דתנינן תפילת הערב אין לה קבע "The Sages said: They learned the [obligation of the] prayers from the [daily] perpetual offerings [and instituted them as their replacement]. The morning prayer [was learned from] the morning *tamid*... and the afternoon prayer from the twilight offering. They did not encounter anything to support the evening prayer and simply decreed it. This is why we learned that the evening prayer has no fixed obligation." Rabbi Tanhuma attempted to find some connection to the Temple offerings, suggesting a reference to the remainder of the offerings, which burned at night on the altar until they were totally consumed. In bBerakhot 26b the attributions are reversed. Rabbi Yose b. Hanina states: תפלות אבות תקנום "The Patriarchs

Temple, whose nature and composition we do not know, were performed concurrently with the sacrificial worship,[261] and the Gemara decided that

---

instituted the prayers." [It is interesting to observe the difference here from the Y. T. version: there, the Sages learned the custom or obligation of three prayers from the behaviour of the Patriarchs, whereas the B. T. version asserts that the Patriarchs instituted the prayers)." Rabbi Yehoshua b. Levi states: תפלות כנגד תמידין תקנום "The prayers were instituted [by the Sages] corresponding to the [daily] perpetual offerings." Two baraitot are then cited in the B. T., one supporting the first declaration and the other the second. The citation maintaining that the Patriarchs instituted the prayers is founded upon a homiletic reading of the same biblical texts as in the Y. T. version. The intention of this midrash, in my opinion, was to retroject the use of prayer to the Patriarchs, to bestow upon it the aura of an ancient tradition and enhance its significance. In fact, after a rhetorical discussion of, and challenge to, this opinion, the B. T. declares: תפלות אבות תקנום ואסמכינהו רבנן אקרבנות "The Patriarchs instituted the prayers and the Sages associated them with the sacrifices." Positing a patriarchal idea, however, does not offer a reasonable solution for the מוסף prayer, for which the homily has not indicated any scriptural support. The second opinion, in contrast, is founded upon a factual phenomenon: the times fixed for each prayer correspond precisely to the times when the relevant sacrifices were offered in the Temple. (The evening prayer is associated with the burning of the residues of the sacrifices during the night, to bestow upon it some relevance to the sacrifices). The established halakhah therefore considers the evening prayer as a voluntary one. I wish to emphasize that the dispute refers solely to the prayer of eighteen blessings (שמונה עשרה), not to the recitation of שמע, the pronouncement of God's unity; the latter is obligatory both morning and evening, as it is written: ודברת בם בשבתך בביתך ובלכתך בדרך ובשכבך ובקומך "Talk about them when you sit at home and when you walk along the road, when you lie down and when you get up [Deut 6: 7]." The motive for the institution of the evening prayer is disputable. I postulate that it was added at some time as an extension to the obligatory שמע, as was the case with the other instituted prayers; these were expanded during a long period of time until they attained their current configuration. I. Elbogen, התפילה בישראל, p. 77, writes: הצורך הטבעי בתפילת לילה הוא שהוליד את תפילת ערבית "The natural need for a nightly prayer engendered the evening prayer."

261 See Josephus, *Ag. Ap.* 2: 23, who asserts that there were prayers during the offering of the sacrifices. Luke 1: 10 reports that the people prayed outside the Temple at the time of the incense burning ceremony. The ceremony of the incense burning was performed between the sprinkling of the blood of the *tamid* offering and the burning of its flesh on the altar, as recorded in bYoma 33a: ודם התמיד קודם להטבת שתי נרות והטבת שתי נרות קודם לקטורת וקטורת קודם לאברים "the [sprinkling of the] blood of the perpetual offering [on the altar] precedes the preparation of the two candles [on the lampstand] and the preparation of the two candles precedes the incense [burning] and the incense precedes the [raising of the sacrificial] parts [upon the altar]. From tPesahim 4: 2, one can deduce the same order of the celebration, though it is not expressed as explicitly as in bYoma. In yBerakhot 4: 1, 7b, Rabbi Yose states: לא הוקשה תפילת המנחה לתמיד של בין הערבים אלא לקטורת "The afternoon prayer is not connected with the twilight offering, but rather with the incense celebration." This is deduced from the connection of the terms "prayer" and "incense" in Ps 141: 2: תכון תפילתי קטורת לפניך משאת כפי מנחת ערב "May

the halakhah was contrary to Rabban Gamaliel's opinion. We also have no indication as to the conflicting conceptions behind each position. I postulate that Rabban Gamaliel, conscious of the importance of a unified ritual for the survival of the Jewish people, was concerned that if the evening prayer were considered non-obligatory, this would create a division among the Jewish people; some communities would perform it and others would not. Less significant differences in custom and cult can engender divisions in a pious society, and this was the character of the Israelite people at the time of Rabban Gamaliel, and for a long period of its history. I conjecture, therefore, that Rabban Gamaliel insisted that the prayer should be obligatory, and thus be performed identically in all communities.

Rabban Gamaliel displayed a similar attitude to the idea of a formal system of prayer. It is not within the scope of this study to examine the complex and much-debated issue of the time and the manner in which public prayer was instituted in Israel. There is, however, textual evidence as to when the תפלת עמידה,[262] "the prayer to be performed while standing," the eighteen blessings that are the core of the system of daily prayers, was instituted. We read in mBerakhot 4: 3: "Rabban Gamaliel says: A man must pray the eighteen blessings every day; Rabbi Yehoshua says: [He must pray] an abstract [of them - that is, an abridged version]; Rabbi Aqiba says: If he is competent in his prayers he should pray the eighteen blessings, and if not competent, he should only pray an abridged version." It is evident that an abridged version of the blessings would not be uniform,[263] and Rabbi Aqiba's solution would definitely create at least two divergent systems of prayer. Neither R. Yehoshua nor R. Aqiba, however, considered the uniformity of prayer a meaningful requirement.

---

my prayer be set before you like incense; may the lifting of my hands be like the evening sacrifice."

262 This name was given later, in view of the homily found in yBerakhot 4 :1, 7a and (in a different literary style) bBerakhot 26b (see n. 260): תפילת השחר מאברהם אבינו וישכם אברהם בבוקר אל המקום אשר עמד שם לפני ה' ואין עמידה אלא תפילה "We learned the obligation of the morning prayer from Abraham [as is said, in Gen 19: 27]: 'Early the next morning Abraham got up and returned to the place where he had stood before the Lord,' and standing means praying ."

263 In yBerakhot 4: 3, 8a, and bBerakhot 29a, Rab and Samuel dispute about the contents of this abridged version. In the Y. T. version, we read: אית תניי תני שבע מעין שמונה עשרה ואית תניי תני שמונה עשרה מעין שמונה עשרה "There is a Tanna who understands the term 'abstract' in the mishnah to mean seven [blessings], representing the eighteen, and another Tanna considers it an abridgement of all the eighteen blessings." This dispute, and the great differences regarding the contents and texts of the prayers suggested by the Amoraim, substantiate the assumption that an abridged version could not ensure uniformity. The dispute confirms, moreover, that in the period of the early Amoraim Rab and Samuel, there was as yet no final decision regarding the character of the obligatory daily prayer or its wording.

Rabban Gamaliel is the only Tanna who insisted on a standardized prayer; as is evident in a baraita quoted in bBerakhot 28b, he was actually the initiator of the fixed daily prayer consisting of the typical number of eighteen blessings.[264] We read there: "We learned in a baraita: Simeon ha-Paqoli arranged [composed] eighteen blessings before Rabban Gamaliel at Yabneh." This fundamental standard prayer was thus the initiative of Rabban Gamaliel and composed under his supervision. He was also concerned with standardizing an additional blessing against heretics, as we observe from the succeeding passage: "Rabban Gamaliel said to the Sages: Is there someone [among you] who is able to compose[265] a blessing against the heretics? Samuel ha-Qatan stood up and composed it. In the next year, he forgot it."[266]

But I propose that the dispute concerning the fixed form of prayer was of an even greater scope and consequence. In mBerakhot 4: 4, we read: "Rabbi Eliezer says: If one makes his prayer into a fixed form, his prayer is not considered supplicating." This dictum is vague, and there are a number of attempts in the Gemara to understand the intent of the expression "fixed." One Amora declares that Rabbi Eliezer had in mind "whoever deems the prayer to be a burden." Another suggests "a prayer expressed not in a supplicating manner," while two others declare: "whoever is unable to add something [to the standard prayer]."[267] Most of the traditional commentators do not clarify whether, in their opinion, Rabbi Eliezer disputes or simply adds to the dicta of the other Tannaim in the Mishnah. I think that his declaration, if interpreted as requiring the addition of something to one's prayer, is indeed conflicting with the

---

[264] In yBerakhot 4: 3, 8a, there are an array of homilies explaining the origin of the number eighteen for the blessings.

[265] From the context, one must interpret the term לתקן in this narrative as "to prepare, establish, institute" rather than as "to repair." The rabbinic term תקנה, used for new decrees in religious matters, also corroborates this interpretation. R. Kimelman, "Birkat Ha-Minim," pp. 226-7, mentions recent studies arguing that Rabban Gamaliel reformulated an older blessing.

[266] Although it is not within the scope of this study to elaborate upon the existence of different versions of the same narratives in the two Talmudim, it is interesting to note the similarities and differences between the records in the Y. T. and the B. T. with respect to Samuel ha-Qatan's involvement in this prayer. The Y. T. version in Berakhot 5: 3, 9c does not record who composed the blessing, but records that Samuel ha-Qatan forgot it: שמואל הקטן עבר קומי תיבותא ואשגר מכניע זדים בסופה "Samuel ha-Qatan acted as reader of the prayers and forgot to recite the blessing against the heretics." Thus, in both versions, there is the same event of Samuel ha-Qatan forgetting the blessing, and the same generous and forgiving attitude on the part of the congregation; but there is no conformity regarding the composition of the prayer and Gamaliel's initiative.

[267] This is Rashi' s interpretation: "... דהיינו לשון קבע כהיום כן אתמול כן מחר what is intended is fixed language: the same today as yesterday and tomorrow."

others,[268] and indicates his opposition to Rabban Gamaliel's standardized prayer. I assume that Rabban Gamaliel, too, was cognizant of the deficiency of fixed prayer, but considered such standardization an absolute necessity for the preservation of the Israelites as a united people.[269]

This desire for unity is also revealed in Rabban Gamaliel's dictum in mRosh HaShanah 4: 9: "The public reader [who blows the *shofar*] absolves the public of their obligation [to blow the *shofar*]." He maintains the same opinion regarding the individual obligation for prayer, in his statement in tRosh HaShanah 2: 18. The Sages, in contrast, state in both occurrences: "Everyone must fulfill his own obligation." In the course of the discussions attributed to the Sages and Rabban Gamaliel on both issues, it is revealed that the Sages do agree that the public reader absolves those members of the congregation who do not know how to pray or blow the *shofar*. The dispute refers to those who are competent to perform the rituals: the Sages maintained that these were not absolved by the public reader and must recite the prayers themselves, while Rabban Gamaliel put the entire community on the same level. This confirms his extreme concern to avoid the creation of separate groups within the bosom of the communities; a unified custom with respect to every aspect of communal life was his preeminent consideration.

A further example indicates Rabban Gamaliel's interest in avoiding the creation of non-standardized applications of rules. In yShevi'it 1: 1, 33a and (with a different literary style) in bMo'ed Qatan 3b, we read in the name of Rabbi Yohanan: "Rabban Gamaliel and his court revoked the [previous] prohibition in the first two chapters." This passage refers, as the Gemara interprets it, to the rule that forbids plowing a field or orchard for a certain period prior to the beginning of the seventh year, when the land must remain unplowed (mShevi'it 1: 1 and 2: 1). The purpose of this extension is to ensure that work done in the field before the seventh year will not have its effect during the seventh year. Questions arose on how to assess this period: by a fixed term, or by estimating whether a task could be considered relevant to the condition of the field in the sixth year, or whether its benefit would be realized in the seventh year. In tShevi'it 1: 1, it is stated explicitly: "Rabban Gamaliel and his court decreed that it is

---

268 Ch. Albeck, ששה סדרי משנה, סדר זרעים, quotes on p. 331 the opinion of a traditional scholar, who affirms that Rabbi Eliezer disputes the fixed character of the prayer, as declared in mishnah 3, cited above. Indeed, we find the following in yBerakhot 4: 4, 8a: רבי אלעזר היה מתפלל תפילה חדשה בכל יום "Rabbi Eliezer offered a new prayer every day."

269 Rabbi Eliezer's alleged dictum requiring personal additions to the fixed prayer was not accepted, and Jewish communities recite the fixed prayer. In mAvot 2: 13 there is an assertion in Rabbi Simeon's name: אל תעש תפלתך קבע אלא רחמים ותחנונים לפני המקום "Do not make your prayer like a fixed recital, but like a supplication for divine mercy."

permitted to work the fields [right up] until Rosh Hashanah," that is, without any restriction in the sixth year.

We observe inconsistencies between the three texts reporting Rabban Gamaliel's decision, hinting that there was some doubt with respect to its precise intent. In both the Y. T. and B. T. versions, the question is posed: How is it possible that Rabban Gamaliel decided against the declarations of Beit Shammai and Beit Hillel, who do prohibit work in the fields for some additional time before the New Year? Attempts are made to reconcile this deviation from the norm, but only succeed in creating further difficulties. The B. T. concludes that Rabban Gamaliel considered the extension to be required only during the existence of the Temple, and therefore he annulled it; in the Y. T., however, this reasoning is not cited. Such a distinction with respect to a particular aspect of agricultural labour, in fact, makes no sense. One could comprehend a pre- and post-Temple distinction applying to the entire law of *shevi'it* (seventh year); but this law did remain in force after the Temple's destruction. The justifications for the repeal of the extension period are also tenuous.[270] I postulate that the rules concerning the extension of the prohibition were perplexing and confusing; each type of crop and plant likely had its own rule. On one occasion, in fact, Rabbi Simeon protested the lack of precision as to when

---

[270] Rav Ashi, who concludes the discussion in the B. T., declares that the extension of the prohibition is a "halakhah [given] to Moses from Sinai" that is effective only during the period of the Temple, like the water libation on Sukkot: וכי גמירי הלכתא בזמן שבית המקדש קיים דומיא דניסוך המים אבל בזמן שאין בית המקדש קיים לא "When do we declare it [the extension of the prohibition]? During the time of the Temple, similar to the precept of the water libation [at Sukkot], but after the Temple's destruction, this extension is not valid." This refers to a declaration (disputed in bSukkah 44a) that three particular precepts that have no biblical basis are nonetheless valid because of such a tradition (see the discussion in chap. 3, at n. 88). In yShevi'it 1: 5, 33b, these three traditions are said to have been מיסוד הנביאים הראשונים "originated by the first prophets," and this dictum is also disputed there. This suggestion by itself makes no sense; simply because they were declared together in the name of a single Sage (see n. 272) does not justify their simultaneous abrogation. Moreover, the declaration refers to a specific rule regarding ten young plants spread in a field, which one is allowed to plow until the beginning of the seventh year, and not to the extension of the prohibition against performing work before the seventh year in other circumstances, which is the subject of Rabban Gamaliel's edict. We would also have to assume that the extension of the period of forbidden work declared by Hillel and Shammai in mShevi'it 1: 1 would be valid only at the time of the Temple, and this was their intention. The further suggestion that their rule was initially conceived as a voluntary decree, and each person could decide whether to obey it, indicates the frailty of all the proposed solutions. A similar solution is proposed in the discussion in the Y. T. to justify Rabban Gamaliel's repeal, with the additional twist that the original tradition was forgotten and then re-established; this solution is no more reasonable. We need not extend the arguments on this issue, as each additional comment would add to the confusion.

the prohibition would come into force, declaring (mShevi'it 2: 1): "You left to each one [farmer] to assess [whether for his particular land and crop, work will affect the current crop, or next year's]."[271] Rabban Gamaliel thus desired to avoid a situation in which the proliferation of different rules had the potential to create dissimilar customs within Israelite society. The mishnayot in tractate Shevi'it that decree the extension of the prohibition have as their rationale the logical consideration that work done in the preceding period will almost certainly benefit the crop in the seventh year. Although in mishnah 1: 4 a scriptural hermeneutic is supposed to be the foundation of this extension, it is not alleged that the extension is a Torah precept.[272] I suppose that Rabban Gamaliel considered it a rabbinic edict, and he revoked it with the sweeping and straightforward edict that is cited in Tosefta. Though unity

---

[271] Rabbi Simeon refers to the rules in the mishnah: עד אימתי חורשין בשדה הלבן ערב שביעית עד שתכלה הליחה כל זמן שבני אדם חורשים ליטע במקשאות ובמדלעות "Until what time may one plow a field of grain on the eve of the seventh year? Until moisture ceases. In fields of cucumbers and pumpkins [one may plow] as long as people plow."

[272] Rav Ashi's closing answer in bMo'ed Qatan 4a, which seems to be the solution accepted by the editor of the Gemara, assumes that Rabban Gamaliel considers that the extension is a הלכה למשה מסיני "a halakhah [given] to Moses from Sinai," as Rabbi Ishmael declared. I have written in section 3.5 on the issue of whether a precept with this attribute is considered a Torah precept or a rabbinic edict. In most instances, it is considered a rabbinic edict. It is interesting to observe that many of the citations of the three rules in the name of Rabbi Yohanan, recorded in the B. T. with the attribute הלכה למשה מסיני, indicate רבי נחוניא איש בקעת בית חורתן as the source of this dictum. In the parallel citations in yShevi'it (cited in n. 270) and ySukkah 4: 1, 54b, the source is רבי חונייא דבקעת חוורן, evidently the same person; but here the rule is characterized as מיסוד הנביאים הראשונים "originated by the first prophets." Hence, they are not Torah precepts. This declaration would also go against the dictum that prophets must not institute new rules, discussed earlier in the study (Introduction, n. 73). I also wish to remark that Rabbi Ishmael's declaration in mShevi'it 1: 4, מה חריש רשות אף קציר רשות יצא קציר העומר שהוא מצוה, is vague, and does not indicate his opinion regarding the extension of the prohibition. In bMo'ed Qatan 4a Rav Ashi assumes that since he needs the interpretation of this verse to allow the reaping of the barley for the *omer* on Sabbath, he likely holds that the extension is a "halakhah [given] to Moses fromt Sinai." This is not proven at all, and I would assume that in R. Ishmael's opinion there is no extension at all forbidding work before the arrival of the seventh year. Just as the apodosis, which permits the reaping of the *omer* on Sabbath, must be a Torah precept to override the Sabbath law, so must the protasis, which allows working the field until the beginning of the seventh year. In ySheqalim 4: 1, 47d, it is alleged that Rabbi Ishmael utilizes the interpretation of this verse for another purpose: רבי ישמעאל אמר אין העומר בא מן הסוריא "Since Rabbi Ishmael declared that one must not bring the *omer* from Syria [it must be of Israelite origin]." There is nothing to indicate his opinion with respect to the extension of the seventh year prohibition. The harmonization process defies any hurdle.

in the Israelite way of life was a primary consideration, it is also possible that Rabban Gamaliel had a more immediate concern; shortly after the Temple's destruction, the people likely faced financial difficulties, inducing him to adopt a more lenient position and permit work to continue until the New Year.[273]

Rabban Gamaliel as the leader of the people perceived the necessity of addressing broad and far-reaching problems. We read, in mRosh Hashanah 1: 6, his concern that a legitimate decision might entail harmful repercussions in the future, and should therefore be overridden:[274] "If you prevent the majority [to go now to give evidence, because it is an unnecessary profanation of the Sabbath] it will cause them to fail [in their obligation] in future." His consideration of the public interest is also reflected in his declaration as to when to start the prayer for rain, because of his responsibility for the welfare of the pilgrims from abroad: "...to enable the last of the pilgrims [from Babylon] to reach the river Euphrates [their home, before the start of the rainy season]."[275] A similar concern for

---

[273] See end of section 1.7.

[274] We read there: מעשה שעברו יותר מארבעים זוג ועכבן רבי עקיבא בלוד "It happened that there were over forty pairs of witnesses [who were on their way on a Sabbath to testify on the new moon before Rabban Gamaliel's court] and Rabbi Aqiba held them up from proceeding further." The people who saw the new moon were allowed to profane the Sabbath and walk to the seat of the court to deliver the testimony necessary for the pronouncement of the new moon. Rabbi Aqiba prevented these witnesses from proceeding, since there were already sufficient witnesses and he wanted to avoid unnecessary profanation of the Sabbath. He was correct from the narrow point of view of that particular circumstance, but Rabban Gamaliel perceived the broader aspect of the problem and its possible harmful consequences. He, therefore, decided that it was preferable to profane the Sabbath, in order to ensure the correct calendar and fixing of the holidays in future.

[275] We read in mTa'anit 1: 3: בשלשה במרחשון שואלין את הגשמים רבן גמליאל אומר בשבעה בו חמשה עשר יום אחר החג "On the third day of the month of Marheshvan one starts to recite the prayer for rain. Rabban Gamaliel says: On the seventh [of the month], that is fifteen days after the last day of the Feast of Tabernacles." While the mishnah discloses the reason for Rabban Gamaliel's rule, it does not reveal the motive behind the anonymous conflicting dictum. A close analysis of this dispute reveals the subtle distinctions in the philosophical foundations of the contenders. The B. T. does not elaborate on the dispute in this mishnah, except to quote an amoraic declaration that the halakhah is according to Rabban Gamaliel (bTa'anit 4b). In yTa'anit 1: 3, 64a, on the other hand, an investigation is attempted. It is assumed that the anonymous dictum corresponds to the opinion of Rabbi Meir, who says: הבכירה בשלשה והבינונית בשבעה והאפילה בשבעה עשר "The first rain starts on the third [day of the month], the middle one on the seventh and the late one on the seventeenth." There follows an amoraic declaration that the established halakhah is to start the prayer on the third of the month. This decision conflicts with that in the B. T. We observe that the approach of Rabban Gamaliel was of an entirely different nature than that of the anonymous Sage. He considered the welfare of the entire Israelite people, including the pilgrims from Babylon, as the first priority, while

the public welfare is evidenced in the following pronouncement, which I believe should be ascribed to Rabban Gamaliel, though it is usually attributed to Rabban Simeon ben Gamaliel.[276] The passage refers to a debate regarding the exercise of the death penalty, and the viewpoint, probably that of Rabban Gamaliel, that one must employ it to avoid an increase in the number of murderers.[277] Thus his decision to establish a unified halakhah also had the purpose of ensuring an efficient and coherent internal administration. Standardized applications of rules would avoid the incitement of agitation and tension in society and sentiments of flawed or even unfair justice, especially with respect to financially sensitive issues.

4.2.2.2 The Reaction of the Sages to Rabban Gamaliel's "Reform"

I believe the above passages substantiate the attempt of Rabban Gamaliel to establish a unified halakhic system, in contrast to the autonomy and unrestricted liberty of the Sages before 70 to decide

---

Rabbi Meir (the anonymous Sage of the mishnah) regarded the start of the rains as the most significant event requiring the initiation of the prayer for rain. The talmudic maxim רבי... לשיטתו ורבי... לשטתו "Rabbi X made his declaration according to his principle, and Rabbi Y according to his principle" is certainly appropriate here. Rabban Gamaliel adhered to his principle, his responsibility for the entire people. We also observe, incidentally, the unfriendly attitude of the people of Judah toward the Jews of Babylon, nicknamed בבלאי טפשאי "the stupid Babylonians" in many occasions in the Talmud. The B. T. decided that the halakhah was according to Rabban Gamaliel, who concerned himself with pilgrims' welfare; the Y. T. ignored them and took the start of the rains as the priority.

276 At mMakkot 1: 10, another narrative in which Rabbi Yehoshua and Rabban Simeon ben Gamaliel are mentioned, the מסורת הש"ס suggests changing the text to read "Rabban Gamaliel."

277 We read in mMakkot 1: 10: רבי טרפון ורבי עקיבא אומרים אילו היינו בסנהדרין לא נהרג אדם מעולם רבן שמעון בן גמליאל אומר אף הן מרבין שופכי דמים בישראל "Rabbi Tarfon and Rabbi Aqiba say: If we were [members of] the Sanhedrin, no-one would ever be executed. Rabban Simeon ben Gamaliel says: But they would have increased the number of murderers in Israel." This discussion is supposed to have taken place between Rabban Simeon ben Gamaliel and Rabbi Aqiba and Rabbi Tarfon. This could be neither Rabban Simeon ben Gamaliel the First nor the Second, because the two contenders were not contemporaries of either one, but of Rabban Gamaliel. There are no recorded disputes and debates between Rabbi Aqiba or Rabbi Tarfon and Rabban Simeon ben Gamaliel, but we encounter numerous such occurrences between Rabbi Aqiba and Rabbi Gamaliel. The discussion as such is theoretical, since at that period, the Jewish courts likely had no jurisdiction to impose capital punishment (see above n. 70).

halakhah according to their personal convictions.[278] We may now examine the reaction of the Sages to this profound change.

We may note again the baraita in yBerakhot 4: 1, 7d, and bBerakhot 28a (cited above)[279] describing Rabban Gamaliel's removal as head of the Academy. The vehement opposition of the Sages to the Patriarch's leadership and to his determination to impose his views,[280] which induced his dismissal,[281] is evident from the narrative. The complaint concerning prior clashes with him,[282] revealed in the course of the Sages'

---

278 E. E. Urbach, "Class-Status and Leadership in the World of the Palestinian Sages," writes on p. 58 that the clashes between Rabban Gamaliel and the Sages "testify to the intensification of the conflict between divergent principles: the freedom of halakhic decision against the claim on the part of the Patriarch to the right of supervision and organization, that is, the concept of the Patriarch's jurisdiction as national leader." We observe that Urbach does not question Gamaliel's status as Patriarch.

279 I have cited the narrative from the B. T., as it contains certain details absent in the Y. T. version. Since the authenticity of the details of the story in both sources is doubtful, as I shall argue, the Y. T. is not, in this case, a more reliable source than the B. T.

280 It is recorded in mRosh HaShanah 2: 9 that Rabbi Yehoshua was definitely aware, on the basis of factual evidence, that Rabban Gamaliel erred in his fixing of the day of the new moon. The Day of Atonement according to Rabbi Yehoshua would not be a holiday according to Rabban Gamaliel's decision, and he insisted that Rabbi Yehoshua accept his decision: שלח לו רבן גמליאל גוזרני עליך שתבא אצלי במקלך ובמעותיך ביום הכפורים שחל להיות בחשבונך "He sent him a command: You must come to me, with your cane and money, on the Day of Atonement that is according to your assessment [to demonstrate that you profane it, and accept the day fixed by my court's decision]." See also chap. 1, n. 65.

281 The ousting of Rabban Gamaliel is discussed at more length in nn. 282-3, 285, and 300.

282 We read in yBerakhot 4: 1, 7c, yTa′ anit 4: 1, 67d, and, with one slightly different detail, in bBerakhot 27b and bBekhorot 36a that Rabban Gamaliel punished and insulted Rabbi Yehoshua, after a discussion regarding a halakhic dispute between them: והיה רבן גמליאל יושב ודורש ורבי יהושי עומד על רגליו עד שרינגו כל העם ואמרו לרי חצפית התורגמן הפטר את העם "Rabban Gamaliel was sitting and lecturing and Rabbi Yehoshua was standing on his feet [all that time] until all the people muttered and said to Hutzpit the translator: Discharge the people [close the session]." The Y.T and B.T versions then diverge. In the Y. T. we read: כי על מי לא עברה רעתך תמיד הלכו ומינו את רבי אלעזר בן עזריה בישיבה "Who has not suffered from your continuous viciousness! And they nominated Rabbi Eleazar [to the head of] the Yeshiva." In the B. T. version, the Sages state: בראש השנה אשתקד צעריה בבכורות במעשה דרבי צדוק צעריה הכא נמי צעריה תא ונעבריה "Last year, he annoyed him [Rabbi Yehoshua] with the fixing of the New Year [see n. 280], then he chastised him at the incident of Rabbi Tzadoq [a narrative in bBekhorot 36a describes the same kind of penalty imposed by Rabban Gamaliel on Rabbi Yehoshua]; here too he castigated him; let's dismiss him." See also text at n. 289 on this narrative.

deliberations, also indicates the continuing struggle between the Sages[283] and the Patriarch. Alon[284] and other scholars[285] portray this situation as a

[283] Although the narratives concerning Rabban Gamaliel's dismissal refer to an incident between Rabbi Yehoshua and Rabban Gamalilel, we must assume that the stories represent a constant struggle by the entire body of Sages against Rabban Gamaliel's manner of imposing his opinions and his personal authority. The repetition of three identical incidents and the same castigation of Rabbi Yehoshua does not vouch for their absolute authenticity, but rather conveys the idea of a constant conflict and its ultimate climax that caused Rabban Gamaliel's dismissal. The narrative indicates that this grave decision was taken unanimously, and that both Rabbi Yehoshua and Rabbi Aqiba were considered as replacements. For various reasons, Rabbi Eleazar ben Azaryah was chosen; it seems that none of them would have declined the offer to replace Rabban Gamaliel. Hence, we observe the opposition of the entire body to Rabban Gamaliel. G. Alon, *The Jews*, vol. 1, p. 318 writes: "A close look at the story reveals that what it describes was actually a confrontation between the Patriarch and the Sanhedrin." For modern scholarly views on the reliability of the terms "Sanhedrin" and "Patriarch" and the scope of their functions and authority, see section 3.6 and the Excursus in this chapter, "The Title and Authority of the Patriarch (Nasi) and the President of the Academy/Court (Av Beit Din)."

[284] G. Alon, *The Jews*, vol. 1, pp. 308 ff.

[285] Robert Goldenberg, "The Deposition of Rabban Gamaliel II," writes in his conclusion, p. 190: "Some serious disturbance interrupted the period of Gamaliel's leadership...it is highly plausible that an intense power struggle should have revolved around these three men [Gamaliel, Eleazar and Yehoshua]." I do not intend to comment on this statement, but I would like to express my doubts about another of his declarations. Goldenberg perceives "one major difference" between the Y. T. and B. T. versions (p. 175): according to the Y. T., the political aspect is the root of the struggle, whereas in the B. T., it is deemed a personal dispute, and Yehoshua's honour is the sole motive for Gamaliel's removal. While it is true that the general style of the Y. T. narrative tends to this outlook, I doubt whether these differences really indicate a motivation by the redactor of the B. T. narrative to change certain relevant details of the Y.T. text in order to exhibit Rabban Gamaliel in a better light (p. 189). As matters stand, the authenticity of the details of the narrative are more than dubious; they are not coherent, and many versions may have been in circulation, as Goldenberg also notes. Considering its entire context, the Babylonian version does not, in my opinion, reflect only a personal struggle. It is obvious that the redactor, or even the tradents of the narrative, attempted to conceal the true motive behind the leader's demotion, which was an extremely grave, exceptional, and almost inconceivable act in the social environment of the rabbinic world. As I have argued above (n. 282), the alleged behaviour of Yehoshua that caused his "punishment" by Gamaliel is devoid of any sensible rationale. The deliberation of the Sages in the B. T., missing in the Y. T., indicates their judgment of Gamaliel's character and demeanor. They were afraid that he would punish Rabbi Aqiba, if the latter replaced him; they decided to appoint Rabbi Eleazar, simply because they assumed Gamaliel would not dare to punish him. The dramatic increase in the number of students also indicates their opposition to Gamaliel's exclusive practices. Yehoshua's acerbic accusation, regarding Gamaliel's insensitivity to the plight of the Sages, is similarly a grave censure, implying that he did not fulfill his duties. The last episode, recording the hesitation about whom to send to inform the Sages, and their reluctance to open the door to the messenger in order to prevent harassment by Rabban Gamaliel's servants, unmistakably indicates the opposition of all the Sages to Gamaliel's

conflict between an autocratic leader who, as the bearer of authority, attempted to centralize all power in his hands, and the Sages, who believed that halakhic authority was grounded in the entire assembly. I do not deny that such circumstances could have been (or even actually were) in effect during Rabban Gamaliel's Patriarchate. Similar conditions pertain in every society to differing degrees and with varying outcomes depending on the personalities involved; thus, such a conflict probably was a factor in the clash between the Patriarchs and the Sages. In our case, however, I think that the ideological conflict between the Patriarch and the assembly of Sages contributed to a great extent to the severity of the clash. Rabban Gamaliel wished to impose one halakhic system, curtailing the authority of the Sages to decide and judge independently. In both versions of the narrative in the Y.T. and B. T., the conflict originates in a halakhic question regarding the integration into the community of an Ammonite convert. In the B.T version, a halakhic decision leads to a judgment:[286] "Immediately they permitted him to join the [Israelite] community." The Y. T. version does not mention this *finale*, but tYadayim 2: 18 does record the acceptance. The Sages perceived this as an attempt to control their minds and judgments, a situation that they opposed.

In contrast, the Sages did not oppose the administrative prerogatives of judges and courts.[287] I have noted above that three grave altercations between Rabban Gamaliel and Rabbi Yehoshua, the speaker of the Sages,

conduct. Thus I do not see that Rabban Gamaliel is more positively portrayed in the B. T. version; I do agree, however, that as with every literary analysis, different opinions may subsist side by side. See further chap. 1, n. 65, as well as Introduction, n. 29 regarding my preference for the B. T. version of this narrative.

[286] We read in mYadayim 4: 4: בו ביום בא יהודה גר עמוני ועמד לפניהן בבית המדרש אמר להם מה אני לבא בקהל "On the same day [after having put the same question previously, in private, to Rabban Gamaliel and Rabbi Yehoshua], Yehudah, a converted Ammonite, came and, standing before them [the Sages] in the academy, asked: Can I be integrated into the community [of Israel]?" The judgment came after Rabban Gamaliel's dismissal, according to the B. T. version. In mYadayim 4: 4, there is no mention of Rabban Gamaliel's dismissal. The mishnah records the dispute and discussions between the contenders, and finally the successful opinion: התירוהו לבא בקהל "they allowed him to be integrated into the community," without any further details of the course of events.

[287] Alon himself perceives the more general aspect of this struggle, unconnected to the particular collision between the assembly of the Sages and the Patriarch: "the full right of the individual Sage to give guidance, on the one hand; and the requirements of good order and centralized authority on the other" (*The Jews*, vol. 1, pp. 308-9). See mRosh HaShanah 2: 9, which declares that whatever Rabban Gamaliel's court has done is done, and delivers a comprehensive rule that every court of three appointed judges is equal to the court of Moses (citations quoted in Introduction, n. 84, chap. 3, end of section 3.2, and n. 293 below). It is interesting to note that Rabbi Aqiba, who took an active part in the deposing of Rabban Gamaliel, made the first statement confirming his decision.

were cited in the decision to dismiss Rabban Gamaliel (yBerakhot 4: 1 7c, yTa'anit 4: 1, 67d, and bBerakhot 27b).[288] Yet we observe differences in the Sages' attitude regarding these three occurrences. In bBekhorot 36a, in which Rabbi Tzadoq relied on Rabbi Yehoshua for an exemption regarding a wounded animal and was contradicted by Rabban Gamaliel, there is no indication of the result; we do not know whether the halakhah was established according to Rabbi Yehoshua or to Rabban Gamaliel.[289] In bBerakhot 28a,[290] regarding the Ammonite's conversion, the assembly decided against Rabban Gamaliel's opinion and rendered judgment, as noted above.[291] In the Rosh HaShanah narrative,[292] regarding Rabban Gamaliel's order to Rabbi Yehoshua to profane what was for him the Day of Atonement, the Sages[293] advised Rabbi Yehoshua to obey the

---

288 The Y. T. versions of this narrative in Berakhot and Ta'anit record only the dispute about the obligation for the evening prayer. I have therefore used the more extended B. T. version, which allows a wider consideration of the various aspects of the narrative.

289 The issue refers to a blemish that occurred to a first-born animal, and one suspects that the owner might have caused it intentionally to allow it to be slaughtered, for his financial advantage. The question arose with respect to an accident to an animal belonging to Rabbi Tzadoq himself. Rabbi Yehoshua believed that different treatment should be reserved for this case, since a Sage is not suspected of having done something wicked. Rabban Gamaliel decided that there should be equal treatment for all; this again offers evidence of Rabban Gamaliel's desire to avoid distinctions in law between different classes. The traditional commentators such as Maimonides and Tosafot maintain that the halakhah follows Rabban Gamaliel.

290 Tosefta at Yadayim 2: 18 records the acceptance, but only in connection with an inquiry unrelated to Rabban Gamaliel's dismissal.

291 Although this decision does not appear in the Y. T. versions, it is recorded in mYadayim 4: 4 with the same wording. In tYadayim 2: 17, the dispute between Rabbi Yehoshua and Rabban Gamaliel is recorded, but not the outcome.

292 See chap. 1, text at nn. 65 ff.

293 Both Rabbi Aqiba and Dosa ben Arhinos, the senior Tanna of the first generation, gave him this advice. We read in mRosh HaShanah 2: 9 that Rabbi Aqiba said: יש לי ללמוד שכל מה שעשה רבן גמליאל עשוי "I have to learn that whatever Rabban Gamaliel has done is done." Dosa, who emphasized that the witnesses accepted by Rabban Gamaliel were עדי שקר הן "false witnesses," went further and stated: אם באין אנו לדון אחר בית דינו של רבן גמליאל צריכין אנו לדון אחר כל בית דין ובית דין שעמד מימות משה ועד עבשיו "If we question the legitimacy of Rabban Gamaliel's court, we would likewise have to question all [the decisions pronounced] by every court from Moses until now." Hence one has to accept the court's decisions. One may deduce from Rabbi Aqiba's scriptural support that his acceptance of the court's decision is limited to the fixing of the calendar and the dates of the holidays, as a traditional commentator suggests (see n. 295). It could also be perceived as simply Rabbi Aqiba's common practice of finding biblical support for every decision, and we must not consider it as a limitation of the validity of judicial decisions. His concept would then be equivalent in its consequences to Rabbi Dosa's

Patriarch's command and accept his decision. Analysis of these three occurrences indicates a difference in attitude with respect to the last incident; the distinction in that case was that it was the court that decided the calendar issue. In that case, the Sages respected the decision of the court as a *fait accompli*,[294] even when they were convinced of its erroneous judgment.[295] The rationales of the Tannaim presented to Rabbi Yehoshua clearly reveal their belief in the absolute necessity of endorsing a court's decision, in order to maintain the integrity of the legal system.[296] In contrast, the other two issues were still in stages of discussion within the Academy. We may also perceive an attitude of compromise on the part of the Sages, a *modus vivendi* we have also noted in other instances. Further, the issue cited in Bekhorot substantiates Rabban Gamaliel's

---

opinion, but declared in a different manner, a common practice in rabbinic deliberations. Scholars attempt to assess from this narrative whether Rabban Gamaliel's authority was limited to the calendar issue. This topic, as I have indicated, is beyond the scope of this study.

[294] See E. E. Urbach, "Class-Status and Leadership in the World of the Palestinian Sages," p. 59.

[295] This account of Rabbi Yehoshua's desecration of the Day of Atonement (as he judged it to be) apparently conflicts with the dictum in mHorayot 1: 1: הורו בית דין וידע אחד מהן שטעו או תלמיד והוא ראוי להוראה והלך ועשה על פיהן.. . הרי זה חייב מפני שלא תלה בבית דין "If the court delivered a decision and one of them [the judges], or a disciple capable of delivering a decision, knew that they erred, and nevertheless acted according to the [erroneous] decision ...he is liable for a sin offering because he did not rely on the court." This justification is on its face illogical, since the individual relied on the court's decision. The traditional commentators, however, as well as the Gemara at yHorayot 1: 1, 45d, and bHorayot 2b, explain that the individual erred by incorrectly interpreting the decree to abide by the Sages' decisions, even when they were patently wrong. In our case, Rabbi Yehoshua was induced to desecrate the Day of Atonement despite his absolute conviction that the court's decision was wrong. Inconsistencies in the rabbinic legal corpus are not uncommon, as argued earlier, and it seems that this is one of those occurrences. It is also plausible that the exception in this specific case was due to the particular significance of the calendar, and the necessity for fixed dates for holidays. In fact, one of the traditional commentators emphasizes Rabbi Aqiba's justification by an interpretation of Lev 23: 4: אלה מועדי ה' מקראי קודש אשר תקראו אתם בין בזמנן בין שלא בזמנן "'These are the Lord's appointed feasts, the sacred assemblies you are to declare' - whether at their correct time or at their incorrect time." Rabbi Aqiba would accept an incorrect court decision only with respect to a calendar issue, whereas Rabbi Dosa would not attempt to repeal any previous court decision. See further the discussion in n. 293.

[296] This resolution was a compromise between, on the one hand, the autonomy of each Sage to interpret the law according to his best understanding, limited by the admission that there is no absolute truth in any human's conception, and, on the other hand, the vital necessity to reach decisions. The court's decisions were accepted for pragmatic reasons, without deducing from this any indication that one opinion was more correct than another.

policy of standardization and inclusiveness. Rabbi Yehoshua maintained: "We discriminated between a Sage and an illiterate person," while Rabban Gamaliel upheld the opposite, faithful to his primary goal of avoiding divisions among the people.

We must also examine the role of Rabban Gamaliel in the excommunication of Rabbi Eliezer. I have already mentioned[297] the "oven of Akhnai" incident, and the excommunication of Rabbi Eliezer due to his reluctance to accept the majority decision in matters of halakhah and his persistence in his own opinion. The record of the event portrays a debate between Rabbi Eliezer and a number of unidentified Sages. Various expressions are used: "they did not accept his opinion," "he said to them," and "they said to him." At a later stage, after the court's verdict of pollution, Rabbi Yehoshua becomes the speaker, disputing with heaven, not with Rabbi Eliezer. The decision to excommunicate Rabbi Eliezer was taken by majority vote: "and they voted and excommunicated him,"[298] and Rabbi Aqiba offered to perform the disagreeable task of informing him of this dreadful sentence. Rabban Gamaliel the Patriarch is not mentioned at all in the course of events, and from the narrative it seems that he was not even present in Yabneh at that time; he was on a boat trip on the high seas. The narrative continues: "[Rabbi Eliezer's great anger is reported, as well as the dire consequences that were to befall anyone who came into his sight]. And even as Rabban Gamaliel boarded the boat, and a great wave came up to drown him, he said: It seems that this [punishment] came upon me because of [what happened with] Rabbi Eliezer ben Hyrcanos." We observe that although Rabban Gamaliel was not even present at the debate and the excommunication, he was considered responsible for Rabbi Eliezer's torment, because he instituted the mandate to impose a single halakhic system.

---

[297] See Introduction, text at nn. 31 ff., and chap. 1, text at nn. 58 ff..

[298] G. Alon, *The Jews*, Vol. 2, pp. 467 ff. contemplates that the issue of the right of the individual to oppose the decision of the majority was at the core of the contention. He assumes that the voting on a disputed issue, expressed in the rabbinic literature with the phrase נמנו וגמרו, was the turning point, after which the individual had to accept the majority's decision. Rabbi Eliezer refused to accept the majority decision after the vote, and was therefore excommunicated. My thesis is, to all intents and purposes, the same as Alon's theory but we differ with respect to the crucial issue of whether a court decision or a vote constituted the determining factor in imposing a rule against the opinion of an individual Sage, commanding his obedience. I believe that the text indicates that the vote was taken for Rabbi Eliezer's excommunication. Alon quotes the phrase נמנו וגמרו "they voted and decided the halakhah," terminology used with respect to an abstract decision on a disputed halakhah; but our text clearly affirms: ונמנו עליו וברכוהו "and they voted and excommunicated him," emphasizing that the vote referred to the excommunication, not to the question of establishing the correct halakhah.

Most significant in this narrative is Rabban Gamaliel's "confessional" utterance, declared in a moment of awe and anxiety, when he was in fear for his life. His supplication to God at that dramatic moment offers us a clue to his philosophy and the justification for his deeds: "He stood up on his feet and said: Master of the World, it is manifest to you that I have not done this for the sake of my honour or the honour of my family; I have done this for the sake of Your honour, to prevent the growth of conflicts in Israel." The last words of his plea make evident what he has "done": the prevention of conflicts, that is, the imposition of a single halakhic codex. Further analysis of this utterance enables us to elaborate upon his goal. He did not indicate that his purpose was to avoid conflicts between the Sages. Such disputes would not insult the divine honour; we read in mAvot 5: 17 that a conflict between Sages is a conflict for the sake of heaven, and is praiseworthy.[299] His intention was to avoid conflicts between the Israelites in general - that is, a situation in which the towns or provinces of the Diaspora would come to observe disparate customs and rules, each following the decisions of the local Sages. Such a situation would, as we know from historical evidence, engender severe friction and division among the Israelite people. Such a phenomenon would be injurious to God's honour, because the divine Torah revealed to the Israelites would be the cause of strife and hostility, not of peace and harmony. The story continues: נח הים מזעפו "[God accepted Rabban Gamaliel's defence, and] the sea calmed its fury."

Rabbi Eliezer was also aware that it was only Rabban Gamaliel who was ultimately culpable. He did not retain any resentment against the Sages who voted for his excommunication, nor against Rabbi Aqiba, the bearer of that horrible sentence; he did, however, maintain uncontrolled rage against Rabban Gamaliel. The narrative relates that Rabban Gamaliel's sister was Rabbi Eliezer's wife, and she prevented him from prostrating himself for a certain prayer, knowing that the consequence might be the death of her brother. Through an unexpected occurrence, she did not succeed, and Rabban Gamaliel died instantly.

299 We read there: כל מחלוקת שהיא לשם שמים סופה להתקיים ושאינה לשם שמים אין סופה להתקיים איזו היא מחלוקת שהוא לשם שמים זו מחלוקת הלל ושמאי ושאינה לשם שמים זו מחלוקת קרח וכל עדתו "Every controversy that is for the sake of heaven [that has at its core a pious issue] will ultimately subsist, but a controversy that does not have a pious purpose will not subsist. [This declaration is somewhat odd, as it suggests approval of conflicts; commentators have attempted various interpretations in order to adapt this pronouncement to their own philosophical backgrounds. It is not within the scope of our study to elaborate on the different opinions; for our purpose, it suffices to emphasize the second part of the declaration.] What is a controversy for the sake of heaven? That is the controversy between Hillel and Shammai. [What is a controversy] not for the sake of heaven? The controversy of Korah and his group." We observe that the halakhic controversies between Hillel and Shammai are highly valued and praised.

The real motive behind this dramatic narrative and the alleged steps leading to Eliezer's excommunication and Gamaliel's supernatural death are more than questionable,[300] but it is obvious that the narrative had a

---

[300] The fact that the identical narrative detailing the same harsh confrontation between Rabban Gamaliel and Rabbi Yehoshua is recorded with respect to three separate issues, is in itself peculiar. Moreover, from the simple understanding of the story one would perceive that Rabbi Yehoshua did not tell the truth, to express it mildly, on three occasions. We read that Rabban Gamaliel came to the academy, after the person who asked the question regarding the evening prayer received opposing answers from Rabbi Yehoshua and Rabban Gamaliel, and stated that Rabbi Yehoshua opposed him: עמד השואל ושאל תפלת ערבית רשות או חובה אמר לו רבן גמליאל חובה אמר להם רבן גמליאל לחכמים כלום יש אדם שחולק בדבר זה אמר ליה רבי יהושע לאו אמר לו והלא משמך אמרו לי רשות אמר ליה יהושע עמוד על רגליך ויעידו בך "The inquirer [the person who asked the question of both Sages] stood and asked: Is the evening prayer a voluntary or an obligatory prayer? Rabban Gamaliel answered: It is an obligatory prayer. Rabban Gamaliel said to the Sages: Is there anyone who disputes this [my declaration that the evening prayer is an obligatory prayer]? Rabbi Yehoshua said: No! Then [Rabban Gamaliel] said to him: [How is that], since I have been told that you said: It is a voluntary prayer? [And] he said to him: Yehoshua, stand up, and testimony will be given against you [that you said otherwise]." The narrative continues that only after an imposed confrontation with the person to whom Rabbi Yehoshua had said that it was a voluntary prayer, did he retract his prior statement. The narrative raises a host of inexplicable questions. First, it is not reasonable to assume that Rabbi Yehoshua attempted to lie. But even if we do so assume, it would have been illogical for him to give a false declaration in front of the witness, who would certainly contradict him. He certainly also was aware of the talmudic axiom: כל מילתא דעבידא לאיגלויי לא משקרי בה אינשי "Men do not lie about things that will become known [bBekhorot 36a]."(I did not find such an explicit statement in the Y.T. In yRosh HaShanah 2: 1, 57d, we find: שנייא היא הכא שאין את יכול לעמוד עליו. This seems out of context, and is corrected by the commentators to read: שנייא היא הכא שאת יכול לעמוד "Here it is different [and one accepts the testimony of one witness] because it is possible to verify it [soon afterwards]," and therefore one would not give false information.) Another oddity is that despite his bad experience the first time, Rabbi Yehoshua repeated the same absurd behaviour twice more. Further, if he had acted in such a dishonest way, such outrageous comportment would have justified Rabban Gamaliel's harsh conduct, and not his dismissal. Rashi was aware of the problem regarding the appearance that Rabbi Yehoshua lied; indicating his astonishment, he explains in his commentary in bBekhorot 36a that Rabbi Yehoshua actually said (though it is not mentioned explicitly): "Nobody maintains differently, because I [Rabbi Yehoshua] have now changed my mind and agree with Rabban Gamaliel." This is a very far-fetched solution, and is not accepted even by the traditional Tosafot commentary.
I have chosen for my analysis the B. T. version of this narrative, as it is the more elaborate, thus enabling more extensive speculation on many aspects. In the Excursus "The Title and Authority of the Patriarch (Nasi) and the President of the Academy (Av Beit Din)," I have discussed the differences between the B.T. and Y. T. versions and mentioned scholarly views on the authenticity of the narratives. In my opinion, consistent with the general consensus, we must accept the kernel of truth revealed in the story, with respect to Rabban Gamaliel's actions to impose his opinion on the

strong message to convey regarding the establishment of a unitary system against the will and resolution of individual Sages. Rabban Gamaliel's objective was in stark opposition to the maxim "Both [conflicting declarations] are the words of the living God." It is possibly not by chance that the homily in bHagigah 4b that defends, or even praises, the growth of different and opposing halakhic decisions is recorded as having been declared by Rabbi Eleazar ben Azaryah;[301] the latter was nominated to the head of the Academy after the deposing of Rabban Gamaliel because of his quarrel with Rabbi Yeshoshua. As we have seen, this incident was triggered by a decision of Rabbi Yeshoshua that conflicted with a halakhic statement of Rabban Gamaliel. We observe that Rabban Gamaliel's resentment was personal - provoked by the fact of confrontation rather than by any concern that the halakhah was incorrect. It appears that Rabban Gamaliel desired this public confrontation with Rabbi Yehoshua, to make his point and demonstrate his authority to fix a unitary halakhah. This is confirmed by the text in yBerakhot; Rabban Gamalilel inspired the disciple to come into the Academy the next day and pose his question, being eager to confront the opposing opinion. It is possible that Rabbi Yehoshua attempted to avoid this public confrontation, and therefore denied his previous decision - a bizarre situation, as I noted above. The B. T. version is yet more emphatic regarding Rabban Gamaliel's attitude. He is recorded as saying to the disciple: "Wait until the next morning [and we shall see who dares to contradict me]." Both versions indicate that Rabban Gamaliel expected no opposition to his provocative question: "Is there anybody who opposes this decision"? Rabbi Eliezer and Aqabyah ben Mahalalel[302] may have been the only renowned Sages tenacious enough to

---

Sages of the academy. I conjecture that this "kernel" had to do with the fixing of a single halakhic system. We observe that the narrative of Rabban Gamaliel's death is related to his opposition to Rabbi Eliezer's objections to a unified halakhah. I have also deduced this assumption from my analysis of the scope of Mishnah tractate Eduyyot, as argued in section 4.1.2, and this conclusion is also linked to this narrative. See J. Neusner, *Biography*, pp. 121 ff., who scrutinizes this narrative under the heading "The Eliezer of Legend." Neusner deduces various concealed motives behind the composition, but similarly concludes (p. 127): "[The probability] that any of these materials goes back to events in Eliezer's own life seems to me unlikely."

301 We read there: שמא יאמר אדם היאך אני למד תורה מעתה תלמוד לומר כולם נתנו מרעה אחד אל אחד נתנן "Lest someone say: How can I now learn Torah [if certain Sages render decisions that conflict with others], [the homily] comes to teach us that all [opinions] were given by one shepherd, one God gave them." The passage goes on: אף אתה עשה אזניך כאפרכסת וקנה לך לב מבין לשמוע את דברי מטמאים ואת דברי מטהרים "Make your ear like the hopper [to receive all the teachings] and prepare your heart to listen to the decisions of the ones who declared [something] polluted and those who declared it pure" - that is, listen to all conflicting decisions, which are all God-given.

302 See citations in nn. 131-3.

continue their opposition to the bitter end, but many others mitigated their strong opposition and compromised on a *modus vivendi* that I shall delineate later on. Others may have been convinced of the correctness of Rabban Gamaliel's view, at least in specific instances.

J. Rubenstein,[303] who has extensively examined the Akhnai narrative to extrapolate its cultural context, also utilizes the B. T. text, with all its additions and embellishments that are absent in the other rabbinic sources. He disapproves of those scholarly approaches that interpret only the first part of the narrative, and alleges that such a method "runs the risk of misinterpretation." Although he investigates the narrative in its entirety, as I did, and reaches generally similar conclusions (pertinent to his goal), I would like to mention certain points on which we differ.

Rubenstein wonders why Rabbi Eliezer was so severely punished, and the reason for burning (apparently in public) the objects he had declared pure. My interpretation of the narrative, associated with my postulate regarding the introduction of a new and revolutionary halakhic system, offers a plausible explanation for these apparently eccentric actions. After the divine intervention in the Academy, which related to the discussion stage, the matter at issue still remained undecided. A hint of this circumstance can be deduced from the fanciful suggestion that the walls did not fall because of the honour of Rabbi Yehoshua, and did not return to their upright position because of the honour of Rabbi Eliezer. The literary style of the narrative,[304] and its chronological sequence, indicate that the miraculous events occurred before the court's final decision. Rabbi Eliezer and the Sages, apparently acknowledging Rabbi Yehoshua's sweeping pronouncement denying God's interference in the interpretation of the Torah, remained adamant in their views. It seems that only subsequent to the divine admission of defeat did an official court decision take place. We read at the beginning of the relevant narrative in bBava Metzi'a 59b: "What was the story of Akhnai? [Or, what does the term Akhnai mean?] Rav Yehudah said in the name of Samuel: They twisted arguments around [the oven] and polluted it."[305] The latter expression

303 *Talmudic Stories*, pp. 34 ff.

304 The verbs used in the narratives, מטהר and מטמאין, are present participles, and indicate a theoretical discussion, not a record of what had already happened. A debate and an attempt to convince usually precede a court's decision.

305 When one examines the literary style of the other records of this event, in mKelim 5: 10, and particularly tEduyyot 2: 1, which states: שעליו רבו מחלוקות בישראל "...an event on which many disputes occurred in Israel," it is clear that they refer to a dispute. Only later, after the debates and the divine intervention, which revolved around the question "what is the correct halakhah," did the Sages render judgment. They declared polluted the sacred matter that Rabbi Eliezer had declared pure, and burned it, as we read in the Y. T. version (Mo'ed Qatan, 3: 1, 81d): לא הקפיד אלא על ידי ששרפו טהרותיו בפניו "Rabbi Eliezer was not angry until they burned the

conveys the idea of a judicial verdict. This fact is, incomprehensibly, not mentioned in the narrative in its chronological order, but rather at the beginning of the narrative, in opposition to Rabbi Eliezer's judgment in his court; to demonstrate the finality of this decision, Rabbi Eliezer's objects were burned. The burning and the subsequent[306] excommunication occurred because he persisted in his judgments,[307] not because he persisted in his opinions; this is similar to the rule of the "rebellious elder," who was allowed to teach but not to deliver judgment according to his opinion.

Rabbi Eliezer's action constituted a challenge to the system. This was not a case of a halakhic dispute; disputes abound in all rabbinic literature and were legitimate. The reference to the incident in mKelim 5: 10 does not indicate any specific events leading up to this dispute, and gives the impression that it was simply a common halakhic discussion about a specific type of oven. It is only tEduyyot 2: 1 that adds: "with respect to which many disputes occurred." The Gemara no longer knows what the term "Akhnai" represents. The B. T. asks: "What is Akhnai?" and responds: "They surrounded him [Whom? Or perhaps this refers to the oven] with words like a snake."[308] This association with a snake is pure imagination; all B.T. versions of this passage read "Akhnai's oven," and the name in Y.T. appears as Hakhinai, a person's name, with no connection to a snake.[309]

My postulate offers a sensible explanation of these oddities. Like Rubenstein, I have questioned the threat against Rabban Gamaliel, who is not mentioned earlier in the narrative.[310] I have linked the plausible solution to my wider thesis, which is that Rabban Gamaliel's goal was the reform and imposition of a fixed halakhah. Rubenstein also assumes that Gamaliel "as Patriarch and leader, signifies rabbinic authority and bears primary responsibility for the ban," but I think that my proposition is more focused on Gamaliel's particular initiative regarding the halakhah and his responsibility for all its ensuing implications. Rubenstein postulates that the narrative "focuses on the tension between the legal process and human

---

matter that he had declared pure."

306 The passage states: אותו היום הביאו כל טהרות שטיהר רבי אליעזר ושרפום באש ונמנו עליו וברכוהו "On that day, they brought all the matters declared pure by Rabbi Eliezer and burned them, and voted and excommunicated him."

307 See previous note. The phrase כל טהרות שטיהר "all the matters that he declared pure," stands in juxtaposition to the Sages' judgment: וטמאוה "and they declared it [them] polluted."

308 The term עכינין for snakes appears in Yalqut Shimoni, *Ha'azinu* 945, and in the form עכנא in bBava Qamma 117b, bBava Metzi'a 84b, ySanhedrin 10: 2, 28d, and in various Midreshei Aggadah.

309 A Tanna named Hananyah b. Hakhinai is mentioned numerous times.

310 *Talmudic Stories*, p. 44; see my discussion above, text at n. 298.

feelings, emotion, dignity,"[311] whereas my interpretation tends in another direction, as suggested. It is obvious that both our assumptions rely on speculation, and there is no way to ascertain exactly what the authors of this complex narrative had in mind. I shall simply draw attention to Rubenstein's assertion that while God is concerned with the law He "cares more for the feelings of the creatures."[312] The divine intervention in the story occurs prior to the harsh treatment of Rabbi Eliezer, antecedent to the burning of the matters he had declared pure, and his excommunication. Rabbi Eliezer's ire and its grim consequences are not the work of God, but suggest instead magical powers; it thus seems to me that divine involvement in the teaching of compassionate behaviour is not evident in this narrative. In any event, both Rubenstein and I agree that the message of the narrative refers to issues regarding the legal process; we differ in its details.

The attempt to establish the halakhah according to Beit Hillel, and thus settle one of the leading disputes, must also be attributed to Rabban Gamaliel. We have noted the talmudic statement that a "Voice of Heaven" pronounced this resolution. Apart from the obvious fact that this decision by a human authority was disguised as divinely inspired, I have demonstrated the logical flaws of this and similar declarations, as well as their failure in practice. In his quest for the unity of the halakhah, Rabban Gamaliel attempted to put to rest this dispute, which had taken on serious proportions, as we can deduce from the descriptions of grim encounters between the two groups,[313] and the contrasting portrayals of an amicable relationship[314] that indicate attempts at reconciliation. Although this decision is not quoted explicitly as originating from Rabban Gamaliel, we must deduce that it was his initiative. There is evidence that this occurred at Yabneh, as we read in yYevamot 1: 6, 3b: "From where did the Voice of Heaven issue? Rabbi Bibi said in the name of Rabbi Yohanan: It issued from Yabneh." There is also ample evidence that Rabbi Yehoshua, the leading contender against Rabban Gamaliel, did not accept this decision: "And this [declaration] is according to Rabbi Yehoshua, who said: One does not obey the Voice of Heaven [bBerakhot 52a]."[315] Rabbi Yehoshua

[311] *Talmudic Stories*, p. 47.

[312] Ibid., p. 48.

[313] In the description of the eighteen edicts; see chap. 3, nn. 65-6 and related text.

[314] See, e.g., chap. 1, n. 55.

[315] Rabbi Yehoshua did not actually make this declaration. In the Akhnai narrative, the primary source for this pronouncement, Rabbi Yehoshua said only: לא בשמים היא "It [the Torah] is [no longer] in heaven" (yMo'ed Qatan 3: 1, 81d, and bBava Metzi'a 59b). It was Rabbi Yirmeyah who, in Babva Metzi'a, explained Rabbi Yehoshua's utterance and its consequence as follows: שכבר נתנה תורה מהר סיני אין אנו משגיחין בבת קול "Since the Torah was already given at Sinai, we do not have to

thus used the same fictional expression "Voice of Heaven" to pronounce his opposition to the imposition of a unified halakhah.

The Sages opposed this severe curtailing or entire annulment of their independence and freedom of decision, as we observe from Rabbi Yehoshua's protest. Many other talmudic passages indicate a similar reaction. The Y. T. in Mo'ed Qatan 3: 1, 81d, addressing the majority rule, contains a slightly different version of the Akhnai passage concerning Rabbi Eliezer ben Hyrcanos[316] cited above:[317] "Did not Rabbi Eliezer know the maxim that one must follow the majority [i.e. how can one explain his obstinacy in opposing this rule]? [Answer:] He disregarded it, until they burned [as polluted] the things he considered pure." This answer makes no sense, and the commentators have difficulty in explaining it. In my opinion, it indicates Rabbi Eliezer's opposition to having a halakhah imposed simply on the grounds that it was the majority decision. We have seen, in fact, that this attribution of a halakhah to a majority decision is in many cases purely fictional.[318] The subsequent narrative in the Y. T. gives an explicit indication of Rabbi Yehoshua's philosophy and explains his opposition to Rabban Gamaliel's scheme. Following the supernatural intervention of heaven to endorse the halakhah according to Rabbi Eliezer,[319] we read: "Rabbi Yehoshua said to them [the inclined walls]: If the Sages fight among themselves, it is not your business [to intervene]. And a Voice of Heaven came out and said: The halakhah is as my son Eliezer [declares]. Rabbi Yehoshua said: [The Torah] is [no longer] in heaven [and it is not within any one person's competence to fix the halakhah]." Rabbi Yehoshua rejected the existence of any prerogative to impose halakhah under the pretense of divine intervention or inspiration. It is obvious that we must accept Rabbi Yehoshua's declarations as revealing his fundamental ideas, though we may ignore the particulars of the narrative in which they are recorded; it is thus irrelevant whether they

abide by the Voice of Heaven." On the basis of this statement, there are a number of occurrences in the B. T. of the above statement alleging that Rabbi Yehoshua expressed himself in this manner. In other occurrences, as for example bEruvin 7a, the record is more precise, and we read: ורבי יהושע היא דלא משגח בבת קול "and [the declaration] is according to Rabbi Yehoshua, who does not abide by the Voice of Heaven."

316 In MS Leiden the name appears in yMo'ed Qatan 3: 1, 81d as אליעזר (ליעזר), though an insert has אלעזר; in B.T. it appears as אליעזר.

317 n. 305.

318 See especially section 3.1.

319 The Y. T. narrative is slightly different than that in the B. T; only the uprooting of the carob tree is mentioned in the discussion with Rabbi Eliezer. The bending of the walls as a result of Rabbi Eliezer's anger is recorded; the Voice of Heaven indicates the purpose of endorsing the halakhah according to Rabbi Eliezer.

were said to be declared in opposition to allegations of divine inspiration made by Rabban Gamaliel or by Rabbi Eliezer.

4.2.3 Later Development

We perceive the opposition of the Sages to Rabban Gamaliel's intention to establish a unitary halakhic system, and we have observed, in our earlier investigation, the long and intricate path necessary to accomplish this goal. The authorization to follow all the rulings (both lenient and severe) of either Beit Shammai or Beit Hillel[320] was extended in bEruvin 7a[321] to include conflicting halakhic decisions of the later Tannaim and even of the Amoraim. The development of fixed rules for the establishment of halakhic decisions was a slow process, stretching over hundreds of years.[322] Even Rabbi, with his exceptional authority,[323] did not fully succeed in accomplishing this scheme initiated by his great predecessor Rabban Gamaliel[324] at least one hundred years earlier; and the Amoraim still disputed halakhot in their day.[325] Even after the acceptance of a decision regarding a disputed halakhah, the result was not necessarily

---

320 See citation in chap. 1, text at n. 54.

321 We read there: ואיבעית אימא הכי קאמר כל היכא דמשכחת תרי תנאי ותרי אמוראי דפליגי אהדדי כעין מחלוקת בית שמאי ובית הלל לא ליעבד כי קוליה דמר וכי קוליה דמר ולא כחומריה דמר וכי חומריה דמר אלא או כי קוליה דמר וכחומריה עביד או כקוליה דמר וכחומריה עביד "Or, you may say, this is the correct interpretation of the dictum: Whenever one encounters a dispute between two Tannaim or two Amoraim, of a similar character as the disputes between Beit Shammai and Beit Hillel, you must not act according to the lenient or stringent decisions of both, but you must carry out both the lenient and stringent decisions of one or the other." Further, there is evidence that in the first amoraic period this "liberal" attitude was still preserved; there was no objection to conflicting customs in different towns. In Rab's district, Samuel did not impose his own opposing halakhah, and Rab did not impose his view in Samuel's community (bEruvin 94a; bHullin 53b; bPesahim 30a). One still honoured the opinion of one's opponent, perceiving as legitimate any practice based on his decision.

322 See section 3.3.

323 D. Goodblatt, *The Monarchic Principle*, p. 133, writes that Rabbi had a "king-like status," and, employing the alleged prerogatives of the idealized Sanhedrin, imposed his will and curtailed the independence of the Tannaim.

324 D. Goodblatt's point in *The Monarchic Principle*, p. 141 about the Patriarch's prerogative of exercising supreme judicial authority and imposing legal rules refers to later periods (end of the 3rd century and most of the 4th), as is evident from his citations.

325 See section 4.1.1. See also C. Hezser, *Social Structure*, pp. 240 - 251 ("Conflicts and Agreements"), regarding conflicting declarations in the Gemara with respect to pluralism, tolerance and opposing opinions.

the establishment of a fixed halakhah. Amoraim of the third generation still disputed whether a rule was fixed halakhah, and therefore to be obeyed, or whether it was simply a recommendation to decide in a particular way because it seemed more likely to be correct (see citation, p. 194). The precise limits of rabbinic authority, which was obviously a cornerstone of the Sages' influence, seem to have remained unsettled, and were the subject of deliberation and contention on the part of both Sages and commentators even in the Middle Ages and later.[326] This circumstance confirms the broad range of opinions that dominated the Sages' cultural and halakhic environment, and its pluralistic perspective. The above-cited dispute between Rabban Gamaliel and the Sages as to whether the evening prayer was obligatory or voluntary was still disputed between Abbaye and Raba,[327] in bBerakhot 27b: "Abbaye said the halakhah is according to the one [Tanna] who said [the evening prayer] is obligatory, and Raba said the halakhah is according to [the Tanna] who said it is a voluntary [prayer]." Rules regarding the resolution of disputes between these two Amoraim were only later established by Rav Ashi,[328] as we read in a dictum in his name in bBava Qamma 73a: "And the halakhah [in disputes between

---

[326] We may note on the one hand the passage in Sifre and Midrash Tannaim, cited in chap. 1, text at n.50: מנין שאם יאמר לך על שמאל שהיא ימין ועל ימין שהיא שמאל שמע לדבריהם ת״ל ככל אשר יורוך "How do we know that if he [the judge] tells you left is right and right is left, you must obey them [the priests and the Levites of the central courts]? Scripture states 'whatever they may instruct you.'" This dictum seems to demand absolute obedience to the courts even when it is evident that their decisions are wrong. The Y. T. at Horayot 1: 1, 45d, on the other hand, explicitly indicates the opposite: יכול אם יאמרו לך על ימין שהיא שמאל ועל שמאל שהיא ימין תשמע להם תלמוד לומר ללכת ימין ושמאל שיאמרו לך על ימין שהוא ימין ועל שמאל שהיא שמאל "Is it possible that if they [the judges] proclaim that right is left and left is right, you should [nevertheless] listen to them? [The biblical verse] teaches us that the obligation of obedience is only valid when they tell you that right is right and left is left." Mishnah Horayot 1: 1 declares implicitly its opposition to a court's unrestricted authority and to blind obedience: הורו בית דין וידע אחד מהן שטעו או תלמיד והוא ראוי להוראה והלך ועשה על פיהן בין שעשו ועשה עמהן בין שעשו ועשה אחריהן בין שלא עשו ועשה הרי זה חייב מפני שלא תלה בבית דין. This may be summarized as follows: If one knew that the court erred, he is liable if he followed the court's wrong decision. This declaration disagrees with the maxim in Sifre that one must obey the court even if it declares that right is left (that is, a manifestly incorrect decision), and concurs with the Y. T. dictum. See my discussion of the Y.T. provision in n. 295 above; for further details on this important issue and its later developments, see Z. Safrai and A. Sagi, סמכות, pp. 11 ff.

[327] Rabban Gamaliel lived at the turn of the second century C. E., and Abbaye and Raba were active in the first half of the fourth century C. E.

[328] Rav Ashi was active in the editing of the Babylonian Talmud, at the end of the fourth and in the first quarter of the fifth centuries.

Abbaye and Raba] is according to Abbaye, in [six disputes, which are summarized in an acronym, and according to Raba in all others]." As a further example, the dispute cited above as to whether the public reader absolves the rest of the people from their obligation to pray was also left in limbo for a long period. We read in bRosh HaShanah 34b: "Rabba bar bar Hana said in the name of Rabbi Yohanan: The Sages agreed to Rabban Gamaliel's statement, but Rab[329] said: It is still in dispute."[330]

We note the extended period, and the "changing of the guard" from the talmudic Sages to the Geonim, that were required for the accomplishment of Rabban Gamaliel's initiative. Such facts reflect the reluctance of the Sages to establish a unitary, fixed halakhah; it is otherwise difficult to provide a reasonable explanation for these odd phenomena.

---

[329] Both Amoraim were active in the third century C. E.

[330] A narrative dealing with this issue in yRosh HaShanah 4: 10, 59d also states in the name of Rabbi Yohanan that the halakhah is according to Rabban Gamaliel. A review of the narrative, however, leaves some doubt as to whether the halakhah was definitely established. In this case, it is possible that Rav Hisda offered his own prayer after listening to the prayer of the public reader because he had not initially intended to complete his obligation by listening to the reader, as is recorded in the Gemara; it is also possible that he was not sure of the correct halakhah, as there was not yet any definite decision on the matter.

Conclusion

I have portrayed in this study the methods of deliberation and exegesis utilized by the Sages to create the halakhah, according to their views and beliefs. Thanks to their intellectual flexibility, and to the unsystematic nature of their legal decision-making, they succeeded in bridging the apparently insurmountable theological gap between the immutable divine decrees and the necessity of adapting these decrees to changing circumstances. Based on my scrutiny and analysis of the relevant rabbinic citations, I believe that I have substantiated the main points of my postulate, as set out in the Introduction, and which may be summarized as follows:

Before 70, the entire legal process, in both its legislative and judicial aspects, was *ad hoc*. Each Sage rendered his decision according to his understanding[1] of the Torah and to the exigencies[2] of the moment. This period constituted the first developmental stage of the halakhah. The pluralism of the earlier period not only tolerated divergent decisions with respect to the interpretation of biblical precepts, but also permitted different practices.[3] There was no pressure for the establishment of one fixed halakhah, and similarly no coercion to fulfill rabbinic preventative edicts.[4] As validation of the above claim, I offered the example of Rabbi

---

1 A dictum in tEduyyot 1: 5 confirms that one Sage would decide halakhot contrary to another. See citation in chap. 4, text at n. 81.

2 I have quoted (chap. 4, n.4) the discussion between Yehudah ben Tabai and Simeon ben Shetah, who were active at the turn of the first century B. C. E, regarding their differences concerning the method of capital punishment (tSanhedrin 6: 6). Ben Tabai's justification for his unorthodox conviction was בשביל לעקור מליבן של ביתוסין "to contradict the opinion of the Boethusians." I have also cited certain extraordinary convictions of Simeon ben Shetah שהיתה השעה צריכה לכך "because it was required in the circumstances."

3 My postulate stands in antithesis to S.J.D. Cohen's assertion in "The Significance of Yavneh." See chap. 4, n. 77.

4 S. Safrai, *The Literature of the Sages*, p. 36, discussing the place and influence of oral Torah in Second Temple Jewish society, asserts that the oral Torah was not "a monolithic body of teachings - on the contrary, it allowed for a great deal of diversity. It allowed diversity and flexibility within the framework of generally accepted attitudes and concepts."

Yose ha-Gelili,[5] who did not accept the prohibition against eating fowl with milk, and induced the inhabitants of the town where he resided to follow his decision, without censure from other Sages.

Rabban Gamaliel initiated a reform with a view to establishing a system of fixed halakhah, that is, a unified codex. Mishnah tractate Eduyyot[6] attests to the formal inception of this process, which represents the second developmental stage of the halakhah. The Sages opposed this infringement upon their independence and aspired to maintain their unconstrained freedom of deliberation and decision.

We then observe a slow development in the direction delineated by Rabban Gamaliel, that is, a process, beginning with Rabbi, of establishing the correct halakhot as between contested opinions. This course of events culminated in the substantial curtailment of halakhic pluralism at the end of the rabbbinic era. This extended process constituted the third developmental stage.

The last stage encompassed various phases. The first phase began with Rabbi's composition of the Mishnah, and his attempt to influence the establishment of halakhah by his particular style of quoting his preference anonymously, or in the name of חכמים, "Sages." This greatly advanced the accomplishment of his forefather's vision. But this arduous task could be achieved only through a compromise between the interests and beliefs of the Sages and those of the Patriarchate, and the pursuit of a functional *modus vivendi* between the contesting parties. The paradoxical maxim that the halakhah is to be decided according to Beit Hillel, but at the same time all conflicting opinions are the words of the Living God, and thus are trustworthy and absolutely legitimate, was a suitable solution to this "Gordian knot."

This compromise created an atmosphere in which every Sage could express his opinion, and attempt to convince others of the correctness of his views. As we have seen,[7] the members of Beit Hillel were praised for their serious consideration of and respect for their opponents' statements, and we may assume that such an attitude characterized the debates in the academy.[8] An additional device, one that seems to me the most significant and decisive procedure in the direction of accommodation, was the preservation of all opinions in the same manner and with the same degree of reverence.[9] There is no explicit distinction in the Mishnah between the

---

5 Although this Tanna was active in the initial post-70 period, we may assume that he would not have confronted the majority of his peers, were this not common, ingrained practice.

6 See chap. 1, n. 45.

7 See, e.g. chap. 1, text at n. 47.

8 See chap. 3, n. 31.

9 See chap. 4, n. 19 and related text.

statements that were preferred by the editor as the final halakhah and the opposing declarations;[10] nor can one detect any denigrating references to the rejected opinions. I would speculate that Rabbi's method of concealing his preference for one proclamation against another under cover of a majority pronouncement[11] may have also been an element of this particular system, to avoid causing embarrassment to the authors of rejected opinions. That is, attributing a preferred opinion to some undefined majority was less likely to antagonize a defeated party than if the opinion were attributed to a particular individual[12].

I would also speculate that there must have been great difficulty in establishing suitable criteria for deciding whose opinion was more appropriate, and who had the authority to establish such criteria.[13] This issue likely constituted another enormous stumbling block in the path of fixing halakhot. I have cited a great number of occurrences in which the final halakhah was not clear or was not universally accepted. In most of the occurrences in which it is stated that the halakhah follows the dicta of one Sage and not those of his contender, no reason is given for this decision. As we have seen, Rabbi attempted to empower himself with the authority to establish the correct halakhah (through his use of anonymous quotations, or attributions to a majority), but gave no indications of the reasons for his decisions. It is possible that his authority in this respect was questioned, and therefore his decisions were not always accepted by the later Sages.[14] (In fact, as we have seen, the Amoraim proceeded vigorously in establishing halakhot. The source of their entitlement to decide which opinions were more appropriate is unclear; they too did not inform us of the motives for their decisions. There is occasionally some tentative rationalization, such as "[one Sage's] motive is intelligible [or rational]," or "his depth is with him [i.e. his reasons are penetrating]," but these are not consistently applied;[15] in many instances the halakhah actually follows not the praised opinion, but another opinion, quoted anonymously or attributed to the majority, or "Sages."[16])

I have already cited[17] the extraordinary rule of the "rebellious elder," who may continue with his legislative pronouncements against the

---

10 See H. H. Cohn, "Methodology," p. 129, heading "Fifth."

11 This was effected either as an anonymous declaration or under the guise of וחכמים אומרים. See section 3.1

12 See, e.g., the discussion of tBerakhot 5: 2, at the end of section 3.1.

13 See, e.g., chap. 3, n. 74.

14 See chap. 3, n.13.

15 See more on this issue and such declarations in sections 3.3 and 4.1.6.

16 See section 3.1.

17 See section 2.3.1.

decisions of the majority, but not with his judicial pronouncements.[18] This exceptional rule can be understood only within the above-postulated situation of compromise. We must also consider as unusual the preservation for eternity of all dissenting and rejected declarations, particularly given that this would have been accomplished through the difficult system of memorization. We cannot compare this procedure to the archiving of all the discussions of a modern legislative body; nor did other ancient legal codices record opposing ideas, though we must assume that there were always dissenting views. The question perplexed even the mishnaic sages, as we read in mEduyyot 1: 5 and 6: "Why does one mention the opinion of the individual among [those of] the many, since the halakhah is according to the many"? The answers proffered in the Mishnah are, to say the least, disappointing,[19] and indicate the difficulty in resolving the issue by traditional conceptions. Since the Mishnah does not indicate that the rejected opinions are in any way inferior, the Amoraim conscientiously examined all the quoted statements with equal attention and esteem, regardless of the final halakhah; they attempted to reveal the origin of and to rationalize every statement in the Mishnah with the same zeal, with no indication of why they ultimately preferred one or the other opinion. This apparently peculiar preoccupation with rejected declarations of law is the result of the above-postulated compromise, and testifies to its effectiveness in practice. The proclamation by the Voice of Heaven, "Both [opinions] are the words of the Living God [yBerakhot 1: 4, 3b, bEruvin 13b and many other occurrences]," granted this compromise divine legitimacy.

This system of compromise thus allowed the establishment and acknowledgement of final halakhot, to ensure the stability of the system, while granting at the same time the utmost freedom of expression to each individual Sage, allowing him to uphold and defend his personal convictions. It is probable that initially each Sage was allowed not only to communicate his opinion, but also to act according to his views. I have cited the maxim that if one wishes to conduct himself according to Beit Shammai, he may do so, and if according to Beit Hillel, he may also do so. We have also seen that a great number of disputes were not finally determined for a long period.[20]

As noted, the process of adjustment from total "anarchy" to a fixed and unified legal system was naturally a slow process. The first step constituted the recognition of judicial decisions as binding. The Sages

---

[18] See chap. 2, text at n. 105.

[19] See the discussion in chap. 3, n. 5.

[20] See also chap. 1, n. 55, regarding the discussion of whether Beit Shammai themselves acted according to their own opinions, even after the determination that the halakhah was to follow Beit Hillel.

perceived that for the sake of good order in society, the supremacy and authority of the courts must be maintained, at all costs, even if a decision was founded upon an erroneous assumption. At the same time, they devised a security valve against the continuing consequences of a wrong judgment, by the creation of a mechanism of repeal.[21] We have observed that Rabbi Yehoshua agreed to this fundamental principle despite his conviction that he would desecrate the Day of Atonement.[22] Rabbi Aqiba acknowledged the formal principle of the finality of judicial decisions: what the court has done, is done.[23] But Rabbi Dosa, who had declared that the witnesses on whom Rabban Gamaliel had relied in a decision were false, and so convinced Rabbi Yehoshua,[24] added another aspect to the issue. Although he was convinced that the court's decision in this case was wrong, he realized that one must not question its judgment, lest one put into doubt all previous court decisions and destroy confidence in the entire judicial system. This reasoning allowed a separation between legislative and judicial decisions.[25] As a result of such separation, the "rebellious elder" could remain a dignified member of the legislative body, but had to accept the final decisions of the court though they conflicted with his own. He was prevented only from pronouncing judgments after judicial decisions were given against his views. Rabbi Eliezer's excommunication was proclaimed because he opposed the court's decision concerning the Akhnai oven.[26] The narrative does not refer to a discussion in the academy, but to Rabbi Eliezer's reluctance to accept the decision that had been confirmed, and his attempt to overturn it by his appeal to a superhuman authority. With respect to the case of the converted Ammonite who wished to be accepted into the community (mYadayim 4: 4), we observe that, initially, it concerned a private inquiry to the Sages and then, a discussion in the academy.[27] The decision to accept the Ammonite's conversion was rendered only after Rabban Gamaliel's dismissal, and was not revoked after Rabban Gamaliel's reinstatement as the head of the Academy.

---

21 See section 3.2.

22 See chap. 1, n. 65, and chap. 4, n. 293.

23 Ibid.

24 We read Rabbi Dosa's statement in mRosh HaShanah 2: 8: עדי שקר הן היאך מעידים על האשה שילדה ולמחר כריסה בין שיניה אמר לו ר׳ יהושע רואה אני את דבריך "They are false witnesses. How can one testify that a woman already gave birth and see her the next day still pregnant? Rabbi Yehoshua said to him: I see your point."

25 See section 2.3.1.

26 See chap. 4, n. 298.

27 See chap. 4, n. 223.

Another variation of the problem was observed in tDemai 5: 24.[28] Rabbi Aqiba had set aside tithes from vegetables cultivated by *Kutim*,[29] contrary to the prevailing custom, and Rabban Gamaliel reproached him: "How did you dare to contravene the declarations of your colleagues, or who granted you authority to set aside tithes? [He] replied: I did not establish halakhah in Israel, I just set aside tithes with respect to my own purchase. [Rabban Gamaliel] retorted: Be aware that you have established halakhah in [the entire community of] Israel by the tithing of your vegetables." The story gives the impression that the Sages went purposely to examine and evaluate the procedure with respect to the precept of tithing, and this explains Rabban Gamaliel's statement that Rabbi Aqiba had established halakhah by his public act. Rabbi Aqiba justified his procedure as his personal right to act according to his own opinion; in view of the particular circumstances, however, Rabban Gamaliel deemed his actions, performed in public, as equal to a court decision. This passage again illustrates the distinction between opposing a specific court judgment and maintaining the right to hold a dissident opinion, and the privilege to act in accordance with it.

We also encountered a similar distinction between a halakhic decision in the academy and a court judgment in tTa'anit 2: 5.[30] Rabbi Yehoshua wanted to reverse a decision of Rabban Gamaliel concerning fasts, after the latter's death; Rabbi Yohanan ben Nuri objected, stating: "I see that the body follows its head; during Rabban Gamaliel's lifetime, we have established the halakhah as he declared, and now after his death, you wish to repeal it. Rabbi Yehoshua said: We listen to you; the halakhah was established according to Rabban Gamaliel and nobody objected to it."[31] The precise circumstances in which Rabban Gamaliel's decision was declared are not clear from the text; it is likely that, as Patriarch, he had proclaimed various fasts. We may assume that the dispute between Rabbi Yehoshua and Rabbi Yohanan ben Nuri concerned whether Rabban Gamaliel's proclamation should be deemed a court decision, to which

---

[28] See chap. 3, n. 85.

[29] The narrative records a visit of a group of Sages, including Rabban Gamaliel and Rabbi Aqiba, to villages of *Kutim*. There are many opinions on the precise identification of the people called *Kutim*, but in this case, it seems to apply to Samaritans, who observed many Israelite laws, including tithing, but were not entirely trustworthy. Their vegetables were therefore considered as dubious with respect to tithing. But Rabbi Aqiba took the initiative and set aside tithes in the manner to be used for vegetables that one is certain have not been tithed.

[30] See chap. 2, n. 220.

[31] There is a parallel to this passage in bEruvin 41a, but with different wording: יהושע אין שומעין לך שכבר נקבעה הלכה כרבן גמליאל "We do not listen to you, because the halakhah was already established according to Rabban Gamaliel." The differences have no effect on our deductions from this narrative.

specific repeal provisions applied,[32] or an academic decision, which could be altered. The Gemara discusses whether Rabban Gamaliel's declaration was indeed enacted during his lifetime. At any rate, we observe the flexibility of the halakhah in the tannaitic period. Rabbi Yehoshua did not hesitate to change a rule promulgated by the Patriarch. He did not consider this illegal, or against any halakhic principle; he ultimately desisted from changing the rule because of Yohanan ben Nuri's opposition, or because the latter convinced him that an abrogation of the decree of a prior Patriarch might damage the prestige of the Patriarchate.

The final phase in the gradual creation of an established codex began with the amoraic period. As I have characterized them,[33] the Amoraim had a different approach to the creation of halakhah. The Tannaim were convinced that they possessed the authority to decree laws and rules without deriving them explicitly and directly from Scripture, and this philosophy allowed them to create law within a wide range of contingencies. One may assume that, in many occurrences, they were well aware of the feebleness of the hermeneutic method for the creation of halakhah. The cognizance of their own broad authority facilitated their acceptance of the conflicting opinions and decisions of their fellow Tannaim. They thus flourished within an environment in which each Tanna could declare his ideas without the necessity of establishing the "correct" halakhah.[34] The Amoraim, on the other hand, did not consider themselves as possessing the authority to create halakhah, and perceived themselves as acting within very narrow limits. In practice, they considered their task and authority to be restricted to investigating the biblical sources of the tannaitic declarations,[35] understanding the motives behind tannaitic disputes,[36] resolving discrepancies between different sources,[37] and deciding the correct halakhah to the best of their understanding,[38] or according to certain rules that became standard.[39]

Talmudic sources offer striking evidence of this difference between tannaitic and amoraic attitudes. We have seen that in spite of disputes on such crucial matters as purity and family law, the members of Beit Hillel and Beit Shammai intermarried, and tolerated the decisions of

---

32 See the discussion of repeal provisions in section 3. 2.

33 See especially sections 2.3.2 and 4.1.7.

34 Except for the requirement to accept a court decision; see section 2.3.1.

35 See section 2.3.2.

36 Ibid.

37 Ibid.

38 Ibid.

39 See section 4.1.6.

their opponents in matters of purity.[40] The Amoraim, in contrast, could not accept such an all-inclusive approach to halakhah, and perceived this right of individual action as entailing an utter transgression of established halakhah. In this connection, yYevamot 1: 6, 3b and bYevamot 14a record disputes between two Amoraim.[41] In each case, one Amora (in the B. T. it is Rabbi Yohanan) declares that Beit Shammai indeed acted according to their own declarations, despite the fact that the halakhah was decided according to Beth Hillel. In each case, a discussion follows with the purpose of reconciling this statement with the amoraic assumption that no-one would have disobeyed the halakhah established according to Beit Hillel

Yet within this passage in the B. T., we find indications that decisions of both Houses were deemed legitimate, and probably followed concurrently even in periods later than that of the Amoraim who disputed with respect to this issue. Abbaye permitted the co-existence of courts that followed Beit Shammai and those following Beit Hillel, as long as they were in different locations. Raba also did not object to such diversity, and objected only to a court within which some members decided according to Beit Shammai and others according to Beit Hillel.[42] These conditions seem to have prevailed during the period of these Amoraim (first half of the fourth century C.E.) - that is, about two hundred years after the alleged decision that the halakhah was always according to Beit Hillel. Moreover, in addition to the amoraic approval of opposing court decisions, we have real evidence of divergent customs in different towns.[43] Though the evidence refers to an earlier period, and we do not know to what extent such customs were still relevant in the later period, we observe that such disparity was common during the early stages of Rabban Gamaliel's reform. Such a situation lends additional support to my proposition that the path to a fixed halakhah was protracted.

The amoraic attitude toward halakhah was conducive to the implementation of the reform that had begun with Rabban Gamaliel. We perceive in the Gemara a much greater interest in establishing final halakhot than we find in the Mishnah. As with every reform, and particularly with respect to a decisive revision of a system that is not enforced by the coercive power of a state but rather by voluntary obedience, the accomplishment of the reform was a complex affair. Based on bEruvin 7a,[44] we observe that even in the late amoraic period, there

---

[40] In mEduyyot 4: 8 this attitude is praised with great emphasis. See the text, translation, and explanation of the concepts in chap. 1, n. 55.

[41] See citation and discussion in chap. 3, nn. 72-3.

[42] See citations and discussion in chap. 3, nn. 82-3 and related text.

[43] See relevant citations in chap. 3, n. 78.

[44] See chap. 4, n. 321.

was an assumption that one was allowed to follow the declarations of one Sage, whether a Tanna or an Amora, as long as one followed them consistently, and without consideration as to how the final halakhah was established - indeed, even contrary to the final halakhah. The question of how to proceed in the face of such "non-conformity" had already been discussed with respect to disputes between the highly-respected schools of Shammai and Hillel, and the principle continued to be applied to conflicting halakhot between Sages of lesser esteem, in later periods.

Thus, in contrast to the drastic and apparently swift change, following the closing of the Mishnah by the influential Rabbi, between the status of the Tannaim and that of the Amoraim, the institution of a fixed halakhah after a great period of pluralism was a slow process. Even the authoritative Rabbi had not fully succeeded in accomplishing the scheme initiated by his great predecessor Rabban Gamaliel at least one hundred years earlier. The Amoraim, centuries later, still deliberated about halakhot disputed in earlier generations and not finally established, as illustrated above.[45] The development of a fixed halakhic system stretched over hundreds of years.

The reform followed a typical path: the more that members of a particular generation attempted to fix a unitary halakhah, the more they suppressed tolerance to opposing opinions. The Sevoraim and the later Geonim accomplished the final transition, from the open and tolerant pre-70 situation,[46] which was able to accommodate divergent opinions

---

[45] See, e.g., section 4.2.3.

[46] I must note here that it is extremely odd that we do not have any trace of a critical declaration against the Jewish Christians from pre-70 Sages. This strange fact cannot be attributed to later censorship; any derogatory talmudic texts expunged from the Talmud are available today in special collections, and no such declarations are evident. We encounter, in fact, an almost inconceivable declaration attributed to "Gamaliel" in Acts 5: 33 - 40 with respect to Christian ideology. J. Neusner, *Pharisees*, p. 373 declares that the Gamaliel mentioned in Acts 5: 34 is presumably identical with Rabban Gamaliel the Elder. We read there: "For if this plan or this undertaking is of men, it will fail; but if it is of God, you will not be able to overthrow them. You might even be found opposing God [NIV transl. vv. 39 - 40]." One may of course question the historicity of Gamaliel's speech, as many scholarly writings do (see for example, Ernst Haenchen, *The Acts of the Apostles*, pp. 256 - 8). Moreover, we perceive a certain favourable bias in Luke's writings toward the Pharisees in Acts, in contrast to the manifestly hostile attitude towards them in Luke 11: 37 - 44, 12: 1, 16: 14 and 18: 10 - 11, and in other NT writings. In addition to the absence of criticism pre-70, there is the fact that the blessing against heretics was instituted only post-70 (see chap. 4, text at nn. 265-6). These circumstances should lend some credence to the narrative, and allow us to suppose an extremely broad-minded and tolerant environment in the pre-70 period. Gamaliel's alleged declaration that Christian ideology may be "of God" (C. B. Williams, *New Testament*, translates: "if it has its origin in God") reflects the utmost boundary of tolerance. Even if "the speech of Gamaliel is most likely a creation of Luke," as G. Lüdemann assumes (*Early Christianity*, pp. 68 -73), we must still consider Luke's opinion that such a declaration by Gamaliel was plausible. Luke wrote Acts for his generation, and would not have

through creative examination and deliberation, to a conclusive, closed, and inflexible system, which attempted to impose a single viewpoint upon the entire Jewish community.[47] Along with this decisive shift, the prohibition against writing halakhot was abrogated,[48] as it no longer had any purpose; since halakhot were now fixed with no contemplation of later change, they could be preserved indefinitely in writing.

Ultimately, the gaonic practice of suppressing and invalidating opposing opinions would constitute one of the factors leading to the creation of the Karaite movement. It seems that Rabban Gamaliel and the followers of his philosophy were more tolerant of and accommodating to divergent opinions in the pursuit of their goal than were the Geonim. Rabban Gamaliel's reform was effected over a long period, but engendered no divisions within Israelite society. The Geonim proceeded in

---

written something that would sound utterly improbable or even preposterous to his readers (as the statement would appear today in an orthodox environment). We must therefore acknowledge a kernel of truth in Luke's statement and the possibility of such a tolerant attitude on the part of Gamaliel. This would indicate that certain leading Pharisees were not utterly negative toward Jesus and his followers; this, in turn, suggests that there were different opinions among the Pharisees with respect to the initial phases of their belief. See also W. J. Lyons, "The Words of Gamaliel (Acts 5.38-39)," on this specific subject. Joseph B. Tyson, *Luke, Judaism, and the Scholars,* quotes a number of scholarly writings about Luke's attitude toward Judaism and the Jews. Judaism does not object to or oppose questions and speculations on even the most significant matters of faith. In *The Guide of the Perplexed,* written by Maimonides and addressed to his disciple, he undertakes to make clear to this disciple "certain things pertaining to divine matters," because he was "perplexed" and "stupefaction had come over" him (Dedicatory Epistle, pp. 3 - 4). Maimonides respected his disciple's perplexity and did not consider it a fault. He wrote to him that "my purpose in this [treatise] was that the truth should be established in your mind." Asking questions and professing doubt became part of the characteristic conduct of the Jews. Primo Levi, the author of books about the comportment of the Jews during the Holocaust and their tribulations during the last world war, portrays the behaviour and thoughts of Mendel, a typical Diaspora Jew (*If Not Now? When?).* He always doubts the correctness of what is done, and sometimes professes admiration for the Gentiles and for the Jewish Zionist girl Line, considering them as having no doubts. Piotr, the Polish soldier, rebukes him for this trait and says: "But you're strange people, all the same...if a man reasons too much, in the end he can't shoot straight, and you people always reason too much. May be that's why the Germans kill you."

47 Cf. S. J. D. Cohen, "The Significance of Yavneh," who perceives an opposite trend. In his opinion, the pre-70 Pharisees did not tolerate disagreements, and this was the reason for the pre-70 "sectarianism." The Yabneh assembly created a tolerant environment, as he portrays it: "For the first time Jews 'agreed to disagree.'" I believe that I have substantiated my opposing thesis with respect to the transition from the pre-70 to the post-70 era, and I leave it to the reader to decide which argument seems more plausible.

48 I would postulate that a similar process occurred with respect to prayers; the writing of prayers ended the era of the spontaneous individual prayer and introduced the fixed style.

a heavy-handed manner in their quest to impose their philosophy, and provoked an irreversible ideological split.

We thus observe the lengthy path from the open-mindedness and tolerance of the pre-70 Sages to the conservative and intolerant attitude of the Geonim.[49] It is a well-known psychological fact that a person who possesses self-confidence in his judgment and opinion is more tolerant to opposing ideas. A folk aphorism declares that one who vociferously attacks the opinions of others indicates thereby his own vacillation. He needs first to assure himself of the validity of his own allegations; the obliteration of opposing ideas grants him such confidence in his propositions. The ancient Sages, with their profound confidence in the correctness of their decisions (to the best of their judgment), had no need to impose a fixed halakhah. At the same time, they appreciated their philosophical-theological limitations. A crucial element of Jewish faith is the conviction that only God is omniscient; no human idea is definite and no-one is in possession of the absolute truth.[50] The early Sages thus believed only that their ideas were closer to the categorical truth than those of their opponents. The Tannaim were well aware that their decisions and declarations merely reflected their opinions of what God might have intended, and, therefore, naturally accepted that another opinion might be the correct one. This is the philosophical foundation of the apparently paradoxical utterance "Both [opinions] are the words of the Living God." For such a Tanna to desire to fix halakhah according to his own particular understanding would contradict this basic philosophy; it would imply that only he had divined God's intention and that the divergent opinions of the other Sages were wrong. Their *Weltanschauung* and personal modesty

---

[49] Cf. S. J.D. Cohen, *From the Maccabees to the Mishna*, p. 136, who perceives this development from another aspect. He suggests there was an attempt by the Sages convened at the assembly recorded in tractate Eduyyot to assume the role of the central authority; in fact, the later Karaite split occurred in opposition to such an attempted imposition of central authority. My reading of the relevant texts about this assembly at Yabneh, as well as of the relevant scholarly citations, considers the establishment of a unique, fixed halakhah as the aim of the assembly, and the later Karaite objection as relating to the utterly rigid application of this fixed halakhah. It is evident that the rabbinic narrative cited in the *Sefer ha-Kabbalah* of Abraham ibn Daud (1161), relating that Anan created the Karaite movement out of personal rancor at not being elected Exilarch, does not record the real cause of this split. A personal grievance could not have provoked such a deep schism and a separation of a significant fraction of the people. Many studies have been published about the Karaite movement and the underlying motives of that schism, and it is not within the scope of this study to elaborate upon them. I do not dispute that many factors provoked this split, but I perceive the halakhic contention from a different perspective than S. Cohen. In any event, our two views would appear to complement each other.

[50] We read Job's confession following God's reproof of his ignorance: לכן הגדתי ולא אבין נפלאות ממני ולא אדע "Surely I spoke of things I did not understand, things too wonderful for me to know [Job 42: 3]."

would not allow such an inference. This was the foundation of their tolerance for opposing opinions.[51] Subsequent generations gradually lost this self-confidence,[52] and with this loss grew their urgent need for fixed halakhah and consequently their intolerance to opposing ideas. This loss of confidence, in other words, initiated a need for more self-assurance and a movement toward the conviction that their own ideas were the only truth. This, in turn, engendered arrogance toward contrary opinions and less humility toward God. They were obviously not conscious of this decadence in their veneration of God, and likely imagined that they were implementing God's mandate with utmost punctiliousness.

Another crucial factor influenced the "Great Divide" between the two earlier stages (the pre-70 and Tannaitic) and the amoraic attitudes toward the law, in the third stage. The pre-70 Sages, and still to a great extent the Tannaim, believed themselves to possess the wisdom and authority to be creative in their halakhic decisions.[53] They could, therefore, regenerate and reform the law, adapting it to contemporary necessities. They proclaimed and promulgated legal decisions apparently in total conflict with the simple understanding of scriptural laws, in some cases adopting a lenient stance and in others a more strict interpretation. I have already cited examples corroborating the wide range of tannaitic authority. The unequivocal *lex talionis* of Exod. 21: 24 - 25, "an eye for an eye," was drastically limited to a pecuniary retribution.[54] The Sages neutralized the numerous death penalties for various transgressions quoted in Scripture, by requiring the prior warning of the offender. The conditions of the admonition were such as to practically eliminate any possibility of carrying out the death penalty; the warning had to be given to the offender by two witnesses before he committed the offence, and had to inform him of the precise punishment he would face by performing the evil deed.[55] On the strict side, we have also seen the extension of works prohibited on the Sabbath.[56] Hillel, as we have noted,[57] in effect abrogated the cancellation of debts in the seventh year. He also created certain new precepts; for

---

[51] See the examples cited in chap. 4, n. 61 regarding the tolerance shown by the early Tannaim for opposing decisions.

[52] See below an explanation for this radical change.

[53] M. Fishbane, *Biblical Interpretation in Ancient Israel*, p. 4, writes that the Sages' exegesis must be seen "as a natural theological consequence of the notion that the contents of interpretation *are part of* [italics are the author's] the written divine revelation (implicitly or explicitly)."

[54] Concerning the talmudic deliberations on this issue see chap. 2, nn. 73 ff. and related text.

[55] See chap. 2, n. 82.

[56] See mHagigah 1: 8, cited in chap. 2 n. 26.

[57] See chap. 2, nn. 151-59 and related text.

example, he established hygienic rules for the well-being of the body as a divine command.[58]

At the same time, the Sages' sense of creativity directed them to respect the creativity of other scholars, thus generating an atmosphere of tolerance and flexibility. Rabbi's closing of the Mishnah constituted the "watershed" in this respect, and initiated the third stage.[59] The succeeding Amoraim were given notice, explicitly or implicitly, by this event that the era of creativity had come to an end. Whereas a Tanna could unrestrictedly oppose and repudiate the dicta of another Tanna, an Amora could not challenge or contradict the opinion of a Tanna. A two-tier classification of the Sages thus resulted; the amoraic function and authority was from then on restricted to the interpretation of the Mishnah, the conclusive law, and the reconciliation of its apparent or real inconsistencies. The almost unlimited resourcefulness of the Tannaim was drastically contracted by Rabbi's opus, and consequently future amoraic deliberations were squeezed into a straitjacket. The Tannaim put forward the principles of the law, but did not reveal their rationale. The Amoraim often preferred not to interpret such principles and extend them. They likely were concerned that they might overstep their authority, if their consideration of logical principles were too free. As we have seen above, they interpreted the Mishnah by assuming that the tannaitic dicta were founded upon interpretations of Scripture, and thus the disputes among the Tannaim were perceived simply as the result of divergent hermeneutics. This method was patently contrary to the tannaitic viewpoint. The narrowly-confined powers of thought and decision of the Amoraim did not allow them to be creative, except in one manner: to interpret the mishnaic decrees restrictively and proclaim more stringent regulations. Thus started the period of decadence in creative halakhic thought; the Amoraim believed that the road to leniency was utterly blocked for them, and the only way to exercise creativity led in the opposite direction.

These circumstances also had a negative impact on the previously tolerant environment. The quality of tolerance is the outcome of freedom of thought, which consequently initiates a symmetrical respect for the same freedom for opposing concepts. The curtailing of one's own freedom undermines the tolerance for any ideas apart from the narrow consensus, and engenders, at the same time, the pursuit of strict and rigid rules. This process was further impelled by the conservative philosophy that no one had the authority to change the rules established by the previous generations; this philosophy continues to prevail even in our own days. As we have noted,[60] this supreme reverence for the opinions of prior

---

58 See Introduction, n. 97.

59 See discussion in sections 2.3.2 and 4.1.7.

60 Chap. 2, n.112.

generations was almost unlimited. Even the opinions of such illustrious sages as Hillel and Shammai were rejected because of an alleged conflicting halakhic declaration by the earlier sages Shemayah and Abtalion. The range of individual creativity became continuously smaller and took the metaphorical shape of a funnel leading in one narrow direction.

The issue of authority thus became the major impediment to legal development. Although it is not within the scope of the study, I would like to state briefly my perceptions of the later developmental stages of the rabbinic law - that is, the fourth stage. I wish to emphasize that my book does not have as its goal the preaching or promotion of shifts or modifications in the contemporary approach to the halakhah (although it is my hope that scholars of Jewish theology and law may draw certain practical conclusions from the rabbinic approach to halakhah that has been exposed in this study). On the other hand, I certainly revealed in my interpretations of rabbinic literature a definite process of adaptation and alteration in the development of rabbinic law in its initial stages. At that primary stage, logical and practical considerations, within the boundaries of the Torah, dominated the halakhic disputes and decisions, allowing creative legislation in all directions: lenient and strict, tolerant and exclusive, flexible and rigid, pluralistic or with fixed halakhot, according to the circumstances. The Sages were not fundamentalists - that is, they did not perceive the literal text of Scripture as binding. They believed they had the privilege, indeed the duty, to interpret Scripture in the appropriate way. Intimate knowledge of the Torah served them as a blueprint and guideline for understanding the divine will and commands, and gave them the ability and authority to accomplish this goal.

The Tannaim left a legacy of creative interpretation of Scripture in its broadest sense, a technique of overriding biblical precepts and rules, and a decisive belief in the human authority to apply these criteria for the practical implementation of the *Grundnorm*, the general philosophy of the Bible.[61] Most importantly, they indicated the technique whereby their decisions could be seen as assiduously complying with the divine commands expressed in the Torah, without changing or repelling them.

There is continual development in all aspects and expressions of intellectual thought, and this also occurred in the development of halakhic concepts. Without any external influence or impact, modifications will often follow an evolutionary path; but I perceive a dichotomy in the developmental stages of the halakhah between the tannaitic and amoraic periods. I think that the transition from the tannaitic to the amoraic concepts constituted a real cut-off between two distinct types of theories

[61] I refer the reader to my conjecture (chap. 3, nn. 184 ff. and related text) that the Sages saw themselves as analogous to the prophets, and as possessing their privileges.

and convictions. Nevertheless, though this transition represented a radical change in the underlying halakhic philosophy, we should not lose sight of the common theology that guided the two classes of Sages. We perceive in this respect a paradox of coexistence between diversity and uniformity, as is prevalent in religious matters. This is analogous to the transition from the "miraculous" oral prophets to the "ethical" written prophets and ultimately to the rabbinic Sages.

Rabbi's closure of the independent and authoritative Mishnah terminated a significant stage in the development of Jewish law. The later Amoraim, "degraded" by their own account, were deprived explicitly or implicitly of the authority enjoyed and applied by the Tannaim. They were intimidated against utilizing the prerogative in fact granted to them as erudite scholars, a prerogative categorically exercised by the antecedent Sages. Consequently, they practised restraint in their decisions, which relieved them of the awesome[62] responsibility, as they perceived it, of eventually having to repudiate a divine edict with a lenient decision. The hesitation to utilize the prerogative of authority reversed the previous flexibility of Jewish law, and became the foremost impediment for its continued progress in that direction. The issue of authority thus became the pivotal obstacle in the development of Jewish law. A belief grew that there was a constant decline in status, knowledge, and authority. The prerogative of interpreting the Torah to establish halakhah was off-limits for the Amoraim and the succeeding generations of Rabbis. The Amoraim could interpret the Mishnah, as stated above, but could not contradict a Tanna, nor suggest an interpretation of the Torah other than the ones alleged to have been used by the Tannaim. The later commentators could interpret only the Gemara, and so on until our days. Each generation would never dare to decide a halakhah on the basis of its own interpretation of a Torah precept, or contradict a decision by a Sage of a previous generation.

As an illustration of this state of affairs, I would like to offer a striking example of tannaitic creativity, and compare it to a modern rabbinic response. We read in bBerakhot 28b: "Simeon ha-Pakoli arranged [the prayer of] eighteen blessings before Rabban Gamaliel in Yabneh. Rabban Gamaliel said to the Sages: Is there someone who knows how to compose a blessing against the heretics? Samuel ha-Qatan stood up and composed it." Though there is a question as to when these eighteen blessings were actually introduced into the daily prayers, including conflicting dicta in rabbinic literature as to who instituted the prayers and with respect to the interpretation of the term הסדיר, "arranged," this issue does not affect our investigation. What is evident is that the nineteenth blessing against

---

62 See J. Roth's assumption that their apprehension was reflected in the declaration that their opinions are the will of God (chap. 2, n. 122).

heretics was created in Yabneh at that period, to accommodate a prevailing exigency.[63] In contrast, the modern Chief Rabbi of Israel is deemed to lack the authority to decree the addition of a blessing on Independence Day,[64] when hymns of praise from the Book of Psalms are recited to thank God for His benevolent support of Israel's redemption. One notes this extreme reversal in rabbinic attitude: from self-confidence and almost unlimited authority, to an influence limited to more severe interpretations of the pronouncements of previous Sages. We have observed this gradual process extending from the pre-70 period, when there were no bounds to the Sages' freedom, through the somewhat more restricted tannaitic period, through the amoraic period, and finally to the total dogmatism of the Geonim.

The rigidity of the halakhah, and the conviction that only an "infallible" leader knows God's will, undermine all tolerance to divergent opinions and exacerbate divisiveness. Although contemporary Jewish history is outside the scope of this study, I shall briefly cite certain instances that illustrate the continuity of this conception. The "separatists" who constituted the community of the Dead Sea Scrolls contended that only their leader possessed the true divine revelation; only he correctly understood God's commands, and it was only the group under his leadership that constituted the true Israel. Though there are no such blunt declarations by the Geonim, they too insisted that the only way to fulfill the divine commands was through the observance of the halakhah as decided by them. One consequence of this attitude was the Karaite split. We encounter a similar drastic division with the formation of the Hassidic movement in the 18th century. The followers of each Rabbi believed that only their own leader had an exclusive channel of communication with the Deity and could secure for them communion and salvation. The Gaon of Vilna, the renowned and acclaimed leader of "intellectual" Judaism, believed the Hassidic movement to be a great danger to the Jewish community, and went so far as to request the usually hostile Czarist authorities to intervene against them. It was only with the rise of the Enlightenment movement in Jewish society, and the consequent realization of the danger to their collective faith and way of life, that the prevailing enthusiasm for internecine struggles between the different Hassidic groups, and against their opponents, was dampened. Yet the fundamental belief that only one's own leader possesses divine enlightenment and the true knowledge of God's will persists, erupting occasionally, as circumstances allow. It is a jest of fate that modern

---

63 See J. Heinemann, *Prayer in the Talmud*, p. 225.

64 Rabbi Lau's decision and instruction in this respect was reported in the reputable Israeli newspaper *Ha'aretz*, 11May 2000.

ultra-orthodox groups,[65] the self-appointed followers of the Pharisees, accuse their non-conformist opponents of the same misdemeanor of which the Pharisees were accused by the "separatists" of the Dead Sea Scrolls community. It is only their own Rabbis, like the Righteous Teacher of the ancient community, who are deemed to know the divine intent and will, and only those who obey their particular interpretations constitute the true Israel.

It is plausible that the pluralistic and *ad hoc* attitude of the early period was also the result of a lack of any organized institution for the establishment of a unique and universally binding codex of law. The activity of the Sanhedrin in this field is more than questionable and a matter of dispute. I have also demonstrated the fallibility of the rabbinic narratives with respect to the alleged involvement of the Sanhedrin in halakhic decisions in the pre-70 period. The Yabneh convention, summoned by Rabban Gamaliel for the purpose of fixing halakhah, is presented as a first-time occurrence,[66] and demonstrates the absence of such activity before the Temple's destruction. One may deduce from this episode that the Patriarch, the only acknowledged authority at that time (as there was no longer a High Priest), had a greater influence on the Sages after the Temple's destruction than before. He could summon the Sages - and it seems that they complied - to a meeting intended to accomplish a radical alteration of legal procedures. We observe here the interaction between political, sociological and legal issues.

I should like to add a final note on methodology. I have cited and examined a number of talmudic citations to substantiate my thesis, but am aware that there are other citations that may be interpreted in such a manner as to reach a contrary deduction. We must keep in mind, however, the intentional lack of systematic organization in the Talmud, and its pluralistic nature. Given such circumstances, I propose that the existence of apparently conflicting dicta does not invalidate a thesis that is based upon the examination of the development of the rabbinic legal system over an extended period, and substantiated by an array of appropriate citations. We must also be aware of the uncertainty of any deduction founded upon talmudic quotations in general, due to the vagaries of oral tradition. I wish

---

[65] See Z. Safrai and A. Sagi, סמכות, p. 15, where it is asserted that this doctrine of divine inspiration held by contemporary Rabbis is a relatively recent belief, originating only shortly before our time.

[66] The record in mShabbat 1: 4 of a meeting of members of the Houses of Hillel and Shammai in the upper chambers of a certain Hananyah, and of the halakhic decision reached there, does not contradict the above assumption. This meeting, if it actually took place as recorded, was convened for the promulgation of special regulations, deemed necessary due to extraordinary circumstances. These rules are known by the specific name "the eighteen edicts," and have no connection with a meeting to decide disputed halakhot. See further on this passage section 3.4.

to quote one such example that seems to me weightier than so many others that abound in the Talmud. We read in mEruvin 10: 10: "A door bolt which has, on its top, a movable fastener - Rabbi Eliezer prohibits its use [on Sabbath], and Rabbi Yose permits its use.[67] Rabbi Eliezer said: In Tiberias, they were using this device until Rabban Gamaliel and the elders prohibited its use, [but] Rabbi Yose said: They were not using it [because it was considered prohibited] until Rabban Gamaliel and the elders came and permitted its use." This narrative decisively demonstrates the problematic of oral tradition. The passage refers to a significant decision of the Patriarch, which was still disputed between two contemporary Sages. All the more must we question the authenticity and accuracy of oral traditions generated centuries earlier. We must also consider in our investigation the possibility of intentional changes in the composition of talmudic narratives, effected so as to emphasize their particular message rather than the exact course of events.

While it is difficult to be confident of the authenticity of the various dicta with respect to transmission errors, I assume that any such inaccuracies would not invalidate my postulates with respect to rabbinic methods of consideration and resolution, as I have deduced them from the cited passages. Further, we need not suspect a deliberate misrepresentation of every rabbinic narrative. We must ask ourselves whether a tradent would have had a valid reason to alter the facts or conceal the real particulars of an event in order to convey a message appropriate to his particular philosophy. I have attempted to unearth any such motives where it has appeared relevant; in the absence of any "suspicious" motive, however, I think the rabbinic narratives should be assumed to be authentic, or at the very least to contain a plausible kernel of truth.

Conversely, I must reiterate my overall doubt about the possibility of fashioning a trustworthy account of the actual circumstances of the period. To our great disappointment, as I have noted, we do not possess any authentic data about the real and manifold circumstances of the relevant period. Scholarly comparison of the halakhic declarations of 4QMMT with the parallel rabbinic halakhot, attempting to identify the groups involved in the anonymous "dissident" writings, may be methodologically unsound. This approach contrasts writings and opinions of the pre-70 era with pronouncements of the post-70 era, notwithstanding the general consensus that the Temple's destruction provoked dramatic changes in all spheres of Jewish life. Some scholars have indeed remarked upon this methodological flaw. Moreover, scholars have lately advanced serious

67 The exact meaning of this mishnah is disputed, and we encounter two interpretations. One maintains that the prohibition refers to the use of the gadget as a separate device for the performance of tasks involving various objects that one must not use or touch on Sabbath. The other argues that plugging the device into the door-closing mechanism is prohibited, because it is considered equal to building a structure.

doubts with respect to the rabbinic image of uninterrupted continuity in exegesis and tradition, and the supposition that the Pharisees were the forerunners of rabbinic Judaism. A fundamental division is now perceived between the two periods,[68] and scholars do not concur in the transplanting of the pre-70 *Sitz im Leben* to the post-70 circumstances in the rabbinic period. I have attempted, in contrast, only a limited reconstruction, that of the halakhic circumstances of the pre-70 period, by an extrapolation backwards from the post -70 state of affairs, having noted a continuous pattern in the development of the Jewish legal system. In addition to the restricted scope of my investigation, the conclusions are founded upon punctilious analysis of specific dicta and narratives, not upon broad generalizations. P. R. Callaway[69] coined the concept of "micro-compositional strategy," and I believe that this systematic approach reduces the use of theoretical speculation and allows a better understanding of the individual laws and edicts. I thus believe that the application of the above-cited strategies has enabled a more appropriate comparison and contrast between the pre- and post-70 periods with respect to the halakhic environment.

It must be emphasized that the use in this study of the term "pluralism," and the assumption of a concept of nationality-ethnicity, do not constitute an attempt to impose a modern reading on ancient data. These terms are indeed modern, but the concepts as such are ancient ideas, perceived *de facto*, even if not expressed in philosophically precise definitions. The pluralism of the halakhah is patently displayed and substantiated in the many citations and phenomena quoted in the study, and in particular by the maxim "Both [opposing opinions] are the words of the Living God." The unity of the people and its survival as a distinct ethnic and cultural unity is equally well corroborated as historical fact, in the ethnically inspired rules and procedures of Ezra and Nehemiah, as well as in the rabbinic citations I have quoted concerning the perils of sectarianism.

To summarize the circumstances and shifts in the developmental stages of the rabbinic law in contemporary terminology, I would conclude my study with the following statement. The Tannaim, and - as I endeavoured to demonstrate - certainly their alleged intellectual forefathers, the Pharisees, opposed a hegemonic reading of the Torah, and were convinced of the plurivocality of the biblical text. The Amoraim, though conscious of this phenomenon through their analysis of the tannaitic declarations, preferred an authoritative reading, and for practical motives, chose the application of fixed halakhot. The subsequent

---

[68] See L. L. Grabbe, "Hellenistic Judaism."

[69] P. R. Callaway, "Extending Divine Revelation: Micro-Compositional Strategies in the Temple Scroll."

generations of rabbinic commentators and leaders asserted a hegemonic reading of the amoraic text, the Gemara, in all its halakhic and ideological aspects. We have lately experienced a marked opposition by scholars to the hegemonic reading of the Bible, but it seems to me there is as yet no resolute voice of objection to the hegemonic reading of the Gemara, even in academic circles. The plurivocality of Scripture was assumed by its redactors, whose dialectical editing intentionally left contradictions and inconsistencies and attested to the openness of the text to diversified readings. I believe this plurivocality should be applied to the entirety of Jewish post-biblical literature. I hope that my study will contribute to the initiation of serious scholarly debate with respect to the plurivocality of the Talmud itself.

Appendix: Who Were Beit Hillel and Beit Shammai?

We have noted throughout this work the numerous references to disputes between Beit Hillel and Beit Shammai, including exceptions to the well-known maxim that the halakhah is always according to Beit Hillel.[1] In this Appendix, I shall propose that the attribution of disputes to these schools may have been a fiction, the result of an attempt to organize and classify a miscellany of customs and anonymous halakhic decisions. I shall analyze the particular case of a number of mishnayot in mShabbat chap. 1, and propose a plausible explanation for the different concepts that seem to characterize these disputed rules. I shall then relate these types of disputes to the rabbinic disputes with the "dissidents," in an attempt to explain why the disputes between the Houses did not generate the type of sectarianism that occurred in the late Second Commonwealth period.

Oddities and Inconsistencies

a) absence of attributions

Our first task is to comment on the odd talmudic usage concerning these two schools, which avoided giving the names of the individual Sages in the disputes between them.[2] Undoubtedly, many of the Sages had schools of

---

1 See, e.g., chap. 1 n. 55, and section 3.4.

2 Cf. B. Z. Bacher, אגדות התנאים part 1, pp. 1-17, who offers a complex explanation for this phenomenon. He suggests that after the destruction "the name of the person responsible for a saying could win acceptance for the saying." He asserts that before the destruction, the authority of the Sanhedrin assured the acceptance of halakhic declarations. As I have argued in section 3.6, the Sanhedrin's presumed involvement in the promulgation of halakhic decisions is fictitious. Moreover, we observe that with respect to ethical sayings, the name of a pre-70 Sage was considered significant, and was transmitted. The circumstances of the first three mishnayot in tractate Eduyyot, if we consider them as authentic, in fact contradict Bacher's theory of the role of the Sanhedrin. Though the names of Hillel and Shammai are quoted in these disputes, the halakhah was established differently than either of their opinions. In the first two mishnayot, the opinion of anonymous חכמים was preferred to the great names of Hillel and Shammai. In mishnah 3, an opposing tradition attributed to Shemayah and Abtalion was declared correct; this was because their reputations were considered superior to those of Shammai and Hillel, not because of a decision by the Sanhedrin.

disciples who approved of and followed their opinions and decisions; yet, in most cases, halakhic and other pronouncements are still attributed to a particular Sage, and not to a group. This oddity is even more perplexing when we consider that a number of Sages who were known to be members of Beit Shammai,[3] or who consistently followed the opinions of this school, are otherwise identified by their own names.[4]

b) leniency versus strictness

Mishnah tractate Eduyyot reveals a particular problem regarding the nature of these disputes. I have already discussed the numerous oddities[5] in this tractate regarding the first three disputes between Hillel and Shammai, in which the halakhah was decided according to neither opinion. The succeeding disputes between Beit Shammai and Beit Hillel, in contrast, are recorded without any decision as to the final halakhah. Other declarations regarding the character of the halakhic disputes between Beit Shammai and Beit Hillel then follow. In chap. 4 of this tractate, the anonymous redactor classifies the halakhot in which Beit Shammai's decisions are lenient and Beit Hillel's decisions are stricter. Mishnah 4: 1 begins: "These are Beit Shammai's lenient declarations and Beit Hillel's stricter ones"; this style suggests a perception that, in general, one would expect Beit Hillel to be more lenient. Chap. 5 then quotes the attestations of individual Sages on this issue that are similarly apparently unexpected.[6] Yet in fact such a general trend is difficult to prove. In the first chapter of the tractate there are four minor halakhot[7] in which Beit Shammai seem to be stricter than Beit Hillel; in mishnayot 12 and 13, on the other hand, there are three significant issues in which Beit Shammai were initially the lenient party and Beit Hillel the stricter one. In mishnah 14, Beit Hillel initially held a more lenient opinion in a matter of ritual cleanness, and in the end, adopted Beit Shammai's stricter view. Hence, there is no consistent evidence in tractate Eduyyot of a generally stricter attitude on the part of Beit Shammai.

---

3 See Ch. Albeck, מבוא למשנה, pp. 218- 219 who lists a number of Sages described as disciples of Beit Shammai, and the relevant rabbinic quotations.

4 We do not have the names of many of Hillel's disciples. There is only a passage in yNedarim 5: 6, 39b, and bSukkah 28a with the names of two of his alleged eighty disciples: the greatest was Jonathan b. Uzziel, and the least important, Yohanan ben Zakkai.

5 Chap 3., n. 5.

6 These disputes are attributed to the Houses, in contrast to certain disputes attributed in chap. 1 to Shammai and Hillel themselves.

7 I consider the disputes in mishnayot 9 and 10 as a single controversy. In addition, one may doubt whether the consequences of this conceptual disagreement may be considered as strict or lenient. Beit Shammai's decision may appear stricter but it should not be logically classified as such; it is simply a conceptual disagreement.

c) did the halakhah always follow Beit Hillel?

We have, throughout this work, noted instances even in later talmudic disucssions in which Beit Shammai still followed their own decisions, or where public opinion followed Beit Shammai, despite the sweeping ruling in favour of Beit Hillel.[8] We may note here several more such inconsistencies. In tTerumot 3: 12, according to Rabbi Yehudah, the halakhah in this particular instance follows Beit Shammai, but the majority of the people following the opinion of Beit Hillel.[9] A similar pronouncement appears in yTerumot 3: 2, 42a.[10] Yet another unusual point is encountered in parallel passages in ySukkah 2: 8, 53d and bEruvin 13b. Each passage contains an explanation of the motive for the general establishment of the halakhah according to Beit Hillel, but each ends differently.[11] The Y. T. passage concludes with the significant phrase: "...and moreover, they [seriously] consider Beit Shammai's declarations and [being convinced of their correctness,] reverse their own opinions." This dictum is ambiguous, and does not elaborate upon the situations in which Beit Hillel consented to the opposing opinions, or the reason for such altruism. The simple meaning of this text seems to point to a sweeping about-face. In the B. T. parallel, no such statement appears. Instead we find: "They [Beit Hillel] declare both their own opinions and those of Beit Shammai; they also declared those of Beit Shammai before their own." The most remarkable feature of these parallels is the fact that, despite this explicit explanation of the worthiness of Beit Hillel, the deliberation in ySukkah, regarding the relevant Mishnah dispute between Beit Shammai and Beit Hillel, ends by deciding the halakhah according to Beit Shammai.[12]

Such irregularities suggest that we must explore the rabbinic objective behind these mentions of two conflicting groups called Beit Hillel and Beit Shammai.

Hypothesis: A Plausible *mise en scène*

I shall offer an explanation of this riddle that is based, first, on the discrepancy between actual facts and their presentation in rabbinic

---

8 See, e.g., chap. 1 n. 55.

9 We read there: אמר ר׳ יהודה הלכה כדברי בית שמיי אלא שנהגו הרבים כדברי בית הלל.

10 There we observe another twist. The anonymous חכמים declare that the halakhah is neither according to Beit Hillel, nor according to Beit Shammai, similar to the pronouncements in mEduyyot 1: 1 - 3.

11 See B.T. citation in chap. 1, text at n. 47.

12 We read there: מה זכו בית הלל שתיקבע הלכה כדבריהן

literature, a fact acknowledged to varying degrees by many scholars, and, second, on my portrayal of the developmental stages of pharisaic-rabbinic law.

Pre-70, we have observed[13] that there are almost no identifiable halakhic declarations. Though there is no doubt that many such rules were declared in that period by various Sages, I have argued that the ideological objective of preserving the flexibility and pluralism of the law rendered it unimportant to memorize such rules to serve as precedents. The recollection of the names of the authors of these declarations was therefore of no interest;[14] it was the practical application of a great number of these halakhic decisions in everyday life that kept them alive within Israelite society. As we have noted, many of these decisions were not unanimous, and conflicting procedures and practices coexisted easily among the people.

As I have argued, Rabban Gamaliel attempted[15] to change this state of affairs by creating a unified codex of law; Mishnah tractate Eduyyot serves as evidence of this crucial enterprise.[16] It is significant that the task of this assembly is recorded as: "[To avoid a situation in which] one declaration of Torah [law] is not the same as another." The first step in this process is described as follows (tEduyyot 1:1): "They said: Let us start with [the disputes between] Hillel and Shammai."

Post-70, I propose the following *mise en scène*.[17] The Sages who had assembled in Yabneh for the purpose of organizing the existing laws into a fixed halakhah encountered a great number of conflicting customs with no identifiable origins. Their first task was to classify these into two general groups: lenient and strict halakhot. As we gather from various rabbinic narratives, Shammai was perceived to have had a strict and severe personality, while Hillel was perceived as compassionate and easy-going;[18] the Sages therefore decided to attribute a batch of strict halakhot to

---

[13] See chap. 4, text at nn. 13 ff., on the lack of identification of the authors of halakhot alleged to originate from the pre-70 period.

[14] E. Schürer, *History*, II, I, pp. 351 ff., and II. Ii, 4 ff., discussing the individual names of the Sages enumerated in mAvot 1: 1 - 18, asserts: "It is likely that just ten names were known."

[15] See section 4.2.2.1 on his accomplishment in this respect.

[16] See section 4.1.2.

[17] J. Neusner, *Pharisees, Part I*, pp. 22-23 writes with respect to a similar *ex post facto* joining of two unrelated circles of disciples: "For the later rabbinic continuators of the Pharisees what happened had to be revised into what ought to have happened." He goes on to say that when the historical circumstances "were not palatable ... new facts had to be invented both to improve the picture, and to fill out its blank spaces."

[18] As it is stated in bShabbat 30b: לעולם יהיה אדם ענותן כהלל ולא יהיה קפדן כשמאי "One should always be kind, like Hillel, and not hot-tempered, like Shammai." See also n. 44 below regarding the alleged bias concerning the personality of Shammai.

Shammai's school, while another collection of lenient customs was attributed to Hillel's school. As the implementation of a fixed halakhah proceeded, however, the flaws in this imprecise classification were revealed.[19] As we have seen, certain halakhot attributed to Beit Shammai were in practice more lenient than those attributed to Beit Hillel, and vice-versa. As yet another example of the difficulties resulting from this broad classification into lenient and strict decrees, we may note the dispute between Beit Shammai and Beit Hillel regarding the minimum value required for the betrothal of a woman (mQiddushin 1: 1). Beit Shammai require a coin or other object of the value of a *dinar*, whereas Beit Hillel maintain that a coin or object of the value of a *perutah* (a lesser value) is sufficient. Though the opinion of Beit Hillel appears more lenient, mEduyyot 4: 7 classifies this dispute among the lenient decisions of Beit Shammai and among the stricter ones of Beit Hillel, demonstrating the shortcomings of this sweeping classification.

A further dilemma was created by the decision in Yabneh to establish a general rule that the halakhah is always according to Beit Hillel. In some instances, the Sages preferred, for legitimate reasons, to establish the halakhah contrary to the presumed opinion of Beit Hillel. An elaborate mechanism was thus instituted to allow reversals of the previous classification. In some cases in which it was deemed advisable to establish the halakhah according to Beit Shammai, it was declared that Beit Hillel had changed their minds and accepted the opinion of their opponents. In other instances, the maxim that the halakhah was always to follow Beit Hillel was simply ignored, with no justification,[20] and in express conflict with another maxim to the effect that the halakhah could never follow Beit

---

19 Often these editors did not perceive the precise extent of the dispute allegedly reflected in the different declarations. J. Neusner, "Attributions," quotes such an example on pp. 134 ff. The example concerns a dispute between Beit Shammai and Beit Hillel in mBetzah 1: 6, and the subsequent deliberations and disagreements on the underlying circumstance of that dispute. Neusner comments: "The second-century authorities are alleged to have three distinct 'traditions' on what is the issue between the Houses" (p. 136). In *Pharisees, Part III*, Neusner writes on p. 230: "The attributions of laws and disputes to the pre-70 Pharisees are apt in the main to be reliable"; a review of his study, however, indicates that this statement is pertinent only to the topics of the disputes, but not necessarily to details, which were more often altered.

20 We read in yBerakhot 8: 5, 12d: שבית שמאי אומרי׳ בשמי׳ ומאור ובית הלל אומרי׳ מאור ובשמים רבי בא ורב יהודה בשם רב הלכה כדברי מי שאומר בשמים ואחר כך מאור "... Beit Shammai say : First the blessing of the spices [must be said] and then of the light; and Beit Hillel say: First the blessing of the light and then of the spices. Rabbi Ba and Rav Yehudah in the name of Rab say that the halakhah follows the one who says: First the [blessing of] spices and then the [blessing of] the light [i.e. Beit Shammai.]"

Shammai.[21] Occasionally, it seems the Mishnah left matters deliberately vague; we find the ambiguous phrase "after they conceded," with no indication of whether Beit Shammai yielded to Beit Hillel or vice-versa.[22]

In mEduyyot 3: 10, we are told that Rabban Gamaliel acted strictly according to Beit Shammai's decisions. In contrast, the antecedent mishnah 9 records a strict decision of Rabban Gamaliel, and disputed by the anonymous חכמים "Sages"; this decision is not attributed to Beit Shammai, and we do not know its origin.[23]

The list of stricter decisions of Beit Hillel that are enumerated in Eduyyot also suggests a revision of an earlier assumption that Beit Shammai's decisions were always stricter. One may also postulate that the Sages of later generations who decided that the halakhah was always to be decided according to Beit Hillel may have reversed the attributions of specific declarations. This was not considered inappropriate, since initially these declarations had been attributed more or less at random to one or the other of the schools. We have seen that Rabbi also used the fiction of attributing the declaration of a particular Sage to the anonymous "Sages," thus establishing a majority opinion for the halakhah he considered advisable.[24] We should, therefore, not be reluctant to assume that a similar fictional method may have been used by the initiators of the concept of the schools of Beit Shammai and Beit Hillel, in the interests of establishing an

---

21 A rhetorical question is posed in yEruvin 1: 2, 19a: ויש הלכה כבית שמאי ולא כבית הלל "Is there [such a thing as] halakhah according to Beit Shammai and not according to Beit Hillel?"

22 In mTerumot 5: 4, after an alleged debate regarding a dispute between Beit Shammai and Beit Hillel, we read: לאחר שהודו. In yTerumot 5: 2, 43c, it is asked: אחר שהודו מי הודה למי בית שמאי לבית הלל או בית הלל לבית שמאי "[It says in the Mishnah] 'after they conceded.' Who yielded to whom? Beit Shammai to Beit Hillel, or Beit Hillel to Beit Shammai?" An extensive inquiry into this question follows, with arguments for both possibilities; in the course of this discussion, it is proposed that Beit Hillel conceded to Beit Shammai, because Beit Shammai's response in the mishnah to Beit Hillel's position seems decisively more logical than that of their opponents.

23 S. Safrai, "ההכרעה כבית הלל ביבנה," refers to the sweeping rabbinic statement לעולם הלכה כדברי בית הלל "The halakhah is always according to Beit Hillel," allegedly declared in Yabneh, and questions its authenticity. He maintains that the halakhah was not indiscriminately fixed according to the views of Beit Hillel in a wholesale manner, but rather each halakhah was decided separately, mostly according to Beit Hillel, but in some cases according to Beit Shammai. Thus Safrai too assumes, although not explicitly, that the report of a unitary decision regarding an entire corpus of halakhot is really a fiction; this alleged corpus of halakhot had to be disaggregated in order to establish the halakhah. I hypothesize, similarly, that such an aggregate structure had never really existed.

24 See section 3.1.

illustrious pedigree for the generally-accepted customs and laws of Jewish society.[25]

This device of the assigned pedigree continued to remain useful. This is illustrated in an interesting, but fictive, narrative about a supposed dispute between the two schools with respect to a philosophical issue.[26] The fictitious character of this narrative is beyond doubt; its literary structure indicates its fantastic nature, and its conclusion contrasts with the prevalent assumptions concerning the attributes of the two schools and the approval of the Hillelite way. The number of oddities in this short narrative is substantial, and I shall mention a few. The first peculiarity is the record of philosophical disputes between the two schools, whose discussions were usually confined to halakhic issues. It is even more bizarre that a vote was taken on such an issue. One may appreciate the utility of a practical procedure for establishing a definite halakhah, but a vote with the intent to impose a philosophical perspective is totally against the rabbinic style. The record that the dispute continued for "exactly" two and one-half years enhances the impression of oddity. The text does not identify which school maintained each view. We might assume that Beit Shammai, mentioned first,[27] are the authors of the first, pessimistic[28] maxim; yet this is doubtful,

---

[25] This is a common occurrence in Israelite biblical and post-biblical literature. J. Neusner, *Pharisees, Part III*, pp. 340 ff. questions L. Ginzberg's assumption "that the decrees were made by those to whom they were attributed."

[26] We read in bEruvin 13b: שתי שנים ומחצה נחלקו בית שמאי ובית הלל הללו אומרים נוח לו לאדם שלא נברא יותר משנברא והללו אומרים נוח לו לאדם שנברא יותר משלא נברא נמנו וגמרו נוח לו לאדם שלא נברא יותר משנברא "Beit Shammai and Beit Hillel disputed during two and one half years [about the following issue]. These said: It would be better if humans had not been created, and these said: It is better that humans were created than not. [Then] they voted and decided that it would have been preferable if humans had not been created."

[27] Certain scholars, for example, S. Hoenig, *The Great Sanhedrin*, p. 184, and Ch. Tchernowitz, תולדות ההלכה vol. 4, pp. 99- 124, 277 - 340, draw conclusions from the fact that Beit Shammai are quoted first in their disputes with Beit Hillel. The first scholar assumes that this indicates their conservative tendency, while for the second this attests that the Beit Shammai group was older than Beit Hillel. I suggest that the editor was simply following the known rabbinic maxim that Beit Hillel displayed esteem toward Beit Shammai by first quoting the others' declarations. As noted above (text at n. 11), it is stated in in ySukkah 2: 8, 53d, and bEruvin 13b that the halakhah was established according to Beit Hillel precisely because of this attitude: ולא עוד אלא שמקדימין דברי בית שמאי לדבריהן "Moreover they quoted Beit Shammai's declarations first." In mSukkah 2: 8 (to which the above statement in Y. T. Sukkah responds) there is an example of this common structure: כאותה ששנינו מי שהיה ראשו ורובו בסוכה ושלחנו בתוך הבית בית שמאי פוסלין ובית הלל מכשירין "As we learned [elsewhere] in the Mishnah: Beit Shammai declare that someone who had his head and the bulk of his body in the Sukkah but had his table in the house has not fulfilled the precept of eating in the Sukkah, and Beit Hillel maintain that he has performed his duty." It is obvious that it was due to this custom of Beit Hillel in

since the style differs from the usual method of identifying clearly who said what. The style here indicates, in my opinion, the intent of the editor to conceal the origin of each utterance. Moreover, if we assume that Beit Shammai were the source of the pessimistic philosophy, it would seem strange that their viewpoint was accepted as the binding one,[29] in contrast to the common maxim that the halakhah was always according to Beit Hillel. I propose that a later debate among Israelite intellectuals on this philosophical issue was attributed by the editor to a noble source, and he attempted to justify his own pessimistic philosophy by mentioning a non-existent vote that appeared to confirm it. This editor, probably aware of the previous fictitious attributions of anonymous halakhic decisions to Beit Shammai and Beit Hillel, took the liberty of acting similarly.

The Nature of the Disputes between Beit Shammai and Beit Hillel

As we have seen, there is a general assumption throughout the Talmud regarding the severity of Beit Shammai regarding the law (as well as the supposed rudeness of Shammai himself).[30] We have seen, however, that this assumption has no basis; contrary to the stereotype, in a great number of instances Beit Shammai were actually more lenient in their halakhic decisions.

Yet it is still a remarkable fact that the existence of these two schools, however much the record about them has been altered, did not engender the sort of sectarian split as occurred between the Pharisees and the "dissidents." Identifiable groups with differing opinions on such an array of

---

quoting their opponents' opinion first, and not for any other purpose, that the editor of the Mishnah quoted the declarations of Beit Shammai first. Although this explanation appears in the Gemara, we may assume that since it appears in both Talmudim, it was known by the last editor of the Mishnah (whenever this redaction occurred). Even if we assume, in contrast, that it was the authors of the explanation in the Talmudim who deduced their opinion from the fact that Beit Shammai's opinions regularly appear in the Mishnah before those of Beit Hillel, we may still assume that their judgment in this respect was more acute than that of modern scholars.

28 There are no indications of Beit Shammai maintaining a pessimistic philosophy.

29 It seems that this philosophy is in its essence contrary to Israelite theology and blatantly contradicts Scripture. One must not criticize God's decision to create humans (Gen 1: 26) and His emphatically favourable opinion concerning this creation: וירא אלהים את כל אשר עשה והנה טוב מאד "God saw all He had made and it was very good [Gen 1: 31]."

30 See n. 44 below regarding J. Neusner's perception of the bias of the mishnaic redactor against Shammai's personality and the halakhic decisions of his school, Beit Shammai.

halakhot would naturally have created rival leaders.[31] The desire for accurate implementation of the Torah precepts was undoubtedly a strong impulse in Israelite society during the last period of the Second Temple. In such circumstances it is unlikely that two distinct groups guided by resolute leaders[32] could have cooperated in the friendly and practical manner portrayed in the rabbinic literature.[33]

We have in fact noted that the rabbinic record regarding the relationship between the schools is inconsistent.[34] I must mention particularly the narrative, utterly in conflict with the usual portrayal of relations between the two schools, which records a hostile encounter between them regarding the promulgation of the "eighteen decrees."[35] The

---

[31] A. Saldarini, *Pharisees,* p. 210, characterizes Beit Shammai and Beit Hillel as "factions," not sects. This, however, is a semantic exercise that does not explain the reason behind their division.

[32] Ch. Albeck, מבוא למשנה, pp. 218-219 lists prominent Tannaim who were members of Beit Shammai. It is also assumed that Rabbi Eliezer ben Hyrcanos, known for his adamant stance against the majority of the Sages with respect to the event of the Akhnai oven (see chap. 1, text at nn. 58 ff.), was also a member of Beit Shammai.

[33] See the relevant citation in chap. 1, n. 55. I. Ben Shalom, בית שמאי, p. 234, questions why the disputes between the schools did not provoke a real split between them. He suggests that they had separate organizations, meeting places and courts, and met only occasionally on matters of mutual agreement. He assumes that they were separated *de facto* but not *de jure*. I cannot conceive of such circumstances existing during a period in which a pluralistic spirit dominated Israelite society and halakhic disputes were the order of the day. The discrepancies in the talmudic narratives concerning the relations between the schools may either demonstrate the want of reliability of the rabbinic literature with respect to historical events, or portray different occurrences. Friendly relations dominated the halakhic disputes, while hostile accounts likely refer to debates on political issues (see section 3.4 on this issue). It is plausible that, in political matters, unity of leadership is of crucial importance, and pluralism is not a practical solution. This is not to exclude the possibility that political debates and contentions were attributed to these groups, as were conflicting halakhic pronouncements. The specific passage describing hostile relations refers to the proclamation of the eighteen decrees; it seems (ibid.) that at least some of these had, or are assumed to have had, a political context with respect to relations with the Romans. An antagonistic environment would be plausible with respect to such a consequential political issue.

[34] I shall briefly reiterate the instances. We have records of harsh relations between Beit Shammai and Beit Hillel, such as that "they drew swords in the school," or even that the disciples of Shammai actually killed those of Beit Hillel (see chap. 3, nn. 65-6). There is, on the other hand, the statement that "truth and peace prevailed among them" (see chap. 4, text at n. 143). We have noted the criticism that the schools of Shammai and Hillel had too many unlearned disciples, and this was the reason for the increase in conflicts (quoted in chap. 3, n. 132). This, however, is in manifest contradiction to the utterance in mAvot 5: 17 that the conflict between Beit Shammai and Beit Hillel was a controversy for the sake of heaven - that is, a virtuous struggle (see chap. 4, text at n. 299).

[35] Concerning the decisive vote between the members of Beit Shammai and Beit Hillel (quoted in chap. 3, text at nn. 65-6), tShabbat 1: 16 adds to the record in mShabbat 1: 4

circumstances of these decrees are also perplexing; there are different versions of the list of the eighteen decrees in several talmudic texts, which are unclear. In bShabbat 17a it is recorded that one of the supposed eighteen decrees[36] had already been disputed personally between Shammai and Hillel, and the same strained relations are imputed to them.[37] The Gemara states ambiguously:[38] "And Hillel and Shammai promulgated this decree, and [the people] did not accept it from them; their disciples decreed it and they accepted it." This explanation is logically not tenable, and adds to the many questions[39] regarding the authenticity of the narratives

---

a description of the mood on that day of confrontation between the two groups: והיה אותו היום קשה להם לישראל כיום שנעשה בו העגל "And that day was as distressing to the people of Israel as the day on which the golden calf was made." We note that the narrative regarding the eighteen decrees recounts that the event had taken place at the dwelling of Rabbi Hananyah ben Hizkiyyah ben Garon, who was a great conciliator. He is quoted in bHagigah 13a and bMenahot 45a as the person who succeeded in reconciling the conflicting dicta in the Pentateuch and the book of Ezekiel, thereby avoiding the suppression of the latter. Thus his association with this event may be fictitious; his known aptitude in reaching a consensus between conflicting opinions may have been intended to bestow upon the decrees a greater chance of acceptance.

36 This refers to the issue of הבוצר לגת, that is, the cutting of grapes for the wine press. Fruit does not become unclean before it is touched by a liquid. Hillel considers the grapes put into the wine press as not yet touched by liquid and therefore not fit to become unclean, but Shammai considers them as fit.

37 We read there: אמר לו אם תקניטני גוזרני טומאה אף על המסיקה נעצו חרב בבית המדרש אמרו הנכנס יכנס והיוצא אל יצא ואותו היום היה הלל כפוף ויושב לפני שמאי כאחד מן התלמידים והיה קשה לישראל כיום שנעשה בו העגל "[As we have seen in the preceding note, Hillel considers grapes in the winepress not fit to become unclean, but Shammai considers them as fit. Hillel retorts with the logical question: Why are olives put in the olive press treated differently than the grapes in the wine press? This is an apparently undermining argument; Shammai] replied: If you enrage me I will also decree that olives put into the olive press are fit to become unclean. [A vote was to take place; in order to win, the disciples of Shammai] drew swords in the school, and said: Whoever is to go in, go in, and whoever is to go out shall not go out [in order to achieve a majority]. And on that day Hillel sat bowed in subordination to Shammai like one of the disciples, and that day was as distressing to the people of Israel as the day in which the golden calf was made." The parallel narrative in yShabbat 1: 4, 3c, has a different portrayal of the grim events connected with the dispute between the Houses.

38 From the succeeding rhetoric in the Gemara, it is not clear whether this phrase is a statement or a question. Rashi seems to consider it a statement.

39 In bShabbat 14b there is a similar discussion with respect to the uncleanness of the hands; a quote from a baraita, however, states that: שמאי והלל גזרו טומאה על הידים "Shammai and Hillel [by mutual agreement, in contrast to the issue of the grapes] declared the hands unclean." A similar allegation, but with different details, appears in yShabbat 1: 4, 3d, with respect to a decree regarding the obligation to wash the hands. We read there: הלל ושמאי גזרו על טהרת הידים רבי יוסי בי רבי בון

regarding the eighteen decrees and the relations between the two Sages and their disciples.

It must be noted that there are other passages in which the authenticity of alleged declarations of Shammai is questionable. I shall quote one characteristic occurrence. In mOrlah 2: 4 we read: "[Usually a tiny quantity of an unclean substance that is mixed with a clean substance does not render the whole thing unclean. The dispute in this mishnah involves a situation in which a tiny quantity does produce a distinct effect, as for example sourdough or yeast that leavens the dough, or spices that modify the taste of food]. Beit Shammai consider that even a small quantity [of such an unclean substance] makes the entire material unclean. Beit Hillel maintain that even in that case an unclean substance does not render all the material unclean, if it is less than the size of an egg." The subsequent mishnah 5, however, contains a conflicting statement: "Dostai of Kefar Yatmah was a disciple of Shammai and said: I have heard from Shammai the Elder who declared that [an unclean substance] less than the size of an egg never renders unclean [all the material in which it was mixed]." We thus observe that the list of halakhot attributed to Beit Shammai is questioned by one of Shammai's identified disciples.[40] Such phenomena[41]

בשם רבי לוי כך היתה הלכה בידן ושכחוה ועמדו השנים והסכימו על דעת הראשונים "Hillel and Shammai decreed the duty to keep the hands clean [by washing them]. Rabbi Yose ben Rabbi Bun [said] in the name of Rabbi Levi: This halakhah was [already] a prior tradition, [but] was forgotten, and the two [Hillel and Shammai] agreed to the decision of the antecedent Sages [and renewed it]." At any rate, both versions indicate problems with this decree and with the identity of its authors. The same question arises as to why their followers, Beit Hillel and Beit Shammai, had to decree this again. The puzzle is more perplexing in this case, since according to the baraita in the B.T. both Sages proclaimed this decree in full agreement. The B.T. attempts to attribute the quotation in the baraita in the name of Hillel and Shammai as having been proclaimed by the Sages together with their schools, but this solution is not acceptable, and other possibilities are put forward. It is noteworthy that a new term, הלל וסיעתו שמאי וסיעתו "Shammai and his faction, Hillel and his faction" is used in this deliberation instead of the previously used term תלמידיהו "his disciples," or the common "Beit Hillel and Beit Shammai." The use of three different terms for the same entity indicates the perplexity surrounding the schools of Shammai and Hillel.

40 We must note that this Tanna lived at the time of the Temple, that is, much before the conference at Yabneh, when we assume there was an attempt to establish the halakhah according to Beit Hillel. It is, therefore, odd that the editor of the Mishnah would have attributed a halakhah to Beit Shammai despite the contrary evidence of one of his personal disciples. This inconsistency can only be explained by assuming this attribution has resulted from the sweeping classification of all strict pronouncements as originating from Beit Shammai.

41 We read in mShevi'it 4: 2: בית שמאי אומרים אין אוכלין פירות שביעית בטובה ובית הלל אומרים אוכלין בטובה ושלא בטובה רבי יהודה אומר חלוף הדברים זו מקולי בית שמאי ומחומרי בית הלל "Beit Shammai say that one may not eat the fruits of the seventh year from a field when one has [done the owner of the

add to the skepticism concerning the existence of distinct groups called Beit Hillel and Beit Shammai and the dialogues between them.[42]

Such conflicting narratives regarding the nature of the relationship between the two schools certainly do little to affirm the authenticity of the entire record of these schools. We observe another oddity in bShabbat 14b: "But Hillel and Shammai disputed on only three issues." Although the Gemara marvels: "Are there no more?" only one additional dispute is recorded. This is still far-removed from the three hundred and sixteen disputes attributed to Beit Shammai and Beit Hillel.[43] It is difficult to accept that the disciples of Hillel and Shammai disagreed on such a multitude of halakhot on which their leaders agreed; this is especially so given that the disputes between the schools do not refer for the most part to new problems, but relate to such everyday issues as the Sabbath laws; these had likely already been raised during the lives and leadership of Hillel and Shammai. The fictional character of the above declaration is thus evident, and leads us to a different conclusion than that intimated by the talmudic portrayal of these two schools and the nature of their disputes.[44]

Again, I suggest that the scenario I have posited above - that is, the fictive nature of the classification - would explain this lack of consistency, and more importantly, why the existence of these two schools engendered no sectarian split. Though I have no explicit evidence to substantiate this hypothesis,[45] I maintain that the transition from an open and free method of

---

field a] favour. Beit Hillel say that one may eat irrespective of whether one has [done a] favour [for the owner] or not. Rabbi Yehudah says: It is the opposite [Beit Shammai allowed this and Beit Hillel prohibited it, and] that [decree] is one of those in which Beit Shammai held the lenient position and Beit Hillel the stricter." We note the impasse that results from the fictitious attribution of all strict decrees to Beit Shammai and all lenient ones to Beit Hillel.

42 See further section 3.4 regarding doubts as to the authenticity of the debates between the Houses.

43 M. D. Gross, אבות הדורות, p. 29. According to his count, Beit Shammai give the lenient decision in fifty-five disputes out of the total.

44 J. Neusner, *Pharisees, Part I*, pp. 208 ff. critically scrutinizes a great number of rabbinic narratives about Shammai, both positive and negative, and notes the biased approach toward him in all the narratives in which he is juxtaposed to Hillel. On p. 230, he writes: " Evidently Judah the Patriarch deliberately excluded evidence on Hillel's relationship to the House of Hillel similar to that of Shammai to the House of Shammai." On p. 294, he again questions the authenticity of the Hillel traditions, declaring: "Indeed, the whole corpus of Tannaitic literature was shaped by Hillelites." If we agree with Neusner's assessment of the credibility of all rabbinic records of the Hillel and Shammai controversies, we may also question, in my opinion, the authenticity of those reports detailing the odd structure and alleged utterances of both Houses.

45 The authenticity of dicta attributed to earlier Sages is now being questioned even by tradition-oriented scholars. We may note, for example, that D. Weiss-Halivni, *Midrash, Mishna and Gemara*, states on p. 19: "Can we be sure that the *drashoth* attributed to

decision-making to a closed and fixed process, which I have portrayed and corroborated in this work, allow us to consider this scenario as plausible.[46] The many inconsistencies with respect to the two Houses add to the skepticism regarding that structure and strengthen the plausibility of my proposition. There is, as far as I know, no attempt to explain logically and historically[47] the motive for this exceptional literary creation of two anonymous groups.[48] I have therefore considered it opportune to present my proposition as a basis for further scholarly deliberations.[49]

---

rabbis who lived long before the times of the editors of the Mishna and the Midrashei Halakha were actually stated by them and are not later additions by the editors?" He then cites a pronouncement in mSheqalim 6: 6: זה מדרש דרש יהוידע כהן גדול "Yehoyada the High Priest gave this exposition," a statement that is obviously devoid of any authenticity. Halivni then elaborates on the editorial activities that added or omitted earlier declarations. S. Stern, "Attribution and Authorship in the Babylonian Talmud," agrees in principle that the attributions are problematic, but attempts to consider this phenomenon in a more positive light. He perceives it (p. 51) as a tension between "individual innovative authority" and "collective tradition." Although the title of his essay refers to the Babylonian Talmud, one may apply the same assumptions to other rabbinic sources. It is definitely more effective to attempt to substantiate such a phenomenon through analysis of the wealth of citations in the Gemara, than through analysis of the sparse mishnaic text. L. Jacobs, who also relates to the problem of attributions in "How Much of the Babylonian Talmud is Pseudepigraphic?" and proffers evidence from B. T. citations, writes (p. 46): "Pseudepigraphic Rabbinic statements are not limited, of course, to the Babylonian Talmud, but it will be argued that in this work the pseudepigraphic element is prevalent to a remarkable degree." We should therefore not hesitate *a priori* to attribute to later editors the "creation" of the two opposing but undefined groups Beit Shammai and Beit Hillel.

46 I have cited in chap. 4, text following n. 79, Josephus' declaration that the Sadducees, as against the Pharisees, "dispute with the teachers" (*Ant.* 18: 16). Hence, it is implied that the Pharisees did not dispute with their teachers over views and halakhot. If there were such conflicts between the two Schools of Shammai and Hillel as are portrayed in the rabbinic literature, this would utterly contradict Josephus' description of the Pharisees.

47 There have been a great number of scholarly attempts to understand the underlying cause of the creation and persistence of the two groups, including L. Finkelstein, *Pharisees,* Vol. 2, pp. 619 ff.; L. Ginzberg, *On Jewish Law and Lore*, pp. 102 ff.; and I.D. Gilat, "כוונה ומעשה במשנת תנאים" pp. 104 - 116. A. Guttmann, "Hillelites and Shammaites - a Clarification," refers to the problematic and attempts to classify the leading Tannaim as Hillelites or Shammaites. As far as I know, however, no-one has addressed the question of why halakhic declarations were attributed to the schools, rather than to the individual tradents.

48 There is, on the other hand, scholarly skepticism about the precision of details and attributions in rabbinic literature. In addition to J. Neusner's assumptions, cited in n. 44, I wish to quote a number of declarations by E. P. Sanders on this subject. In *Jewish Law from Jesus to the Mishna,* p. 169, Sanders cites the above-quoted mOrlah 2: 4 (see text at n. 40) and asserts: "In the end we do not know what Shammai said on the topic, and there will always be uncertainty about this and many other details. We see, however, the relative indifference towards attributions and opinions." Regarding an attribution in mYevamot 15: 1 - 2, he declares that it "cannot be correct, since the

Analysis of Mishnah Shabbat - Attempts at Classification

Rabbinic literature records three hundred and sixteen disputes between Beit Shammai and Beit Hillel. It is naturally beyond the scope of this study to analyze all of them, and I shall thus attempt to examine some of the principles that seem to have been at the heart of the controversies between the two schools. I shall then contrast these with the principles of the dissident sects.

In deriving such principles, I must again emphasize the processes of rabbinic reasoning that I have portrayed above. The Mishnah rarely indicates the reason for any tannaitic decision. The Amoraim speculated about these reasons, and usually proposed various, often conflicting, ideas. We must critically evaluate their deliberations, and proffer other speculations that may seem to us more plausible. The Amoraim conceived that the Tannaim were restricted in their decisions to appropriate interpretations of Scripture;[50] they thus based their justifications of tannaitic dicta on such scriptural precedents, or on certain acknowledged principles. We should not consider ourselves-confined to these amoraic perceptions, and should attempt to reveal the principles that guided the Tannaim in their declarations. Although I have proposed that the Tannaim resolved to preserve their freedom of decision-making without being confined to rigid rules, I am of the opinion that they were nonetheless guided by certain principles that were applied to similar occurrences. They might, in some cases, have deviated from the primary principle for perfectly logical reasons, but generally maintained a coherent approach to similar cases.[51]

Houses of Hillel and Shammai preceded Rabbi Judah, and the passage has them enter a discussion after him...this shows clearly that there were editorial confusions, and consequently the possibility of incorrect attribution." He goes even further on p. 170 and states: "A major issue in rabbinic tradition is the overall date and reliability of the Houses material....there are, however, post 70 traditions among the Houses material." Sanders asserts on p. 171: "Uncertainty in detail is almost the rule rather than the exception.... Sometimes, what is attributed to a House in one source is attributed to a later Rabbi in another." This again indicates the great uncertainty regarding the authenticity of attributions of halakhic declarations to the Houses.

49 L. L. Grabbe, "4QMMT and Second Temple Jewish Society," p. 89, declares: "There is nothing more dangerous to good scholarship than the comfortable consensus which lies unchallenged...questioning the consensus can only be salutary...we need to take account of all sources and possibilities."

50 See sections 2.3.2 and 4.1.7.

51 For example, with regard to Sabbath laws, we have encountered the principle regarding מלאכה שאינה צריכה לגופה "a work not required for its essential purpose" (see chap. 2, n.8). Digging a hole because one needs the hole is a prohibited work; but if one digs a hole because he needs the earth, it is not considered a work deserving punishment. The same principle appears in the Y.T. with a different expression: עד שיהא לו צורך בגופו של דבר "[One is not liable for punishment or a sin offering]

The disputes recorded in Mishnah tractate Shabbat between Beit Shammai and Beit Hillel provide in some occurrences a clear indication of the different principles that guided the two schools, but at the same time attest to the difficulty in discerning a consistent classification. Chap. 1 of this tractate discusses work that is completed after the commencement of the Sabbath, either automatically without intervention by the "owner" of the work, or by a gentile who is not commanded to obey the Sabbath laws. The first three mishnayot of this chapter set out crucial principles on which Beit Shammai and Beit Hillel agree.[52] In mishnah 1, there is a list of eight examples of the primary prohibition against moving things from a private domain to a public domain on Sabbath. Mishnayot 2 and 3 list ten acts that are prohibited by virtue of the preventative principle סייג לתורה "a fence [or hedge] to the Torah" - that is, the interdiction of an otherwise permitted act lest one is induced involuntary or erroneously to perform a similar but prohibited act.[53]

Mishnayot 5 - 8 then set out a number of disputes between the two schools. At first glance, these seem to be of the same character, since they refer to work that starts before Sabbath and is completed during Sabbath; Beit Shammai prohibit them and Beit Hillel permit them. Upon further analysis, however, we note their different characters: certain of the examples deal with the automatic continuation of tasks begun with respect to an Israelite's property, while others refer to occurrences in which gentiles are involved. Other considerations must thus be involved in Beit Hillel's decision to permit them. There then follow examples in mishnayot 9 - 11, on which Beit Shammai and Beit Hillel are assumed to agree (though this is explicitly stated for only two of the examples cited in mishnah 9).

The editor of the Mishnah has put together all these apparently similar rules. We do not know, however, whether he assumed that both parties founded their rules upon the same principles, or in contrast, did not consider it necessary to stress the different principles that guided the

---

unless he requires the essence of the work." We may note another principle (in this case with the opposite consequence): פסיק רישיה ולא ימות "If you cut off the head [the living being] must die." (This principle is found in bAvodah Zarah 61a in the abridged form פסיק רישיה; Rashi and Tosafot, explaining its meaning, add the last two words.) The principle applies with respect to an act that must be prohibited because its consequences are inevitable; thus, the dictum providing that an unintentional act is different than an intentional one does not apply in this case.

52 This is the implication of mishnah 4. For our purpose, it is of no significance whether the agreement on these halakhot was included in the eighteen decrees or not; see the discussion above (nn. 35 ff. and related text) on this topic.

53 See discussion in section 4.1.7.

contenders.[54] The Tosefta[55] and Talmudim attempt to reveal the reasons behind the disputed halakhot in mishnayot 5 - 8 and 9b. In tShabbat 1: 21

[54] Cf. S. Zeitlin, "Les principes." Zeitlin assumes the following four principles to have been contested between the schools. 1. The authority of the Rabbis to interpret the law and effect adjustments even by the convention of a legal fiction. 2. The method of interpretation of Scripture, according to both the letter and the spirit. 3. Building a fence around the law. 4. The evaluation of intention in the application of the law. I disagree with his classification. Both Beit Hillel and Beit Shammai concur with respect to the authority of the Sages to interpret the law and adjust it. We have no record that Shammai or Beit Shammai opposed the institution of the *prosbul*, an obvious manipulation of the law through a legal fiction. See also E. S. Rosenthal, מסורת-הלכה, pp. 324 ff. regarding the concurrence of Beit Shammai and Beit Hillel on the principles of interpretation of the law. Both schools consented to the principle of building a fence around the law, and only differed occasionally as to its degree. Finally, there is no evidence that Beit Shammai denied the significance of intention. Intention is a factor, for instance, in questions involving work on Sabbath. As an example, we read in mShabbat 12: 2 of someone who splits a branch from a tree with the intention of improving the plant. (Rashi and other traditional commentators understand the term המלקט, which indicates, in other instances, the act of picking up something that is detached, as implying a splitting off. Ch. Albeck, in his commentary to this mishnah in ששה סדרי משנה, follows Rashi. Accordingly, the term לתקן refers to the intention of the person to repair or improve the tree, by pruning. Maimonides in his commentary to the mishnah understands המלקט to refer to the act of picking up fallen branches, and the term לתקן to refer to the preparation of the soil for plowing by removing any branches.) The mishnah deems such a person liable for a violation of the Sabbath, even for cutting a tiny branch; but if he intended to use the branch for making a fire, he is only liable if he cuts off a quantity sufficient for cooking an egg. Yet we do not encounter a dispute between Beit Shammai and Beit Hillel with respect to this and similar Sabbath laws in which the relevant intention is an element of the work, and accordingly governs whether a prohibited work has been performed on the Sabbath. Further, the dispute between Beit Shammai and Beit Hillel in mBava Metzi'a 3: 12, with respect to the responsibility of the bailee of an object if he declares that he will seize the object, does not involve the issue of intention. It refers to the question of when an object is deemed to be transferred to another owner. Beit Shammai maintain that if one declares in the presence of two witnesses (as Rashi explains) that he will take possession of an object legally in his charge, this formalizes the change of ownership, and he is therefore responsible for any damage from that moment onwards. Beit Hillel require a physical act of appropriation to complete the transfer of ownership. Nor does the dispute in mNazir 5: 1, concerning an erroneous dedication of *heqdesh*, revolve around an issue of intention. It does not relate to the effectiveness of a statement of intention versus a physical action, but to the relationship between one's verbal expression and one's intention. As we see from the alleged debate between the contending parties, Beit Shammai maintain that the relevant dedication in this case was originally erroneously expressed. Moreover, the real motive for the dispute remains a matter of speculation, and we see that in the deliberation of the Gemara in bNazir 31a, it is alleged that the dispute refers to the comparison of a mistaken dedication to a case in which there has been a substitution of dedicated materials, in which the validity of an erroneous expression is not disputed. Beit Shammai compare the dedication procedure to an act of substitution, and therefore consider a mistaken dedication as valid, whereas Beit Hillel do not approve of the

and yShabbat 1: 5, 3d, it is suggested that each group interpreted the relevant biblical verses differently;[56] this led to Beit Shammai's conclusion that the task must be totally completed before Sabbath, and Beit Hillel's perception that the automatic continuation of a task initiated before the beginning of Sabbath is not prohibited. In bShabbat 18a,[57] an entirely different motive is alleged to be the core of the dispute: the precept requiring "the resting of [an Israelite's] vessels."[58] According to the Gemara, Beit Shammai would declare this rule of rest even when there is no work involved, while Beit Hillel would maintain that there is no precept of rest for vessels.

Both of these proposed explanations offer a reasonable motive for the prohibition or permission of activities enumerated in mishnayot 5-8 and 9b;[59] but some inconsistencies remain. The discussion of Beit Shammai's

---

comparison, considering the act of substitution as *sui generis*. Finally, there is the dispute between Beit Shammai and Beit Hillel in mMikva'ot 4: 1, regarding the disqualification for the ritual bath of "collected" water - in this case, rain water that is collected in a receptacle and left forgotten under a drain pipe. Again, there is no indication that Beit Shammai negated the significance of intent. Rabbi Meir asserts in the mishnah that it was decided by vote to acknowledge the halakhah according to Beit Shammai. If one forgot the receptacle in the yard, however, and not under the drain, Beit Shammai agreed that the water was not disqualified; they maintained that, in this case, it is certain that there was no intention to collect the water. Hence, even according to Beit Shammai intention affects the application of this law; they simply dispute whether inattentiveness can be deemed to indicate a real lack of intention.

55 The Tosefta cites an alleged debate between the two parties, but I think that this portrayal does not bear the mark of authenticity. As we shall see (text at nn. 57-8), bShabbat 18a sets out another motive for Beit Shammai's prohibitions, the precept of שביתת כלים "the resting of [an Israelite's] vessels." If the Gemara had considered the alleged debate in Tosefta authentic, this motive would not have been brought up in the deliberations. This simulated debate between Beit Shammai and Beit Hillel in the Tosefta casts doubt on the entire issue of the disputes between these two "generic" groups, and further corroborates my assessment of their fictitious character.

56 We read in Tosefta: שבית שמיי אומ' ששת ימים תעבוד ועשית כל מלאכתך שתהא כל מלאכתך גמורה מערב שבת ובית הלל או' ששת ימים תעבד מלאכה עושה אתה כל ששה "Beit Shammai say: It is written 'Six days you should labour and do all your work [Exod 20: 8; v. 9 in KJV]' and that means all your work should be complete on the eve of Sabbath. And Beit Hillel say [the passage] means you may work all the six days [that is, you must not work on the seventh day, but the task may be completed of its own accord on the seventh day]."

57 We read there as part of a baraita: ובכל אשר אמרתי אליכם תשמרו לרבות שביתת כלים "'Be careful to do everything I have said to you' [Exod 23: 13; this apparently superfluous verse] comes to add [the precept requiring] the resting of [the Israelite's] vessels."

58 This precept is deduced through suitable exegesis of a scriptural verse in Mekilta d'Rabbi Ishmael, *Mishpatim* 20 and *Bo* 9 (see n. 65).

59 The text of mishnah 9b: ושוין אלו ואלו שטוענין קורת בית הבד ועגולי הגת "Both [Beit Shammai and Beit Hillel, who dispute in mishnah 9a] agree on the issue of

prohibition offered in Y. T. and Tosefta does not indicate whether Beit Shammai considered the rule regarding automatic continuation of a process to be a Torah command or a rabbinic decree. In bShabbat 18a, however, the precept of "the resting of [an Israelite's] vessels" is stated in the rhetorical deliberations to be a Torah command, according to both Beit Shammai and Beit Hillel, or perhaps only according to Beit Shammai.[60]

Further, neither of the rationales offered in the Tosefta and Talmudim is applicable to the dispute cited in mishnayot 7 and 8, in which gentiles are involved. Nor are the circumstances of mishnah 7 (involving a sale to a gentile) and mishnah 8 (involving articles given to a gentile who is to do work on them) exactly the same, [61] and none of the rabbinic literature reflects any attempt to investigate the dispute regarding these two circumstances. The later commentators[62] state that Beit Shammai insisted a sale had to be completed a sufficient time before the Sabbath to allow the gentile buyer to reach his destination,[63] to preclude any assumption that he was carrying the goods on Sabbath as an agent for the Israelite. Beit Hillel

---

the [continuous dripping of the juice from] the oil and wine press on Sabbath," is not in its appropriate place. It seems to be interjected as an opening for mishnah 10, as part of the range of Sabbath work with respect to which Beit Shammai and Beit Hillel agree. The text of this statement is rather ambiguous as to whether the relevant activity is permitted or prohibited. The Gemara in bShabbat 19a understands it to mean that both schools agree that the activity is permitted, and questions Beit Shammai's consent in this case. The question is resolved by positing that the schools are in agreement when the fruit was crushed before Sabbath; there is no longer any work involved in this process, since the real work, the crushing of the fruit, occurred before Sabbath

60 We read there: מאן תנא שביתת כלים דאורייתא בית שמאי היא "Who is the Tanna [that declares the precept] of the resting of the vessels a Torah command? It is Beit Shammai."

61 Mishnah 7 refers to the sale of goods (without any specification of their nature) to a gentile shortly before the commencement of Sabbath. Beit Shammai require that the sale and the tasks involved in its execution must be concluded in time to allow the buyer to reach his destination before Sabbath. Mishnah 8 refers to the belongings of an Israelite, which are given to a gentile so that he may do work on them. Beit Shammai require that the items must be given to the gentile before Sabbath in time to allow the completion of the work before Sabbath, while Beit Hillel permit this as late as Friday before sundown.

62 Rabbenu Nissim, in his commentary on Alfasi, states that neither of the motives used to explain the antecedent mishnayot - the precept that a work must be completed before Sabbath and the precept of rest for the vessels - is applicable in this occurrence.

63 I have not encountered in the Gemara an explicit clarification of Beit Shammai's requirement - that is, whether the Israelite must actually insist that the gentile buyer reach his destination before dawn, or simply complete the transaction ahead of Sabbath with enough time to allow the buyer to reach his destination. I would argue that the Israelite cannot be held responsible for the buyer actually reaching his home, and hence, his duty is restricted to the completion of the sale at the appropriate time before Sabbath. One of Maimonides' commentators, מגיד משנה, confirms this assumption in his comments to *Mishneh Torah, Hilkhot Shabbat* 6: 12.

were not concerned about the issue. It is not clear, however, whether the same reasoning is at work in mishnah 8, with respect to work performed by a gentile on Sabbath for an Israelite. The traditional commentators, including Maimonides, considered that Beit Shammai's requirement to allow for appropriate time before Sabbath for the gentile to complete the required work on the Israelite's goods was, again, to avoid any assumption that the gentile performed the work as the Israelite's agent.[64]

We read in Mekilta d'Rabbi Ishmael,[65] however, that the prohibition of work on Sabbath also includes work performed for an Israelite by a gentile. It is plausible that the application of this rather more conventional rule is at the root of the dispute. Beit Shammai conceived that if one assigns a task to a gentile shortly before the commencement of Sabbath, one is deemed to have instructed him to perform the work promptly, and this is prohibited; therefore, the task must be commissioned in ample time to be completed before Sabbath. If the gentile then performs it on Sabbath, he does it of his own will and on his own account, not as a consequence of the Israelite's instruction, and this is not prohibited. Beit Hillel maintained that work done by a gentile on a contractual basis severs the link between the two parties, and it is entirely within the gentile's control[66] when to perform the work. It is, therefore, permitted to commission a gentile to perform work for an Israelite even right before sundown on Friday.

Continuing with chapter 1 of tractate Shabbat, mishnah 10[67] concerns the automatic continuation on Sabbath of a roasting or baking process started before Sabbath, a halakhah supposedly acknowledged by both Beit

---

64 Ch. Albeck, *ששה סדרי משנה, סדר מועד*, links this dispute to the previous mishnayot and proposes the same three motives for all; he does not perceive the difference in circumstances, as I have suggested, and as the commentators perceived them.

65 Mekilta d'Rabbi Ishmael, *Bo* 9. We read there: כל מלאכה לא יעשה בהם לא תעשה אתה ולא יעשה חברך ולא יעשה גוי מלאכתך "[It is written in Exod 12:16:] 'Do not work at all in these days' [this verse refers to the Passover holiday, not to Sabbath, but it is then deduced to be relevant to the Sabbath by an argument *a fortiori*], and this means that neither you, nor your friend, nor an alien should do your work."

66 The commentators correctly emphasized that this permission is only valid when the work is performed at the gentile's location. It is prohibited to perform the work at the Israelite's premises, consistent with their view that the dispute refers to the problem of how the act might be viewed by society. It is nevertheless conceivable that, according to my assumption, Beit Hillel would also prohibit performing the work on Sabbath at the Israelite's premises, because in this case, the link between the two would not be deemed disconnected.

67 We read there: אין צולין בשר בצל וביצה אלא כדי שיצולו מבעוד יום אין נותנין פת לתנור עם חשכה ולא חררה על גבי גחלים אלא כדי שיקרמו פניה מבעוד יום "One must not roast meat, egg and onion [on Friday afternoon], unless it will be roasted before sundown. One must not place dough in the oven before sundown or a cake on the coals, unless the surface will become crusted before sundown."

Shammai and Beit Hillel.[68] Again, questions arise as to the originator of this rule. This issue, we must agree, is of the same character as the cases cited in mishnayot 5 and 6: the automatic completion of work begun before the Sabbath. If Beit Hillel allow the bleaching of flax in the oven to continue on Sabbath (as in mishnah 6), one would also expect them to allow the roasting of meat to continue, if started before. Similarly, if Beit Shammai prohibit the continuation of bleaching, the same prohibition should apply to the baking of bread, and the formation of a crust should not imply the completion of the baking process; bread should be completely baked before the commencement of Sabbath. Agreement on this point is therefore not the expected result. Further, there is an alleged discussion between Beit Shammai and Beit Hillel recorded in tShabbat 1: 20, in which Beit Shammai claim that Beit Hillel also prohibit the continuation of roasting on Sabbath, and question why they nonetheless permit the continuous soaking of ink and similar substances (as in mShabbat 1: 5). There is no logical answer to this question in the Tosefta. In tShabbat 1: 21, Beit Hillel retort by posing their own question: Why do Beit Shammai permit the loading of the beams of the oil press and the round mold of the wine press at Friday dusk, while prohibiting the continuous soaking process? Again, no answer is proffered in the Tosefta, which states only: "These remained resolute in their answer, and these remained resolute in their answer [that is, each group persisted in its position]." This phrase suggests that the contenders in fact gave answers;[69] but the structure of the Tosefta passage indicates that the succeeding explanation given for the dispute was offered by the toseftan editor, and is not a record of an actual deliberation between the two Houses. The explanation given is that Beit Shammai require the completion of a work before Sabbath and Beit Hillel permit its automatic continuation during Sabbath. Yet this reasoning is not satisfactory, since it does not address the specific questions asked by the contenders. In bShabbat 19a,[70] the question posed by Beit Shammai is cited, and a logical explanation offered based on the different circumstances of the cases; but the question posed by Beit Shammai to Beit Hillel, regarding their prohibition of the completion of the roasting process, remains without answer.

In bShabbat 18b, a baraita is recorded that appears to originate in Beit Shammai's principle that prohibits the continuation of an automatic

---

68 The mishnah does not indicate the author of the prohibition against this automatic completion of work, or the reason for the prohibition. It is cited anonymously, a mode that implies it was considered the final halakhah; this does not, however, preclude the possibility of an initial dispute.

69 The expression בתשובתן indicates an answer; a persistence in one's position should have been expressed by דבריהן, as in mEduyyot 1: 3.

70 See n. 59, which cites the answer.

process: a woman is prohibited from putting on a pot of beans, which require an extended cooking time, to cook before the Sabbath. Nonetheless, the Gemara attempts to demonstrate that the rule may also be derived from Beit Hillel's opinion. In order to vindicate this clearly unworkable conjecture, a rabbit is pulled from the hat: the act is stated to be prohibited by Beit Hillel for a different motive, to prevent the contingency that the woman might rake the coals to intensify the heat and speed up the cooking. This reasoning is immediately challenged, since it obviously conflicts with Beit Hillel's decision to permit the similar process of bleaching on Sabbath. As is common, various imaginative devices are brought forward to reconcile the irreconcilable.

Two rabbinic sources thus attempt to attribute to Beit Hillel a rule utterly conflicting with their clear principle. I have the impression that these speculations in tShabbat 1: 20 and in bShabbat 18b result from Rabbi's decision to quote the prohibition of mishnah 10 anonymously, thus indicating his intent to establish it as the final halakhah. Since the halakhah is also assumed to follow the opinion of Beit Hillel, intellectual acrobatics must be utilized to harmonize the decision with that opinion, despite the evident defiance of common sense.

We may deduce certain inferences from the scrutiny of these halakhot. As we have seen, the Tannaim, the authors of the mishnaic decrees, created their rules in various ways (often on the basis of logical principles), though bound within the framework of the Torah. These rules and principles were disputed among the Sages, as is common in every intellectual society; in contrast to contemporary scholars, however, who consider themselves free of any restrictions in their considerations, the framework of the Torah bound the Sages. The editor of the Mishnah, as we have seen in other instances,[71] disregarded those principles likely used by the authors of these halakhot in reaching their decisions; he attempted to impose his own opinions, by attributing the rules he preferred to the anonymous "Sages" or to a majority. Thus it was he who considered it appropriate to prohibit the continuous cooking by the housewife - possibly as a preventative measure[72] - and therefore quoted this rule as an anonymous declaration, to establish it as the final halakhah. The harmonization impulse of the Sages completely obliterated any remaining logical structure. The preventative nature of the

---

71 See section 3.1.

72 This is a reasonable conjecture, since in the succeeding mishnah, there is a contrasting, more lenient approach to a similar topic, the roasting of the Passover lamb and the upkeep of the fire in the Temple. In these circumstances, it seemed less likely than in the case of a housewife or an individual baker that the people deployed for the tasks would forget the Sabbath laws and commit a transgression. Such an opinion is suggested in yShabbat 1: 8, 4b: חבורות זריזות הן "The groups [who prepare the Passover sacrifice] are scrupulous [and may be trusted not do something prohibited]," and in bShabbat 20a, in a slightly different literary style: דבני חבורה זריזין הן.

prohibition of continuous cooking was brought up in a rhetorical discussion; the later commentators fully acknowledged this preventative measure as the motive for this prohibition, and went on to establish[73] a complex group of halakhot.[74] Yet, they still had to attempt to reconcile the alleged prohibition by Beit Hillel with the necessity of preparing food for Sabbath in the traditional manner: putting uncooked food into an oven on the eve of Sabbath and taking it out Sabbath morning, a custom widespread in all rabbinic communities. The halakhic consequences of such dialectical acrobatics are remarkable.

With respect to our particular investigation, it is significant to note how ideas and decisions are attributed in retrospect to authors who did not declare them. This method served the goal of harmonizing apparently conflicting utterances. We observe that debates, as for example the discussions between Beit Shammai and Beit Hillel in the above-cited tShabbat 1: 20, are devised by rabbinic literature, though they evidently did not take place.[75] We have also noted how later Sages ascribed their own

---

[73] They also considered the fact that the prohibition is quoted anonymously in the mishnah.

[74] See Maimonides, *Mishneh Torah*, *Hilkhot Shabbat* 3: 3 - 18 and *Tur Shulhan Arukh*, *Orah Hayim* 253-4.

[75] We should similarly regard the alleged personal intervention of Shammai in disputes between Beit Shammai and Beit Hillel, recorded in mEduyyot 1:7, 8, 10, 11. For disciples to dispute with their master, in whose name they were supposed to continue his teachings against Beit Hillel, would be extraordinary. At least two rabbinic sources contradict such an occurrence. We have noted above (p. 366) a statement in bShabbat (by Rav Huna) that Hillel and Shammai disputed on only three halakhot (recorded in mEduyyot 1: 1, 2 and 3): אמר רב הונא בשלשה מקומות נחלקו שמאי והלל. The Gemara than scrutinizes this statement and finds two other disputes, but does not refer to the above interventions of Shammai. Although we do not encounter Hillel's personal opinion in these mishnayot, we may assume that Beit Hillel expressed his views, and hence in effect the dispute was between the heads of the schools. Further, we read the following description of the disputes in tHagigah 2: 9 and ySanhedrin 1: 4, 19c: משם הלכה יוצא ורווחת בישראל משרבו תלמידי שמיי והלל שלא שימשו כל צרכן הרבו מחלוקות בישראל ונעשו שתי תורות "[Previously] the halakhah was established from there [the Superior Court in the Temple] and spread to all of Israel. When there was an increase in the number of disciples of Shammai and Hillel, who did not attend sufficiently to their needs [of the scholars, i.e. they did not learn sufficiently], disputes increased in Israel and this generated two Torot." The simple interpretation of this narrative would indicate that the disputes between the disciples, that is, between Beit Shammai and Beit Hillel, started after the destruction of the Temple and the cessation of the Sanhedrin, and after the death of the heads of the schools. It would not be logical to assume that the disciples started this conflict at a time when their leaders agreed upon these issues. With respect to the dispute concerning the laying of hands on the offerings, recorded in mHagigah 2:3 and tHagigah 2:10-12 (see chap. 3, n. 147), there are doubts as to the authenticity of the narrative. See I. Ben Shalom, בית שמאי, pp. 234 -5, who maintains that the dialogues

opinions and motives to the pronouncements of earlier Sages. Thus tShabbat 1: 21 sets out the motives for particular Sabbath laws within an alleged debate between Beit Shammai and Beit Hillel, as if these were the authentic opinions of the two schools. (As we have seen, bShabbat 18a offers another motive for their dispute.) The liberty taken by the Sages and editors in devising imaginary debates and attributing alleged opinions and motives correlates with my hypothesis regarding the arbitrariness of classifying strict declarations as originating from Beit Shammai and lenient ones as originating from Beit Hillel. The prohibition against completing the cooking on Sabbath was probably initially attributed, as a strict rule, to Beit Shammai; but since it was decided (by whom remains unclear) to establish this stricter halakhah as the rule, the editor quoted it anonymously; Tosefta, and the baraita quoted in bShabbat 18b, more audacious, attributed it to Beit Hillel, to conform with the maxim that the halakhah is always to follow Beit Hillel.

Comparison and Contrast between Rabbinic and Dissident Halakhic Rules

The analysis of these disputes confirms that the real nature of the disagreements between the Houses was divergent approaches to and evaluations of the principles underlying halakhic issues.[76] As we have noted, it is remarkable that such divergences did not engender sectarian conflict. Thus, as the final point in this Appendix, it is interesting to compare certain rabbinic rules (in some case, reflected in supposed disputes between Beit Shammai and Beit Hillel) with the opinions expressed by the

---

between Beit Shammai and Beit Hillel are a later literary arrangement, and do not attest to real conversations. See also chap. 2, n. 107.

76 This conclusion contradicts the attempts by some scholars to detect other motives, and to propose typological classifications of the schools according to non-halakhic criteria, as the key to understanding the disputes between them. Numerous such categorizations have been proposed, such as a Babylonian school versus a Jerusalemite, leniency versus strictness in the application of the law, gentleness versus rudeness, moderate versus restrictive, peace-loving as against intensely unbending ultra-nationalists, progressives versus conservatives, plebeians versus patricians, townspeople versus provincial communities, conceptual diversity versus conceptual unity, innovative versus rigid approach to the established law, and similar classifications (see also the section on "leniency versus strictness" above). The fact that the Sages themselves were compelled to adjust their initial stereotype, admitting many exceptions to it, negates any attempt to classify the disputes on the basis of such general characteristics. This fact also highlights the arbitrary nature of the attribution of halakhot to one school or the other. L. Ginzberg, *On Jewish Law and Lore*, pp. 102 ff., has already contested this assumption and demonstrated its flaws.

"dissidents" of the Dead Sea sects.[77] I shall examine three such instances, which I have classified according to the principles I deem to underlie these rules.

a) Difference in Principle, Agreement in Practice

I postulate that the motive behind all the prohibitions in the above-cited rules in Mishnah tractate Shabbat, whether attributed to Beit Shammai or to anonymous origin, was the rabbinic practice of decreeing preventative rules, as discussed in section 4.1.7. The dispute between the contenders is restricted to the issue of whether the enumerated cases are all susceptible to the same degree of erroneous transgression. The stricter approach requires all cases to be treated equally, whereas the more lenient one conceives a difference between them and exempts some cases from preventative restrictions. We often encounter in connection with similar cases the rabbinic maxim: "We must not consider such a farfetched [contingency]."[78]

Comparing the acts prohibited in mishnayot 2 and 3, which are characterized as undisputed, and comparing them with those acts whose prohibition was disputed, we may perceive the differences that justify a distinct approach. The first mishnayot refer to occurrences in which the individual is engaged in some absorbing activity that may cause him to overlook the commencement of Sabbath; there was therefore no disagreement with respect to the sensible requirement of a preventive prohibition. In the circumstances specified in mishnayot 5 and 6, on the other hand, the persons involved were not performing any work at the start of the Sabbath; they had in effect completed their relevant tasks, by placing the beans in the water, the flax in the oven, the wool in the kettle, and the trap in the water. The lenient group therefore thought it extremely unlikely that the owners would forget the Sabbath and attempt to hasten the work by tampering with their utensils.

The remaining two mishnayot, covering a sale to a gentile and work done by a gentile for an Israelite, may also be regarded as within the category of preventative decrees, just as the traditional commentators supposed. The concern in this case is not that one might perform a prohibited act, but that others might assume that a transgression had been committed. Such an apprehension is found elsewhere to justify the rabbinic

---

77 I have preferred to use comparisons with halakhot of the Dead Sea Scrolls, as these are primary evidence of the rules of these sects, whereas the Sadducees' declarations, as cited by the Rabbis, likely do not reflect their genuine and unaltered viewpoint; moreover, the Rabbis presented the Sadducees' conceptions in a biased manner, adapted to their own purposes.

78 In most of the relevant occurrences, the text is not so concise; in the rhetorical deliberation, it is explained that in a contention, some argue that one must consider such an eventuality and others argue that it is unnecessary.

prohibition of an action.[79] There might also have been a desire to prevent the Israelite from instructing the gentile to perform the task without delay; such a stipulation, concluded shortly before the commencement of the Sabbath, would be tantamount to an explicit mandate to perform the work for the Israelite on the Sabbath, which is unquestionably prohibited.[80] In either case, the strict view would decree a restriction, while the lenient view would follow its customary routine and consider such a contingency too remote to require a prohibition. I thus suggest that all the episodes relate to the identical topic of preventative decrees. This principle bestows a logical organization on the mishnayot of this chapter, in contrast with the jumble of issues suggested by the traditional commentators.

As we have noted, there is no reliable data from a primary source as to the motive that induced the stricter group to prohibit this type of conduct. Although I would not completely exclude the Tosefta's speculation that the prohibition in mishnayot 5 and 6 stems from the opinion that any work must be entirely completed before the Sabbath, or that the vessels of an Israelite must rest on Sabbath, I tend to reject these explanations. Such conceptions would compel us to treat these prohibitions as Torah commands,[81] and would not fit into the general rabbinic philosophy. They would conform rather with the dissident view expressed in the Damascus Scroll 4Q266, Col. X: 22: אל יאכל איש ביום השבת כי אם המוכן "A person must eat on Sabbath only what was ready-made before [Sabbath]." The dissident groups did not accept the concept of distinct legal statuses for Torah precepts and human decrees, a cornerstone of rabbinic legal theory, or a two-tiered system of rules of divine and human origin.[82] Such a prohibition also conflicts with the permission for the automatic continuation of work that is declared in mishnayot 5 and 6; there is no logical difference between these works and the cooking process. The rabbinic restrictions are the outcome of the concept of preventive prohibitions, סייג לתורה "a fence [or hedge] to the Torah," whereas the dissident concept originates from a different theory.[83] The prohibition

---

79 We read in yKil'ayim 3: 4, 28b: מה שאסרו חכמים לא גזרו אלא מפני מראית עין "What the Sages had prohibited was decreed only for the sake of appearances [i.e. to prevent someone getting the wrong impression]."

80 See n. 65. Although the Mekilta deduces this prohibition through scriptural exegesis, it is considered a rabbinic restriction, not a Torah edict (bEruvin 67b).

81 This issue is discussed earlier, text at nn. 59-60.

82 See S. Talmon, "בין מקרא ובין משנה," particularly p. 26, regarding the attitude of the Qumran community with respect to the rabbinic distinction between written and oral Torah.

83 Interestingly, the antecedent exhortations in the Damascus Scroll Col. X are expressed as explicit prohibitions of various acts, except with respect to food. The wording of the Scroll does not specifically prohibit the acts of cooking or preparing the food in the

against proceeding with the cooking, as expressed in mishnah 10 and in the baraita, which allegedly was accepted by the lenient group, also stems from the rabbinic concept of preventative decrees and has no theoretical affinity with the dissident rule.[84] We do not know, as discussed above, whether this rule is authentic; if it was, it is plausible to assume that the particular circumstances induced the lenient group to agree on the application of a preventative restriction in this case.[85]

b) Differences in Practice, Agreement in Principle

With respect to the immediately preceding issue, the Pharisees/Sages and the dissidents seem to have agreed as to practice, but disagreed as to principle. Let me now scrutinize an example of the opposite case, in which there is no agreement between the pharisaic-rabbinic view and the dissident view on practice, but in which both sides base their decisions on the same principle. This is the much-discussed issue of the law of the נצוק *nitzoq*,

---

same way as it prohibits (for instance) walking outside one's location: אל יתהלך איש "a man should not go..."; it simply stresses that the food must be ready before Sabbath.

84 I do not agree entirely with L. Schiffman, *The Halakhah at Qumran,* p. 98, who compares the rabbinic prohibition in our mishnah, and in bBetzah 6b, with the CD rule. He perceives that there were different origins, but does not specify the legal distinctions. The topic in Betzah is of an entirely different character; there the rabbinic prohibition stems from the rule of מוקצה, regarding a substance not reserved or dedicated for use before Sabbath.

85 The same character is apparent with respect to the prohibition against trading on Sabbath. I conceive that the text in CD XI: 15, אל יחל איש את השבת על הון ובצע בשבת, refers to trading; as Martinéz and Tigchelaar have translated it: "No one should profane the Sabbath for riches or gain on the Sabbath." L. H. Schiffman, *The Halakhah at Qumran,* p. 125, indicates, as one of two possibilities for the explanation of this passage, that it refers to trading, but fails to note the use of the term יחל solely in this particular prohibition. As we know, the dissident authors used phrases or terms from Scripture to stress the linkage of their declarations to the biblical source; hence, we should correlate the term יחל with Nehemiah's reproach concerning trading on Sabbath. We read in Neh 13: 17: מה הדבר הרע הזה אשר אתם עושים ומחללים את יום השבת "What is this wicked thing you are doing - desecrating the Sabbath day?" The use of the same term as Nehemiah used in his censure indicates the nature of the profanation: trading on Sabbath. I presume that the many other apparently odd rules connected to the holiness of the Sabbath, such as not to discuss business (CD X: 16 - 17), pronounce stupid words (X: 17 - 19), or wear dirty clothes (XI: 3) are connected to the concept of חילול שבת, avoiding the desecration of the Sabbath. The Pharisees also prohibited trading on Sabbath, but only as a preventative decree; the punishment is also different for the transgression of a rabbinic rule than for the violation of a Torah command, for which one is liable to capital punishment. See chap. 2, text at n. 11, on this particular issue.

"liquid stream," in mYadayim 4: 7,[86] and its counterpart in 4QMMT Fragment 8 Column IV.[87] The principle that a substance poured from one vessel to another makes a connection between the two, and can pollute the clean contents of the upper vessel, is acknowledged by all parties: the Pharisees/Sages, both Beit Shammai and Beit Hillel, as cited in the mishnah, and the dissident author of MMT. All agree that a viscous, sticky substance like honey creates a connection;[88] Beit Shammai concur with the dissidents that such a connection is created by "even a thick soup of split beans [Jastrow] [mMakhshirin 5: 9]."[89] The dissension between the Pharisees/Sages and MMT consists solely in the evaluation of the physical properties of water, or other non-viscous liquid, and whether or not such a liquid creates a connection between two vessels.

c) Differences in Both Practice and Principle

Let me now analyze a third type of conflict between the Pharisees/Sages and dissidents, in which we note both different concepts and different practical implications. This example involves a dispute regarding the rabbinic concept of ברא ירך אם "the fetus is an element of its mother" and its legal implications. I have chosen this topic for the following reasons: a) it is both a universal and a contemporary problem, b) it will indicate certain lenient implications of an apparently strict standpoint, c) it will demonstrate

---

86 We read there: אומרים צדוקין קובלין אנו עליכם פרושים שאתם מטהרים את הנצוק "The Sadducees say: we reproach you, Pharisees, because you declare the flow of liquid [from a pure vessel] as pure." The mishnah presents the dispute concerning defilement of a flow of liquid as a debate between the Sages and the Sadducees; we also encounter this argument expressed from the view of a "dissident" party in 4QMMT Fragment 8 Column IV, cited in the next note. There is thus confirmation of a dispute between Judean groups with respect to this issue; yet the dilemma regarding the identification of the different groups remains. Was this a controversy between the Pharisees and Sadducees, as appears in mYadayim 4: 7, or was another dissident group, associated with the Dead Sea Scrolls, involved? The ambiguity of terms in these sources confirms the thesis that the Sages did not grant any significance to the precise identification of their opponents. These texts also suggest that the rabbinic narratives do not attest to real debates with specific groups, but rather reflect theoretical arguments against concepts attributed to these groups.

87 We read there: ו]אף על המצוקות אנחנו אומר[ים] שהם שאין בהם [ט]הרה המוצקות אינם מבדילות בין הטמא [ל]טהור כי לחת המוצקות והמקבל מהמה כהם לחה אחת "...and also concerning liquid streams, we say that in these there is no purity, and also that flows of liquid streams can not separate impure from pure, because the liquid of the liquid streams and their vessels is alike" (text and translation from Martínez and Tigchelaar).

88 We read in mMakhshirin 5: 9: כל הנצוק טהור חוץ מדבש הזיפין והצפחת "Any flow of liquid leaves [what remains in the outpouring vessel] clean except [two types of] honey."

89 We read there in continuation: בית שמאי אומרים אף המקפה שלגריסין ושלפול.

the Sages' "modern" opinion on this acrimonious issue, and d) it will emphasize the conceptual, rather than the halakhic, character of certain pharisaic/rabbinic - dissident disputes. 4Q396, MMT^{c}, Col I: 2 - 4, which is in poor condition, is interpreted as referring to a living (animal) fetus found within its slaughtered mother; it may not be slaughtered on the same day, because of the prohibition in Lev 22: 28.[90] This law is based on the dissident concept that the fetus is a separate living being, and is not a component of its mother like her body parts. Consistent with the same principle, we read in the Temple Scroll 11QT L: 10 - 11: "And if a woman is pregnant and her child dies in her womb, all the days which he is dead within her she shall be impure like a grave."[91] There follow precise details concerning the gravity of her uncleanness. This law too is founded upon the principle that the fetus is a separate person; hence its mother is, metaphorically and legally, its grave.

The rabbinic rule, in contrast, states: "the fetus is an element of its mother" (bYevamot 78a and others).[92] In mHullin 4: 5 it is thus provided:[93] "And the Sages say: The [ritual] slaughter of the mother [animal] purifies it [the offspring found inside the mother, and it does not need to be ritually slaughtered]." We read similarly in mArakhin 1: 4: "When a pregnant

---

90 We read there: ושור או שה אתו ואת בנו לא תשחטו ביום אחד "Do not slaughter a cow or a sheep and its young on the same day."

91 We read there: ואשה כי תהיה מלאה וימות ילדה במעיה כול הימים אשר הוא בתוכה מת תטמא כקבר. Text and translation from Martínez, p. 1269.

92 I did not find a parallel rabbinic rule regarding the uncleanness of the mother carrying a dead fetus, but there is an indirect reference to this topic. In mNazir 7: 2, there is a list of unclean substances for which a Nazir must interrupt his vow and shave. Among them is ועל מלא תרווד רקב "for a spoonful of dirt containing decayed human remains." In bNazir 51a, it is explained that in order to effect this outcome, the dirt must contain only human remains, without being mixed with any other substances such as pieces of cloth or wood. In addition, it must originate from one person only; a spoonful of dirt from two persons does not cause this effect. The Gemara then discusses the following issue: עובר במעי אשה כיון דאמר מר עובר ירך אמו הלכך גופה הוא כיון דסופו לצאת מיפרש פריש מינה "What about [a spoonful of dirt originating from] a woman with a fetus in her womb? Since one Sage said that a fetus is an element of its mother, is it deemed to be one body, and thus causes pollution, or, since it was supposed eventually to be separated, is it deemed to be a separate body [and thus considered two persons]." A complex discussion follows. Maimoinides, *Mishneh Torah, Hilkhot Tum'at Met* 3: 5, concludes: אשה מעוברת ועוברה במעיה אין להם רקב "A pregnant woman [buried] with a fetus in her womb does not produce dirt [that pollutes the Nazir]." Hence we see that the principle עובר ירך אמו הוא "the fetus is an element of its mother" is also incorporated in rabbinic law within rules of cleanness.

93 The mishnah refers to finding living young within the womb of the slaughtered animal. Rabbi Meir maintains that it is a separate animal and must be slaughtered, but the Sages oppose this. The halakhah follows the majority.

woman has to be executed, one does not wait until she gives birth [because the fetus is an element of its mother]. But when she is already sitting on the birthing chair, one waits until she gives birth." The Gemara in bArakhin 7a explains the motive for the second case: "Since it [the fetus] moved from its place, it becomes a distinct body [human being]" and must not be killed for the sins of its mother. We note that these differing opinions are not the result of any halakhic dispute regarding how to interpret Scripture.[94] The dilemma involves, as it does in our day, a lack of agreement on the precise nature of human conception. Regarding the halakhic implications of this dispute, we note that the dissident rule would be more lenient in the case of the woman awaiting execution than the rabbinic halakhah.[95] One may assume that the life of the fetus, as a separate living creature, would be safeguarded, and the execution postponed until after its birth.[96]

---

94 Although the Gemara in bArakhin 7a attempts in its usual rhetorical manner to reveal a scriptural support for this decision, I think the tannaitic decree was based on the principle עובר ירך אמו הוא "the fetus is an element of its mother." The dictum that, once the mother has sat upon the travailing chair, the fetus must be saved indicates the use of this principle. The rhetoric in the Gemara starts with a question regarding the apparent superfluity of the mishnah statement: פשיטא "This [the decision not to postpone the execution] is a clear case [therefore why is the pronouncement in the mishnah necessary?]" The Gemara then attempts to demonstrate that the mishnah had to declare the rule because we might have deduced from the phrase in Deut 22: 22, ומתו גם שניהם "Both [the man and the woman] must die," that in this case too both the mother and the fetus must die. This maxim is also the basis of mBava Qamma 5: 1, where there is definitely no connection to the exegesis of a scriptural verse. The mishnah deals with the case of an ox that gored a pregnant cow; one finds both dead without knowing whether the goring occurred before the cow gave birth, and the calf died because of the goring, or whether the calf was gored after its delivery. In the first case, the owner of the ox would not be liable to pay for the loss of the calf, since it was a part of its mother at the time of the goring. In the second case, the owner would also have to pay for the loss of the calf. Rav Yehudah declares in bBava Qamma 46a that while the Sages dispute the decision of the mishnah, they do not repudiate the principle that the fetus is an element of its mother. The contention relates to another general legal principle: המוציא מחברו עליו הראיה "When one claims damages from his neighbour, he must provide the evidence." In this case, since the precise fact of when the goring occurred is unknown, and there is no evidence, there is no legal basis for demanding compensation for the calf.

95 An even more appalling rule is quoted in bArakhin 7a: אמר רב יהודה אמר שמואל האשה היוצאה ליהרג מכין אותה כנגד בית הריון כדי שימות הוולד תחילה כדי שלא תבא לידי ניוול "Rav Yehudah said in the name of Samuel: One hits a [pregnant] woman going to her execution on her uterus in order that the death of the fetus precedes the execution of its mother. This is done in order to avoid disgrace to her [i.e. so that she does not give birth in public during her execution]." The dissident halakhah is here definitely more lenient.

96 It is only fair to remark here that, on the other hand, the dissidents do not allow the desecration of the Sabbath for saving a life, whereas the Sages prescribe this. We read in tShabbat 15: 11: מפקחין פקוח נפש בשבת והזריז הרי זה משובח ואין צריך

d) Conclusion

We have scrutinized three types of dissension between the pharisaic-rabbinic halakhah and that of the dissidents. We may summarize our comparisons as follows:

1. Some Sabbath laws demonstrate the same operative rules, but different underlying concepts.

2. The rules of *nitzoq*, regarding the polluting effect of a poured liquid, reflect the same legal principle but different practical implications, due to conflicting opinions regarding the physical qualities of various substances.

3. The laws with respect to the status of the fetus show contradictory theoretical opinions concerning this "mystical" topic and, in consequence, divergent rules and practical applications.

I believe that the analysis of halakhic disputes between the Pharisees/Sages and the "dissidents" constitutes a fascinating subject. Scholars have limited their research on this topic primarily to a comparison between the halakhic declarations of the opposing groups. I have attempted an analysis of the conceptual foundations of the different groups that ultimately generated the divergent halakhic decisions. I hope that my initial undertaking on a restricted number of conflicting halakhot will arouse an interest in this particular segment of research; this type of analysis will, in my opinion, reveal many other aspects of the motives and circumstances of the sectarian division in the last period of the Second Commonwealth.

ליטול רשות מבית דין "One opens up a heap of debris to save a life on Sabbath, and the faster one does this the more praiseworthy it is. One does not need to receive permission [to do this] from the court." There is a scholarly debate regarding the correct interpretation of CD XI: 16 - 17 on this issue; see, e.g., Joseph M. Baumgarten, "The Relevance of Rabbinic Sources to the Study of Qumran Law," who maintains that the dissidents did not allow the desecration of the Sabbath in this case. See also L. Schiffman, *The Halakhah at Qumran*, pp. 125 - 128, and his suggestions on the interpretation of these verses in the Damascus Scroll.

Bibliography

Aderet, A. "מסכת עדויות כעדות לדרכי השיקום והתקומה." In יהודים ויהדות בימי בית שני המשנה והתלמוד, מחקרים לכבודו של ש. ספראי, pp. 251 - 265. Edited by I. Gafni, A. Oppenheimer, M. Stern. Jerusalem, 1993. [מסכת עדויות]

Albeck, Ch. ששה סדרי משנה. 6 vols. Jerusalem, 1952-7.

-------- מבוא למשנה. Jerusalem, 1959.

-------- מבוא לתלמודים. Tel Aviv, 1969.

Albeck, S. "Law and History in Halakhic Research." *In Modern Research in Jewish Law*, pp. 1 - 20. Edited by Bernard S. Jackson. Leiden, 1980.

Alon, G. תולדות היהודים בא"י בתקופת המשנה והתלמוד. Vol. I. Tel Aviv, 1967.[תולדות]

——— *Jews, Judaism and the Classical World, Studies in Jewish History in the Times of the Second Temple and Talmud.* Translated by Israel Abrahams. Jerusalem, 1977. [*Jewish History*]

-------- *The Jews in their Land in the Talmudic Age*. 2 vols. Translated and edited by Gershon Levi. Jerusalem, 1980, 1984. [*The Jews*]

Alter, Robert. *The Art of Biblical Narrative*. New York, 1981.

Bacher, Wilhelm (Binyamin Ze'ev). *Die Exegetische Terminologie der jüdischen Traditionsliteratur*. 2 parts. Leipzig, 1899, reprinted Hildesheim 1965. [*Terminologie*]

——— *Tradition und Tradenten in den Schulen Palästinas und Babyloniens*. Leipzig, 1914. [*Tradition*]

-------- אגדות התנאים. 2 parts. Translated from German by A. Z. Rabinowitz. Jerusalem, 1922.

Baer, Y.F. "היסודות ההיסטוריים של ההלכה." *Tsiyon* 17/1 (1952), 1-55

Bakhos, Carol. Book Review. *JBL* 120/4 (2001), 784 - 792.

Baumbach, G. "The Sadducees in Josephus. " In *Josephus, the Bible and History*, pp.173 - 195. Edited by L. H. Feldman and Gohei Hata. Detroit, 1989.

Baumgarten, Joseph M. "A Response to the Discussion on DJD XVIII." In *The Dead Sea Scrolls at Fifty, Proceedings of the 1997 Society of Biblical Literature, Qumran Section Meetings*, pp. 199 - 201. Edited by R. A. Kugler and E. M. Schuller. Atlanta, GA, 1999.

-------- "The Relevance of Rabbinic Sources to the Study of Qumran Law." In *Proceedings of the Twelfth World Congress of Jewish Studies*, Division A, pp. 73 - 78. Jerusalem, 1999.

Beckwith, R.T. *Calendar and Chronology, Jewish and Christian*. Leiden,1996.

Ben Shalom, I. בית שמאי ומאבק הקנאים נגד רומי. Jerusalem, 1993. [בית שמאי]

Bentham, J. An Introduction to the Principles of Morals and Legislation. Edited by J.H. Burns and H.L.A. Hart. Methuen, 1982.

Berger, M.S. *Rabbinic Authority*. New York, 1998.

Bernstein, M. "The Employment and Interpretation of Scripture in 4QMMT: Preliminary Observations." In *Reading 4QMMT, New Perspectives on Qumran Law and History*, pp. 29-51. Edited by J. Kampen and M. J. Bernstein. Atlanta, 1996.

Boccaccini, G. "History of Judaism: Its Periods in Antiquity." In *Judaism in Late Antiquity. Part 2, Historical Syntheses*, pp. 285 - 308. Edited by J. Neusner. Leiden, 1995. ["History of Judaism"]

Büchler, A. הסנהדרין בירושלים ובה"ד הגדול שבלשכת הגזית. Translated from German by N. Ginton. Jerusalem, 1974.[הסנהדרין]

Bultmann, R. *Primitive Christianity in its Contemporary Setting*. New York, 1965.

Callaway, P. R. "Extending Divine Revelation: Micro-Compositional Strategies in the Temple Scroll." In *Temple Scroll Studies*, pp. 149 - 162. Edited by G. J. Brooke. Sheffield, 1989.

Cazelles, H. "Biblical and Pre-biblical Historiography." In *Israel's Past in Present Research, Essays on Ancient Israelite Historiography*, pp. 98 - 128. Edited by V. Philips Long. Winona Lake, Indiana, 1999.

Cohen, S.A. *The Three Crowns, Structures of Communal Politics in Early Rabbinic Jewry*. Cambridge, 1990.[*Three Crowns*]

Cohen, S.J.D. *Josephus in Galilee and Rome, his Vita and Development as an Historian*. Leiden, 1979. [*Josephus*]

------- "The Significance of Yavneh: Pharisees, Rabbis, and the End of Jewish Sectarianism." *HUCA* 55 (1984), pp. 27 - 54. ["The Significance of Yavneh"]

------- *From the Maccabees to the Mishna*. Philadelphia, 1987.

------- "Judaism to the Mishna 135 - 220 CE." In *Christianity and Rabbinic Judaism, A Parallel History of their Origins and Early Development*, pp. 195 - 223. Edited by H. Shanks. Washington DC, 1992. ["Judaism"]

------- *The Synoptic Problem in Rabbinic Literature*. BJS 326. Providence, 2000.

Cohn, H.H. "The Methodology of Jewish Law, A Secularist View." In *Modern Research in Jewish Law*, pp. 123 - 135. Edited by Bernard S. Jackson. Leiden, 1980. ["Methodology"]

Daube, D. "Rabbinic Methods of Interpretation and Hellenistic Rhetoric." *HUCA* 22 (1949), 239 - 264.

Davies, P. R. "Qumran and the Quest for the Historical Judaism." In *The Scrolls and the Scriptures, Qumran Fifty Years After*, pp. 24 - 42. Edited by S. E. Porter and C. A. Evans. Sheffield, 1997.

------- *Scribes and Schools*. Louisville, Ky, 1998.

Efron, J. *Studies of the Hasmonean Period*. Leiden, 1987.

Elbogen, I. התפילה בישראל בהתפתחותה ההיסטורית. Translated from German by J. Amir, and complemented by J. Heinemann et al. Tel Aviv, 1972.

Elon, M. המשפט העברי, תולדותיו, מקורותיו, עקרונותיו. 3 vols. Jerusalem, 1973.

------- *Jewish Law, History, Sources, Principles*. 4 vols. Translated from Hebrew by B. Auerbach and M. J. Sykes. Jerusalem, 1994. [*Jewish Law*]

Encyclopedia Judaica.
S.v. "Maimonidean Controversy," by H. H. Ben-Sasson. Vol. 11, 745-754
S.v. "Oral Law," by M. D. Herr. Vol. 12, 1439-1442.
S.v. "Yose ha-gelili," by I.M. Ta-Shma.

Englard, I. "Research in Jewish Law." In *Modern Research in Jewish Law*, pp. 21-65. Edited by Bernard S. Jackson. Leiden, 1980.

Epstein, J. N. מבואות לספרות התנאים. 2 vols. Edited by E. Z. Melamed. Jerusalem, 1957.[תנאים]

Falk, Z. W. "Binding and Loosing." In *Studies in Jewish Legal History, Essays in Honour of David Daube*, pp.92 - 100. Edited by B. S. Jackson. London, 1974.

Feinstein, D.M. אגרות משה, אורח חיים. Vol. 1. New York, 1959.

Finkelstein, L. The Pharisees, The Sociological Background of their Faith. 2 vols. Philadelphia, PA, 1940. [Pharisees]

------- "The Ethics of Anonymity among the Pharisees." In *Pharisaism in the Making, Selected Essays*, pp. 187 - 198. Ktav Publishing, 1972.

------- *Sifra on Leviticus*. 5 vols. New York, 1989. [Sifra]

Fishbane, M. *Biblical Interpretation in Ancient Israel*. Oxford, 1985.

Fitzpatrick-McKinley, A. *The Transformation of Torah from Scribal Advice to Law*. JSOT Supplement Series 287. Sheffield, 1999. [*The Transformation of Torah*]

Fox (Lebeit Yoreh), Harry. "Jaffee's *The Talmud of Babylonia: Horayot*." *JQR* 79/2-3 (Oct. 1988 - Jan. 1989), 235 - 242. ["*Horayot*"]

------- "Neusner's *The Bavli and its Sources*, A Review Essay." *JQR* 80 (January-April, 1990), 349 - 361.["*Bavli*"]

-------- "Introducing Tosefta." In *Introducing Tosefta: Textual, Intratextual and Intertextual Studies*, pp. 1-37. Edited by H. Fox and T. Meacham. New York, 1999.

Fox, Marvin. "Maimonides and Aquinas on Natural Law."*Dine Israel* 3 (1972), v-xxxvi.

Frankel, Z. דרכי המשנה . Warsaw, 1923.

Frymer-Kensky, T. "The Emergence of Jewish Biblical Theologies." In *Jews, Christians, and the Theology of the Hebrew Scriptures*, pp. 109 - 121. Edited by A. O. Bellis and J. S. Kaminsky. Atlanta 2000.

Gadamer, H.G. *Truth and Method*. Translated from German by G. Barden and J. Cumming. New York, 1975.

Gafni, I. 'ישיבה' ו'מתיבתא'' *Tsiyon* 43 (1978), 12 - 37.

-------- "היצירה הרוחנית-ספרותית." In ארץ-ישראל מחורבן בית שני ועד הכיבוש המוסלמי, Vol. 1, pp. 473 - 494. Edited by Z. Baras et al. Jerusalem, 1982.

-------- "' שבט ומחוקק' - על דפוסי מנהיגות חדשים בתקופת התלמוד בארץ ישראל ובבבל". In כהונה ומלוכה יחסי דת ומדינה בישראל ובעמים, pp. 79 - 91.Edited by I. Gafni and G. Motzkin. Jerusalem, 1987. [שבט ומחוקק]

-------- "Talmudic Research in Modern Time: Between Scholarship and Ideology." In *Jüdische Geschichte in hellenistich-römischer Zeit, Wege der Forschung, vom alten zum neuen Schürer*, pp. 133 - 148. Edited by A. Oppenheimer and E. Müller - Luckner. München, 1999. ["Talmudic Research"]

Gaster, T.H. *Myth, Legend and Custom in the Old Testament*. N. Y. 1969.

Geiger, Abraham. *Urschrift.und Ubersetzungen der Bibel*. Frankfurt, 1928. [*Urschrift*]

Gerhardsson, Birger. *Memory and Manuscript, Oral Tradition and Written Transmission in Rabbinic Judaism and Early Christianity*. Grand Rapids, Mi. 1961. [Memory and Manuscript]

Gilat, I.D. "להשתלשלותם של איסורי שבות בשבת." In מחקרי תלמוד, Vol. 2, pp. 197 - 219. Edited by M. Bar-Asher and D. Rosenthal. Jerusalem, 1993. [איסורי שבות]

-------- "כוונה ומעשה במשנת תנאים." *Bar-Ilan* 4-5 (1967), 104-116.

-------- פרקים בהשתלשלות ההלכה . Ramat Gan, 1992.

Ginzberg, L. "Tamid. The Oldest Treatise of the Mishna." *Journal of Jewish Lore and Philosophy* 1 (1919), 33 - 44, 197 - 209, 265 - 295.

-------- *On Jewish Law and Lore*. Meridian, 1962.

Goldberg, A. "דרכו של רבי יהודה הנשיא בסידור המשנה." *Tarbits* 28 (1958), 260-9.

Goldenberg, Robert. "The Deposition of Rabban Gamaliel II: an

Examination of the Sources." *JJS* 23/2 (1972), 167 -190. ["The Deposition of Rabban Gamaliel II"]

Goodblatt. D. *Rabbinic Instruction in Sassanian Babylonia*. Studies in Judaism in Late Antiquity 9. Leiden , 1975.

-------- "The Origin of Roman Recognition of the Palestinian Patriarchate." In *Studies in the History of the Jewish People and the Land of Israel*, Vol. IV, pp. 89 - 102. Haifa, 1978. ["Roman Recognition"]

-------- "The Babylonian Talmud." In *Aufstieg und Niedergang der Rőmischen Welt II*, pp. 257 - 336. Edited by H. Temporini and W. Haase. Berlin, 1979.

------- "על ספור ה"קשר" נגד רבן שמעון בן גמליאל השני." *Tsiyon* 49 (1984), 349 - 374. [קשר]

------- "The Place of the Pharisees in First Century Judaism: The State of the Debate." *JSJ* 20/1 (1989), 12 - 30. [" The Place of the Pharisees"]

------- *The Monarchic Principle, Studies in Jewish Self-Government in Antiquity*. TSAJ 38. Tübingen, 1994. [*The Monarchic Principle*]

------- "Iudaea between the Revolts." In *Jüdische Geschichte in hellenistich-römischer Zeit, Wege der Forschung, vom alten zum neuen Schürer*, pp. 101 - 118. Edited by A. Oppenheimer and E. Müller - Luckner. München, 1999.

Goodman, M. *State and Society in Roman Galilee, A. D. 132 - 212*. Totowa, N. J., 1983. [*Roman Galilee*]

Grabbe, Lester L. "Hellenistic Judaism." In *Judaism in Late Antiquity. Part 2, Historical Syntheses*, pp. 53 -83. Edited by J. Neusner. Leiden, 1995.

-------- "4QMMT and Second Temple Jewish Society." In *Legal Texts and Legal Issues, Proceedings of the Second Meeting of the International Organization for Qumran Studies, Cambridge 1995*. Vol. XXIII: *Studies on the Texts of the Desert of Judah*, pp. 89 - 108. Edited by M. Bernstein, F. G. Martínez, J. Kampen. Leiden, 1997.

Green, W.S. "What's in a Name - The Problematic of Rabbinic 'Biography.'" In *Approaches to Ancient Judaism: Theory and Practice*, pp. 77-96. Brown Judaic Studies 1. Atlanta, GA, 1978. ["Biography"]

Gross, M.D. אבות הדורות. Tel Aviv, 1957.

Guttmann, A. "Hillelites and Shammaites - a Clarification." *HUCA* 28 (1957), 115 - 126.

Haenchen, Ernst. *The Acts of the Apostles: A Commentary*. Revised translation by R. McL. Wilson. Oxford, 1971.[*The Acts of the Apostles*]

Halbertal, Moshe. מהפכות פרשניות בהתהוותן: ערכים בשיקולים פרשניים במדרש הלכה. Jerusalem, second revised edition, 1999. [מהפכות]

Halevy, Isaac. דורות הראשונים 6 vols. Jerusalem 1966.

Halperin, B."The State of Israelite History." In *Reconsidering Israel and Judah*, pp. 540 - 565. Edited by G. N. Knoppers and J. Gordon McConville. Winona Lake, Ind., 2000.

Handelman, S. A. *The Slayers of Moses, The Emergence of Rabbinic Interpretation in Modern Literary Theory*. Albany, N. Y., 1982. [*Interpretation*]

Harris, Jay M. *How Do We Know This?* New York, 1995.

-------- "From Inner-Biblical Interpretation to Early Rabbinic Exegesis." In *Hebrew Bible/Old Testament, The History of its Interpretation*, Vol. I, pp. 256 - 269. Edited by Magne Sæbo. Gőttingen, 1996.

Harvey, V. A. *The Historian and the Believer: A Confrontation between the Modern Historian's Principles of Judgment and the Christian's Will-to-Believe*. New York, 1966. [*Confrontation*]

Havlin, S.Z. על החתימה הספרותית. In ,מחקרים בספרות התלמודית יום עיון לרגל מלאת שמונים שנה לשאול ליברמן, pp. 148 - 192. Jerusalem, 1983.

Heger, Paul. "Tosefta and Historical Memory." In *Introducing Tosefta: Textual, Intratextual and Intertextual Studies*, pp. 277 - 301. Edited by H. Fox and T. Meacham. N.Y, 1999. ["Tosefta"]

------- *The Three Biblical Altar Laws*. BZAW 279. Berlin, 1999. [*Altars*]

Heinemann, Joseph. *Prayer in the Talmud*. Studia Judaica 9. Berlin, 1977.

Herr, M. D. "לבעיית הלכות מלחמה בשבת בימי בית שני ובתקופת המשנה והתלמוד" *Tarbits* 30 (1960-61), 242 - 256.[מלחמה]

-------- "The Historical Significance of the Dialogues between Jewish Sages and Roman Dignitaries." *Scripta Hierosolymitana* 22 (1971), 123 - 150. ["Dialogues"]

-------- "תפיסת ההיסטוריה אצל חז"ל" In *Sixth World Congress of Jewish Studies*, Vol. 3, pp. 129 - 142. Jerusalem 1977.

Hezser, C. *The Social Structure of the Rabbinic Movement in Roman Palestine*. Tübingen, 1997. [*Social Structure*]

Hoenig, S. *Great Sanhedrin, A Study of the Origin, Development, Composition and Functions of the Bet Din Ha-Gadol during the Second Jewish Commonwealth*. Philadelphia, 1953.[*The Great Sanhedrin*]

Instone Brewer, David. *Techniques and Assumptions in Jewish Exegesis before 70 CE*. Texte und Studien zum Antiken Judentum 30. Tűbingen, 1992. [*Techniques*]

Jacobs, L."How much of the Babylonian Talmud is Pseudepigraphic?" *JJS* 28/1 (1977), 46 - 59.

Jacobs, M. *Die Institution des jüdischen Patriarchen*. Tübingen, 1995.

Jaffee, M. "The Taqqanah in Tannaitic Literature: Jurisprudence and the Construction of Rabbinic Memory." *JJS* 41/2 (1990), 204 - 225.["Taqqanah"]

Kadushin, Max. *Understanding the Rabbinic Mind.* 3rd edition. New York, 1972.

Kahane, A. הספרים החיצונים . Tel Aviv, 1959.

Kaiser, O. *Einleitung in das Alte Testament*. Revised edition. Gütersloh, 1984.

——— *Studien zur Literaturgeschichte des Alten Testamentes.* Forschung zur Bibel 90. Würzburg, 2000.

Kaminka, A. "Hillel's Life and Work." *JQR* 30 (1939-40), 107 - 122.

Kapah, J. D. משנה עם פירוש רבינו משה בן מימון . 7 vols. Jerusalem, 1963.

Kaplan, Lawrence. "דעת תורה: תפישה מודרנית." In בין סמכות לאוטונומיה במסורת ישראל, pp. 95 - 145. Edited by Z. Safrai and A. Sagi. Tel Aviv, 1997.

Kasher, R. "Interpretation" In Mikra. Text, Translation, Reading and Interpretation of the Hebrew Bible in Ancient Judaism and Early Christianity. Edited by M. J. Mulder and H. Sysling. Assen, 1988.

Kimelman, R. "Birkat Ha-Minim and the Lack of Evidence for an Anti-Christian Jewish Prayer in Late Antiquity." In *Jewish and Christian Self-Definition*, Vol. II, pp. 226 - 244. Edited by E. P. Sanders et al. Philadelphia, 1981. [" Birkat Ha-Minim"]

Lapin, H. "Early Rabbinic Civil Law and the Literature of the Second Temple Period." *Jewish Studies Quarterly* 2 (1995), 149 - 183.

Levi, Primo. *If Not Now? When?* Translated from Italian by W. Weavers. New York, 1985.

Levinas, E. *Nine Talmudic Readings*. Translated from French by A. Aronowicz, Bloomington, Indiana,1994.

Levine, Lee. *The Rabbinic Class of Roman Palestine in Late Antiquity*. New York, 1989

-------- "Judaism from the Destruction of Jerusalem to the End of the Second Jewish Revolt 70 - 135 C. E." In *Christianity and Rabbinic Judaism, A Parallel History of their Origins and Early Development*, pp. 125 - 149. Edited by H. Shanks. Washington DC, 1992. ["Judaism"].

Levinson, B.M. *Deuteronomy and the Hermeneutics of Legal Innovation*. New York, 1997.

Lewin, B.M. אגרת רב שרירא גאון. Reprinted Jerusalem, 1972.

Lieberman, S. *Hellenism in Jewish Palestine.* Texts and Studies of the

Jewish Theological Seminary of America 18. New York, 1950. [*Hellenism*]

------- *Greek in Jewish Palestine*. New York 1965. [*Greek*]

Lightstone, Jack N. "Sadducees versus Pharisees, The Tannaitic Sources." In *Christianity, Judaism and other Greco-Roman Cults: studies for Morton Smith at sixty*. Part 3: *Judaism before 70*, pp. 206 -217. Edited by J. Neusner. Leiden, 1975. ["Sadducees versus Pharisees"]

------ *Yose the Galilean. I. Tradition in Mishna-Tosefta.* Leiden, 1979. [*Yose the Galilean*]

Lüdemann, G. *Early Christianity According to the Traditions in Acts: A Commentary*. Minneapolis, MN, 1989. [*Early Christianity*]

Lyons, W. J. "The Words of Gamaliel (Acts 5.38-39)." *JSNT* 68 (1997), pp. 23 - 49.

Maimonides. *The Guide of the Perplexed.* Translated by S. Pines. Chicago, Ill, 1963.

Mantel, H.D. *Studies in the History of the Sanhedrin*. Harvard Semitic Studies XVII. Cambridge, MA, 1961. [*Sanhedrin*]

Margaliot, M., ed. אנציקלופדיה לחכמי התלמוד והגאונים . 2 vols. Tel Aviv, 1962.

Martinéz, F.G. and E. J. C. Tigchelaar. *The Dead Sea Scroll Study Edition.* Vol. 1: 1Q1 - 4Q273. Leiden, 1997.

Moore, G.F. *Judaism*. 3 vols. Cambridge, 1927

Neusner, Jacob. Development of a Legend, Studies on the Traditions Concerning Yohanan ben Zakkai. Studia Post-Biblica 16. Leiden, 1970. [Yohanan ben Zakkai]

------ *The Rabbinic Traditions about the Pharisees before 70. Part I, The Masters.* [*Pharisees, Part I*] *Part III, Conclusions.* [*Pharisees, Part III*] Studies in Ancient Judaism 1. Leiden, 1971.

------- Eliezer ben Hyrcanus, *The Tradition and the Man*. 2 vols. Leiden, 1973. [*Eliezer ben Hyrcanus*]

------ *A History of the Mishnaic Law of Purities, Part XIV* and *Part XXI* . Leiden, 1977. [*Purities*]

------- The History of Earlier Rabbinic Judaism; Some New Approaches. HR16. 1977. [History]

------- "The Use of the Later Rabbinic Evidence for the Study of First-Century Pharisaism." In *Approaches to Ancient Judaism: Theory and Practice*, pp. 215 - 227. Brown Judaic Studies 1. Atlanta, GA, 1978. ["Evidence"]

------- "The Formation of Rabbinic Judaism; Yavneh (Jamnia) from A.D. 70 to 100." In *Aufstieg und Niedergang der Römischen Welt II*, pp. 3 - 42. Edited by H. Temporini and W. Haase. Berlin, 1979. ["Yavneh"]

------ *From Politics to Piety, The Emergence of Pharisaic Judaism*. New

York, 1979. [*From Politics to Piety*]

------- "Scripture and Tradition in Judaism." In *Approaches to Ancient Judaism, Volume II*, pp. 173-193. Brown Judaic Studies 9. Edited by W. S. Green. Atlanta, GA, 1980.

-------- "Rabbinic Sources." In *Approaches to Judaism 3*, pp. 1 - 17. Brown Judaic Studies 11. .Edited by W. S. Green. Ann Arbor, 1981.

——— *Judaism, The Evidence of the Mishnah*. Chicago, 1981.[*Judaism*]

——— *In Search of Talmudic Biography. The Problem of the Attributed Sayings*. Brown Judaic Studies 70. Chico, CA, 1984. [*Biography*].

——— *Sifra. An Analytical Translation*. 3 vols. Brown Judaic Studies 138-140. Atlanta, 1988. [*Sifra*]

——— *Judaic Law from Jesus to the Mishna*. Atlanta, GA, 1993. [*Judaic Law*]

------- "Rabbinic Judaism: History and Hermeneutics." In *Judaism in Late Antiquity, Part Two, Historical Synthesis*, pp. 161 - 228. Leiden, 1995. ["Hermeneutics"]

------- "Evaluating the Attributions of Sayings to Named Sages in the Rabbinic Literature." In *Approaches to Ancient Judaism, New Series*, Vol. 7, pp. 125-141. Studies in the History of Judaism 110. Atlanta, 1995. ["Attributions"]

——— *From Scripture to 70, Pre-Rabbinic Beginnings of the Halakha*. Atlanta, Ga,. 1998. [*From Scripture to 70*]

Newman, L.E. Past Imperatives, Studies in the History and Theory of Jewish Ethics. New York, 1998.

Nielsen, E. *The Ten Commandments in New Perspective*. Translated from German by D. J. Bourke. London, 1968.

Noth, M. *Exodus, A Commentary*. The Old Testament Library. Translated from German by J. S. Bowden. Philadelphia, 1962. [*Exodus*]

Oppenheimer, A. "Gedaliah Alon- zwischen der jüdischen Historiographie des 19. Jahrhunderts und der modernenen historischen Forschung." In *Jüdische Geschichte in hellenistich-römischer Zeit, Wege der Forschung, vom alten zum neuen Schürer*, pp. 165 - 180. Edited by A. Oppenheimer and E. Müller - Luckner. München, 1999. ["Gedaliah Alon"]

Otto, E. *Wandel der Rechtsbgründungen in der Gesellschaftsgeschichte des Antiken Israel: Eine Rechtsgeschichte des Bundesbuches Ex. 20, 22 - 23, 13*. Studia Biblica 3. Leiden, 1988. [*Rechtsbgründungen*]

Patrick, Dale. "Studying Biblical Law as a Humanities." *Semeia* 45 (1989), 27 - 47.

Porton, Gary G. *The Traditions of Rabbi Ishmael, Part Four, the Materials as a Whole*. Leiden, 1982. [*Rabbi Ishmael*]

Preuss, H. D. *Old Testament Ideology*. Vol.1. Translated by Leo G.

Purdue. Louisville, KY, 1955.

Rajak, T. *Josephus, the Historian and his Society*. London, 1983

Regev, Eyal. "How did the Temple Mount Fall to Pompey." *JJS* 45/2 (1994), 276 - 289.

-------- "Jose ben Joezer and the Qumran Sectarians on Purity Laws. Agreement and Controversy." In *The Damascus Document. A Centennial of Discovery, Proceedings of the Third International Symposium of the Orion Center for the Study of the Dead Sea Scrolls and Associate Literature, 4 - 8 February, 1998*. Vol. 34: *The Studies on the Texts of the Desert of Judah*, pp. 95 - 107. Edited by J. M. Baumgarten, E. G. Chazon, A. Pinnick. Leiden 2000. ["Purity Laws"]

Rendtorff, R. "The Paradigm is Changing: Hopes - and Fears." In *Israel's Past in Present Research, Essays on Ancient Israelite Historiography*, pp. 51 - 68. Edited by V. Philips Long. Winona Lake, Indiana, 1999. ["Paradigm"]

Rivkin, E. "Defining the Pharisees: The Tannaitic Sources." *HUCA* 40 - 41 (1969-70), 205 - 249.

Rokeah, D. *Jews, Pagans and Christians in Conflict*. Leiden, 1982. [*Conflict]*.

Rosenfeld, B. Z. "Sage and Temple in Rabbinic Thought after the Destruction of the Second Temple." *JSJ* XXVIII/4 (1997), 437 - 464. ["Sage and Temple"]

Rosenthal, A. "תורה שעל פה ותורה מסיני- הלכה ומעשה" In מחקרי תלמוד , Vol. II, pp. 448 - 487. Edited by M. Bar-Asher and D. Rosenthal. Jerusalem, 1993. [תורה]

Rosenthal, E.S. "מסורת -הלכה וחידושי-הלכות במשנת חכמים" *Tarbits* 63 (1994), 321-74. [מסורת-הלכה]

Roth, J. *The Halakhic Process, A Systemic Analysis*. New York, 1986. [*Halakhic Process]*

Rubenstein, J. *Talmudic Stories: Narrative Art, Composition, and Culture*. Baltimore/London, 1999. [*Talmudic Stories*]

Safrai, S. בשלהי הבית השני ובתקופת המשנה. Jerusalem, 1981.

-------- "ההכרעה כבית הלל ביבנה." In *Proceedings of the Seventh World Congress of Jewish Studies, Studies in the Talmud, Halacha and Midrash*, pp. 21 - 44. Jerusalem, 1981.

-------- "התאוששות היישוב היהודי בדור יבנה, נשיאותו של רבן גמליאל". In ארץ-ישראל מחורבן בית שני ועד הכיבוש המוסלמי, היסטוריה מדינית, חברתית, ותרבותית, pp. 30 - 33. Edited by Z. Baras, S. Safrai, M. Stern, Y. Tsafrir. Jerusalem 1982. [התאוששות]

——— "הלכה למשה מסיני - היסטוריה או תיאולוגיה" In מחקרי תלמוד, pp. 11 - 38. Edited by Y. Sussman and D. Rosenthal. Jerusalem, 1990.["הלכה למשה מסיני"]

——— *The Literature of the Sages, First Part*. Assen /Philadelphia, 1987.

Safrai, Z. and A. Sagi "בין סמכות לאוטונומיה במסורת ישראל." In בין סמכות לאוטונומיה במסורת ישראל, pp. 9-31. Tel Aviv, 1997.[סמכות]

Sagi, Avi. "Both are the Words of the Living God, A Typological Analysis of Halakhic Pluralism." *HUCA* 65 (1994), 105 - 136.[" Pluralism"]

Saldarini, A.J. "The Adoption of a Dissident: Akabiah ben Mahalalel in Rabbinic Tradition." *JJS* 33 (1982), 547 - 556. [" The Adoption of a Dissident"]

——— *Pharisees, Scribes and Sadducees in Palestine Society, A Sociological Approach*. Wilmington, Delaware, 1988. [*Pharisees*]

Sanders, E.P. *Jewish Law from Jesus to the Mishna; Five Studies*. London, 1990.

Schäfer, P. *Studien zur Geschichte und Theologie des Rabbinischen Judentums*. Arbeiten zur Geschichte des Antiken Judentums und des Christentums X V. Leiden, 1978. [*Studien*]

——— "Johanan b. Zakkai und Jabneh." In *Aufstieg und Niedergang der Römischen Welt II*, pp. 43 - 101. Edited by H. Temporini and W. Haase. Berlin, 1979.

——— "Research into Rabbinic Literature: An Attempt to Define the Status Quaestionis." *JJS 37* (1986), 139 - 152. ["Status Quaestionis"]

——— "Der Vorrabbinische Pharisäismus." In *Paulus und das Antike Judentum*, pp. 125 - 175. Edited by M. Hengel and U. Heckel. Tübingen, 1991.

Schechter, Solomon. אבות דרבי נתן. New York, 1967. [ARN]

Schiffman, L. H. *The Halakhah at Qumran*. Studies in Judaism in Late Antiquity16. Edited by J. Neusner. Leiden, 1975,

——— *Reclaiming the Dead Sea Scrolls*. Philadelphia, PA, 1994.

——— "The Place of 4QMMT in the Corpus of Qumran Manuscripts." In *Reading 4QMMT, New Perspectives on Qumran Law and History*, pp. 81 - 98. Edited by J. Kampen and M.J. Bernstein. Atlanta, 1996. ["The Place of 4QMMT"]

——— "The Contribution of the Dead Sea Scrolls." In *Jüdische Geschichte in hellenistich-römischer Zeit, Wege der Forschung, vom alten zum neuen Schürer*, pp. 205 - 219. Edited by A. Oppenheimer and E. Müller - Luckner. München, 1999. ["Contribution"]

——— "The Zadokite Fragments and the Temple Scroll." *Studies on the Texts of the Desert of Judah* 34 (2000),133 -145.

Schlüter, M. *Auf welche Weise wurde die Mishna geschrieben*? Tűbingen,

1993. [*Mishna*]

Schürer, E. *A History of the Jewish People in the Time of Jesus Christ*. 3 vols. Translated by S. Taylor and P. Christie. Edinburgh, 1885. [*History*]

Smith, M. "A Comparison of Early Christian and Early Rabbinic Tradition." *JBL* 82 (1963), 169 - 176.

Stemberger, Günter. *Das Klassische Judentum, Kultur und Geschichte der rabbinischen Zeit (70 n. Chr. Bis 1040 n. Chr.)*. München, 1979. [*Das Klassische Judentum*]

------- *Jewish Contemporaries of Jesus, Pharisees, Sadducees, Essenes*. Translated from German by A. W. Mahnke. Minneapolis, 1995. [*Jewish Contemporaries of Jesus*]

------- "Die innerrabbinische Überlieferung von Mishna Abot." In *Geschichte-Tradition-Reflexion, Festschrift für Martin Hengel zum 70. Geburtstag, I Judentum*, pp. 511 - 527. Edited by P. Schäfer. Tűbingen 1996. ["Abot"]

------- *Introduction to the Talmud and Midrash*. 2nd edition. Translated and edited by Morris Bockmuehl. Edinburgh, 1996.

------- "Die Umformung des palästinensischen Judentums nach 70." In *Jüdische Geschichte in hellenistich-römischer Zeit, Wege der Forschung, vom alten zum neuen Schürer*, pp. 85 - 99. Edited by A. Oppenheimer and E. Müller - Luckner. München, 1999. ["Judentums"]

Stern, M., ed. *Greek and Latin Authors on Jews and Judaism*. Vol. I. Jerusalem, 1976,

Stern, S. "Attribution and Authorship in the Babylonian Talmud." *JJS* 45/1 (1994), 28 - 51.

Strugnell, J. "The Qumran Scrolls: A Report of Work in Progress." In *Jewish Civilization in the Hellenistic-Roman Period*, 94-106. Journal for the Study of the Pseudepigrapha, Supplement Series 10. Edited by S. Talmon. Sheffield, 1991. ["The Qumran Scrolls"]

Sussmann, Y. "The History of Halakha and the Dead Sea Scrolls, Preliminary Observations on Miqṣat Ma'ase Ha-Torah (4QMMT)." *Tarbits* LIX 1-2 (1990), 11 - 76. ["4QMMT"]

Talmon, S. "בין מקרא ובין משנה" In מגילות מדבר יהודה, ארבעים שנות מחקר, pp. 10 - 39. Edited by M. Broshi et al. Jerusalem, 1992.

Tchernowitz , Ch. תולדות ההלכה 4 vols. New York, 1950.

Thoma, C. "Der Pharisäismus,." In *Literatur und Religion des Frühjudentums*, pp. 254 - 272. Edited by I. Maier and J. Schreiner. Würzburg, 1973.

Tyson, Joseph B. *Luke, Judaism, and the Scholars, Critical Approaches to Luke-Acts*. Columbia, SC, 1999. [*Luke, Judaism, and the Scholars*]

Ulrich, E. "The Scrolls and the Study of the Hebrew Bible." *In The Dead Sea Scrolls at Fifty, Proceedings of the 1997 Society of Biblical Literature, Qumran Section Meetings*, pp. 31 - 42. Edited by R. A. Kugler and E. M. Schuller. Atlanta, GA, 1999.

Urbach, E.E.. בעלי התוספות. Jerusalem, reprint 1968.

-------- מעמד והנהגה בעולמם של חכמי א"י, דברי האקדמיה הלאומית הישראלית למדעים Jerusalem, 1969. [מעמד]

-------- ההלכה, מקורותיה והתפתחותה והתלמוד. Tel Aviv, 1984. [ההלכה]

-------- מעולמם של חכמים. Jerusalem, 1988. [חכמים]

-------- "סמכות ההלכה בימינו" In בין סמכות לאוטונומיה במסורת ישראל, pp. 457 - 463. Edited by Z. Safrai and A. Sagi. Tel Aviv, 1997. [סמכות]

-------- מחקרים במדעי היהדות. Vol.1. Edited by M. D. Herr and Y. Frenkel. Jerusalem, 1998. [מחקרים]

-------- "Class-Status and Leadership in the World of the Palestinian Sages." In *Proceedings of the Israel Academy of Sciences and Humanities*, Vol. 2, pp. 38 - 74. Jerusalem, 1968.

Vermes, G. *Post-Biblical Jewish Studies*. Studies in Judaism in Late Antiquity 8. Leiden, 1975. [*Studies*]

Vincent, L. H. and A. M. Steve. *Jérusalem de l'Ancien Testament* I. Paris, 1954.

von Rad, G. *Deuteronomy, A Commentary*. Translated from German by D. Barton. Philadelphia, 1966. [*Deuteronomy*]

Weiss, H. "The Sabbath in the Writings of Josephus." *JSOT* 29/4 (1998), 363 - 390.

Weiss, I. H. דור דור ודורשיו. Jerusalem.1965.

Weiss, M. "האותנטיות של השקלא וטריא במחלוקות בית שמאי ובית הלל" *Sidra* 4 (1988), 53 - 66. ["האותנטיות"]

Weiss-Halivni, D. *Midrash, Mishnah and Gemara. The Jewish Predilection for Justified Law*. Cambridge, 1986.[*Midrash, Mishnah and Gemara*]

Williams, C. B. *New Testament in the Language of the People*. Chicago, 1963.[*New Testament*]

Wintermute, O. S. "Jubilees." In *The Old Testament Pseudepigrapha*, Vol. 2, pp. 35-142. Edited by James H. Charlesworth. New York, 1985.

Wise, M., M. Abegg and E. Cook. *The Dead Sea Scrolls. A New Translation*. San Francisco, 1996.

Yaron, R. "Biblical Law: Prolegomena." In *Jewish Law in Legal History and the Modern World*, pp. 27 - 44. Edited by B. S. Jackson. Leiden, 1980.

Zeitlin, S. "Les principes des controverses halachiques entre les écoles de Schammai et de Hillel." *REJ* 93 (1932), 3 - 83.["Les principes"]

-------- "The Pharisees and the Gospels." *In Essays and Studies in Memory of Linda R. Miller*, pp. 235 - 286. Edited by I. Davidson. New York, 1938.

------- *Studies in the Early History of Judaism*. Vol 4. *History of Early Talmudic Law*. New York, 1978.[*Studies*]

Subject Index

Halakhot, by Topic

Hierarchy of Precepts

Ideology

Citations Index

CPSIA information can be obtained at www.ICGtesting.com
Printed in the USA
LVOW05*2308201114

414765LV00016B/568/P

9 783110 176360